Contributions to Management Science

The series *Contributions to Management Science* contains research publications in all fields of business and management science. These publications are primarily monographs and multiple author works containing new research results, and also feature selected conference-based publications are also considered. The focus of the series lies in presenting the development of latest theoretical and empirical research across different viewpoints.

This book series is indexed in Scopus.

More information about this series at http://www.springer.com/series/1505

Vahid Jafari-Sadeghi • Hannan Amoozad Mahdiraji • Léo-Paul Dana
Editors

Empirical International Entrepreneurship

A Handbook of Methods, Approaches, and Applications

Springer

Editors
Vahid Jafari-Sadeghi
School of Strategy and Leadership
Coventry University
Coventry, UK

Hannan Amoozad Mahdıraji
Leicester Castle Business School
De Montfort University
Leicester, UK

Léo-Paul Dana
Montpellier Business School
Montpellier, France

ISSN 1431-1941 ISSN 2197-716X (electronic)
Contributions to Management Science
ISBN 978-3-030-68971-1 ISBN 978-3-030-68972-8 (eBook)
https://doi.org/10.1007/978-3-030-68972-8

This Springer imprint is published by the registered company Springer Nature Switzerland AG.
The registered company address is: Gewerbestrasse 11, 6330 Cham, Switzerland

Acknowledgements

We would like to thank all the authors for their contribution to this book. They brought experience, dedication, and specialism which led to a collection of chapters with a wide range of methodologies as to address the objective of this book.

We would like to have a special thanks to the reviewers, who brought knowledge and expertise to international entrepreneurship and methodological insights. Without their valued and respected reviews, this book would not have had the same robustness in methods as well as quality in the international entrepreneurship debate.

We would like to thank the Springer for this opportunity, the editor, Prashanth Mahagaonkar, and his team for their constant support and guidance in the process from the very first beginning of idea formulation to final editing and publication.

Finally, we would like to take this opportunity to thank our families who kept us motivated and stood by us in this journey. We dedicate our sincere gratitude and love for them.

Vahid Jafari-Sadeghi
Hannan Amoozad Mahdiraji
Léo-Paul Dana

Contents

Editors and Contributors

About the Editors

Vahid Jafari-Sadeghi is currently a lecturer in business strategy in the School of Strategy and Leadership at Coventry University. He holds his PhD in international entrepreneurship from the University of Turin where he has served as a post-doctoral fellow. Also, he has been a visiting research scholar at the University of Regina and contributed to different research projects with various scholars and universities. He has published papers in several international journals and publications such as Journal of Business Research, International Business Review, Journal of International Entrepreneurship, Research in International Business and Finance, etc. He is a member of the editorial board at British Food Journal and acted as guest editor and reviewer for several academic journals and performed as track chair and presenter for a number of international conferences.

Hannan Amoozad Mahdiraji is currently a senior lecturer in business and management of faculty of business and law and researcher at the centre of enterprise and innovation at De Montfort University. He cooperated as a lecturer with Coventry University and as an assistant professor for the University of Tehran, previously. He graduated with his PhD in operations and manufacturing management in 2012 from the University of Tehran. His main interest areas include multiple-criteria decision-making methods, optimisation, game theory, and supply chain management. His H-index is currently 15, i-10 index 17, and with nearly

600 citations. Since 2012 he has published 43 research papers in famous international journals including expert systems with the application, applied mathematical modelling, cleaner production, knowledge management, etc.

Léo-Paul Dana is professor at Dalhousie University and at Montpellier Business School, Montpellier Research in Management. He is also member of the Entrepreneurship and Innovation Chair, which is part of LabEx Entreprendre at the Université de Montpellier and visiting professor at Kingston University. A graduate of McGill University and HEC-Montreal, he has served as Marie Curie Fellow at Princeton University and visiting professor at INSEAD. He has published extensively in a variety of journals including Entrepreneurship Theory and Practice, International Business Review, International Small Business Journal, Journal of Business Research, Journal of Small Business Management, Journal of World Business, Small Business Economics, and Technological Forecasting and Social Change.

Contributors

Niloofar Ahmadzadeh Kandi Department of Business and Law, University of Wollongong, Sydney, NSW, Australia

Hannan Amoozad Mahdiraji Faculty of Business and Law, Leicester Castle Business School, De Montfort University, Leicester, UK

Iuliia Andreeva School of Business and Management, Lappeenranta-Lahti University of Technology, Lappeenranta, Finland

Mostafa Azari Faculty of Management, University of Tehran, Tehran, Iran

Nikta Babakhani Department of Industrial Management, Faculty of Management, University of Tehran, Tehran, Iran

Nataliia Bartkiv Ivano-Frankivsk Chamber of Commerce and Industry, Ivano-Frankivsk, Ukraine

Paolo Pietro Biancone Department of Management, University of Turin, Turin, Italy

Davide Calandra Department of Management, University of Turin, Turin, Italy

María del Carmen García Centeno San Pablo CEU University (CEINDO), Law and Economics Program, Madrid, Spain

Léo-Paul Dana Rowe School of Business, Dalhousie University, Halifax, NS, Canada
Montpellier Business School, Montpellier, France

Antonio Daood Department of Management, University of Bologna, Bologna, Italy

Amir Hosein Ebrahimi Department of Industrial Management, Faculty of Management, University of Tehran, Tehran, Iran

Anisur Faroque School of Business and Management, LUT University, Lappeenranta, Finland

María de las Mercedes Barrachina Fernández San Pablo CEU University (CEINDO), Law and Economics Program, Madrid, Spain

Alberto Ferraris Department of Management, University of Turin, Turin, Italy

Luciano Fratocchi Department of Industrial and Information Engineering & Economics, University of L'Aquila, L'Aquila, Italy

Nima Garousi Mokhtarzadeh Faculty of Management, University of Tehran, Tehran, Iran

Miguel Angel Gil Robles Accounting and Finance Department, Tecnológico de Monterrey, Monterrey, Mexico

Shide Sadat Hashemi Saramadan Andishe Avina Co, Science, and Technology Park of TarbiatModares, Tehran, Iran

Elaheh Heydari Department of Management, IA University, Mashhad, Iran

Seyed Hossein Hosseini Model-Based Management Systems Institute (SAMAM), Tehran, Iran

Daniel Iannaci Department of Management, University of Turin, Turin, Italy

Maria Ivanova-Gongne Åbo Akademi, Turku, Finland

Vahid Jafari-Sadeghi Faculty of Business and Law, School of Strategy and Leadership, Coventry University, Coventry, UK

Ismail Jafarpanah Faculty of Management, University of Tehran, Tehran, Iran

Zahra Jamshidi New Business Department, Faculty of Entrepreneurship, University of Tehran, Tehran, Iran

Sepideh Khavarinezhad Department of Management, University of Turin, Turin, Italy

Amir Hossein Khorasgani School of Economy, Finance and Accounting, Faculty of Business and Law, Coventry University, Coventry, UK

Ignat Kulkov Åbo Akademi, Turku, Finland

Hasan Mahmud School of Business and Management, LUT University, Lappeenranta, Finland

Oksana Malynka Ivano-Frankivsk National Technical University of Oil and Gas, Ivano-Frankivsk, Ukraine

Kaveh Moghaddam School of Business Administration, University of Houston-Victoria, Katy, TX, USA

Vincenza Odorici Department of Management, University of Bologna, Bologna, Italy

Denis Odlin Department of International Business, Strategy & Entrepreneurship, Auckland University of Technology, Auckland, New Zealand

Arto Ojala School of Marketing and Communication, International Business, University of Vaasa, Vaasa, Finland

Carmen Calderón Patier San Pablo CEU University (CEINDO), Law and Economics Program, Madrid, Spain

Manuela Presutti Department of Management, University of Bologna, Bologna, Italy

Vesa Puhakka Department of Marketing, Management and International Business, University of Oulu Business School, University of Oulu, Oulu, Finland

Seyed Hossein Razavi Hajiagha Department of Management, Faculty of Management and Finance, Khatam University, Tehran, Iran

Philippe Régnier School of Management-Freiburg, University of Applied Sciences (HES-SO), Fribourg, Switzerland

Mojtaba Rezaei Department of Management, University of Turin, Turin, Italy

Shahrbanou Rezaei Department of Industrial Engineering, Sajjad University, Mashhad, Iran

Sami Saarenketo School of Business and Management, LUT University, Lappeenranta, Finland

Seyed Mojtaba Sajadi New Business Department, Faculty of Entrepreneurship, University of Tehran, Tehran, Iran

Silvana Secinaro Department of Management, University of Turin, Turin, Italy

Arun Sukumar International Centre for Transformational Entrepreneurship, Coventry University, Coventry, UK

Mohammadreza Taghizadeh-Yazdi Department of Industrial Management, Faculty of Management, University of Tehran, Tehran, Iran

Kambiz Talebi New Business Department, Faculty of Entrepreneurship, University of Tehran, Tehran, Iran

Richard Tomlins International Centre for Transformational Entrepreneurship, Coventry University, Coventry, UK

Lasse Torkkeli School of Business and Management, LUT University, Lappeenranta, Finland
Turku School of Business, University of Turku, Turku, Finland

Nigel Walton Faculty of Business and Law, School of Strategy and Leadership, Coventry University, Coventry, UK

Thomas Weber Romain College of Business, University of Southern Indiana, Evansville, IN, USA

Pascal Wild School of Management-Freiburg, University of Applied Sciences (HES-SO), Fribourg, Switzerland

Sivakumar Velayutham Faculty of Business, Hospitality, and Humanities, Nilai University, Nilai, Malaysia

Anna Vuorio School of Business and Management, LUT University, Lappeenranta, Finland

Ali Zamani Babgohar Faculty of Management, University of Tehran, Tehran, Iran

Introduction: International Entrepreneurship from Methodological Perspectives

Vahid Jafari-Sadeghi, Hannan Amoozad Mahdiraji, and Léo-Paul Dana

1 Introduction

The global business environment has witnessed enormous internationalisation practices that suggest untapped opportunities for both businesses and entrepreneurs (Jafari Sadeghi et al. 2019b). In a rapidly evolving economic environment, it is inevitable for ventures to adopt an integrated policy for presence in global markets (Dana 2001; Sukumar et al. 2020). However, internationalisation is the most intricate strategy that can be undertaken by particularly small ventures (Fernández and Nieto 2005; Jafari Sadeghi et al. 2019a). In recent years, although constantly changing (international) business environment created complex circumstances for firms to enter the global markets (Acs et al. 2003; Dana and Wright 2009; Etemad et al. 2001; Jafari Sadeghi et al. 2018), technological evolution and reduction of barriers across borders through regional trade agreements have facilitated the market globalisation (Jafari Sadeghi et al. 2019b; Leonidou 2004). In this context, entrepreneurship can play the role of mediator in propelling ventures into global markets

V. Jafari-Sadeghi (✉)
Faculty of Business and Law, School of Strategy and Leadership, Coventry University, Coventry, UK
e-mail: Vahid.Jafari-Sadeghi@coventry.ac.uk

H. Amoozad Mahdiraji
Faculty of Business and Law, Leicester Castle Business School, De Montfort University, Leicester, UK
e-mail: Hannan.AmoozadMahdiraji@dmu.ac.uk

L.-P. Dana
Rowe School of Business, Dalhousie University, Halifax, NS, Canada

Montpellier Business School, Montpellier, France
e-mail: lp762359@dal.ca

V. Jafari-Sadeghi et al. (eds.), *Empirical International Entrepreneurship*,
Contributions to Management Science,
https://doi.org/10.1007/978-3-030-68972-8_1

and thus facilitating the country's growth in the economy (Acs et al. 2012; Jafari-Sadeghi 2020). Focusing on the internationalisation of small- and medium-sized enterprises (SMEs), Oviatt and McDougall-Covin (2005) shed the light on the field of international entrepreneurship (IE) and define it as "the discovery, enactment, evaluation, and exploitation of opportunities—across national borders—to create future goods and services". In this vein, taking advantage of wealth material of entrepreneurship and internationalisation, international entrepreneurship is seen as a hybrid phenomenon that has increasingly attracted scholars globally.

2 Structure

Given the importance of IE, the aim of this book is to provide key analytical themes of what it means to internationalise entrepreneurially. This is a collection of prominent chapters that gives an understanding of types of methods which can be used in the field of international entrepreneurship. Chapters are clustered into qualitative and quantitative articles. The qualitative stream covers articles that investigated international entrepreneurship, conceptual and empirical methods, as well as literature reviews. Chapters in quantitative stream analyse IE through a broad range of statistical methods such as regressions, panel data, structural equational modelling, as well as decision-making and optimisation models in certain and uncertain circumstances.

2.1 *Stream A: Qualitative Research Methods*

The first stream of this book looks at qualitative methods, in which they disentangle prior knowledge, propose new ideas for the conceptualisation of IE, and investigate the topic qualitatively. Therefore, Stream A includes a total number of twelve chapters in three parts of Conceptualisation, Literature Reviews, and Empirical Methods. Figure 1 depicts the qualitative categories of this book.

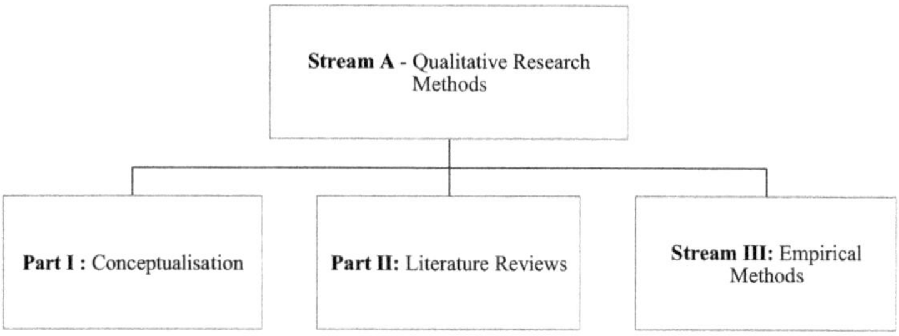

Fig. 1 Qualitative streams

Part I includes four chapters, providing more conceptual insights for international entrepreneurship. Chapters in this stream explore topics such as networking for SME internationalisation in distant markets, dynamic capabilities for immigrant entrepreneurs, technology transformation, and the concept of Belief-Actions-Results (BAR) for international entrepreneurial investments. Moreover, in Part II, chapters review IE literature from different perspectives including entrepreneurial decision-making and technology as well as topic modelling. Finally, Part III consists of five chapters, which take advantage of empirical methods to explore new insights into IE.

2.2 Stream B: Quantitative Research Methods

In Stream B, quantitative methods and their applications in international entrepreneurship have been illustrated. Quantitative methods include a wide range of methods and techniques using mathematical or/and statistical equations to solve a problem or deal with a challenge. In Stream B, three categories of quantitative methods have been implemented in international entrepreneurship encompassing Applied Statistics, Multiple-Criteria Decision-Making (MCDM), and Optimisation Methods. These three categories cover eleven chapters of this book. The contributors have presented interesting researches in employing quantitative methods in international entrepreneurship. Figure 2 demonstrates the methods covered in this book in the second stream.

In the applied statistics section (Part IV), SEM, CFA, Delphi, and hypothesis testing have been employed by the contributors to research in international entrepreneurship. Internationalising ventures facing ageing and sizing by considering international growth, entrepreneurial and market orientation; internationalising entrepreneurially from the low-tech emerging market by considering the role of international entrepreneurial capability and orientation in early internationalising firms from Bangladesh; leaders navigating institutional on female international entrepreneurship in emerging economies; investigating the barriers to the internationalisation of SMEs in Iran; and eventually, shaping effectuation and causation international entrepreneurial decision-making logic concerning the role of big data in an emerging market have been analysed with statistical methods.

In the decision-making section (Part V), a combination of multi-criteria decision-making methods has been applied to investigate international entrepreneurship problems, challenges, and dilemmas. Methods including WASPAS, BWM, SAW, VIKOR, and TOPSIS have been applied. Moreover, in this category, a novel uncertain approach in decision-making entitled interval-valued intuitionistic fuzzy has been employed in IE challenges. Considering uncertainty in international markets, applying the IVIF approach in decision-making problems in IE could be productive in the relevant literature. In this category, location selection in the international entrepreneurial ecosystem for medical tourism start-ups and team member selection of international entrepreneurs' problems have been addressed by the contributors.

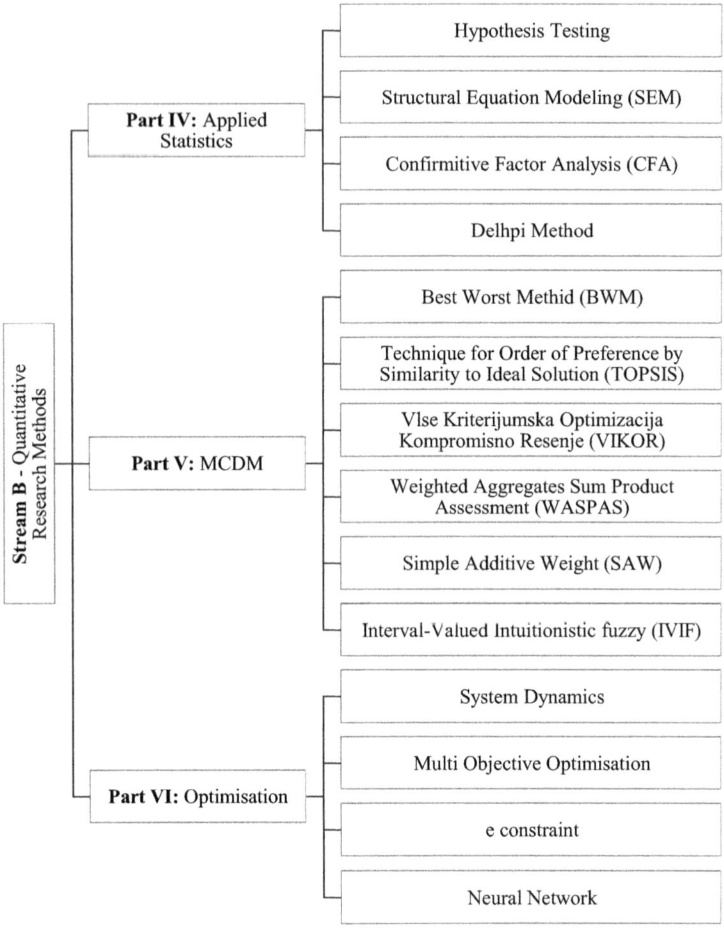

Fig. 2 Quantitative streams

In the last category of the quantitative part (Part VI), multi-objective optimisation and mathematical modelling alongside systems dynamics simulation and neural networks have been employed by the contributors. The authors have applied these methods to address IE challenges such as introducing new products to international markets using green entrepreneurial supply chain optimisation; analysing the impact of international networking capability on international performance by considering the mediating role of dynamic entrepreneurship capabilities; applying a system dynamic approach to modelling growth engines in international entrepreneurship era; and ultimately, entrepreneurship rate prediction.

References

Acs ZJ, Dana L-P, Jones MV (2003) Toward new horizons: the internationalisation of entrepreneurship. J Int Entrep 1:5–12

Acs ZJ, Audretsch DB, Braunerhjelm P, Carlsson B (2012) Growth and entrepreneurship. Small Bus Econ 39(2):289–300

Dana L-P (2001) Networks, internationalization & policy. Small Bus Econ 16(2):57–62

Dana L-P, Wright RW (2009) International entrepreneurship: research priorities for the future. IJGSB 3(1):90–134

Etemad H, Wright RW, Dana L-P (2001) Symbiotic international business networks: collaboration between small and large firms. Thunderbird Int Bus Rev 43(4):481–499

Fernández Z, Nieto MJ (2005) Internationalization strategy of small and medium-sized family businesses: some influential factors. Fam Bus Rev 18(1):77–89

Jafari Sadeghi V, Biancone PP, Giacoma C, Secinaro S (2018) How does export compliance influence the internationalization of firms: is it a thread or an opportunity? J Glob Entrep Res 8(1):3

Jafari Sadeghi V, Biancone PP, Anderson RB, Nkongolo-Bakenda J-M (2019a) International entrepreneurship by particular people 'on their own terms': evidence of universal attributes of entrepreneurs in evolving economies. Int J Entrep Small Bus 37(2):288–308

Jafari Sadeghi V, Nkongolo-Bakenda J-M, Anderson RB, Dana L-P (2019b) An institution-based view of international entrepreneurship: a comparison of context-based and universal determinants in developing and economically advanced countries. Int Bus Rev 28(6):101588

Jafari-Sadeghi V (2020) The motivational factors of business venturing: opportunity versus necessity? A gendered perspective on European countries. J Bus Res 113(May 2020):279–289

Leonidou LC (2004) An analysis of the barriers hindering small business export development. J Small Bus Manag 42(3):279–302

Oviatt BM, McDougall-Covin PP (2005) Defining international entrepreneurship and modeling the speed of internationalization. J Int Entrep 29(5):537–554

Sukumar A, Jafari-Sadeghi V, Garcia-Perez A, Dutta DK (2020) The potential link between corporate innovations and corporate competitiveness: evidence from IT firms in the UK. J Knowl Manag 24(5):965–983

Vahid Jafari-Sadeghi is currently a lecturer in business strategy in the School of Strategy and Leadership at Coventry University. Vahid holds his PhD in international entrepreneurship from the University of Turin where he has served as a post-doctoral fellow. Also, he has been a visiting research scholar at the University of Regina and contributed to different research projects with various scholars and universities. Vahid has published papers in several international journals and publications such as the *Journal of Business Research*, *International Business Review*, *Journal of International Entrepreneurship*, *Research in International Business and Finance*, etc. He is a member of the editorial board at the *British Food Journal* and acted as guest editor and reviewer for several academic journals and performed as a track chair and presenter for a number of international conferences.

Hannan Amoozad Mahdiraji is currently a senior lecturer in business and management of faculty of business and law and researcher at the centre of enterprise and innovation at De Montfort University. He cooperated as a lecturer with Coventry University and as an assistant professor for the University of Tehran, previously. Hannan graduated with his PhD in operations and manufacturing management in 2012 from the University of Tehran. His main interest areas include multiple-criteria decision-making methods, optimisation, game theory, and supply chain management. His H-index is currently 15, i-10 index 17, and with nearly 600 citations. Since 2012 he has published

43 research papers in famous international journals including expert systems with the application, applied mathematical modelling, cleaner production, knowledge management, etc.

Léo-Paul Dana is Professor at Dalhousie University and at Montpellier Business School, Montpellier Research in Management. He is also a member of the Entrepreneurship and Innovation Chair, which is part of LabEx Entreprendre at the Université de Montpellier, and Visiting Professor at Kingston University. A graduate of McGill University and HEC-Montreal, he has served as Marie Curie Fellow at Princeton University and Visiting Professor at INSEAD. He has published extensively in a variety of journals including *Entrepreneurship: Theory and Practice*, *International Business Review*, *International Small Business Journal*, *Journal of Business Research*, *Journal of Small Business Management*, *Journal of World Business*, *Small Business Economics*, and *Technological Forecasting & Social Change*.

Part I
Qualitative Research Streams: Conceptualisation

Immigrants and International Entrepreneurship: Transnational Dynamic Capability and Dual Social Network Embeddedness

Kaveh Moghaddam and Thomas Weber

1 Introduction

In recent years, accelerating changes in the international business environment have created new circumstances favourable for small firms to enter global markets (Alon et al. 2009; Bayfield et al. 2009; Etemad et al. 2001; Jafari Sadeghi and Biancone 2018). In particular, the relaxation of trade barriers and availability of low-cost telecommunications and transportation have provided smaller firms with the chance to enter the global market which was once thought to only be possible for large multinational firms (Dana 2017; Dana et al. 2009a; Sadeghi et al. 2019). In addition, the global economy provided a plethora of opportunities for entrepreneurs to pursue internationalisation activities (Jafari Sadeghi et al. 2019).

In particular, international entrepreneurship (as a hybrid of internationalisation and entrepreneurship) contains exploring opportunities and exploiting scarce resources and network ties across international boundaries (Dana et al. 2009b). International entrepreneurship literature has emphasised the importance of the entrepreneur in the international development of new ventures and examined entrepreneurs' general attitude, orientation, experience, and social network (Jafari-Sadeghi et al. 2019). "The contribution of migrant and ethnic entrepreneurs to local economies is also of interest within international entrepreneurship" (Acs et al. 2003: 6). In particular, immigrant entrepreneurs with unique characteristics, experiences, and networks have become an influential group of entrepreneurs actively engaging in

---

K. Moghaddam (✉)
School of Business Administration, University of Houston- Victoria, Katy, TX, USA
e-mail: moghaddamk@uhv.edu

T. Weber
Romain College of Business, University of Southern Indiana, Evansville, IN, USA
e-mail: thomas.weber@usi.edu

V. Jafari-Sadeghi et al. (eds.), *Empirical International Entrepreneurship*, Contributions to Management Science,
https://doi.org/10.1007/978-3-030-68972-8_2

international entrepreneurship (Moghaddam et al. 2018). The availability of inexpensive means of communication (e.g. email and the Internet) and affordable transportation (e.g. air travel) are significant drivers for immigrants to engage in transnational entrepreneurship (Drori et al. 2009). Transnational Entrepreneurs (TEs) are "individuals that migrate from one country to another, concurrently maintaining business-related linkages" with their former country of origin (COO) and adopted country of residence (COR). TEs use their dual embeddedness in their COO and COR to grow their entrepreneurial firms (Drori et al. 2009: 1001). For example, some Chinese Canadians have goods manufactured in China that they import to Canada while exporting Canadian products to Asia (Sadeghi et al. 2018; Wong and Ng 2002). These TEs earn profits in both countries because they are embedded in China and Canada, and they understand the cultures, legal systems, and economic systems of both countries.

There have been a number of studies focused on the transnational economic activities of immigrants such as direct investment in the COO (Vaaler 2011); however, there has been little investigation into the process of transnational entrepreneurship (Dimitratos et al. 2016) and the competitive advantages TEs have (Sequeira et al. 2009; Yeung 2009). Therefore, this chapter focuses on transnational entrepreneurship and its simultaneous contribution to the COO and COR (Moghaddam et al. 2018).

While prior studies have highlighted the positive effect of social networks on firm performance, this relationship has remained in a *black box* with little understanding of the organisational processes by which such positive effect may become realised (Garousi Mokhtarzadeh et al. 2020b). Based on the dynamic capability perspective (Teece et al. 1997; Teece 2007) and the relational theory of social networks (Granovetter 1973), this chapter offers a theoretical framework to explain how TEs develop their competitive advantage to succeed in a global market. This theoretical framework suggests that TEs recognise opportunities and benefits from the social networks in their COO and COR. It also explains how TE use their ethnic and nonethnic ties to improve firm performance through the mediating effects of their dynamic capabilities (Teece 2007; Winter 2003) and the moderating effect of the institutional distance between the COO and the COR.

2 Theoretical Background

The research on transnational entrepreneurship was originated by immigration scholars in the late 1990s, and it was mostly limited to case studies (Itzigsohn et al. 1999; Kyle 1999; Landolt et al. 1999; Portes et al. 2002). In the past two decades, transnational entrepreneurship researchers have studied ethnic ties (e.g. Chand and Ghorbani 2011) and ethnic market knowledge (e.g. Shinnar et al. 2011) as important resources to understand the success factors of TEs. "Ethnic is an adjective that refers to differences between categories of people" and implies "a common origin and culture" (Aldrich and Waldinger 1990: 112). Ethnic ties refer to those social ties between individuals or firms with a common COO and culture (Moghaddam et al. 2018). Unfortunately, the extant literature does not provide theoretical insight into how TEs' unique resources may affect firm performance and how TE's processes create competitive advantage (Lin and Tao 2012).

2.1 *Ethnic Advantage*

Ethnic advantage refers to the notion that TEs "possess relative knowledge and social capital advantages" compared to other competitors (Nielsen and Riddle 2007: 5). Their advantages are based on the idea that TEs face less risk because they understand their COO market preferences and the COO's business environment better than foreign competitors (Gillespie et al. 1999). TEs "are unique in that they are socially embedded in both their home and host environment" an advantage that benefits "these entrepreneurs in opportunity recognition, start-up, and maintenance of new ventures" (Sequeira et al. 2009: 1023). However, empirical studies examining the effect of ethnic advantage on firm performance report mixed findings. While some studies emphasise the positive effect of ethnic ties on TEs' firm success (Chand and Ghorbani 2011), other studies report no significant effect (Heilbrunn and Kushnirovich 2007; Zimmer and Aldrich 1987), and other studies report a negative effect (Fregetto 2004). It is important to note that ethnic advantage is a necessary but not sufficient condition in creating a competitive advantage for TEs (Moghaddam et al. 2018).

2.2 *Dynamic Capability Perspective*

The *dynamic capability perspective* is a useful framework to examine why some TEs succeed and others (with the same level of access to market knowledge or social network privileges) fail (Zafarullah et al. 1997). We suggest that it is TEs' dynamic capabilities of *opportunity sensing* and *opportunity seizing* (explained below) not the TEs' resources, per se (Adner and Helfat 2003), that result in TEs' success in creating a competitive advantage. Dynamic capability is defined as "the firm's ability to integrate, build, and reconfigure internal and external competences to address rapidly changing environments" (Teece et al. 1997: 516). Dynamic capabilities are difficult to imitate because their development depends on the path taken to create them as well as firm technological, financial, and social asset positions (Moghaddam et al. 2016). A social network-based model of creating dynamic capabilities may explain how TEs develop organisational processes in both the COO and COR which result in their unique competitive advantage. TEs' success depends on developing unique organisational dynamic capabilities which allow them to compete against established firms (Arthurs and Busenitz 2006; Sapienza et al. 2006).

2.3 TE's Dynamic Capability Development

Dynamic capabilities are considered active reconfigurations of a firm's intangible and tangible assets and can be disaggregated into the abilities to sense opportunities and seize opportunities (Teece 2007). Therefore, we suggest that TEs must develop two key organisational processes: (1) the *opportunity sensing process* to identify opportunities and (2) the *opportunity seizing process* to take advantage of such opportunities.

2.4 Opportunity Sensing

Entrepreneurial opportunities include introducing products or services to new markets or offering existing products and services in new ways (Eckhardt and Shane 2003; Smith et al. 2019). Opportunity sensing can be considered the essence of entrepreneurship (Dana 1987; Hitt et al. 2001) because the ability to recognise and seize opportunities others do not perceive is one of the characteristics that differentiates entrepreneurs from others (Shane and Venkataraman 2000). The ability to sense opportunities is vital to take advantage of foreign market opportunities (Lu et al. 2010). Often, entrepreneurial opportunities that are not equally recognisable to everyone exist because of asymmetries in market information (Moghaddam et al. 2017b; Shane and Venkataraman 2000).

TEs have unique information and knowledge of their COO and COR that is not readily available to other rivals which helps them to sense opportunities that may be a source of competitive advantage. Van Gelderen (2007) examined the entrepreneurial activities of former USSR immigrants in the Netherlands and Israel and found that knowledge of the COO may aid TEs in recognising unique opportunities. For example, if a TE started a travel agency, the TE has the knowledge to provide tours to their COO inhabitants to visit their COR or provide inhabitants of the COR with tours to explore the COO. Another example of an opportunity TEs are well suited to take advantage of is importing and exporting of hand-made products (e.g. Persian hand-woven carpets).

While one individual in a firm may have the "necessary cognitive and creative skills" to sense some opportunities, it is more fruitful to "embed scanning, interpretative, and creative processes inside the enterprise itself" (Teece 2007: 1323). In other words, the firm will be "vulnerable" if opportunity sensing is "left to the cognitive traits of a few individuals". Therefore, we argue that TEs need to develop opportunity sensing processes such as internal research and development activities (Teece 2007) to systematically pursue sensing opportunities.

2.5 *Opportunity Seizing*

In addition to the opportunity sensing processes, TEs also need to develop their opportunity seizing processes. In particular, developing a set of gestation activities such as "developing a [business] model", "hiring committed employees", and "engaging in promotional efforts" may significantly affect firm performance (Newbert 2005: 67). For instance, the marketing process, defined as the "capacity to formulate effective marketing mix strategies", can be considered an opportunity seizing capability (Weerawardena et al. 2007: 301) contributing to competitive advantage development (Kor and Mahoney 2005) and positively affecting firm performance (Knight et al. 2004). Another example would be product portfolio optimisation and product-technology alignment capabilities (Garousi Mokhtarzadeh et al. 2020a) which are important skills to develop opportunity seizing and create a firm's competitive advantage. In the same vein, a firm's innovative capability is an important organisation opportunity seizing process which may help a firm develop more effective business models, products, services, or technologies (Sukumar et al. 2020). Employing a product differentiation strategy (based on unique product features and high quality) has been recognised to positively affect the internationalisation of small firms (Ayob and Dana 2017). Effective employment of such a differentiation strategy can be considered another example of an opportunity seizing capability.

We consider opportunity seizing to be a process of strategically managing and leveraging tangible and intangible resources. It includes business model development, establishing decision-making protocols, establishing control and monitoring mechanisms, and building loyalty and commitment (Teece 2007).

3 Transnational Entrepreneurship: A Theoretical Framework

Opportunity sensing when combined with opportunity seizing leads to growth and wealth creation (Ireland et al. 2003). Improperly bundled resources "lead to poorly coordinated and often chaotic attempts to create maximum value by using the firm's capabilities" (Ireland et al. 2003: 979). Therefore, we posit that in order to assure optimal firm performance, both opportunity sensing and opportunity seizing processes are required (Teece 2007) for the development of TEs' dynamic capabilities. Furthermore, TEs' transnational dynamic capabilities play a mediating role between the ethnic advantage and social capital of TEs and their firm performance.

3.1 TEs' Dual Social Embeddedness

Social networks refer to "a web of personal connections and relationships for the purpose of securing favours in personal and/or organisational action" (Zhou et al. 2007: 674). Social networks are an important resource for entrepreneurial firms in general (Aldrich and Kim 2007) and for immigrant start-ups in particular (Chung and Whalen 2006; Chung and Tung 2013). Entrepreneurial firms have limited resources, and social networks provide complementary resources essential to establish and run a new venture (Greve and Salaff 2003). Considering that small entrepreneurial firms have limited resources, access to social networks becomes even more essential when these firms engage in internationalisation (Ratten et al. 2007). In a recent qualitative study of Italian small firm internationalisation, all the entrepreneurs specified that they developed international networks and established connections with international partners or representatives (Jafari-Sadeghi et al. 2020a).

The advantages of social ties are often referred to as social capital (Rezaei et al. 2020) which can be considered TEs' most valuable resource (Acquaah 2007; Prashantham 2011). Social embeddedness is defined as "the density and strength" of an immigrant's social ties within their local ethnic community and their COO (Nielsen and Riddle 2007: 5). Social embeddedness "not only helps in the founding of organisations, but also provides access to support during the entrepreneurial process" (Zaheer, Lamin, and Subramani 2008: 953).

In their study of immigrants from three Latin American countries with firms in the USA, Portes et al. (2002) found that the majority of TEs rely heavily on their social ties in both their COO and COR. TEs are in a unique position to develop *dual social embeddedness* because they have a deep understanding of the cultures of both their COO and COR because of their experiences in both countries. Because the TEs spend a great deal of time in the COO and the COR learning the culture, language, and social norms of both countries, this results in TEs being integrated into both countries and gives them a high degree of social embeddedness in the two countries. It would be very difficult, if not impossible, for a non-immigrant entrepreneur to develop such a high level of social embeddedness.

4 The Mediating Role of TEs' Dynamic Capabilities

In order to understand the effect of TEs' dual social embeddedness on firm performance, we argue that TEs' dynamic capabilities play a mediating role in this relationship. Drawing on the relational theory of social networks (Granovetter 1973), we suggest that TEs' social ties (ethnic and nonethnic ties in the COO and COR) may positively affect firm performance through integrating and reinforcing the TEs' opportunity sensing and opportunity seizing organisational processes.

The relational theory of social networks characterises social networks in terms of strong and weak ties (Granovetter 1973). The strength of a tie can be defined as a combination of "the amount of time, the emotional intensity, the intimacy (mutual confiding), and the reciprocal services which characterise the tie" (Granovetter 1973: 1361). Strong ties are costly to build and maintain, but they are more trustworthy because of the smaller scope. Weak ties, on the other hand, are not as expensive to build and maintain, but they have a broader scope that is better suited to transfer more, better, and novel information (Sharma and Blomstermo 2003; Uzzi 1997).

Social networks "facilitate the acquisition of knowledge and the discovery of opportunities" and contribute "to lowering risk and uncertainty inherent in international operations" (Weerawardena et al. 2007: 301). Multiple studies have established the significant benefits of social networks providing access to information and knowledge (Sharma and Blomstermo 2003; Zhou et al. 2007). In regard to the opportunity-seeking process, the relational theory of social networks suggests that *weak ties* are "more likely to link members of different small groups than are strong ties, which tend to be concentrated within particular groups" (Granovetter 1973: 1376), whereas *strong ties* "lead to overall fragmentation" (Granovetter 1973: 1378) which may isolate individuals from the novel information flow. In other words, weak ties provide more access to information than strong ties (Chung and Whalen 2006) and strengthen the opportunity sensing process in entrepreneurial firms.

In particular, TEs' ethnic ties in their COO allow them to acquire fresh and timely information directly from reliable sources (Lu et al. 2010). Most TEs originate in developing countries which are associated with a "high level of uncertainty due to the ineffective nature of market-supporting institutions in facilitating economic exchange and access to information, resources, and knowledge" (Acquaah 2007: 1239). This uncertainty in the business environment especially in developing countries makes TEs' weak ethnic ties more important to secure access to current information and knowledge.

In the COR, TEs may utilise their weak ethnic and nonethnic ties to gain information about "permits, laws, management practices, reliable suppliers, and promising business lines" (Aldrich and Waldinger 1990: 127). Several studies suggest that TEs experience a lower growth rate, or possibly failure if they do not develop a social network outside their ethnic communities (Prashantham and Dhanaraj 2010). TEs' nonethnic weak ties in the COR also aid the TEs in overcoming unfamiliarity with the COR's culture and institutions.

Key Point 1a: A higher degree of TEs' ethnic weak ties in the COO is positively associated with higher effectiveness of their opportunity sensing capability.

Key Point 1b: The simultaneous development of a higher degree of TEs' ethnic and nonethnic weak ties in the COR is positively associated with higher effectiveness of opportunity seizing capability.

The relational theory of social networks (Granovetter 1973) suggests that the entrepreneur's social ties are important for implementing strategy (Andersson and Wictor 2003) and seizing opportunities. The main differentiator between weak and strong ties is trust (Granovetter 1973). Entrepreneurs who use strong ties, which are built on trust, instead of costly formal contracts to seize opportunities are more likely to succeed (Uzzi 1997; White et al. 2018). To build trust among partner organisations, entrepreneurs must use strong ties (Lu et al. 2010; Rezaei et al. 2020). In addition, the entrepreneur's networks are vital to acquire essential complementary resources and capabilities to seize opportunities (Blyler and Coff 2003; Wu 2007). TEs may use their strong social ties with top managers in buyer or supplier organisations, government officials, and community leaders (Acquaah 2007) to access the resources they require to successfully seize opportunities (Mesquita and Lazzarini 2008).

TEs heavily depend on strong ties with their ethnic community and network relationships especially their ties to their COOs (Portes et al. 2002). Social activities such as participation in "hometown associations", "political activity", "sports clubs", and "charity organisations" develop strong ties between TEs and their COO which are instrumental in building strategic resources for their transnational business (Sequeira et al. 2009: 1035). Ethnic ties significantly affect where TEs choose to locate their new ventures and "serve as an important mechanism that ensures access to resources and key stakeholders, such as venture capitalists, the local government or local union leaders and employees" (Zaheer et al. 2008: 953). Strong social ties also support TEs in recruiting the human capital they need to seize opportunities and manage the business in the COO (Acquaah 2007). In other words, social networks are "instrumental for resource acquisition and eventual success" (Drori et al. 2009: 1011). Therefore, firms with high levels of social embeddedness are expected to outperform their competitors (Acquaah 2007; Nahapiet and Ghoshal 1998).

On the other hand, the strong ties which TEs develop in the COR may provide them with endorsement, financial capital, and committed human resources. Typically, TEs' entrepreneurial pursuits lack legitimacy, and TEs require endorsement in the COR to overcome this deficit (Lin et al. 1981). Being endorsed by nonethnic social networks provides stronger legitimacy than an endorsement by ethnic social networks. TEs may use ethnic rotating credit associations (Aldrich and Waldinger 1990) or ethnic venture capital (Zhang et al. 2016) to raise the required financial resources to seize opportunities (Moghaddam et al. 2017a). Strong social ties also allow TEs to develop the human capital (Acquaah 2007; Boudlaie et al. 2020; Leana and Van Buren 1999) they need to seize opportunities and manage the business in the COR. Newbert (2005: 67) describes the hiring process as an important part of the opportunity seizing process, and Yang et al. (2011) suggest that strong ethnic ties are important to hire committed and trustworthy employees. In a study of Chinese TEs in Canada, Wong and Ng (2002) found family networks were vital critical contributors to TEs' success. In a qualitative study of Indian TEs in the USA (Moghaddam 2015), successful entrepreneurs reported that they simultaneously established their strong ties with both ethnic and nonethnic communities in the COR.

Key Point 2a: The use of TEs' ethnic strong ties in the COO positively reinforces the effectiveness of the opportunity seizing capability.

Key Point 2b: The simultaneous use of TEs' ethnic and nonethnic strong ties in the COR positively reinforces the effectiveness of the opportunity seizing capability.

5 The Moderating Role of Institutional Distance

Understanding the context of an entrepreneurial firm is essential to understand the institutional forces that affect its entrepreneurial activities especially when there are transnational activities across developed and developing countries (Jafari-Sadeghi et al. 2020b; Jafari Sadeghi et al. 2019; Tabesh et al. 2019; Welter 2011). Institutional differences can "accentuate variations in the types and rates of the firms being created, why and how they are created, and how they evolve over time" (Zahra and Wright 2011: 73).

There are three institutional pillars: (1) the regulative pillar, which refers to the enforcement of rules; (2) the normative pillar which describes the code of conduct that must be followed to gain legitimacy; and (3) the cognitive pillar which refers to the mindset and understanding schema of individuals (Scott 1995). Institutional distance is defined as the extent of the dissimilarity "between the regulatory, cognitive, and normative institutions of two countries" (Kostova and Zaheer 1999: 71). A high institutional distance would exist when all three pillars are significantly different in different countries. The international business literature suggests that when there is a high institutional distance, transnational enterprises encounter serious challenges to become legitimate in the target country and to transfer strategic routines from the home country to foreign subsidiaries. A high institutional distance is viewed as a threat to creating an international firm with a competitive advantage.

International business mainstream literature considers institutional distance as a barrier that negatively affects internationalisation (Ghemawat 2001; Xu and Shenkar 2002). In contrast to that dominant narrative, we argue that higher institutional distance between the COO and the COR increases the value of TEs' dual embeddedness and allows them to explore opportunities not possible to other competitors (Drori et al. 2009) because institutional distance can be "an opportunity for arbitrage, complementarity or creative diversity"(Zaheer et al. 2012: 26). Other, more traditional, competitors may not be able to identify the opportunities TEs recognise because the TEs' exposure to and understanding of the institutional differences in both the COR and the COO allow the TEs to analyse the environment from a different perspective and recognise different opportunities.

Generally, TEs come from developing countries and migrate to developed countries (Riddle 2008), and the institutional distance between the COO and the COR tends to be large. Often, developing countries have weaker institutions, and "the role of social ties in facilitating access to resources is likely to be even stronger" (Zaheer et al. 2008: 953). When a TE from a COO with weak institutions starts a business in a COR with strong institutions, this creates what Griffith and Harvey (2001: 600) describe as a "market knowledge gap" (i.e. the knowledge difference between international partners related to the local market). Therefore, when there is a high institutional distance between the COO and the COR, TEs are more likely to sense opportunities because of their dual embeddedness.

The understanding context may also help us enrich our understanding of the actions entrepreneurs take (Clarysse et al. 2011; Zahra and Wright 2011). In order to successfully exploit an opportunity, a firm needs resources such as access to low-cost distribution networks, financial resources, and competent personnel; however, in many developing countries these resources are not "readily available because of the underdeveloped nature of the institutional structures" (Acquaah 2007: 2141). Most developing countries suffer from poor business infrastructure and a nontransparent legal and governance climate (Li et al. 2004); however, TEs may have an advantage because they can use their ethnic social networks in their COO as a substitute for the institutional infrastructure (Mesquita and Lazzarini 2008).

Key Point 3a: The higher the degree of the institutional distance between the COO and the COR, the more positive the effect of TEs' dual social embeddedness on the opportunity sensing capability.

Key Point 3b: The higher the degree of the institutional distance between the COO and the COR, the more positive the effect of TEs' dual social embeddedness on opportunity seizing capability.

6 Theoretical Implications and Conclusion

Entrepreneurship as a field of study is growing rapidly, but there is a criticism that it lacks commonly accepted and well-developed research paradigms (Aldrich 2000; Hitt et al. 2001). As a field, "we know little about how to incorporate the different dimensions of entrepreneurial activities into theory building and testing" (Zahra and Wright 2011: 72). Furthermore, entrepreneurship scholars tend to examine complex constructs such as internationalisation and capability development "without carefully recognising their micro-foundations" (Zahra and Wright 2011: 77). Transnational entrepreneurship literature is not an exception and is also characterised as fragmented (Lin and Tao 2012). In this chapter, we have briefly reviewed the transnational entrepreneurship literature from the past two decades and suggested a theoretical framework to better understand how TEs create competitive advantage. Figure 1 summarises how the dual embeddedness of TEs affects their firm performance through the mediating effect of opportunity sensing and opportunity seizing and the moderating effect of institutional distance between the COO and the COR. While ethnic ties play the key role in the COO, the *simultaneous use* of ethnic and nonethnic ties in the COR is essential for the success of transnational entrepreneurship. In other words, we suggest that ethnic and nonethnic ties of transnational entrepreneurs should be considered as complements (not as substitutes for each other) in the pursuit of successful transnational entrepreneurship.

The suggested theoretical framework contributes to the transnational entrepreneurship literature in several ways. First, we offer a theoretical framework to address a theoretical void in the transnational entrepreneurship literature. Table 1 lists some examples of the concepts included in our suggested theoretical framework. Second, the relationship between TEs' social network embeddedness and their firm performance is examined in terms of how strong and weak social ties may affect different dynamic capabilities in different ways. Based on the dynamic capability perspective, we explain how TEs may create a competitive advantage that is different from a

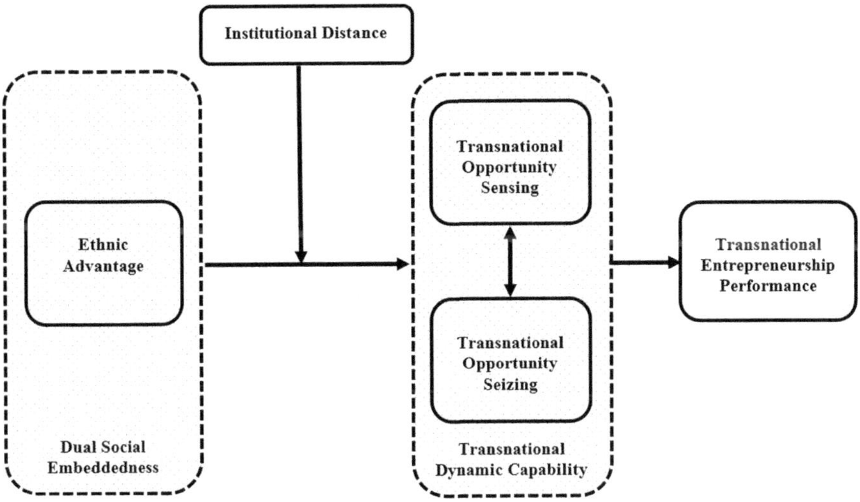

Fig. 1 Transnational entrepreneurship theoretical framework

Table 1 Examples of theoretical framework concepts

Theoretical perspective	Concept	Examples
Dual social embeddedness	COR ethnic weak tie	Ethnic community events (Rusinovic 2008)
	COR nonethnic weak tie	COR professional associations (Rusinovic 2008)
	COO ethnic weak tie	COO professional associations (Sequeira et al. 2009)
	COR ethnic strong tie	Ethnic rotating credit associations (Aldrich and Waldinger 1990)
	COR nonethnic strong tie	Nonethnic partners/suppliers (Aldrich and Waldinger 1990)
	COO ethnic strong tie	Community leaders (Acquaah 2007)
Dynamic capability perspective	Opportunity sensing process	Research and development (Teece 2007)
	Opportunity seizing process	Building employee loyalty (Teece 2007)
	Transnational dynamic capability	New product development (Eisenhardt and Martin 2000)
Institutional theory	Institutional distance	Regulative dissimilarity (Kostova and Zaheer 1999)
Strategic entrepreneurship perspective	Transnational performance	International sales (Wang and Liu 2015)
	Transnational entrepreneurship	Travel agency (Van Gelderen 2007)

traditional entrepreneur. The framework presented in Fig. 1 is consistent with the notion that "without dynamic capabilities to transform entrepreneurial resources into future advantages, entrepreneurial resources do not translate into start-up performance" (Wu 2007: 551).

Finally, our suggested theoretical framework is a response to Zahra and Wright's (2011) call to consider the context in developing theoretical models in the entrepreneurship field. Despite the recognition of the importance of the context in entrepreneurial activities (Shane and Venkataraman 2001), scholars search for general rules of entrepreneurship that ignore context (Zahra and Wright 2011). However, context is essential to theory building and meaningful theory testing (Whetten 1989). In our transnational entrepreneurship theoretical framework (Fig. 1), the contextual factor of institutional distance is theorised as a positive moderator which is interestingly in contrast to the common application of institutional distance as a negative moderator in international business literature (Kostova and Zaheer 1999; Xu and Shenkar 2002).

TEs are new important players in today's competitive global market, and they can benefit from a better understanding of how social networks may impact their international market development (Chen and Tan 2009). TEs should not solely focus on their ethnic social ties. That is why we suggest that ethnic ties in the COO and the COR may lead to higher firm performance when they are used in conjunction with nonethnic ties in the COR. Furthermore, it is crucial for TEs to understand the importance of dynamic capabilities in developing and sustaining their competitive advantage.

The trends of soaring immigration, especially of immigrants from developing countries to developed countries, the rapid globalisation process, and the rise in international business, indicate an upward trend in transnational entrepreneurship. Therefore, both theoretical and empirical research of transnational entrepreneurship will be needed to uncover the important aspects of transnational entrepreneurship.

References

Acquaah M (2007) Managerial social capital, strategic orientation, and organizational performance in an emerging economy. Strateg Manag J 28(12):1235–1255

Acs Z, Leo-Paul D, Jones MV (2003) Toward new horizons: the internationalisation of entrepreneurship. J Int Entrep 1(1):5

Adner R, Helfat CE (2003) Corporate effects and dynamic managerial capabilities. Strateg Manag J 24(10):1011–1025

Aldrich HE (2000) Learning together: national differences in entrepreneurship research. In: Sexton DL, Landström H (eds) Handbook of entrepreneurship. Blackwell Publishers, Oxford, U.K., pp 5–25

Aldrich HE, Kim PH (2007) Small worlds, infinite possibilities? How social networks affect entrepreneurial team formation and search. Strateg Entrep J 1(1/2):147–165

Aldrich HE, Waldinger R (1990) Ethnicity and entrepreneurship. Annu Rev Sociol 16:111–135

Alon I, Dana L-P, Jenkins A (2009) International business by SMEs: empirical findings from New Zealand. JIBE 10(2):59–78

Andersson S, Wictor I (2003) Innovative internationalisation in new firms: born globals–the Swedish case. J Int Entrep 1(3):249–275
Arthurs J, Busenitz L (2006) Dynamic capabilities and venture performance: the effects of venture capitalists. J Bus Ventur 21(2):195–215
Ayob AH, Dana L-P (2017) Product strategies for export ventures: an empirical investigation among SMEs in an emerging economy. Jurnal Pengurusan 50:25–33
Bayfield R, Dana LP, Stewart S (2009) Firm characteristics and internationalisation strategies: an empirical investigation of New Zealand exporters. IJGSB 3(3):275–287
Blyler M, Coff R (2003) Dynamic capabilities, social capital, and rent appropriation: ties that split pies. Strateg Manag J 24(7):677–686
Boudlaie H, Mahdiraji HA, Shamsi S, Jafari-Sadeghi V, Garcia-Perez A (2020) Designing a human resource scorecard: an empirical stakeholder-based study with a company culture perspective. JEMI 16(4):113–147
Chand M, Ghorbani M (2011) National culture, networks and ethnic entrepreneurship: a comparison of the Indian and Chinese immigrants in the US. Int Bus Rev 20(6):593–606
Chen W, Tan J (2009) Understanding transnational entrepreneurship through a network lens: theoretical and methodological considerations. Entrep Theory Pract 33(5):1079–1091
Chung HFL, Tung RL (2013) Immigrant social networks and foreign entry: Australia and New Zealand firms in the European Union and Greater China. Int Bus Rev 22(1):18–31
Chung E, Whalen K (2006) The embedded entrepreneur: recognizing the strength of ethnic social ties. NEJE 9(1):49–59
Clarysse B, Bruneel J, Wright M (2011) Explaining growth paths of young technology-based firms: structuring resource portfolios in different competitive environments. Strateg Entrep J 5 (2):137–157
Dana L-P (1987) Evaluating policies promoting entrepreneurship: a cross-cultural comparison of entrepreneurship case study: Singapore and Malaysia. J Small Bus Entrep 4(3):36–41
Dana L-P (2017) International entrepreneurship research: how it evolved and directions for the future. Int J Entrep Small Bus 30(4):477–489
Dana LP, Grimwood S, William G (2009a) Export incentives and international entrepreneurship in New Zealand firms. J Int Bus Entrep Dev 4(1–2):1–21
Dana LP, Hamilton RT, Wick K (2009b) Deciding to export: an exploratory study of Singaporean entrepreneurs. J Int Entrep 7(2):79–87
Dimitratos P, Buck T, Fletcher M, Li N (2016) The motivation of international entrepreneurship: the case of Chinese transnational entrepreneurs. Int Bus Rev 25(5):1103–1113
Drori I, Honig B, Wright M (2009) Transnational entrepreneurship: an emergent field of study. Entrep Theory Pract 33(5):1001–1022
Eckhardt J, Shane S (2003) Opportunities and entrepreneurship. J Manag 29(3):333–349
Eisenhardt K, Martin J (2000) Dynamic capabilities: what are they? Strateg Manag J 21 (10):1105–1121
Etemad H, Wright RW, Dana LP (2001) Symbiotic international business networks: collaboration between small and large firms. Thunderbird Int Bus Rev 43(4):481–499
Fregetto E (2004) Immigrant and ethnic entrepreneurship: a US perspective. In: Welsch HP (ed) Entrepreneurship: the way ahead. Routledge, New York, pp 253–268
Garousi Mokhtarzadeh N, Amoozad Mahdiraji H, Jafari-Sadeghi V, Soltani A, Abbasi Kamardi A (2020a) A product-technology portfolio alignment approach for food industry: a multi-criteria decision making with z-numbers. Br Food J 122(12):3947–3967
Garousi Mokhtarzadeh N, Amoozad Mahdiraji H, Jafarpanah I, Jafari-Sadeghi V, Cardinali S (2020b) Investigating the impact of networking capability on firm innovation performance: using the resource action-performance framework. J Intellect Cap 21(6):1009–1034
Ghemawat P (2001) Distance still matters. Harv Bus Rev 79(8):137–147
Gillespie K, Riddle L, Sayre E, Sturges D (1999) Diaspora interest in homeland investment. J Int Bus Stud 30(3):623–634
Granovetter MS (1973) The strength of weak ties. Am J Sociol 78(6):1360–1380

Greve A, Salaff JW (2003) Social networks and entrepreneurship. Entrep Theory Pract 28(1):1–22
Griffith D, Harvey M (2001) A resource perspective of global dynamic capabilities. J Int Bus Stud 32(3):597–606
Heilbrunn S, Kushnirovich N (2007) Immigrant and indigenous enterprises: similarities and differences. Int J Bus Perform Manag 9(3):344–361
Hitt M, Ireland R, Camp S, Sexton D (2001) Guest editors' introduction to the special issue strategic entrepreneurship: entrepreneurial strategies for wealth creation. Strateg Manag J 22(6):479–491
Ireland R, Hitt M, Sirmon D (2003) A model of strategic entrepreneurship: the construct and its dimensions. J Manag 29(6):963–989
Itzigsohn J, Cabral C, Medina E, Vazquez O (1999) Mapping Dominican transnationalism: narrow and broad transnational practices. Ethn Racial Stud 22(2):316–339
Jafari Sadeghi V, Biancone PP (2018) How micro, small and medium-sized enterprises are driven outward the superior international trade performance? A multidimensional study on Italian food sector. Res Int Bus Financ 45:597–606
Jafari Sadeghi V, Nkongolo-Bakenda J-M, Anderson RB, Dana L-P (2019) An institution-based view of international entrepreneurship: a comparison of context-based and universal determinants in developing and economically advanced countries. Int Bus Rev 28(6):101588
Jafari-Sadeghi V, Kimiagari S, Biancone Paolo P (2019) Level of education and knowledge, foresight competency and international entrepreneurship: a study of human capital determinants in the European countries. Eur Bus Rev 32(1):46–68
Jafari-Sadeghi V, Dutta Dev K, Ferraris A, Del Giudice M (2020a) Internationalisation business processes in an under-supported policy contexts: evidence from Italian SMEs. Bus Process Manag J 26(5):1055–1074
Jafari-Sadeghi V, Nkongolo-Bakenda J-M, Dana L-P, Anderson RB, Biancone PP (2020b) Home country institutional context and entrepreneurial internationalization: the significance of human capital attributes. J Int Entrep 18(2):165–195
Knight G, Madsen T, Servais P (2004) An inquiry into born-global firms in Europe and the USA. Int Mark Rev 21(6):645–665
Kor Y, Mahoney J (2005) How dynamics, management, and governance of resource deployments influence firm-level performance. Strateg Manag J 26(5):489–496
Kostova T, Zaheer S (1999) Organizational legitimacy under conditions of complexity: the case of the multinational enterprise. Acad Manag Rev 24(1):64–81
Kyle D (1999) The Otavalo trade diaspora: social capital and transnational entrepreneurship. Ethn Racial Stud 22(2):422–446
Landolt P, Autler L, Baires S (1999) From hermano lejano to hermano mayor: the dialectics of Salvadoran transnationalism. Ethn Racial Stud 22(2):290–315
Leana CR, Van Buren HJ (1999) Organizational social capital and employment practices. Acad Manag Rev 24(3):538–555
Li S, Park S, Li S (2004) The great leap forward: the transition from relation-based governance to rule-based governance. Organ Dyn 33(1):63–78
Lin X, Tao S (2012) Transnational entrepreneurs: characteristics, drivers, and success factors. J Int Entrep 10(1):1–20
Lin N, Ensel WM, Vaughn JC (1981) Social resources and strength of ties: structural factors in occupational status attainment. Am Sociol Rev 46(4):393–405
Lu Y, Zhou L, Bruton G, Li W (2010) Capabilities as a mediator linking resources and the international performance of entrepreneurial firms in an emerging economy. J Int Bus Stud 41 (3):419–436
Mesquita LF, Lazzarini SG (2008) Horizontal and vertical relationships in developing economies: implications for SMEs' access to global markets. Acad Manag J 51(2):359–380
Moghaddam K (2015) The ingredients of a success recipe. SAJGBR 4(2):162–189
Moghaddam K, Bosse D, Provance M (2016) Strategic alliances of entrepreneurial firms: value enhancing then value destroying. Strateg Entrep J 10(2):153–168

Moghaddam K, Aidov A, DuVal C, Azarpanah S (2017a) High-growth entrepreneurial firm funding: a qualitative study of native-born and immigrant entrepreneurs. Ventur Cap 19 (1–2):75–94
Moghaddam K, Tabesh P, Weber T, Azarpanah S (2017b) The effect of culture on opportunity recognition: a qualitative study of immigrant and native-born entrepreneurs. Int J Entrep Small Bus 31(2):309–324
Moghaddam K, Rustambekov E, Weber T, Azarpanah S (2018) Transnational entrepreneurship, social networks, and institutional distance: toward a theoretical framework. NEJE 21(1):45–64
Nahapiet J, Ghoshal S (1998) Social capital, intellectual capital, and the organizational advantage. Acad Manag Rev 23(2):242–266
Newbert S (2005) New firm formation: a dynamic capability perspective. J Small Bus Manag 43 (1):55–78
Nielsen, T. M., & Riddle, L. (2007). Why diasporas invest in the homeland: a conceptual model of motivation. In *Academy of Management annual meeting*. Philadelphia, PA
Portes A, Guarnizo L, Haller W (2002) Transnational entrepreneurs: an alternative form of immigrant economic adaptation. Am Sociol Rev 67(2):278–298
Prashantham S (2011) Social capital and Indian micromultinationals. Br J Manag 22(1):4–20
Prashantham S, Dhanaraj C (2010) The dynamic influence of social capital on the international growth of new ventures. J Manag Stud 47(6):967–994
Ratten V, Dana L-P, Han M, Welpe I (2007) Internationalisation of SMEs: european comparative studies. Int J Entrep Small Bus 4(3):361–379
Rezaei M, Jafari-Sadeghi V, Bresciani S (2020) What drives the process of knowledge management in a cross-cultural setting: the impact of social capital. Eur Bus Rev 32(3):485–511
Riddle L (2008) Diasporas: exploring their development potential. ESR Review 10(2):28–36
Rusinovic K (2008) Moving between markets? Immigrant entrepreneurs in different markets. Int J Entrep Behav Res 14(6):440–454
Sadeghi VJ, Biancone PP, Giacoma C, Secinaro S (2018) How does export compliance influence the internationalization of firms: is it a thread or an opportunity? J Glob Entrep Res 8(3):1–15
Sadeghi VJ, Biancone PP, Anderson RB, Nkongolo-Bakenda J-M (2019) International entrepreneurship by particular people 'on their own terms': a study on the universal characteristics of entrepreneurs in evolving economies. Int J Entrep Small Bus 37(2):288–308
Sapienza H, Autio E, George G, Zahra S (2006) A capabilities perspective on the effects of early internationalization on firm survival and growth. Acad Manag Rev 31(4):914–933
Scott WR (1995) Institutions and organizations. Foundations for organizational science. A Sage Publication Series, London
Sequeira J, Carr J, Rasheed A (2009) Transnational entrepreneurship: determinants of firm type and owner attributions of success. Entrep Theory Pract 33(5):1023–1044
Shane S, Venkataraman S (2000) The promise of entrepreneurship as a field of research. Acad Manag Rev 25(1):217–226
Shane S, Venkataraman S (2001) Entrepreneurship as a field of research: a response to Zahra and Dess, Singh, and Erikson. Acad Manag Rev 26(1):13–16
Sharma D, Blomstermo A (2003) The internationalization process of born globals: a network view. Int Bus Rev 12(6):739–753
Shinnar RS, Aguilera MB, Lyons TS (2011) Co-ethnic markets: financial penalty or opportunity? Int Bus Rev 20(6):646–658
Smith AW, Moghaddam K, Lanivich SE (2019) A set-theoretic investigation into the origins of creation and discovery opportunities. Strateg Entrep J 13(1):75–92
Sukumar A, Jafari-Sadeghi V, Garcia-Perez A, Dutta Dev K (2020) The potential link between corporate innovations and corporate competitiveness: evidence from IT firms in the UK. J Knowl Manag 24(5):965–983
Tabesh P, Tabesh P, Moghaddam K (2019) Individual and contextual influences on framing effect: evidence from the Middle East. J Gen Manag 45(1):30–39

Teece DJ (2007) Explicating dynamic capabilities: the nature and microfoundations of (sustainable) enterprise performance. Strateg Manag J 28(13):1319–1350
Teece D, Pisano G, Shuen A (1997) Dynamic capabilities and strategic management. Strateg Manag J 18(7):509–533
Uzzi B (1997) Social structure and competition in interfirm networks: the paradox of embeddedness. Adm Sci Q 42(1):35–67
Vaaler PM (2011) Immigrant remittances and the venture investment environment of developing countries. J Int Bus Stud 42(9):1121–1149
Van Gelderen M (2007) Country of origin as a source of business opportunities. Int J Entrep Small Bus 4(4):419–430
Wang Q, Liu C (2015) Transnational activities of immigrant-owned firms and their performances in the USA. Small Bus Econ 44(2):345–359
Weerawardena J, Mort GS, Liesch PW, Knight G (2007) Conceptualizing accelerated internationalization in the born global firm: a dynamic capabilities perspective. J World Bus 42(3):294–306
Welter F (2011) Contextualizing entrepreneurship—conceptual challenges and ways forward. Entrep Theory Pract 35(1):165–184
Whetten DA (1989) What constitutes a theoretical contribution? Acad Manag Rev 14(4):490–495
White GO, Hemphill T, Weber T, Moghaddam K (2018) Institutional origins of WOFS formal contracting: a judicial arbitrariness perspective. Int Bus Rev 27(3):654–668
Winter S (2003) Understanding dynamic capabilities. Strateg Manag J 24(10):991–995
Wong LL, Ng M (2002) The emergence of small transnational enterprise in Vancouver: the case of Chinese entrepreneur immigrants. Int J Urban Reg Res 26(3):508–530
Wu L (2007) Entrepreneurial resources, dynamic capabilities and start-up performance of Taiwan's high-tech firms. J Bus Res 60(5):549–555
Xu D, Shenkar O (2002) Institutional distance and the multinational enterprise. Acad Manag Rev 27 (4):608–618
Yang C, Colarelli SM, Han K, Page R (2011) Start-up and hiring practices of immigrant entrepreneurs: an empirical study from an evolutionary psychological perspective. Int Bus Rev 20 (6):636–645
Yeung HW (2009) Transnationalizing entrepreneurship: a critical agenda for economic geography. Prog Hum Geogr 33(2):210–235
Zafarullah M, Ali M, Young S (1997) The internationalization of the small firm in developing countries—exploratory research from Pakistan. J Glob Mark 11(3):21–40
Zaheer S, Lamin A, Subramani M (2008) Cluster capabilities or ethnic ties? Location choice by foreign and domestic entrants in the services offshoring industry in India. J Int Bus Stud 40 (6):944–968
Zaheer S, Schomaker MS, Nachum L (2012) Distance without direction: restoring credibility to a much-loved construct. J Int Bus Stud 43(1):18–27
Zahra SA, Wright M (2011) Entrepreneurship's next act. Acad Manag Perspect 25(4):67–83
Zhang J, Wong PK, Ho YP (2016) Ethnic enclave and entrepreneurial financing: Asian venture capitalists in Silicon Valley. Strateg Entrep J 10(3):318–335
Zhou L, Wu W, Luo X (2007) Internationalization and the performance of born-global SMEs: the mediating role of social networks. J Int Bus Stud 38(4):673–690
Zimmer C, Aldrich H (1987) Resource mobilization through ethnic networks: kinship and friendship ties of shopkeepers in England. Sociol Perspect 30(4):422–445

Kaveh Moghaddam is an Associate Professor of International Strategy and Entrepreneurship at the University of Houston—Victoria. His primary research interests are strategic entrepreneurship and internationalisation strategies of emerging market firms. He has published his research in several academic journals including *Strategic Entrepreneurship Journal*, *Journal of International Management*, and *International Business Review*. He has served on the *Journal of International Management* editorial board.

Thomas Weber is an Associate Professor of Management at the University of Southern Indiana. His research interests include strategic management, caring, and innovation. He has published his research in several academic journals including *Entrepreneurship, Theory and Practice*, *Journal of International Management*, and *International Business Review*.

Internationalisation of SMEs and Distant Markets: The Networking and Service Functions of Global Cities

Philippe Régnier and Pascal Wild

1 Introduction

Internationalisation is the most intricate strategy that can be undertaken especially by SMEs (Dana 2017; Dana and Wright 2009; Fernández and Nieto 2005; Jafari Sadeghi et al. 2019a). Since the early 2000s, about 100 cities are ranked annually as global cities. This chapter explores conceptually and empirically as a frontier research issue whether the world service functions of global cities play a role in the internationalisation of SMEs and globally born start-ups.

Most studies in international business management (IBM) have been devoted so far to the status, motivation, pace, and networking capacity of SMEs before and during their internationalisation. We know little about their modes of identifying and localising external resources and advanced services to explore and access foreign markets, and even less in the case of so-called globally born start-ups.

Economic history and geography, international development economics, and urban sociology have demonstrated for long that "world cities" play a significant business development and intermediation role. More recent literature shows that these cities, renamed and ranked as global cities since the beginning of the twenty-first century, provide a high concentration of advanced producer services (APS) offering various types of support to multinational corporations and large firms (Acs 2002; Acs and Armington 2004; Acs et al. 2008; Currid 2006; Doel and Hubbard 2002; Friedmann 1986; Sassen 2001; Taylor 2004). This may also apply to the internationalisation of SMEs and start-ups, at least through similar or different modes. However, this assumption should be empirically validated and lead to

P. Régnier (✉) · P. Wild
School of Management-Freiburg, University of Applied Sciences (HES-SO), Fribourg, Switzerland
e-mail: Philippe.Regnier@hefr.ch; Pascal.Wild@hefr.ch

V. Jafari-Sadeghi et al. (eds.), *Empirical International Entrepreneurship*, Contributions to Management Science,
https://doi.org/10.1007/978-3-030-68972-8_3

additional inputs to theories dealing with the economic functions of global cities. Therefore, this chapter begins by introducing an interdisciplinary conceptual research framework, which combines inputs from international business management (IBM) devoted to the internationalisation of firms and inputs from other disciplines (history, geography, economics, sociology) studying the economic functions of global cities in particular.

Secondly, it reviews how recent studies and rankings of global cities are based on mixed research methods, which measure the concentration of international business activities in these major urban hubs and their interconnectivity in support of global finance, innovation, technology, trade, and other ventures. These methods enable (1) to quantify the size of manufacturing and tertiary activities carried by multinational firms in global cities and (2) to qualify the variety of advanced producer services (APS) concentrated there to facilitate business flows at regional, continental, and intercontinental levels. They stop short of studying other categories of firms except for MNCs, and they have completely neglected the case of internationalising SMEs and their possible linkages with global cities.

The authors suggest going beyond existing knowledge of SME internationalisation. They consider the supportive functions of global cities as equally applicable to this category of firms. Some research methods can be used to demonstrate that global cities act as advanced entrepreneurial ecosystems, which promote not only large firms but also SMEs and globally born start-ups. Some empirical work results are presented to illustrate this research objective.

2 Interdisciplinary Conceptual Research Framework

This section suggests an interdisciplinary approach to analyse how and how far global cities may foster internationalisation of firms and SMEs and start-ups in particular. The construction of a conceptual research framework needs to combine contributions from management sciences and SME internationalisation knowledge more specifically on the one hand, and from disciplines such as history, geography, economics, and sociology, on the other hand.

2.1 Management and SME Internationalisation

This subject has been studied conceptually and empirically since the 1970s, but no single management theory has been able to capture all the dimensions of SME internationalisation (Che Senik et al. 2011; Coviello and McAuley 1999; Gankema et al. 2000; Fujita 1998; Jafari-Sadeghi et al. 2020b; Rialp and Rialp 2001; Zahra and George 2002; Zucchella and Scabini 2007).

2.2 *Limitations in the Use of MNC Theories*

Theories dealing with the internationalisation of multinational corporations (MNCs) cannot be fully applied to SMEs (Ruzzier et al. 2006). The reasons rely on differences in terms of size, resources, outreach strategy, and management. However, they draw attention to some essential factors, for instance, the high transaction costs to internationalise. As SMEs have limited internal capacities, the optimal combination of internal/external resources is crucial.

2.3 *Incremental Theory*

The so-called Uppsala theory has made a considerable contribution by suggesting that firms and especially SMEs go international through continuous foreign market learning (Johanson and Vahlne 1977, 1990). Accessing incrementally new "psychic distant" markets involves the understanding of differences in language, behaviour, and business practices.

Since the late 1990s, a new type of SMEs has been identified as "born global" (Bell et al. 2003; Oviatt and McDougall 1994; Schueffel and Baldegger 2008). They have global activities since the very early phase of their creation (i.e. starts-up in ICTs) and seem to skip essential stages of the gradual process, such as described by the Uppsala theory. Thanks to specific skills and/or proprietary technologies used as a competitive advantage (Garousi Mokhtarzadeh et al. 2020; Sadraei et al. 2018), globally born start-ups internationalise rapidly and do not fear "psychic" distance (McDougall-Covin et al. 2014).

2.4 *Network and Resource-Based Approaches*

"Internal" and "external" resources represent the total assets of SMEs (Ruzzier et al. 2006; Zucchella et al. 2007; Zucchella and Scabini 2007). To develop competitive advantages overseas, SMEs need to combine both. The external ones correspond to the capacity to access international business networks and advanced services abroad, as suggested by the revision of the Uppsala Model by its original authors (Johanson and Vahlne 2009).

2.5 *Support of Advanced Producer Services*

SME internationalisation relies on external business facilitation provided by advanced producer services (APS), also called business development services (BDS) (Fujita 1998; Bell et al. 2003). A clear distinction is necessary between financial services (such as accounting, banking, insurance) and technical ones (such as certification, marketing, logistics, packaging, transportation). It also refers to strategic B2B partnerships and various formal/informal inputs provided by interpersonal networks. When SMEs target distant markets, the distance is not only geographic but also linguistic, cultural, behavioural, and psychological, resulting in uncertainties and risks. To minimise them, SMEs have to enter relevant networks (Schweizer 2013; Mokhtarzadeh et al. 2020; Sadeghi et al. 2017). This process contains four phases:

1. Recognition of the liability of outsidership (not being part/inside the relevant networks in the foreign market of destination)
2. Identification of the relevant network(s)
3. Mobilisation of internal capabilities and corresponding
4. Accessing, managing, and leveraging opportunities identified in the relevant network(s)

Empirically, existing data is mostly limited to SME exports and is systematically collected in OECD countries and in a few emerging ones. Most SMEs tend to expand overseas gradually and cautiously, and more rapidly in the case of globally born start-ups. SMEs tend to internationalise first in trans-frontier markets and other markets of proximity. Accessing distant foreign markets is more difficult due to high risks and transaction costs.

In conclusion, SMEs need to identify both functional and social networks to access reliable business information and APS to penetrate foreign markets. Such facilities are even more crucial in the case of emerging and unknown markets, where institutional voids and business conditions' instability prevail. It is anticipated that urban hubs and global cities, in particular, provide a high concentration of such facilitation services.

3 Global Cities and SME Internationalisation

The study of world cities has generally focused on the role of urban centres during various historical waves of globalisation, especially since colonial times (Abu-Lughod 1989; Braudel 1984). However, the concept of global cities is very recent. Geographers and sociologists have introduced it since the 1990s (Castells 1996, 2011; Sassen 1991, 2001; Taylor 2004, 2011). Subsequent empirical research has led to the construct of annual rankings of about 100 global cities during the last 15 years. Global cities are viewed as a global city network of major nodes in the world economic system.

3.1 Cities as Economic Command and Control Centres

Throughout history, cities have been urban centres where important decisions would be taken at national, regional, and even continental levels. Capital cities can play this role but also other types of cities controlling major economic and financial flows. Under various modes of the international division of labour, interlinkages among cities lead to a hierarchical categorisation between core/primary and peripheral/ secondary cities, depending mainly on their economic articulations (Friedmann 1986. Taylor 2004).

3.2 The Concentration of Entrepreneurship and Supportive Services

Global cities are dynamic centres concentrating human skills, manufacturing activities and services, with a high propensity for innovation and international exchange (Amin Moghadasi et al. 2017; Boudlaie et al. 2020; Gill et al. 2017; Jacobs 1984; Jafari-Sadeghi et al. 2019; Sassen 1991). Due to globalisation, Sassen has introduced the concept of interconnected cities.

Thanks to ICTs, products and services can be connected across borders, independently from their spatial location, and global cities take leadership in this transnational process. Such interconnectivity stimulates highly entrepreneurial ecosystems based on information, knowledge, and creativity in global cities (Acs and Armington 2004; Acs et al. 2008; Currid 2006, Fritsch and Falck 2007; Rezaei et al. 2020).

Based on over 70 national country reports, *the Global Entrepreneurship Monitor* (various years) permits to gather data on the role of selected global cities as facilitators of corporate internationalisation, mainly MNCs. Global cities offer top quality entrepreneurial environments, which facilitate smaller firms and even SMEs to venture into domestic, regional, and intercontinental markets. Micro processes interconnect different spaces, time zones, and both real and virtual flows. Using global cities as market entry points (Zucchella and Scabini 2007), a firm can benefit strategically from reliable business information services, rapid access to value-chain B2B linkages, highly specialised professionals, innovation hubs and knowledge spin-offs, first-class infrastructure, and logistics.

4 Proposal for a Conceptual Research Framework

As territorial nodes essential to world trade and economic, financial, and knowledge flows, global cities are major hubs for MNCs and their affiliates and provide an exceptional density of APS and specialised networks (functional and social ones)

Table 1 Interdisciplinary conceptual research framework

	SME internationalisation	Global cities
Role of business networks	Increased theoretical and empirical applications of network approaches explain the internationalisation process (Johanson and Vahlne 2009)	Global cities as products of the increasingly intertwined global economy, as "nodes and hubs" in the global network of economic flows (Castells 1996, Sassen 1991, 2001)
Role of specialised services	APS/BDS facilitate SME internationalisation processes, in particular, when considering their lack of resources and knowledge	Supply of highly specialised and globally operating APS/BDS is a core function of global cities, which are considered as "global service centres" (Sassen 1991, 2001; Taylor 2001)
Role of market distance	The scientific community argues that geographic and psychic distance decrease SME's capacity to access local markets	Global cities have a strong embedded relationship with their nearby hinterland. The "hinterworld" defines the much wider area in which global cities' APS provide their services
Tentative interdisciplinary research hypothesis	Global cities' APS and BDS facilitate SME process of internationalisation	

linking hinterlands to regional and world markets. The authors suggest that empirical research can show that global cities also serve transnational SMEs and globally born start-ups. For them, high costs to access APS concentrated in global cities may be compensated by a secured reduction of business risks and downstream transaction expenses. For start-ups, global cities may be the only locations to find appropriate incubation services and funding opportunities.

The proposed conceptual framework (see Table 1) adopts an interdisciplinary approach combining:

1. SME internationalisation processes based on the use of APS and professional networks
2. And the specialisation of such networks and services concentrated in global cities to help SMEs and start-ups to access foreign markets, and especially distant ones

5 Exploring the Economic Functions of Global Cities: A Research Methodology

The collection and analysis of data on SME internationalisation and their functional use of global cities can proceed from a methodology using mixed research methods.

- Quantitative research methods help to gather information on (1) the numbers and directions of SME internationalisation and on (2) the numbers and size of corporate activities and related APS/BDS concentrated in global cities.
- Qualitative research methods enable to select (1) specific direct or indirect routes adopted by internationalising SMEs, with a possible focus on distant and non-traditional markets versus classical markets of proximity, and (2) the typology of APS/BDS concentrated in global cities and utilised by SMEs for various market diversification purposes.

The use of mixed research methods to study the service functions of global cities will be clarified thereafter.

Quantitative and qualitative tools to analyse SME internationalisation and the use of global cities will be exposed in the third section of this chapter.

6 Research on Classification and Rankings of Global Cities

The concept of "global city" was first introduced at Princeton University by sociologist Saskia Sassen in her book *The Global City: New York, London, Tokyo* (Sassen 1991). The term "world city" goes back to the nineteenth century. It was used to describe the control of a disproportionate amount of global business as suggested by the *Illustrated London News* related to the port of Liverpool in 1886.

The first attempt to categorise and rank global cities was made in 1998 by British academics (Beaverstock et al. 1999). They established *the Globalisation and World Cities Research Network* (GaWC) as a kind of roster ranking cities based on their connectivity through four APS: accountancy, advertising, banking/finance, and law.

The GaWC research network conducts research focused on the external relations of global cities. Until its inception, most research efforts went into studying the internal structures of individual cities and comparative analyses between a few cities. Special attention was also devoted to studying the connectivity of each major city with the global network of cities (Taylor et al. 2009). The GaWC selected 316 cities to cover all world regions. It included APS firms with a minimum of 15 offices with at least one in each prime region: North America, Western Europe, and Pacific Asia. The "extra-locational functions" and size of such firms in each city such as regional headquarters or a subsidiary office are recorded by giving each firm value numbers between 0 and 5, whereas an ordinary presence is accounted with a 2, extra-size with a 3, and a regional headquarter with a 4 (Taylor 2001). Thus, a matrix with 316 cities multiplied by 100 firms was constructed, in which the world city network can be interpreted as the combination of the number of service firms as major actors producing various types of global networking flows (Sassen 1991, 2001; Taylor 2001, 2004).

The GaWC inventory identifies three levels of global cities and several sub-ranks (Taylor 2001; GaWC 2021). Since 2004, it has included additional indicators, which put more weight on economic factors than on cultural or political

Table 2 Classification of global cities by ranking group

Group	Description
Alpha ++	Cities fully integrated into the global economy (such as London, New York, Tokyo) compared to other cities
Alpha +	Cities providing advanced service niches to the global economy
Alpha/alpha –	Cities linking major economic regions to the global economy
Beta	Cities linking moderate economic regions to the global economy
Gamma	Cities linking smaller economic regions to the global economy
Sufficiency	Cities offering a sufficient concentration of services so as not to depend on other global cities

Source: Taylor (2001), GaWC (2021)

ones. Since 2008, it has led to the annual classification of about 100 global cities (Table 2).

In 2008, in conjunction with the Chicago-based consulting firm A.T. Kearney and the Chicago Council on Global Affairs, *Foreign Policy* published a ranking of global cities (Global Cities Index and Emerging Cities Outlook 2012). The main parameters are "Business activity" (30%), "Human capital" (30%), "Information exchange" (15%), "Cultural experience" (15%), and "Political engagement" (10%).This index has been updated every 2 years.

In all rankings, New York, London, and Tokyo rank first, and the majority of global cities are concentrated in the OECD economies. However, emerging economies are also present, especially in East Asia: Beijing, Hong Kong, Singapore, and Tokyo are among the top ten global cities, whereas Seoul (12th), Shanghai (18th), Kuala Lumpur (39th), and Bangkok (42nd) are among the top 50. However, only 3 first ranking global cities are present in Africa: Cairo, Casablanca, and Johannesburg (with Lagos emerging as a potential fourth one).

On the economic front, the density of business activities, human capital, and information exchange are key research parameters to differentiate global cities from others. Empirical research tends to focus on the numbers of MNCs and their affiliates concentrated in global cities, including their legal status, the size of their paid-up capital and workforce, their annual turnover, the type and measure of their local and external transactions in commodity trading, manufacturing, or services. The top 12 global cities host about 70% of MNC headquarters, and the top 4 counts for 46% (Clark 2013).

In practice, rankings are regularly scrutinised by policymakers to maintain the attractiveness of global cities and to promote both competitiveness and interconnectivity among them. This is the case, for example, in the financial sector, between London and Frankfurt in Europe, or between Dubai, Mumbai, Hong Kong, Singapore, and Tokyo in East Asia. Another example is Casablanca, where municipal authorities have decided to construct a brand new financial city to attract more foreign investment and remain among the top three global cities in Africa.

7 Research on Advanced Producer Services (APS)

The strong presence of MNCs and their affiliates in global cities generate a specific density of APS and BDS serving these corporations and other large firms producing goods and/or services. APS and BDS contribute to corporate globalisation through worldwide connections among global cities (i.e. between financial markets) and through their respective articulation functions between global and regional markets (Clark 2013).

Contrary to MNCs and large firms, the physical presence of foreign SMEs in global cities is seldom, except for small numbers of so-called transnational SMEs and globally born start-ups. However, this significant difference does not mean that smaller firms do not use global cities to access regional and global markets. Recent research trends (e.g. Jafari Sadeghi et al. 2019b; Dana et al. 2009a, b; Ratten et al. 2017) go in several directions, such as exploring SME internationalisation to distant emerging markets and the resolution of institutional voids and other types of risks, or such as exploring various modes of SME internationalisation along with cognitive or technical sets of global value chains.

7.1 APS and SME Internationalisation

APS concentrated in global cities are major facilitators for SME integration in both cognitive and technical modes of the international division of labour. They provide critical support to access reliable business information, market intelligence, first-class knowledge, specialised human skills, and other unique inputs. They supply appropriate communication tools, financial and technical logistics, marketing/delivery functions, transportation networks, after-sale, and maintenance. APS concentrated in global cities are not for free, especially for SMEs with limited financial resources, but they are indispensable to reduce distance vis-a-vis markets of final destination and to minimise risks and full transaction costs (Fig. 1).

Most internationalising SMEs are primarily active in trading. They look for their own performance through dynamic exports. In this context, a variety of APS concentrated in global cities supply three types of services addressing motivations,

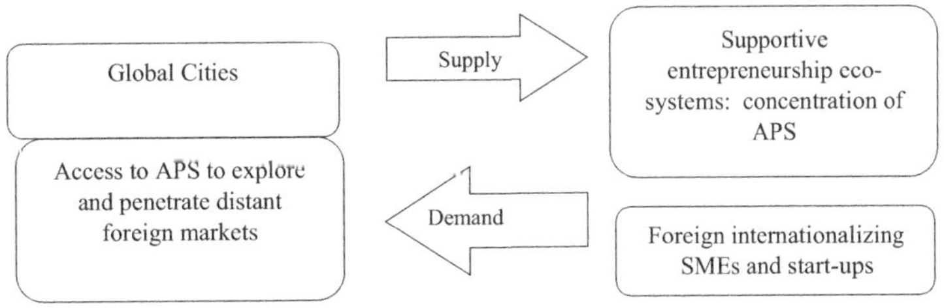

Fig. 1 Demand and supply of APS based in global cities

information, and operations of SMEs. Motivation and information services are needed to identify not only business opportunities but also market entry barriers (Jafari-Sadeghi 2020). Operational services are supplied to compensate for the absence of SME internal resources to conduct transactions overseas. The agglomeration of APS providers in global cities contributes to reducing distance vis-à-vis markets of final destination (Goerzen et al. 2013). The more expensive international transaction costs are, the more SMEs rely on external services to keep control and maximise business trust vis-à-vis both suppliers and clients—what APS can offer. Furthermore, global cities are more than once exclusive providers of highly specialised services such as telecoms, digitalisation, financial and legal counsel, lab control and testing, certification, after-sale, and maintenance.

Internationalising SMEs may also decide to proceed beyond exports and enter various types of financial and technological ventures with overseas partners (Dana et al. 2016). Sometimes, they opt for the direct majority or full ownership investment to produce and sell on regional and global markets. Such deals are long term and imply sophisticated operations compared to import-export transactions. They need a wide variety of APS, mostly concentrated in global cities.

7.2 Advanced Producer Services and Globally Born Start-Ups

Thanks to specific skills and/or proprietary technologies used as a competitive advantage, globally born start-ups internationalise rapidly (McDougall-Covin et al. 2014). Within a couple of years after incubation, their agility permits to expand at least into two different continents.

According to the data, as derived from the GEM (Global Entrepreneurship Report) project, global cities act as highly advanced entrepreneurship ecosystems (Acs et al. 2008). Their accumulation of knowledge and sophisticated human capital lead to innovation dynamics. Their modes of governance promote competitive systems of innovation to anticipate international processes of R&D, creative destruction, and production of new products and services (Jafari-Sadeghi et al. 2020a; Sukumar et al. 2020). The introduction of ICTs and industry 4.0 more recently reinforce the role of central and interconnected innovation hubs played by global cities.

Thanks to various types of APS, BDS, and public-private partnerships, global cities have become key actors in the incubation and launch of start-ups. First-class labs and universities, science and technology parks, MNC affiliates and subsidiaries, para-public institutions, business angels, and venture capitalists provide an appropriate environment for start-up creation and outreach of global markets. Globally born start-ups can emerge in one global city and connect right away to the world. Some of them are even initiated between two or several global cities at the same time by accessing and combining various segments of human, financial, and technical capital and instant communication/digital services in each of them.

As shown in the third section of this chapter, empirical research methods do not target any more only classical patterns of SME internationalisation but also new modes of internationalisation among young globally born start-ups, which are mainly micro and small enterprises in their first years of life. Recent studies in various OECD economies indicate the rapid rise of this new category of firms in national surveys dealing with SME internationalisation. This phenomenon is also observed in emerging economies, and their global cities in particular such as the urban triangle Hong Kong-Guangzhou-Shenzen denominated as China's Silicon Valley.

8 Research Focus on SME Internationalisation and the Role of Global Cities

As announced in the introduction, a research methodology is presented thereafter to envisage whether and how internationalising SMEs utilise the economic nodding functions of global cities to access distant markets. Contrary to markets of proximity as the first and most frequent destinations of SMEs, distant markets require sophisticated strategies and substantial internal and external resources (Régnier and Wild 2017, 2018; Sadeghi and Biancone 2018).

Mixed methods can be used here and combine quantitative and qualitative research tools to reach two objectives:

1. A first and mainly quantitative research objective aims to survey at the national or infra-national level representative samples of internationalising SMEs. A distinction has to be made between classical SMEs using gradual modes of internationalisation (in terms of pace, scope, and timing) and globally born start-ups internationalising rapidly to several continents in parallel.
2. A second research objective (of a quantitative and qualitative nature) needs the design of national or infra national SME internationalisation surveys in such a way that SME market destinations (proximity versus distant ones) are clearly documented. Also, the research work must identify and specify the end market role or the final market intermediation functions of the 100 global cities ranked worldwide, in particular those localised distantly from the SME country of origin. Precise qualitative research questions can clarify what kind of financial and non-financial services are occasionally or more regularly utilised by internationalising SMEs.

Several quantitative and qualitative research adjustments can complement these two objectives:

- Numbers, density, and specialisation of SMEs may vary among countries, being, for instance, much higher in Western Europe and Japan compared to Australia, Canada, and the USA or emerging countries in Africa, Asia, Latin America, and the Middle East.

- Numbers and profiles of internationalising SMEs to markets of proximity versus distant ones may also vary, small-sized economies (especially in Europe) being much more export-oriented than larger economies benefiting from large domestic markets.
- The degree, pace, and scope of internationalisation may be very different from one SME to the next. For some, internationalisation is just a small portion of their annual turnover. For others, it is their main performance driver due to their full export-orientation and/or niche specialisation. Their family or non-family business status may also play a differentiated role, some family-based SMEs not targeting growth necessarily.
- Non-internationalised SMEs represent the bulk of any domestic economy. A portion of them may be interested in expanding abroad and express focused informational, and service needs to be met by global cities.
- The profile and strategy of globally born start-ups are different from classical SMEs and are fully oriented towards rapid internationalisation. This is why they must be studied as a distinct sub-group when conducting SME internationalisation surveys.
- The entrepreneurial ecosystems of global cities may vary in their organisation and distribution of APS and BDS. Global cities also proceed under different socio-economic regimes at national and local government levels, in both industrialised and emerging countries.
- SME and start-up internationalisation may benefit from APS concentrated in global cities existing in countries of SME origin and countries of SME market destination. This can be of significant competitive advantage, especially in case of SME proximity to such cities, such as in small, highly export-oriented economies in Europe or neighbour emerging countries close to city-states (such as Dubai, Hong Kong, or Singapore).

Since the 2000s, SME internationalisation surveys have appeared primarily in the OECD countries. However, most reviews have focused on international management strategies of SMEs and on their capacity to create competitive products and adopt successful business models to penetrate foreign markets. Yet, a minority of studies have addressed so-called SME externalities, meaning how SMEs can identify and use external services and resources, available domestically or/and abroad, to internationalise beyond trans-border markets. Even though most, if not all, APS are concentrated in urban centres both at home and overseas, the service provider role of global cities vis-à-vis internationalising SMEs has been rarely studied so far.

There are a few recent exceptions initiated either by small-sized and highly export-oriented nations in Europe (Austria, Belgium, Finland, the Netherlands, Sweden, Switzerland) and Asia (Hong Kong, Malaysia, Taiwan, Singapore, South Korea), or by dynamic provinces or states of larger countries such as Canada, Germany, and Japan.

The study of global cities combined with the study of SME internationalisation brings new and valuable insights into the analysis of the scope of SME internationalisation and the facilitating role such cities can play. Whereas the presence of APS firms, all of them being multinationals, serves as predictors for the identification of a global city and enables the measurement of their importance, it is not yet studied what kind of supportive role they play vis-à-vis foreign internationalising SMEs. The rankings of global cities, most prominently provided by the GaWC, serve as a grid to be applied in a variable that measures whether internationalising SMEs are connected to these cities through services provided by APS firms, or but more rarely through direct or indirect SME presence locally (for instance, through a representation office, a trade agent, or a local distributor).

In contrast to multinational firms, most internationalising SMEs are widely dispersed over different world economic regions and do not fully cover markets on a global scale. Their presence in global cities needs to be analysed in relation to their overall presence in global cities' hinterlands, which correspond to different world economic regions. For example, two consecutive studies conducted in 2016 and 2019 demonstrated the role of global cities for Swiss internationalising SMEs vis-à-vis distant emerging markets. Three global cities were ranked in first position, namely, Tokyo, Mexico City, and Singapore (Baldegger et al. 2016; Baldegger et al. 2021). The Swiss SME samples studied in 2016 and 2019 contained over 20% of global start-ups, a number in expansion from 17% in 2016 to 24% in 2019.

Based on such recent empirical surveys to be replicated in other OECD economies, it may be tentatively concluded that:

1. Global cities do play various functions in SME and start-up internationalisation, even if less or not visible compared to the cases of multinational corporations and large firms.
2. SME priorities go for professional/sectoral business hubs and service networks concentrated in global cities to collect reliable information about distant and unknown foreign markets. Transnational corporations providing specialised APS services play a significant enabling role in this process, in addition to more localised and smaller-sized BDS and related networks.
3. Among BDS services localised in global cities, most of them cover regional markets, such as bankers, lawyers, HR specialists, scientists, technicians, translators, and transporters. They master business communication and professional practices, and compliance with norms and standards (formal and informal) of doing business locally and in neighbour regional markets.

References

Abu-Lughod JL (1989) Before European hegemony: the world system a.D. 1250–1350. Oxford University Press, New York

Acs Z (2002) Innovation and the growth of cities. Edward Elgar, Cheltenham

Acs Z, Armington C (2004) Employment growth and entrepreneurial activity in cities. Reg Stud 38 (8):911–927

Acs Z, Bosma N, Sternberg R (2008) The entrepreneurial advantage of world cities: evidence from global entrepreneurship monitor data. Global Entrepreneurship Monitor research paper

Amin Moghadasi M, Derakhshandeh B, Ferdosi M, Jafari Sadeghi V (2017) Organizational conformity as an entrepreneurial response to the changes in internationalization process: a study of IT-oriented firms in Saveh. World J Account Financ Eng 1(1):53–64

Baldegger R, Schüffel P, Hammer M (2016) Hub internationalization. In: Proceedings of the Academy of International Business (AIB) 2016 Annual Meeting (No. CONFERENCE). 27–30 June 2016

Baldegger R, Wild P, Schueffel P (2021) The effects of entrepreneurial orientation in a digital and international setting. In: Entrepreneurial orientation: epistemological, theoretical, and empirical perspectives (Advances in entrepreneurship, firm emergence and growth, vol 22), Emerald Publishing Limited, pp 145–174

Beaverstock J, Smith R, Taylor PJ (1999) A roster of world cities. Cities 16(6):445–458

Bell J, McNaughton R, Young S, Crick D (2003) Towards an integrative model of small firm internationalisation. J Int Entrep 1(4):339–362

Boudlaie H, Mahdiraji HA, Shamsi S, Jafari-Sadeghi V, Garcia-Perez A (2020) Designing a human resource scorecard: an empirical stakeholder-based study with a company culture perspective. J Entrep Manag Innovat 16(4):113–147

Braudel F (1984) The perspective of the world. Collins, London

Castells M (1996) The rise of network society, 2nd edn. Blackwell, Oxford

Castells M (2011) The rise of the network society: the information age: economy, society, and culture, vol 1. John Wiley & Sons, London

Che Senik Z, Scott-Ladd B, Entrekin L, Adham KA (2011) Networking and internationalization of SMEs in emerging economies. J Int Entrep 9(4):259–281

Clark P (ed) (2013) The Oxford handbook of cities in world history. OUP, Oxford

Coviello NE, McAuley A (1999) Internationalisation and the smaller firm: a review of contemporary empirical research. Manag Int Rev 39(3):353–356

Currid E (2006) New York as a global creative hub: a competitive analysis of four theories on world cities. Econ Dev Q 20(4):330–350

Dana L-P (2017) International entrepreneurship research: how it evolved and directions for the future. Int J Entrep Small Bus 30(4):477–489

Dana L-P, Wright RW (2009) International entrepreneurship: research priorities for the future. Int J Global Small Bus 3(1):90–134

Dana L-P, Grimwood S, William G (2009a) Export incentives and international entrepreneurship in New Zealand firms. J Int Bus Entrep Develop 4(1/2):1–21

Dana L-P, Hamilton RT, Wick K (2009b) Deciding to export: an exploratory study of Singaporean entrepreneurs. J Int Entrep 7(2):79–87

Dana L-P, Grandinetti R, Mason MC (2016) International entrepreneurship, export planning and export performance: evidence from a sample of winemaking SMEs. Int J Entrep Small Bus 29 (4):602

Doel M, Hubbard P (2002) Taking world cities literally: marketing the city in a global space of flows. City 6(3):351–368

Fernández Z, Nieto MJ (2005) Internationalization strategy of small and medium-sized family businesses: some influential factors. Fam Bus Rev 18(1):77–89

Friedmann J (1986) The world city hypothesis. Dev Chang 17(1):69–83

Fritsch M, Falck O (2007) New business formation by industry over space and time: a multidimensional analysis. Reg Stud 41(2):157–172

Fujita M (1998) The transnational activities of small and medium-sized enterprises. Kluwer Academic Publisher, Boston

Gankema HGJ, Snuif HR, Zwaart PS (2000) The internationalization process of small and medium-sized enterprises: an evaluation of stage theory. J Small Bus Manag 38(4):15–27

Garousi Mokhtarzadeh N, Amoozad Mahdiraji H, Jafari-Sadeghi V, Soltani A, Abbasi Kamardi A (2020) A product-technology portfolio alignment approach for food industry: a multi-criteria decision making with z-numbers. Br Food J 122(12):3947–3967

GaWC (2021) The world according to GaWC 2020. From https://www.lboro.ac.uk/gawc/world2020t.html. Accessed on January 2, 2021
Gill A, Gurău C, Dana L-P, Sánchez CR (2017) Human capital, financial strategy and small firm performance: a study of Canadian entrepreneurs. Int J Entrep Small Bus 31(4):492
Goerzen A, Asmussen CG, Nielsen BB (2013) Global cities and multinational enterprise location strategy. J Int Bus Stud 44(5):427–450
Jacobs J (1984) Cities and the wealth of nations. Random House, New York
Jafari Sadeghi V, Biancone PP, Anderson RB, Nkongolo-Bakenda J-M (2019a) International entrepreneurship by particular people 'on their own terms': a study on the universal characteristics of entrepreneurs in evolving economies. Int J Entrep Small Bus 37(2):288–308
Jafari Sadeghi V, Nkongolo-Bakenda J-M, Anderson RB, Dana L-P (2019b) An institution-based view of international entrepreneurship: a comparison of context-based and universal determinants in developing and economically advanced countries. Int Bus Rev 28(6):101588
Jafari-Sadeghi V (2020) The motivational factors of business venturing: opportunity versus necessity? A gendered perspective on European countries. J Bus Res 113:279–289
Jafari-Sadeghi V, Kimiagari S, Biancone PP (2019) Level of education and knowledge, foresight competency and international entrepreneurship: a study of human capital determinants in the European countries. Eur Bus Rev 32(1):46–68
Jafari-Sadeghi V, Dutta DK, Ferraris A, Del Giudice M (2020a) Internationalisation business processes in an under-supported policy contexts: evidence from Italian SMEs. Bus Process Manag J 26(5):1055–1074
Jafari-Sadeghi V, Nkongolo-Bakenda J-M, Dana L-P, Anderson RB, Biancone PP (2020b) Home country institutional context and entrepreneurial internationalization: the significance of human capital attributes. J Int Entrep. https://doi.org/10.1007/s10843-019-00264-1
Johanson J, Vahlne JE (1977) The internationalization process of the firm—a model of knowledge development and increasing foreign market commitments. J Int Bus Stud 8(1):23–32
Johanson J, Vahlne JE (1990) The mechanism of internationalization. Int Mark Rev 7(4):11–25
Johanson J, Vahlne J-E (2009) The Uppsala internationalization process model revisited: from liability of foreignness to liability of outsidership. J Int Bus Stud 40(9):1411–1431
McDougall-Covin P, Jones MV, Serapio MG (2014) High-potential concepts, phenomena, and theories for the advancement of international entrepreneurship research. Entrep Theory Pract 38 (1):1–10
Mokhtarzadeh N, Amoozad Mahdiraji H, Jafarpanah I, Jafari-Sadeghi V, Cardinali S (2020) Investigating the impact of networking capability on firm innovation performance: using the resource-action-performance framework. J Intellect Cap 21(6):1009–1034
Oviatt BM, McDougall PP (1994) Toward a theory of international new ventures. J Int Bus Stud 25:45–64
Ratten V, Dana L-P, Ramadani V (2017) Internationalisation of family business groups in transition economies. Int J Entrep Small Bus 30(4):509–525
Régnier P, Wild P (2017) The geoeconomics of global cities: exploring new avenues for expanding business internationalization. In: Advances in Geoeconomics. Routledge, New York/London, pp 29–45
Régnier P, Wild P (2018) SME internationalisation and the role of global cities: a tentative conceptualisation. Int J Export Market 2(3):158–179
Rezaei M, Jafari-Sadeghi V, Bresciani S (2020) What drives the process of knowledge management in a cross-cultural setting: the impact of social capital? Eur Bus Rev 32(3):485–511
Rialp A, Rialp J (2001) Conceptual frameworks on SMEs' internationalization: past, present and future trends of research. Adv Int Mark 11(1):49–78
Ruzzier M, Hisrich RD, Antoncic B (2006) SME internationalization research: past, present, and future. J Small Bus Enterp Dev 13(4):476–497
Sadeghi VJ, Biancone PP (2018) How micro, small and medium-sized enterprises are driven outward the superior international trade performance? A multidimensional study on Italian food sector. Res Int Bus Financ 45:597–606

Sadeghi V, Biancone PP, Giacoma C, Secinaro S (2017) Export compliance: a missing component of international entrepreneurship. Int J Bus Manag 12(11):103–110
Sadraei R, Jafari Sadeghi V, Sadraei M (2018) Biotechnology revolution from academic entrepreneurship to industrial: chemo-entrepreneurship. Biomet Biostat Int J 7(6):546–550
Sassen S (1991) The Global City. Princeton University Press, New York
Sassen S (2001) The Global City. Princeton University Press, New York, London, Tokyo
Schueffel PE, Baldegger RJ (2008) The process model of internationalization and the international new venture framework. Growth Publisher, Liebefeld/Bern
Schweizer R (2013) SMEs and networks: overcoming the liability of outsidership. J Int Entrep 11 (1):80–103
Sukumar A, Jafari-Sadeghi V, Garcia-Perez A, Dutta DK (2020) The potential link between corporate innovations and corporate competitiveness: evidence from IT firms in the UK. J Knowl Manag 24(5):965–983
Taylor PJ (2001) Specification of the world city network. Geogr Anal 33(2):181–194
Taylor PJ (2004) World City network: a global urban analysis. Routledge, London
Taylor PJ, Ni P, Derudder B, Hoyler M, Huang J, Lu F, Chen W (2009) Measuring the world city network: new results and developments. GaWC Res Bull 300
Taylor P (2011) Measuring the world city network: new results and developments. In: ICTS for mobile and ubiquitous urban infrastructures: surveillance, locative media and global networks. IGI Global, pp 15–23
Zahra SA, George G (2002) International entrepreneurship: the current status of the field and future research agenda. In: Strategic entrepreneurship: creating a new mindset. Blackwell Publisher, Oxford, pp 255–288
Zucchella A, Scabini P (2007) International entrepreneurship - theoretical foundations and practices. Palgrave, London
Zucchella A, Palamara G, Denicolai S (2007) The drivers of the early internationalization of the firm. J World Bus 42(3):268–280

Philippe Régnier is Full Professor, Dean (Applied Research and Development), School of Management, Freiburg, University of Applied Sciences Western Switzerland (HES-SO). He is specialised in entrepreneurship, private sector, and development in emerging economies, with most of his field research work in Asia and Africa. He served as an associate professor at the Graduate Institute of International and Development Studies, Geneva, Switzerland, and as a full professor at the School of International Development and Global Studies, University of Ottawa, Canada. His current research deals with the internationalisation of Western SMEs to emerging markets and with the entrepreneurship ecosystems of global cities.

Pascal Wild is Associate Professor, School of Management, Freiburg, University of Applied Sciences Western Switzerland (HES-SO). He is specialised in the study of SMEs' internationalisation and global entrepreneurship. He holds a PhD in socioeconomics from the University of Geneva. His current research deals with the role of East and Southeast Asian global cities as hubs in the internationalisation process, speed, scope, and success of internationalising firms and their entrepreneurial orientation.

International Entrepreneurship Within Service Ecosystems: Applying Service-Dominant Logic and the BAR Framework in Research Design

Denis Odlin

1 Introduction

Understanding how small, often poorly resourced firms succeed as they expand internationally is important practically as well as theoretically because these firms represent sources of new economic value (Haltiwanger et al. 2012; OECD 2013) and are often the pioneers of new industries and markets (Abernathy and Utterback 1978). While small- and medium-sized enterprises (SMEs) have traditionally been the backbone of domestic economic systems, these firms now actively compete internationally with larger firms (Dabić et al. 2019). Entrepreneurs play an important role as a catalyst for developing this new value across borders, although the popular view of the heroic risk-taking entrepreneur as the central actor in the process does not match empirical reality (Venkataraman et al. 2012). Accordingly, starting from the assumption that entrepreneurs are the primary drivers of small firm internationalisation is a flawed approach to international entrepreneurship (IE) research. Nonetheless, this is the primary logic of the field and derives from the highly cited definition of international entrepreneurship as "the discovery, enactment, evaluation, and exploitation of opportunities—across national borders—to create future goods and services", and with research oriented towards the individuals that pursue these opportunities (Oviatt and McDougall 2005, p 540).

Reviewing IE literature, Keupp and Gassmann (2009) identified a lack of definitional rigour, with the consequence that IE studies predominantly focused on the phenomenon of small firm internationalisation and relied on international business theory for explanatory power—or no theory at all. Further weaknesses they

D. Odlin (✉)
Department of International Business, Strategy & Entrepreneurship, Auckland University of Technology, Auckland, New Zealand
e-mail: denis.odlin@aut.ac.nz

V. Jafari-Sadeghi et al. (eds.), *Empirical International Entrepreneurship*, Contributions to Management Science,
https://doi.org/10.1007/978-3-030-68972-8_4

identified were the lack of a process perspective in understanding how entrepreneurial efforts intersected with firm internationalisation and an overemphasis on small firms, whereas entrepreneurship is independent of firm size. These scholars argued that such problems needed to be overcome to achieve the necessary theoretical rigour for IE to become a legitimate research field.

This chapter highlights three criticisms of IE research and methodology; ontological problems in the opportunities construct, limitations created by a focus on the individual or firm level of analysis, and hindsight bias in research design. It argues that to ensure methodological rigour, IE researchers should avoid prematurely narrowing their conceptual and theoretical perspectives to the entrepreneurs (or their firms) when initially designing research to investigate a phenomenon or research gap. The chapter introduces service-dominant logic (SDL) (Vargo and Lusch 2011; Whalen and Akaka 2016; Wieland et al. 2017) as a theoretical framework for IE that not only takes a process perspective, it emphasises the creation of value (representing the fundamental process in Shane and Venkataraman's (2000) conception of entrepreneurship). SDL highlights that both value and markets are co-created, so entrepreneurial actions must be understood in relation to the other actors in an ecosystem (Whalen and Akaka 2016). Entrepreneurs do not create value on their own, so Foss and Klein's (2018) beliefs-actions-results (BAR) framework offers a sound alternative to the "discovery, enactment, evaluation, and exploitation of opportunities" in the IE definition.

The chapter first details the methodological difficulties created by the definition of IE and then presents how the beliefs-actions-results framework (Foss and Klein 2018) can be operationalised in IE research by focusing on value rather than the opportunity construct. The chapter then shows how service-dominant logic (Vargo and Lusch 2016) within an institutional framework (Wieland et al. 2017) can be used to investigate how value is co-created across borders without requiring IE researchers to start from the individual or firm level of analysis. It concludes by proposing how to avoid hindsight bias in research design.

2 Issues in the Conception of International Entrepreneurship

This section reviews Oviatt and McDougall's definition of IE and its implications for IE research methodology.

2.1 Critiquing "Opportunities"

Scholarly developments in recent years mean that defining IE as "the discovery, enactment, evaluation, and exploitation of opportunities" (Oviatt and McDougall

2005, p 540) may limit the theoretical contribution IE research makes. "Opportunities" is a contested concept in entrepreneurship (Wright and Phan 2018) and may be inadequate as the construct on which an entire field of study is based (Davidsson 2015)—indeed Foss and Klein (2018) argue it should be abandoned:

> Opportunities can at best be manifest *ex-post* when entrepreneurial outcomes are successful. What entrepreneurship scholars mean by "opportunity" is simply a business idea, plan, or belief, which may or may not turn out as the entrepreneur imagines. (p.4)

In other words, if an "opportunity" did not lead to a successful outcome, then it was not an opportunity and could not have existed in the first place. This creates a success (hindsight) bias in IE research by locking the researcher into a retrospective analysis of those business ideas that succeeded.

Oviatt and McDougall's (2005) definition of IE also suggests that opportunities exist independently of the entrepreneurs—that the environment is full of hidden opportunities awaiting "discovery". We are left with the same ontological difficulty—do those individuals that discover "opportunities" get transformed into entrepreneurs while individuals who search but cannot discover opportunities are not entrepreneurs? Or do we have a success bias that only individuals that discover opportunities that prove successful are entrepreneurs?

Because of these ontological problems, a shift is underway in understanding opportunities as being created, rather than being discovered (Whalen and Akaka 2016). This perspective treats opportunities as "created endogenously through the actions, reactions and enactment of entrepreneurs exploring ways to create new products or services" (Alvarez and Barney 2007, p 15). That is, rather than being seeded from existing markets, or formed through exogenous change, the source of opportunities is the entrepreneurs themselves who bring the opportunity into being. Seeking a middle road between opportunities as objective entities that may be discovered and opportunities as a created outcome, other scholars have used a realist philosophical framing to propose that opportunities are propensities (potential) that the entrepreneur actualises (Ramoglou and Tsang 2016). Taking the creation perspective further, proponents of an ecosystem view of entrepreneurship argue that opportunity (and the value associated with it) is co-created between the customer and the entrepreneur (at a minimum, although other actors may be involved) so that an entrepreneur cannot create value independently (Whalen and Akaka 2016). This perspective of opportunities as co-created is consistent with the emerging marketing perspective of value as co-created through service-for-service transactions (Vargo and Lusch 2008), and markets as socially constructed configurations determined by market actors (Storbacka and Nenonen 2011).

Opportunities have been the central concept underpinning entrepreneurship; however, whether opportunities are alternatively discovered, created, co-created, or are propensities fundamentally changes the way IE research is designed and operationalised. Oviatt and McDougall's (2005) definition reflects the discovery perspective, but this potentially holds IE research back from embracing more recent theoretical developments. The next section examines the concept of the entrepreneur and its implications for IE research.

2.2 Critiquing "Entrepreneurship"

Oviatt and McDougall stressed their agreement with Shane and Venkataraman (2000) "that entrepreneurship has two parts: (1) opportunities; and (2) individuals who strive to take advantage of them" (Oviatt and McDougall 2005, p.539). In somewhat of a contradiction, Oviatt and McDougall then tied their conception of IE to "internationally entrepreneurial actors", identified as organisations, groups, as well as individuals (Ibid., p 540). One branch of IE investigates "those actors, how they act and the effects of their actions" (Ibid), while another branch compares entrepreneurial systems across national borders. The effect of Oviatt and McDougall's conception is to tie IE research to either the individual level or firm level (organisational) of analysis. This is reflected in Keupp and Gassmann's (2009) finding that most IE research investigated small firms and did not take a broader perspective of entrepreneurship.

The implication of this focus on the level of the individual or firm is demonstrated in the IE domain ontology and thematic analysis by Jones et al. (2011) which deliberately excluded SME internationalisation papers that did not include elements of entrepreneurship. Thus, their domain ontology did not include research about factors that may influence whether individuals or firms can successfully internationalise, such as industry and competitors, ecosystems, technological innovation, and the international environment, unless directly linked to the entrepreneur. Other influences on how future products and services are created across borders are not considered, suggesting that the Oviatt and McDougall (2005) definition of IE creates a very narrow field of study.

Given that the expansion of entrepreneurial SMEs into international business was driven by external factors such as reduced trade barriers and developments in transportation and telecommunications (Dana 2017), and that continuing growth is particularly influenced by external factors such as government support programs and the saturation of domestic markets (Ratten et al. 2007; Alon et al. 2009), the continued emphasis on the individual and firm levels of analysis is misplaced. Despite the study of the personal characteristics of individual entrepreneurs being identified as a "dead end" in 1987 (Dana 2017), the publication of research on these aspects continues. More surprisingly, of eleven questions for future IE research proposed by Dana (2017), nine were at the firm level, one was a firm-level view of networks, and only one identified issues beyond the firm.

Oviatt and McDougall's definition, Jones et. al's subsequent domain ontology, and Dana's future IE research questions imply that IE is based on two foundational presumptions: a) that the phenomenon of firms crossing borders is primarily driven by entrepreneurs and b) that the success or failure outcomes of these enterprises in creating "future products and services" are primarily a consequence of the actions of these entrepreneurs. As will be explicated later in the chapter, this is contrast to research that highlights that value—as the foundation of entrepreneurial activity (Shane and Venkataraman 2000)—is co-created with other market actors and that no firm (or entrepreneur) is able to act independently. That is, these presumptions are not clearly proven to be valid, and, based on Jones et al.'s (2011) domain ontology, any research that found to the contrary would not be considered IE research.

2.3 *Critiquing Hindsight Bias in IE Research*

While these critiques of the framing of "opportunities" as a primary construct of IE, the level of analysis of IE, and unproven presumptions about the influence of entrepreneurs on the creation of future goods and services across borders are theoretical, they nevertheless influence IE research methods. Further, they create a fundamental hindsight bias in theoretical framing of IE—researchers typically start from the analysis of consequences, such as the creation of products and services in international markets, and then work backwards to an entrepreneurial cause. This hindsight bias affects the understanding of opportunities and the treatment of success and can lead researchers to theorise simplistic causal explanatory links for processes that are vastly more complex and random (Chandra and Wilkinson 2017).

Hindsight bias is especially evident when IE is the framing for studies of rapid internationalisation, a topic addressed in the second part of Oviatt and McDougall's 2005 paper and which has become a mainstay of IE research (Keupp and Gassmann 2009). Rapid internationalisation research has created various categories of organisations, such as born globals (BGs), international new ventures, and rapidly internationalising ventures, where the primary definitional difference from other internationalising firms is their rapid growth in international markets (Cesinger et al. 2012). Accordingly, these firms can only be recognised post hoc once their performance is known. Effectively, unsuccessful BGs cannot exist because these firms only come into being once they exceed various speed, scope, and age thresholds. Firms that may have attempted to internationalise rapidly but failed to achieve the thresholds (Cesinger et al. 2012) are classified as traditionally internationalising firms. Welch et al. (2016) described the BG concept as "reified", that is, treating as an empirical fact that "born global" is a distinct organisational form, rather than a theoretical abstraction to be improved through research. Welch et al. (2016) showed that researchers had stopped including all the original elements of the BG concept and simply relied on age at first internationalisation as the only dimension for identification. Hennart (2014) proposed that the phenomenon of rapid internationalisation was nothing more than a rational response to a firm's market context, based on facilitating factors in the modern business environment, while Dow (2017) provided evidence to support this. Leading scholars in the field argued that categories based on firm age at internationalisation, such as born global, were no longer leading to theoretical development and that researchers should address context, dynamics, and variety (Reuber et al. 2017). Such critiques of rapid internationalisation research reflect problems of hindsight bias as well as the problem created by IE's two foundational presumptions.

Hindsight bias also distorts the design of empirical research where—because more data is available—researchers investigate successful industries, firms, or phenomena (Denrell and Kovács 2008). This is particularly evident in case study research, which is a research design used extensively in IE in part because of difficulty accessing useful quantitative data sets. Small firms are usually privately held and are not required to publish data like listed firms. Further, small entrepreneurial firms typically do not gain the attention of industry analysts, regulatory bodies, or other industry actors in their early stages of business development or entry into international markets. Indeed, the strategy of small firms is often to "fly under radar" and gain a foothold in specialist markets before competitors are aware of their presence (Audretsch et al. 1999, 2018), so there is little publicly available data on these firms' actions, meaning few reliable or comparable quantitative data sets exist. Consequently, researchers tend to focus on successful cases and overlook failure cases.

Further hindsight bias can be added in the data-gathering stage. IE researchers often use retrospective accounts of entrepreneurs to make sense of cause-effect relationships, yet these accounts often are the individual seeking to rationalise what happened (Golden 1992). The testimony of these respondents contains unconscious hindsight bias and may not reflect how they made decisions at the time.

Using a qualitative design like case studies is not problematic in itself, although it limits the generalisability of findings. Nevertheless, researchers must be careful not to create a research design that presumes the cause of the identified outcome. For example, using case studies to identify the characteristics of rapidly internationalising firms requires comparison with gradually internationalising firms to find differences. Unfortunately, many early studies only investigated firms that had rapidly internationalised, and accordingly their findings confounded those firm behaviours with SMEs in general. For example, many studies claim that rapidly internationalising firms target niches (e.g. Cannone and Ughetto 2014; Cavusgil and Knight 2015; Gabrielsson et al. 2008), yet this is a strategy of almost all SMEs (Audretsch et al. 1999).

The above critiques of the opportunity concept, the level of analysis limitations, and hindsight bias in research design suggest fundamental problems in the conceptualisation and practice of IE research. Nonetheless, we must be careful not to lose sight of the importance of studying IE and "throw the baby out with the bathwater", as the old idiom warns. Resolving definitional problems contributes to the development of scholarly fields (Wright and Phan 2018). The remainder of the chapter addresses how researchers can overcome these potential problems in their IE research designs.

3 Focusing on Value Instead of Opportunities

Despite starting from the logic of opportunities, Shane and Venkataraman (2000) explained entrepreneurship as based on variations in people's beliefs about the value of resources. For example, when people believe that the price of a resource is set too low and act on that belief by buying the resource and then selling it at a higher price in another location or time or in a modified form, they earn an entrepreneurial profit. For different beliefs to exist there also has to be variations in the information available to the market participants as a consequence of either more (or less) accurate information, access to new information or educated guesses (Shane and Venkataraman 2000). Thus, entrepreneurial behaviour is based on the asymmetry of both beliefs and information about value.

Information alone is insufficient—action is required before entrepreneurial profit is possible. Potentially, many people can identify variations in resource values, but the action is the necessary connection between having a belief and gaining an entrepreneurial profit. International entrepreneurs act to apply asymmetries of beliefs and information about the value of resources across borders. Shane and Venkataraman (2000) specifically note the entrepreneurial act of reselling a resource in a different location, which is a key element of IE.

Value can be understood as a utility or benefit (Vargo and Lusch 2004). Thus, value is not the same as price, and modern marketing scholars have come to understand the value in terms of an exchange of service, rather than in economic terms, as will be expanded later in the chapter (Vargo and Lusch 2011). Accordingly, asymmetries of beliefs and information as the foundation of entrepreneurial action are more than just arbitrage, where traders act on short-term price disparities within existing markets.

Given the ontological, epistemic, and methodological critiques of the opportunity construct in entrepreneurship research, Foss and Klein (2018) propose that "entrepreneurs are individuals who seek to combine heterogeneous resources in the pursuit of profit under genuine uncertainty" (p 11). This requires entrepreneurs to apply judgement when making decisions about how to act because, under conditions of genuine uncertainty, rational analysis of future conditions is not possible. Because judgement is costly to articulate, entrepreneurs must take ownership of the key resources and combine these with the resources of others (Foss and Klein 2018). The entrepreneur combines multiple resources, which further distinguishes entrepreneurship from arbitrage. The unit of analysis in entrepreneurship research, therefore, becomes "investment" rather than an opportunity—how entrepreneurs assemble "resources in the present in anticipation of uncertain receipts in the future" (Foss and Klein 2018, p 16).

The consequent beliefs-actions-results framework proposed by Foss and Klein reflects the process of entrepreneurial investment. Beliefs include the entrepreneur's beliefs about the present, such as the availability of resources and their values, technological possibilities, and customer preferences, and possible futures, such as customer demand, regulatory issues, and technological change. Importantly, it also includes the entrepreneur's beliefs about their own abilities to create different futures. Actions include all the activities required to implement the investment, including the creation of new firms, products or services, development of relationships with other actors, and activities to influence institutional factors (such as changing regulations or modifying the "rules of the game"). It also includes decisions (an action) not to act, such as to curtail investment. Results include objective profits or losses from the entrepreneurial investment as well as non-financial outcomes such as achievement of social goals, learning, and adaptation.

3.1 Application of BAR Framework in IE Studies

Although "international opportunity" is the central theme of IE, according to Oviatt and McDougall's definition, IE researchers need to move beyond a reliance on opportunities as a conceptual element of their research design. In operationalising their research, this means separating what respondents may refer to as an opportunity into its processual elements. This is not to discard actors' perspectives of opportunity, because the word is widely used and understood, but to acknowledge the limitations of "opportunity" as a research concept and avoid the trap of using it as the central organising theme.

When operationalising the BAR framework, researchers will recognise that each element is at a different level of analysis, with Beliefs at the individual level. This is because beliefs are a cognitive element that only exists in the mind of the individual and cannot be independently verified—beliefs are what the individual says they are. A researcher may document the reported beliefs of a team, although these represent the negotiated outcomes of individual beliefs and various information flows so are not the same as entrepreneurial beliefs. A team is not an entrepreneur (Casson 2003). International aspects of culture, norms, and language can be expected to impact beliefs in the BAR framework because these are taken-for-granted aspects of informal institutions (North 1990).

Actions may be at the level of the individual or the firm and represent identifiable behaviours. A documented decision to act represents an action as an identifiable behaviour yet is not the same as the action itself. Actions can be verified—this separates them from beliefs or intentions. Internationally entrepreneurial actions typically involve the movement of various resources—including financial, knowledge, and physical resources—across borders.

Results represent outcomes that can be analysed in terms of financial and non-financial value. Financial (economic) results will be denominated in a currency, which varies across borders and often is verifiable. Non-financial value, such as reputation, knowledge, or network position change (Johanson and Vahlne 2009), may not be able to be reliably measured or verified. International elements of results represent the movement of this value across borders. The operationalisation of the BAR framework for IE is shown in Table 1.

Analysing value within the results of entrepreneurial investments requires IE researchers to reconsider "value". A new paradigm in marketing explains how value is transferred through service, rather than through goods (Vargo and Lusch 2004). This "service-dominant logic" (SDL) represents a new paradigm for understanding entrepreneurship and the process of creating value (Vargo and Lusch 2014).

Table 1 Applying the BAR framework in IE research

BAR Elements	Beliefs	Actions	Results
Level of analysis	Individual	Individual or firm	Firm
Unit of analysis	Cognitive aspects	Identifiable behaviours	Financial value Non-financial value
Verifiable	No	Yes	Sometimes
International elements	Norms Culture Language	Movement of resources across borders	Movement of value across borders

4 IE Within a Broader Context: An Ecosystem Perspective

The simple framework of IE derived from Oviatt and McDougall's definition focused on entrepreneurs developing future goods and services across national boundaries belies the multi-layered complexity of practice. In short, entrepreneurs are neither the decision-makers nor even key influencers for many of the aspects that determine the success or failure of entrepreneurial investment. As discussed above, the presumption that they do is unhelpful to progressing rigorous IE research.

Instead, entrepreneurs act within systems, and while they play their part in determining the direction of systems, entrepreneurs must also respond to the system (Sarason et al. 2006). Markets are examples of such systems. Rather than being independent entities existing to bring supply and demand into equilibrium, as in the economic perspective, markets are better understood as socially created by market actors such as sellers, buyers, institutions, and sales intermediaries (Storbacka and Nenonen 2011). Markets represent configurations of interdependent actors who introduce new market practices, such as new ways to exchange services and goods, development of norms that guide these transactions, and shared symbols and language to facilitate market communication. From this system perspective, entrepreneurial acts cannot be researched in isolation.

A system perspective is not new to entrepreneurship. Categories of ecosystems, and the nature of the entrepreneurial thinking required to create them, were proposed by Zahra and Nambisan (2012). Clusters act as ecosystems to encourage knowledge and value creation, and entrepreneurs relocate to participate in clusters when they can appropriate part of their value (Pitelis 2012). The pursuit of opportunity in global ecosystems has also been proposed as a new research direction for IE (Reuber et al. 2018). What these approaches lack is an integrated framework that links entrepreneurial actors, value co-creation, resource integration, and institutional systems.

The SDL perspective provides such a framework. Previously, the goods-dominant logic of economics assumed that sellers added value to their products as it proceeded along the value chain, and the value was transferred to the buyer as the economic exchange value. Producers created value and consumers destroyed value, so once the money was exchanged, the value was lost (Vargo and Lusch 2011). This economic logic pervades traditional entrepreneurship scholarship, with the entrepreneur seen as a producer of new opportunities which are then sold to customers for an entrepreneurial profit. It is also evident in Oviatt and McDougall's definition of IE.

In contrast in service-dominant logic (SDL), value creation is assumed to occur when customers integrate the various resources of sellers. More specifically, service—the application of resources for the benefit of another party—is exchanged for service (Vargo and Lusch 2008). Actors transact to acquire the benefits of specialised competencies (knowledge or skills) in the form of service (Vargo and Lusch 2004). Buyers do not want products; they want the service a product provides. Buyers potentially integrate services from multiple vendors and repay using money as a fungible resource that can be transferred to gain other services. Buyers also transfer non-financial services to sellers, such as the reputation value of a customer reference site or the knowledge gained by the seller to better understand the customer application and develop better products. Value is not destroyed in the transaction—it is created.

In SDL, the nomenclature of producers and consumers is discarded in favour of actor to actor transactions, with customers one type of actor providing service (Vargo and Lusch 2011), and emphasises the earlier point that value is always co-created (Vargo and Lusch 2008).

Factors influencing value co-creation processes are market practices (as described above), technologies (understood as useful knowledge rather than in a narrow sense of artefacts), and business models (Wieland et al. 2017). Business models contain sets of decision variables about strategy (Wieland et al. 2017), reflecting the design of the structure, content, and governance of transactions between firms and other market actors (Zott and Amit 2008). Business models represent the ways actors integrate resources to create new value (Storbacka and Nenonen 2011). In an entrepreneurship sense, business models represent how entrepreneurs reconfigure the resources available to them to transact with other market actors, often by selling resources in another location or time or in a modified form.

Value co-creation processes occur within nested and overlapping ecosystems of actors involved in resource integration and service exchange that is both enabled and constrained by institutions and institutional arrangements (Wieland et al. 2017). These value co-creation processes establish the ecosystems in the first place so are recursive and dynamic.

Institutions and institutional arrangements might include commonly shared yet informal understandings among market actors, such as the "rules of the game" in competition and legitimate organisational forms, as well as formal institutions such as regulations and technical standards (North 1990; Peng et al. 2009; Vargo and Lusch 2016). Service ecosystems of market actors operate at the firm-to-firm transactional level as well as nesting within meso- and macro-level institutions (Vargo and Lusch 2016; Vargo et al. 2020) and provide a sound framework for unravelling complexities in international contexts (Akaka et al. 2013). The service ecosystems framework is shown in Fig. 1.

The SDL ecosystem framework provides a robust foundation for IE researchers because it:

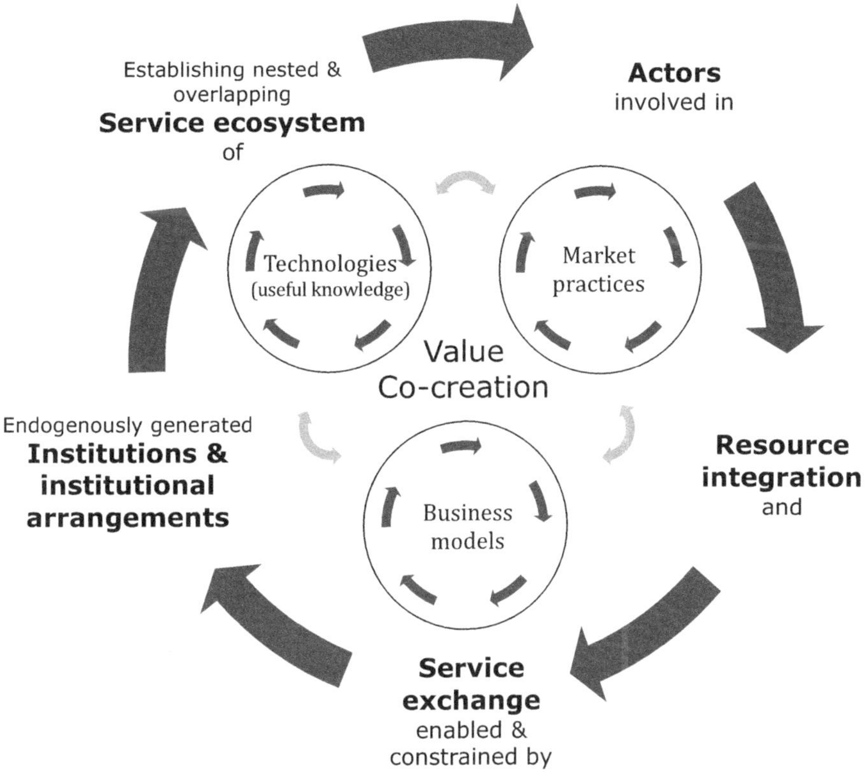

Fig. 1 Service ecosystems perspective. (Source: Wieland et al. (2017))

- Is process-oriented and dynamic, overcoming the criticism of the static nature of much of IE research (Keupp and Gassmann 2009)
- Does not presume cause-effect relationships
- Focuses on value, which is the underpinning of entrepreneurial investment and how value is created (Shane and Venkataraman 2000)
- Includes the institutions and the influence of entrepreneurs on institutions (institutional entrepreneurship) (Sarason et al. 2006; Battilana et al. 2009)
- Includes multiple actors (in addition to the entrepreneur) within ecosystems
- Includes resource integration—a key process of entrepreneurship (Shane and Venkataraman 2000; Foss and Klein 2018)
- Represents interrelationships between markets (as practices), technology (understood as useful knowledge), and business models as the realisation of value delivery

Although SDL contains no overt international dimension, it is implicit in market practices, service exchange, and institutional arrangements, just as the entrepreneur is implicit within actors. The next section expands on how SDL can be applied in IE research.

4.1 Application of SDL Ecosystems Framework in IE Studies

The SDL ecosystem framework provides a structure that accommodates entrepreneurship research across borders. The five concepts in the outer (process) ring of the framework all have international dimensions.

Ecosystem actors, whether defined at the individual or firm level, may be located in multiple countries, and the mix of actors involved in entrepreneurial investments represents a key IE dimension for future study. Not all ecosystem actors will be entrepreneurial actors (as in Oviatt and McDougall 2005) yet may still contribute to the process of value co-creation. Actors are involved in resource integration which also may cross borders, such as when an entrepreneur moves a raw material from one country to another for further processing. Oviatt and McDougall (1994) identified geographically focused and global start-ups as types of international new venture that integrate resources across countries, such building design capabilities in one country and production facilities in another.

A service exchange is clearly an action that may cross borders. Service transactions may also include domestic activity supporting international exchange, and understanding these may be necessary to fully understand international entrepreneurship.

The study of institutions and institutional arrangements has been a mainstay of international business research (Peng et al. 2008) and represents a body of work relevant to the study of value co-creation in service ecosystems. This can contribute to studies of the effect of home country culture, language, and norms on entrepreneurial processes as well as the overarching impact of national politics, policies, and regulation on IE (Jafari Sadeghi et al. 2019). This might also include the impact of supranational bodies such as the UN or WTO on entrepreneurial processes. Importantly, institutions and institutional arrangements include how actors may develop micro-level structures to cooperate in cross-border networks (Akaka et al. 2013).

Service ecosystems represent complex social and economic systems that influence and are influenced by exchange, with dyadic service exchanges at a micro-level embedded in meso-level local and organisational systems, which are themselves embedded in macro-level national, regional, and global systems (Akaka et al. 2013). Service ecosystems, therefore, represent the context of actors involved in internationally entrepreneurial exchanges.

Technologies, market practices, and business models also include cross-border elements. How ideas and technologies are managed across borders is fundamental to internalisation theory, another mainstay of international business research (Buckley and Casson 2009). Market practices vary by location as well as by ecosystem and institutional arrangement (Akaka et al. 2013). Business models represent the way an internationally entrepreneurial actor configures resource integration across borders.

The SDL framework locates entrepreneurial processes within a broader ecosystem to make sense of how entrepreneurs develop international businesses. Accordingly, it provides a theoretical perspective that overcomes the limitations in the economic goods-dominant logic of traditional entrepreneurship studies. The next section addresses the final problem of hindsight bias.

5 Overcoming Hindsight Bias in Research Design

Fundamental to overcoming hindsight bias in research design is ensuring that alternative explanations have been explored. Designs that investigate a process in isolation, without reference to alternatives, risk hindsight bias.

For example, Gabrielsson et al.'s (2008) paper "Born Globals: Propositions to help advance the theory" provided a useful and insightful study of the phases of BG development. It was based on semi-structured interviews of senior managers from eight BGs drawn from four countries and across different industries that included software, machinery, mobile entertainment, apparel, and food. The selected firms needed to have "demonstrated the capability for accelerated internationalisation" (Gabrielsson et al. 2008, p 389), that is, by successfully internationalising early and rapidly. The paper develops multiple propositions about the actions required for creating a successful (sustainable) BG in the longer term.

The paper's research design contains elements of hindsight bias that call its findings into doubt. We cannot be sure whether the actions of these successful rapidly internationalising SMEs might also have been followed by unsuccessful SMEs or SMEs that were ultimately successful but took longer to internationalise because there is no comparison with these alternatives. For example, when the researchers propose that "Sustainable BGs seek financing from venture capitalists domestically and/or abroad" (Gabrielsson et al. 2008, p 395), this would appear to be an action common to multiple organisation types and not unique to BGs. Does this mean that unsustainable BGs or gradually internationalising SMEs do not seek capital from venture capitalists? If we have no means of comparison to alternative forms, how can we conclude anything about the special characteristics of sustainable BGs? To avoid hindsight bias, in addition to the eight successful BGs, the research design could have included case firms that were unsuccessful as well as those that took longer to internationalise in order to identify the unique features of the BGs.

The other problematic aspect of this design is that it presupposes, like much of IE, that the only level influencing the behaviour of these firms is the intentions of individual (entrepreneurial) managers. Institutional influences such as the country of origin or the industry rules of the game are assumed to be immaterial by comparing BGs from multiple counties and industries. That is, the BGs are plucked out of their ecosystems, networks, and institutional environments and examined in isolation.

A research design that avoids these hindsight bias problems is "Domestic competitor influence on internationalising SMEs as an industry evolves" (Odlin 2019). To investigate the competitive strategies of internationalising SMEs, it follows the competitive interactions of an industry segment of thirteen firms over a decade and a half of development, thereby ensuring both a dynamic perspective and contextualisation of firm-level actions (Zahra et al. 2014). Rapidly and gradually internationalising SMEs are compared, as well as successful and unsuccessful firms. The paper further compares SMEs with large firms. It selects a single country as the focus, thereby comparing firms within a common macro-institutional context, in addition to the common industry institutional context. Nevertheless, the design is not without its limitations and still contains potential hindsight bias by interviewing managers about their recollections years after the events occurred (particularly in relation to the emergence and growth phases of their industry).

Despite the relevance of competitive strategies to entrepreneurs in internationalising SMEs, Odlin (2019) would be unlikely to be classified as IE research because its focus is not the entrepreneur. The research project was originally conceived as an extension to Gabrielsson et al. (2008) to understand the competitive strategies of BGs. As the design evolved, and particularly after gathering secondary data on the research context, it became evident that additional firms needed to be studied in order to make sense of the strategies of the rapidly internationalising firms. By the close of the data gathering phases, every internationalised firm that had ever participated in the industry segment in NZ had been studied. The findings showed that rapidity of internationalisation after the firm start-up was not relevant to understanding firm competitive strategy—the critical factor was the time of internationalisation relative to the stage of the industry evolution. Therefore, what started as an IE research project studying BGs was no longer IE by its conclusion. This suggests that IE research itself may have a hindsight bias—that an objective researcher of a particular phenomenon cannot determine whether their study is in the field of IE until they have analysed their results.

For readers to trust research findings, the key task in presenting empirical papers is "ruling out alternative explanations of the phenomenon under investigation" (Cuervo-Cazurra et al. 2016, p 882). Particularly in qualitative research, which is an important method in IE, this requires clearly delineating the contextual boundaries of any theoretical claims, identifying why a particular location or sample has been selected and clarifying how the data analysis navigates cultural and linguistic limitations while reporting on cases that do not fit the overall pattern or interpretation proposed by the researchers in their paper (Cuervo-Cazurra et al. 2016). For IE researchers, this means paying particular attention to avoiding hindsight bias.

6 Conclusion

This chapter has identified three definitional and methodological issues in IE research and proposed solutions to them. The post hoc ontological difficulty with the opportunities construct can be resolved by focusing instead on the beliefs, actions, and results of investments by entrepreneurial actors. Avoiding the presumptions that the phenomenon of SME internationalisation is driven by entrepreneurs and that the success of IE investments is primarily a consequence of their actions means a new perspective is needed. The SDL framework provides such a perspective because it takes a process view of how value is co-created and logically integrates actors, resources, institutions, systems, market practices, business models, and technology. Hindsight bias can be minimised by careful research design and avoiding analysis of phenomena in isolation.

References

Abernathy WJ, Utterback JM (1978) Patterns of industrial innovation. Technol Rev 80:41–47

Akaka MA, Vargo SL, Lusch RF (2013) The complexity of context: a service ecosystems approach for international marketing. J Int Mark 21:1–20

Alon I, Dana LP, Jenkins A (2009) International business by SMEs: empirical findings from New Zealand. J Int Bus Econ 10:59–78

Alvarez SA, Barney J (2007) Discovery and creation: alternative theories of entrepreneurial action. Strateg Entrep J 1:11–26

Audretsch DB, Prince YM, Thurik AR (1999) Do small firms compete with large firms? Atl Econ J 27:201–209

Audretsch DB, Lehmann EE, Schenkenhofer J (2018) Internationalization strategies of hidden champions: lessons from Germany. Multinat Bus Rev 26:2–24

Battilana J, Leca B, Boxenbaum E (2009) How actors change institutions: towards a theory of institutional entrepreneurship. Acad Manag Ann 3:65–107

Buckley PJ, Casson MC (2009) The internalization theory of the multinational enterprise: a review of the progress of a research agenda after 30 years. J Int Bus Stud 40:1563–1580

Cannone G, Ughetto E (2014) Born globals: a cross-country survey on high-tech start-ups. Int Bus Rev 23:272–283

Casson MC (2003) The entrepreneur, 2nd edn. Edward Elgar, Cheltenham

Cavusgil ST, Knight GA (2015) The born global firm: an entrepreneurial and capabilities perspective on early and rapid internationalization. J Int Bus Stud 46:3–16

Cesinger B, Fink M, Madsen TK, Kraus S (2012) Rapidly internationalizing ventures: how definitions can bridge the gap across contexts. Manag Decis 50:1816–1842

Chandra Y, Wilkinson IF (2017) Firm internationalization from a network-centric complex-systems perspective. J World Bus 52:691–701

Cuervo-Cazurra A, Andersson U, Brannen M et al (2016) From the editors: can I trust your findings? Ruling out alternative explanations in international business research. J Int Bus Stud 47:881–897

Dabić M, Maley J, Dana LP et al (2019) Pathways of SME internationalization: a bibliometric and systematic review. Small Bus Econ. https://doi.org/10.1007/s11187-019-00181-6

Dana LP (2017) International entrepreneurship research: how it evolved and directions for the future. Int J Entrep Small Bus 30:477

Davidsson P (2015) Entrepreneurial opportunities and the entrepreneurship nexus: a re-conceptualization. J Bus Ventur 30:674–695

Denrell J, Kovács B (2008) Selective sampling of empirical settings in organizational studies. Adm Sci Q 53:109–144

Dow D (2017) Born global firms and accidental internationalists: has Hennart (2014) opened a can of worms? Rev Int Bus Strategy 27:286–307

Foss NJ, Klein P (2018) Entrepreneurial opportunities: who needs them? Acad Manag Perspect 34 (3):366–377

Gabrielsson M, Kirpalani VHM, Dimitratos P et al (2008) Born globals: propositions to help advance the theory. Int Bus Rev 17:385–401

Golden BR (1992) Research notes: the past is the past—or is it? The use of retrospective accounts as indicators of past strategy. Acad Manag J 35:848–860

Haltiwanger J, Jarmin RS, Miranda J (2012) Who creates jobs? Small versus large versus young. Rev Econ Stat 95:347–361
Hennart J-F (2014) The accidental internationalists: a theory of born globals. Entrep Theory Pract 38:117–135
Jafari Sadeghi V, Nkongolo-Bakenda JM, Anderson RB, Dana LP (2019) An institution-based view of international entrepreneurship: a comparison of context-based and universal determinants in developing and economically advanced countries. Int Bus Rev 28:1–16
Johanson J, Vahlne J-E (2009) The Uppsala internationalization process model revisited: from liability of foreignness to liability of outsidership. J Int Bus Stud 40:1411–1431
Jones MV, Coviello NE, Tang YK (2011) International entrepreneurship research (1989-2009): a domain ontology and thematic analysis. J Bus Ventur 26:632–659
Keupp MM, Gassmann O (2009) The past and the future of international entrepreneurship: a review and suggestions for developing the field. J Manag 35:600–633
North DC (1990) An introduction to institutions and institutional change. In: Eggertsson T (ed) Institutions, *Institutional Change and Economic Performance,* e-book. Cambridge University Press, pp 3–10
Odlin D (2019) Domestic competitor influence on internationalizing SMEs as an industry evolves. J World Bus 54:119–136
OECD (2013) Entrepreneurship at a glance. OECD Publishing, Paris
Oviatt BM, McDougall PP (1994) Toward a theory of international new ventures. J Int Bus Stud 25:45–64
Oviatt BM, McDougall PP (2005) Defining international entrepreneurship and modeling the speed of internationalization. Entrep Theory Pract 29:537–553
Peng MW, Wang DYL, Yi J (2008) An institution-based view of international business strategy: a focus on emerging economies. J Int Bus Stud 39:920–936
Peng MW, Sun SL, Pinkham B, Chen H (2009) The institution-based view as a third leg for a strategy tripod. Acad Manag Perspect 23:63–81
Pitelis C (2012) Clusters, entrepreneurial ecosystem co-creation, and appropriability: a conceptual framework. Ind Corp Chang 21:1359–1388
Ramoglou S, Tsang E (2016) A realist perspective of entrepreneurship: opportunities as propensities. Acad Manag Rev 41:410–434
Ratten V, Dana L, Han M, Welpe IM (2007) Internationalisation of SMEs: European comparative studies. Int J Entrep Small Bus 4:361–379
Reuber AR, Dimitratos P, Kuivalainen O (2017) Beyond categorization: new directions for theory development about entrepreneurial internationalization. J Int Bus Stud 48:411–422
Reuber AR, Knight GA, Liesch PW, Zhou L (2018) International entrepreneurship: the pursuit of entrepreneurial opportunities across national borders. J Int Bus Stud 49:395–406
Sarason Y, Dean TJ, Dillard JF (2006) Entrepreneurship as the nexus of individual and opportunity: a structuration view. J Bus Ventur 21:286–305
Shane S, Venkataraman S (2000) The promise of entrepreneurship as a field of research. Acad Manag Rev 25:217–226
Storbacka K, Nenonen S (2011) Markets as configurations. Eur J Market 45:241–258
Vargo SL, Lusch RF (2004) Evolving to a new dominant logic for marketing. J Mark 68:1–17
Vargo SL, Lusch RF (2008) From goods to service(s): divergences and convergences of logics. Ind Mark Manag 37:254–259
Vargo SL, Lusch RF (2011) It's all B2B and beyond: toward a systems perspective of the market. Ind Mark Manag 40:181–187
Vargo SL, Lusch RF (2014) Inversions of service-dominant logic. Mark Theory 14:239–248
Vargo SL, Lusch RF (2016) Institutions and axioms: an extension and update of service-dominant logic. J Acad Mark Sci 44:5–23
Vargo SL, Akaka MA, Wieland H (2020) Rethinking the process of diffusion in innovation: a service-ecosystems and institutional perspective. J Bus Res 116:526–534

Venkataraman S, Sarasvathy S, Dew N, Forster WR (2012) Reflections on the 2010 AMR decade award: whither the promise? Moving forward with entrepreneurship as a science of the artificial. Acad Manag Rev 37:21–33
Welch C, Rumyantseva M, Hewerdine LJ (2016) Using case research to reconstruct concepts. Organis Res Methods 19:111–130
Whalen PS, Akaka MA (2016) A dynamic market conceptualization for entrepreneurial marketing: the co-creation of opportunities. J Strateg Mark 24:61–75
Wieland H, Hartmann NN, Vargo SL (2017) Business models as service strategy. J Acad Mark Sci 45:925–943
Wright M, Phan P (2018) Opportunity: is there a future in the construct? Acad Manag Perspect. https://doi.org/10.5465/amp.2018.0162
Zahra SA, Nambisan S (2012) Entrepreneurship and strategic thinking in business ecosystems. Bus Horiz 55:219
Zahra SA, Wright M, Abdelgawad SG (2014) Contextualization and the advancement of entrepreneurship research. Int Small Bus J 32:479–500
Zott C, Amit R (2008) The fit between product market strategy and business model: implications for firm performance. Strategic Manag J 29:1–26

Denis Odlin is a Lecturer in the Department of International Business, Strategy and Entrepreneurship at Auckland University of Technology, which is ranked in the top 1% of universities in the world. He teaches master's level courses in IB, and his research investigating the competitive strategies of internationalised SMEs has been published in the *Journal of World Business* and *International Business Review*. Prior to AUT, Denis taught at the University of Auckland Graduate School of Management and the Hong Kong Polytechnic University. Denis also has industry experience in Australia and Asia, holding regional and global marketing management roles in high-technology firms. As an entrepreneur, he started up and successfully ran two businesses of his own. Denis holds a PhD in International Business from the University of Auckland and a master's degree from the University of Melbourne.

Entrepreneurs, Platforms, and International Technology Transformation

Nigel Walton

1 Introduction

This chapter analyses how entrepreneurs have, over 40 years, developed a technology infrastructure that has acted as a building block for a new type of firm and business model known as the platform company. It explains the three waves of innovation that made the platform business model a reality and how this impacted the evolution of the modern business ecosystem. This is followed by a critical review of business model theory and the relevance of the dynamic perspective of business models and the role of business model innovation. This includes a critical appraisal of Voelpel et al.'s (2004) Wheel of Business Model Reinvention and Lecoq et al.'s (2006) RCOV model.

The unique characteristics of platforms and how they can leverage core competencies (Prahalad and Hamel 1990) and enter multiple markets and industries are also explored using RBV theories. The Knowledge-Based View (Spender 1996; Grant 2016) and the use of data and information as a source of competitive advantage through the application of Datafication and Big Data analytics capabilities are considered using the "core competencies tree" (Prahalad and Hamel 1990). The chapter concludes with an analysis of the international nature of the modern platform

A major portion of the chapter has been part of the author's dissertation: Walton, N. (2018) *The Extent to Which Data-Rich Firms Operating Two-Sided Platform-Ecosystem Business Models Are Able to Use Data to Gain an Innovation Advantage over Established One-Sided Companies*. PhD Dissertation: Coventry University. January 2018.

N. Walton (✉)
Faculty of Business and Law, School of Strategy and Leadership, Coventry University, Coventry, UK
e-mail: ad0006@coventry.ac.uk

V. Jafari-Sadeghi et al. (eds.), *Empirical International Entrepreneurship*, Contributions to Management Science,
https://doi.org/10.1007/978-3-030-68972-8_5

companies and how the World Wide Web and market aggregation characteristics have made these companies into born global firms.

2 Ecosystem Theory, the Entrepreneur, and the Waves of Technological Change

Before analysing the waves of entrepreneurial innovation and technological change that made the platform business model reality, the chapter will begin with a definition of the term platform and why this has been selected for the analysis.

According to Gawer (2009: 3–4), a platform is defined as "… . .a building block, which can be a product, a technology or a service that acts as a foundation upon which other firms can develop complementary products, technologies or services".

As far as this analysis is concerned, the platform is a "technology" or technological building block which acts as a foundation upon which other firms can develop complementary products, technologies, or services. This technology is the Internet and digitisation. The platforms we will be analysing are also what is commonly referred to as two-sided marketplaces or multi-sided businesses (Gawer 2009; Van Alstyne et al. 2016).

The infrastructure that enabled the platform business model to become a reality was the result of three waves of entrepreneurial innovation (Case 2017). These consisted of Wave 1, the birth of the Internet and the personal computer (PC) industry (1969–1990); Wave 2, Web 1.0 (1990–2000); and Wave 3, Web 2.0. (2000–2011).

During the first wave, the ARPANET (the original Internet) and microprocessor chip were conceived, but more importantly between 1977 and 1990 an industry standard for personal computers was established following a standards war (Shapiro and Varian 1999) involving Apple-Motorola and Microsoft, Intel, and IBM. The second wave of technology evolution began with the roll-out of the World Wide Web in 1992 based on the pioneering work of Tim Berners-Lee. This second wave of evolution also saw the dot-com boom and what became known as Web 1.0. This witnessed the widespread diffusion of personal computers using compatible standards that were linked together via the Internet, creating a global communications network. The third wave saw the rise of social media and was built on the earlier waves by harnessing new technologies and entrepreneurial innovations such as 3G and 4G wireless capabilities, digitisation, the smartphone, cloud computing, and GPS (Walton and Pyper 2019).

This was driven by high levels of recombinant innovation (Henderson and Clark 1990; Weitzman 1998) and created the four key infrastructural components needed for the building of the platform business model (Davidson et al. 2018). These consisted of (1) the Internet and digitisation (the building block of today's platforms): (2) cloud computing (global infrastructure); (3) smartphones and apps (infrastructure connection); and (4) search and social media (connecting people and information).

This era of technological disruption was driven by entrepreneurs. Schumpeter defined entrepreneurs as innovative individuals who linked innovation to "new combinations" of new or existing knowledge, resources, and equipment (Schumpeter 1934: 65). These entrepreneurs were also opportunity-oriented (Aparicio et al. 2016). It was also a period during which ecosystems emerged as a means of value creation. The term ecosystem originated from the biological sciences and was defined by Tansley (1935) as an interactive system between a group of living creatures and the environment in which they lived (Walton 2017).

The concept of a business ecosystem was introduced by James Moore (1993, 1996) who defined an ecosystem as an economic community of interacting organisations and individuals which produced goods and services of value. This included key stakeholders such as customers, suppliers, lead producers, competitors, etc. (Moore 1996: 26). Important features of the ecosystem concept included the co-evolution of products, services, and capabilities by ecosystem members who were aligned with one or more central companies. Business ecosystems also consist of firms from a variety of industries, and like biological ecosystems, they evolve with implications for their members in terms of innovation, cooperation, and competition (Kapoor and Lee 2013; Hannah and Eisenhardt 2017; Adner 2017; Jacobides et al. 2018).

In Moore's original ecosystem there were three layers consisting of the core business at the centre, surrounded by an extended enterprise layer (layer 2) and the wider business ecosystem layer (layer 3). Later research on ecosystems by Iansiti and Levien (2004) identified that business ecosystems, unlike natural biological ecosystems, did not self-organise. Moore's reference to the alignment of ecosystem members to a central company was therefore very important. These central companies were what Iansiti and Levien (2004) referred to as "keystones" or platform leaders (Gawer and Cusumano 2002). During the three waves of the technological advancement outlined above, different keystones or platform leaders emerged to drive the entrepreneurial innovation.

In Wave 1, Steve Jobs and Steve Wozniak started the PC revolution through the launch of the Apple 1 and Apple 2 computers (1976–1977), but it was two other entrepreneurs, Bill Gates at Microsoft and Andy Grove at Intel, who won the standards battle. These entrepreneurs were successful because of how they developed a large installed base of users by leveraging complementarities (Kapoor 2014) in software and hardware development through an open architecture (Davidson et al. 2018). The second wave saw two new entrepreneurs emerge with Michael Dell selling low-cost PCs and hardware and John Chambers at Cisco providing the "plumbing" upon which the Internet would ultimately connect the PCs and other forms of hardware and software. These four firms, therefore, became the keystones or platform leaders who created the building blocks for the roll-out of Tim Berners-Lee's World Wide Web. This comprised a compatible industry standard for PCs (Microsoft and Intel), low-cost affordable hardware (Dell), and Internet infrastructure (Cisco). This drove the Web 1.0 revolution and ultimately led to the dot-com boom and crash in 1999–2000 (Gawer and Cusumano 2002).

However as new technologies evolved (digitisation, 3G/4G, and the smartphone) and as computing prices fell, a third wave unfolded (Web 2.0) where a new group of entrepreneurs and technology firms started to gain traction such as Jeff Bezos's Amazon (e-commerce and cloud computing), Sergey Brin and Larry Page's Google (search), Mark Zuckerberg's Facebook (social media), and the re-emergence of Steve Jobs and Apple as a mobile handset producer. These firms did not only become the new "keystones" in developing the foundations of the multi-sided platform company, they also changed the nature of how ecosystems worked.

As mentioned earlier, Moore's (1993) original ecosystem model featured the business at the core and an extended enterprise layer and ecosystem in its outer layers. Since Moore's work was produced before the Internet gained any traction, it was largely based on traditional brick-and-mortar companies such as Wal-Mart. Wave 1 of the technological transformation was also based primarily upon the development of hardware and software products, and Wave 2 only saw a relatively basic application of the Internet compared to today.

Using Gawer's (2009) typology of ecosystems, Wave 1 and Wave 2 would be classified as "Industry Ecosystems" consisting of several firms or organisations that didn't necessarily buy or sell from one another but whose products/services functioned together as part of a technological system driven by high levels of symbiosis and co-development (Fransman 2010). This didn't necessarily entail any form of Internet connectivity. It wasn't until Wave 3 that Gawer's (2009) multi-sided market or two-sided platform emerged. These platforms consisted of several firms transacting with each other through an intermediary technology (the Internet) that represented the marketplace.

Instead of a traditional business forming the core ecosystem (Moore 1993), this had now changed to a technology. The new ecosystems were no longer populated by traditional brick-and-mortar companies but had become platform-powered (Reillier and Reillier 2017) with Internet companies forming the core component of the ecosystems with other digital platforms and smartphone-enabled individuals developing complementary products (Kapoor and Agarwal 2017).

The four components of the platform business model infrastructure were now complete, namely, the Internet and digitisation, cloud computing, smartphones and apps, and search and social media (Choudary 2013). These technologies spawned a new global ecosystem of Internet-based companies including Alibaba, Tencent, and Baidu in China, Gojek and Grab in South-East Asia, and the new "Jio Platforms in India" (Leavy 2016). This is in addition to the North American Internet giants (mentioned earlier) as well as platform companies in Europe such as Spotify, Deliveroo, Adyen, Revolut, etc.

The chapter will now analyse the theories of business model innovation and how entrepreneurs have used new platform-based business models to disrupt traditional markets and industries globally.

3 Platforms and Business Model Innovation

In recent years, the business model has been the focus of substantial attention from both academics and practitioners. Since 1995, there have been over 1200 articles published in peer-reviewed academic journals in which the business model concept has been addressed (Wirtz et al. 2016).

The term business model can be traced back 60 years and was first used by Bellman et al. in 1957. The business model started to gain greater significance following the advancement of information technology and electronic business particularly in the 1990s (Hedman and Kalling 2002). The uptake of the term grew exponentially during the "new economy" boom (Wirtz et al. 2010). While the term "business model" had hardly been used before 2000, the dot-com boom caused it to become highly relevant and widespread in practice.

Nevertheless, despite a number of emerging themes, the literature is still very fragmented, and many authors have commented on the existence of research silos (Zott et al. 2011). Three research fields were identified by Wirtz et al. (2016) which they classified as technology-oriented, organisation theory-oriented, and strategy-oriented business models. According to Wirtz et al. (2016), from 2000 to 2002, the technologically oriented business model article predominated with regard to electronic business, but from 2002 onwards more strategy-oriented articles were published. In comparison, the organisation-oriented articles played a subordinate role.

The level of abstraction used to view business models was also very important, and this ranged from the detailed product level, the business and company level, and the aggregated industry level. Authors of the early technology-orientation school (Amit and Zott 2001; Eriksson and Penker 2000) considered the business model to represent only a small part of a company. However, this is no longer the view of authors of the modern technological orientation in the "new economy", who now see business models representing whole companies (Osterwalder and Pigneur 2010; Garousi Mokhtarzadeh et al. 2020). This view is also shared by the organisation-orientation school. Meanwhile, the authors of the strategy orientation school viewed business models from the perspective of providing a picture of a company's competitive situation or position (Hamel 2000).

Moreover, when defining the business model, it is also worth noting that existing literature has mostly adopted a static perspective (Lindner et al. 2010; Van Putten and Schief 2012). Nevertheless, the dynamic perspective of business models (Casadesus-Masanell and Ricart 2010; Cavalcante et al. 2011; Demil and Lecoq 2010; Van Putten and Schief 2012) is particularly relevant to platform companies and the "new age" economy, and it is this perspective that will form the basis of the ongoing analysis.

Osterwalder and Pigneur (2010) define a business model as:

> …….the rationale of how an organisation creates, delivers, and captures value.

This is a commonly held definition, and it is underpinned by a range of interacting components which they mapped out using a business model canvas. This builds on earlier work by Chesbrough and Rosenbloom (2002) who formulated a checklist of key business model functions which included the articulation of the value proposition; identifying a market segment and specifying the revenue generation mechanism; defining the structure of the value chain detailing the revenue mechanism; estimating the cost structure and profit potential; describing the position of the firm within the value network; and formulating the competitive strategy.

Meanwhile, Baden-Fuller and Mangematin (2013) were critical of the fact that most research on business models focused on their role as descriptors of an actual phenomenon often by reference to taxonomic categories, i.e. cognitive instruments, rather than a real phenomenon. The authors, therefore, proposed a typology that consisted of four elements. These included (1) identifying the customers and the number of separate customer groups, (2) customer engagement or customer proposition, (3) monetisation, and (4) value chain and linkages.

Moreover, when analysing the customer identification and customer engagement components of their typology, Baden-Fuller and Mangematin (2013) included "project-based" (taxi) and "pre-designed" (bus) systems. Business models using the "project-based" (taxi) approach created value by interacting with customers to solve specific problems such as innovation platforms including Innocentive and GitHub (Davies and Brady 2000; Jafari-Sadeghi et al. 2020a; Sukumar et al. 2020; Nightingale et al. 2011; Hobday 2000). Alternatively, those firms utilising the "pre-designed" (bus) system (transaction platforms such as ad placements on Google and Facebook) add value by producing "one size fits all" goods or services repetitively via standardised mass production/service processes (Hounshell 1985; Chandler 1990; Nightingale 2000). According to Demil and Lecoq (2010), Google appeared to be deploying a "bus-based" user engagement system for search engine users but a "taxi-based" user engagement system for its advertisers (who could tailor their advertising offering and set the price they were willing to pay).

Baden-Fuller and Mangematin (2013) were also critical of the different approaches to classifying business models. They stated that taxonomic approaches were inappropriate because they simply served as exemplars. These were not as useful as typological categorisations which were conceptually derived. When using taxonomies, it was not possible to fully understand how the nature of the categorisation might influence the results. However, considering typologies of business models, this emphasised the configuration possibilities that transcend time and industry boundaries and helps to delve into fundamental questions behind business models and the ability to manipulate and adapt them. The typological business model approach also made it possible to model and articulate different activities within the firm. Baden-Fuller and Mangematin (2013) also revealed what they considered to be a new category of the business model previously un-noticed called the multi-sided (two-sided) model where engagement and value creation involved several customer groups and a whole new dynamic. It is this category of a business model that will be the focus of this analysis.

As mentioned earlier, the dynamic perspective of business models has been adopted for this analysis, and this is exemplified by Voelpel et al. (2004) who researched the business model's dynamic nature and made a distinction between what they referred to as business model change and business model reinvention. Voelpel et al. (2004) said that new sources of competitive advantage could be obtained through business model reinvention that was based on disruptive innovation instead of incremental change or continuous improvement.

Voelpel et al. (2004) also pointed out that the newly emerging environment (Kelly 1998; Hitt et al. 2003) had three distinguishing features. It was vastly globalised, it favoured intangible things (ideas, information, relationships, knowledge), and it was intensely interlinked with ubiquitous networks (Voelpel et al. 2004: 4). According to the authors, these attributes created a new type of marketplace and society often referred to as the "new economy", "knowledge economy", or the "networked economy" (Tapscott 1997). This was due to a shift from the industrial-based to knowledge and information-based economy with human imagination and ingenuity being the main source of value.

Voelpel et al. (2004: 8) highlighted the important role played by business ecosystems in the new economy and that these operated across industries, thereby requiring a systemic perspective not restricted to traditional boundaries. The authors said that organisations needed to shift from traditional industry-focused mechanistic thinking to ones that were systematic, holistic, and new-value configuration-focused in nature. The need for organisations to constantly create new business models was also emphasised as a result of these changes (Tucker 2001) by experimenting with a portfolio of strategies. This is what Davenport et al. (2006) referred to as "poised" strategies.

Finally, when pursuing business model reinvention, two kinds of innovation were also identified. The first concerned innovation with respect to the firm's own historic strategy, and the second related to a firm's industry and its competitors (proactively reinventing the industry). In terms of historic strategy, the platform company does not utilise the traditional single-sided linear business model, where the organisation inputs resources, processes them into a final product and/or service, and then distributes the outputs via a physical distribution channel or retail outlet.

Instead, platforms adopt Baden-Fuller and Mangematin's (2013) multi-sided business model. Pure platform companies do not actually make anything. Their role is to create connections between buyers, sellers, and other users such as software developers (apps) and companies wishing to advertise. Their role is to manufacture connections between users. Therefore, ownership of the means of connection [to the Internet] is more important than ownership of the means of production (Moazed and Johnson 2016) that was the key source of competitive advantage during the industrial age (Choudary 2015).

Secondly, platform companies have played a major role in proactively re-inventing markets and industries and disrupting incumbent firms (competitors). Apple, Spotify, YouTube, Amazon, and Netflix have all disrupted the media industry through the disintermediation of the supply chain (Parker et al. 2016). The adoption of digital download and streaming technologies resulted in the removal of physical products (DVDs and CDs) and the need for physical infrastructures such as manufacturing plants, warehousing, and brick-and-mortar retail outlets. Meanwhile, platforms have asset-light business models and are cheap to set-up.

In the sharing economy, ride-hailing companies use free or low-cost technologies to run their platforms such as free maps from Google, free GPS, orders submitted via users' smartphones, and low-cost cloud computing. There are also low fixed costs since vehicles and bikes are provided by the contractors (drivers and riders) and in the case of Airbnb, so is the real estate. This is what Van Alstyne et al. (2016) referred to as the delinking of assets from value. Financial technology platforms (Fintech) are also able to do away with costly brick-and-mortar branch networks, while e-commerce marketplaces such as Alibaba, eBay, and Shopify do not have to maintain expensive retail and delivery infrastructure, and this has disrupted the major high street retail and shopping mall brands.

Platforms have therefore changed the economics of the industries that they have entered by lowering costs and prices but providing enhanced value. Google and Facebook have transformed advertising through programmatic trading of ads over their Internet platforms. This is made possible by free user-generated content such as videos, photos, messages, and data in general. This is what Kotler (1986) referred to as the "prosumer", a consumer who also produces a "product".

Platforms are also able to reduce the transaction costs (Coase 1937; Williamson 1981) of doing business. Two-sided platforms create new efficiencies by aggregating unorganised markets (Parker et al. 2016). This is the process whereby the platforms provide centralised markets to serve widely distributed individuals and organisations. Market aggregation provides information and power to users who previously engaged in interactions in a haphazard fashion often without access to reliable or up-to-date market data and/or infrastructure.

A transaction cost consists of three core activities or costs: (1) search and information costs, (2) bargaining costs, and (3) policing and enforcement costs. Search and information costs are the costs involved in determining that the required good is available on the market at the lowest price. This information is available free, 24/7 due to the powerful search capabilities of the Internet and comparison websites.

Meanwhile, bargaining costs are the costs required to come to an acceptable agreement with the other party to the transaction. These are also lowered because Internet users now have more information available to them, thereby strengthening their bargaining power. Policing and enforcement costs involve the costs of making sure the other party sticks to the terms of the contract and taking appropriate action where necessary. This is ensured through escrow accounts and digital audit trails and records.

There is also greater price transparency as platforms have created a new layer of reputational information by leveraging social feedback about producers. Platforms like Yelp, Angie's List, and Trip Advisor have created an entirely new industry based on certifying the quality of the product and service providers. This means that the search and information costs, bargaining costs, and policing and enforcement costs for platform participants are minimal compared to traditional vertically integrated one-sided businesses. As the transaction costs of doing business using a two-sided business model have fallen dramatically, this has led to a transitioning of value away from internal hierarchies to external markets (the make or buy decision) causing significant disruption in traditional industries (Coase 1937; Williamson 1981).

Finally, platforms enjoy the benefits of near zero-marginal cost growth dynamics (Rifkin 2014). Due to the Internet and connected technology, digitised information goods have a zero marginal cost of distribution. This means that the cost of serving one additional customer is close to zero. Alternatively, a linear business selling physical products is limited to how far it can scale due to high fixed costs. In order to serve more customers, it needs to employ more people, acquire more raw materials, increase the number of production facilities and offices, etc.

In order to operationalise and measure the development of new business models, Voelpel et al. (2004: 26) also proposed a four-dimensional framework called the "Wheel of Business Model Re-invention". This was a four-stage model comprising customer sensing, technology sensing, business infrastructure sensing, and economics/profitability sensing stages. The model was also iterative and dynamic with an emphasis on speed and fast responsiveness.

"Customer Sensing" involved sensing the potential for change in customer or user behaviour and developing new customer value propositions. This is where two-sided firms are very adept due to the vast troves of data that they accumulate from the strong network relationships and connections they develop. Two-sided firms such as Amazon and Alibaba are able to use sentiment analysis to determine the attitude of consumers with respect to a topic, interaction, or event.

Meanwhile, "Technology Sensing" indicates the ability of the firm to sense the relative strength and impact of technology in creating new customer value and business networks. Since the large industry platform companies have been the pioneers of the new technologies including the Web 1.0 and Web 2.0 infrastructure, they are always well-positioned as the innovators of new technologies. The two-sided platforms were early adopters of cloud computing, apps, and GPS. This is now being extended to include artificial intelligence (AI) and the Internet-of-Things (IoT).

"Business System Infrastructure" involved sensing the potential for value system (re)configuration including organisational structures. The world's leading Internet platforms (Amazon, Apple, Google, Facebook, Microsoft, Alibaba, and Tencent) are all platform leaders (Gawer and Cusumano 2002) or keystones (Iansiti and Levien 2004) in their respective fields, but they are continuously extending the reach of their platforms into new markets and industries including cloud computing, financial services, health, and transportation. Many platforms are now becoming "super apps" such as We Chat, Gojek, Grab, Meituan Dianping, and Uber, as they seek to enter multiple markets using a single app and technology platform to sell a wide range of virtual products and services.

The "Economics and Profitability" dimension of the model entails sensing the economic feasibility and profitability of proposed business models. Platform companies such as Amazon, Alibaba, and Tencent are able to test concepts and business models in both the virtual and real worlds and analyse digital feedback to assess future potential. In financial services, Alipay and WeChat Pay are able to develop credit ratings and credit scores based on data accumulated from users during their e-commerce transactions and from their social media feeds. Amazon, meanwhile, spends on average 18 months pilot testing new concepts and gathering online feedback before deciding on whether to launch a new business model. This influenced its decision to enter into grocery deliveries. Finally, the "Economics and Profitability" dimension is clearly illustrated by the fact that the world's most valuable companies, in terms of profits, market capitalisation, and brand equity, are the big technology platforms mentioned earlier (Walton 2018; Walton and Pyper 2019).

Casadesus-Masanell and Ricart (2010) also analysed the dynamic interrelations between elements or components in business models, but they also considered the influence of globalisation, deregulation, and the advancement in information and communications technology (ICT) as key drivers of business model innovation. Cavalcante et al. (2011) went a step further by elaborating on the previously missing links between business model dynamics and innovation. They conceptualised business models from a process-oriented viewpoint and emphasised the key role of the actors or agents in the dynamics of the business model. They also differentiated between four types of business model change, namely, business model creation, extension, revision, and termination. They established a direct connection between these types of business model change and the corresponding degree of innovation.

According to Henry Chesbrough (2010), business model innovation presented both opportunities and barriers to modern firms. For example, technology by itself had no single objective value, and the economic value remained latent until it was commercialised in some way via a business model. He also said that a mediocre technology within a great business model may be more valuable than a great technology exploited via a mediocre business model. Chesbrough (2010) used the example of Xerox Parc in the 1970s to illustrate this phenomenon. Although Xerox was innovating, it didn't know how to deploy and commercialise its new technologies. For example, the company produced the Alto personal computer (PC) in 1973 but decided that there was no market for a PC. Most of the key components from the Alto reappeared several years later in the Apple Macintosh.

Companies, therefore, need to commercialise new ideas and technologies through their business models. Moreover, the same idea or technology taken to market through two different business models is likely to yield two different economic outcomes. These views were reinforced by Teece (2010: 192) who said that great technological achievements commonly failed commercially because no proper attention had been given to designing a business model to take the technologies to market properly.

Meanwhile, Demil and Lecoq (2010) in their article, *Business Model Evolution: In Search of Dynamic Consistency*, developed the transformational approach further when they proposed the use of the RCOV model as well as drawing upon earlier research by Penrose (1959). Penrose's work adopted a dynamic view of organisational growth as well as highlighting the dynamics that occurred between the different components. The Penrosian (1959) approach also underlined the ongoing dimension of change as a permanent rather than a transient state. This was reinforced by Lecoq et al.'s (2006) research that viewed the organisation as

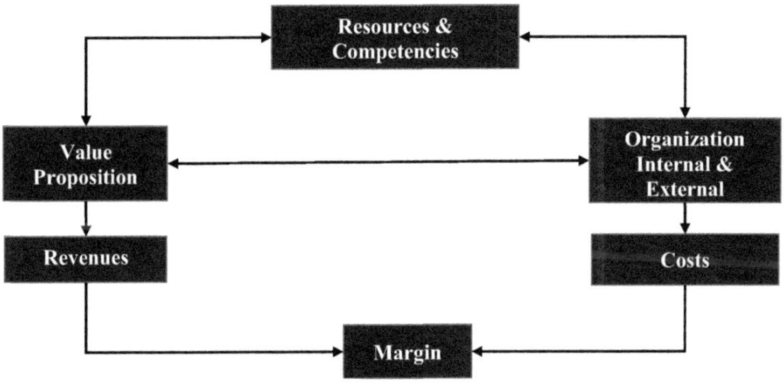

Fig. 1 The RCOV model: the main business model components and their relationships (Adapted from Lecoq et al. 2006)

being dependent upon its ability to anticipate and react to the consequences of evolution in any given business model component. This is what they referred to as "dynamic consistency", which enabled the firm to change while maintaining sustainable performance.

Penrose argued that the growth of the firm resulted from the interaction between its *resources*, its *organisation*, and its capacity to propose new *value propositions* in markets. Using a business model perspective, Demil and Lecoq (2010) linked this to three core business model components consisting of resources and competencies, organisational structure, and the proposition for value delivery. The *resources* could come from external markets or they could be developed internally, while the *competencies* represented the ability and knowledge to improve or recombine the services that the resources could offer.

The *organisational structure* incorporated the organisation's activities and its relations with other organisations to combine and exploit its resources. This would include the value chain or value network of activities with external stakeholders. The business model also included the *value proposition* that the company delivered to customers such as products and services (see Fig. 1).

When analysing two-sided platform companies, the RCOV model provides a more flexible framework than Porter's (1985) Value Chain and other RBV frameworks. The fact that resources can be sourced externally is very important since the platform business model inverts the RBV theory. For example, resources are sourced from an external ecosystem of providers and suppliers and not internally from the organisation itself (Parker et al. 2016). The reference to "competencies that represented the ability and knowledge to improve or recombine the services the resources could offer" was also very relevant. Since data is at the core of everything that two-sided firms do, this can be recombined to produce a range of diverse products and services (Lycett 2013) in a broad range of market sectors and industries. User data can be leveraged to market products relating to media, health, financial services, transport, food, accommodation, etc.

The data-rich nature of the platform companies has also influenced the type of organisation structure that two-sided firms operate. The structures are asset-light and leverage external network effects (Van Alstyne et al. 2016). The two-sided firms operate across a value network (Peppard and Rylander 2006), not through a value chain. They leverage the benefits of market mechanisms by lowering transaction costs which are made possible through the utilisation of low-cost cloud computing. This has led to the shrinkage of the core resource base and structure at the centre of the platform ecosystem and the expansion outwards towards the periphery (Van Alstyne et al. 2016). This asset-light organisation structure has resulted in a very low-cost base leading to a performance advantage over traditional brick-and-mortar companies such as banks, high street retailers, hotels and taxi companies, etc. As mentioned earlier, since the marginal cost of scaling a digital platform is close to zero (Rifkin 2014), the two-sided firms have also changed the economic models of many industries such as music and advertising, etc. This has also impacted positively on the profit margins of the world's leading technology platform-based firms.

The cost benefits and the ability of platforms to reduce transaction costs have also resulted in new value propositions. Content is often given away free in order to gain traffic to a website or smartphone app so that advertising streams can be monetised (Google). The content on a vast proportion of social media sites is provided free-of-charge enabling the social media firms to focus on enhancing user experiences (Rifkin 2014). Two-sided markets, therefore, offer high levels of interactivity and engagement for large audiences that cannot be replicated by one-sided firms. Services can also be provided on-demand and in real-time 24/7. This has resulted in both new and higher value propositions that one-sided firms are not able to match due to their structure.

The ability to scale rapidly using the World Wide Web as a global platform and the availability of cloud infrastructure (platform as a service, software as a service, and infrastructure as service), plus an ecosystem of apps and smartphones, means that the two-sided platform companies can also generate high revenues and a large number of users through network effects (Walton and Pyper 2019).

Finally, Amit and Zott (2012), in their article entitled "Creating Value Through Business Model Innovation", stated that due to environmental pressures, more firms were resorting to business model innovation rather than product/service or process innovation in order to enhance performance and/or their chances of survival. They claimed that changing how a company did business was often easier than changing the products or services themselves.

In the article, the authors use the example of how Apple defeated HTC using business model innovation rather than product innovation following the launch of the iPod music player and the iTunes music store. This illustrated how difficult it is for a company to imitate or replicate an entire ecosystem rather than a single product or process. Apple's innovation at the business model level was too much of a competitive challenge for HTC as well as other handset makers such as Nokia and Blackberry. This ecosystem advantage was also illustrated in a famous "burning platform" speech by Stephen Elop (as CEO of Nokia) in 2011 when he said that Nokia was not being put out of business by another handset (Apple iPhone) but by an entire ecosystem of content. He said that the battle of devices had become a war of ecosystems and that competitors were taking Nokia's market share not with devices but with an entire ecosystem—Apple's app store and Google's marketplace (Savitz 2011).

4 The Resource-Based View (RBV) of Technological Transformation

The origins of the resource-based view (RBV) can be traced back over 60 years to the work of Joseph Schumpeter and Edith Penrose. It was Joseph Schumpeter who laid the foundations for a resource-based theory in his *History of Economic Analysis* (1954), which highlighted the importance of resource differences in generating innovation, entrepreneurship, and economic growth. In her work, *The Theory of the Growth of the Firm* (1959), Penrose applied Schumpeter's theory to the industrial organisation. Schumpeter also made a distinction between innovation and discovery on the one hand and innovation and commercialisation on the other. This reflected the nineteenth-century model of innovation where independent inventors offered their inventions to entrepreneurs for commercialisation.

Penrose (1959) reinterpreted Schumpeter's theory of the modern firm and noted the necessity for innovation, discovery commercialisation, and entrepreneurship all taking place *within* the firm's boundaries. Penrose, therefore, highlighted the importance of in-house research and development and anticipated the growing importance of organisational learning, technological change, flexibility, diversification, collaboration, networks, shared capabilities, and internationalisation.

It is generally agreed that an organisation's resources are the productive "assets" that it owns and controls and which the firm uses to make a product or deliver a service. These resources are normally classified as tangible resources (such as cash, equipment, or land), intangible resources (such as patents, reputation, and culture), and human resources (such as skills and motivation) (Jafari-Sadeghi 2020; Jafari-Sadeghi et al. 2020a).

According to Grant (1991), however, on their own resources are not productive, and if any competitive advantage is to be achieved, the resources have to be combined to form capabilities. Capabilities emerge from the cooperation and coordination of a team of resources within a firm, and therefore a capability is the capacity of a team of resources to perform some task or activity. The simple possession of resources is therefore not enough. The strategic assets of a firm also represent another important RBV concept. Strategic assets are another way of describing those resources, capabilities, or competencies that are particularly valuable to the firm and are critical to its strategic objectives and its ability to sustain competitive advantage. This competitive and advantage will also be enhanced if the resources and capabilities meet all of the VRIO criteria and are valuable, rare, inimitable, and effectively operationalised (Grant 1991).

However, as discussed by Voelpel et al. (2004) earlier in the chapter, markets and industries had experienced a shift away from an industrial-based to knowledge and information-based economy. This new economy had three distinguishing features. It was vastly globalised, it favoured intangible things (ideas, information, relationships, knowledge), and it was intensely interlinked with ubiquitous networks. This has had significant implications regarding the resources needed to compete in the "new economy" and the factors of production. The traditional factors of production in the industrial era were land, labour, and capital, whereas the new factors of production in the Internet age are data and information. The land was the crucial raw material and source of competitive advantage in the agrarian revolution, iron ore was the crucial raw material and source of competitive advantage in the industrial revolution, and data has now become the crucial raw material and source of competitive advantage in the knowledge and information age (Walton and Pyper 2019: 1; Rezaei et al. 2020; Jafari-Sadeghi et al. 2019).

The chapter will now analyse the extent to which data and information have become the core competency driving the platform business model and how this may be contributing to a new source of competitive advantage. Using Prahalad and Hamel's (1990) definition, a core competency results from a specific set of skills that deliver additional value to the customer, and these enable an organisation to access a wide variety of markets. In fact, core competencies fulfil three criteria:

1. They provide potential access to a wide variety of markets.
2. They should normally make a significant contribution to the perceived customer benefits of the end product.
3. They are difficult to imitate by competitors.

The core competency of the two-sided platform companies is the ability to capture vast amounts of data and then to process this into information and to perform predictive and prescriptive analytics. Predictive analytics enables the platform to predict future behaviour based on past performance, and prescriptive analytics allows it to make timely responses and interventions.

This ultimately leads to high levels of organisational knowledge and innovation. This is normally referred to as Big Data analytics, but this is now being extended into the areas of artificial intelligence (AI) and machine learning. The collective learning does not only extend across the organisation but also externally to include suppliers and buyers that interact with the technology platform. It also includes structured data and unstructured/semi-structured data as well (Sharda et al. 2014).

This also fulfils Prahalad and Hamel's (1990) three core competency criteria outlined above. First, access to a wide variety of markets is achieved. Since the main processing activities of modern service companies consist of information and customers, the digital platform firms can enter a diverse range of markets by targeting customers using Big Data algorithms based on previous search histories and online profiles. The dematerialisation of products through digitisation (payments, music, books, magazines newspapers, movies, finance, insurance, etc.) has also meant that platform companies can sell to a broad range of industries. This has given rise to the new "super app" mentioned earlier.

For example, Apple does not just sell computers and mobile hardware devices but also distributes music, books, films, and software apps as well. The same applies to Amazon and Alibaba with more than 400 million products (each) on their platforms including taxi-hailing and financial services. Google, Facebook, and Microsoft are also more than just search engines, social media sites, and/or software companies, respectively. They sell media products and run cloud computing platforms as well as software applications and digital assistants all based on the leveraging of the vast troves of data that they have accumulated.

Second, they also make a significant contribution to the perceived customer benefits of the end product. Customers now receive products and services either free or at very low prices via the Internet often "on-demand" with minimal delays in waiting times. Amazon is now able to guarantee same day or next day delivery, a vast selection of products and services to choose from, and very low prices. Spotify (and YouTube) offer free music or a low-price subscription alternative plus a massive range of songs that can be streamed instantly. Alibaba and other "Fintech" companies also offer loans and money transfers at very low rates of commission (with very short lead times) compared to the banks and other established one-sided financial institutions. Due to the data-rich nature of the two-sided business model, these firms are able to deliver products and services at significantly lower transaction costs to one-sided businesses.

Third, the core competency is difficult for competitors to imitate. Over 90% of data today is generated over the Internet (Sharda et al. 2014), and it is in an unstructured or semi-structured format. In order to mine and analyse the data, specialist resources and capabilities are required such as Natural Language Processing (NLP) and Big Data analytics. A large cloud computing capability is also required. These resources and capabilities are not only valuable, but they are also strictly confined to the large technology platforms making them rare and inimitable (VRIO) to traditional linear companies.

Another perspective that can be used to analyse the core competencies of the two-sided platform firms is Prahalad and Hamel's (1990) "core competency tree" framework (see Fig. 2).

The routes of the tree consist of the competencies which in this case are the "Big Data" and "Datafication" (Normann 2001; Lycett 2013) capabilities that the two-sided platforms have. The "Big Data" competencies comprise the ability to gather vast troves of data from both structured and unstructured sources (i.e. internally within an organisation as well as from the World Wide Web) and to perform predictive and prescriptive analytics. Meanwhile, "Datafication" consists of three highly interlinked stages: dematerialisation, liquification, and density. Dematerialisation is the ability to reduce physical products down into a digital format. Liquification is the capability to manipulate and move/transfer the dematerialised information. Finally, density is the recombination of the dematerialised information as an end-user product or output (Normann 2001; Lycett 2013).

Meanwhile, the core product (the link between the core competencies and the end product) is the Internet platform infrastructure. Management of the data is performed

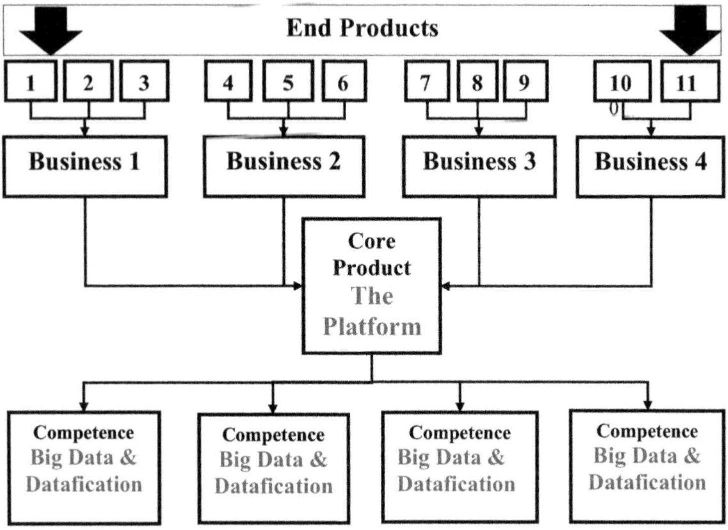

Fig. 2 Prahalad and Hamel's (1990) "The Core Competency Tree"

by the actual businesses, and this produces the end products which may include streamed media content, social media relationships, targeted advertisements, fulfilled e-commerce transactions, money transfers, room bookings, fast food deliveries, taxi rides, etc. The main difference between the one-sided and two-sided models is that the two-sided platforms view the firm as a portfolio of competencies, not as a portfolio of businesses. Competences (in this case Datafication) are the routes of the tree (company), so they are not visible and are difficult to replicate. Moreover, single-sided firms do not generally have Big Data and Datafication competencies. Finally, unlike physical assets, core competencies do not deteriorate as they are applied and shared—they grow, i.e. in this instance data generates more data creating a data flywheel effect (Brynjolfsson and McAfee 2011).

Therefore, more data and better algorithms and machine learning (artificial intelligence) serve to enhance the innovation capabilities of the two sided-firms resulting in exponential scale and revenue growth (Ismail et al. 2014) based on the law of accelerating returns (Kurzweil 2008). This has been driven by Moore's Law and the doubling of computing power every 18–24 months (Moore 1965). This is a further innovation advantage that the platform firms have over more traditional one-sided businesses with high physical fixed asset-based infrastructures.

This also builds on the knowledge-based theory of the firm (KBV) where knowledge is considered to be the most strategically significant resource that an organisation has (Spender 1996; Grant 1996) and is the result of being able to process data into information and perform advanced analytics. However, the ability of platform companies to scale rapidly and to leverage data as a core competency are not their only distinctive characteristics. These firms have also demonstrated an ability to internationalise and expand globally very quickly. This is a phenomenon that has become known as the born global company (Cavusgil and Knight 2009). This concept will be analysed in more detail in the final section of the chapter.

5 Born Global Firms

Global markets were previously dominated by large multi-national corporations (MNCs), whereas SMEs were locally based. However, the removal of political barriers and the advent of the Internet has resulted in more SMEs internationalising (Dabic et al. 2019; Jafari-Sadeghi et al. 2020b) and even becoming born global firms. Many years ago, internationalisation was a gradual and incremental process. The Uppsala Model (Johanson and Wiedersheim-Paul 1975) identified four stages of progressive entry into international markets. Similar stage models of internationalisation were developed by Bartlett and Ghoshal (1989); Bilkey and Tesar (1977); Cavusgil (1980); Johanson and Vahlne (1977); Dana et al. (2016) and Newbould et al. (1978).

A problem when applying the stage model is that it assumes a considerable span of time during which a firm can gain experience, accumulate resources, and develop the managerial capabilities required for international operations (Ratten et al. 2007; Dana et al. 2009a, b). However, the rapid globalisation of markets over the last 20 years (Levitt 1983; Ohmae 1989) and the growth of the Internet have dramatically reduced that time span and enabled small start-up firms to become born globals. In the contemporary global business environment, time has become a critical strategic weapon (Stalk 1988; Stalk and Hout 1990). In such an environment, time-delayed models, such as the stages theory, are therefore considered to be inappropriate. Coviello and Martin (1999) concluded that small, high-tech firms rarely followed a stepwise approach to internationalisation. Oviatt and McDougall (2005) developed a model of the forces influencing the speed of internationalisation. They argued that speed was enabled by technology, motivated by competition, and moderated by the knowledge intensity of the opportunity and the firm's international networks. Internationalisation could, therefore, be summarised as the discovery, execution, assessment, and exploitation of business opportunities that add value to the business (Ferreira et al. 2017). Finally, the stage process was relevant for the internationalisation of physical goods but not digital products and services delivered by platform companies.

Meanwhile, the speed at which a platform scales and creates a network effect and critical mass is crucial to its success (Moazed and Johnson 2016; Mokhtarzadeh et al. 2020). Being the first to scale is even more important than having a first-mover advantage (Hoffman 2018; Gill et al. 2017). A network effect creates a competitive "moat" around the platform similar to a barrier to entry. Achieving this is what is known as a winner-takes-all or winner-takes-most strategy (Parker et al. 2016). Therefore, platform firms may have no choice other than to become "instant internationals" (or born globals) in order to survive (Oviatt and McDougall 1999; Knight and Cavusgil 1996; Jafari Sadeghi et al. 2019a). The platform companies also utilise the World Wide Web as their core resource base which makes early internationalisation almost inevitable. The Internet could therefore be classed as a universal factor that influences the internationalisation of SMEs (Audretsch 2003; Dana and Wright 2009) regardless of the location of the firm, i.e. the Internet is location-agnostic (Dana 2017; Jafari Sadeghi et al. 2019b).

According to Oviatt and McDougall (2005) and Mort and Weerawardena (2006), firm internationalisation tends to happen more quickly for ventures that leverage extensive international networks, and since the Internet is a global network, this partly explains the born-global nature of early-stage platform companies. A born global company has been defined as a "business organisation that, from inception, seeks to derive significant competitive advantage from the use of resources and the sale of outputs in multiple countries" (Oviatt and McDougall 1994).

Other definitions include:

> Management views the world as its marketplace from the outset. (Knight and Cavusgil 1996)

If one considers the early vision statements of Google and Amazon, one realises that these had a global market view: "To organise the world's information and make it universally accessible and useful" (Google) and to be the "Earth's biggest book store" and to be "the earth's most customer centric-company" (Amazon). In addition to viewing the world as a marketplace from the outset, the leading platform companies derive well over 25% of their sales from overseas activities 2 to 3 years after formation, which was another condition of being a born global company set by London Business School (2008).

Meanwhile, Gabrielsson et al. (2008) stated that born global firms had four channels available to them to assist in rapid international growth from an early stage. These included (1) multinational enterprises (MNEs) acting as systems integrators or global customers; (2) multination enterprises (MNEs) distributing or licensing born global products or services; (3) networks of supportive firms and/or business associates; and (4) the Internet or some combination of two or more of the variables mentioned.

The platform companies are able to benefit from all four variables outlined by Gabrielsson et al. (2008). First and foremost, the platform companies are Internet-based, and due to the global nature of the World Wide Web, they can reach anyone who has an Internet connection.

This enables the platform companies to achieve high levels of market aggregation across international borders from "day one". Market aggregations are the process whereby platforms provide centralised markets to serve widely dispersed individuals and organisations. Market aggregation across international boundaries provides information and power to platform users who normally engage in interactions in a haphazard fashion often without access to reliable or up-to-date market data (Parker et al. 2016). Amazon marketplace, Alibaba, and Etsy provide online sites where vendors of thousands of products from around the world can offer their wares to consumers. Meanwhile, service platforms such as Upwork can bring thousands of skilled professionals under a single roof from anywhere in the world making it easy for potential employers to evaluate, compare, and hire people.

Platforms also act as systems integrators and serve global customers. Amazon, Microsoft, Google, Alibaba, and Tencent all have cloud computing platforms serving multi-national customers, while open-source platforms such as Linux, Android, and GitHub attract software developers on a global scale. Platforms also have rich networks of supportive firms due to the large ecosystems which support the delivery of a wide range of products and services. As the platforms move into more markets and industries (becoming "super apps"), these ecosystems increase in size. Finally, platforms are good at distributing born global products or services. Born global firms generally pursue a differentiation strategy, with relatively distinctive products that are targeted at niche markets (Porter 1985). Often these niches are too small to be of interest to larger firms. However, due to the digitised nature of the products that are distributed online, platform companies can micro-segment and micro-target customers with customised offerings. The platform companies are therefore able to deliver differentiated-specialised products at a lower cost and price than traditional competitors (Ayob and Dana 2017: 30).

Digital rather than physical inventories also enable platforms to serve a "long tail" (Anderson 2009) of consumers normally overlooked by traditional manufacturers and retailers. An example of this is Revolut, which initially targeted frequent international travellers by promising to save them money on foreign transaction fees. This was a specialised niche market nationally but a relatively large market globally. All these factors have contributed to a large swathe of platform start-ups becoming born global companies very quickly. Over the years these have included well-known brands such as Amazon, Google, Airbnb, Uber, Spotify, Netflix, Skype, and a whole range of Fintech companies, particularly those offering payments services. Meanwhile, as the Covid-19 pandemic undermines the global supply chains of traditional companies that produce and deliver physical goods and services, the digital platforms created within the last 2–3 years are now seeing exponential international growth as users seek new ways of communicating, working, and buying goods and services. This has meant that platforms created in the shadow of the pandemic have the potential to become "born globals" and/or to reinforce their born global credentials as more people migrate online and remain loyal to the new services they have adopted post-Covid-19.

6 Conclusion

It can be seen from the preceding analysis the important role played by entrepreneurs in the building of disruptive technologies and ecosystems as the foundations of a new means of delivering value to global consumers. Business model innovation, driven by new platform Internet companies using data and information as a new factor of production and source of competitive advantage, has changed the competitive landscape for incumbent firms on an international scale. The platform business model that originated in North America has now expanded into Europe and Asia as these companies have become born global firms. As global supply chains are threatened by potential fragmentation from the Covid-19 pandemic, the current Internet business models of the platform companies are likely to enjoy even greater success as more citizens migrate online to fulfil personal and work-based needs. This provides exciting opportunities for further research to evaluate the ongoing impact of the platform companies as new technologies are adopted going forward including artificial intelligence (AI), Industry 4.0, and the Internet-of-Things (IoT).

References

Adner R (2017) Ecosystem as structure: an actionable construct for strategy. J Manag 43(1):39–58

Amit R, Zott C (2001) Value creation in E-business. Strateg Manag J 22(6/7):493–520

Amit R, Zott C (2012) Creating value through business model innovation. MIT Sloan Manag Rev 53(3). Spring 2012

Anderson C (2009) The longer long tail: how endless choice is creating unlimited demand. Random House, London

Aparicio S, Urbano D, Audretsch D (2016) Institutional factors, opportunity entrepreneurship and economic growth: panel data evidence. Technol Forecast Soc Chang 102:45–61

Audretsch D (2003) SMEs in the age of globalisation. Edward Elgar Publishing, Cheltenham

Ayob AH, Dana L (2017) Product strategies for export ventures: an empirical investigation among SMEs in an emerging economy. Jurnal Pengurusan 50:25–30

Baden-Fuller C, Mangematin V (2013) Business models: a challenging agenda. Strateg Organ 11 (4):418–427. Sage Publishing

Bartlett CA, Ghoshal S (1989) Managing across borders: the transnational solution. Harvard Business School Press, Boston

Bilkey WJ, Tesar G (1977) The export behaviour of smaller sized Wisconsin manufacturing firms. J Int Bus Stud 8(1):93–98

Brynjolfsson E, McAfee A (2011) The big data boom is the innovation story of our time. The Atlantic. November 2011

Casadesus-Masanell R, Ricart JE (2010) From strategy to business models and on to tactics. Long Range Plan 43(2–3):195–215

Case S (2017) The third wave: an entrepreneur's vision of the future. Simon and Schuster, London

Cavalcante S, Kesting P, Ulhoi J (2011) Business model dynamics and innovation: (re)establishing the missing linkages. Manag Decis 49(8):1327–1342

Cavusgil ST (1980) On the internationalisation process of firms. Eur Res 8:273–281

Cavusgil ST, Knight GA (2009) Born global firms: a new international enterprise. Business Expert Press, New York

Chandler AD (1990) Scale and scope. Harvard University Press, Cambridge, MA

Chesbrough H (2010) Business model innovation: opportunities and barriers. Long Range Plan 43:354–363

Chesbrough H, Rosenbloom RS (2002) The role of the business model in capturing value from innovation: evidence from Xerox Corporation's technology spin-off companies. Ind Corp Chang 11(3):529

Choudary SP (2013) Platform power: secrets of billion-dollar internet start-ups. Platform Thinking Labs

Choudary SP (2015) Platform scale: how a new breed of start-ups is building large empires with minimum investment. Platform Thinking Labs

Coase R (1937) The nature of the firm. Economica 4(16):386–405

Coviello NE, Martin KA-M (1999) Internationalization of service SMEs: an integrated perspective from the engineering consulting sector. J Int Mark 7(4):42–66
Dabic M, Maley J, Dana L, Novak I, Pellegrini MM, Caputo A (2019) Pathways of internationalisation: a bibliometric and systematic review. Small Bus Econ. Springer
Dana L-P (2017) International entrepreneurship research: how it evolved and directions for the future. Int J Entrep Small Bus 30(4):477–489
Dana L-P, Wright RW (2009) International entrepreneurship: research priorities for the future. Int J Glob Small Bus 3(1):90–134. https://doi.org/10.1504/IJGSB.2009.021572
Dana L-P, Grimwood S, William G (2009a) Export incentives and international entrepreneurship in New Zealand firms. JIBED 4(1/2):1–21. https://doi.org/10.5367/000000006775870497
Dana L-P, Hamilton RT, Wick K (2009b) Deciding to export: an exploratory study of Singaporean entrepreneurs. J Int Entrep 7(2):79–87. https://doi.org/10.1007/s10843-008-0032-8
Dana L-P, Grandinetti R, Mason MC (2016) International entrepreneurship, export planning and export performance: evidence from a sample of winemaking SMEs. Int J Entrep Small Bus 29 (4):602. https://doi.org/10.1504/IJESB.2016.079965
Davenport TH, Leibold M, Voelpel SC (2006) Strategic management in the innovation economy: strategic approaches and tools for dynamic innovation capabilities, 1st edn. Publicis, Bremen
Davidson S, Giesen E, Harmer M, Marshall A (2018) How industry leaders enhance the value of ecosystems. Strat Leader. Emerald Publishing 46(2):26–33
Davies A, Brady T (2000) Organizational capabilities and learning in complex product systems: towards repeatable solutions. Res Policy 29:931–953
Demil B, Lecoq X (2010) Business model evolution in search of dynamic consistency. Long Range Plan 43:227–246
Eriksson HE, Penker M (2000) Business modelling with UML: business patterns at work. Wiley, New York
Ferreira JJ, Fernandes CI, Ratten V (2017) International entrepreneurship research: mapping and cognitive structures. Int J Entrep Small Bus 30(4):545–566
Fransman M (2010) The new ICT ecosystem: implications for policy and regulation. Cambridge University Press, Cambridge
Gabrielsson M, Manek Kirplanai VH, Dimitratos P, Solberg CA, Zucchella A (2008) Born globals: propositions to help advance the theory. Int Bus Rev 17:385–401
Garousi Mokhtarzadeh N, Amoozad Mahdiraji H, Jafari-Sadeghi V, Soltani A, Abbasi Kamardi A (2020) A product-technology portfolio alignment approach for food industry: a multi-criteria decision making with z-numbers. Br Food J. https://doi.org/10.1108/BFJ-02-2020-0115
Gawer A (2009) Platform dynamics and strategies: from products to services. Edward Elgar, Cheltenham
Gawer A, Cusumano MA (2002) Platform leadership: how Intel, Microsoft, and Cisco drive industry innovation. Harvard Business School Press, Boston
Gill A, Gurău C, Dana L-P, Sánchez CR (2017) Human capital, financial strategy and small firm performance: a study of Canadian entrepreneurs. Int J Entrep Small Bus 31(4):492. https://doi.org/10.1504/IJESB.2017.085428
Grant RM (1991) The resource-based theory of competitive advantage: implications for strategy formulation. Calif Manag Rev 33(3):114–135
Grant RM (1996) Toward a knowledge-based theory of the firm. Strateg Manag J 17:109–122
Grant RM (2016) Contemporary strategy analysis, 9th edn. Wiley, Chichester
Hamel G (2000) Leading the revolution. Harvard Business School Press, Boston
Hannah DP, Eisenhardt KM (2017) How firms navigate cooperation and competition in nascent ecosystems. Strateg Manag J 39(12):3163–3192. https://doi.org/10.1002/smj.2750
Hedman J, Kalling T (2002) IT and business models: concepts and theories. Copenhagen Business School, Copenhagen
Henderson R, Clark K (1990) Architectural innovation: the reconfiguration of existing product technologies and the failure of established firms. Adm Sci Q 35:9–30

Hitt MA, Ireland RD, Hoskisson RE (2003) Strategic management: competitiveness and globalisation. Thomson-South-Western, Mason, OH
Hobday M (2000) The project-based organization: an ideal form for managing complex products and systems? Res Policy 29(7–8):871–893
Hoffman R (2018) Blitzscaling: the lightning-fast path to building massively valuable companies. Harper Collins, New York
Hounshell DA (1985) From the American system to mass production: 1800–1932. Johns Hopkins University Press, Baltimore, MD
Iansiti M, Levien R (2004) Strategy as ecology. Harv Bus Rev 82(3):68–78. 126
Ismail S, Malone MS, Van Geest Y (2014) Exponential organizations: why new organizations are ten times better, faster and cheaper than yours. Diversion Books, New York
Jacobides MG, Cennamo C, Gawer A (2018) Towards a theory of ecosystems. Strateg Manag J 39 (8):2255–2276. https://doi.org/10.1002/smj.2904
Jafari Sadeghi V, Biancone PP, Anderson RB, Nkongolo-Bakenda J-M (2019a) International entrepreneurship by particular people 'on their own terms': a study on the universal characteristics of entrepreneurs in evolving economies. Int J Entrep Small Bus 37(2):288–308. https://doi.org/10.1504/ijesb.2019.100109
Jafari Sadeghi V, Nkongolo-Bakenda JM, Anderson RB, Dana L (2019b) An institution-based view of international entrepreneurship: a comparison of context-based and universal determinants in developing and economically advanced countries. Int Bus Rev 28(2109):101588
Jafari-Sadeghi V (2020) The motivational factors of business venturing: opportunity versus necessity? A gendered perspective on European countries. J Bus Res 113(May):279–289. https://doi.org/10.1016/j.jbusres.2019.09.058
Jafari-Sadeghi V, Kimiagari S, Biancone PP (2019) Level of education and knowledge, foresight competency and international entrepreneurship: a study of human capital determinants in the European countries. Eur Bus Rev 32(1):46–68. https://doi.org/10.1108/EBR-05-2018-0098
Jafari-Sadeghi V, Dutta DK, Ferraris A, Del Giudice M (2020a) Internationalisation business processes in an under-supported policy contexts: evidence from Italian SMEs. Bus Process Manag J. https://doi.org/10.1108/BPMJ-03-2019-0141
Jafari-Sadeghi V, Nkongolo-Bakenda J-M, Dana L-P, Anderson RB, Biancone PP (2020b) Home country institutional context and entrepreneurial internationalization: the significance of human capital attributes. J Int Entrep. https://doi.org/10.1007/s10843-019-00264-1
Johanson J, Vahlne J-E (1977) The internationalization process of the firm: a model of knowledge development and increasing foreign market commitments. J Int Bus Stud 8(1):23–32
Johanson J, Wiedersheim-Paul F (1975) The internationalization of the firm. J Manag Stud 12 (3):305–323
Kapoor R (2014) Collaborating with complementors: what do firms do? In: Adner R, Oxley JE, Silverman BS (eds) Collaboration and competition in business ecosystems, Advances in strategic management, vol. 30. Emerald Group Publishing Limited, pp 3–25
Kapoor R, Agarwal S (2017) Sustaining superior performance in business ecosystems: evidence from application software developers in the iOS and android smartphone ecosystems. Organ Sci 28(3):531–551
Kapoor R, Lee JM (2013) Coordinating and competing in ecosystems: how organizational forms shape new technology investments. Strateg Manag J 34(3):274–296
Kelly K (1998) New rules for the new economy – 10 radical strategies for a connected World. Viking Penguin, New York
Knight G, Cavusgil ST (1996) The born global firm: a challenge to traditional internationalization theory. Adv Int Mark 8:11–26
Kotler P (1986) The Prosumer movement: a new challenge for marketers. In: Lutz RJ (ed) NA—advances in consumer research volume 13. Association for Consumer Research, Provo, UT, pp 510–513
Kurzweil R (2008) The law of accelerating returns. Springer Publishing, New York

Leavy B (2016) The next wave of global disruption and the role of China's entrepreneurs. Strat Leader. Emerald Publishing 44(3):27–37
Lecoq X, Demil B, Warnier V (2006) Le business model, un outil d'analyse strategique. L'Expansion Manag Rev 123:96–109
Levitt T (1983) The globalization of markets. Harv Bus Rev, May–June, pp 92–102
Lindner MA, Vaquero LM, Rodero-Merino L, Caceres J (2010) Cloud economics: dynamic business models for business on demand. IJBIS 5(4):373–392
London Business School (2008) Born global. London Bus Sch Rev. 1 Dec 2008
Lycett M (2013) Datafication: making sense of (big) data in a complex world. Eur J Inf Syst 22:381–386
Moazed A, Johnson N (2016) Modern monopolies: what it takes to dominate the 21st century economy. St. Martin's Press, New York
Mokhtarzadeh N, Amoozad Mahdiraji H, Jafarpanah I, Jafari-Sadeghi V, Cardinali S (2020) Investigating the impact of networking capability on firm innovation performance: using the resource-action-performance framework. J Intellect Cap. https://doi.org/10.1108/JIC-01-2020-0005
Moore GE (1965) Cramming more components onto integrated circuits. Electronics 38(8)
Moore JF (1993) Predators and prey: a new ecology of competition. Harv Bus Rev, May–June, pp 75–86
Moore JF (1996) The death of competition: leadership & strategy in the age of business ecosystems. Harper Collins, New York
Mort GS, Weerawardena J (2006) Networking capability and international entrepreneurship: how networks function in Australian born global firms. IMR. Emerald Group Publishing Limited 23 (5):549–572. https://doi.org/10.1108/02651330610703445
Newbould GD, Buckley PJ, Thurwell JC (1978) Going international: the experience of smaller companies overseas. John Wiley & Sons, New York
Nightingale P (2000) The product-process-organisation relationship in complex development projects. Res Policy 29(7–8):913–930
Nightingale P, Baden-Fuller C, Hopkins MM (2011) Projects, project capabilities and project organizations. In: Cattini G, Ferriani S, Taube F (eds) Project-based organizing and strategic management, Advances in strategic management, vol 28. Emerald Group Publishing Ltd, Bingley, pp 215–234
Normann R (2001) Reframing business when the map changes the landscape. John Wiley & Sons, Chichester
Ohmae K (1989) The global logic of strategic alliances. Harv Bus Rev, March–April, pp 143–154
Osterwalder A, Pigneur Y (2010) Business model generation: a handbook for visionaries, game changers and challengers. Wiley, Hoboken, NJ
Oviatt BM, McDougall PP (1994) Towards a theory of international ventures. J Int Bus Stud 25 (1):45–64
Oviatt BM, McDougall PP (1999) A framework for understanding accelerated international entrepreneurship. In: Wright RW (ed) International entrepreneurship: globalization of emerging businesses. JAI Press, Stamford, CT, pp 23–40
Oviatt BM, McDougall PP (2005) Defining international entrepreneurship and modeling the speed of internationalization. ETP:537–554. https://doi.org/10.1111/j.1540-6520.2005.00097.x
Parker GP, Van Alstyne MW, Choudary SP (2016) Platform revolution: how networked markets are transforming the economy and how to make them work for you. Norton, New York
Penrose ET (1959) The theory of the growth of the firm, 4th edn. Oxford University Press, Oxford
Peppard J, Rylander A (2006) From value chain to value network: insights for mobile operators. Eur Manag J 24:128–141
Porter ME (1985) Competitive advantage. Free Press, New York
Prahalad CK, Hamel G (1990) The Core competence of the corporation. Harv Bus Rev 68(3):79–91
Ratten V, Dana L, Han M (2007) Internationalisation of SMEs: European comparative studies. Int J Small Bus 4(3):361–379

Reillier L, Reillier B (2017) Platform strategy: how to unlock the power of communities & networks to grow your business. Routledge, Abingdon
Rezaei M, Jafari-Sadeghi V, Bresciani S (2020) What drives the process of knowledge management in a cross-cultural setting: the impact of social capital? Eur Bus Rev 32(3):485–511. https://doi.org/10.1108/EBR-06-2019-0127
Rifkin J (2014) The zero marginal cost society: the internet of things, the collaborative commons and the eclipse of capitalism. Palgrave Macmillan, Basingstoke
Savitz E (2011) "Burning platform" memo highlights Nokia's woes. Forbes. 9 Feb 2011. https://www.forbes.com/sites/ericsavitz/2011/02/09/ceos-burning-platform-memo-highlights-nokias-woes/#5bce11118296
Schumpeter J (1934) The theory of economic development: an inquiry into profits, capital, credit, interest and the business cycle. Transaction Publishers, New Brunswick
Shapiro C, Varian HR (1999) The art of standards wars. Calif Manag Rev 41(2):8–32
Sharda R, Delene D, Tutban E (2014) Business intelligence: a managerial perspective on analytics, 3rd edn. Pearson, Harlow
Spender JC (1996) Making knowledge the basis of a dynamic theory of the firm. Strateg Manag J 17:45–62
Stalk G (1988) Time: the next source of competitive advantage. Harv Bus Rev, July–August, pp 41–51
Stalk G, Hout TM (1990) Competing against time. Free Press, New York
Sukumar A, Jafari-Sadeghi V, Garcia-Perez A, Dutta DK (2020) The potential link between corporate innovations and corporate competitiveness: evidence from IT firms in the UK. J Knowl Manag. https://doi.org/10.1108/JKM-10-2019-0590
Tansley AG (1935) The use and abuse of vegetational concepts and terms. Ecol 16(3):284–307
Tapscott D (1997) Strategy in the new economy. Strateg Leadersh 25(6):8–14
Teece DJ (2010) Business models, business strategy and innovation. Long Range Plan 43 (2–3):172–194
Tucker R (2001) Strategy innovation takes imagination. J Bus Strateg 22(3):23–27
Van Alstyne MW, Parker GG, Choudary SP (2016) Pipelines, platforms and the new rules of strategy. Harv Bus Rev 94(4):54–62
Van Putten B, Schief M (2012) The relation between dynamic business models and business cases. Electron J Inf Syst Eval 15(91):138–148
Voelpel SC, Leibold M, Tekie EB (2004) The wheel of business model reinvention: how to change your business model to leapfrog competitors. J Chang Manag 4(3):259–276
Walton N (2017) The internet as a technology-based ecosystem: a new approach to the analysis of business, markets and industries. Palgrave Macmillan Pivot, London
Walton N (2018) The extent to which data-rich firms operating two-sided platform-ecosystem business models are able to use data to gain an innovation advantage over established one-sided companies. PhD dissertation, Coventry University. January
Walton N, Pyper N (2019) Technology strategy. Red Globe Press, London
Weitzman ML (1998) Recombinant growth. Q J Econ 113(2):331–360
Williamson OE (1981) The economics of organization: the transaction cost approach. Am J Sociol 87(3):54–577
Wirtz BW, Schilke G, Ullrich S (2010) Strategic development of business models: implications of the web 2.0 for creating value on the internet. Long Range Plan 43(2–3):216–226
Wirtz BW, Pistoia A, Ullrich S, Gottel V (2016) Business models: origin, development and future research perspectives. Long Range Plan 49:36–54
Zott C, Amit R, Massa L (2011) The business model: recent developments and future research. J Manag 37(4):1019–1042

Nigel Walton is Assistant Professor in Business Strategy at Coventry Business School, Coventry University. He is also an Associate Lecturer in Strategy at the Open University Business School as well as being a founder and Chief Editor of the Journal of Platform Economics (JPE). He was previously a Senior Lecturer in Innovation and Entrepreneurship at the University of Worcester. His research interests are in entrepreneurship, platform strategies, ecosystems, digital disruption, and technology innovation. He has written two books on platform Internet companies and technology strategy titled: "The Internet as a Technology Based Ecosystem: A New Approach to the Analysis of Business, Markets and Industries (2017)" and "Technology Strategy (2019)".

Part II
Qualitative Research Streams: Literature Reviews

A Review of International Entrepreneurship as Part of Broader Opportunity Research: Topic Modelling Approach

Vesa Puhakka and Arto Ojala

1 Introduction

International Entrepreneurship (IE) research plays a vital role in understanding the internationalisation of new, fast-growing, and born global companies (Oviatt and McDougall 2005; Reuber et al. 2018). IE also plays an essential role in research on entrepreneurs and entrepreneurship in a globalising, multicultural, and technological world (Dana 1999, 2001; Mainela et al. 2018), and especially in the exploration of entrepreneurial opportunities (Mainela et al. 2014). Jones et al. (2011) pointed out in their IE review that a significant part of research examines entrepreneurial internationalisation focusing on the type of venture (e.g. Madsen and Servais 1997; Oviatt and McDougall 1994), the process of internationalisation (e.g. Autio et al. 2000; Nummela et al. 2004; Sadeghi et al. 2018), networks and social capital (e.g. Coviello and Munro 1995; Presutti et al. 2007), as well as knowledge and capabilities (e.g. Weerawardena et al. 2007; Zahra et al. 2005). According to Jones et al. (2011), the previous research has also focused on cross-country and cross-cultural comparisons of entrepreneurship (e.g. Anderson et al. 2006; Baker et al. 2005; Jafari-Sadeghi et al. 2019a). The least attention they consider has been given to research that draws directly from opportunity theories of entrepreneurship and examines how to discover or create international opportunities.

V. Puhakka (✉)
Department of Marketing, Management and International Business, University of Oulu Business School, University of Oulu, Oulu, Finland
e-mail: vesa.puhakka@oulu.fi

A. Ojala
School of Marketing and Communication, International Business, University of Vaasa, Vaasa, Finland
e-mail: arto.ojala@univaasa.fi

V. Jafari-Sadeghi et al. (eds.), *Empirical International Entrepreneurship*, Contributions to Management Science,
https://doi.org/10.1007/978-3-030-68972-8_6

This study aims to complete the picture of earlier IE reviews by examining IE's influence and impact on broader entrepreneurial opportunity research. The research corpus utilised in this study is 1326 published journal articles on opportunities in time between 1958 and 2016. We are not looking at dedicated IE articles as such but rather broadly opportunity articles where IE is one of the key themes. Opportunity research is being considered because it has been the main research area for entrepreneurship for the last 20 years (see seminal papers by Dana 1995; Gaglio and Katz 2001; Shane and Venkataraman 2000). Also, in IE's influential articles, the opportunity is a crucial concept (Dana 1994; McDougall and Oviatt 2003; Oviatt and McDougall 1994). This study applies topic modelling (Blei and Lafferty 2006; Blei et al. 2003) in the analysis. Topic modelling is an unstructured, algorithm-based analysis of sizeable naturalistic text data, which looks at the use of words with their context. It can bring out the below-the-surface embedded deep structures of a great mass of text and display. For example, how science is organised differently is usually seen as structuring.

This study contributes in two ways. First, the study aims to show how science is polyphonic. The diversity of topics reveals how IE's construction is a dynamic, contingent, and always an unfinished area of human activity. The research involves and is connected with various discourses, perspectives, and ideologies at the same time. Second, the study aims to open up a path for computer-aided, algorithm-based analysis of large text masses. This study highlights a way to analyse a large mass of articles as a polyphonic discussion, immersed in a wide variety of even contradictory topics, without polyphony or contradiction being seen as a problem but as a natural part of science. The study reveals how language produces the reality that we see as research on opportunities and IE within it.

The rest of the study is structured as follows. We start by explaining the topic modelling approach, the article corpus, and examining it. Then we analyse and determine what influence and impact IE have on the broader opportunity research. We then suggest how the IE theme can evolve as part of broader opportunity research. We finally conclude with a discussion of implications for IE research regarding the use of the topic modelling approach. In the following, the topic and theme are used interchangeably.

2 Methodology

2.1 Topic Modelling Approach

Topic modelling is about mining texts to find a probabilistic model arranging a corpus of documents. We define a topic as "a distribution over a fixed vocabulary" (Blei 2012: 3), that is, how likely particular words coexist in a text. Probabilistic topic modelling is a set of algorithms whose task is to find thematic structures immersed in a text data corpus (Steyvers and Griffiths 2007). Probabilistic topic modelling focuses on the whole corpus, not individual texts. Topic model algorithms statistically analyse words in the documents under consideration to find topics that produce the documents' text, the links between the topics, and the change of topics over time (Blei et al. 2003).

The main idea is that the human use of words is not random, but the words are used in specific contexts (e.g. scientific research), which constitute the broader topics. The benefit of topic modelling is that it does not require any prior classification or code trees or qualitative coding of the data, and the algorithms can handle masses of information quickly and efficiently (Newman et al. 2010). The algorithms produce the latent topics emerging from the original documents based on the use of words.

This study uses the LDA (latent Dirichlet allocation) topic model approach, a probabilistic model of texts (Blei 2012; Blei et al. 2003). The LDA is based on the idea that each document consists of many topical themes (Blei et al. 2003). Thus, articles are blends of many topics. The LDA is an unsupervised statistical method that takes advantage of this thinking and tries to find what kind of latent topics there are and how documents blend the various topics. It aims to reveal the below-the-surface embedded generating process that produces the observed text corpus (Blei 2012). Therefore, it is not based on the idea that there are ex-ante categories in which texts or parts of texts should be placed. Instead, it is looking—by the words and about their use to each other—for the classification through which texts are produced as a blend of various topics (Blei and Lafferty 2007).

Thus, the approach regards texts as naturalistic and unstructured. Naturalistic linguistic data is data sampled from a natural context, as it is without manipulation and so that the researcher has not affected its production. In the LDA, the algorithms go through the text space to find possible topics and weights for documents to present the data's best possible representation (Blei et al. 2003). For this to be possible, the topic model requires that only a few words are likely to be part of the topic and that each document is attached as little as possible to topics. Through these rules, the LDA double-checks the texts and sets the optimal structure of topics. The LDA, therefore, inversely looks for the generative process that produces the detected text corpus (Blei 2012). In sum, the topics consist of a network of words in which the words appear together more often than would happen randomly.

2.2 *Identification of the Relevant Literature*

Articles were selected for analysis via a three-step process. Keyword searches carried out the first stage. The search used the ABI/INFORM Complete database. The criteria used were peer-reviewed scientific publications written in English and published in scholarly journals. The specific date range, quality requirements from the journals (e.g. impact factor), and thematic scoping (e.g. business and management) were not set because the aim was to bring the opportunity research as widely and comprehensively as possible.

The keywords for searches were "opportunity" and its different versions in the title or abstract and "entrepreneurship", "small business", "SME", or "new venture" and their various forms at any point in the publication. These following keywords were included in closing out the kind of research that uses the word "opportunity" in any sense other than linking it to entrepreneurship and its various forms. To make sure that these constraints did not rule out relevant articles, the manual analysis was done on a thousand articles that did mention the word "opportunity" but not the word "entrepreneurship", "small business", "SME", or "new venture". The investigation showed that the procedure did not rule out entrepreneurship's opportunity articles, which this study is particularly interested in.

In the second stage, we moved our attention to how the articles use the opportunity concept. The articles included standard scientific articles, commentaries, editorials, and essays. All paragraphs with the word "opportunity" were searched for in these articles. The opportunity is defined was broadly defined to be about value creation in order for the different ways to see an upcoming opportunity were included in the analysis. The aim was to find those articles that explicitly use the opportunity concept as part of the research problem, the constitution of theoretical arguments, a variable or theme in data collection, or the context of the conceptual modelling based on empirical data. Those articles that used the opportunity word as a general expression or in a single sentence were excluded from the analysis. Excluded articles were reviewed for the second time, and it was confirmed that only those articles in which the opportunity was not an essential concept were excluded.

The third phase confirmed that it is not lost articles that should be covered by the analysis. This stage was deliberately broad and open. Confirmation was done by analysing manually back and forth the references of the found articles, doing searches using Google Scholar, studying the number of journals in core entrepreneurship, management and organisation, marketing, and international business journals, as well as by examining the articles citing the seminal Dana (1994), Oviatt and McDougall (1994), and Shane and Venkataraman (2000) articles. The search revealed very few articles that corresponded to the required criteria. This stage confirmed that the phases one and two procedure functions—and that for the analysis—could form a reliable and comprehensive corpus of the entrepreneurship's opportunity research.

As a result, we identified 1326 articles. The defined article corpus is from the years 1958–2016. The corpus contains 790 articles from the 2010s, 594 articles from the 2000s, 75 articles from the 1990s, 13 articles from the 1980s, one article from the 1970s, two articles from the 1960s, and four articles from the 1950s. The use of the opportunity word in the articles ranged from 1 time to 603 times. On average, the opportunity word was mentioned 52 times in the examined articles. All in all, the opportunity word was used 73,013 times.

2.3 Analysing Scientific Impact

The articles' LDA exploration was carried out by utilising the Topic Modelling Tool (TMT) (see https://code.google.com/archive/p/topic-modeling-tool/). The TMT topic modelling tool applies MALLET, which is a full, Java-based program family "for statistical natural language processing, document classification, clustering, topic modelling, information extraction, and other machine learning applications to text" (http://mallet.cs.umass.edu/) in a graphical user interface. Andrew McCallum has written the MALLET. The toolkit is Open Source Software released under the Common Public License (see http://mallet.cs.umass.edu/index.php).

The exploration was done in the following three steps: In the first stage, the full-text corpus was fed in its entirety into the TMT program. Each article was one document. It set boundaries so that the program searched for ten main topics and removed from the analysis the most common stop words, it did not preserve the case, and it made 300 training cycles to find the most suitable model. The number of topics was tested with different options, but the ten best distinguish between various +topics. The first phase yielded output.csv and output.html folders for the ten central topics. These folders have both CSV- and HTML-formatted documents of (1) the main research topics and the articles the topics appear in, (2) a numbered listing of topics, and (3) the listing of the documents (the articles) and the topics appearing in each document. This step aims to find which specific topics the research area consists of and what articles and their parts belong to these particular topics.

The second step was to take a closer look at the topics and give titles describing their content. The program does not directly provide meaningful headers to the topics, but they are displayed as a list of keywords that the algorithm thinks to belong to best describe the topics. It is the task of the researcher to interpret and decide what their common denominator is. This was done by reading each topic and examining their key themes, concepts, keywords, and methods, and cross analysing the articles to unite and distinguish them. By delving into the articles in each of the topics, looking for common denominators within the topic, considering the program's word list in the title of the topic, and comparing the topics to each other, we could give each of the ten topics a meaningful heading.

The third step was to move into a more in-depth analysis of the IE topic as part of the broader opportunity research. The first was to examine the influence of various opportunity research topics and, in particular, the IE theme throughout the whole scientific discussion. Topic modelling enables this by generating an influential figure on each article's topic, which tells you how much of the article's text belongs to each topic. Each topic's influence, including IE, was calculated as follows: the sum of the influential figures in each topic of the articles in the period, multiplied by the number of articles for that particular topic in the period, and then divided by the number of all articles in the period. This calculation method considers both the volume and the number of articles in a given topic concerning all articles. Second, the impact of articles with citations where IE was a central topic was examined. The goal was to find the most cited and least cited articles and what topics and blends they contain.

Also, the topics and journals around which the most influential articles and researchers intertwine were analysed. Third, we analysed the typical combinations of different topics in the articles and, in particular, with which topics IE appears. The top 20% of the topics in the article in question were chosen as the article's main topics. Thus, typically, an article has two to five topics that are the focus of its discussion. The size of each of the main topic's support topics shows from what perspective the main topic can be published and which other topics remain marginal despite their importance. The analysis seeks to reveal a broader, embedded structure. The productive structure of the phenomenon is essential, not the individual paper per se.

Topic modelling analysis and standard qualitative analysis—in which the researcher's observations and interpretation play a significant role, and where theory and data analysis are continuously discussed—have clear points of convergence (Hannigan et al. 2019). Topic modelling analysis often proceeds through the following process: searching for data by criteria, converting data to .txt format, running topic modelling, and manually transferring topics in the doc to Excel while simultaneously writing memos. These will then be followed by a more detailed qualitative analysis and reflection on what is relevant and interesting. One way or another, this is how most social scientists use topic modelling analysis. It is not a mechanical analysis, but the researcher's theoretical knowledge and understanding of the phenomenon and the material play a key role. The key is to be able to ask the right questions and find the answers through the analysis.

3 Findings

The findings below are observations of the immersed structure of the entire scientific discussion. This generative structure cannot be detected by reading the articles alone, but it leads to a debate that we as researchers see as opportunity research. The following will first introduce the topics of all opportunity research. Secondly, we analyse the most influential topics, the place of IE, and how the topics emerge relative to one another. Thirdly, we look at the impact of topics and articles that focus on IE and identify the scientific journals that have had an impact on the IE theme. Fourthly, we explore the themes with IE that have made the most impact. Fifthly, we examine the combinations of IE with other themes and whether they deal with a particular theme or are combinations of different topics and in what respect.

3.1 Topics on Broader Opportunity Research

Opportunity research, as a whole, appears to be utterly polyphonic. Polyphony emerges in the diversity of topics and fragmentation of discussion. The key is to understand that topic modelling analysis does not categorise articles by topics but instead reveals that articles blend many topics within them. Table 1 below highlights various topics, ranging from internationalisation to cognition and again from finance to culture. In polyphonic opportunity research, the research topics are related to each other more or less equally, in which case, there is no single prevailing perspective in the research. Opportunity research typically addresses issues related to the phenomenon's nature, emergence processes, actors and characteristics, contexts and influential external factors, and the final outputs. In this case, the emergence of topics as diverse in the research is also central to its future development. However, voices with a requirement for consistency in the topic's content can also be located in the research.

However, the abundance of topics speaks to the vivid research area and its centrality as a research concept. The concept of opportunity has been applied in many ways. The topic modelling analysis brought up the following topics (in alphabetical order): (1) cognition and learning, (2) external determinants, (3) growth and capital, (4) individual qualities, (5) international entrepreneurship, (6) knowledge and information, (7) local and cultural embeddedness, (8) process and practice perspective, (9) social and institutional context, and (10) technology entrepreneurship. These were subjected to topic modelling analysis within them. Table 1 illustrates all the opportunity topics and sub-topics. These topics represent a diversity of voices, different ways of thinking about the central feature of opportunity, ideologies, and interpretive frameworks. However, this is not a weakness of the research area but rather a resource. It can be argued that opportunity research has varied and diverse approaches. This is the way science evolves.

Therefore, opportunity research is not clear in its definitions or methods. The topic modelling analysis of opportunity research highlights the reason why there is an active debate in entrepreneurship about whether the concept of opportunity works and is sufficiently exact as a starting point for research. Based on our analysis, voices representing external determinants, growth, and capital—or knowledge and information—require standard definitions and methods. On the other hand, more permissive and flexible approaches include international entrepreneurship, local and cultural embeddedness, process and practice perspective, and approaches with a social and institutional context. However, this is why our analysis emphasises that the use of the opportunity in research is inevitably ambiguous, complex, and multidimensional.

For this reason, it is also natural that it is vague, abundant, and inconsistent. On the other hand, the concept must be criticised and questioned. In this way, the topics that make the phenomenon understandable and produce the scientific dialogue phenomenon evolve and change. From this study's perspective, it is essential to observe that the use of the concept of opportunity is naturally polyphonic. Through this, researchers can view entrepreneurship in many ways. It helps scientists talk about the phenomenon, not limit it. International entrepreneurship is part of this diverse and vibrant debate on entrepreneurship, contributing to a cross-border and cross-cultural perspective.

The analysis shows that opportunity research is overall diverse and meaningful. The research of the subject interweaves diverse views on the nature of the

Table 1 Synthesis of topics

Topics	Cognition and learning	Growth and capital	Individual qualities	International entrepreneurship	Knowledge and information	Local and cultural embeddedness	Processual and practice perspective	Regional and national determinants	Social and institutional contexts	Technology entrepreneurship
Genre 1										
Sub-topic 1 2 3 4 5	Knowledge Recognition Process information Cognitive	Capital market Entrepreneurial risk Industry entry Public costs Accounting	Entrepreneurs Entrepreneurial Venture Information management	**International business Internationalisation Network Foreign markets Global**	Knowledge Market Resources Business Entrepreneurs	Company history American British relations Time	Narrative Story Life Social Context	Growth Innovation rate Economic Urban market Sector	Entrepreneurship Institutional Economic Institutions Entrepreneurial activity	Technological management Innovation Technology Industry Number analysis
Genre 2										
Sub-topic 1 2 3 4 5	Experience Search Research capital Entrepreneur	Growth Performance Strategic Corporate venturing Firms	Risk Failure Decision Affect Emotions	**Marketing Market Small firms Export Business**	Firm Business costs Economic Capital Information Theory	Political Poverty Change Power Group	Theory Process Entrepreneurial opportunities Action Entrepreneurs	Entrepreneurship Countries Economic Country-level National	Local Small Informal market Community Networks	Innovation process Product Entrepreneurial knowledge Business opportunities Opportunity development
Genre 3										
Sub-topic 1 2 3 4 5	Effectuation Family Entrepreneurial ties Networks	Investment Partners alliance Foreign investors Relationship	Performance Efficacy Positive Focus Model	**Subsidiary Corporate Managers Family Knowledge**	Resources Equilibrium Market economy Activity Entrepreneurship	Women Family Gender Social Work	Change Organisational Power Institutional Market actors	Growth Capital Business Entry Venture	Social entrepreneurship Entrepreneurial learning Business Education Entrepreneur	International markets Business strategy Sales Capabilities Venture
Genre 4										
Sub-topic 1 2 3 4 5	Learning Students Education Entrepreneurial development Social	Political entrepreneurial institutions Government Rights Power	Knowledge Social Cognitive Individual capital	**Performance Entrepreneurial orientation Firm innovation Strategic model Results**	Search Uncertainty Risk Information Decision	Ethnic Local Community Immigrant entrepreneurs International markets	Social process Entrepreneurship Venture theory Research Individuals	Start Regional level Knowledge Entrepreneurship Regions	Sustainable family business Entrepreneurial opportunities Organisational Academic	Academic knowledge Research University Venture development Engineering

Genre 5										
Sub-topic 1 2 3 4 5	Model Venture devel-opment Time Product Market	Resources Ties Networks Relationships Information	Students Edu-cation Women Inten-tions Behaviour	**Business theory Risk Management Capabilities Research**	Entrepreneurship Opportunity the-ory Discovery pro-cess Kirzner Entrepreneur	Development Small entrepre-neurial world Growth	Entrepreneurship research Knowl-edge field University Science Economic	Firms Employ-ment Firm size Small Experience	Women Entrepre-neurship Entre-preneurs Growth Capital	Brand Business Entre-preneurship World marketing Small

opportunity. IE is available as one of the focal points for productive discussions on opportunity research. IE has an extensive influence on opportunity research, and its tip is very sharp in terms of influence and impact. On the other hand, IE also appears as relatively traditional IB research within opportunity research: its main research areas are internationalisation processes, internationalisation of SMEs, and international market opportunities. These themes are essential, but IE could bring the meaning of globalisation and crossing borders—socially, physically, mentally, and culturally—more broadly and deeply into the research as part of its contribution to opportunity research.

3.2 Most Influential Topics in Opportunity Research and Relationships Between Them

Second, opportunity research was considered in its entirety and IE's place in it. Topic modelling analysis highlighted the above ten topics through which opportunity research was formed. These topics can be found in articles in different proportions. These topics, in order of influence, are processual and practice perspective, knowledge and information, cognition and learning, social and institutional context, external determinants, growth and capital, technology entrepreneurship, individual qualities, international entrepreneurship, and local and cultural embeddedness. The articles combine the themes and are most often combinations of three to five topics. However, some of these topics are more influential than others, and influence changes over time. These are shown in Fig. 1.

Overall, the most influential topics have been processual and practice perspective, knowledge and information, and cognition and learning. The least influential topics have been individual qualities, international entrepreneurship, and local and cultural

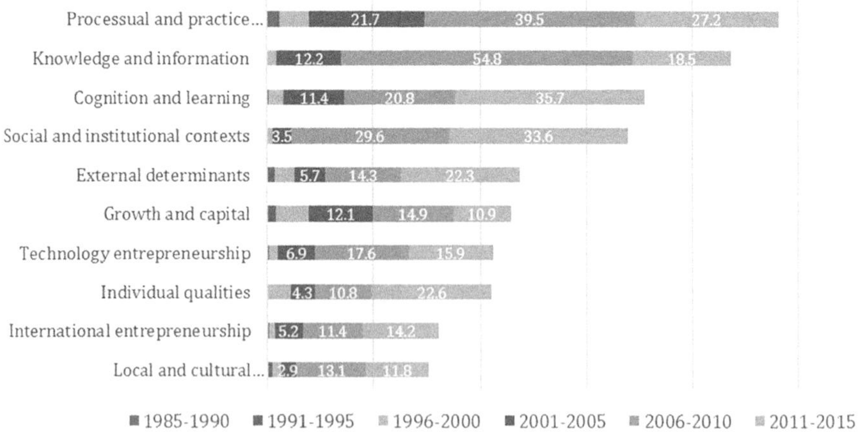

Fig. 1 The most influential topics in opportunity research

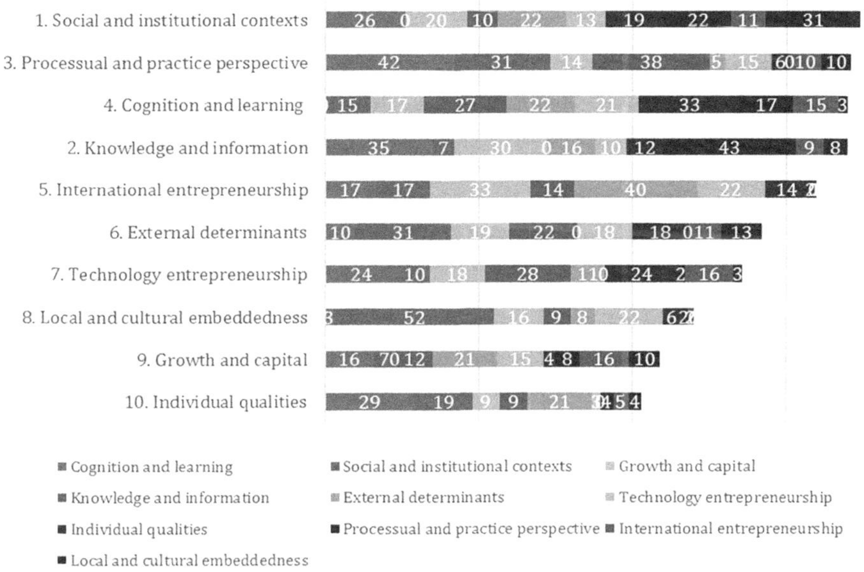

Fig. 2 The emergence of topics relative to each other

embeddedness. This is not to say that themes are not necessary per se; the issue is how strongly they come to the fore in articles on the subject. This finding is in line with the development of entrepreneurship research, where the concept of entrepreneurship and its processual nature have been central. On the other hand, especially in the early 2000s, knowledge and information and cognition and learning were popular explanatory models in all social sciences. However, it is particularly interesting that their role and influence is weakening. Alongside them, and even beyond their influence, is the theme of social and institutional context.

The role of IE has also increased significantly in the 2010s. Especially in the 2010s, international entrepreneurship has established itself as an essential theme in opportunity research (see Fig. 1). This suggests that the explanatory models for opportunity research have started to move towards more contingent, contextual, and learning-based models. Indeed, processuality and cognition are still influential, but knowledge and information, in particular, is rapidly dripping from the place of the most influential topics and is in the most recent period of analysis only slightly more influential than the IE theme. IE is part of this new trend and provides a theoretical and methodological basis for understanding the entrepreneurial opportunity phenomenon as a global, multicultural, and cross-border activity.

Figure 2 below further illustrates how the topics emerge relative to one another. The longer the bar, the more diverse the central theme is. The social and institutional context attaches itself most strongly to different themes. This may explain its growing influence. When looking at topics relative to one another, the furthest apart is the processual and practice perspective and the external determinants; they do not readily coexist. Correspondingly, the highest amount of support is sought from cognition and learning and growth and capital. The least support is found from international entrepreneurship and local and cultural embeddedness. It is a challenge for IE to get broader opportunity research to take advantage of IE. However, this also illustrates the research orientation. Processuality, cognition, growth, and knowledge—together and separately—dominate the discussion. Processuality is a major central theme but less significant as a supportive topic. Anything related to social, community, or people-to-people issues has little consideration in the discussion, although their role in a globalising and complex world is continually rising.

Furthermore, the size of each central theme's support themes is an indication of the angle at which the central theme is published. However, those with little conversation, such as cognition and locality, should be allowed to interact with each other, as these places could be important for contributions. Strong connections, such as knowledge and information and cognition and learning, on the other hand, could be drawn from elsewhere, and representatives of these angles could also accept and open up other perspectives to the phenomenon. IE mostly uses external explanatory factors as a support theme, and all the more so IE could use a broader theoretical basis. Locality and social institutionalism are strongly intertwined. Conversely, like IE, the roles of communities and technology are also potent drivers of economies and entrepreneurship, and therefore their role in research should be highlighted in the future. Their rich tradition of theory and methodology is still underused.

In sum, for the IE theme to gain influence in the opportunity research, it should make itself applicable to other themes and broadly link itself to different themes. Isolation as an independent branch of research with independent definitions or scientific journals does not alone promote IE as a research field. For example, IE could learn from the social and institutional context theme, as its importance has snowballed. It has strongly influenced the theorising of entrepreneurship during the last years while at the same time engaging with other themes. To increase its influence, IE could combine many themes, open up more broadly how IE benefits entrepreneurship research, seek to develop entrepreneurship theory (and not just international entrepreneurship theory), and publish in the most respected entrepreneurship journals.

Furthermore, the above shows opportunity to research as rather one-sided in its orientation. As a researcher, if one wanted to publish, he or she may want to base a study on processuality, knowledge, or cognition and publish it in the four most dominant journals. Still, contextualism, cultures, internationality, or technology have not earned the attention they deserve from researchers (and here, this refers precisely to how much of the themes are addressed in those articles where opportunity is a key concept). However, the analysis of the influence above suggests that a change may be happening. The influence of themes is already changing, which is likely to affect the future in the form of impact. This is also a good trend for IE, as it enables its theoretical and methodological heritage to be more strongly incorporated into entrepreneurship research. IE is generally seen too much as an external variable or a new business abroad in opportunity research. Instead, IE can bring a wealth of heritage and expertise to the understanding of the birth of a multicultural, cross-border, cross-cultural, evolving, and transformational new business.

The attention that processuality receives in opportunity research is focused on the challenges of defining the opportunity phenomenon. This is understandable, and the work has been valuable. However, it may be suggested that now is the time to take inspiration from other themes, such as IE, since the opportunity phenomenon is partly stuck with definition debates and because the global economy is changing radically with artificial intelligence, globalisation, climate issues, and people's unbound interactions. The phenomenon can no longer be understood simply by analysing the individual or the company as an opportunity producer but rather in context. However, what makes it challenging is that the most cited articles and topics that researchers have pressure to refer to are explicitly based on the theorising or empirical analysis of individuals or firms, not cultures, processes, or collectives, in the most influential journals.

3.3 Impact of IE Theme as Part of Opportunity Research

Third, the impact of the topics, particularly the effects of IE, was analysed. The implication here refers to the impact that the topic has had on the conceptualisation, theory, methodology, and understanding of the whole phenomenon of opportunity research. Impact analysis began by examining the impact of all topics on opportunity research. The citation counts of the articles based on Google Scholar were used to calculate the impact (all 1326 articles citation counts were searched). In total, these articles have received 311,152 citations.

Each topic's impact was calculated as follows: the sum of the articles' citations with that theme, multiplied by the number of articles' text shares in the theme and divided by the number of these articles. This brings up the theme's proportion of the impact. In this way, it was found that the processual and practice perspective has had the most significant impact on opportunity research (see Fig. 3). Knowledge and information and cognition and learning have also played a vital role in the research. International entrepreneurship, technology entrepreneurship, and local and cultural embeddedness have been the least affecting.

Moreover, if we look at the impacts of the above topics relative to one another, on average, each topic produces one-tenth of the total effect. Above this average are the processual and practice perspective (18.6% by the impact), knowledge and information (11.9% by the impact), and cognition and learning (11.5% by the impact). This means that the opportunity articles that deal with these three themes have created almost half of the total impact. Also, the mere consideration of the opportunity phenomenon's processual nature and the type of practice it involves has received nearly a quarter of all attention. Below average, nonetheless, a significant impact has been created by individual qualities (9.8% by the impact), external qualities (9.6% by the impact), growth and capital (9.3% by the impact), and social and institutional context (8.7% by the impact). The articles with the least impact

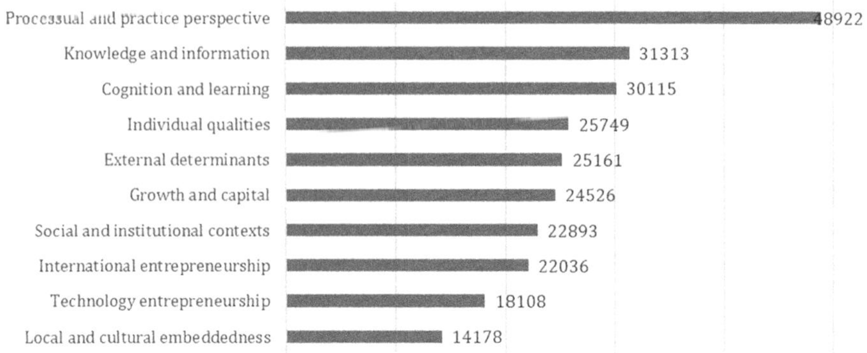

Fig. 3 Citation impact of the topics

were articles on international entrepreneurship (8.4% by the impact), technology entrepreneurship (6.9% by the impact), and local and cultural embeddedness (5.4% by the impact).

The impact analysis was followed by a review of the journals where opportunity articles with IE were published and the number of citations these articles received in each journal (see Fig. 4; journals with at least 100 citations). In total, the articles with the IE theme have received 80,620 citations. Based on the analysis, the *Journal of Business Venturing* is an essential journal to make an impact. The articles published in this journal have received nearly 20,000 citations, which is almost a quarter of all IE citations. The next most relevant journals have been *Journal of International Business Studies* (7889 citations), *Journal of Management* (6517 citations), and *Entrepreneurship Theory and Practice* (5067 citations). These four journals are about half as likely to be referenced. This tells how focused the impact building is.

Other relevant journals for IE impact-building as part of opportunity research have been *International Business Review* (3519 citations), *Journal of Management Studies* (3226 citations), *Journal of Business Research* (2771 citations), *Journal of World Business* (2261 citations), *Strategic Entrepreneurship Journal* (2337 citations), and *Small Business Economics* (2113 citations). The dedicated journal of IE, *Journal of International Entrepreneurship*, has also produced a fair impact (1361 citations). All in all, IE has been involved as a theme in producing about a quarter of all citations in opportunity research. This is more than IE's more general influence or impact.

3.4 The Impact of IE Theme with Other Topics

Fourth, the impact was examined in more detail, and specifically from the perspective of IE. First, we looked at how many citations come from the articles, with IE being one of the eight essential topics in the article. Table 2 below shows that the

Fig. 4 The number of citations received by articles featuring an IE theme in each journal

articles in which IE is one of the eight most essential themes have generated 79,176 citations. There is a total of 424 IE articles, with an average of 138 citations. The 10% most cited articles have 23,783 citations, and the average citation for these most cited articles is 559 citations. Of these 424 articles, IE articles as the central theme have returned 40,172 citations (50.7%). There is a total of 168 of these articles. Citations are even more concentrated when we find that 10% of the most cited articles with IE as the main topic have generated over 20,000 citations (26.2%). Therefore, in practice, less than 20 articles have produced a large part of IE's impact on opportunity research. This confirms that IE is a reasonably self-determining topic within the opportunity research having a narrow theme with a sharp tip.

This also indicates that the IE theme within opportunity research is divided into two groups in terms of impact. On the one hand, the IE theme is the central theme in a relatively small number of articles as a whole, but their impact is high. These articles are ground-breaking articles that have theorised international entrepreneurship as a phenomenon from an opportunity perspective. They have also added value

Table 2 The importance of IE in opportunity articles

How important is IE in an opportunity article?	The number of articles	Citations in total	Citations per article on average	Citations of 10% most cited	Citations per article on average of 10% most cited
Main theme	168	40,172	239	20,671	1216
Second most important	53	7372	139	3444	574
Third most important	60	10,824	180	6312	1052
Fourth most important	72	9780	136	5848	731
Fifth most important	44	9063	206	6091	1218
Sixth most important	22	2099	95	1758	586
Seventh most important	4	400	100	303	303
Eighth most important	1	6	6	6	6
Sum/average	424	79,716	138	23,783	559

to a broader focus on entrepreneurship. The second group is articles where IE is a theme but does not play a central role. These articles have not created as much impact on the research as IE's central theme. This indicates that IE is still a relatively unknown theme in opportunity research, thus its rich research tradition has not been utilised. Only a small number of top articles create a significant impact, probably more in IE and IB research than in entrepreneurship. This is one of the significant challenges of IE research: how to have an impact so that a wide range of entrepreneurship and IB research can take advantage of IE research tradition, theory, and findings.

The following looks at the most- and least-cited topics with IE and what mixes are in the articles. This tells us what topics the most remarkable IE articles wrap around. The results especially indicate that the ten most cited articles are different from all others. Figure 5 first reveals that the ten most-cited IE articles (IE is the central theme) within opportunity research are intertwined with growth and capital, cognition and learning, and knowledge and information. Very little attention is given to the social and institutional context and local and cultural embeddedness, which is not discussed in the most cited articles. The more articles are included, the more topics other than the above will be covered. It is noteworthy that the role of growth and capital is diminishing and that the importance of the social and institutional context is increasing as we move from the most cited articles to a broader range of articles. Cognition and learning continuously play an important role despite the citation category.

Taken together, the results suggest that opportunity studies somewhat safely combine familiar and powerful themes. This is the best way to get attention by

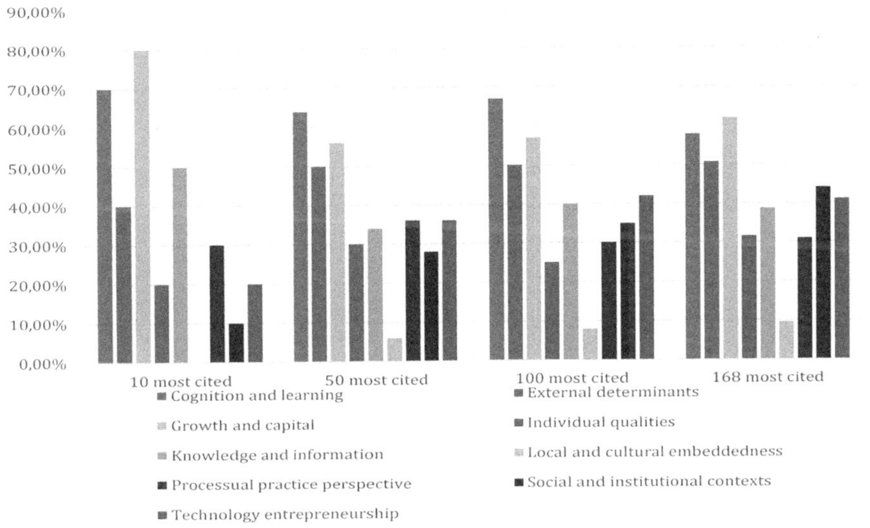

Fig. 5 The volume IE combines with other topics in different citation categories

referring. If, on the other hand, research is at the interface of more than one theme or combines newer themes, research will not quickly receive attention in the form of citations, even though the development of the phenomenon as a subject of study would need it. However, articles often combine so many different themes that purity is almost impossible. Nevertheless, research artificially simplifies the phenomenon in publications. This is important because future research always builds on previous research. It is tempting for researchers to build on research that receives much attention. In this case, a paper may also receive citations.

Nonetheless, this does not advance science. Science should also have other types of impact measures because, according to this analysis, research seems to be one-sided if one looks at the most influential articles for citations and does not value versatility, new perspectives, and the combination of different discourses. The IE theme is quite one-sided and needs a broader theme if you look at IE's impact with citation categories.

3.5 *The Development of Topics in Articles with IE as the Main Topic*

Last, the following is a look at the combinations of themes with IE's central theme. In Fig. 6, the bar length indicates the number of articles where IE is the central theme; this second theme is included. Overall, IE was the central theme in 160 articles out of 1326 opportunity articles, which is 12%. The IE theme is typically intertwined with external determinants (40 articles) and growth and capital

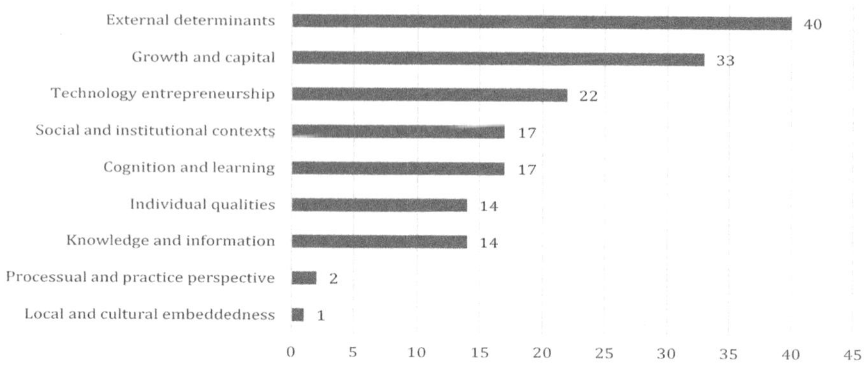

Fig. 6 The combinations of themes of the IE primary topic

(33 articles). Technology entrepreneurship and IE also often coexist (22 articles). The least IE theme seeks support from the processual and practice perspective (two articles) and local and cultural embeddedness (one article). In general, it seems that IE is more intertwined with hard variables than with soft human and social issues. The result is quite surprising because IE is often related to things like context, networks, or ethnicity.

This suggests that opportunity research uses IE as a background variable or technology market-related opportunities in the international market. In particular, it is surprising that processuality and practice and local and cultural embeddedness are the least relevant. It is surprising because processuality is at the core of internationalisation and its core articles. Nonetheless, while embeddedness is usually an essential role in IE research, its importance is almost non-existent in opportunity research. It is also possible to notice that IE is not linked to the dominant themes of opportunity research, namely, cognition and learning, knowledge and information, and the processual and practice perspective. For this reason, it is not surprising that IE is the second least prominent theme in opportunity research. The preceding implies that IE research is not broadly concerned with entrepreneurship research, although its critical IE articles conceptualise opportunity as its core but are suggestively part of IB research.

The above also implies that IE researchers are still IB researchers in their identity and are not involved in entrepreneurship research but in international business research. Indeed, researchers involved in entrepreneurship research, especially opportunity research, use IE to research external influences, growth and capital, and technology's commercialisation. However, this is an excellent opportunity for IE research: truly combining entrepreneurship and internationalisation. By bringing the central ideas of internationalisation about processuality, embeddedness, and crossing borders, it might be possible to reform entrepreneurship theory to better reflect the increasingly globalised world in which business is born and built.

Furthermore, Fig. 7 below shows that in articles where IE is the central theme, 21–25% of the text is related to IE. This means that IE is a clear central theme in

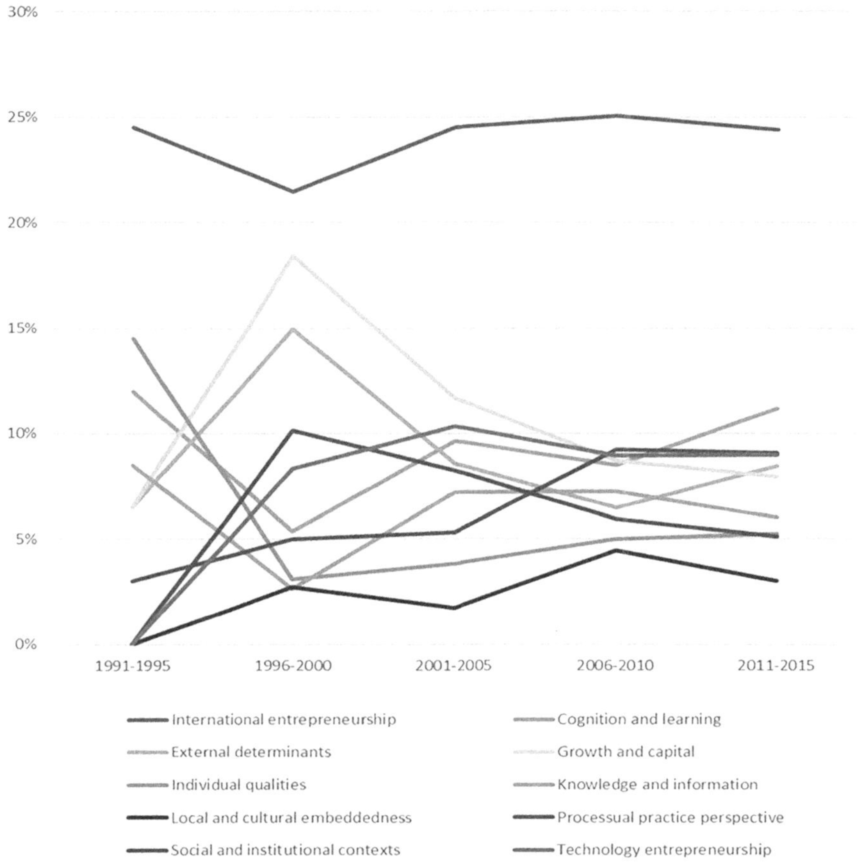

Fig. 7 The development of topics in articles with IE

these articles and that its share has remained almost the same since the 1990s. Furthermore, the first opportunity articles with IE as the central theme were published in the early 1990s. Figure 7 also shows how the importance of other themes supporting IE has changed over time. The main support themes in the early 1990s were individual qualities, cognition and learning, and knowledge and information. By the late 1990s, support themes had changed, and IE was interwoven with growth and capital, external determinants, and the processual and practice perspective. At the turn of the twenty-first century, support themes have diversified, and almost all of the other themes appear in IE articles. This trend will strengthen in the late 2000s, and most support topics will be roughly equal. Interestingly, however, support themes are reduced, and the IE theme as a standalone theme is strengthened. As we enter the 2010s, cognition and learning and growth and capital will increase, and all other themes will be reduced where IE is the central theme.

If we look at the general trends from Fig. 7, the central IE theme from 1990 to 2000 applied for support on fewer support themes, while the 2000–2015 one has many other themes, but with less weight than before. From the IE theme's point of view, it is a bit worrying that it is positioned so strongly today as a standalone theme. The reason may be that IE opportunity research draws gradually from its own IE theory. On the other hand, it can also be suggested that the central IE theme should benefit from a reliable and more extended theory base of different themes. Trends also show that the role of growth and capital, knowledge and information, process and practice perspectives, and local and cultural embeddedness in IE articles is diminishing significantly. On the other hand, cognition and learning and technology entrepreneurship are growing.

In sum, the articles are not pure; they deal with a particular theme and combinations of different topics. As research progresses over time and the more it becomes, the more it blends. The requirement of purity, i.e. precise definitions and a common agenda, is not realistic. Research lives as any other object of human activity: it is diverse, building on existing networks, and expands. It makes the subject a living, not a lousy, research area. It enables new creative points of view and innovative research results. Consistency does not promote innovation; it stops it. In this respect, opportunity research is going in the right direction. The reduction in the dominance of some topics and the discussion and amalgamation of topics make an exciting future, not the other way around. It is essential to embrace and support the IE theme in this process of diversification.

4 Suggestions for Future Research

The analysis above elucidates how the opportunity phenomenon comes out as a dynamic process. However, until now, opportunities as a whole have been examined in two ways. The modern discovery view posits that the identification of an opportunity is built on its birth and remains about the same over time. It will be developed better and aims to make it possible for it to be more efficiently tackled to be exploited, particularly in markets. Again, the understanding of social-cognitive shaping underlines the opportunity to be socially constructed in relation to others. In this case, the opportunity emerges through the interaction between the entrepreneur's capabilities and the surrounding society's characteristics. The difficulty with both of these situations is that the approaches presume the ex-ante existence of elements (building materials), of which being fitted together in a new way is viewed as giving birth to the opportunity. Instead, this study's analysis shows the research to be multidimensional, blending perspectives, and naturally contradictory on the subject. Here, the challenge is that the traditional approaches striving for purity poorly correspond to today's noisy, unpredictable, experimental, and even chaotic research reality. The above analysis has the following implications for future research.

First, IE and opportunities, in general, do not have fixed or permanent identifications; instead, they continue to take shape and expand in the research. In this case, opportunities encompass contents that are mixed and drawing in different directions. Therefore, the identification of opportunities will vary continuously. The first suggestion of this study is that future research should explore the shaping of opportunities as evolving in social interaction and immersed in the particular historical and cultural contexts of research (see Dana 1994, 1995; Sadeghi and Biancone 2018). This enables research in a broad range of cross-border organisational situations and does not require the starting point to be the emergence of a new company or the detection of an international market. Thus, future research should pay more attention to the contextually immersed and processual nature of IE as part of opportunity research.

Secondly, IE research needs a conceptual extension to respond to the everyday practical dynamism and complexity of the phenomenon (Young et al. 2003). In this case, opportunity stems from a cultural-historically immersed collective dialogue in which the arguments based on a mediating artefact and the subsequent counterarguments are discussed and compete and depend on the cultural-historical context (Dana 1994, 1995). Here, mediating artefacts refer to different culture-specific symbols, tools, and activities to communicate and transform individuals' understanding into a community's knowledge and vice versa. Individuals' perceptions are externalised, stabilised, and institutionalised into meaning structures, such as opportunities, the production of which, in a particular community, consists of a set of rules and regulations. This cultural space, in turn, refers to the activities and boundary conditions of IE and the effect of the constitutive norms and regulations on the dialogue between people. The dialogue between entrepreneurs, customers, financiers, and other key players in the shaping of opportunities is not just a dialogue between them; instead, the mediating historical and cultural mechanisms are involved in the debate to the extent that the unique production of individuals or firms may be questioned (Nayak and Maclean 2013). Thus, the study's second suggestion is that future IE research should examine opportunities as a culturally and historically regulated phenomenon.

Thirdly, IE, as part of opportunity research, often talks about social interaction and cooperation. But in the end, however, the research looks at the individual or the firm's transformation. In the case of opportunities, this most often concerns a single company or a single (observed) (international market) opportunity. However, such an approach would be a formal analysis of the phenomenon's elements and not an understanding of the whole (cf. Tsoukas and Chia 2002). The third suggestion of this study is that future research should also focus on the historical conditions that allow specific ways of thinking about opportunities. These historically institutionalised conditions structure the broader system of thought and produce opportunities in specific historical circumstances (Holt 2008, Jones and Holt 2008; Rezaei et al. 2020). The boundaries of ways of thinking about opportunities always depend on the rules of activity in a given situation, and these are born and change historically and constitute the activities and thinking (see, e.g. Alon et al. 2009; Anderson et al. 2006; Jafari-Sadeghi et al. 2019b; Sadeghi et al. 2019). On this basis, this paper contends that future research should better account for the historical production of the conditions under which something can be seen as an opportunity (Mainela et al. 2018).

Fourthly, according to traditional business thinking, actors must learn to find useful answers and the ways and means to enable the correct operations in the context in question. Against this background, much of the research on opportunities based on the above analysis can approach learning through expert knowledge, resources, competencies, and information. The situation is seen as analysable, and a solution to the situation can be derived from the analysis and via the elements of the solution. The challenge here relates to how the actors learn, based on the skills and resources that make this possible. Such research has been very influential. The problem here is that the learner is separated from the learning context. However, when this is the case, embedded knowledge and learning also exist below the surface, associated with the context itself. A hidden truth resides in this situation, whereby people have gradually produced historical and contextual knowledge. This requires a learning experience, living and being in the context (Jafari-Sadeghi 2020). Such research is helpful because it anchors the learning and knowledge in human contexts. In turn, the problem of such research is that it continues to see knowledge and learning as being free of ideologies and hegemonies. Hence, the fourth suggestion of the present study is that learning opportunities also involve questioning and dealing with contradictions (Hjorth 2004, 2013). The conflict between the actor and the situation creates a situation whereby the actor must exceed the learned limits to create something new. An entrepreneur needs to detach herself or himself from her or his immediate context, even if it provides the necessary resources because a new opportunity can only be created by questioning the familiar. On this basis, this study suggests that it is useful for research on IE to examine learning in addition to breakout (Engeström 2006).

5 Concluding Remarks

A literature review is a form of scientific activity in which researchers organise existing knowledge insightfully. In the social sciences, particularly, it emphasises the organising in a new creative way and the dialogical outlining of future research avenues. Distinctive of the literature reviews in the social sciences is that they do not expect straightforwardly the accumulation of knowledge, in which the researcher has an instrumental role in piling up, appraising, and transferring knowledge forward. Preferably, it sees the definitions, the arguments on the nature of a phenomenon, and the manifestations of the phenomenon as taking place through active dialogue in a scientific community. Building on this, this study aimed to analyse previous international entrepreneurship research as part of broader opportunity research from the social science perspective.

Social science is immersed in its specific functioning, including a literature review, habitually attached to the natural scientific world view. In most cases, this means that previous research is placed in categories, as defined by previous research or emerging from the data, despite researchers habitually making human errors. For example, when researchers see something taking place a few times in previous research, they might find confirmation for it, even if, in reality, the finding is based on their cognitive bias as human beings to draw such hasty conclusions. However, the above taxonomic categorisation has been a critical modern scientific method to perceive, understand, and explain the world. Nevertheless, for social sciences, this is a significant problem. In reality, humans frame, blend, and transform concepts quickly and continually.

Concepts produced by humans as linguistic meaning systems do not fall easily into alleged natural categories. This is so because concepts are formed and exist in relation to other concepts, their meanings are subject to constant change, and concepts in actual human use unpredictably blend with other concepts. Therefore, social science phenomena are by nature polyphonic. Consequently, the deeper structure of a social phenomenon, like science, might conflict with its emerging manifestations (literature reviews). Thus, science is instead multi-centred, nonlinear, and intersubjective activity. This study suggests that social science's inherent polyphonic nature can adequately be understood when supported by digital resources and computer-assisted text analysis (DiMaggio 2015). The digitalisation of publications, the development and application of search engines, and the maturation of machine-vision-based text analysis tools have made it possible for researchers to explore large quantities of publications quickly, efficiently, and reliably (Blei et al. 2003).

References

Alon I, Dana LP, Jenkins A (2009) International business by SMEs: empirical findings from New Zealand. JIBE 10(2):59–78

Anderson RB, Dana LP, Dana TE (2006) Indigenous land rights, entrepreneurship, and economic development in Canada: "opting-in" to the global economy. J World Bus 41(1):45–55

Autio E, Sapienza HJ, Almeida JG (2000) Effects of age at entry, knowledge intensity, and imitability on international growth. Acad Manag J 43(5):909–924

Baker T, Gedajlovic E, Lubatkin M (2005) A framework for comparing entrepreneurship processes across nations. J Int Bus Stud 36(5):492–504

Blei DM (2012) Probabilistic topic models. Commun ACM 55(4):77–84

Blei DM, Lafferty JD (2006) Dynamic topic models. In: Proceedings of the 23rd international conference on machine learning. ACM, pp 113–120

Blei DM, Lafferty JD (2007) A correlated topic model of science. Ann Appl Stat 1(1):17–35

Blei DM, Ng AY, Jordan MI (2003) Latent dirichlet allocation. J Mach Learn Res 3:993–1022

Coviello NE, Munro HJ (1995) Growing the entrepreneurial firm: networking for international market development. Eur J Mark 29(7):49–62

Dana LP (1994) On the internalization of a discipline: research and methodology in cross-cultural entrepreneurship and small-business studies. J Small Bus Entrepreneur 11(2):61–76

Dana LP (1995) Entrepreneurship in a remote sub-Arctic community. Entrep Theory Pract 20 (1):57–72

Dana LP (1999) Entrepreneurship in Pacific Asia: past, present and future. World Scientific, Singapore

Dana LP (2001) Networks, internationalization & policy. Small Bus Econ 16(2):57–62
DiMaggio P (2015) Adapting computational text analysis to social science (and vice versa). Big Data Soc 2(2):1–5
Engeström Y (2006) Development, movement and agency: breaking away into mycorrhizae activities. In: Yamazumi K (ed) Building activity theory in practice: toward the next generation. Center for Human Activity Theory, Kansai University, Osaka, pp 1–43
Gaglio CM, Katz JA (2001) The psychological basis of opportunity identification: entrepreneurial alertness. Small Bus Econ 16(2):95–111
Hannigan T, Haans R, Vakili K, Tchalian H, Glaser V, Wang M, Kaplan S, Jennings PD (2019) Topic modeling in management research: rendering new theory from textual data. Acad Manag Ann 13(2):586–632
Hjorth D (2004) Creating space for play/invention–concepts of space and organizational entrepreneurship. Entrep Reg Dev 16(5):413–432
Hjorth D (2013) Public entrepreneurship: desiring social change, creating sociality. Entrep Reg Dev 25(1–2):34–51
Holt R (2008) Using activity theory to understand entrepreneurial opportunity. Mind Cult Act 15 (1):52–70
Jafari-Sadeghi V (2020) The motivational factors of business venturing: opportunity versus necessity? A gendered perspective on European countries. J Bus Res 113:279–289
Jafari-Sadeghi V, Kimiagari S, Biancone PP (2019a) Level of education and knowledge, foresight competency and international entrepreneurship: a study of human capital determinants in the European countries. Eur Bus Rev 32(1):46–68
Jafari-Sadeghi V, Nkongolo-Bakenda JM, Dana LP, Anderson RB, Biancone PP (2019b) Home country institutional context and entrepreneurial internationalization: the significance of human capital attributes. J Int Entrep. https://doi.org/10.1007/s10843-019-00264-1
Jones O, Holt R (2008) The creation and evolution of new business ventures: an activity theory perspective. J Small Bus Enterp Dev 15(1):51–73
Jones MV, Coviello N, Tang YK (2011) International entrepreneurship research (1989–2009): a domain ontology and thematic analysis. J Bus Ventur 26(6):632–659
Madsen TK, Servais P (1997) The internationalization of born globals: an evolutionary process? Int Bus Rev 6(6):561–583
Mainela T, Puhakka V, Servais P (2014) The concept of international opportunity in international entrepreneurship: a review and a research agenda. Int J Manag Rev 16(1):105–129
Mainela T, Puhakka V, Sipola S (2018) International entrepreneurship beyond individuals and firms: on the systemic nature of international opportunities. J Bus Ventur 33(4):534–550
McDougall PP, Oviatt BM (2003) Some fundamental issues in international entrepreneurship. Entrep Theory Pract 18:27
Nayak A, Maclean M (2013) Co-evolution, opportunity seeking and institutional change: entrepreneurship and the Indian telecommunications industry, 1923–2009. Bus Hist 55(1):29–52
Newman D, Noh Y, Talley E, Karimi S, Baldwin T (2010) Evaluating topic models for digital libraries. In: Proceedings of the 10th annual joint conference on digital libraries. ACM, pp 215–224
Nummela N, Saarenketo S, Puumalainen K (2004) Rapidly with a rifle or more slowly with a shotgun? Stretching the company boundaries of internationalising ICT firms. J Int Entrep 2 (4):275–288
Oviatt BM, McDougall PP (1994) Toward a theory of international new ventures. J Int Bus Stud 25 (1):45–64
Oviatt BM, McDougall PP (2005) Defining international entrepreneurship and modeling the speed of internationalization. Entrep Theory Pract 29(5):537–553
Presutti M, Boari C, Fratocchi L (2007) Knowledge acquisition and the foreign development of high-tech start-ups: a social capital approach. Int Bus Rev 16(1):23–46
Reuber AR, Knight GA, Liesch PW, Zhou L (2018) International entrepreneurship: the pursuit of entrepreneurial opportunities across national borders. J Int Bus Stud 49(4):395–406

Rezaei M, Jafari-Sadeghi V, Bresciani S (2020) What drives the process of knowledge management in a cross-cultural setting. Eur Bus Rev 32(3):485–511

Sadeghi VJ, Biancone PP (2018) How micro, small and medium-sized enterprises are driven outward the superior international trade performance? A multidimensional study on Italian food sector. Res Int Bus Financ 45:597–606

Sadeghi VJ, Biancone PP, Giacoma C, Secinaro S (2018) How does export compliance influence the internationalization of firms: is it a thread or an opportunity? J Glob Entrep Res 8(3):1–15

Sadeghi VJ, Nkongolo-Bakenda JM, Anderson RB, Dana LP (2019) An institution-based view of international entrepreneurship: a comparison of context-based and universal determinants in developing and economically advanced countries. Int Bus Rev 28(6):101588

Shane S, Venkataraman S (2000) The promise of entrepreneurship as a field of research. Acad Manag Rev 25(1):217–226

Steyvers M, Griffiths T (2007) Probabilistic topic models. Handbook of latent semantic analysis 427(7):424–440

Tsoukas H, Chia R (2002) On organizational becoming: rethinking organizational change. Organ Sci 13(5):567–582

Weerawardena J, Mort GS, Liesch PW, Knight G (2007) Conceptualizing accelerated internationalization in the born global firm: a dynamic capabilities perspective. J World Bus 42(3):294–306

Young S, Dimitratos P, Dana LP (2003) International entrepreneurship research: what scope for international business theories? J Int Entrep 1(1):31–42

Zahra SA, Korri JS, Yu J (2005) Cognition and international entrepreneurship: implications for research on international opportunity recognition and exploitation. Int Bus Rev 14(2):129–146

Vesa Puhakka is a Professor of Management and Entrepreneurship at the University of Oulu Business School, Finland. His research focuses on international entrepreneurship, entrepreneurial opportunity creation processes, growth-generating mechanisms, and strategy practices. His latest research has been published, for example, in Journal of Business Venturing, Industrial Marketing Management, and International Journal of Management Reviews. The Academy of Management and the NFIB Education Foundation awarded his doctoral dissertation for outstanding research in entrepreneurship and independent business in 2003.

Arto Ojala is a Professor of International Business at the University of Vaasa. His research interests include cross-section of international business, entrepreneurship, and information systems. His current research projects focus on the evolution and internationalisation of digital platforms, digital business models, and digital transformation. His research has been published, for example, in International Business Review, Journal of International Marketing, Journal of Small Business Management, and Journal of World Business.

Entrepreneurial Decision-Making Process Optimisation: A Literature Review and Future Research Agenda

Iuliia Andreeva

1 Introduction

Previous research literature shows great attention to entrepreneurial decision-making and entrepreneurial opportunity research in both theoretical considerations and practical implications. Research on entrepreneurial decision-making and entrepreneurial opportunities are valuable because entrepreneurial decision-making process generates entrepreneurial opportunities (Maine et al. 2015; Gabrielsson and Politis 2011) and opportunity discovering and evaluation is of great importance to understand the decision-making process (Shepherd et al. 2015). Entrepreneurial decisions and opportunity discovering and evaluation are considered as central concepts for international entrepreneurship research (Shepherd et al. 2015; Short et al. 2010; Collinson and Houlden 2005; Perks and Hughes 2008; Kontinen and Ojala 2011; Mainela et al. 2014; Glavas et al. 2017). Research literature explores interrelations between entrepreneurial decision-making and entrepreneurial opportunities across various concepts (Andersson 2011; Chandra 2017; Perks and Hughes 2008; Endres and Woods 2006; Clark et al. 2018; Gabrielsson and Politis 2011; Sarasvathy et al. 2014).

International external environment and new technologies constantly require to optimise entrepreneurial decision-making process in a way (Foroudi et al. 2017; Zhu and Lin 2019; Lee et al. 2008), to seize a most appropriate set of opportunities for moving forward to successful results of entering the new international market (Jafari-Sadeghi et al. 2020) and growth decisions. Entrepreneurship research explores the optimisation through various theoretical concepts. Existent research considers optimisation as resource distribution (Desa and Basu 2013; Liu and Liang

I. Andreeva (✉)
School of Business and Management, Lappeenranta-Lahti University of Technology, Lappeenranta, Finland

V. Jafari-Sadeghi et al. (eds.), *Empirical International Entrepreneurship*, Contributions to Management Science,
https://doi.org/10.1007/978-3-030-68972-8_7

2015), evolutionary algorithms using mathematical operations (Sieja and Wach 2019). Several researches explore the concept of optimisation as decision-makers choice (Milkman et al. 2009), the process of entrepreneurial behaviour for ranking and selecting of most appropriate alternatives (Gans et al. 2019). This concept also used as entrepreneurial behaviour of discovering and exploitation a set of opportunities to increase the profit in conjunction with entrepreneurial decision-making process (Endres and Woods 2006).

There has been a lack of views on the concept of optimisation related to the entrepreneurial decision-making process, which enables to seize a more appropriate set of opportunities. The reasons why the theory of this scientific area should be developed are to realise how decision-making process optimisation works, to explain the constructs of decision-making process optimisation, to create a unified measurement, and to lead to practical implications for entrepreneurs and SMEs. This study provides the framework of entrepreneurial decision-making process optimisation based on six components and two decisions in conjunction with multiple criteria for evaluating opportunities and entrepreneurial decisions.

New web technologies transform business (Demir et al. 2017; Büyüközkan 2004; Foroudi et al. 2017), require to use new channels for seizing opportunities (Zhu and Lin 2019), influence decision-making processes, require to reconsider decision-making process, and offer opportunities to overcome barriers (Lee et al. 2008; Taiminen and Karjaluoto 2015). New technologies need to be applied by small- and medium-sized companies (SMEs) to achieve goals and increase productivity (Mokhtarzadeh et al. 2020) and seize more opportunities (Jafari-Sadeghi and Biancone 2018). Despite some researchers consider technological changes as the assistance for SMEs in their international activity (Dana 2017), many studies highlight that SMEs have a lack of resources, time, finance, capital, and expertise (Taiminen and Karjaluoto 2015; Desa and Basu 2013; Bruneel and De Cock 2016). Simultaneously, many factors such as economic, political, social, and cultural (Jafari-Sadeghi et al. 2019b) also influence the decisions of SMEs to enter new market and growth. Therefore, it can be quite difficult for SMEs to adopt new technologies, exploit new opportunities (Desa and Basu 2013), and evaluate what set of opportunities are mostly required to achieve business goals.

This study strives to achieve several purposes. The first purpose is to examine existing research in entrepreneurial decision-making and entrepreneurial opportunity dimensions by combining them in the international context, underlining main concepts, processes, and interrelations. The other purpose is to develop a conceptual framework for entrepreneurial decision-making process optimisation. The further purpose is to provide a set of propositions based on literature review and conceptual model. The last but not the least purpose is to offer directions for future research agenda related to propositions.

The study begins with describing the methodology. Then, this study develops an overall review of the concepts in the entrepreneurial decision-making process and entrepreneurial opportunity, explains the concept of optimisation, and builds the list of key definitions. Further, the study offers a conceptual framework for the decision-making process optimisation and provides a set of propositions. Thereafter, the study develops a detailed future research agenda in accordance with a set of propositions.

2 Methodology

This study uses a systematic literature review which follows a transparent methodology to analyse literature in a systematic manner, select relevant literature by ranking its quality, and combine literature domains to build new theoretical construct (Kraus et al. 2020; Snyder 2019). The study collects relevant research articles focusing on entrepreneurial decision-making, entrepreneurial opportunity, and international entrepreneurship areas and analyses them for the purposes of the research. The review process included two main processes: (1) data collection and (2) data cleaning. The process of data collection was divided into the following steps: defining keywords for searching corresponding literature, identifying criteria for including and excluding articles for final review, initial articles collection, and additional searching. The process of data cleaning decreased the number of articles by applying including and excluding criteria. Data cleaning continued further with coding procedures. The pilot coding was conducted with a number of articles to determine potential contradictions and necessary adjustments for further coding. Further, articles were coded manually according to journals, method, key definitions of entrepreneurial decision-making, opportunity, and optimisation.

2.1 Data Collection

Articles for conducting literature review were gathered in the Scopus database. According to the purpose of this research, I built the list of keywords, which were included in the title, abstract, or keywords of articles, and identified including and excluding criteria. The study focuses on articles published in the high ranking (Kraus et al. 2020), academic international journals and excludes articles from other types of publications such as book review, conference proceedings, and regional journals. Articles included in the final review were limited to not only entrepreneurial decision-making, entrepreneurial opportunity, international entrepreneurship, and SME but also to entrepreneurial orientation, entrepreneurial marketing, international entrepreneurial activity, and psychological points of entrepreneurship-related with decision-making. Table 1 represents the full range of keywords and including and excluding criteria.

Collection of articles started with the following keywords: "entrepreneurial decision-making" *and* "opportunity" *and* "SME". To observe the dimension of online and offline entrepreneurial opportunities, more detailed, further, searching was conducted with the keywords: "online and offline opportunities" *and* "digital channels". To examine streams in entrepreneurial decision-making optimisation

Table 1 Criteria for selecting articles

	Including criteria	Excluding criteria
Publication type	Academic international high-ranking journal	Book reviews, conference proceedings, unknown journals, regional journals
Database	Scopus	
Keywords	Entrepreneurial decision-making, opportunity, SME, online and offline opportunities, digital channels, optimisation, entrepreneurial	
Additional research areas	• Entrepreneurial marketing • Entrepreneurial orientation • International entrepreneurial activity • Psychological points of entrepreneurship-related with decision-making	• Other types of decision-making but not entrepreneurial • Entrepreneurial decision-making or opportunities for large companies not for SMEs • Research focus on SME is not related to entrepreneurial decision-making or opportunity

research, I used "decision-making process" *and* "optimisation" *and* "entrepreneurial" keywords. This searching yielded 318 articles as total. Further, additional searching was conducted by manual cross-referencing (Bruneel and De Cock 2016). To do this, some articles from the previous searching were identified as key articles in the entrepreneurial decision-making and entrepreneurial opportunity areas. The searching added 32 articles derived from the list of references of these key articles with the total number of 350 articles included in the review before selection.

2.2 Data Cleaning

Data cleaning was provided by applying including and excluding criteria. Primarily, I screened out articles which had not contained keywords in the abstract, title, author's keywords, and those which were not published in high-ranking, international journals. Then, to confirm that the chosen articles match for the objectives of this research, the theoretical part with research questions or hypotheses of the paper was examined. The article was included in the final literature review if it had been related to entrepreneurial decision-making, entrepreneurial opportunity, and international entrepreneurship areas. The articles of international entrepreneurship area combine articles of entrepreneurial decision-making and entrepreneurial opportunity research and were included in international entrepreneurship dimensions because focusing on international context. After taking cleaning procedures, 105 articles were included in the literature review, in which 40 articles were selected in the area of entrepreneurial decision-making, 24 articles related with entrepreneurial opportunity, and 41 articles were selected in international entrepreneurship.

The articles were coded by the method used in the research into conceptual and empirical within three dimensions: entrepreneurial opportunity (EO), entrepreneurial

Table 2 Articles classification by used methodologies

	EDM	EO	IE	Total
Conceptual	12	6	8	26
Empirical				
Qualitative	21	7	20	48
Quantitative	5	11	9	25
Mixed	2	–	4	6

decision-making (EDM), and international entrepreneurship (IE). This research includes conceptual and empirical articles, which are divided into qualitative, quantitative, and mixed articles (see Table 2).

Conceptual articles were included in the review if theoretical considerations concerned entrepreneurial decision-making, entrepreneurial opportunity, and international entrepreneurship, their interrelations and overlapping, simultaneously taking into account requirements of excluding and including criteria. Empirical articles were included and examined if the papers consider research problems in entrepreneurial decision-making, entrepreneurial opportunity, and international entrepreneurship focusing on SMEs. In total, the literature review includes 26 conceptual articles and 79 empirical articles, among which 48 are qualitative, 25 are quantitative, and 6 are mixed articles.

3 Results Overview

3.1 Entrepreneurial Decision-Making and Opportunities in International Entrepreneurship

Combining entrepreneurship research and international business research as mutual research streams (Dana 2017), international entrepreneurship research considers decision-making and opportunity as main concepts (Chandra 2017; Dimitratos et al. 2014) and pays great attention for exploring international activities of SMEs (Alon et al. 2009; Bayfield et al. 2009). International entrepreneurship research emphasises the role of risk and uncertainty (Andersson 2011; Aharoni et al. 2011; Mainela et al. 2014; Sadeghi et al. 2018), international environment (Jafari-Sadeghi et al. 2019b), time (Aharoni et al. 2011; Kontinen and Ojala 2011) and network (Jafari-Sadeghi et al. 2020; Dana 2017), alertness, and international entrepreneurial culture (Dimitratos et al. 2012).

3.2 Entrepreneurial Opportunities: Discovering and Evaluation

Researchers in entrepreneurship area pay great attention for investigation the concept of opportunity (Lassalle and McElwee 2016; Ardichvili et al. 2003; Baron 2006), which enables to recognise opportunity (Lassalle and McElwee 2016). This concept includes market dimensions focusing on market conditions and non-market dimensions focusing on croup characteristics (Lassalle and McElwee 2016), set of resources, and competitive shortcoming (Alvarez and Barney 2007; Ardichvili et al. 2003). The concept of opportunity likewise involves behaviour and economic activity focusing on innovation and arbitrage (Mainela et al. 2014; Sukumar et al. 2020). The opportunity can be changed through time and national, regional, and local levels (Lassalle and McElwee 2016). Within factors that influence on the entrepreneurial opportunities or paly an important role for discovering opportunities can be identified such criteria as active searching (Baron 2006), alertness (Baron 2006; Ardichvili et al. 2003; Endres and Woods 2006), and discovering process (Ardichvili et al. 2003). Considering opportunity-related processes, previous research literature presents different concepts. Some researches investigate opportunity development in relation to the processes of sensing, discovering, and creation (Ardichvili et al. 2003). Others examine opportunity discovery and creation (Mainela et al. 2014), recognition (Baron 2006; Kontinen and Ojala 2011; Stouraitis et al. 2017), identification and exploitation (Perks and Hughes 2008), and opportunity discovery involving search and recognition (Hsieh et al. 2007).

Opportunity evaluation is considered as a very important process for entrepreneurship, strategy, and decision-making (Scheaf et al. 2020; McMullen and Shepherd 2006; Perks and Hughes 2008), enables to recognise the new opportunity or adjust current opportunities to changing circumstances, and should be made at different stages of opportunity development (Ardichvili et al. 2003). There are many studies applying different criteria to evaluate opportunities. Opportunity evaluation can be conducted through feasibility analysis (Ardichvili et al. 2003; McMullen and Shepherd 2006; Scheaf et al. 2020) to assess the profitability of a set of resources, and stage-gate procedure (Ardichvili et al. 2003) to estimate opportunities at each stage of development. Scheaf et al. (2020) analysed 49 criteria for opportunity evaluation and categorised them into four main dimensions: gain and loss estimation, perceived desirability, and feasibility. Research on entrepreneurial opportunity also explores the external environment, technology (Stouraitis et al. 2017), and resource mobilisation (Lassalle and McElwee 2016) as criteria for opportunity evaluation. Some researches develop dimensions of international entrepreneurial culture, which include international market, networking and learning orientation, international innovation propensity, international risk attitude, and international motivation for measuring opportunities (Dimitratos et al. 2012). Growth and profitability can be used as factors to measure opportunities (Steffens et al. 2009; Ghannad and Andersson 2012; Gabrielsson et al. 2014).

3.3 Online and Offline Entrepreneurial Opportunity

A great massive of researches investigate opportunities through particular channels (Shaltoni 2017; Jones et al. 2015) by comparing online and offline channels (Kiani 1998), studying the balance between them (Wentrup 2016), and examining the impact on small- and medium-sized companies (Jones et al. 2015). Researches also explore online and offline channels separately from each other (Foroudi et al. 2017; Jones et al. 2015; Taiminen and Karjaluoto 2015) and the impact of a selected channel on opportunities (Zhu and Lin 2019; Wentrup 2016). Comparisons of online and offline channels demonstrate that online channels are more accessible, flexible and addressable, less expensive, and more rapidly (Kiani 1998). According to Taiminen and Karjaluoto (2015), the classification of online channels offers one and two ways with two levels of company control. One-way online channel includes such tools as websites, e-mail newsletters, banner adverting, and online directories, which are characterised by high company control, and search engine optimisation and search engine advertising with low company control. Two-way online channel involves the company's blogs and communities with a high level of company control and social media with low company control (Taiminen and Karjaluoto 2015).

Previous researches list various opportunities and represent the different classifications of opportunities for SMEs. Researchers identify such opportunities as improving growth, efficiency, communication and knowledge, decreasing costs (Taiminen and Karjaluoto 2015), and overcoming lack of time and financial resources (Jones et al. 2015; Foroudi et al. 2017). Opportunities for marketing (Shaltoni 2017), communication (Kiani 1998; Jones et al. 2015), and consumers (Kiani 1998; Jones et al. 2015; Foroudi et al. 2017) are also highlighted in the research literature. Experience and knowledge of international market enable to seek and evaluate opportunities (Jafari-Sadeghi et al. 2019a) and select and seize the appropriate set of opportunities.

Some researchers classify online opportunities with three levels: communication, transaction, and transformation (Shaltoni and West 2010). Online opportunities have specific dimensions to assess their effectiveness and necessity. The success of usability of online opportunities can be measured through sales and profit, satisfied and repeated customers, occupancy rate, and growth (Jones et al. 2015). Research also develops dimensions of external environment and collaboration, planning, and operation through which online opportunities can be measured (Zhu and Lin 2019). Digital tools used for the evaluation of online opportunities depend on the type of digital channels applied by the company (Taiminen and Karjaluoto 2015).

3.4 Entrepreneurial Decision-Making Process

The analysis of entrepreneurial decision-making process as a core element concerning every part of entrepreneurial processes (Gabrielsson and Politis 2011) passes through different levels based upon employees (Blauth et al. 2014; Douglas 2005) and entrepreneurs (Douglas 2005; McVea 2009), personal and company levels (Clark et al. 2018), and industry and country levels (Bruneel and De Cock 2016). Some researchers examine entrepreneurial decisions from the side of discovering and using opportunity, and consider entrepreneurial decision-making process based on neoclassical, Austrian, and behavioural theories (Endres and Woods 2006). The main body of research is based on effectual and causal approaches to investigate entrepreneurial decision-making process (Sarasvathy et al. 2014; Perry et al. 2012; Dew et al. 2009; Chandler et al. 2011; Chandra 2017; Maine et al. 2015; McVea 2009; Eyana et al. 2018).

Research literature in entrepreneurial decision-making area includes various concepts through which researchers explore the entrepreneurial decision-making process. Some researchers consider entrepreneurial decision-making in relation to personality traits such as creativity (Blauth et al. 2014); sensemaking and confidence (Cunningham and Anderson 2018); experience and career motives (Gabrielsson and Politis 2011); positive emotions and rationality (Zhu 2015); and moral imaginations (McVea 2009). The entrepreneurial decision-making process is also explored from the side of opportunities regarding new product development (Kester et al. 2011). The major part of researches considers the entrepreneurial decision-making process according to the primary activities associated with entrepreneurship (Shepherd et al. 2015).

Entrepreneurial decision-making research differentiates entrepreneurial decisions from non-entrepreneurial (Shepherd et al. 2015; Nouri and Ahmady 2018). Entrepreneurial decisions based on behavioural perspectives include growth, process, and reaction decisions (Douglas 2005). Entrepreneurial decisions can be related with predicting or creating the future (Engel et al. 2017), the ability of the company to risk change (Cunningham and Anderson 2018), career, and ethics (Gabrielsson and Politis 2011; McVea 2009). Entrepreneurial decisions are closely related to marketing including marketing mix decisions, core marketing decisions, and market entry decisions (Nouri and Ahmady 2018). Entry mode decisions represent antecedents, process and outcomes, decisions to create new ventures (Shepherd et al. 2015; Dew et al. 2009), and decisions to be or not to be entrepreneurs (Bruneel and De Cock 2016; Shepherd et al. 2015). The huge part of entrepreneurial decisions related to opportunities defining opportunity assessment decisions (Shane and Venkataraman 2000), decisions about exploiting opportunities, the impact of environment, and exit decisions (Shepherd et al. 2015).

3.5 *Market Entry and Growth Decisions*

Studies in international entrepreneurship research pay attention to investigating the market entry decisions because this type of decisions influences on an entrepreneurial strategy to internationalise (Perks and Hughes 2008) and growth decisions due to this type of decisions reflects the necessity of changes for business (Douglas 2005).

International entrepreneurship research considers market entry decisions as critical and crucial for international strategy (Perks and Hughes 2008; Ojala and Tyrväinen 2008). Market entry decisions are defined as the selection of countries for international activity (Ojala and Tyrväinen 2008), as combined decisions of what market to choose and when and how to enter into the international market (Perks and Hughes 2008; Gaba et al. 2002), and as a decision to start an international activity (Andersson 2011). Growth decisions are determined as a development process (Douglas 2005), expanding business through phases in size and in international line (Gabrielsson et al. 2014). Some studies examine growth decisions as entrepreneurial marketing decisions including decisions of market penetration and development, product expansion, diversification, and segmentation (Nouri and Ahmady 2018).

Market entry and growth decisions are influenced by various factors through which researches explore these concepts. Market entry decisions are influenced by a set of external factors such as industry and home country environment (Perks and Hughes 2008) and internal factors like lack of resources, prior knowledge (Ojala and Tyrväinen 2008; Perks and Hughes 2008), and international experience (Perks and Hughes 2008). Research has also identified such influencing factors as cultural and geographical distance, size of market, and country risk (Ojala and Tyrväinen 2008). While external factors can make a great sense to pursue opportunities, internal factors constrain the market entry decision (Perks and Hughes 2008). The research investigates new market entry and growth decisions through risk, profitability (Lévesque and Schade 2005), and uncertainty (Andersson 2011; Douglas 2005; Harms and Schiele 2012). Risk attitude, market orientation and proactiveness, international learning, and networking influence the growth across the early phase of entry new market (Gabrielsson et al. 2014) and might be examined through entry new market and growth decisions.

4 The Concept of Optimisation in Entrepreneurship Research

There have been several approaches to studying optimisation processes based on various theories in the research literature. An approach based on the resource-based view (Desa and Basu 2013; Liu and Liang 2015) and resource-dependence theory (Desa and Basu 2013) includes materials, labour, and skills as critical dimensions and considers optimisation in relation with adjustment resource mobilisation and allocation. Optimisation from resource-based theory means making decisions to increase types of resources and to reduce resource dependencies (Desa and Basu 2013). Optimisation from resource-based perspectives explains cases and periods of usage to seek potential market opportunities (Desa and Basu 2013; Liu and Liang 2015). Another approach based on neoclassical, Austrian, and behavioural theories depicts optimisation as a set of sequential actions, which leads to optimal decisions and profitability (Endres and Woods 2006).

Researchers explore the optimisation process in comparison with other processes such as bricolage (Desa and Basu 2013) and the choice itself (Gans et al. 2019). While the process of choice implies the selection of unclassified alternatives, the optimisation process means cancellation of unprofitable alternatives (Gans et al. 2019). Whereas optimisation attracts definite resources, bricolage means using various combinations of resources (Desa and Basu 2013). Both studies consider these processes as different but complementary to each other (Desa and Basu 2013; Gans et al. 2019).

Scholars of optimisation literature represent models supported by mathematical equations (Lévesque and Schade 2005; Liu and Liang 2015; Sieja and Wach 2019; Gans et al. 2019) and descriptive process (Endres and Woods 2006; Desa and Basu 2013) to examine and evaluate the process of optimisation. The research focused on mathematical proof of optimisation develops mathematical equations based on cost, time, quality, and flexibility (Liu and Liang 2015), and relations between time, profit, and risk (Lévesque and Schade 2005). Research based on resource-based theory and which considered materials, labour, and skills as main dimensions of optimisation examines optimisation through revenue, Human Development Index, and Global Competitiveness Index (Desa and Basu 2013). Another stream of research regarding optimisation builds sequential actions for optimisation and notes alertness as critical ability, cost decreasing, and revenue (Endres and Woods 2006).

5 Key Definitions

This study integrates entrepreneurial decision-making and entrepreneurial opportunity research streams in the international context to build the conceptual framework for decision-making process optimisation leveraging online and offline opportunities. Following this purpose, the study focuses on the following three main definitions: entrepreneurial decision-making, entrepreneurial opportunity, and optimisation.

According to considerations of entrepreneurial decision-making, research literature represents the array of definitions of entrepreneurial decision-making (see Table 3).

Based on the focus of the investigation to the concept of entrepreneurial opportunity and opportunity-related processes, research literature presents various types of entrepreneurial opportunity definitions (see Table 4).

Entrepreneurship research identifies various definitions of optimisation grounded on the theory or framework being a basis of scientific research. The set of definitions of optimisation spread from entrepreneurship to mathematics and evolutionary dimensions (see Table 5).

Table 3 Definitions of entrepreneurial decision-making

Definition of entrepreneurial decision-making	Source of definition
Process of exploiting new opportunities to create economic value	Gabrielsson and Politis (2011)
Method to increase entrepreneurial creativity	Blauth et al. (2014)
The decision about the process of entering a new market (how and when) to seize an opportunity	Perks and Hughes (2008)
Entrepreneurs respond to the environment and determine whether opportunities are created or recognised in the environment	Maine et al. (2015)
Elaborating on the content and meaning of career management for entrepreneurship scholarship and, more specifically, explaining how career management can drive causal and effectual decision-making	Engel et al. (2017)
Decisions made by the owner include a number of initiatives to organisational changes	Douglas (2005)
Decisions made in consequences of uncertainty, which require a range of balancing considerations about market, environment, culture	Clark et al. (2018)
Identifying opportunities by decision-makers focusing on innovations, profitable venture, and effectiveness in situations of uncertainty, information overload, and time pressure	Nouri and Ahmady (2018)

Table 4 Definitions of entrepreneurial opportunity

Definition of entrepreneurial opportunity	Source of definition
"Chance to meet a market need through a creative combination of resources to deliver superior value"	Ardichvili et al. (2003, p. 108)
The core process of entrepreneurship including opportunity recognition, evaluation, and exploitation	Shepherd et al. (2015)
"Idea or dream that is discovered or created by an entrepreneurial entity and that is revealed through analysis over time to be potentially lucrative"	Short et al. (2010, p. 55)
Multi-levelled structure combining market and non-market Dimensions	Lassalle and McElwee (2016)
Entrepreneurial behaviour to generate new economic activity	Mainela et al. (2014)
Potentially viable match between the means of the entrepreneur and an existing or future target market	Maine et al. (2015)

6 Conceptual Framework

This study represents the conceptual framework of decision-making process optimisation to catch online and offline opportunities supported by the literature review of the entrepreneurial decision-making, entrepreneurial opportunity, and international entrepreneurship research relating to new market entry and growth decisions. For this study, the conceptual framework was built upon the model by Chandra (2017) who conceptualised the entrepreneurial decision-making process combining with three types of opportunity evaluation based on four internationalisation models. The conceptual framework encompasses six components, which are explained in detailed in this section (see Fig. 1). Based on the literature review and conceptual framework,

Table 5 Definitions of optimisation

Source	Theory/Framework	Definition of optimisation
Gans et al. (2019, p. 737)	Entrepreneurial choice process	"Deselection of less preferred alternatives"
Desa and Basu (2013)	The resource-based view (RBV)	Searching a resource advantage
	Resource dependence theory (RDT)	The process of increasing the number and diversity of resources and, simultaneously, the process of decreasing resource dependencies
Liu and Liang (2015)	Resource-based strategy; sense and respond (S&R) methodology	Sustainable development of operational competitiveness
Endres and Woods (2006)	Neoclassical, Austrian, and behavioural theories of entrepreneurial decision-making	The special type of behaviour to exploit a profit set of opportunities
Sieja and Wach (2019)	Evolutionary algorithms	Algorithms with mathematical operations

some propositions were formulated in conjunction with components of the framework.

Discovering opportunities include data about the external environment and informational channels which required to obtain a clear comprehension of online and offline opportunities. The research examines multiple external factors of environment considering them as determinants for decisions to seek opportunities (Perks and Hughes 2008; Shepherd et al. 2015). Conditions of the external environment include political, economic, and legal factors, which influence on entrepreneurial decisions in SMEs in conjunction with seeking new opportunities (Stouraitis et al. 2017; Sciascia et al. 2006). Several studies use the terms of dynamism and heterogeneity of the environment to explore external conditions (Sciascia et al. 2006).

Channels include three main groups: online, offline, and Omni channels. Each group of channels includes tools to discover online and offline opportunities (Taiminen and Karjaluoto 2015; Zhu and Lin 2019; Wentrup 2016). Online channels involve such tools as websites, usage of new technologies, adds, network, and blogs. Two-way online channel involves the company. Offline channels represent traditional ways for entrepreneurial activities. Omni channel combines a range of tools from offline and online channels.

Conditions of the external environment and selected channels lead to leverage offline opportunities such as resources, knowledge, and experience (Taiminen and Karjaluoto 2015; Jones et al. 2015; Shaltoni 2017; Foroudi et al. 2017; Jafari-Sadeghi et al. 2019a) and online opportunities as e-commerce growth, online activities, and network (Jones et al. 2015; Jafari-Sadeghi et al. 2020; Dana 2017). These considerations lead to the first proposition.

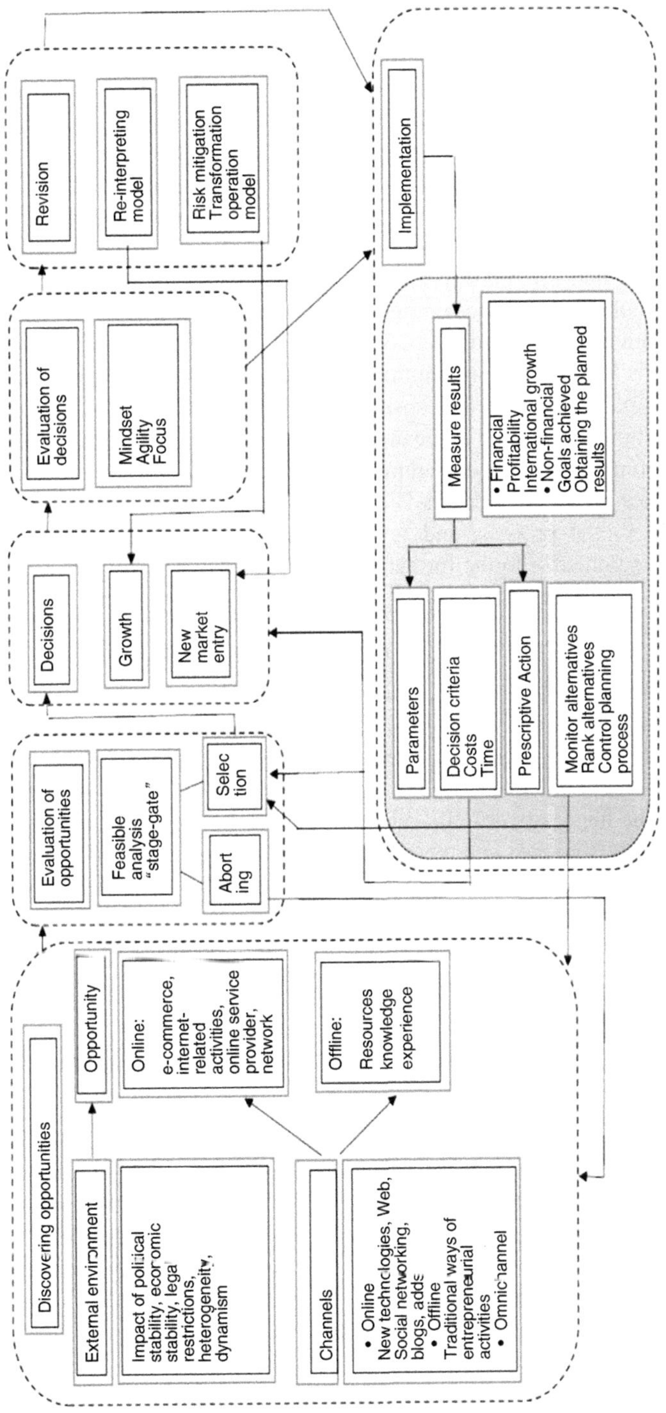

Fig. 1 Framework for decision-making process optimisation

Proposition 1 *External environment and selected channels influence on the process of discovering opportunities.*

Evaluation opportunities as a core process for decision-making and opportunity development (Scheaf et al. 2020; McMullen and Shepherd 2006; Perks and Hughes 2008). The whole vision of how entrepreneurial decisions are related to entrepreneurial opportunity discovering and evaluation is of great importance for entrepreneurship research area (Shepherd et al. 2015; Ardichvili et al. 2003; Short et al. 2010). Evaluation opportunities include two types of analysis to select the appropriate opportunities and abort inappropriate ones. A feasibility analysis focuses on evaluating how the set of opportunities fits the company's goals (Ardichvili et al. 2003; McMullen and Shepherd 2006; Scheaf et al. 2020). The main aim of "stage-gate" analysis is to evaluate opportunities through a wide range of criteria to select suitable opportunities and to refuse unsuitable opportunities (Ardichvili et al. 2003). Selected opportunities are used in the decision-making process to achieve set results. Aborted opportunities cannot be used in the decision-making process, and if most of the opportunities were rejected, this is a reason to go back to the first stage, check channels used in the process, and rethink combination of opportunities. These considerations summarise to the further proposition.

Proposition 2 *Discovering and evaluation opportunities are associated with entrepreneurial decisions for selecting the appropriate set of opportunities.*

Decisions introduce two types of decisions: growth decisions and new market entry decisions. Market entry and growth decisions are of great importance for the entrepreneurial decision-making process to meet new opportunities during the process of internationalisation (Perks and Hughes 2008; Ojala and Tyrväinen 2008). From one hand, opportunity-related processes give entrepreneurs new abilities to overcome the risk and uncertainty related to market entry and growth decisions (Biancone and Jafari Sadeghi 2016; Perks and Hughes 2008; Andersson 2011). From the other hand, opportunities can be recognised or discovered based on the decision-making process (Andersson 2011; Dew et al. 2009; Chandler et al. 2011; Sarasvathy et al. 2014). According to the above considerations, this study offers the following proposition.

Proposition 3 *The process of making new market entry and growth decisions requires a corresponding set of opportunities.*

Evaluation of decisions should be made through criteria allowing to evaluate the level of compliance with the company's purposes (Kester et al. 2011). According to Kester et al. (2011), evaluation the effectiveness of decisions can be conducted with mindset, agility and focus criteria (Kester et al. 2011). Mindset means that decision-makers have a vision of the whole process. Agility indicates a willingness to changes and ability to reflect potential opportunities. Focus implies concentrating on actions to achieve the main goals. If the results meet the short-term goals, the style of decision-making with a corresponding set of opportunities can be implemented for further usage.

Revision part follows the evaluation of decisions and is based on the evaluation results. Decisions should be made according to the purposes of the company (Kester et al. 2011). Revision starts in the case if the company did not achieve short-term purposes and includes an action for every decision. Revision procedures enable to re-interpret model of new market entry decision. Regarding growth decision, revision leads to transformation of operational model and decreasing risks.

Proposition 4 *Evaluation and revision processes of entrepreneurial decision-making are associated with types of entrepreneurial decisions and provided with particular criteria.*

Implementation is a final component, which is divided into implementation and optimisation part. Initially, the decision-making process including new market entry and growth decisions in conjunction with a set of opportunities is implemented and measured. Measurement of the results gives an overview of whether the company achieved planned results. Financial and non-financial criteria can be used to measure performance results (Eyana et al. 2018). Financial criteria include two performance indicators: profitability and international growth in sales (Eyana et al. 2018). Non-financial criteria represent the achievement of goals and planned results (Kester et al. 2011; Eyana et al. 2018).

Optimization enables to support entreprenerial decision-making process, to react effectively to changes in environment and technology (Schiavone 2011), to correct any deviations and improve the quality of the process of decision-making. The optimisation includes prescriptive actions and parameters. Parameters aim to increase the chances to find the appropriate combination of opportunities and, simultaneously, decrease risks. This study examines the decision-making process through decision criteria, costs, and time (Lévesque and Schade 2005; Andersson 2011; Douglas 2005; Harms and Schiele 2012). These parameters enable us to make changes in decision process according to a set of opportunities. Prescriptive actions help to improve the quality of the process by defining which set of decision criteria can be more suitable to get better alternatives for opportunities. Prescriptive actions involve monitoring and ranking alternatives and controlling planning processes where opportunities are discovered and evaluated (Andersson 2011). The considerations of the decision-making process optimisation lead to the final proposition.

Proposition 5 *Optimisation of entrepreneurial decision-making process increases the likelihood of selecting the most appropriate set of opportunities.*

7 Discussion

This study considered a topic of entrepreneurial decision-making process optimisation. The literature review explored entrepreneurial decision-making and entrepreneurial opportunity research streams combining them in an international context. This study examined key definitions, main concepts and their characteristics regarding entrepreneurial decision-making process, entrepreneurial opportunities and optimization. The literature review identified various dimensions and processes of the entrepreneurial decision-making process and entrepreneurial opportunities (Chandra 2017; Perks and Hughes 2008; Endres and Woods 2006) and factors of environment considering them as determinants of decisions to seek opportunities (Perks and Hughes 2008; Jafari-Sadeghi et al. 2019a). The literature review examined great diversity of interrelations and mutual influence between main concepts of entrepreneurial opportunities, entrepreneurial decision-making process, and international entrepreneurship (Chandra 2017; Mainela et al. 2014, 2014; Dimitratos et al. 2014, 2012; Kontinen and Ojala 2011; Glavas et al. 2017; Lassalle and McElwee 2016; Short et al. 2010). The literature review revealed various dimensions and processes of entrepreneurial decision-making and entrepreneurial opportunities to investigate them separately from each other, and in interrelations (Chandra 2017; Perks and Hughes 2008; Endres and Woods 2006) based on models and theories as a basis for opportunity development and evaluation (Chandra 2017; Gabrielsson and Politis 2011; Sarasvathy et al. 2014). Opportunity discovering and evaluation processes were explored as very important for decision-making (Scheaf et al. 2020; McMullen and Shepherd 2006; Perks and Hughes 2008).

Researches represent the decision-making process as complicated, involving numbers of decision-makers, striving to find reasonable solutions and quite different from optimisation (Andersson 2011). Theoretical underpinnings of this study reflected in the literature review revealed a lack of considerations of how entrepreneurial decision-making process can be optimised for leveraging a more appropriate set of online and offline opportunities.

8 Future Research Agenda and Limitations

This study presents the directions for the future research agenda formulated in general terms and is detailed in accordance with propositions. Despite the number of theoretical and practical implications, this study has several limitations, which can be simultaneously considered as directions for future research. This research does not cover studies, which consider concepts and interrelations of entrepreneurial opportunity, entrepreneurial decision-making, and international entrepreneurship from individual perspectives. This research does not involve studies regardless of psychological determinants, cognitive aspects of individuals, or entrepreneurial personality of decision-makers to make decisions to pursue new opportunities. Future research can focus on investigating the role of the logic of entrepreneurial decision-making process and comparison between types of logic. For the purpose of this study, all concepts are considered for SMEs, but future research can be made for large companies or for special industries.

Based on the considerations underpinning the framework offered, this study presented a set of propositions to expand the directions for future research. Proposition 1 underlines the role of the external environment and channels for discovering entrepreneurial opportunities. Future research can explore the role of another combination of external environmental factors and their role in discovering opportunities. It is valuable to investigate internal factors such as policy, network, and resources (Ratten et al. 2007) regarding discovering opportunities and entrepreneurial decision-making process. Future research also can focus on relations between internal and external factors, their interaction with selected channels, and influence on discovering opportunities. Environmental factors can be explored in connection with their impact on opportunity creation, recognition, development, or other opportunity-related processes. Future research can focus on technology selection (Mokhtarzadeh et al. 2020) to choose better channels and tools in conjunction with seizing opportunities.

The next direction for future research is connected with processes related to entrepreneurial opportunity. Proposition 2 highlights discovering and evaluation processes as a basis in the entrepreneurial decision-making process for selecting the appropriate set of entrepreneurial opportunities. Future research can explore other processes such as opportunity creation, recognition, development, and their importance in the entrepreneurial decision-making process for selecting a better set of opportunities.

The third direction for future research relates to interrelations between a special set of entrepreneurial opportunities and the types of entrepreneurial decisions, as outlined in Proposition 3. This study focuses only on new market entry and growth decisions and considers them in connection to entrepreneurial opportunities. Future research can investigate other types of entrepreneurial decisions in relation to a more suitable combination of opportunities for the effective decision-making process.

Proposition 4 outlines close relations between evaluation and revision processes of entrepreneurial decisions and types of decisions, and the impact of these processes on the level of entrepreneurial decisions. Future research can consider different criteria to evaluate entrepreneurial decisions, define a set of criteria needed for a particular type of a decision, and identify what kind of revision procedures is required for a specific type of entrepreneurial decision.

Proposition 5 relates to the final results of entrepreneurial decision-making process optimisation, which increase the likelihood of selecting the most suitable set of entrepreneurial opportunity. Antecedents of the entrepreneurial decision-making process, which lead to the necessity of optimisation, can be analysed in future research. Future research can explore whether export incentives (Dana et al. 2009) influence on optimisation of entrepreneurial decision-making process and compare the level of impact in developing and developed countries. This study is theoretical, which represents the model of how entrepreneurs can optimise their decision-making processes based on two entrepreneurial decisions. The further research can analyse theoretical framework with a practical side by conducting empirical research and checking the process and results over time (Dana 2017) that enable to make adjustments for the model.

9 Conclusion

The main purposes of this paper were to examine previous studies on entrepreneurial decision-making, entrepreneurial opportunities, and international entrepreneurship, offer a theoretical framework for optimisation of the entrepreneurial decision-making process, and provide directions for future research based on a set of propositions. The majority of previous studies on entrepreneurial decision-making and entrepreneurial opportunity within international entrepreneurship examine the relationships between entrepreneurial decision-making and opportunity creation and recognition through various characteristics. The goal of this research was to focus on the optimisation of the entrepreneurial decision-making process for leveraging online and offline opportunities. The contributions of this study to theory related to extending current studies on entrepreneurial decision-making and entrepreneurial opportunities combining with the international context. The theoretical framework enables us to explain how to optimise an entrepreneurial decision-making process to achieve the most appropriate set of opportunities and, eventually, better outcomes.

This study offers practical implications for small- and medium-sized companies, decision-makers, and entrepreneurs of small business. Lack of resources and informal style of decision-making process influence on entrepreneurial decisions. Optimisation of decision-making process helps to overcome the effect of lack of resources and pursue the appropriate set of online and offline opportunities.

References

Aharoni Y, Tihanyi L, Connelly B (2011) Managerial decision-making in international business: a forty-five-year retrospective. J World Bus 46:135–142

Alon I, Dana L-P, Jenkins A (2009) International business by SMEs: empirical findings from New Zealand. J Int Bus Econ 10(2):59–78

Alvarez SA, Barney J (2007) Discovery and creation: alternative theories of entrepreneurial action. Strateg Entrep J 1(1/2):11–26

Andersson S (2011) International entrepreneurship, born globals and the theory of effectuation. J Small Bus Enterp Dev 18(3):627–643

Ardichvili A, Cardozo R, Ray S (2003) A theory of entrepreneurial opportunity identification and development. J Bus Ventur 18(1):105–123

Baron RA (2006) Opportunity recognition as pattern recognition: how entrepreneurs "Connect the Dots" to identify new business opportunities. Acad Manag Perspect 20:104–119

Bayfield R, Dana L-P, Stewart S (2009) Firm characteristics and internationalization strategies: an empirical investigation of New Zealand exporters. IJGSB 3(3):275–287

Biancone PP, Jafari Sadeghi V (2016) Risk management in export compliance: concepts, procedures, and solutions. In: Cantino V, De Vincentiis P, Racca MG (eds) Risk management: perspectives and open issues. McGraw-Hill, London, UK, pp 64–78

Blauth M, Mauer R, Brettel M (2014) Fostering creativity in new product development through entrepreneurial decision making. Creat Innov Manag 23(4):495–509

Bruneel J, De Cock R (2016) Entry mode research and SMEs: a review and future research agenda. J Small Bus Manag 54:135–167

Büyüközkan G (2004) Multi-criteria decision making for e-marketplace selection. Internet Res 14 (2):139–154
Chandler GN, DeTienne DR, McKelvie A, Mumford TV (2011) Causation and effectuation processes: a validation study. J Bus Ventur 26(3):375–390
Chandra Y (2017) A time-based process model of international entrepreneurial opportunity evaluation. J Int Bus Stud 48(4):423–451
Clark DR, Li D, Shepherd D (2018) Country familiarity in the initial stage of foreign market selection. J Int Bus Stud 49:442–472
Collinson S, Houlden J (2005) Decision-making and market orientation in the internationalization process of small and medium-sized enterprises. Manag Int Rev 45(4):413–436
Cunningham J, Anderson AR (2018) Inspired or foolhardy: sensemaking, confidence and entrepreneurs' decision-making. Group Decis Negot 27(3):393–415
Dana L-P (2017) International entrepreneurship research: how it evolved and directions for the future. Int J Entrep Small Bus 30(4):477–489
Dana L-P, Grimwood S, William G (2009) Export incentives and international entrepreneurship in New Zealand firms. J Int Bus Entrep Dev 4(1/2):1–21
Demir H, Yozgat U, Demirbag O, Artan I (2017) New pace of impression management tactics in digital age. J Glob Strat Manag 11(1):27–34
Desa G, Basu S (2013) Optimization or bricolage? Overcoming resource constraints in global social entrepreneurship. Strateg Entrep J 7:26–49
Dew N, Read S, Sarasvathy SD, Wiltbank R (2009) Effectual versus predictive logics in entrepreneurial decision-making: differences between experts and novices. J Bus Ventur 24(4):287–309
Dimitratos P, Voudouris I, Plakoyiannaki E, Nakos G (2012) International entrepreneurial culture-toward a comprehensive opportunity-based operationalization of international entrepreneurship. Int Bus Rev 21(4):708–721
Dimitratos P, Amorós JE, Etchebarne MS, Felzensztein C (2014) Micro-multinational or not? International entrepreneurship, networking and learning effects. J Bus Res 67(5):908–915
Douglas D (2005) The human complexities of entrepreneurial decision making: a grounded case considered. Int J Entrep Behav Res 11(6):422–435
Endres A, Woods C (2006) Modern theories of entrepreneurial behavior: a comparison and appraisal. Small Bus Econ 26:189–202
Engel Y, Burg EV, Kleijn E, Khapova SN (2017) Past career in future thinking: how career management practices shape entrepreneurial decision making. Strateg Entrep J 11(2):122–144
Eyana SM, Masurel E, Paas LJ (2018) Causation and effectuation behaviour of Ethiopian entrepreneurs: implications on performance of small tourism firms. J Small Bus Enterp Dev 25 (5):791–817
Foroudi P, Gupta S, Nazarian A, Duda M (2017) Digital technology and marketing management capability: achieving growth in SMEs. Qual Mark Res Int J 20(2):230–246
Gaba V, Pan Y, Ungson GR (2002) Timing of entry in international market: an empirical study of U.S. fortune 500 firms in China. J Int Bus Stud 33(1):39–55
Gabrielsson J, Politis D (2011) Career motives and entrepreneurial decision-making: examining preferences for causal and effectual logics in the early stage of new ventures. Small Bus Econ 36 (3):281–298
Gabrielsson M, Gabrielsson P, Dimitratos P (2014) International entrepreneurial culture and growth of international new ventures. Manag Int Rev 54(4):445–471
Gans J, Stern S, Wu J (2019) Foundations of entrepreneurial strategy. Strateg Manag J 40:736–756
Ghannad N, Andersson S (2012) The influence of the entrepreneur's background on the behaviour and development of born globals' internationalisation processes. Int J Entrep Small Bus 15 (2):136–153
Glavas S, Mathews S, Bianchi C (2017) International opportunity recognition as a critical component for leveraging internet capabilities and international market performance. J Int Entrep 15:1–35

Harms R, Schiele H (2012) Antecedents and consequences of effectuation and causation in the international new venture creation process. J Int Entrep 10(2):95–116
Hsieh C, Nickerson JA, Zenger TR (2007) Opportunity discovery, problem solving and a theory of the entrepreneurial firm. J Manag Stud 44:1255–1277
Jafari-Sadeghi V, Biancone PP (2018) How micro, small and medium-sized enterprises are driven outward the superior international trade performance? A multidimensional study on Italian food sector. Res Int Bus Financ 45:597–606
Jafari-Sadeghi V, Kimiagari S, Biancone PP (2019a) Level of education and knowledge, foresight competency and international entrepreneurship: a study of human capital determinants in the European countries. Eur Bus Rev 32(1):46–68
Jafari-Sadeghi V, Nkongolo-Bakenda J-M, Anderson RB, Dana L-P (2019b) An institution-based view of international entrepreneurship: a comparison of context-based and universal determinants in developing and economically advanced countries. Int Bus Rev 28:1–16
Jafari-Sadeghi V, Dutta DK, Ferraris A, Del Giudice M (2020) Internationalisation business processes in an under-supported policy contexts: evidence from Italian SMEs. Bus Process Manag J. https://doi.org/10.1108/BPMJ-03-2019-0141
Jones N, Borgman R, Ulusoy E (2015) Impact of social media on small business. J Small Bus Enterp Dev 22(4):611–632
Kester L, Griffin A, Hultink EJ, Lauche K (2011) Exploring portfolio decision-making processes. J Prod Innov Manag 28:641–661
Kiani GR (1998) Marketing opportunities in the digital world. Internet Res 8(2):185–194
Kontinen T, Ojala A (2011) International opportunity recognition among small and medium -sized family firms. J Small Bus Manag 49(3):490–514
Kraus S, Breier M, Dasi-Rodriguez S (2020) The art of crafting a systematic literature review in entrepreneurship research. Int Entrep Manag J. https://doi.org/10.1007/s11365-020-00635-4
Lassalle P, McElwee G (2016) Polish entrepreneurs in Glasgow and entrepreneurial opportunity structure. Int J Entrep Behav Res 22(2):260–281
Lee SH, DeWester D, Park SR (2008) Web 2.0 and opportunities for small business. Serv Bus 2:335–345
Lévesque M, Schade C (2005) Intuitive optimizing: experimental findings on time allocation decisions with newly formed ventures. J Bus Ventur 20:313–342
Liu Y, Liang L (2015) Evaluating and developing resource-based operations strategy for competitive advantage: an exploratory study of Finnish high-tech manufacturing industries. Int J Prod Res 53(4):1019–1037
Maine E, Soh P, Dos Santos N (2015) The role of entrepreneurial decision-making in opportunity creation and recognition. Technovation 39–40(1):53–72
Mainela T, Puhakka V, Servais P (2014) The concept of international opportunity in international entrepreneurship: a review and a research agenda. Int J Manag Rev 16(1):105–129
McMullen JS, Shepherd DA (2006) Entrepreneurial action and the role of uncertainty in the theory of the entrepreneur. Acad Manag Rev 31(1):132–152
McVea JF (2009) A field study of entrepreneurial decision-making and moral imagination. J Bus Ventur 24(5):491–504
Milkman KL, Chugh D, Bazerman MH (2009) How can decision making be improved? Perspect Psychol Sci 4(4):379–383
Mokhtarzadeh NG, Mahdiraji HA, Jafari Sadeghi V, Soltani A, Kamardi AA (2020) A product-technology portfolio alignment approach for food industry: a multi-criteria decision making with z-numbers. Br Food J 122(12):3947–3967
Nouri P, Ahmady A (2018) A taxonomy of nascent entrepreneurs' marketing decisions in high-tech small businesses. J Small Bus Strateg 28(3):69–79
Ojala A, Tyrväinen P (2008) Market entry decisions of US small and medium-sized software firms. Manag Decis 46(2):187–200
Perks KJ, Hughes M (2008) Entrepreneurial decision-making in internationalization: propositions from mid-size firms. Int Bus Rev 17(3):310–330

Perry JT, Chandler GN, Markova G (2012) Entrepreneurial effectuation: a review and suggestions for future research. Entrep Theory Pract 36(4):837–861
Ratten V, Dana L-P, Han M, Welpe I (2007) Internationalisation of SMEs: European comparative studies. Int J Entrep Small Bus 4(3):361–379
Sadeghi VJ, Biancone PP, Giacoma C, Secinaro S (2018) How does export compliance influence the internationalization of firms: is it a thread or an opportunity? J Glob Entrep Res 8(3):1–15
Sarasvathy S, Kumar K, York J, Bhagavatula S (2014) An effectual approach to international entrepreneurship: overlaps, challenges, and provocative possibilities. Entrep Theory Pract 38:71–93
Scheaf DJ, Loignon AC, Webb JW, Heggestad ED, Wood MS (2020) Measuring opportunity evaluation: conceptual synthesis and scale development. J Bus Ventur 35:1–26
Schiavone F (2011) Strategic reactions to technology competition: a decision-making model. Manag Decis 49(5):801–809
Sciascia S, Naldi L, Hunter E (2006) Market orientation as determinant of entrepreneurship: an empirical investigation on SMEs. Int Entrep Manag J 2(1):21–38
Shaltoni AM (2017) From websites to social media: exploring the adoption of internet marketing in emerging industrial markets. J Bus Ind Mark 32(7):1009–1019
Shaltoni AM, West DC (2010) The measurement of e-marketing orientation (EMO) in business-to-business markets. Ind Mark Manag 39:1097–1102
Shane S, Venkataraman S (2000) The promise of entrepreneurship as a field of research. Acad Manag Rev 25:217–226
Shepherd DA, Williams TA, Patzelt H (2015) Thinking about entrepreneurial decision making: review and research agenda. J Manag 41(1):11–46
Short JC, Ketchen DJ Jr, Shook CL, Ireland RD (2010) The concept of "Opportunity" in entrepreneurship research: past accomplishments and future challenges. J Manag 36(1):40–65
Sieja M, Wach K (2019) The use of evolutionary algorithms for optimization in the modern entrepreneurial economy: interdisciplinary perspective. Entrepreneurial Bus Econ Rev 7 (4):117–130
Snyder H (2019) Literature review as a research methodology: an overview and guidelines. J Bus Res 104:333–339
Steffens P, Davidsson P, Fitzsimmons J (2009) Performance configurations over time: implications for growth- and profit-oriented strategies. Enterp Theory Pract 33(1):125–148
Stouraitis V, Boonchoo P, Harun M, Kyritsis M (2017) Entrepreneurial perceptions and bias of SME exporting opportunities for manufacturing exporters: a UK study. J Small Bus Enterp Dev 24(4):906–927
Sukumar A, Jafari-Sadeghi V, Garcia-Perez A, Dutta DK (2020) The potential link between corporate innovations and corporate competitiveness: evidence from IT firms in the UK. J Knowl Manag 24(5):965–983
Taiminen HM, Karjaluoto H (2015) The usage of digital marketing channels in SMEs. J Small Bus Enterp Dev 22(4):633–651
Wentrup R (2016) The online–offline balance: internationalization for Swedish online service providers. J Int Entrep 14(4):562–594
Zhu Y (2015) The role of Qing (positive emotions) and Li 1 (rationality) in Chinese entrepreneurial decision making: a confucian Ren-Yi wisdom perspective. J Bus Ethics 126(4):613–630
Zhu Z, Lin S (2019) Understanding entrepreneurial perceptions in the pursuit of emerging e-business opportunities: the dimensions and drivers. Comput Hum Behav 95:252–261

Iuliia Andreeva is a PhD student at the School of Business and Management at Lappeenranta-Lahti University of Technology, Finland. Her research interests include international entrepreneurship, international business, international marketing, internationalisation, SME internationalisation strategies, and decision-making process.

International Entrepreneurship and Technology: A Structured Literature Review

Paolo Pietro Biancone, Silvana Secinaro, Daniel Iannaci, and Davide Calandra

1 Introduction

The scientific debate under the international entrepreneurship field is under investigation by several authors. However, this field is evolving with the spread of technology, and companies are facing with new challenges in the global world in terms of the development of new technological solutions (Leonidou 2004; Maignan and Lukas 1997; Vadana et al. 2019; Zou and Stan 1998). The global economy involves enormous internationalisation activities that provide untapped opportunities for entrepreneurs and businesses (Acs et al. 2003; Dana 2017; Jafari-Sadeghi et al. 2019c, 2020).

With market internationalisation, business activities are evolving towards new interests both for small- and medium-sized enterprises and for large multinationals, also considering growing economies (Jafari-Sadeghi et al. 2019a, c; McDougall and Oviatt 2000). Additionally, entrepreneurs could look for technological changes quickly and with less financial resources than ever (Dabić et al. 2019; Dana 2017).

The scientific debate of how international entrepreneurship faces with technology is still evolving. As stated by the European Commission and Lackéus and Williams Middleton (2015), it is essential to prepare entrepreneurs able to act on the international market with new technological skills.

For all these premises, this chapter aims to analyse the literature on the relationship between international entrepreneurship and technology. Additionally, this essay seeks to provide a critical discussion of the technology elements that entrepreneurs should consider facing new international markets.

P. P. Biancone · S. Secinaro · D. Iannaci · D. Calandra (✉)
Department of Management, University of Turin, Turin, Italy
e-mail: paolo.biancone@unito.it; silvana.secinaro@unito.it; daniel.iannaci@unito.it; davide.calandra@unito.it

V. Jafari-Sadeghi et al. (eds.), *Empirical International Entrepreneurship*, Contributions to Management Science,
https://doi.org/10.1007/978-3-030-68972-8_8

Authors will provide an in-depth analysis of the literature using the approach proposed by Massaro, Dumay, and Guthrie. Notably, the Structured Literature Review (STL) is an approach which combines several research methods and approaches with a rigorous research protocol and allows the replicability of results (Massaro et al. 2016). The process joins together the rules of content and bibliometric analysis, which would enable to minimise errors in the collection and interpretation studies. Therefore, as suggested by Zaheer et al. (2019), SLR allows creating interdisciplinary, rigorous, and emerging research stream-oriented reviews. Furthermore, the bibliometric review is implemented using "Bibliometrix" package with R software (Aria and Cuccurullo 2017). The analysis also considers the co-occurrence network, which allows creating codes and the emergence of significant research flows (van Eck and Waltman 2014).

Additionally, all sources were validated by verifying the definition of technological ecosystems of Adomavicius et al. (2006). Therefore, after this first step, authors continue the reading of the title and abstract considering only scientific paper which deals with technology and its role with the component, product, application, support, and infrastructure. After these phases, researchers can analyse 253 scientific papers.

This chapter has several implications. In terms of theoretical contribution, we introduce an SLR in the entrepreneurship field, which could be useful for a future summary of the literature by researchers. Additionally, authors provide an in-depth discussion of the results giving the tools for future research to educate entrepreneurs on technology for international markets. In a practical perspective, this chapter can be consulted by entrepreneurs to understand the level of internationalisation of their company and to focus new investments in technology for medium-to-long-term policies of achieving new markets.

This chapter shows a comprehensive state-of-the-art literature about international entrepreneurship and technology. Despite the growing research in this field, this essay provides insights to entrepreneurs to reach new markets using IT skills and opportunities. The chapter concludes the journey with a structured research agenda for future challenges in this field.

Finally, the rest of the essay is structured as follows. The next section will assess an in-depth analysis of the method employed. In the third section, researchers will present the results and the discussion section. Moreover, Section 4 discusses the main results obtained from the analysis. The last section concludes the chapter considering the main results obtained and providing a structured future research agenda for researchers.

2 Methodology

This chapter is based on the Structured Literature Review (SLR) method of Massaro et al. (2016). According to D'Adamo and Rosa (2019), Dal Mas et al. (2019), Secundo et al. (2020), and Zaheer et al. (2019), this method allows a rigorous and reliable analysis of sources under study. Additionally, SLR will enable researchers to

Table 1 SLR review protocol

Review protocol elements	Authors' consideration
What is already known?	Based on the need, there is the potential for a structured literature review investigating how international entrepreneurship faces with technologies
Research topic	The chapter deals with two essential streams of literature. On one side, the entrepreneurship literature highly investigated by several authors and the technology and innovation literature
Motivation	Disruptive technologies also face conventional entrepreneurship methods. Additionally, for an international entrepreneur, the link with new technologies is even vital for market survival
Journals' research	We have decided not to limit research to individual scientific journals because of the still young scope

investigate main research trends contributing to highlight young stream. SLR starts from the premises of Tranfield et al. (2003), who stated that review, in general, should require structured and replicable processes. Despite different literature review methods exist, we think that SLR is the best option because it joins multiple ways and allows to create research protocol; it is particularly interesting applying in the accounting field studies. Therefore, our chapter, considering these essential elements, considers SLR as a valid method which ensures these elements avoiding researcher biases. As reported by Massaro et al. (2016), the analysis is based on ten essential steps:

1. Write a literature review protocol.
2. Define the questions that the literature review is setting out to answer.
3. Determine the type of studies and carry out a comprehensive literature search.
4. Measure article impact.
5. Define an analytical framework.
6. Establish a literature review reliability.
7. Test literature review validity.
8. Code data using the developed framework.
9. Develop insights and critique through the analysis of the results extracted.
10. Develop future research paths and questions.

The rest of this point will develop the first eight points. Point nine will be the next section, and point ten will be implemented in the conclusion section.

The first elements to address consider the development of a rigid research protocol based on the following items shown in Table 1.

This essay will use SLR and bibliometric analysis to investigate the theme thoroughly. Additionally, these two methods allow us to avoid problems in results interpretations. As stated by Zupic and Čater (2015), bibliometric analysis in the business and management introduces "measured of objectivity into the evaluation of scientific literature" increasing rigour of study and decreasing review's biases.

Secondly, considering research questions selection, this chapter is based on previous literature review and bibliometric analysis (Secinaro et al. 2020; Zaheer et al. 2019). Therefore, we identified three research questions:

RQ1. *What are the characteristics of the literature for the international entrepreneurship within technology?*
RQ2. *What is the focus of this literature in terms of key concepts?*
RQ3. *What are the future directions in this field considering new topics and methodologies?*

Thirdly, considering the determination of article in the analysis, the authors used the Scopus database to retrieve all the relevant sources. This database includes relevant and updated references, especially in the information system (IS) research stream (Oakleaf 2010; Okoli and Schabram 2010). To avoid missing relevant literature, researchers have compared the most cited paper in the Scopus database with the Web of Science (WOS) database. The results suggest what Oakleaf (2010) suggested. Therefore, our analysis is implemented considering the Scopus database.

To select the appropriate scientific flow, we consider a keywords analysis including "*international entrepreneurship*" AND "*technology*" on the Scopus database. The study also includes relevant search limitations. For instance, researchers selected only peer-review articles on the business, management, and accounting area. The analysis was conducted in May 2020.

Besides to ensure the inclusion of relevant articles, three authors independently verified that the extracted articles were related to the scope of the study (Grafton et al. 2011). The first analysis reveals 997 documents; after the application of research limitations, we consider only 426 peer-reviewed articles; and then only the areas of business, management, and accounting are considered. Therefore, the final sample consists of 253 scientific articles.

Fourthly, considering the selection of article with an impact in the field of analysis, this chapter will start viewing the most cited papers. Therefore, at the same time, researchers believe that quantitative and qualitative research data could suggest impressive results for future studies. Additionally, with bibliometric analysis, it is possible to avoid biases in the data selection because of the quantitative analysis which could help researchers to focus on the primary and relevant papers (Zupic and Čater 2015).

Fifthly, we develop a coding framework based on the previous literature (Dal Mas et al. 2019; Massaro et al. 2015; Sadeghi and Biancone 2017; Secinaro and Calandra 2020; Secundo et al. 2020; Zaheer et al. 2019). Mainly, this chapter starting from the review protocol and research questions analysed considering primary information as timespan evolution, authors' citations and collaborations, journals, keywords, and their occurrences. Furthermore, the paper by Zaheer et al. (2019) allowed the authors to obtain relevant codes such as the background of the authors and thus experiment with more adventurous research. Finally, an essential system comes from the paper of Adomavicius et al. (2006) which aims to investigate relevant technologies implemented in the international entrepreneurship research stream. Table 2 shows the analytical framework created for the analysis.

Table 2 Analytical framework

Category	Variables	Specifications
Bibliometric data	Main information	Years
	Authors	Citations
		Collaborations
	Sources	Journals
		Citations
	Keywords	Occurrences
	Authors	Collaboration
Coding analysis ($a = 0.667$)	Authors' background	Mixed
		Practitioner
		Scholar
Coding analysis ($a = 0.795$)	Research methods	Qualitative
		Quantitative
		Mixed
		Review
		Conceptual
Coding analysis ($a = 0.667$)	Patterns of technology evolution	Influence in the technology ecosystem
		Product development
		Product and infrastructure alignment
		Feed-forward evolution
		Feed-Back evolution
		Incremental evolution
		Not applicable

Sixthly, to establish literature review reliability, researchers refer to Krippendorff (Krippendorff 2011). This method allows researchers to determine reliability in the coding analysis. Therefore, a variable with an amount between $a = 0.667$ and $a = 0.800$ indicates a reliable variable with the same meaning.

Seventhly, to test literature review validity, researchers should verify the internal, external, and constructive validity of their results. As performed by Broadbent and Guthrie (2008), our chapter proceeds using a preliminary classification of results obtained. Subsequently, the analysis continues with the codes' creation framework already used in the literature. Therefore, we can affirm that the study of the results through the created codes follows a structured process of internal validity of the research field.

Eighthly, to proceed with the coding process, the researchers used some specialised software. For the analysis of the quantitative data, we used R and the Bibliometrix package (Aria and Cuccurullo 2017). Also, we used VOSviewer software to conduct the keywords' analysis. Additionally, this software is used for keywords' cluster analysis (van Eck and Waltman 2014). In the end, for qualitative coding analysis, researchers use the Dedoose software.

The last paragraph will develop insights and critique from the analysis. Finally, the conclusion section will develop future research paths and questions for researchers.

3 Results

This section aims to present the results retrieved from the analysis of the pools of paper under investigation according to point nine of Massaro et al.'s (2016) methodological paper. Thus, researchers here answer the following two research questions: RQ1. What are the characteristics of the literature for the international entrepreneurship within technology? RQ2. What is the focus of this literature in terms of key concepts?

3.1 Descriptive Analysis of the Literature

Table 3 identifies the primary information concerning the data under analysis.

As indicated, the starting year of the scientific field is 1982. However, as shown in Fig. 1, the highest increase in terms of articles produced occurred between 2018 and 2019. Interestingly, the research flow has been flattened for many years. However, considering the whole period under analysis, the research area shows an annual growth rate of 7.71%. The table then indicates other relevant information. The articles are published in 106 scientific sources. Considering the period of publication, the average publication rate is seven articles per year. Also, each document has been cited about 20 times. The authors then used 14,190 references from other authors and 821 keywords. Besides, the number of articles by multiple authors confirms that the scope of research is highly collaborative. Only 53 have single author signatures.

3.2 Authors' Citations Analysis

Considering now the average quotations received from the 253 documents (Fig. 2), some interesting results emerge. From 1982 to 2002, the number of citations per paper was very high due to the low number of published articles. From 2003 to 2020, on the other hand, the average number of citations decreased, a sign of an increasing number of documents produced by researchers.

Table 4 shows the ten most cited articles written between 1989 and 2010. The most cited papers were written for at least 10 years ago and are now considered by

Table 3 Main information about data

Description	Results
Timespan	1982–2020
Sources	106
Documents	253
Average years from publication	7.38
Average citations per documents	20.19
Average citations per year per documents	1.927
References	14.190
Keywords plus (ID)	329
Author's keywords	821
Authors	565
Authors appearances	611
Authors of single-authored documents	53
Authors of multi-authored documents	512
Single-authored documents	58
Document per author	0.448
Author per document	2.23
Co-authors per documents	2.42
Collaboration index	2.63

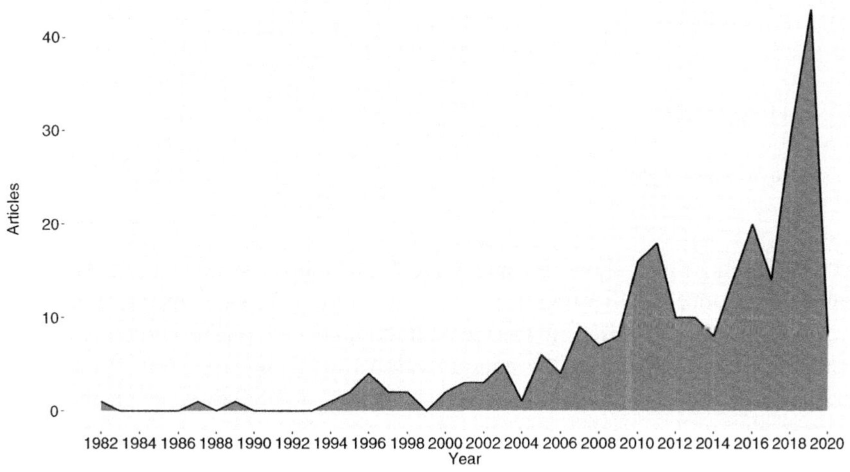

Fig. 1 Annual scientific production

researchers all over the world as the essential starting point for the analysis of this area. Total citations per year represent the average of citations for each paper. Interesting is that the contribution of Burgel and Murray (2000) received more citations than the second paper of Knight (1997). It is possible due to the innovative topic and discussion about technological international entrepreneurs and start-ups investigating organisational perspectives.

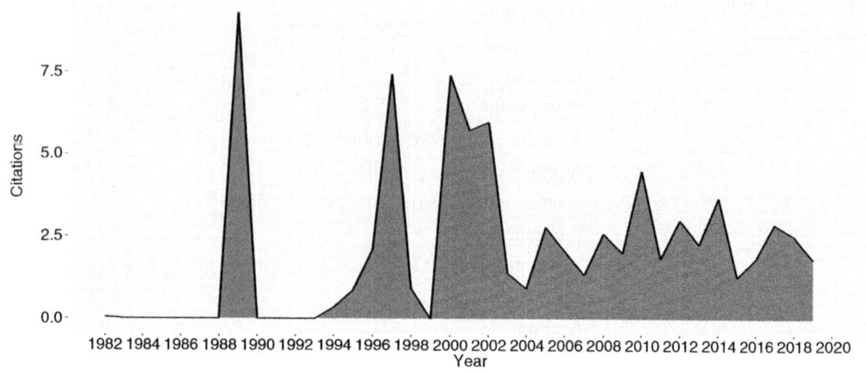

Fig. 2 Average citations per year

Table 4 Most global cited documents

Paper	Total citations	Total citations per year
Cantwell et al. (2010)	362	32.9091
Knight (1997)	304	12.6667
Burgel and Murray (2000)	296	14.0952
McDougall (1989)	288	9.0000
Manolova et al. (2002)	184	9.6842
Fillis (2001)	144	7.2000
Desa (2012)	134	14.8889
Dodd and Patra (2002)	128	6.7368
Jones (2001)	102	5.1000
Matlay and Westhead (2005)	96	6.0000

The following Fig. 3 shows the authors' collaborations. As we can see, the most significant collaboration between the authors takes place between the USA and the European area. Besides, England has the highest number of collaborations compared to other countries. However, the analysis allows for some reflection. Within the collaborations, entire continents such as Asia, Africa, and South America are weak and even absent. The explanation may derive from two elements. First, research institutes and universities in Europe and the USA promote collaboration between researchers both internally and externally (Gazni et al. 2012). Therefore, they could be more attracted to cooperation. Second, European and American countries could have more active policies to encourage entrepreneurship (Renault 2006). Additionally, as discussed by Román et al. (2013), incentives for youth entrepreneurship aimed at technology transfer have become a hot topic on the European agenda.

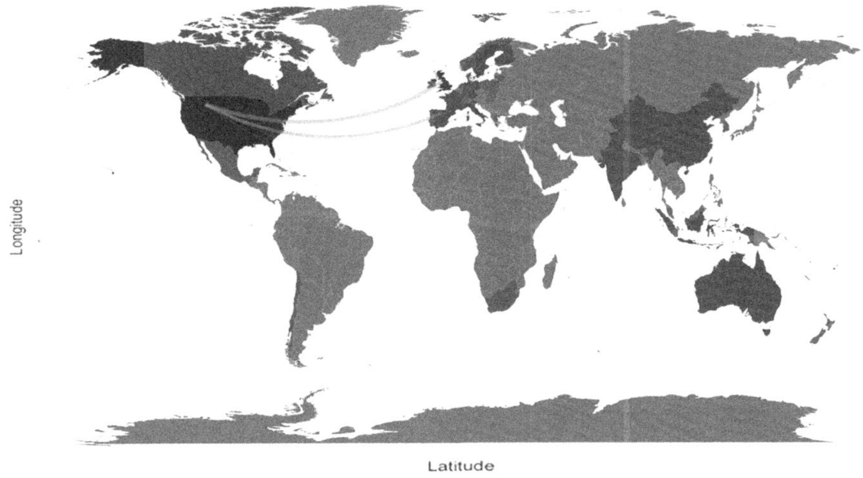

Fig. 3 Collaboration World Map

Table 5 Most relevant sources

Sources	Articles
International Journal of Scientific and Technology Research	19
Journal of International Entrepreneurship	13
Journal of Small Business Management	9
International Journal of Entrepreneurship and Innovation Management	8
Entrepreneurship and Sustainability Issues	7
Journal of Small Business and Enterprise Development	7
Journal of Technology Transfer	7
Emerald Emerging Markets Case Studies	6
Small Business Economics	6
Technovation	6

3.3 Sources Analysis

The following paragraph presents the primary sources and publication interests of the international journals about this research topic. As shown in Table 5, the highest number of published articles is 19 from the *International Journal of Scientific and Technology Research*. Subsequently, further journals interested in the field are the *Journal of International Entrepreneurship* with 13 publications and the *Journal of Small Business Management* with nine publications.

Moving on local citations, Table 6 shows the primary sources, in terms of scientific relevance articles published in the *Journal of International Business Studies*, *Journal of Business Venturing*, and *Strategic Management Journal* with 486, 440, and 333 citations, respectively.

Table 6 Most local cited sources

Sources	Articles
Journal of International Business Studies	486
Journal of Business Venturing	440
Strategic Management Journal	333
Entrepreneurship Theory and Practice	232
Research Policy	228
International Business Review	227
Academy of Management Journal	190
Small Business Economics	188
Academy of Management Review	181
Journal of International Entrepreneurship	160

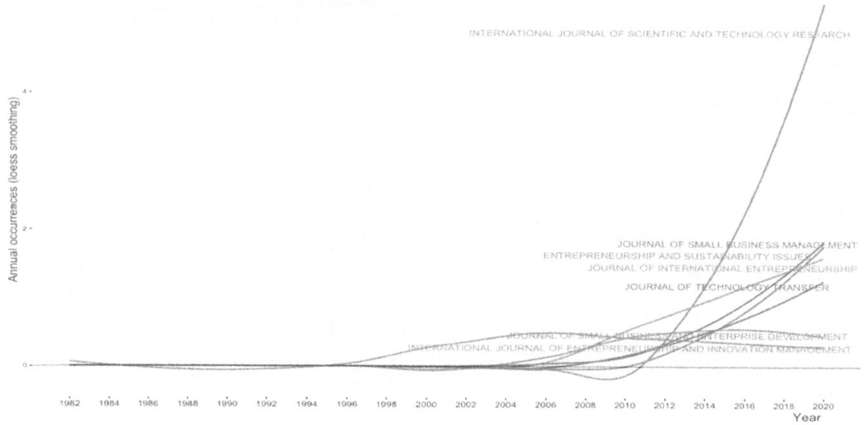

Fig. 4 Source dynamics

Finally, Fig. 4 illustrates the distribution frequency of articles. As we can see, the increase in cumulative growth has taken place since 2008. It is possible to notice a remarkable growth in sources, especially in terms of interest from the International Journal of Scientific and Technology Research. The rest of the journals have had a more limited but significant growth in terms of publication dynamics, a sign of the general increase in publications in this field of research.

3.4 Keywords Analysis

This paragraph aims to investigate keywords, and their co-occurrence presents in the title, abstract, and keywords used by authors. As shown in Fig. 5, the most commonly used keyword "entrepreneurship" coincides with the field of research. However, as shown, the analysis reveals the difficulty of growth from 2015 in the field of

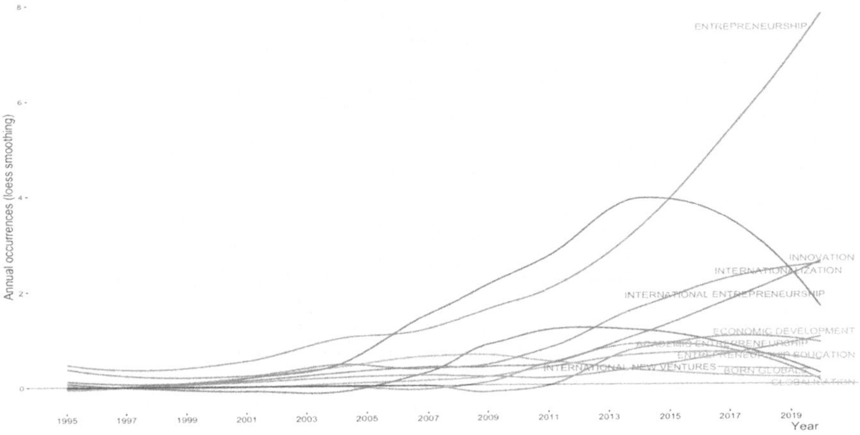

Fig. 5 Keywords growth

"international entrepreneurship". The results are in line with Dana's enlightening paper (2017) in which she stressed the challenge of internationalisation to more classical theories by invoking a higher propensity abroad for small businesses without outsourcing but using new telecommunication services. This challenge is, therefore, still, minimal. Moreover, the graph shows how the role of technologies as we have been looking for is included in the innovation research strand.

Figure 6 below shows the evolution of the research topics by the density of discussion and centrality. On the lower right side, the level of centrality is standard as it derives from the research topics set by us. More interesting is the field of education that can be seen from the analysis, as well as the potential of technology transfer that international entrepreneurs can exploit for their business. Within this field, the highest density is given by the industrial possibility of technology exchange both at the level of small and large companies.

To further investigate the structure of knowledge in this research field, researchers examined the keywords of the published articles, intended as central components of the study network, using the VOSviewer software (van Eck and Waltman 2014; Secinaro et al. 2020; Su and Lee 2010). To develop more in-depth insights, Fig. 7 finds out four research streams.

As we can see, the purple area of the figure focuses on academic spin-off as a means of technology transfer. As discussed by Mikhailova and Olsen (2016), one of the problems of entrepreneurship is related to the construction of social networks. As indicated by their case study, learning and understanding of technological processes are often more immediate in the academic field. This is due to the many stages and skills required. Similarly, the results of Pettersen and Tobiassen (2012) on three case studies show that in the period of academic spin-offs, they benefited from financial, knowledge, innovation, resources, technology, marketing, and reputation resources. The founders, therefore, benefited by receiving incentives for internationalisation and technology (Dana et al. 2009). Contributions by Boudlaie et al. (2020), Franco-

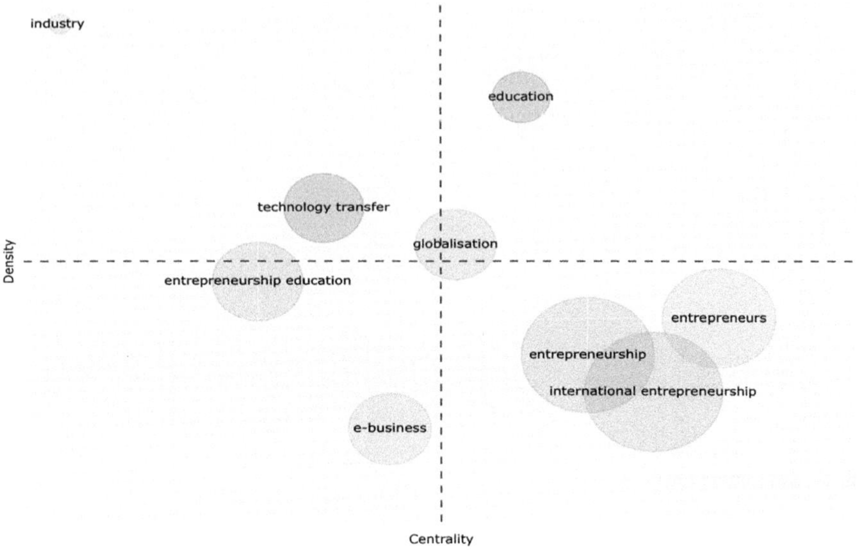

Fig. 6 Thematic map

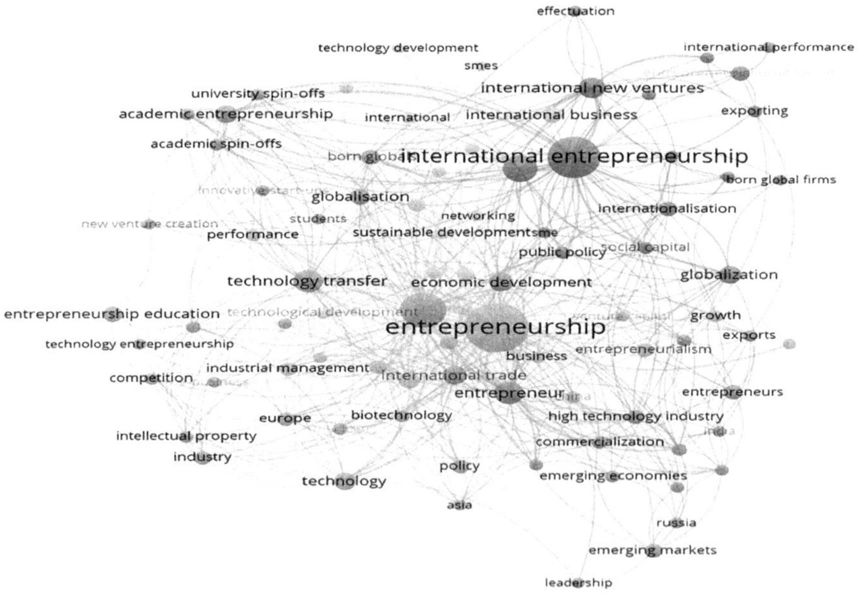

Fig. 7 Co-occurrence keywords

Leal et al. (2016), Jafari-Sadeghi et al. (2019b), and Styles and Genua (2008) also extend that while idea and innovation are essential elements in academia; however, the role of non-academics is equally crucial to support the internationalisation of spin-offs.

Further studies such as the contribution of Scuotto et al. (2019) analyse the degree of diffusion of innovation between universities, entrepreneurship, and technology. Their analysis shows that entrepreneurship induces more innovation at the university level, primarily benefiting students. Subsequently, it enables university systems to improve their national and international positioning and thus attract new talent and research funding.

Interesting are the results derived from the second strand of research (yellow area, Fig. 7) concerning the growth of technology and the need for social sustainability. According to Alon et al. (2020), this role falls to social enterprises (SE) as hybrid organisations that combine financial and social objectives. Hybrid organisations are starting to play an essential role in international entrepreneurship because of the social impact of their actions (Amin Moghadasi et al. 2017; Secinaro et al. 2019). As indicated by Agrawal and Kumar (2018) in the India case study analysis, entrepreneurs often combine elements of technology with the global marketplace by considering aspects of social impact. The second line of research concerns the opportunity for social enterprises to make their social networking available to the business. Thus, according to Jaiswal-Dale et al. (2019), social networking allows international technology companies to obtain new capital, even when launching their business idea.

Also, the third strand of research (blue area, Fig. 7) analyses the role of high technology in international enterprises. According to Zhang and Dodgson (2007), global enterprises benefit from more knowledge about the technical standards of technology sectors. However, the authors themselves warn of the possibility of failure due to specific social and cultural factors that could limit internationalisation (Bayfield et al. 2009). The opposite case is reported by Todd et al. (2007), which indicate the situation of Indian small- and medium-sized enterprises (SMEs). High technology and advanced technological infrastructure enable companies to participate in global markets with new, highly innovative products and services (Alon et al. 2009; Ayob and Dana 2017; Biancone and Jafari-Sadeghi 2016; Mokhtarzadeh et al. 2020). Rao's case study (2007) also shows the role of technology in international business development for SMEs.

Finally, the fourth strand of research (Green Area, Fig. 7) analyses technology and the competitive role for international entrepreneurs. Starting from the part of academic spin-offs, the next step comes from Löfgren (2018) and Ratten et al. (2007), who demonstrate the direct and indirect positive effects of technology on international competitiveness through networking and development. As stated by Khakimov et al. (2018) and Sadeghi et al. (2019) competitiveness cannot be without a necessary educational restructuring to prepare IT, specialists, and future international entrepreneurs. On this point, Jafari-Sadeghi et al. (2020) also add how this element is linked to policy. Indeed, a policy context that is not strongly supported induces international entrepreneurs to seek more by exploiting networks and the power of technology in more settings, also increasing their competitiveness.

3.5 Author's Background

This section aims to illustrate the background of the authors who have produced articles in this area. Figure 8 shows that 475 authors derive from the university context as scholars at various levels. Only 59 of the total 565 authors are professionals. Finally, 31 authors have a mixed background.

These results indicate that the level of collaboration between professionals and academics is still shallow. In a research field characterised by a vocation for technology and internationalisation, a broad exchange of views is desirable. As indicated by Bartunek (2007), the creation of collaborations between professionals and academics is essential and encourages researchers to think holistically based frameworks. Scientific authors will, therefore, be able to aspire to a greater exchange of visions, and this will enable dialogue between researchers and practitioners (Romme et al. 2015).

3.6 Research Methods

The paragraph aims to define the research methods used by the researchers in the area analysed. Figure 9 illustrates how most of the papers have adopted qualitative methodologies. The result is in line with the contribution of Zaheer et al. (2019). Of the qualitative papers, 33 relate to case studies on global companies and industrial contexts including, for example, biotech. Additional articles use interview-based methods. Subsequently, quantitative methods are also used by applying analysis models on large scale data.

A smaller number of items concern action/design research with field analysis and application of research to improve technology valorisation processes for SMEs. Finally, eight articles propose mixed methods of study, and three articles review the literature. The scientific contributions review the literature on small enterprises

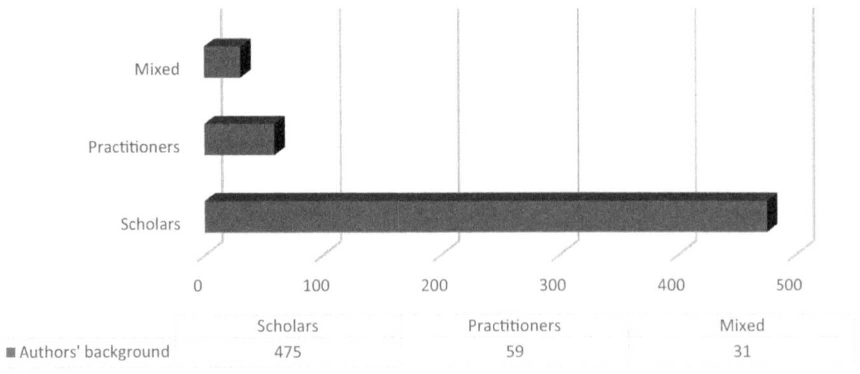

Fig. 8 Author's background

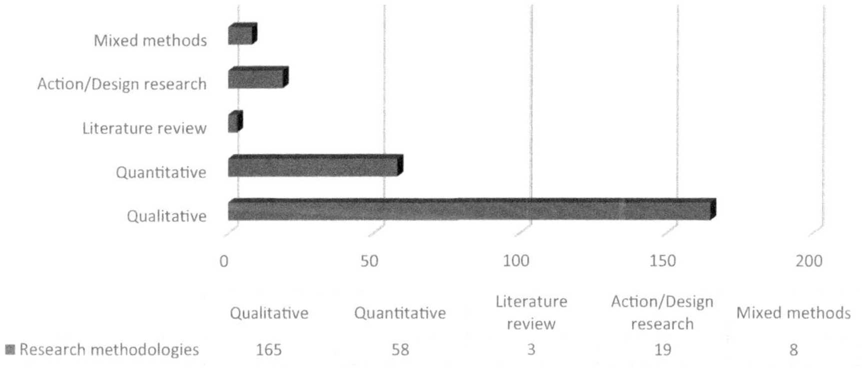

Fig. 9 Methodologies used in the research stream

and internationalisation (Fillis 2001; Mullen et al. 2009), and, finally, on the occasion of the review on the 25 years of publication of the journal *Technovation*, Merino et al. (2006) also focus on the role of technologies for international entrepreneurship.

3.7 *Patterns of Technology Evolution*

The section aims to analyse the ecosystem and the stage of technology indicated by the authors in the research flow of international entrepreneurship and technology. The researchers, to create continuity with the theory, have used as codes the phases of the technological evolution of Adomavicius et al. (2006). According to the authors, it is possible to distinguish between two crucial steps in the technological ecosystem. First, the strategies of influence of technology as an external component. Second, the strategy of technological evolution The last case then presents numerous phases to which companies and managers can refer. Phase 1 (Product Development) concerns the launch of new technologies. Phase 2 (Product and Infrastructure Alignment) includes the alignment of products and infrastructure with already structured technologies. Phase 3 (Feed-Forward Evolution) involves a transversal co-evolution and maturation of the existing technology system. Phase 4 (Feed-Back Evolution) concerns the evolution of product or service technologies that allow the implementation of new projects. Finally, Phase 5 (Incremental Evolution) affects the application of evolutionary models and the continuous development of technologies on already existing products.

The summary of the analysis carried out on the sample of articles is shown in Fig. 10.

The results reveal that the research area benefits positively from the influence of technology. According to Vuorio et al. (2020), technology in international entrepreneurship brings innovation in services. However, technological innovation and

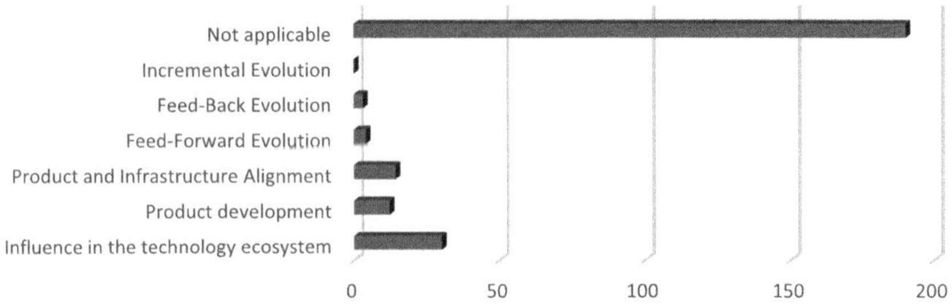

	Influence in the technology ecosystem	Product development	Product and Infrastructure Alignment	Feed-Forward Evolution	Feed-Back Evolution	Incremental Evolution	Not applicable
■ Patterns of technology evolution	30	12	14	4	3	0	190

Fig. 10 Distribution of patterns of technology evolution

internationalisation must be well governed in order not to incur lower profitability. Interesting is the perspective of de la Hoz-Rosales et al. (2019) who discover that technology positively influences international enterprises as well as social progress. Finally, according to Sozinova et al. (2018), technology also has a significant influence on corporate marketing by reducing the burden on international entrepreneurs' balance sheets.

Considering the product development phase, some impressive results can be deduced. For example, according to Dudin et al. (2019), international energy companies benefit from new technologies to raise the level of sustainability of the economic system. Therefore, the introduction of new technologies at the service of electricity (i.e. smart grid) can only benefit companies and citizens (Cheraghi et al. 2019; Hall et al. 2019).

Significant contributions are also made in the analysis of the Product and Infrastructure Alignment phase. In the case of Leiva and Kuschel (2020), the authors refer to the technological use for the removal of arsenic from water. The international business initiative has given the company opportunities to exploit existing infrastructure and technologies to change its business model. Also, according to Pergelova et al. (2019), digital technologies allow international alignment and expansion, especially in the fields of general market knowledge and facilitating iterations between customers and partners. Finally, the same authors hypothesise how female entrepreneurs can use digital technologies even more for greater versatility of resources.

Finally, for phases 3 and 4, some articles have been discovered. Ferri et al. (2020) investigate cloud systems for start-ups. The specific case can be classified as an evolution of technologies at the level of more services that companies can offer. Shapenko et al. (2018) analyse the case of a technology company that over the years has sought in technology an opportunity for service evolution for its international customers. Finally, Alderete (2017) also discusses how broadband in developing and developed countries can evolve companies' technologies and foster their internationalisation.

4 Discussion

Analysing the results of 253 articles, we can highlight some new insights, critiques, and implications that we will summarise in this section. This SLR focused on determining the research knowledge about international entrepreneurs and technologies considering authors, sources, keywords, research methods, and technology evolution. Despite the long story of the entrepreneurship's field, the topic related to the internationalisation and technology is extremely new and low addressed among authors. Researchers could find this topic challenging; therefore, the analysis reveals them the main sources of future publications as *International Journal of Scientific and Technology Research*, *Journal of International Entrepreneurship*, and *Journal of Small Business Management*. Moving on keywords analysis, this paper provides relevant insights. First, the results reveal that few studies considered together with the international entrepreneurship and technology as a unique research stream. Additionally, the analysis of technology patterns distribution demonstrated the previous sentences giving researchers more stimulus for future studies. Second, the analysis finds out four main research streams as academic spin-off as a means of technology transfer, the growth of technology and the need for social sustainability, the role of high technology in international enterprises, and technology and the competitive role for foreign entrepreneurs.

Considering the author's background, the analysis finds that most of the authors are academics. This result in light of the academic role of university spin-offs as a tool of innovation (Scuotto et al. 2019; Sukumar et al. 2020) could be adequate. However, as suggested by Romme et al. (2015), new trading zones should be found in the future to advocate more discussion on this topic. Moreover, despite many quantitative studies, in this research stream, most of the research is qualitative. As suggested by Wiles et al. (2011) design of new methods could be tested to try a distribution of new research experiences. Finally, in terms of patterns of technology evolution, the analysis reveals that the articles so far have been dedicated to discovering the influence that technology has adopted on international entrepreneurship.

5 Conclusion

This section aims to conclude the chapter and answer the RQ3. What are the future directions in this field considering new topics and methodologies? Starting our analysis, we aim to show a comprehensive discussion about international entrepreneurship and technology. To rigorously write this essay, we use the Structured

Literature Review (SLR) method of Massaro et al. (2015) as a reliable and international validate tools.

As discussed by Acs et al. (2003) and Dana (2017), our analysis has started keeping in mind that the flow of research on international entrepreneurship is innovative and continuously seeking new technological combinations. Starting from these considerations, we derive that in addition to international business theory, entrepreneurship literature, the research flow is also linked to the theory of technological innovation. The analysis makes us reflect on some critical future research implications. Starting from the method of Romme et al. (2018), researchers could consider new research perspectives that affect the debate between academics and professionals. Our results dwell only on the academic side. Therefore, in the future, we call for new research goals that compare the academic vision with that of professionals, thus also giving more space in terms of contribution. Further research could be carried out by invoking new interesting case studies. This would allow further participation of professionals and researchers to put in writing problems and solutions required by the international business world.

Our study, like all research, has certain limits. First, we believe that the idea of using the Scopus database could limit the number of sources investigated. Second, more studies in terms of technologies success cases could be considered in this field to inspire enlightened managers to seek new solutions. Third, it would be interesting to investigate further why international entrepreneurs find it challenging to implement technological collaboration. All the limitations represent for us future lines of research that academics may follow in the future.

References

Acs Z, Dana L-P, Jones MV (2003) Toward new horizons: the internationalisation of entrepreneurship. J Int Entrep 1(1):5–12

Adomavicius G, Bockstedt J, Gupta A, Kauffman RJ (2006) Understanding patterns of technology evolution: an ecosystem perspective. Proceedings of the 39th annual Hawaii international conference on system sciences (HICSS'06), Vol. 8, presented at the proceedings of the 39th ANNUAL Hawaii international conference on system sciences (HICSS'06), 189a–189a

Agrawal A, Kumar P (2018) Social entrepreneurship and sustainable business models the case of India. Palgrave Macmillan, London

Alderete MV (2017) Mobile broadband: a key enabling Technology for Entrepreneurship? J Small Bus Manag 55(2):254–269

Alon I, Dana L-P, Jenkins A (2009) International business by SMEs: empirical findings from New Zealand. J Int Bus Econ 10(2):59–78

Alon I, Mersland R, Musteen M, Randøy T (2020) The research frontier on internationalization of social enterprises. J World Bus 55(5):01091

Amin Moghadasi M, Derakhshandeh B, Ferdosi M, Jafari-Sadeghi V (2017) Organizational conformity as an entrepreneurial response to the changes in internationalization process: a study of IT-oriented firms in Saveh. World J Account Financ Eng 1(1):53–64

Aria M, Cuccurullo C (2017) Bibliometrix: an R-tool for comprehensive science mapping analysis. J Inf Secur 11(4):959–975

Ayob AH, Dana L-P (2017) Product strategies for export ventures: an empirical investigation among SMEs in an emerging economy. Jurnal Pengurusan (UKM J Manag) 50(0):25–33
Bartunek JM (2007) Academic-practitioner collaboration need not require joint or relevant research: toward a relational scholarship of integration. Acad Manag J 50(6):1323–1333
Bayfield R, Dana LP, Stewart S (2009) Firm characteristics and internationalisation strategies: an empirical investigation of New Zealand exporters. Int J Globalisation Small Bus 3(3):275
Biancone PP, Jafari-Sadeghi V (2016) Risk Management in Export Compliance: concepts, procedures, and solutions. In: Cantino V, De Vincentiis P, Racca MG (eds) Risk management: perspectives and open issues. McGraw-Hill, London, pp 64–78
Boudlaie H, Mahdiraji HA, Shamsi S, Jafari-Sadeghi V, Garcia-Perez A (2020) Designing a human resource scorecard: an empirical stakeholder-based study with a company culture perspective. Int J Entrep Innov Manag 16(4):113–147
Broadbent J, Guthrie J (2008) Public sector to public services: 20 years of 'contextual' accounting research. Account Audit Account J, Emerald Group Publishing 21(2):129–169
Burgel O, Murray G (2000) The international market entry choices of start-up companies in high-technology industries. J Int Mark 8:33–62
Cantwell J, Dunning JH, Lundan SM (2010) An evolutionary approach to understanding international business activity: the co-evolution of MNEs and the institutional environment. J Int Bus Stud 41(4):567–586
Cheraghi S, Choobchain S, Abbasi E (2019) Investigation of entrepreneurship development barriers in the field of renewable energies technologies in developing countries: a case of Iran. Int J Sci Technol Res 8(3):11
D'Adamo I, Rosa P (2019) A structured literature review on obsolete electric vehicles management practices. Sustain For 11:6876
Dabić M, Maley J, Dana L-P, Novak I, Pellegrini MM, Caputo A (2019) Pathways of SME internationalization: a bibliometric and systematic review. Small Bus Econ. https://doi.org/10.1007/s11187-019-00181-6
Dal Mas F, Massaro M, Lombardi R, Garlatti A (2019) From output to outcome measures in the public sector: a structured literature review. Int J Organ Anal, Emerald Publishing Limited 27 (5):1631–1656
Dana L-P (2017) International entrepreneurship research: how it evolved and directions for the future. Int J Entrep Small Bus 30(4):477
Dana LP, Grimwood S, William G (2009) Export incentives and international entrepreneurship in New Zealand firms. J Int Bus Entrep Dev 4(1–2):1–21
Desa G (2012) Resource mobilization in international social entrepreneurship: bricolage as a mechanism of institutional transformation. Entrep Theory Pract 30(2):299–320. Los Angeles, CA: SAGE Publications
Dodd S, Patra E (2002) National Differences in entrepreneurial networking. Entrep Reg Dev 14:117–134
Dudin M, Frolova E, Protopopova O, Mamedov O, Odintsov S (2019) Study of innovative technologies in the energy industry: nontraditional and renewable energy sources. 6:1704–1713. https://doi.org/10.9770/jesi.2019
van Eck NJ, Waltman L (2014) Visualizing bibliometric networks. In: Ding Y, Rousseau R, Wolfram D (eds) Measuring scholarly impact: methods and practice. Springer International Publishing, Cham, pp 285–320
Ferri L, Spanò R, Tomo A (2020) Cloud computing in high tech startups: evidence from a case study. Tech Anal Strat Manag, Routledge 32(2):146–157
Fillis I (2001) Small firm internationalisation: an investigative survey and future research directions. Manag Decis, MCB UP Ltd 39(9):767–783
Franco-Leal N, Soetanto D, Camelo-Ordaz C (2016) Do they matter? The role of non-academics in the internationalization of academic spin-offs. J Int Entrep 14(3):410–440
Gazni A, Sugimoto CR, Didegah F (2012) Mapping world scientific collaboration: authors, institutions, and countries. J Am Soc Inf Sci Technol 63(2):323–335

Grafton J, Lillis AM, Mahama H (2011) "Mixed methods research in accounting", edited by Grafton. J Qual Res Account Manag 8(1):5–21
Hall J, Matos S, Bachor V (2019) From green technology development to green innovation: inducing regulatory adoption of pathogen detection technology for sustainable forestry. Small Bus Econ 52(4):877–889
de la Hoz Rosales B, Camacho-Ballesta JA, Tamayo-Torres I (2019) Effects of innovative entrepreneurship and the information society on social progress: an international analysis. Entrep Sustain Issues 7(2):782–813
Jafari-Sadeghi V, Nkongolo-Bakenda J-M, Anderson RB, Dana L-P (2019a) An institution-based view of international entrepreneurship: a comparison of context-based and universal determinants in developing and economically advanced countries. Int Bus Rev 28(6):101588
Jafari-Sadeghi V, Biancone PP, Anderson R, Nkongolo-Bakenda J-M (2019b) International entrepreneurship by particular people 'on their own terms': evidence of universal attributes of entrepreneurs in evolving economies. Int J Entrep Small Bus 32:288–308
Jafari-Sadeghi V, Kimiagari S, Biancone PP (2019c) Level of education and knowledge, foresight competency and international entrepreneurship: a study of human capital determinants in the European countries. Eur Bus Rev, Emerald Publishing Limited 32(1):46–68
Jafari-Sadeghi V, Dutta DK, Ferraris A, Del Giudice M (2020) Internationalisation business processes in an under-supported policy contexts: evidence from Italian SMEs. Bus Process Manag J 26(5):1055–1074
Jaiswal-Dale A, Simon-Lee F, Zanotti G, Cincinelli P (2019) The role of social networking in capital sourcing. Glob Bus Rev, SAGE Publications India:0972150919868867
Jones MV (2001) First steps in internationalisation: concepts and evidence from a sample of small high-technology firms. J Int Manag 7(3):191–210
Khakimov A, Karlinskiy V, Rakhmatullin R (2018) Information and communication technologies in SMES: competitiveness analysis. J Entrep Educ, Allied Business Academies 21(2S)
Knight GA (1997) Cross-cultural reliability and validity of a scale to measure firm entrepreneurial orientation. J Bus Ventur 12(3):213–225
Krippendorff K (2011) Computing Krippendorff's alpha-reliability. Departmental Papers (ASC). https://repository.upenn.edu/asc_papers/43
Lackéus M, Williams Middleton K (2015) Venture creation programs: bridging entrepreneurship education and technology transfer. Educ Train, Emerald Group Publishing Limited 57(1):48–73
Leiva F, Kuschel K (2020) HMSolution and the search for product-market fit. Emerald Emerg Market Case Stud, Emerald Publishing Limited 10(1):1–20
Leonidou LC (2004) An analysis of the barriers hindering small business export development. J Small Bus Manag 42(3):279–302
Löfgren A (2018) Potential international competitiveness and co-innovation of technology-based international SMEs. Int J Entrep Innov Manag 22(6):597
Maignan I, Lukas B (1997) Entry mode decisions: the role of managers' mental models. J Glob Mark 10(4):7–22
Manolova TS, Brush CG, Edelman LF, Greene PG (2002) Internationalization of small firms: personal factors revisited. Int Small Bus J Res Entrep 20(1):9–31
Massaro M, Dumay J, Garlatti A (2015) Public sector knowledge management: a structured literature review. J Knowl Manag, Emerald Group Publishing Limited 19(3):530–558
Massaro M, Dumay J, Guthrie J (2016) On the shoulders of giants: undertaking a structured literature review in accounting. Account Audit Account J 29(5):767–801
Matlay H, Westhead P (2005) Virtual teams and the rise of e-entrepreneurship in Europe. Int Small Bus J 23:279–302
McDougall PP (1989) International versus domestic entrepreneurship: new venture strategic behavior and industry structure. J Bus Ventur 4(6):387–400
McDougall PP, Oviatt BM (2000) International entrepreneurship: the intersection of two research paths. Acad Manag J 43(5):902–906

Merino MTG, do Carmo MLP, Álvarez MVS (2006) 25 years of Technovation: characterisation and evolution of the journal. Technovation 26(12):1303–1316

Mikhailova O, Olsen PI (2016) Internationalization of an academic invention through successive science-business networks: the case of TAVI. J Int Entrep 14(3):441–471

Mokhtarzadeh N, Amoozad Mahdiraji H, Jafari-Sadeghi V, Soltani A, Abbasi Kamardi A (2020) A product-technology portfolio alignment approach for food industry: a multi-criteria decision making with z-numbers. Br Food J 122(12):3947–3967

Mullen MR, Budeva DG, Doney PM (2009) Research methods in the leading small business–entrepreneurship journals: a critical review with recommendations for future research. J Small Bus Manag 47(3):287–307

Oakleaf M (2010) Writing information literacy assessment plans: a guide to best practice. Comminfolit 3(2):80

Okoli C, Schabram K (2010) A guide to conducting a systematic literature review of information systems research. SSRN Electron J 26(10):1–49, Sprouts: Working Papers on Information Systems

Pergelova A, Manolova T, Simeonova-Ganeva R, Yordanova D (2019) Democratizing entrepreneurship? Digital technologies and the internationalization of female-led SMEs. J Small Bus Manag 57(1):14–39

Pettersen IB, Tobiassen AE (2012) Are born globals really born globals? The case of academic spin-offs with long development periods. J Int Entrep 10(2):117–141

Rao MN (2007) "Entrepreneurship, globalization, and information technology: a case study of Webject systems, Inc.", edited by V. Eunni, R., G. Brush, C. and R. Kasuganti, R. Int J Emerg Mark, Emerald Group Publishing Limited 2(2):181–197

Ratten V, Dana L-P, Han M, Welpe I (2007) Internationalisation of SMEs: European comparative studies. Int J Entrep Small Bus 4:361–379

Renault CS (2006) Academic capitalism and university incentives for faculty entrepreneurship. J Technol Transf 31(2):227–239

Román C, Congregado E, Millán JM (2013) Start-up incentives: entrepreneurship policy or active labour market programme? J Bus Ventur 28(1):151–175

Romme AGL, Avenier M-J, Denyer D, Hodgkinson GP, Pandza K, Starkey K, Worren N (2015) Towards common ground and trading zones in management research and practice. Br J Manag 26(3):544–559

Romme AGL, Broekgaarden J, Huijzer C, Reijmer A, van der Eyden RAI (2018) From competition and collusion to consent-based collaboration: a case study of local democracy. Int J Public Adm 41(3):246–255

Sadeghi VJ, Biancone PP (2017) Shariah compliant international entrepreneurship: a study of Islamic finance in Europe. Eur J Islamic Financ 8

Sadeghi VJ, Biancone PP, Anderson RB, Bakenda JMN (2019) International entrepreneurship by particular people 'on their own terms': a study on the universal characteristics of entrepreneurs in evolving economies. Int J Entrep Small Bus 37(2):288

Scuotto V, Del Giudice M, Garcia-Perez A, Orlando B, Ciampi F (2019) A spill over effect of entrepreneurial orientation on technological innovativeness: an outlook of universities and research based spin offs. J Technol Transf. https://doi.org/10.1007/s10961-019-09760-x

Secinaro S, Calandra D (2020) Halal food: structured literature review and research agenda. Br Food J. https://doi.org/10.1108/BFJ-03-2020-0234

Secinaro S, Corvo L, Brescia V, Iannaci D (2019) Hybrid organizations: a systematic review of the current literature. Int Bus Res 12(11)

Secinaro S, Brescia V, Calandra D, Biancone P (2020) Employing bibliometric analysis to identify suitable business models for electric cars. J Clean Prod 264:121503

Secundo G, Ndou V, Vecchio PD, De Pascale G (2020) Sustainable development, intellectual capital and technology policies: a structured literature review and future research agenda. Technol Forecast Soc Chang 153:119917

Shapenko A, Korovkin V, Leleux B (2018) ABBYY: the digitization of language and text. Emerald Emerg Market Case Stud, Emerald Publishing Limited 8(2):1–26
Sozinova A, Malysheva N, Zonova AV, Fokina OV, Shchinova RA (2018) Effectiveness of marketing of business structures as a basis of import substitution in Russia: the role of information technologies. Espacios 39
Styles C, Genua T (2008) The rapid internationalization of high technology firms created through the commercialization of academic research. J World Bus 43(2):146–157
Su H-N, Lee P-C (2010) Mapping knowledge structure by keyword co-occurrence: a first look at journal papers in technology foresight. Scientometrics 85(1):65–79
Sukumar A, Jafari-Sadeghi V, Garcia-Perez A, Dutta DK (2020) The potential link between corporate innovations and corporate competitiveness: evidence from IT firms in the UK. J Knowl Manag 24(5):965–983
Todd PR, Javalgi R, Raj G (2007) "Internationalization of SMEs in India: fostering entrepreneurship by leveraging information technology", edited by V. Eunni, R., G. Brush, C. and R. Kasuganti, R. Int J Emerg Mark 2(2):166–180
Tranfield D, Denyer D, Smart P (2003) Towards a methodology for developing evidence-informed management knowledge by means of systematic review. Br J Manag 14(3):207–222
Vadana I-I, Torkkeli L, Kuivalainen O, Saarenketo S (2019) Digitalization of companies in international entrepreneurship and marketing. Int Mark Rev, Emerald Publishing Limited 37 (3):471–492
Vuorio A, Torkkeli L, Sainio L-M (2020) Service innovation and internationalization in SMEs: antecedents and profitability outcomes. J Int Entrep 18(1):92–123
Wiles R, Crow G, Pain H (2011) Innovation in qualitative research methods: a narrative review. Qual Res 11(5):587–604
Zaheer H, Breyer Y, Dumay J (2019) Digital entrepreneurship: an interdisciplinary structured literature review and research agenda. Technol Forecast Soc Chang 148:119735
Zhang MY, Dodgson M (2007) 'A roasted duck can still fly away': a case study of technology, nationality, culture and the rapid and early internationalization of the firm. J World Bus 42 (3):336–349
Zou S, Stan S (1998) The determinants of export performance: a review of the empirical literature between 1987 and 1997. Int Mark Rev, MCB UP Ltd 15(5):333–356
Zupic I, Čater T (2015) Bibliometric methods in management and organization. Organ Res Methods 18:429–472

Paolo Pietro Biancone is a Full Professor in Business Administration at the University of Turin. He is a chartered accountant, a freelance journalist, and an author of numerous publications on accounting, entrepreneurship, and Islamic finance field. He is Editor in Chief of the European Journal of Islamic Finance and the European Journal of Social Impact and Circular Economy. He is the scientific coordinator of the University of Turin team of the European project H2020 Avangard on the electric business model. He promoted research in new technologies within all the research topics interested.

Silvana Secinaro is an associate professor at the Department of Management at the University of Turin, a chartered accountant, a freelance journalist, and an author of numerous publications on public and private accounting, as well as crowdfunding. She has a degree in Accounting from Bocconi University and a PhD in Business and Management at the University of Turin. She is a component of the National Commission of Italian Ministry of finances on IPSAS and a member of the editorial staff of Press, the national magazine of the Chartered Experts Accounting, October 2014. She was reviewer for projects funded by the European Community about Financial Reporting with a 3-year mandate 2018–2020. Her research interest deals with Islamic economy, business models, and new technologies in accounting.

Daniel Iannaci is a PhD in Business and Management at the Department of Management of the University of Turin. His doctoral course focused on new technologies applications in accounting, auditing, and accountability with a focus on financial reporting of financial and non-financial information of the hybrid organisation. Additionally, he is part of the Avangard H2020 Project funded by the European Commission on electric cars' business models. Finally, he studied and published works among non-profit organisation, hybrid organisation, social impact, and financial reporting.

Davide Calandra is a PhD Candidate in Business and Management at the Department of Management of the University of Turin. His doctoral course focuses on new technologies applications in accounting, auditing, and accountability with a particular focus on blockchain and artificial intelligence. Additionally, he is part of the Avangard H2020 Project funded by the European Commission on electric cars' business models. Finally, he studied and published works among business model, Islamic economy, circular economy, and data quality in healthcare fields.

Part III
Qualitative Research Streams: Empirical Methods

The Impact of Diaspora on International Entrepreneurship in Malaysia: A Historical Institutionalism Approach

Sivakumar Velayutham

1 Introduction

In the 1980s, stagflation and high unemployment contributed to renewed interest in supply-side economics and factors determining economic growth. Simultaneously, the 1980s and 1990s have seen a re-evaluation of the role of small and medium enterprises (SMEs) in economic growth and a renewed focus on promoting entrepreneurship (Wennekers and Thurik 1999). Studies indicate that in the 1970s and 1980s, economic activity moved away from large firms to small firms. The 500 largest American firms' employment share dropped from 20 per cent in 1970 to 8.5 per cent in 1996 (Carlsson 1992, 1999). Small firms play an essential role in the economy, serving as agents of change by their entrepreneurial activity, being the source of considerable innovative activity, stimulating industry evolution, and contributing to a significant share of the newly generated jobs (Acs 1992; Audretsch 1993, 1995; Sukumar et al. 2020).

The Malaysian government has also recognised the importance of entrepreneurship to economic growth, as evidenced by the sheer amount and variety of supporting mechanisms and policies for entrepreneurs, including funding, physical infrastructure, and business advisory services. The establishment of a special ministry for entrepreneurs—the Ministry of Entrepreneur Development—in 1995 further highlights the importance the government places upon entrepreneurship and entrepreneur development. The ministry is supposed to act as the lead agency for Malay entrepreneurs' development and co-ordinate entrepreneurship activities.

Parts of this paper has been presented at the Asian Conference on Entrepreneurship 2018 by the author and published in the Proceedings of the Conference edited by the author.

S. Velayutham (✉)
Faculty of Business, Hospitality, and Humanities, Nilai University, Nilai, Malaysia
e-mail: sivakumar@nilai.edu.my

V. Jafari-Sadeghi et al. (eds.), *Empirical International Entrepreneurship*, Contributions to Management Science,
https://doi.org/10.1007/978-3-030-68972-8_9

However, one issue has dominated government initiatives on entrepreneurship promotion and development in Malaysia: the level of Malay participation in small business and entrepreneurship compared to that of other ethnic groups, mainly the Chinese (Omar and Azmi 2015). This has been a hot topic in Malaysia because entrepreneurship is seen as a means of addressing wealth inequality among Malaysia's three different ethnic groups. Successful entrepreneurs are held up as economic heroes and successful role models (Thillainathan and Cheong 2016).

Since 1966, the government has established various agencies and plans to promote Malay entrepreneurial activities in all sectors within Malaysia (Fong 1990). This includes the formation of the Council of Trust for the Indigenous People (MARA) in 1966; the New Economic Policy (NEP) in 1970; and the Bumiputra (Malay) Commercial and Industrial Community (BCIC) programs in the mid-70s. In 2013 the Small Retailer Transformation Programme (TUKAR) was launched.

The results, however, have not been impressive. Farouk (2012) laments the failure of the Malaysian state to create a Bumiputera Commercial and Industrial Class (BCIC):

> While analysts have emphasised the utility of strong states in inventing the bourgeoisie, especially in light of the impressive economic performances of the East Asian newly industrialised economies (NIEs), recent attempts to bring about a BCIC in Penang were unsuccessful, illustrating the extent to which the processes of class formation lie outside the control of even a relatively powerful state (p. 1).

Dana (1987a, b) compares the success of Singapore's entrepreneurship efforts to that of Malaysia and attributes the poor development of Malaysian entrepreneurship to excessive regulation and rules by the government authorities.

The list of 100 Most Influential Young (under 45 years of age) Entrepreneurs (100 MIYE) compiled by Entrepreneur Insight (http://entrepreneurinsight.com.my/100miye, 2019) highlights that more than 80% are Chinese, 15% are Malays, and less than 5% are Indians in contrast to the population ratio (Bumiputera 69%, Chinese 23%, and Indian 7%).

The difference in ethnic entrepreneurship (Bogan and Darity, Jr. 2008; Greene and Owen 2004; Fairlie and Robb 2008) and the question of whether public policies for entrepreneurship make a difference (Sarfati 2012) has not only been a topic of interest in Malaysia but also in other countries. Research into ethnicity and entrepreneurship can be traced back to classic works such as those of Weber (1930), Sombart (1914), and Simmel (1950). These scholars were interested in why certain racial or religious groups were more successful in formalised businesses and, hence, led to capitalism's development. In many countries, particularly the West, government policies have mainly focused on promoting entrepreneurship among minorities (Bogan and Darity, Jr. 2008; Fairlie and Meyer 2003), in contrast to Malaysia.

More recent studies have examined the institutional variations in the national environment using institutional theory to study international entrepreneurship. Wright and Ricks (1994) highlighted the impact of the international environment or settings on entrepreneurial firms' global activities. Research has found that institutional variations in the national environment may cause different levels of entrepreneurship across countries (Busenitz et al. 2000; Casson 1990; Alon et al. 2009; Jafari-Sadeghi et al. 2019a, b, 2020a, b), and among ethnic groups (Acs and Karlsson 2002; Ahlstrom and Bruton 2002; Churchill 2017; Estrin and Mickiewicz 2011; Karlsson and Acs 2002). Studies have also examined the impact of firm-specific variables on firms' internationalisation (Ratten et al. 2007; Bayfield et al. 2009; Jafari-Sadeghi and Biancone 2018; Jafari-Sadeghi et al. 2020c).

As the institutional lens becomes applied to broader ranges of entrepreneurial phenomena, there is a concern that the theory now lacks "scope conditions" or an assessment of the external contingencies under which the theory will or will not apply (Suddaby 2010). Others indicate a need to address core questions that underpin the theoretical foundation of neo-institutionalism but remain unanswered (see Barley and Tolbert 1997; Hallett 2010; Lawrence and Suddaby 2006; Hallett and Ventesca 2006)—What is an institution? How are they formed? How do they change? What role do individual actions play in institutional processes?

Thus, this chapter investigates the historical contexts that have shaped the institutions that have supported Chinese ethnic entrepreneurship dominance in Malaysia. It highlights the historical spread of the institution of Chinese diaspora in South-east Asia and its impact on the internationalisation of Chinese enterprises in Malaysia. It adopts the historical institutionalism approach to address the impact of diaspora on the internationalisation of Chinese enterprises in Malaysia.

This manuscript is divided into four main parts. In the next section, we briefly analyse the 100 MIYE list to provide a breakdown of the 100 young entrepreneurs by ethnicity and then use a sample to highlight the different enterprises the entrepreneurs are involved in and the internationalisation of their activities. Section 3 outlines the features of the historical institutionalism approach and its application in this study. Section 4 reviews the relationship between political economy, diaspora, and Chinese entrepreneurship in Malaysia. In Sect. 5, we discuss the findings within the extant literature contexts and further highlight the contributions of historical institutionalism to the study of international entrepreneurship and opportunities for future research.

2 Malaysia's 100 Most Influential Young Entrepreneurs (100 MIYE) 2019

The 100 Most Influential Young Entrepreneurs (100 MIYE) is an annual event organised by Entrepreneur Insight to honour bold creative and innovative young Malaysian entrepreneurs. Entrepreneur Insight is a brand and online publication covering the local entrepreneurs' movement (http://entrepreneurinsight.com.my/about-us/). In 2019 the then prime minister Tun Dr Mahathir Mohammed presented the awards with the Minister of Entrepreneurship Development in attendance highlighting, thereby, the prominence given to the event.

Table 1 Breakdown of the business activities of the sample entrepreneurs

Main business activity	Bumiputeras	Chinese	Indian
Entertainer (singer, acting)	9		
Education and training	2	1	
Food and health products	3	4	1
Property	1	3	1
Design and construction		5	
Furniture		1	
IT services		2	1
Marketing		2	
Financial advisory services		2	1
Unknown			1
Total	15	20	5

The 100 MIYE is as follows: 80 Chinese, 15 Bumiputras, and 5 Indians. The analysis is based on the names included in the online list. An analysis was made to identify the entrepreneurial activities of the awardees based on a sample. The sample includes all the Bumiputera and Indian awardees as they are a small number and an equivalent 20 random Chinese awardees. The breakdown of the business activities of the sample is provided in Table 1.

Several observations can be made based on the breakdown of the business activities the entrepreneurs from the different ethnic groups are involved in. First, the Bumiputera entrepreneurs are only involved in a few business activities, while the business activities of the non-Bumiputra entrepreneurs are more diverse. Bumiputra entrepreneurs are mainly involved in business activities within local markets where culture, language, and religion can be a significant advantage. For the above reason, the Bumiputra entrepreneurs also have limited ability to internationalise to markets that do not share their culture. In contrast to the above, Chinese entrepreneurs are involved in business activities that are more open to competition from other local and international enterprises. For the above reason, the non-Bumiputra entrepreneurs are more internationalised, either sourcing or marketing their products and services overseas.

3 Historical Institutionalism

As pointed out earlier, institutionalism has been very influential in understanding institutional variations in the national environment. As a theory, institutionalism focuses on the processes of legitimation and social reproduction by emphasising that organisational environments are composed of "taken-for-granted beliefs and widely promulgated rules that serve as templates for organising" (DiMaggio and Powell 1991). They argue that "institutions resulting from these processes are not only constraints on the human agency, but also and foremost the product of human actions" (p. 28). The constraints consist of "both informal constraints (sanctions, taboos, customs, traditions, and codes of conduct), and formal rules (constitutions, laws, property rights)" Jepperson (1991, p. 145).

In general, institutional theory has been employed to explain how firms interact with the environment to secure their positions and legitimacy (Meyer and Rowan 1977; Scott 2007). The international entrepreneurship literature has considered the interaction between (international) entrepreneurial activities and country institutions (Bowen and De Clercq 2008; Muralidharan and Pathak 2017; Nasra and Dacin 2010). Other studies have sought to address how and why entrepreneurial activities vary among different economies and to explain the extent to which the level of business activities is influenced by country-specific institutions (Busenitz et al. 2000; Praveen Parboteeah et al. 2009), and to apply the concept of "institutional distance" to study distinctions in the institutional context among nations, which is deemed to affect the decision of firms regarding whether they should enter a specific market (Bae and Salomon 2010; Garousi Mokhtarzadeh et al. 2020; Salomon and Wu 2012; Zucchella and Magnani 2016).

Most international entrepreneurship studies based on institutional theory are, however, ahistorical. Suddaby et al. (2014) argue that "in their search for scientific legitimacy—i.e., the ability to make broad theoretical generalisations and claims of universal knowledge—contemporary organisational institutionalists have minimised or obscured the role of history" (p. 107). When institutional researchers treat history as an objective, measurable phenomenon, two distinct problems arise. First, research tends to become essentialist—analysis becomes fixed and objective; and second, there is a tendency toward functionalism (Suddaby et al. 2014). "Ahistorical approaches to understanding institutions tend to view issues from the past through the eyes of the present. As a result, they tend to privilege the present by assuming that surviving present-day institutions represent higher standards of legitimacy, adaptability, or superior logic" (Kieser 1994). In sum, new institutionalism limits our understanding of institutions as the outcome of historical processes. It forces us to treat institutions as things rather than processes and encourage the reduction of complex causality into simple variables (Suddaby et al. 2014).

Historical institutionalism is an approach to study politics and social change. "This approach is distinguished from other social science approaches by its attention to real-world empirical questions, its historical orientation and its attention to how institutions structure and shape behaviour and outcomes" (Steinmo 2008). Although the term "historical institutionalism" was not coined until the early 1990s (Longstreth et al. 1992), the approach is far from new. Many of the most exciting and important politics studies—from Karl Polanyi's classic Great Transformations to Theda Skocpol's States and Social Revolutions and Philippe Schmitter's Still a Century of Corporatism?—would be categorised as historical institutionalists (Steinmo 2008).

Historical intuitionalism is a conceptual toolbox for understanding the causal mechanisms that underpin the processes of institutional durability and change (Fioretos et al. 2016). It seeks to explain with greater precision how a particular institutional configuration produced some observable outcome. Historical institutionalism focuses on institutional legacies and temporal effects, especially the timing and sequence of events, to explain the patterns of politics or policy (Fioretos et al. 2016). Historical institutionalists embrace two essential ontological claims about the social world: (1) that causally relevant conditions can combine in varied ways to produce a given outcome, and (2) that the same inputs and causal mechanisms, in different contexts, can yield different outcomes (Falleti and Lynch 2009).

With its emphasis on timing and sequence of events, several concepts dominate the historical institutionalist approach, namely—critical junctures, path dependence, intercurrence, and modes of institutional change (Fioretos et al. 2016). "The first involves arguments about crucial founding moments of institutional formation that send countries along broadly different developmental paths; and the second suggests that institutions continue to evolve in response to changing environmental conditions and ongoing political manoeuvring but in ways that are constrained by past trajectories" (Thelen 1999). Collier and Collier defined critical juncture "as a period of significant change, which typically occurs in distinct ways in different countries (or in other units of analysis) and which is hypothesised to produce distinct legacies" (1991, p. 29).

Within the historical institutionalism literature, there are multiple understandings of path dependence. In one approach, path dependence is defined as "dynamic processes involving positive feedback," or self-reinforcement (Pierson 2004, p. 20). The second approach to path dependence states that the early events that trigger path-dependent processes are accidental ones that were neither anticipated nor intended (Mahoney 2000; Mahoney and Schensul 2006). The extensive attention of historical institutionalist scholars to path-dependent processes has led to characterisations and criticisms of historical institutionalism as a tradition devoted to the study of institutional stability (Fioretos et al. 2016). Orren and Skowronek (1994) encouraged scholars to move beyond the "iconography of order," and introduced the term "intercurrence" to capture the ongoing character of institutional creation, reproduction, and change.

Finally, historical institutionalism brings attention to the causal mechanisms that produce variations in patterns of incremental change. Building on their own (Thelen 2004; Streeck and Thelen 2005), Mahoney and Thelen (2010) identify four modes of gradual institutional change: "displacement or the removal of existing rules and the introduction of new ones; layering or the introduction of new rules on top of or alongside existing ones; drift or the changed impact of existing rules due to shifts in the environment; and conversion or the changed enactment of existing rules due to their strategic redeployment" (pp. 15–22).

The next section will utilise the four methods in the historical institutionalism toolbox to trace the impact of diaspora on Chinese entrepreneurship's international entrepreneurship in Malaysia. Prior studies have identified various environmental dimensions that have an impact on entrepreneurship. Gnyawali and Fogel (1994), based on a synthesis of prior studies, developed a framework with five dimensions: government policies and procedures, socioeconomic conditions, entrepreneurial and business skills, financial support to business, and non-financial support to the business. The framework contains factors related to the individual and the industry (task environment) and dimensions of the institutions of entrepreneurship (general environment). While this study will focus on the institutional dimensions: economic factors, political factors, and socio-cultural factors (Shane 2003), the historical institutionalism approach emphasises that historical process, i.e., the outcomes of past events and interpretations of those events, is underpinned by the interactions of individuals (Suddaby et al. 2014).

4 Political Economy, Diaspora and Chinese Entrepreneurship in Malaysia

As highlighted in Sect. 2, there is a vast difference in entrepreneurs' quantity and quality from the three different ethnic groups (Indians, Malays, and Chinese) in Malaysia. This section aims to identify the interaction of diaspora and the political economy of Malaysia in the evolution of Chinese entrepreneurship in Malaysia. This section consists of a few parts identifying the critical junctures and intercurrence in the political economy that have affected Chinese entrepreneurs' development in Malaysia.

4.1 Historical Factors

Political Economy: While Indians and Chinese are considered migrants to Malaysia, the Bumiputras (Malays) are considered the country's indigenous people. The migration of Chinese to Malaysia can be traced to the opening up of tin mines by Malaysia's colonial administration and the increase in world demand in the second half of the nineteenth century (Lian 1995). The migration of Indians to Malaysia began later (beginning of the twentieth century) due to the extensive development of European-owned rubber estates in the west coast states (Lian 1995). While the Chinese migration was mostly spontaneous and varied in occupations (they were involved in mining, rice trade and milling, and the cultivation of commercial crops such as sugar, pepper, and gambier), Indian migration was regulated and mainly employed as labourers in the plantations (Lian 1995; Kaur 2008). Kaur (2008) also highlights that colonial government policies ensured that Indian labour had less job or residential mobility and remained essentially a circulatory labour force. Hence, compared to Chinese workers, Indian workers had very little bargaining power. In addition to the above differences, the Chinese migration to Malaysia was part of a larger migration to other South-east Asian countries. Indian migration was predominantly to Malaysia and Singapore, which were both British colonies.

Diaspora: The term "diaspora" is frequently traced to Jews living dispersed among the Gentiles after the Captivity (or) to the body of Jewish Christians outside of Palestine (Oxford English Dictionary, 2000, Volume IV: 613; Safran 1991).

Today it has been extended to refer to almost every nameable population that is dispersed in space (Brubaker 2005). Wang (1991) identifies four major phases of migration out of China. The first phase of migration from China is referred to as the Huashang (Chinese trader) phase, consisting of merchants and traders and eventually their families going abroad to establish businesses in the host countries (Wang 1991). The leading destination of Huashang migration was Asian countries, particularly to South-east Asia before 1850 (Fitzgerald 1965; Legge 1886). The above is in line with Lian's (1995) assertion that Chinese migration to Malaysia can be traced to the second half of the nineteenth century.

Poston and Wong (2016) found over 40.3 million overseas Chinese in 148 countries around 2011. Over two-thirds (70 per cent) of the 40.3 million overseas Chinese resided in five countries in descending order: Indonesia, Thailand, Malaysia, the United States, and Singapore. Four of the five countries are located in South-east Asia. Crawford (2000) observes that the vast majority of the Overseas Chinese have roots in the southeastern provinces of Guangdong and Fujian and have maintained, across generations, tight economic and psychological/mythological contact with their home regions. Even during this period, leading Chinese entrepreneurs in Malaysia like Robert Kuok had expanded to other regional countries (Tanzer 2018).

The contribution of diaspora to entrepreneurship is well documented in the literature. The Jewish entrepreneur stands as the archetypal diaspora entrepreneur and as the model for many discussions (e.g., on innovation and opportunity, see Elo and Volovelsky 2017; Kahane 2012). Bonacich (1973) and Waldinger et al. (1990) refer to Jews as middlemen due to their ability to locate customers behind ethnic markets' borders.

While both Chinese and Indian migrants came initially as sojourners (immigrants who do not plan to settle permanently), by the mid-1920s, the Chinese population tended to settle permanently, in contrast to the Indians who remained a transient community. First, it was easier, quicker, and less expensive for Indians to return to their homeland than for the Chinese. The Communist revolution deterred the return of the Chinese to their homeland (Smith 1964). As the "theory of middleman minorities" (Rinder 1958–1959; Bonacich 1973) highlights, middleman entrepreneurs frequently begin as sojourners. It is pointed out that sojourners exhibit essential attributes necessary for successful entrepreneurs—a tendency towards thrift and a concentration in certain occupations.

Sojourners are there to make money, not spend it, and this "future time orientation" enables them to accumulate capital. This orientation contrasts with that of settlers and "natives" who generally wish to live more rounded lives since they do not aim to live elsewhere (Bonacich 1973, p. 585). Besides, Bonacich (1973) also points out that sojourning contributes to a high degree of internal solidarity: "Since they plan to return, sojourners have little reason to develop lasting relationships with members of the surrounding host society.... thus, ethnic and regional associations are strong, mutual assistance is prevalent, and trust retained among members from the same general area" (p. 586).

The difference between the Indians and Chinese migrants to Malaysia was that the Indians achieved their goal of return and invested their savings in India. The

Chinese did not and hence built businesses in Malaysia. The social solidarity of sojourners is still reflected in Malaysia's Chinese community and reflected in the continued strength of Chinese clan associations. After migration, Chinese businesses are also consistent with the literature on middleman minorities (Bonacich 1973). They were frequently traders—a middleman between producers and consumers, agents—a middleman between owner and renter. The businesses depend heavily on the use of unpaid family labour. If wage labour was required, extended family or clan members were preferred (Bonacich 1973). It was also training for the employees to frequently set up their businesses in the future with the employer's assistance.

Before independence, the Bumiputeras dominated mainly by the Malay ethnic group were concentrated mainly in the rural areas and predominantly farmers living in a feudal political system (Wan Husin 2013). In the Malay feudal system, business ownership was controlled by the aristocrats (Wan Husin 2013):

> The trading and agriculture domain were reserved exclusively for the aristocrats, as it was crucial to ensure that the clout to rule remained in their clutch. The trade sector was in the hands of society's upper crust since the Srivijaya Empire era and continued in the succeeding kingdoms in the Malay Peninsula and Sumatra [9]. The peasants were mainly unencumbered from getting involved in the business or trade sector. Their principal breadwinning occupation was to either till the land as farmers or cast their skills as fishermen (p. 361).

The concept of unreciprocated help is also another feature of Malay society that probably discourages entrepreneurship. Selat (2004) points out that the concept of unreciprocated help is an essential element in the Malay community. A person is expected to help another member of the community without expecting anything in return. They believe that he or she will be rewarded by god hereafter. The value of the contribution to society is highly appreciated and renowned by the Malays. Social status is determined by how much contribution is given to the society rather than the wealth or achievement one has. "That is the reason why the Malays have stereotyped the Chinese as greedy and opportunistic people" (Selat 2004, p. 8).

4.2 Post-Independence

Political Economy: At independence, the Malaysian economy was dominated by commodity exports (rubber, tin, then palm oil, and petroleum) (Yusof and Battasali 2008), with the production dominated by large colonial (United Kingdom) owned firms, the small and medium businesses dominated by Chinese, and workers in the plantations and tin mines mainly Indians and Chinese, and the Malays mainly in the villages living on small-scale agriculture and fishing. Therefore, at independence, the Chinese dominated entrepreneurship in Malaysia. Many small and medium enterprises grew to become large food manufacturing and trading companies as part of the more extensive bamboo network, a network of overseas Chinese businesses operating in South-east Asia markets that share common family and cultural ties (Weidenbaum and Hughes 1996).

This was also facilitated by the continuation of the laissez-faire economic policy adopted by the government on independence. The government generally did not interfere in the economy and allowed the markets to function with little interference. Jomo and Sundaram (2004) observe that income distribution in Peninsular Malaysia worsened between 1957 and 1970, with the rich becoming richer and the poor becoming poorer in all ethnic groups, especially among the Malays. The lasses-faire economic policy allowed Chinese entrepreneurs to dominate the economy and facilitated their expansion into regional markets (Gomez 2002).

4.3 May 13, 1969, and the New Economic Policy (NEP)

Political Economy: On May 13, 1969, following the 1969 Malaysian general election when opposition parties made gains at the expense of the ruling coalition, the Alliance Party Sino-Malay sectarian violence broke out around the capital Kuala Lumpur and surrounding areas. Official reports put the number of deaths due to the riots at 196, although Western diplomatic sources at the time suggested a toll of close to 600, with most of the victims being ethnic Chinese (Time 1969). The riots proved to be a watershed moment for Malaysian political and economic institutions. The government declared a state of national emergency by the Yang di-Pertuan Agong (King), the suspension of the Parliament, and governance of the country taken over by the National Operations Council (NOC) between 1969 and 1971. During this period, the first Prime Minister of Malaysia resigned in 1970 to be succeeded by Tun Abdul Razak, the architect of the New Economic Policy.

The NEP was presented when the parliamentary rule was restored in February 1971 and implemented over 20 years. The New Economic Policy was focussed on restricting the scope of laissez-faire capitalism and allowing more significant state intervention in socioeconomic areas to advance Malay welfare. The NEP had two main objectives—the reduction of poverty irrespective of race and the restructuring of Malaysian society to eliminate the identification of race with economic function (Koon 1997). Towards these two ends, state interventionist policies were implemented to raise Malay income through poverty reduction policies such as the establishment of Felda in the rural sector (Sutton 1989); expansion of employment opportunities in the urban sector through recruitment of more Malays in the civil service, and increasing Malay professionals through the expansion of higher education opportunities for Malays (Selvaratnam 1988); and last but not least raising the Malay share of corporate wealth from 2.4% to 30% by 1990 (Koon 1997). One of the main initiatives to raise the Malay share of corporate wealth was to nurture Malay entrepreneurs by MARA mentioned previously in the introduction. Malay entrepreneurs were also given preference in the awarding of Malaysian government contracts, and corporations were asked to reserve 30% of new issues for Malays (Milne 1986).

Koon (1997) observes that the "NEP with its preferential treatment of Malays and its apparent assault on Chinese economic, educational and cultural interest led many to question whether they had a viable interest in the country. However, when the NEP drew to a close, both the Malay and Chinese political and business leadership appeared essentially satisfied with its results" (p. 262). This was a critical juncture for Chinese enterprise, which could have produced distinct legacies (Collier and Collier 1991). So, the critical question is why Chinese business leadership were essentially satisfied with the outcome. Several reasons can be identified for a positive outcome.

A major reason was the steady expansion of the Malaysian economy enabling the government to reduce income inequality without reducing the wealth of the Chinese (Shari 2000). Koon (1997) observes that by the late 1970s, Chinese businesses faced severe Malay competition in their traditional construction, transportation, and distribution sectors. "In the retail sector, for example, the establishment of new Malay firms increased at a faster rate than Chinese ones, growing from 3311 to 32,800 between 1971 and 1981, compared to the Chinese increase from 18,957 to 55,417 over the same period" (p. 274). The Chinese, however, quickly identified that the Industrial Co-ordination Act 1975's (the implementation tool for economic restructuring) equity restructuring requirements could be used to their advantage. The NEP made available a vast new pool of Malay capital that could be tapped through joint ventures. This contributed to the creation of new Chinese entrepreneurs such as William Cheng (Amalgamated Steel Mills) and Vincent Tan (Berjaya) (Koon 1997). At the level of small and medium enterprises, "Ali-Baba" relationships were forged—where the Malays provided the contracts, and the Chinese implemented them (see Chin 2001).

In 1981, Mahathir Mohammed became the prime minister with visions of nurturing new Malay entrepreneurs to be implemented by his finance minister in 1984. Several new Malay entrepreneurs, e.g., Halim Saad (Renong), Tajuddin Ramli (Malaysian Airlines), Yahya Ahmad (HICOM and Proton), and Syed Mokhtar (MMC), emerged through government patronage (Gomez 2009). Patronage included cheap loans, government contracts, and privatisation of government entities.

In 1991 the New Economic Policy (NEP) was replaced by the New Development Policy (NDP). The NDP, while retaining the main objectives of the NEP, eschewed numerical targets and emphasised growth and income raising policies over income distribution policies.

Diaspora: Two primary resources underpin diaspora entrepreneurship—cultural training and ethnic social networks (Boudlaie et al. 2020; Mokhtarzadeh et al. 2020; Velayutham 2008). To a large extent, the two are integrated, i.e., the social networks are the foundation of cultural training. As highlighted earlier, the Chinese social networks and cultural training for new Chinese entrepreneurs are extensive and in-depth, not only in Malaysia but also regionally, allowing them a broader market than other ethnic groups in Malaysia. There was not only a migration of Chinese from the southeastern provinces of China, namely Guangdong and Fujian, to Malaysia but also South-east Asian countries, including Indonesia, Thailand, Philippines, and Singapore (Crawford 2000). While the Chinese from Guangdong might have migrated to different South-east Asian countries, they maintained their social networks of critical importance to entrepreneurship.

Even in a challenging political and economic environment, the Chinese entrepreneurs' social networks reduced economic risks related to the creation of a new business, rendering the decision to become self-employed more attractive from a risk diversification perspective (Rauch 2001). These were of particular importance in South-east Asia because of weak institutional structures related to contract enforcement in these countries. Weak institutional structures related to contract enforcement contribute to increased risks in national and international trade, which can be mitigated by the trust prevalent in social networks (Rauch 2001). Rauch further emphasises that social networks, in addition to being used to transmit information about past opportunistic business conduct, can also be used to transmit information about current opportunities for profitable international trade or investment. In Malaysia's cross-cultural setting, Chinese entrepreneurs' social capital leads to better knowledge and risk management (Rezaei et al. 2020).

Social networks can also act as barriers to entry into particular business areas for outsiders (Spencer and Qiu 2001). In Malaysia, many Bumiputeras complain that there are numerous barriers to entry into many business sectors (Utusan Melayu 2007; Astar 2008). Social networks also provide a learning platform for young entrepreneurs, as pointed out earlier.

4.4 1997 Asian Financial Crisis

Political Economy: The Asian Financial Crisis (AFC) had a significant impact on Malaysia's political and economic institutions. Politically, the Deputy Prime Minister Anwar Ibrahim was sacked and expelled from the ruling party UMNO, and later convicted of sodomy. Economically the value of the Malaysian Ringgit (RM) dropped from 2.52 ringgit to one US dollar in June 1997 to a low of 4.5 ringgit to the dollar in January 1998. This steep descent contributed to a stock market crash—the Kuala Lumpur Composite Index (KLCI) of the Kuala Lumpur Stock Exchange (KLSE) dropped from 1,271 points in February 1997 to a historic low of 262 points on September 1, 1998 (Ping and Yean 2007).

The massive drop in the value of the Ringgit and the stock market had a devastating impact on enterprises that had borrowed extensively, especially from abroad. The AFC had a vastly different impact on Malay and Chinese entrepreneurs in Malaysia. The Chinese entrepreneurs who generally adopted conservative financing escaped the worst impact of the crisis. Companies owned by Malay entrepreneurs (Halim Saad of Renong, Tajuddin Ramli of MAS, and Yahya Ahmad of HICOM) who had borrowed heavily to expand were in deep financial trouble. They had to be rescued by the government (Ping and Yean 2007). *Forbes* magazine published a list of Malaysians with a total wealth of more than one billion US dollars in 1996 featured six Chinese, one Sri Lankan Tamil, and three Malays. A later *Forbes* list of twenty wealthiest businesspeople in Malaysia in 2001 features sixteen Chinese, one Sri Lankan Tamil, and three Malays.

Diaspora: Hamidon (2009) argues that government support and preferential treatment have been counterproductive because they contribute to dependency. The dependency theory was mooted vigorously by researchers from South America as Cardoso and Faletto (1979). This theory advocates that capitalist countries create an unequal relationship between the capitalist countries and the less developed countries. Due to these developed (capitalist) countries' unfavourable practices, the disparity and underdevelopment keep expanding on these less developed countries (James 1997). In addition, developing countries have to continue to rely on aid or donations for their expenses (Cardoso and Faletto 1979). One of the outcomes of this dependency theory is that it creates a welfare mentality among the recipients.

Hamidon (2009) identifies many similarities of the preferential treatment accorded to the Malays to the dependency theory. It is argued that the government's efforts to alleviate or help the Malays from the crutches of economic poverty have contributed to the development of a welfare mentality, continuously seeking help from the government. In the AFC environment, Malay entrepreneurs could no longer depend on the government for help as the government itself needed help and was required to implement austerity policies to mitigate the AFC's effects.

In the aftermath of the AFC, the government also adopted more liberal economic policies. It eliminated many company ownership and employment restrictions to prevent local funds' flight and attract foreign direct investment. Many existing and new Chinese entrepreneurs who had survived the AFC were well placed to grow in the new liberalised economic environment. Many of the Chinese entrepreneurs were in manufacturing, and the weak Ringgit made them more competitive. Ping and Yean (2007) attribute Malaysia recovery from the AFC to its manufacturing exports.

The aftermath of the AFC also coincides with China's emergence as a significant economy culminating in joining the WTO in 2001. Chinese products flooded global markets, and it also became a major market for exports from ASEAN countries, including Malaysia. In 1995 the United States was Malaysia's leading trading partner, followed by Singapore, its closest neighbour. In 2018 Malaysia's main export markets were in the following order: Singapore, China, United States, Hong Kong, and Japan (https://wits.worldbank.org/CountrySnapshot/en/MYS). Ethnic Chinese are the major ethnic groups in 3 of the five main export markets, and hence, Malaysian Chinese entrepreneurs have a significant advantage because they share a common language and culture with the trading partners. From January to September 2019, China was the third biggest source of foreign tourists (2.41 million arrivals), after Singapore (7.8 million) and Indonesia (2.7 million) (Povera and Goh 2020). The above changes in Malaysia's political economy have been very favourable to Chinese entrepreneurs and their ability to expand overseas in contrast to other ethnic groups in Malaysia and are reflected in the number of Chinese in the 100 MIYE.

5 Discussion and Conclusion

Entrepreneurs play an essential role in the economy, serving as agents of change by their entrepreneurial activity, being the source of considerable innovative activity, stimulating industry evolution, and creating an important share of the newly generated jobs (Acs 1992; Audretsch 1993, 1995). In the current globalised and competitive environment, expanding international activities is crucial for firms, especially SMEs, to survive, succeed, and grow (Dikova et al. 2016; Majocchi et al. 2005). Following the recognition that entrepreneurship is critical to economic development, many governments around the world have implemented a variety of supporting mechanisms and policies for entrepreneurs, including funding, physical infrastructure, and business advisory services (OECD 1998; Andersone and Bogdanova 2014; Centre for International Private Enterprise 2014).

In Malaysia, the government is interested in promoting entrepreneurship and, more specifically, among the Bumiputeras (Malays). Towards this end, it has established various entities, e.g., MARA and programmes, e.g., Economic Transformation Programme (ETP) and The Small Retailer Transformation Programme (TUKAR), to develop and grow Malay entrepreneurs. However, the MIYE 100 highlights the limited impact and even failure of Malaysian government programs to develop Malay entrepreneurs as MIYE 100 is continuing to be dominated by Chinese entrepreneurs.

Entrepreneurship (International) research using institutional theory has sought to identify institutional variations in the national environment (Busenitz et al. 2000; Casson 1990; Sadeghi et al. 2019), and among ethnic groups (Acs and Karlsson 2002; Ahlstrom and Bruton 2002; Churchill 2017; Estrin and Mickiewicz 2011; Karlsson and Acs 2002) that influences entrepreneurship. For the most part, international entrepreneurship research based on institutional theory is ahistorical and hence treated institutional variable as fixed and objective, rather than as processes. It encourages the reduction of complex causality into simple variables (Suddaby et al. 2014).

This paper adopts the historical institutionalism approach to study the dominance of Chinese entrepreneurs in the Malaysian economy. Prior studies have identified five dimensions that have a significant impact on entrepreneurship development and success: government policies and procedures (Duran et al. 2017), socioeconomic conditions (Bruton et al. 2008; Jafari-Sadeghi and Biancone 2017), entrepreneurial and business skill (Takyi-Asiedu 1993), financial support to business Young and Weisch 1993), and non-financial support to business (Hawkins 1993; Phillips 1993

A study of the Malaysian political economy from pre-independence to the current time shows that the environment has changed dramatically over the years because of both domestic and global factors, which has, at times, been favourable to Chinese entrepreneurs and at other time unfavourable. Chinese entrepreneurs have, however, maintained their dominance over the Malaysian economy. The diaspora analysis highlights that group solidarity, social networks, and cultural training have enabled

Chinese entrepreneurs to adjust and frequently even convert adverse political and economic environment to their benefit.

The study highlights the importance of history when analysing the impact of institutional variables on entrepreneurship. The research highlights that causally relevant conditions can combine in varied ways to produce a given outcome. The study highlights the ongoing character of institutional creation, reproduction, and change and how individuals adapt to change and frequently convert adverse changes to their advantage.

References

Acs ZJ (1992) Small business economics: a global perspective. Challenge 35(November/December):38–44

Acs ZJ, Karlsson C (2002) Introduction to institutions, entrepreneurship and firm growth: from Sweden to the OECD. Small Bus Econ 19(3):183–187

Ahlstrom D, Bruton GD (2002) An institutional perspective on the role culture in shaping strategic actions by technology-focused entrepreneurial firms in China. Enterp Theory Pract 26(4):53–70

Alon I, Dana LP, Jenkins A (2009) International business by SMEs: empirical findings from New Zealand. J Int Bus Econ 10(2):59–78

Andersone E, Bogdanova O (2014) Export credit guarantees in developing business environment of the European economic area. Procedia Soc Behav Sci 156:322–328

Astar I (2008) Silap Malayu dan tindakan GABEM: Dimanakah silap kota? Warta GABEM 6:23

Audretsch DB (1993) Kleinunternehmen in der Industrieökonomiek; ein neuer Ansatz. Discussion paper FS IV 93–26. Wissenschaftszentrum, Berlin

Audretsch DB (1995) Innovation and industry evolution. MIT Press, Cambridge, MA

Bae J-H, Salomon R (2010) Institutional distance in international business research. In: DeVinney T, Pedersen T, Tihanyi L (eds) The past, present and future of international business & management. Emerald Group Publishing Limited, Bingley, United Kingdom, pp 327–349

Barley SR, Tolbert P (1997) Institutionalization and structuration: studying the links between institutions and action. Organ Stud 18(1):93–117

Bayfield R, Dana LP, Stewart S (2009) Firm characteristics and internationalisation strategies: an empirical investigation of New Zealand exporters. IJGSB 3(3):275–287

Bogan V, Darity W Jr (2008) Culture and entrepreneurship? African American and immigrant self-employment in the United States. J Socio-Econ 37:1999–2019

Bonacich E (1973) A theory of middleman minorities. Am Sociol Rev 38(October):583–594

Boudlaie H, Mahdiraji HA, Shamsi S, Jafari-Sadeghi V, Garcia-Perez A (2020) Designing a human resource scorecard: an empirical stakeholder-based study with a company culture perspective. J Entrep Manage Innovat 16(4):113–147

Bowen HP, De Clercq D (2008) Institutional context and the allocation of entrepreneurial effort. J Int Bus Stud 39(4):747–767

Brubaker R (2005) The 'diaspora' diaspora. Ethn Racial Stud 28(1):1–19

Bruton GD, Ahlstrom D, Obloj K (2008) Entrepreneurship in emerging economies: where are we today and where should the research go in the future. Entrep Theory Pract 32(1):1–14

Busenitz LW, Gómez C, Spencer JW (2000) Country institutional profiles: unlocking entrepreneurial phenomena. Acad Manag J 43(5):994–1003

Cardoso FH, Faletto E (1979) Dependency and development in Latin América. University of California Press

Carlsson B (1992) The rise of small business: causes and consequences. In: Adams WJ (ed) Singular Europe, economy and policy of the European community after 1992. University of Michigan Press, Ann Arbor, MI, pp 145–169
Carlsson B (1999) Small business, entrepreneurship, and industrial dynamics. In: Acs Z (ed) Are small firms important? Kluwer Academic Publishers, Dordrecht
Casson M (1990) Entrepreneurship. Edward Elgar, Aldershot
Centre for International Private Enterprise (2014) Creating the environment for entrepreneurial success. Centre for International Private Enterprise, Washington D.C.
Chin YW (2001) Usahawan Cina Di Malaysia: Interaksi Budaya dan Transformasi Keusahawanan [Chinese enterprise in Malaysia: cultural interaction and entrepreneurial transformation]. Unpublished PhD dissertation, Universiti Kebangsaan Malaysia
Churchill SA (2017) Fractionalization, entrepreneurship, and the institutional environment for entrepreneurship. Small Bus Econ 48(3):577–597
Collier RB, Collier D (1991) Shaping the political arena: critical junctures, the labor movement, and regime dynamics in Latin America. Princeton University Press, Princeton, NJ
Crawford D (2000) Chinese capitalism: cultures, the South-east Asian region and economic globalisation. Third World Q 21(1):69–86
Dana LP (1987a) Evaluating policies promoting entrepreneurship—a cross-cultural comparison of entrepreneurship case study: Singapore and Malaysia. J Small Bus Entrep 4(3):36–41
Dana LP (1987b) Industrial development efforts in Malaysia and Singapore. J Small Bus Manag 25:74
Dikova D, Jaklič A, Burger A, Kunčič A (2016) What is beneficial for first-time SME-exporters from a transition economy: a diversified or a focused export strategy? J World Bus 51 (2):185–199
DiMaggio PJ, Powell WW (1991) Introduction. In: DiMaggio PJ, Powell WW (eds) The new institutionalism in organisational analysis. University of Chicago Press, Chicago, pp 1–38
Duran P, Kostova T, Van Essen M (2017) Political ideologies and the internationalization of family-controlled firms. J World Bus 52(4):474–488
Elo M, Volovelsky EK (2017) Jewish diaspora entrepreneurs-the impact of religion on opportunity exploration and exploitation. Int J Entrep Small Bus 31(2):244–269
Estrin S, Mickiewicz T (2011) Institutions and female entrepreneurship. Small Bus Econ 37 (4):397–415
Fairlie RW, Meyer BD (2003) The effect of immigration on native self-employment. J Labor Econ 21(3):619–650
Fairlie RW, Robb AM (2008) Race and entrepreneurial success: Black-, Asian-, and White-owned businesses in the United States. MIT Press, Cambridge
Falleti TG, Lynch J (2009) Context and causation in political analysis. Comp Pol Stud 49 (9):1143–1166
Farouk AFA (2012) State and entrepreneurship: the failure to create a Bumiputera commercial and industrial community (BCIC) in Penang, Malaysia. Kajian Malaysia 30(1):1–20
Fioretos O, Falleti TG, Sheingate A (2016) Historical institutionalism in political science. In: The Oxford handbook of historical institutionalism. Oxford University Press, Oxford and New York, pp 3–30
Fitzgerald CP (1965) The third China: the Chinese communities in South-East Asia. Angus and Robertson, London, UK
Fong CO (1990) Small and medium Industries in Malaysia: economic efficiency and entrepreneurship. Dev Econ 28(2):152–179
Garousi Mokhtarzadeh N, Amoozad Mahdiraji H, Jafari-Sadeghi V, Soltani A, Abbasi Kamardi A (2020) A product-technology portfolio alignment approach for food industry: a multi-criteria decision making with z-numbers. Br Food J 122(12):3947–3967
Gnyawali DR, Fogel DS (1994) Environments for entrepreneurship development: key dimensions and research implications. Entrep Theory Pract 18(4):43–62

Gomez ET (2002) Chinese business development in Malaysia: networks, entrepreneurship or patronage. In: Gerke S, Menkhoff T (eds) Chinese entrepreneurship and Asian business networks. Routledge, London
Gomez ET (2009) The rise and fall of capital: corporate Malaysia in historical perspective. J Contem Asia 39(3):345–381
Greene PG, Owen MM (2004) Race and ethnicity. In: Gartner WB (ed) Handbook of entrepreneurial dynamics: the process of business creation. Sage, New York
Hallett T (2010) The myth incarnate. Am Sociol Rev 75(1):52–74
Hallett T, Ventesca M (2006) Inhabited institutions: social interactions and organizational forms in Gouldner's patterns of industrial democracy. Theory Soc 35(2):213–236
Hamidon S (2009) The development of Malay entrepreneurship in Malaysia. PhD theses, Massey University, Auckland, New Zealand
Hawkins DL (1993) New business entrepreneurship in the Japanese economy. J Bus Ventur 8:137–150
Jafari-Sadeghi VJ, Biancone PP (2017) Exploring the drivers of gender entrepreneurship: focus on the motivational perspectives in USA, Italy and France. In: Gender and family entrepreneurship. Routledge, pp 138–155
Jafari-Sadeghi VJ, Biancone PP (2018) How micro, small and medium-sized enterprises are driven outward the superior international trade performance? A multidimensional study on Italian food sector. Res Int Bus Financ 45:597–606
Jafari-Sadeghi VJ, Nkongolo-Bakenda JM, Anderson RB, Dana LP (2019a) An institution-based view of international entrepreneurship: a comparison of context-based and universal determinants in developing and economically advanced countries. Int Bus Rev 28(6):101588
Jafari-Sadeghi VJ, Biancone PP, Anderson RB, Nkongolo-Bakenda JM (2019b) International entrepreneurship by particular people 'on their own terms': a study on the universal characteristics of entrepreneurs in evolving economies. Int J Entrep Small Bus 37(2):288–308
Jafari-Sadeghi V, Nkongolo-Bakenda JM, Dana LP, Anderson RB, Biancone PP (2020a) Home country institutional context and entrepreneurial internationalization: the significance of human capital attributes. J Int Entrep 18:165–195
Jafari-Sadeghi V, Kimiagari S, Biancone PP (2020b) Level of education and knowledge, foresight competency and international entrepreneurship. Eur Bus Rev 32(1):46–68
Jafari-Sadeghi V, Dutta DK, Ferraris A, Del Giudice M (2020c) Internationalisation business processes in an under-supported policy contexts: evidence from Italian SMEs. Bus Process Manag J 26(5):1055–1074
James P (1997) Post-dependency: the third world in an era of globalism and late capitalism. Alternat Social Transf Human Govern 22(2):205–226
Jepperson R (1991) Institutions, institutional effects, and institutionalism. In: Powell WW, DiMaggio PJ (eds) The new institutionalism in organisational analysis. University of Chicago Press, Chicago, pp 143–163
Jomo KS, Sundaram JK (2004) The new economic policy and interethnic relations in Malaysia. UNRISD, Geneva
Kahane B (2012) "Tikkun Olam": how a Jewish ethos drives innovation. J Manag Dev 31 (9):938–947
Karlsson C, Acs ZJ (2002) Introduction to institutions, entrepreneurship and firm growth: the case of Sweden. Small Bus Econ 19(2):63–67
Kaur A (2008) International migration and governance in Malaysia: policy and performance. UNEAC Asia Papers No.22
Kieser A (1994) Why organization theory needs historical analyses—and how this should be performed. Organ Sci 5(4):608–620
Koon HP (1997) The new economic policy and the Chinese community in Peninsular Malaysia. Dev Econ 35(3):262–292
Lawrence TB, Suddaby R (2006) Institutions and institutional work. In: Clegg S, Hardy C, Lawrence TB (eds) Sage handbook of organization studies. Sage, London

Legge J (1886) A record of Buddhist Kingdoms: being an account by the Chinese Monk Fahein of his travels in India and Ceylon (A.D. 399–414). In: Search of the Buddhist books of discipline. The Clarendon Press, Oxford, UK
Lian KF (1995) Migration and the formation of Malaysia and Singapore. In: Cohen R (ed) The Cambridge survey of world migration. Cambridge University Press, Cambridge, pp 392–396
Longstreth F, Steinmo S, Thelen KA (eds) (1992) Structuring politics: historical institutionalism in comparative analysis. Cambridge University Press
Mahoney J (2000) Path dependence in historical sociology. Theory Soc 29(4):507–548
Mahoney J, Schensul D (2006) Historical context and path dependence. In: Goodin RE, Tilly C (eds) The Oxford handbook of contextual political analysis. Oxford University Press, New York and London, pp 454–471
Mahoney J, Thelen K (2010) A theory of gradual institutional change. In: Mahoney J, Thelen K (eds) Explaining institutional change: ambiguity, agency, and power. Cambridge University Press, Cambridge, pp 1–37
Majocchi A, Bacchiocchi E, Mayrhofer U (2005) Firm size, business experience and export intensity in SMEs: a longitudinal approach to complex relationships. Int Bus Rev 14 (6):719–738
Meyer JW, Rowan B (1977) Institutionalised organisations: formal structure as myth and ceremony. Am J Sociol 83(2):340–363
Milne RS (1986) Malaysia-beyond the new economic policy. Asian Surv 26(12):1364–1382
Mokhtarzadeh N, Amoozad Mahdiraji H, Jafarpanah I, Jafari-Sadeghi V, Cardinali S (2020) Investigating the impact of networking capability on firm innovation performance: using the resource-action-performance framework. J Intellect Cap 21(6):1009–1034
Muralidharan E, Pathak S (2017) Informal institutions and international entrepreneurship. Int Bus Rev 26(2):288–302
Nasra R, Dacin MT (2010) Institutional arrangements and international entrepreneurship: the state as an institutional entrepreneur. Entrep Theory Pract 34(3):583–609
OECD (1998) Fostering entrepreneurship. OECD, Paris. www.oecd.org
Omar, C. M. Z. C., & Azmi, N. M. N. (2015). Factors affecting the success of Bumiputera entrepreneurs in small and medium enterprises (SMEs) in Malaysia. International Journal of Management Science and Business Administration, 1(9), 40-45.
Orren K, Skowronek S (1994) Beyond the iconography of order: notes for a new institutionalism. In: Dodd L, Jillison C (eds) The dynamics of American politics: approaches and interpretations. Westview Press, Boulder, pp 311–330
Phillips BD (1993) The growth of small firm jobs by state, 1984–1988. Bus Econ 48(2):48–53
Pierson P (2004) Politics in time: history, institutions, and social analysis. Princeton University Press, Princeton
Ping LP, Yean TS (2007) Malaysia ten years after the Asian financial crisis. Asian Surv 47 (6):915–929
Poston DL Jr, Wong JH (2016) The Chinese diaspora: the current distribution of the overseas Chinese population. Chinese J Sociol 2(3):348–373
Povera A, Goh PP (2020) China suspending tour groups will hit Malaysia hard, says Matta president. New Staraits Times, January 27. https://www.nst.com.my/news/nation/2020/01/560062/china-suspending-tour-groups-will-hit-malaysia-hard-says-matta-president
Praveen Parboteeah K, Hoegl M, Cullen J (2009) Religious dimensions and work obligation: a country institutional profile model. Hum Relat 62(1):119–148
Ratten V, Dana LP, Han M, Welpe I (2007) Internationalisation of SMEs: European comparative studies. Int J Entrep Small Bus 4(3):361–379
Rauch JE (2001) Business and social networks in international trade. J Econ Lit 39 (December):1177–1203
Rezaei M, Jafari-Sadeghi V, Bresciani S (2020) What drives the process of knowledge management in a cross-cultural setting. Eur Bus Rev 32(3):485–511

Rinder ID (1958–1959) Strangers in the land: social relations in the status gap. Soc Probl 6 (Winter):253–260
Sadeghi VJ, Biancone PP, Anderson RB, Nkongolo-Bakenda JM (2019) International entrepreneurship by particular people 'on their own terms': a study on the universal characteristics of entrepreneurs in evolving economies. Int J Entrep Small Bus 37(2):288–308
Safran W (1991) Diasporas in modern societies: myths of homeland and return. Diaspora 1 (1):83–99
Salomon R, Wu Z (2012) Institutional distance and local isomorphism strategy. J Int Bus Stud 43 (4):343–367
Sarfati G (2012) Do public policies for entrepreneurship make a difference? Prospective scenarios for Canada, Ireland, and Italy. FSRJ 4(1):114–139
Scott WR (2007) Institutions and organisations: ideas and interests. Sage Publications, Thousand Oaks, CA
Selat N (2004) Malays: a cultural history. In: Harun Y (ed) Malaysia: papers on society and culture. Victoria University of Wellington, Wellington, NZ, pp 1–10
Selvaratnam V (1988) Ethnicity, inequality, and higher education in Malaysia. Comp Educ Rev 32 (2):173–196
Shane SA (2003) A general theory of entrepreneurship: the individual-opportunity nexus. Edward Elgar Publishing
Shari I (2000) Economic growth and income inequality in Malaysia, 1971–95. J Asia Pac Econ 5 (1–2):112–124
Simmel G (1950) The stranger. In: Wolf K (ed) The sociology of Georg Simmel. Free Press, Glencoe Il
Smith TE (1964) Immigration and permanent settlement of Chinese and Indians in Malaya. In: Cowan CD (ed) The economic development of South-East Asia. George Allen and Unwin, London, pp 174–185
Sombart W (1914) The jews and modern capitalism. Transaction, New Brunswick NJ
Spencer BJ, Qiu LD (2001) Keiretsu and relationship-specific investment: a barrier to trade? Int Econ Rev 42:871–901
Steinmo S (2008) Historical institutionalism. In: Porta DD, Keating M (eds) Approaches and methodologies in the social sciences: a pluralist perspective. Cambridge University Press, Cambridge, pp 118–138
Streeck W, Thelen K (eds) (2005) Beyond continuity: institutional change in advanced political economies. Oxford University Press, Oxford
Suddaby R (2010) Challenges for institutional theory. J Manag Inq 19(1):14–20
Suddaby R, Foster WM, Mills AJ (2014) Historical institutionalism. In: Bucheli M, Wadhwani RD (eds) Organizations in time: history, theory, methods. Oxford University Press, Oxford, pp 100–123
Sukumar A, Jafari-Sadeghi V, Garcia-Perez A, Dutta DK (2020) The potential link between corporate innovations and corporate competitiveness: evidence from IT firms in the UK. J Knowl Manag 24(5):965–983
Sutton K (1989) Malaysia's FELDA land settlement model in time and space. Geoforum 20 (3):339–354
Takyi-Asiedu S (1993) Some socio-cultural factors retarding entrepreneurial activity in sub-Saharan Africa. J Bus Ventur 8:91–98
Tanzer A (2018) Robert Kuok A memoir. Landmark Books
Thelen K (1999) Historical institutionalism in comparative politics. Annu Rev Polit Sci 2:369–404
Thelen K (2004) How institutions evolve: the political economy of skills in Germany, Britain, the United States, and Japan. Cambridge University Press, Cambridge
Thillainathan R, Cheong KC (2016) Malaysia's new economic policy, growth and distribution: revisiting the debate. Malays J Econ Stud 53(1):51–68
Time (1969) Race war in Malaysia. Time, May 23. https://web.archive.org/web/20070518061525/http://www.time.com/time/magazine/article/0%2C9171%2C900859%2C00.html

Utusan Melayu (2007) Sejauh mana kekuatan rumpun Melayu. Utusan Malaysia (online), November 8
Velayutham S (2008) Development of personal networking in different societies: Guanxi in China and Wasta in the Middle East. Asian Profile 36(6):547–557
Waldinger R, Aldrich H, Ward R (1990) Opportunities, group characteristics and strategies. In: Waldinger R, Aldrich H, Ward R (eds) Ethnic entrepreneurs: immigrant business in industrial societies. Sage, London, pp 13–48
Wan Husin WN (2013) Business dominance among the Malays and Chinese in Malaysia from a civilizational perspectives. Int J Soc Sci Humanit Stud 3(4):360–364
Wang G (1991) China and the Chinese overseas. Times Academic Press, Singapore
Weber M (1930) The protestant ethic and the spirit of capitalism. Scribner, New York
Weidenbaum ML, Hughes S (1996) The Bamboo network: how expatriate Chinese entrepreneurs are creating a new economic superpower in Asia. Martin Kessler Books, Free Press
Wennekers S, Thurik R (1999) Linking entrepreneurship and economic growth. Small Bus Econ 13:27–55
Wright RW, Ricks DA (1994) Trends in international business research: twenty-five years later. J Int Bus Stud 25(4):687–701
Young EC, Weisch HP (1993) Major elements in entrepreneurial development in central Mexico. J Small Bus Manag 31(4):80–85
Yusof ZA, Battasali D (2008) Economic growth and development in Malaysia: policy making and leadership. Working Paper No. 27. The International Bank for Reconstruction and Development/The World Bank
Zucchella A, Magnani G (2016) International entrepreneurship: theoretical foundations and practices, 2nd edn. Palgrave Macmillan, New York

Sivakumar Velayutham is a professor of accounting and dean of the Faculty of Business at Nilai University. He previously held positions at Charles Darwin University, Australia; and Massey University New Zealand and the University of Sharjah, United Arab Emirates. Sivakumar's research interests include education, accounting, culture, and economic development. He has previously published in the British Accounting Review, Accounting Education, Asian profile and Critical Perspectives in Accounting, Corporate Governance, and the Journal of Islamic Accounting and Business Research.

Internationalisation of Start-Ups: An Institutional Entrepreneurship Perspective

Miguel Angel Gil Robles

1 Introduction

The internationalisation of start-ups has been studied from a financial (Chin et al. 2016), organisational (Han 2007), and economic perspective (Jafari Sadeghi et al. 2019). The current literature defines internationalisation, in the context of start-ups, as a vehicle for growth outside of their domestic market (Barney 2014; Etemad et al. 2001; Hitt et al. 2000). Recent studies assume that start-ups can become international, not only by selling their products abroad but also by establishing business networks, supply chains and acquiring technology from abroad (Cahen 2019; Neubert 2018). To explain why start-ups become international, some studies have focused on analysing the economic context and the institutional environment in which the start-up operates (Gil and Klarner 2020; Neubert 2017; Muralidharan and Pathak 2017).

Unfortunately, little is known about the characteristics of the entrepreneurs who founded the start-up and how such characteristics affect how the start-up internationalises (Dana 2017; Han 2006). More specifically, the current literature has paid little attention to the process in which organisational changes are promoted and actively developed by entrepreneurs who pushed their international agenda (Amin Moghadasi et al. 2017; Mundula and Auci 2019). This paper incorporates the notion of institutional entrepreneurship into the study of internationalisation in start-ups.

Using Tracey et al.'s (2011) theoretical framework of institutional entrepreneurship, this paper intends to incorporate the role of the entrepreneur in institutional change. The framework involves an entrepreneur combining specific aspects of already established institutions in generating organisational change (Burns and

M. A. G. Robles (✉)
Accounting and Finance Department, Tecnológico de Monterrey, Monterrey, Mexico
e-mail: m.gil@tec.mx

V. Jafari-Sadeghi et al. (eds.), *Empirical International Entrepreneurship*,
Contributions to Management Science,
https://doi.org/10.1007/978-3-030-68972-8_10

Scapens 2000). The current literature has used Tracey et al.'s (2011) framework of institutional entrepreneurship to study internationalisation and organisational change, mostly in large enterprises (Greenwood et al. 2011; Pache and Santos 2013). This chapter argues that institutional entrepreneurship permits a rich understanding of how start-ups become international. Moreover, this study uses a qualitative methodology. To be specific, the case studies of two Mexican start-ups that recently became international are analysed (Yin 2017).

The main contribution of this chapter is to incorporate the notions of institutional entrepreneurship in understanding why and how start-ups become international (Jafari Sadeghi et al. 2019). Moreover, by incorporating the role of an entrepreneur in institutional change, this study expands the current understanding of organisational change in start-ups (Cahen 2019). This chapter also contributes to the literature on institutional entrepreneurship by providing a new empirical study in start-ups. Finally, this study of two Mexican start-ups enriches the current understanding of internationalisation in start-ups in the context of an emerging market.

2 Literature Review

Although several studies tried to understand how and why start-ups become international (e.g. Chin et al. 2016; Han 2007),there is still no clear explanation. Based on the current findings of the entrepreneurial literature, there are at least some hints about how and why start-ups become international. For instance, Dana et al. (2009) analysed 47 Singaporean start-ups with the purpose of understanding their reasons for becoming international. Their findings were that most of the studied organisations became international because they identified an opportunity to expand into a new market. Moreover, the authors also found that another significant number of organisations became international due to a negative national context, such as "*domestic market saturation and intense local competition*" (Dana et al. 2009, p. 6). Similarly, Jafari Sadeghi et al. (2020) completed a study on the internationalisation of Italian SMEs. The authors found that in the studied organisations the founder of the organisation played a critical role in the internationalisation of the firm, "*Given the dominant, overarching role of the entrepreneurial founder in nascent ventures, it was expected thatmotivational factors for internationalisation would have a significant impact, which was noted, in the sample of Italian entrepreneurial ventures we studied*" (Jafari Sadeghi et al. 2020, p. 12). Although both studies identified why entrepreneurs decide to become international, it is still not clear *how* they decide to become international, and how they choose the market and strategy to become international (Barney 2014).

To answer the questions of how start-ups become international and what strategy they use to achieve this objective, Fernández and Nieto (2005) analysed Spanish organisations that became international. In their quantitative study, the authors found that the organisations studied focused their efforts on international alliances that would allow them to start operations internationally. The authors concluded that the studied organisations that have alliances "*with another company as a shareholder are more involved in international markets*" (Fernández and Nieto 2005, p: 86). Moreover, in the study of Italian SMEs conducted by Jafari Sadeghi et al. (2020), the authors found that "*international networking capabilities play a critical role in influencing the entrepreneurial venture's opportunity development processes, including internationalisation of operations.*" (p. 12). While the findings from both papers reveal that making alliances with other organisations is a successful strategy for becoming international, it is still not clear how the entrepreneurs in these organisations decide how to complete such alliances.

Moreover, the internationalisation of start-ups in emerging markets has not been studied as intensively as in developed countries. One of the few studies on the internationalisation of start-ups in emerging markets was carried out by Zhu et al. (2006). This research tried to understand how start-ups in emerging markets become international by "*building knowledge and capabilities to enter and compete successfully in international markets*" (Zhu et al. 2006, p. 1). The findings from their study were that start-ups develop new knowledge from other business groups and the government to obtain the required abilities to become international. These findings are in line with Fernández and Nieto (2005), who already stated the importance of alliances with other organisations before internationalisation. The main contribution from Zhu et al.'s (2006) paper is that success in internationalisation is not a matter of completing the alliance or having a relationship with government organisations but on the ability of the organisation to learn from such alliances and relationships. However, the paper is still not clear on how the organisations in developing countries can learn from these alliances and relationships. Similarly, Jafari Sadeghi et al. (2019) studied the internationalisation of SMEs in Italy and Iran. The authors found that SMEs "*need to get along with various exporting challenges, which vary according to the country from which the SME operates*" (Jafari Sadeghi et al. 2019, p. 12). They concluded that in developing economies, SMEs tend to face more internal challenges, while in developed economies the organisations confront external problems. The study of Jafari Sadeghi et al. (2019) underpins the assumption that in the case of Mexican start-ups, the major challenges during internationalisation are internal.

A more recent study on the internationalisation of start-ups points out that there are specific internal and external factors that affect how an organisation sets its internationalisation strategy (Lindsay et al. 2017). Apart from these internal and external factors, the authors also noted that there are host and home institutions that affect how the organisation becomes international. The contribution of this study highlights the relationship between the stated factors and institutions with the organisation's entry mode: "*Our study reveals a novel perspective on SMEs' access to different sources of resources (external vs. internal), and exposure to, and use of, institutions (host vs. home, respectively) relating to their foreign market entry mode*" (Lindsay et al. 2017, p. 12). Similarly, Jeong et al. (2017) studied the relationship between "*network and institutional perspectives, [to] explore patterns of network development and cultivation in SMEs during the internationalisation process*" (Jeong et al. 2017, p. 323).

As the most recent literature focuses more on the importance of institutions and relationships during the internationalisation process of start-ups, it becomes relevant to the role of the entrepreneur in the development of such institutions and relationships (Cahen 2019; Mokhtarzadeh et al. 2020; Neubert 2018). Oviatt and McDougall (2005) highlighted the role of entrepreneurs and how they affect the organisation as it faces internationalisation. The authors stated that to understand internationalisation, it is vital to "*illustrate transnational entrepreneurs' unique positioning and the means by which they structure their environment*" (Oviatt and McDougall 2005, p. 1094). As it becomes evident that the way in which the entrepreneur envisions the world and how internationalisation affects how the organisation becomes international, institutional entrepreneurship becomes an interesting framework to explain how this phenomenon occurs (Rezaei et al. 2020).

As previously stated, institutions and relationships among start-ups are critical when completing their internationalisation process(Etemad et al. 2001). Moreover, the role played by entrepreneurs in the organisations is of relevant interest in understanding why and how start-ups internationalise(Glavas et al. 2014). Due to the aforementioned, institutional entrepreneurship seems to provide a reasonable theoretical framework to study the internationalisation of start-ups.

Institutional entrepreneurship is defined as "*the activities of actors who have an interest in particular institutional arrangements and who leverage resources to create new institutions or to transform existing ones*" (Maguire et al. 2004, p. 657). Moreover, Mundula and Auci (2019) described an institutional entrepreneur as "*an individual who puts an effort into establishing and reorganising property rights and other institutional structures to exploit economic opportunities that are not feasible within the institutional status quo*" (p. 59). Thus, institutional entrepreneurship focuses on understanding how an individual seeks to transform or create institutions in an organisation to impose its agenda.

In the case of the internationalisation of start-ups, institutional entrepreneurship is relevant for at least two reasons. Firstly, institutional entrepreneurship focuses on how the individual envisions the world, its values, and objectives (Terjesen and Elam 2009). This is relevant, as the entrepreneurship literature has already stated that start-ups become international mostly to seek out new opportunities or as a reaction to negative contexts in the local environment (Neubert 2018). By understanding how the entrepreneur envisions the world, it is possible to understand why and how the organisation identifies opportunities abroad or threats in the local market. Secondly, institutional entrepreneurship aims to explain how institutions are formed and transformed in the organisation (Leca and Naccache 2006). This is critical when analysing how entrepreneurs can communicate their ideas and convince the whole organisation to work towards their goal.

To make sense of the empirical findings, this chapter uses the institutional entrepreneurship framework elaborated by Tracey et al. (2011). This framework permits clear analysis of the processes that allow the entrepreneur to create and transform the institutions in the organisation to make it international. The framework considers a multilevel analysis which includes the micro, meso, and macro levels.

With regards to the micro-level, Tracey et al. (2011) established the urge to analyse problem framing and counterfactual thinking. Problem framing relates to the issues that the entrepreneur wants to tackle, and counterfactual thinking are the ideas that underpin the actions taken by the entrepreneur. Regarding the meso level, the framework states the need to build and theorise the organisational template. These two concepts clarify the structure of the organisation. By building the organisational template it is possible to identify the expected actions in the organisation. Theorising the organisational template refers to the values that the organisation has. Finally, the macro-level analysis contemplates connecting with macro-level discourse and aligning this with highly legitimate actors. These two concepts relate to how the entrepreneur legitimates the new or transformed institutions based on external actors.

3 Methodology

To understand how and why start-ups become international, this chapter uses a qualitative methodology (Ahrens and Chapman 2006). To be specific, the chapter uses a comparative case study of two start-up firms based in Mexico (Yin 2017). One of the start-up firms was founded in 2017 and specialises in the creation of audio-visual content. The other start-up firm was founded in 2018 and specialises in designing and installing technology systems in buildings and houses. Both organisations focused on the national market during their first year of existence. During the second year, both organisations started a transformation to become international. The focus of this chapter is to understand this process of change through the lens of institutional entrepreneurship (Parker 2012).

The data collection consisted of semi-structured interviews of individuals in the organisation, collection of private and public documents, and visits to the headquarters of the organisation (Barriball and While 1994). The data collection period took place between February and July 2020. The owners of both start-up organisations agreed to participate in the research project but demanded that their names, the names of the organisations, and any relevant information which would reveal their identities, remain anonymous (Jordan 2014). They argued that due to the high competitiveness in their industries, they prefer not to reveal their managerial processes and experiences. Thus, all the names and relevant data in this chapter have been anonymised.

A total of 26 semi-structured interviews were conducted during the data collection period of this research; 13 semi-structured interviews with each organisation. The interviews were conducted with the two founders (CEOs), senior managers, mid-tier managers, and a few employees. All the interviews were conducted, recorded, and transcribed in Spanish (Halcomb and Davidson 2006). Due to the COVID-19 outbreak, 22 of the 26 interviews were conducted via a phone or Skype call. Once the interviews were transcribed, the researcher translated the transcripts into English before the data analysis period (Chen and Boore 2010). In addition to the interviews, the collected documents were stored on a private hard drive, which the researcher accessed when needed. In total, 35 private documents were collected. The private documents consist of minutes from meetings and emails between senior managers. Finally, the researcher was able to complete two visits to each of the headquarters of the organisations before the COVID-19 emergency that started in February. During the visits, the researcher took notes about his observations. Also, during these visits, the researcher was able to complete four interviews, two with each organisation.

The data analysis period took place between July and October 2020. During the data analysis period, key actors in both organisations were contacted briefly by the researcher to clarify specific points in the case studies (Miles and Huberman 1994). The data analysis was initiated with a timeline of events; focusing on the events that took place to achieve the internationalisation of both start-ups. The key events from the timeline were later analysed using the different levels from the institutional entrepreneurship framework; more specifically, the micro, meso, and macro levels. Later, the researcher prepared a table with the representative data for each of the analysed elements (Ritchie and Spencer 2002). The representative data are quotations from the interviews or excerpts from private documents.

4 Case Study 1: Smart Tech Inc

Smart Tech Inc (hereafter SMI) is a start-up based in Mexico. The organisation was founded in 2017. The founder of the firm is an electrical engineer with 20 years of experience in the industry. SMI specialises in designing and installing technology systems in houses and buildings. Examples of their services are closed-circuit televisions, air conditioning systems, and entertainment installations. According to the founder and CEO, the greatest challenge of the firm is "*to design a new system that is specifically tailored to the needs of our client*" (CEO, Interview). The CEO of the firm is the owner of 90% of the total shares. The other 10% is equally divided between the CFO and COO. The 2019 sales accounted for 2,500,000 USD of which 65% were from international sales. The firm has operations in the USA, Canada, Colombia, and Panama.

During the first year of operations, the company focused on the local market. The CEO explained that before the company was founded, he worked for 17 years at larger American firms that delivered the same services. The CEO explained: "*I worked for more than 17 years in other firms, mostly American, that is where I learned a lot about this industry*" (CEO, Interview). He added that around 2016, one local client asked him if he could do a large project on his own. The CEO explained that the client suggested that he leave the American company and start working on this project on his own. He decided to invite a few friends of his who worked at the American company, including the one who is currently COO at SMI. The COO explained during an interview, "*I was invited by [the CEO] to be part of this new firm, I decided to join becauseI wouldbe a partner and senior manager in this new organisation*" (COO, Interview).

During the first year of existence, STI did relatively well financially. The firm completed two more large projects during their first year which allowed them to become financially stable. However, by the end of 2017, the first client of STI approached the CEO and proposed that he work on a new project in the USA. The CEO explained to the client about the challenges of working abroad. Nevertheless, the client suggested that if the CEO started the new project, he would introduce him to key companies in the USA that could help him to overcome any legal and operational challenges. Although the CEO was certain that the project was a good idea, he had to convince the other senior managers. The CEO explained during an interview:

> *Accepting the project abroad was a good idea because we had a lot of support from the client. The client was willing to introduce us to a full network of companies that would allow us to complete the project. However, the other senior managers were not sure about the decision. And if you ask me about other managers, I might say they were not happy either.* (CEO, Interview)

As stated by the CEO, the initial steps to becoming international had two challenges. Firstly, other senior managers were not entirely convinced about the international project. Secondly, there was not a clear strategy on how to become international. To overcome these two challenges, the CEO decided to set an internationalisation strategy based mainly on networking and alliances. Furthermore, the CEO also stated that he intended to familiarise organisational members with the idea of becoming international. The CFO stated during an interview:

> *I think that [the CEO] had a clear idea about internationalisation. And when he found out that we were not that sure about the idea, he decided to create a strategy that would include everyone in the organisation. I mean, instead of saying something like 'leave if you don't like it' he decided to include us.* (CFO, Interview)

The CEO stated that including everyone in the conversation was a key objective of his plan to become international. Moreover, the strategy to become international was based on developing alliances and working together with experienced organisations. By doing this, the CEO intended to convince others that the internationalisation plan was possible and not as complicated as it seemed. The project manager explained during an interview:

> *[The CEO] talked directly with us about the possibility of starting a project in the United States. However, he complimented that comment with a lot of good insights about his plan. Also, he talked a lot about alliances and friends that he had, who would help us with legal stuff.* (Project Leader, Interview)

Once that it was clear that convincing others and establishing a clear internationalisation strategy was the path to take, the CEO decided to take action towards achieving his objectives.

To include more organisational individuals into the internationalisation plan, the CEO decided to bring the topic into day to day conversations. Specifically, the CEO began to talk about internationalisation opportunities and the benefits of foreign markets during meetings with managers. When the researcher analysed the minutes from meetings from 2017, there was not a single mention of international opportunities. However, the minutes from 2018 showed an intensive focus on internationalisation. By doing this, the topic of internationalisation became a common topic for everyone in the organisation. One of the assistant managers explained during an interview:

> *For us, it became normal to talk about becoming international. We talked a lot about the USA and then South America. But if I think about it, I did not realise when we started to talk about international projects, it just happened, and everyone was on the same topic.* (Assistant Manager, Interview)

To establish a clearer strategy towards becoming international, the CEO shared more detailed data about possible alliances with experienced and foreign organisations. The CEO explained that when he first talked with his colleagues about the internationalisation idea, he observed some tension; he believed that they were scared about starting a business in an unknown market. Thus, the best way to reduce uncertainty was by showing the capability of making alliances. The human resources manager explained during an interview:

> *One day [the CEO] explained to me that there was a company in the USA who would hire all the employees required to work in the American project. He mentioned that we would not be responsible for hiring the employees. We would only have to negotiate the price and characteristics that we required for the project [...] To be honest, that conversation reduced a lot of the stress that I had about becoming international.* (Human Resource Manager, Interview)

Once the company completed their first international project in the USA, senior managers interpreted it as a huge success. Now the organisation was open to working internationally and the topic became popular in the organisation. The CEO then decided to legitimise the idea of internationalisation by completing national and international recognition.

After the company had completed the first international project in the USA at the end of 2018, the CEO decided to become even more international. The CEO explained that the market in Mexico was very competitive and thus had a plan to continue the international activity of the firm. According to the COO, completing international projects for the firm was not that complicated since the firm did not have to move physically to other countries. He explained that it was possible to hire local employees, and indeed, with the help of their allied companies, it became a relatively simple task. After the project in the USA, the company found an opportunity to work with the same client, now in Canada.

When the project in Canada started, the CEO believed that it was the right moment to attain some international certificates that would allow the company to acquire more international clients. Moreover, the CEO claimed that getting such certificates would make everyone in the organisation envision the firm as international. This reasoning was observed when other members of the organisation were interviewed. For instance, one salesperson explained during an interview:

[STI] is a very international firm. We have a lot of revenue coming from projects abroad. Moreover, we have some international certificates relevant in the industry, which allow us to enter easily into new foreign markets. (Salesperson, Interview)

Senior managers also saw the certificates as an important part of the internationalisation strategy. The COO explained during an interview:

"*When we got some international certificates, it was clear that we were capable of competing internationally*" (COO, Interview). When asked if before the certificates he did not think that the firm was capable of internationalisation, the COO answered: "*To be honest, I was never entirely sure until we were certified.*" (COO, Interview)

In the end, the CEO continued pushing the agenda of internationalisation. By 2020, the firm had completed at least one project in each of these countries: the USA, Canada, Colombia, and Panama. The CEO explained that it was always through alliances with foreign organisations that the firm was capable of completing the projects. Finally, he explained that the word "international" became very common within the organisation.

5 Case Study 2: Visuals Inc

Visuals Inc (VI) is a Mexican start-up founded in 2018. The firm specialises in the production of audio-visual content. In general terms, the organisation provides two services. Firstly, the firm produces videos, 2D and 3D animation, post-production, and after-effects. Most of their clients for these services are TV and cinema producers, videogame developers, and other firms in general that produce audio-visual content mostly for marketing objectives. Secondly, the organisation provides video mapping services. This service consists of a projection of video and sound on a specific surface. By using specialised software and hardware, the video and audio projection provides the audience with a full spectacle of music and visuals. According to the CEO, the organisation "*uses the most advanced technologies to deliver the greatest experience to the user*" (CEO, Interview). The CEO is the owner of 80% of the shares of the firm. The other 20% is divided equally between the head of human resources and the project manager, who is also the wife of the CEO.

The organisation started as a business delivering video mapping services to local clients. During the first semester, 95% of the revenue came from video mapping services and 100% of that revenue was from national clients. However, during the second semester of 2018, the firm began to sell digital services, such as after-effects and post-production of audio-visual content. It is also during this period that the firm began to sell internationally. According to the project manager, "*the digital services allowed us to sell internationally quickly and easily*" (Project Manager, Interview). During 2019, the internationalisation of the firm became more intensive. By the end of the year, the firm was also delivering video mapping services in the USA, and 60% of the revenue came from abroad.

The CEO stated that the internationalisation process in the organisation was led "*by a pursuit of clients who are willing to pay more for better quality*"(CEO, Interview). The CEO explained that the first steps into internationalisation came from a suggestion from a client based in Monterrey, a city in the north of Mexico, near the border to the USA. According to the CEO, this client introduced him to an American client who was looking for digital services, such as after-effects and post-production of a video. At that time, the company focused only on video mapping, so delivering these digital services was a new challenge. The CEO then explained that the internationalisation strategy focused on transforming the organisation to deliver digital services to an American client. The CEO explained:

> *When this [internationalisation process] started, the most pressing challenge was to be able to deliver digital services and deliver them to an international client. At that moment, that seemed like a huge challenge, because we had to include new people in the organisation and reframe a lot of the processes that we had in the firm.* (CEO, Interview)

The CEO explained that the internationalisation process initially had two main challenges. Firstly, the firm had to transform to be able to deliver more post-production and after-effects services. This became necessary because previously the firm had only focused on video mapping. One of the project leaders explained during an interview that the expertise of the firm was "*video mapping and events, not postproduction services*" (Project Manager 1, Interview). Moreover, the accountant explained during an interview, that all the assets that the company had by mid-2018 were used for video mapping. The accountant stated during the interview that "*the firm did not have the required software for post-production and aftereffects*" (Accountant, Interview). When the CEO was questioned about how these challenges were overcome, he explained:

> *There were two actions that took place in the organisation. One was to invest in the technical requirements to deliver digital services. We used all the revenue from our past events and at the same time, we got a bank loan. With that money, we were able to buy computers and software. Also, we hired new employees with the required skills. The interesting point is that we realised that we could hire only a couple of full-time employees to lead the project and then hire more freelancers to finish the job.* (CEO, Interview)

Secondly, the CEO explained that apart from being ready to provide customers with digital services, the firm had to envision itself as an international organisation. According to the head of human resources, who is also a partner in the firm, the organisational individuals who were part of the organisation when it was founded, "envisioned the firm as a local organisation" (Head of Human Resources, Interview). Moreover, during an interview with a 2D artist, he explained that in early 2018 there were "*no signs of internationalisation*" (2D Artist, Interview).

Once the CEO had determined that the two main challenges of internationalisation were acquiring the technical capabilities to deliver digital services and envisioning the organisation as an international firm, he proposed an action plan to senior managers. Firstly, the CEO explained that it was necessary to elaborate a strategy to acquire the hardware, software, and human talent required to deliver digital services. He also added the urgency to complete these objectives. In a minute from a meeting collected during this research, it can be read that the CEO stated that the firm had a deadline to be ready to deliver digital services by November 2018 (June 2018). The head of human resources explained during an interview:

> *Although we were conscious of the business opportunity of delivering digital services abroad, we were not sure that we could make it on time, or to be honest, it was not even clear if we could make it at all. There were a lot of things that we had to overcome, and it seemed very difficult.* (Head of Human Resources, Interview)

The CEO explained that the strategy was based on hiring a couple of employees with the correct expertise, acquiring the necessary hardware and software, and forming alliances with lawyers and other firms abroad who would facilitate the transactions. The CEO clarified that two employees were hired based on the recommendation from a client. These two employees became project leaders and they created an investment plan on the required software and hardware. Then, using the earnings from their previous projects and getting a bank loan, the firm was able to acquire the list of software and hardware. At the same time, the head of human resources made the contracts with the freelancers who would work during the projects with the companies abroad. Finally, the CEO contacted a few firms abroad who would take care of all the legal details before signing the contract with the international client. The lawyer of the firm explained during an interview:

> *The whole strategy to provide digital services was based on transforming the organisation and having the correct alliances. I was mostly worried about the legal terms of the contracts in the USA, but one of our clients gave us a recommendation for a firm. That firm, in the end, became a key asset in setting the contracts with all of our clients abroad.* (Lawyer, Interview)

In regard to how the firm envisioned itself as an international organisation, there were at least two key actions that took place during the second semester of 2018. Firstly, the CEO explained that he communicated to senior managers all the opportunities that the firm had abroad. Moreover, he also stated that financially, the firm would benefit from foreign clients as the prices for the provided services could be higher than in Mexico. The manager of the firm stated during an interview:

> *It became evident that internationalisation was the correct path for the firm. There were a lot of potential clients and they would pay in dollars or euros, which makes it a lot when you convert them into Mexican pesos.* (Manager, Interview)

The second action, that according to the CEO was very important during the internationalisation process, was that he invited organisational members to travel with him abroad whenever it was possible. The CEO explained that when he was closing the deals with the foreign client, he had to travel to the USA. Thus, he invited one member of the organisation to travel with him to show him a "*new world of possibilities*" (CEO, Interview). The CEO explained that these trips were seen as a work benefit and performance compensation. He selected the best employees and invited them on the trip. The CEO explained that the trip had a positive effect on the organisational members and when they came back, they had a great attitude towards internationalisation. The head of art was one of the first members of the organisation who completed a trip to the USA. He explained during an interview:

> *Completing the trip had a significant positive effect on how I envisioned internationalisation. I had the chance of meeting the clients and relied on my own experience of negotiating the terms of the contract. In the end, I came back with a very good understanding of being international.* (Head of Art, Interview)

By the end of 2019, the company had clients from the USA, Canada, Spain, and Argentina. The organisation followed a similar strategy as mentioned earlier. The CEO created alliances with key firms abroad who assisted in setting the details of the contracts with each client. Furthermore, during November 2019, the company did its first video mapping show in the USA. The CEO explained that by the end of 2019, the organisation was seen as an international start-up.

The CEO explained that the foreign clients were satisfied with the projects and suggested submitting some of these projects to an international conference of the video visual industry taking place in California. The CEO agreed and stated during an interview that participating in such a conference would allow the organisation to acquire more clients and to convince everyone that they were international. The CEO stated:

> *Participating in an international conference was a good opportunity to acquire new clients. But also, it would send a message to everyone inside and outside of the firm. The message was that we are different from local competitors because we are international.* (CEO, Interview)

Apart from international conferences, the firm also completed a certification process with a national association of audio-visual organisations. The organisation is well known in Mexico and Latin America. One of the project leaders explained that by having such a certificate, the firm was able to do business in Argentina relatively easily. The project manager explained during an interview:

> *Completing it [the certificate] allowed the firm to be more known, not only in Mexico but also in Latin America. We believe that by being part of a larger association it is possible to portray a better image as an international firm.* (Project Leader, Interview)

The company continued with the trend of becoming international. However, due to the COVID-19 international emergency, some projects were paused, especially the ones related to video mapping. The company continued to expand its network of clients with digital services, such as post-production, after-effects, and digital animation.

6 Discussion

The purpose of this research is to understand why and how start-ups become international. As stated earlier in this chapter, it is assumed that institutional entrepreneurship might explain the studied process. Institutional entrepreneurship can explain how the owner of a start-up can take action to institutionalise the idea of becoming international until the point that it becomes a reality (Leca and Naccache 2006). This chapter has two main theoretical contributions. Firstly, through the analysis of a comparative case study of two start-ups that experienced an internationalisation process, this research concludes that the process occurs at three levels: micro, meso, and macro (Tracey et al. 2011). Secondly, there is enough evidence to conclude that the contextual factors of a developing economy make it easier for organisations to envision themselves as local companies (Barney 2014; Dana et al. 2009). Thus, the role of the institutional entrepreneur becomes even more important as one of his or her main tasks is to change the vision of the organisation into a more international version of itself.

In both organisations, the micro-institutional level was key to the internationalisation of the firm. Firstly, framing the problem or challenge faced by the firm in the internationalisation process allowed the owners to plan a specific strategy that would tackle the identified issues. Interestingly, in both cases, one of the problems or challenges identified was the necessity of envisioning the organisation as an international firm. This issue has been highlighted by other authors who explain that, particularly in Latin America, SMEs and start-ups tend to envision themselves as local organisations. Secondly, counterfactual thinking was relevant during the process of designing the strategy to tackle the previously identified issues. In both cases, the CEOs created a plan to convince other institutional members that the idea of internationalisation was possible by taking actions that were not previously considered. In both cases, the CEOs argued that alliances with a foreign organisation and key individuals would pave the way into internationalisation.

In regard to the meso-institutional work, both organisations carried out alliances with key actors that helped them during the internationalisation process. The inclusion of these actors reorganised the template of how the firm looked before and after internationalisation. In the case of SMI, lawyers and human resource firms were critical to the internationalisation process. Moreover, in the case of VI, the hired project leaders and freelancers allowed the firm to provide foreign clients with digital services.

Both organisations carried out activities related to the macro-institutional level. Both organisations legitimised their internationalisation by attending international conferences and acquiring certificates recognised in their industries. With the activities at the macro level, the organisations were envisioned as international by their members and by outsiders. These activities allowed the organisations to facilitate negotiations with new clients or to gain alliances with new key partners.

Regarding the context of a developing economy, there is enough evidence from both cases to state that both organisations were initially seen as local companies (Gil and Klarner 2020). However, the CEOs from both firms focused on changing that perception, internally and externally. Moreover, the testimonies from organisational individuals are in line with this conclusion, as these individuals referred to a change in the way in which they envisioned the organisation from a local firm to an international one. Thus, the role of the institutional entrepreneur in transforming the international perspective in an organisation becomes even more important in an emerging economy context.

7 Conclusion

After the in-depth analysis performed on both organisations, there is enough evidence to conclude that, through the lens of institutional entrepreneurship, it is possible to explain how and why start-ups become international. Moreover, the developing economy context is also relevant through the process of internationalisation. This chapter concludes by stating that the internationalisation process can be analysed through the three levels explained in the case study.

Some of the limitations of this chapter are the small number of physical visits to the companies by the researcher due to the COVID-19 emergency, and the change in the overall economic context that occurred due to the same global threat. In regard to the number of visits to the companies, the original plan included at least six visits per company and the possibility of being present during senior management meetings. However, it was not possible due to the lockdown. Moreover, both firms reduced their international operations drastically due to travel restrictions. This also affected the development of the cases as 2020 was planned as a year of international expansion by both companies.

This chapter should inspire future research on the topics of institutional entrepreneurship and start-up internationalisation. For instance, the key elements found from the case studies can be conceptualised as numerical variables that can be tested in a quantitative study. Variables such as international alliances, being envisioned as an international organisation, and the role of external legitimation like certificates and associations. Moreover, it would be interesting to replicate this study in another developing economy, such as a southern Asian country, to analyse if there are significant differences in how start-ups become international.

References

Ahrens T, Chapman CS (2006) Doing qualitative field research in management accounting: positioning data to contribute to theory. *Handbooks Manag Account Res 1*:299–318

Amin Moghadasi M, Derakhshandeh B, Ferdosi M, Jafari Sadeghi V (2017) Organizational conformity as an entrepreneurial response to the changes in internationalization process: a study of IT-oriented firms in Saveh. World J Account Fin Eng 1(1):53–64

Barney JB (2014) *Gaining and sustaining competitive advantage*. Pearson Higher Education, United States

Barriball KL, While A (1994) Collecting data using a semi-structured interview: a discussion paper. *J Adv Nurs 19*(2):328–335

Burns J, Scapens RW (2000) Conceptualizing management accounting change: an institutional framework. *Manag Account Res 11*(1):3–25

Cahen FR (2019) Internationalization of Brazilian high-tech startups. In: Startups and innovation ecosystems in emerging markets. Palgrave Macmillan, Cham, pp 37–53

Chen HY, Boore JR (2010) Translation and back-translation in qualitative nursing research: methodological review. *J Clin Nurs 19*(1–2):234–239

Chin T, Liu RH, Yang X (2016) 'Reverse internationalization' in Chinese firms: a study of how global startup OEMs seek to compete domestically. *Asia Pac Bus Rev* 22(2):201–219

Dana LP (2017) International entrepreneurship research: how it evolved and directions for the future. *Int J Entrep Small Bus 30*(4):477–489

Dana LP, Hamilton RT, Wick K (2009) Deciding to export: An exploratory study of Singaporean entrepreneurs. *J Int Entrep 7*(2):79–87

Etemad H, Wright RW, Dana LP (2001) Symbiotic international business networks: collaboration between small and large firms. *Thunderbird Int Bus Rev 43*(4):481–499

Fernández Z, Nieto MJ (2005) Internationalization strategy of small and medium-sized family businesses: some influential factors. *Family Bus Rev 18*(1):77–89

Gil M, Klarner H (2020) The impact of an incubation process on management control systems of start-ups. Business practices, growth and economic policies in emerging markets

Glavas C, Pike S, Mathews S (2014) Internet-enabled tourism entrepreneurs. International entrepreneurial values elicited through repertory test and laddering analysis. *Int J Tour Res 16* (1):44–55

Greenwood R, Raynard M, Kodeih F, Micelotta ER, Lounsbury M (2011) Institutional complexity and organizational responses. *Acad Manag Annals 5*(1):317–371

Halcomb EJ, Davidson PM (2006) Is verbatim transcription of interview data always necessary? *Appl Nurs Res 19*(1):38–42

Han M (2006) Developing social capital to achieve superior internationalization: a conceptual model. *J Int Entrep 4*(2–3):99–112

Han M (2007) Achieving superior internationalization through strategic ambidexterity. *J Enterp Cult 15*(1):43–77

Hitt MA, Dacin MT, Levitas E, Arregle JL, Borza A (2000) Partner selection in emerging and developed market contexts: resource-based and organizational learning perspectives. *Acad Manage J 43*(3):449–467

Jafari Sadeghi V, Nkongolo-Bakenda JM, Anderson RB, Dana LP (2019) An institution-based view of international entrepreneurship: a comparison of context-based and universal determinants in developing and economically advanced countries. *Int Bus Rev 28*(6):101588

Jafari Sadeghi V, Dutta DK, Ferraris A, Del Giudice M (2020) Internationalisation business processes in an under-supported policy contexts: evidence from Italian SMEs. *Bus Process Manag J* 26(5)

Jeong SW, Jin B, Chung JE, Yang H (2017) Network evolution and cultivation patterns during the internationalization process: case analyses from Korean SMEs. *Asian Bus Manag 16* (4–5):323–351

Jordan SR (2014) Research integrity, image manipulation, and anonymizing photographs in visual social science research. *Int J Soc Res Methodol 17*(4):441–454

Leca B, Naccache P (2006) A critical realist approach to institutional entrepreneurship. *Organization 13*(5):627–651

Lindsay V, Rod M, Ashill N (2017) Institutional and resource configurations associated with different SME foreign market entry modes. *Ind Mark Manag 66*:130–144

Maguire S, Hardy C, Lawrence TB (2004) Institutional entrepreneurship in emerging fields: HIV/AIDS treatment advocacy in Canada. Acad Manag J 47(5):657–679

Miles MB, Huberman AM (1994) Qualitative data analysis: an expanded sourcebook. Sage

Mokhtarzadeh NG, Mahdiraji HA, Jafarpanah I, Jafari-Sadeghi V, Cardinali S (2020) Investigating the impact of networking capability on firm innovation performance: using the resource-action-performance framework. *J Intellect Cap* 21(6)

Mundula L, Auci S (2019) Institutional entrepreneurship, trust, and regulatory capture in the digital economy. In: *Handbook of research on entrepreneurship and marketing for global reach in the digital economy*. IGI Global, pp 58–79

Muralidharan E, Pathak S (2017) Informal institutions and international entrepreneurship. *Int Bus Rev 26*(2):288–302

Neubert M (2017) Lean Internationalization: how to globalize early and fast in a small economy. *Technol Innov Manag Rev 7*(5)

Neubert M (2018) The impact of digitalization on the speed of internationalization of lean global startups. *Technol Innov Manag Rev 8*(5)
Oviatt BM, McDougall PP (2005) Defining international entrepreneurship and modeling the speed of internationalization. *Entrep Theory Pract 29*(5):537–553
Pache AC, Santos F (2013) Inside the hybrid organization: selective coupling as a response to competing institutional logics. *Acad Manage J 56*(4):972–1001
Parker LD (2012) Qualitative management accounting research: assessing deliverables and relevance. *Crit Perspect Account 23*(1):54–70
Rezaei M, Jafari-Sadeghi V, Bresciani S (2020) What drives the process of knowledge management in a cross-cultural setting. *Eur Bus Rev* 32(3)
Ritchie J, Spencer L (2002) Qualitative data analysis for applied policy research. *Qual Res Comp 573*(2002):305–329
Terjesen S, Elam A (2009) Transnational entrepreneurs' venture internationalization strategies: a practice theory approach. *Entrep Theory Pract 33*(5):1093–1120
Tracey P, Phillips N, Jarvis O (2011) Bridging institutional entrepreneurship and the creation of new organizational forms: a multilevel model. *Organ Sci 22*(1):60–80
Yin RK (2017) *Case study research and applications: design and methods*. Sage Publications
Zhu H, Hitt MA, Tihanyi L (2006) The internationalization of SMES in emerging economies: institutional embeddedness and absorptive capacities. *J Small Bus Strateg 17*(2):1–26

Miguel Angel Gil Robles received the B.A. degree in accounting and finance and the M.A. degree in finance from Tecnologico de Monterrey, Mexico, and the PhD degree in accounting and finance from the University of Manchester, UK. He is currently a Professor of accounting and finance with Tecnologico de Monterrey. His research interests focus on management accounting, organisational learning, and management control systems in hi-tech industries.

Always Trusts, Always Hopes, Always Perseveres? Comparative Discourse Analysis of the Perception of International Entrepreneurship During Pandemic

Lasse Torkkeli, Maria Ivanova-Gongne, Anna Vuorio, and Ignat Kulkov

1 Introduction

International entrepreneurship (IE), as defined by McDougall and Oviatt (2000), is *"...a combination of innovative, proactive and risk-seeking behaviour that crosses national borders and is intended to create value in organisations."* A later definition by Oviatt and McDougall (2005, p. 540) considers IE as *"the discovery, enactment, evaluation and exploitation of opportunities—across national borders—to create future goods and services."* Since then, the IE domain has been found *"diverse but growing incoherence"* (Jones et al. 2011), with review studies on the field developing integrative IE frameworks (e.g., Peiris et al. 2012), meta-analyses of IE-performance relationships (Schwens et al. 2018) and extensive reviews of IE (Dana 2017; Paul and Rosado-Serrano 2019). IE is indeed a proper field of research (Servantie et al. 2016), yet there are several areas where IE can still benefit from, both thematically and (and especially) methodologically.

First, thematically, Jones et al. (2011) called for more IE studies where the empirical context provides opportunities for applying proper methods for conducting comparative studies. Indeed, the main body of research in IE has tended to be

L. Torkkeli (✉)
Turku School of Business, University of Turku, Turku, Finland

School of Business and Management, LUT University, Lappeenranta, Finland
e-mail: Lasse.Torkkeli@lut.fi

M. Ivanova-Gongne · I. Kulkov
Åbo Akademi, Turku, Finland
e-mail: mivanova@abo.fi; Ignat.Kulkov@abo.fi

A. Vuorio
School of Business and Management, LUT University, Lappeenranta, Finland
e-mail: Anna.Vuorio@lut.fi

V. Jafari-Sadeghi et al. (eds.), *Empirical International Entrepreneurship*, Contributions to Management Science,
https://doi.org/10.1007/978-3-030-68972-8_11

dominated by single home country contexts. However, as many concepts relevant for international business and entrepreneurship can be very context-dependent (e.g., networking; see Ivanova-Gongne and Torkkeli 2018), much remains to be done in assessing central IE phenomena cross-contextually through comparative studies.

Second, methodologically, IE research has until recently consisted mainly of case-based qualitative and cross-sectional quantitative studies. However, more methodological plurality in qualitative methods is encouraged for both entrepreneurship (van Burg et al. 2020) and international business (e.g., Buckley 2009) domains. We posit that IE, lying at the intersection of these two domains, can thus also benefit from added methodological plurality, as recent studies employing less-used methods such as biographical data (Fillis 2007) or other historical methods (Colli et al. 2013). Extant research (Dana and Dana 2005) has pointed out that surveys or interviews are insufficient to gain a holistic understanding of the entrepreneurial process unless they are complemented with empirics accounting for the context of entrepreneurial environment as well (Dana and Dana 2005). However, while there is ample discussion in the media globally about international entrepreneurship, to our knowledge no studies yet exist that would employ content or discursive analysis as an empirical lens to explain IE behaviour in a particular country, to begin with. Such an approach has been recommended to be applied especially for comparative IE studies (Terjesen et al. 2016). However, to our knowledge, there still are no studies that would apply discourse analysis and *compare* across different countries. This comparative, methodologically innovative chapter seeks to respond to these omissions in the IE domain of research.

To do so now is particularly timely since, at the time of this writing in early 2020, the COVID-19 pandemic has closed down businesses and entire societies worldwide, impacting the public discussion on IE across countries, and how international entrepreneurs themselves experience that discussion. Entrepreneurs who manage to retain their entrepreneurial self-efficacy and "stay the course" even under highly turbulent developments in their environment (e.g. Bullough et al. 2014) can be characterised as resilient. However, the ways in which entrepreneurs respond to crises can come to depend on a variety of factors (Doern et al. 2019). Thus, it is important to assess the nature and change of public discourse around IE, and the perception of that discourse among international entrepreneurs, now that the IE playing field has suddenly become so challenging for entrepreneurs to engage in.

The research questions we concentrate on in this study therefore are:

- *How have media discourses on IE been changed due to the COVID-19 pandemic?*
- *How do international entrepreneurs themselves experience them?*

We employ discourse analysis (cf. Vaara and Tienari 2002; Vaara and Tienari 2004) to illustrate how the media discussion around IE is during the COVID-19 pandemic, and by employing a comparative study setting across the Finnish and Russian contexts, we respond to both types of research gaps in IE mentioned above methodologically. In addition to analysing the media texts, we supplement the empirical data with interviews from international entrepreneurs from both countries.

Thus, the present study provides a thematically timely and methodologically novel contribution to the IE domain of research.

The study continues as follows: Next, we present a concise review of the literature linking IE to the present COVID-19 pandemic. That is followed by describing the applied research methodology, after which we outline the findings of our analysis. The study concludes with discussing their merits, limitations, and potential avenues for future research.

2 COVID-19 and International Entrepreneurship

Starting in late 2019, the COVID-19 pandemic has been having a major stifling impact on international business and entrepreneurship (Caligiuri et al. 2020) worldwide. For instance in Finland, a country with the small domestic market and a high internationalisation-oriented industry structure—and thus home to a substantial body of extant IE body of research (Nummela and Paavilainen-Mäntymäki 2014; Servantie et al. 2016)—the GDP is expected to drop up to 5% due to the coronavirus pandemic (ETLA 2020), and the onset of the pandemic restrictions in Finland is already resulting in more bankruptcies among Finnish enterprises than in other Nordic countries (Talouselämä 2020). Internationally operating Finnish enterprises, for instance, those operating in China, are particularly hard-hit due to the pandemic (Perälä 2020). The situation is in many ways unique and dwarfs other global developments that have in recent years impacted international business and IE; For instance, upon the decision, Brexit was already expected to have a major impact on IE through declining new venture start-ups and their funding (Cumming and Zahra 2016), and the COVID-19 pandemic is very likely to easily dwarf the implications of Brexit for international entrepreneurs worldwide.

Central to the IE domain have since its inception been international new ventures (INVs), rapidly internationalising young enterprises. The global changes enabling the foundation and success of an increasing number of international new ventures included the increasing flow of information across markets, lowering costs of international travel and communication; increasing amount of international experience possessed be managers; and firms becoming increasingly skilled at employing alternative governance mechanisms should as network relationships (Autio 2005; Zahra 2005). In the coronavirus pandemic, it is, however, possible that the flow of information from foreign markets may slow down; the costs for international travel and communication may again increase; the growth of managers' accumulation of international experience may be constrained due to travel restrictions, and firms skills at employing their governance mechanisms such as international networks will be tested. It is, therefore, a relevant question to consider if the COVID-19 pandemic will slow down IE short term only, or on a longer-term also.

Several studies (Bullough and Renko 2013; Bullough et al. 2014) have highlighted the importance of entrepreneurial resilience in overcoming such challenges. More specifically, when faced with a macroeconomic crisis, nascent entrepreneur tends to engage in adaptive response through delay, disengagement, and compensation (Davidsson and Gordon 2016). From a policy perspective, the policy measures to help start-ups in the COVID-19 pandemic should include both short-term measures in the form of help with the cash flow, as well as long-term measures through strengthening the entrepreneurial ecosystem (Kuckertz et al. 2020). However, it bears noting that the thinking of entrepreneurship in crises has been highly influenced by how researchers themselves define and classify crises (Doern et al. 2019). However, we argue that it is that the COVID-19 pandemic can safely be considered as a crisis in more ways than one and that it also presents a "critical incident" (cf. Flanagan 1954) for international entrepreneurship and entrepreneurs.

The ways in which national media provides discursive and how they frame entrepreneurs are especially critical in such a time when entrepreneurship in general and IE in particular are widely seen as risky endeavours dependent on the passing of the COVID-19 crisis. Thus, this time also presents a fruitful time in history at which to study IE phenomena through media. For this purpose, we conducted a comparative discourse analysis in the context of Finland and Russia, and then supplemented that analysis with interviews of entrepreneurs located in the respective countries. We move next to describing the methodological approach taken.

3 Method

The main methodological approach we apply in this study is discourse analysis using publicly available media sources. By looking at textual discourses about entrepreneurship before and during COVID-19 pandemic, our aim was to interpret the core discursive strategies used by the media in presenting the studied phenomenon. In order to respond to the omissions in literature, we focus on and compare the discursive construction of IE in Finland and Russia—specifically, in the business media of the respective countries. From a Critical Discourse Analysis (CDA) perspective, *"discourse is viewed as a type of social practice. Each discursive event is dialectically tied to society insofar as it both constitutes and is constituted by social phenomena"* (Carvalho 2008). Empirically, we apply a discourse analysis of media texts in the leading Finnish and Russian business journals. In line with Vaara and Tienari (2002, p. 279), we regard discourse as *"a method for analysing the social construction of organisational phenomena in textual form"* with IE being the organisational phenomena to be analysed in this study.

Discourses in media are particularly powerful in shaping the societal context, as well as are itself a product of societal influence (see Vaara and Tienari 2002). Thus, it is crucial to take into account discussions in the media as a viable catalyst in moulding how international entrepreneurship is viewed by society and experienced by the actual international entrepreneurs operating in that society. Furthermore, the empirical setting of Finland and Russia provides a context where we would expect to see the potential differences in IE discourse, considering the distinct context Russia provides for IE (e.g., Volchek et al. 2013) compared to most Western countries such as Finland (cf. Kuivalainen et al. 2015).

We collected textual discourses on the topic of IE from the main Finnish and Russian media outlets. The timeline for the search was the time before COVID-19 started to widely spread in the world, i.e. July–December 2019 and the time during the rise of the pandemic, namely January–June 2020. The Finnish business journals were selected by assessing the sixth-largest business media by subscriptions and then accessing their online archives with the following keywords: "kasvuyrittäjyys" (growth entrepreneurship), "kansainvälinen yrittäjyys" (international entrepreneurship), "yrittäjyys" (entrepreneurship), and "kansainvälistyminen" (internationalisation). Thus, the initial results included also items where IE specifically was not mentioned, from which we included after careful reading those that included discussion on internationally entrepreneurial behaviour. The journals used were:

- *Kauppalehti*, the leading daily business newspapers in Finland
- *Taloussanomat*, Finland's largest financial online media
- *Taloustaito*, One of Finland's largest business magazines, covering topics such as taxes, money, investment, and many others
- *Tekniikka ja talous*, a technical-economic journal dealing with technology and innovation
- *Arvopaperi*, a monthly investment-specialised magazine
- *Talouselämä*, the largest financial weekly in the Nordic countries
- *Helsingin Sanomat*, the largest subscription newspaper in Finland

We then complement this with the respective Russian business media sources, which are commonly considered as the most read ones by businesspeople in Russia. The core keyword used in the search of Russian media sources was "предпринимательство" (entrepreneurship). The reason for such a broad keyword was that the terms "growth entrepreneurship" and "international entrepreneurship" are not widely spread in Russia and a more encompassing keyword, such as entrepreneurship could give us more results. The specific outlets were the following:

- *Kommersant*, daily Russian newspaper mostly specialised in politics and business
- *RBC Money*, business newspaper by RosBusinessConsultin, one of the largest Russian media groups, producing business newspapers and magazine, as well as a TV channel
- *Forbes Russia*, Russian edition of a global journal, focusing on business, investing, technology, entrepreneurship, leadership, and lifestyle
- *Vedomosti*, leading business daily newspaper in Russia

The search resulted in a total of 219 articles in Finnish media and 134 articles in Russian media. More specific details on the number of articles per each search period and per each journal can be found in Table 1. As seen in the table, in both the Finnish and Russian media, overall, the number of items in the media pertaining to IE and entrepreneurship grew bigger as the pandemic restrictions started arriving in Europe in early 2020. After obtaining relevant articles we have examined their

Table 1 Summary of articles amount per journal

Journal	July–December 2019	January–June 2020
Kauppalehti	20	38
Taloussanomat	11	5
Taloustaito	5	8
Tekniikka ja talous	7	40
Arvopaperi	3	1
Talouselämä	10	9
Helsingin Sanomat	27	35
Total Finnish	**83**	**136**
Kommersant	8	6
RBC money	7	15
Forbes Russia	8	9
Vedomosti	39	42
Total Russian	**62**	**72**
Grand Total	**145**	**208**

content and interpreted the core discourses used by the media in the articles during each period. The results of the analysis are presented in the following sections.

In addition, we conducted three semi-structured interviews of international entrepreneurs from both countries in June 2020 (two from Russia and one from Finland). The interviews were conducted via Zoom and Skype, due to the restrictions imposed by the novel coronavirus. The information obtained during the interviews was treated as supplementary to the analysis of media outlets and did not represent the focus of this study. The core aim of the interviews was to understand the entrepreneurs' view on how the discussion in the media reflects the reality of entrepreneurs' situation during the crisis and whether it encourages or discourages people from entrepreneurial activity.

4 Findings

4.1 Finnish Media Discourses Before and During COVID-19

As seen in Table 1, we found the discussion on entrepreneurship and internationalisation to be particularly concentrated in three main media sources: *Kauppalehti*, *Tekniikka ja Talous*, and *Helsingin Sanomat*. By the absolute number of news items pre-COVID (2019) and during COVID (2020), the dispersion of the news items remained even in some sources, while in others we witnessed a rapid increase of entrepreneurship-related items during the pandemic, especially March 2020 onwards: For instance in *Kauppalehti*, the latter half of 2019 included 20 items related to entrepreneurship or IE, while already in the first half of 2020, the amount has been almost doubled to 38. An even more rapid change has been in the trade magazine *Tekniikka ja Talous*, where the mere 7 items in the latter half of 2019 expanded into a total of 40 in 2020.

However, having gone through all of them, we noticed a change to distinctly *positive* items about entrepreneurship when moving from 2019 to 2020. In general, starting in March 2020 (the time at which the COVID-19 pandemic hit Finland), the media included almost exclusively positive portrayals of how entrepreneurs were coping and even succeeding despite the pandemic and its accompanying restrictions for business and social life in the country. Simultaneously, we witnessed a shift from items about *internationalisation* and *international* growth to items about new start-ups related to COVID-19 and success stories of existing small- and medium-sized enterprises (SMEs) coping with the impact of the pandemic on business in general.

More specifically, across the Finnish media sources, we noted thematic changes as the pre-COVID "business as usual" entrepreneurship gave way to an increased discussion on entrepreneurial resilience and "can do" attitude. For instance, *Talouselämä* typically had, until March 2020, news on international expansion by enterprises and discussions on the merits of international investments. For instance, on 19 February, in an item titled *"Superfood chain takes Finnish berries to the Asian market—'The perfect combination,'"* the enterprise in question was assessed as follows:

> 'In connection with the opening of the offices, their concept will be refined, and internationalisation will be prepared. Bär Bar's goal is to brand Finnish berries and export them and other Finnish superfoods to the world, especially to Japan and Southeast Asia. In Japan, we have already made certain openings. There are no written agreements yet, but our concept has aroused interest there. There seem to be a lot of opportunities,' says Ojala. (Talouselämä, 19.01.2020)

Once the coronavirus pandemic hit Finland in March, such items related to internationalisation and international strategy became practically absent, replaced by discussion clearly promoting the importance and value of entrepreneurship—for example on 11 April 2020, an item titled *"Now if ever, an ode to entrepreneurship—everyone can do small and big deeds"*:

> Throughout history, entrepreneurs have struggled with difficult conditions and, contrary to probabilities, even built international growth stories. Many are familiar with Supercell's success story, but few remember that the company was founded in the aftermath of the financial crisis in 2010. Google and Netflix were born in the late 1990s just before the dotcom bubble burst. After the Internet bubble, both had to make their way through a sharp decline. Even in the darkest moments of history, something sustainable has been created... (Talouselämä, 11.04.2020)

Similarly, Kauppalehti interviewed Jouni Hakala, the manager of SMEs in Confederation of Finnish Industries (CFI), about the situation:

> We have gone 10 years back in time. The amount of companies trading internationally has dropped by five thousand. ...however, companies are deft to adapt (to the situation), and many (companies) are now rethinking their business. They are looking for new products, services and customers. (Kauppalehti 2020)

This positive highlighting of entrepreneurship was combined with criticism towards the Finnish government for proper support of the entrepreneurs during the crisis, and we recognised a public pressure for the Finnish government to support especially internationalisation of enterprises as this challenging situation seems to persist globally:

> Hakala demands governmental actions to support SMEs' internationalisation. Business Finland has a key role in this. … The CFI wishes that the government would set also ambiguous, numerical goals for SME exporting. (Kauppalehti 2020)

Moving forward towards the summer of 2020, there also started to appear news items combining the two main themes outlined above (positivity about entrepreneurs managing, combined with direct or indirect criticism towards the governmental support and its reach to Finnish entrepreneurs). For instance, an article in *Tekniikka & Talous* on June 2 expounded on how:

> A Turku-based company developed a rapid test for coronavirus, even though it was denied R&D support—now offering it to airports. . .The company's rapid test is not one of the much publicly available testing methods, which are the PCR test and the antibody test. The ArcDian test is an antigen test that directly detects an active virus. However, ArcDia did not receive state product development support for the development of a new corona test. (Tekniikka & Talous, 02.06.2020)

Overall we noticed a distinct "domestication" of discussion in the Finnish media: stories on international entrepreneurship and internationalisation success were in many sources replaced since early 2020 with stories distinctly lacking on the IE angle, and instead promoting the resiliency of Finnish entrepreneurs and their enterprises in general. An exception to this rule was *Kauppalehti*, which also included some 2020 stories related to how different resources for internationalisation would be available, with a post-COVID-19 regrowth view.

4.2 Russian Media Discourses Before and During COVID-19

The higher number of articles about entrepreneurship in Russia could be found in the daily newspaper *Vedomosti*. This may be however due to the newspaper being a daily edition and the newspaper sometimes referring to other sources, for example to other journals in our selection. Before the pandemic, the discourses about entrepreneurship in the journal consisted mostly of discussions about entrepreneurial education of young people, as well as an entrepreneurial activity among the older generations, rent of real estate by entrepreneurs, overview of various entrepreneurial competitions.

One interesting topic highly covered before and during the pandemic was the criminal liability of entrepreneurs (e.g. in relation to tax crimes) and the risks entailed in leading a business. As a consequence, most of the Russian citizens are not eager to start their own business:

> Russians see that the potential profit and increase in social status (as a result of entrepreneurship) do not compensate the risks of losing property and even freedom due to often-changing rules of the game, the despotism of bureaucracy and law enforcement agents and prefer being hired workers and engage in activity, the aim of which is not the improvement of living standards, but rather the preservation of current living standards. (Vedomosti, 4.10.2019)

Thus, the discourse around the criminal liability of entrepreneurs was also highly tied to the government setting the rules and protecting entrepreneurs from draconian actions from law enforcement agents and mitigating criminal liability for entrepreneurs.

The discourses in RBC Money, Kommersant, and Forbes before the pandemic followed a similar pattern as in Vedomosti but focused mostly on governmental actions of easing the tax burden (especially of micro-businesses), defining terms related to entrepreneurship, such as family entrepreneurship/business and governmental support of various entrepreneurial projects. Similar to Vedomosti the discourse in the other journals was highly focused on lack of belief towards engaging in entrepreneurial activity from the society, as well as overviews of various competitions and business forums. Only a few articles focused on stories of individual entrepreneurs and their achievements. While in relation to international entrepreneurship, the discourse was again focused on governmental support of export in the form of guidelines, consultation, and education. However, discourse on international entrepreneurship was present only in a few articles from all the texts obtained.

The core discourse during the COVID-19 pandemic, especially after mid-March, was to a large extent focused on measures of support towards entrepreneurship. Such support was said to be from the government, various banks, and large corporations. Essentially the media also informed about a large amount of small business bankruptcy and entrepreneurs who seized their activities due to the pandemic. Critics towards governmental support were naturally also present:

> Self-employed citizens cannot count on the government's support package for small and medium-sized businesses that suffered from the pandemic. Their activity does not belong to the area of SMEs. Self-employment has special taxation that does not consider the availability of workplaces and payroll. (Forbes, 21.05.2020)

Thus, the topic of taxes and gaps in legislation related to taxation of entrepreneurs and self-employed was present in the Russian media both before and during the pandemic. Too strict rules of taxation of entrepreneurs are constantly discussed in Russian media through the prism of government critique, but also through the government seemingly easing the taxation rules. Apart from the numerous news about government support of entrepreneurship during the pandemic, random discussions focused on, for example, social entrepreneurship, women in entrepreneurship, and entrepreneurial education. Furthermore, the topic international entrepreneurship during the pandemic appeared only in one article, which informed about the possibility for small businesses specialising in consumer products to export their goods through a well-known Russian online retailer who expanded its business to Eastern Europe.

Finally, while to some extent during the pandemic entrepreneurship began to be more popularised in the media, on the other hand, other articles still displayed entrepreneurs as "crooks," which was largely stated to be the opinion of the government and not that of the society:

> "In a recent edition of a special project by TASS (Russian news agency) the president of Russia, Vladimir Putin stated that according to him "there are certain reasons" to perceive entrepreneurs as "crooks" and agreed that the "society" is also of the same opinion. However, the attitude of the society towards entrepreneurs and entrepreneurship is much more complex..." "...the majority Russians have a positive attitude towards small and medium-sized business." (Vedomosti, 13.03.2020 and 23.03.2020)

Thereby, in general, the discussion surrounding entrepreneurship in the media before and during the pandemic had the same largely negative flavour and focus on the government actions rather than those of the entrepreneurs themselves. In the next section, we present a brief summary and comparison of the discourses in the media about entrepreneurship in Russia and Finland.

4.3 Summary of the Comparative Analysis of Discourses About Entrepreneurship

In general, Russian media focused more on entrepreneurship within the country itself and only a few articles dealt with international entrepreneurship, which confirms the discussion in the Russian media itself of an unwillingness and certain fear of Russian entrepreneurs to expand to foreign markets. Such an attitude may be largely due to a lack of information and support for expanding the business abroad. In comparison, the discussions in the Finnish media before the onset of the COVID-19 crisis (i.e., in 2019) were comparatively more about internationalisation and case studies (and challenges) of international expansion among Finnish enterprises. Since Finland has a small domestic market, with a national industry structure heavily favouring knowledge-intensive high-technology products and services (see Kuivalainen et al. 2015), we consider that discussion to be the "normal"—whereas the Finnish media shifting towards entrepreneurship within the country itself in 2020 as the crisis hit, resembles more closely the Russian media discursive and is, at least by Finnish standards, a novel shift, one that could be called "new normal."

Most of the discourse about entrepreneurship in the Russian media leans towards it is still not being the most favourable choice for developing one's career in Russia and does not represent entrepreneurship in a favourable light. While several articles focus on popularising entrepreneurship by discussing entrepreneurial education, various forums, as well as a few individual stories, most of the media discourse is rather focused on discussing the actions of the government in both supporting entrepreneurship and discouraging from it. Conversely, the Finnish media in 2020 has provided a discursive strongly it *is* the most favourable choice in developing one's career in Finland, despite the difficult times that the world and Finnish economy are going through during the pandemic and its accompanying restrictions for enterprises and international business.

4.4 Illustrative Cases Comparison

In order to also include the viewpoint of entrepreneurs themselves, we supplemented the analysis with semi-structured interviews of three entrepreneurs (one from Finland and two from Russia). Specifically, we wanted to ascertain if entrepreneurs themselves have followed the discussion in the media in their respective country during the pandemic; what they think about the discussion around entrepreneurs and entrepreneurship in the media before and during the pandemic; if the entrepreneurs themselves feel that media has described accurately the situation of entrepreneurs during the crisis; and finally, whether or not they, based on the discussion in the media, think that the discussion has been encouraging or discouraging towards (international) entrepreneurship as a career path. The interviews were conducted in June 2020 by the respective Finnish and Russian scholars involved in the present study and translated in English for the purposes of this study.

The *Finnish entrepreneur*, aged 32, has been operating a digital online enterprise that was founded at the end of 2015 and currently employs seven people. The entrepreneur is of Bangladeshi origin, however, has completed his university degree in Finland, and thus has lived in the country almost a decade; he has five years of experience as an international entrepreneur. He has been following the discussion on entrepreneurship and IE in the Finnish media closely, following the general news as well as keeping a close track on the support systems and measures that the Finnish government has been taking to support entrepreneurs in the country amidst the pandemic restrictions.

The entrepreneur considers the media in Finland has not been describing accurately the situation that entrepreneurs are in during this crisis: "*So far, [based on] the news I have seen, I think the media have been, of course, putting up the bigger picture, what is happening on a broader scale. But I think maybe it could show it industry-wise. At least I didn't see that kind of news. I think that would be a much more precise reality of what is happening.*" This criticism arises from the fact that his enterprise is a born-digital (cf. Vadana et al. 2019) and thus the entrepreneur has noticed that in the media, "*the opinions are very subjective and industry-specific. When I talk to some industry-specific people, they have a different point of view. For example, we are a very digital kind of startup. I think Finland is a very highly industrialised country...I think the discussions and the analysis also highly emphasise that kind of industries. So, I think those are indeed badly impacted. But I think if it is considered for digital products, I have also talked to some other business colleagues who are not entrepreneurs, but they are working in digital platforms, they are saying their sales and activities are going up and they're quite busy....*"

This suggests that the discussion in the Finnish media may be over-generalising, as the experience of individual entrepreneurs within the country seems to depend also on the industry characteristics under which they are operating; digital services can be seen to actually benefit from the increase of telecommuting and similar developments that have been increasing social distancing during the pandemic.

Indeed, the entrepreneur considers the discussion in the Finnish media to potentially discourage entrepreneurship: *"The news I have read is mostly related to the shrinking economy and people losing jobs. At least I didn't see such news which emphasises becoming an entrepreneur. . .mostly reflecting what's happening, like how the economy is suffering, rather than encouraging people to try different things."* However, he does not see this development as purely COVID-led, but rather one endemic of the Finnish culture and social system: *"I was talking to one of my friends just a few days ago, he's a PhD researcher and he said that the Finnish economy is structured in such a nice way that it offers a comfortable and secure life. So, people tend to avoid taking risks. I think that even though people are kind of pushed to their limit because of the coronavirus situation but the economy is so supportive, I do not see people suddenly starting to become entrepreneurs."*

Russian entrepreneur 1 provides customer acquisition service for large telecommunications companies. The entrepreneurial activity started five years ago. Prior to that, the interviewee worked as a manager in the same industry. The company currently employs ten people; most of them are part-time.

Entrepreneur 1 superficially tracked the discussion in the media and, in most cases, read the headlines in key Russian news aggregators. According to the interviewee, the media correctly raised the topic and the main issues, but personally *"I didn't want to follow the discussion due to lack of time. In general, the mood worsened and demotivation was spoiling."* Entrepreneur 1 also did not follow the news extensively since the Telecom industry was recognised as not affected by COVID-19 in Russia. The long-chosen strategy of cooperation with two market leaders (one public and one private company) gave an advantage. The market *"shows a slight decline, but everyone in our company is working as usual."* The main provider of reliable information for entrepreneur 1 are bloggers and social media influencers. However, entrepreneur 1 does not highlight any specific ones, since *"some of them are too panicky and others are too relaxed."*

The interviewee expresses an opinion that entrepreneurs themselves have an important role. They generate a request for support and promote it from the bottom to the top to the policymakers. Entrepreneur 1 ambiguously assesses the role of the media in shaping the image of entrepreneurs: *"On the one hand, people will be afraid to become entrepreneurs. If the market falls, the risks are growing. It is very difficult to predict. Demand is falling, the average check is decreasing. On the other hand, people will be forced to become entrepreneurs due to their inability to find employment. Due to the closure of business, many vacant niches will open."* Simultaneously, the importance of entrepreneurs as potential employers is unlikely to grow: *"There is a neutral attitude towards entrepreneurs in society. There is no attitude as to crooks, as the president said, but will not love us more either."*

Russian entrepreneur 2 has been working in the photo and video services industry for B2B and B2C customers for one year. The total experience as an entrepreneur is five years. There are no other employees in the company.

Entrepreneur 2 actively monitors the discussion in business media issues related to COVID-19: *"I prefer the Internet and do not trust television. I read the news on Yandex, Rambler, and Instagram. I'm interested in the opinion of journalists, some deputies, and doctors. From my point of view, the received information could be divided into pro-government and opposition. According to the pro-government influencers, everything is going well in the country. In turn, the opposition or neutral people say the same as I feel myself, the same as my family and friends. The number of negative information from the opposition is less than the positive from authorities."*

Entrepreneur 2 negatively assesses the government's real support for business: *"All entrepreneurs complain that there is no help. Many of my clients, for example, retail and jewellery business have closed. There was a great demand for support, but nothing has been done."* According to entrepreneur 2, informing citizens was carried out as follows: *"COVID-19 came, people should hide at homes (authorities) will give money and help. In reality, support was provided only to large businesses or to those companies that are associated with officials, all other companies received nothing."*

Entrepreneur 2 negatively evaluates the development of entrepreneurship in the future: *"The level of distrust between people and companies has significantly increased. Businesses do not want to pay taxes. Everyone prefers to make a discount and take cash. Many (companies) work without providing a check."* However, the pessimistic attitude is primarily related to the SME: *"The authorities are trying to destroy SMEs and transfer everything to large business. It is easier to control and talk about in the conditions of existence."*

5 Discussion and Conclusion

Overall, our comparative study of the Finnish and Russian international entrepreneurship discussion preceding and coinciding with the onset of the COVID-19 pandemic in both countries yields several interesting insights. First, the analysis of the media in the respective countries provides a contrasting view into the predominant public discussion on entrepreneurship and IE in each country: Whereas in the Finnish media, we found a strong shift towards discussing entrepreneurship and entrepreneurs at the individual and organisational levels—and doing so in a distinctly positive light highlighting examples of entrepreneurial resiliency and agility despite the pandemic; in Russia, the discussion in the media was more strongly positioned at the societal and political levels.

In sum, the regional, national, and global level responses to the recently emerged COVID-19 pandemic are starting to have a major impact on international business in general, and on IE in particular. However, the emerging situation is also providing new opportunities for scholars to compare national responses and examine the nature and resilience of IE and internationalisation-seeking entrepreneurs under such exceptional times. The combined qualitative methodology applied in this study, combining the discourse analysis of public media data with case-based analysis of interviews of entrepreneurs, provides an innovative and rarely applied approach into studying IE phenomena. Content analysis based on document analysis data collection is a relevant qualitative research approach (Edward and Dana 2019) and has been suggested to be a promising approach for entrepreneurship research in particular (Dana and Dana 2005). However, the field of IE has been lacking in studies that would apply content or discourse analysis, an omission to which this study seeks to respond. The present study responds to that omission and, by illustrating how discourse analysis methods can be used to explain timely IE phenomena, argues for the usefulness and applicability of this methodology—and for applying content and discourse analysis approaches in general—in the IE field.

More specifically, by adopting a comparative empirical setting of Finland and Russia, this study responds to the call by Terjesen et al. (2016, p. 315) to "*Pursue more diverse and sophisticated analytical techniques [in comparative IE studies], such as content analysis of secondary sources*" and, in doing so, adds to the stream of comparative IE, which is a major part of the IE research ontology (Jones et al. 2011) and yet has traditionally been overlooked by most IE scholars. Moreover, research on IE has been prevalently conducted in developed countries, and both emerging markets context and especially comparative studies that would account for the similarities and differences across distinct market contexts are called for (Dabić et al. 2019), since comparative IE studies can help in both theoretical development and providing policymakers tools for developing supportive entrepreneurship programs through the insights gained from examining different national environments in parallel (Terjesen et al. 2016).

An added contribution of the study thus lies in uncovering similarities and differences in the discourses on IE in emerging and developed markets in a very specific and defining time of early 2020, when the COVID-19 pandemic is exerting rapid impact on both entrepreneurship (Kuckertz et al. 2020) and international business (Ratten 2020). The present study has illustrated how discourse analysis and media sources can be used to conduct comparative IE studies and, when supplemented further with primary qualitative data from international entrepreneurs themselves, the perception and experience of IE practitioners can be substantially different from the public discussion in their home country media.

We readily acknowledge that this study also comes with limitations. For one, different online media search engines tend to have different syntax for search terms; thus it is possible that some relevant articles were not found despite our attempt to be as exhaustive as possible with the secondary search. Related to this limitation, there are of course several other media sources that we also could have added to the analysis, such as the Association of Finnish Entrepreneurs or the national broadcast company Yle, as the present study was delimited to the trade magazines and newspapers that typically cover the Finnish IE phenomena. We also acknowledge that generalising from the interviews would require a similarly rich qualitative interview data as we had at our disposal with the over 300 media items from the two countries; we are cognizant of the fact that interviews of only a few entrepreneurs can only provide the basis for supplementary considerations, rather than be used for the primary points of arguments. Nevertheless, in our opinion, the addition of some such "primary data" to supplement our discursive analysis adds to the richness of the discussion of the topic—the perceptions on IE during a time of global crisis.

This study also leads to potentially fruitful avenues for future research. For instance, since *international* entrepreneurs are characterised by their distinct mindset as compared to other types of entrepreneurs—the so-called "global mindset" (Nummela et al. 2004; Torkkeli et al. 2018), it is relevant to shed light on the resiliency of that mindset under duress when the media is rife with examples of entrepreneurs in crisis.

Since the interviews were not the focus of this study, more research is needed in the actual entrepreneurs' perception of international entrepreneurship in crisis times and most importantly a cross-cultural/cross-country view on this phenomenon is required. We also consider that future research could adopt a longitudinal frame to examine how the prevalent discourse pertaining to IE across countries impact international entrepreneurial *behaviour* across time; such an examination would go a long way towards establishing a causal chain from public discursive to IE behaviour, a chain that would further contribute to the IE field and help integrate discursive, content and similar types of analysis to IE across contexts and themes; ours was constrained to two countries and one global crisis, and undoubtedly there remain a multitude of country contexts and situations in which discursive analysis can help enrich the IE domain over the long term.

References

Autio E (2005) Creative tension: the significance of ben Oviatt's and Patricia McDougall's article 'toward a theory of international new ventures'. J Int Bus Stud 36(1):9–19

Buckley PJ (2009) Business history and international business. Bus Hist 51(3):307–333

Bullough A, Renko M (2013) Entrepreneurial resilience during challenging times. Bus Horiz 56 (3):343–350

Bullough A, Renko M, Myatt T (2014) Danger zone: the importance of resilience and self-efficacy for entrepreneurial intentions. Entrepreneurship Theory & Practice 38(3):473–499

Caligiuri P, De Cieri H, Minbaeva D, Verbeke A, Zimmermann A (2020) International HRM insights for navigating the COVID-19 pandemic: implications for future research and practice. J Int Bus Stud 51:697–713

Carvalho A (2008) Media (ted) discourse and society: rethinking the framework of critical discourse analysis. Journal Stud 9(2):161–177

Colli A, García-Canal E, Guillén MF (2013) Family character and international entrepreneurship: a historical comparison of Italian and Spanish 'new multinationals'. Bus Hist 55(1):119–138

Cumming DJ, Zahra SA (2016) International business and entrepreneurship implications of Brexit. Br J Manag 27(4):687–692

Dabić M, Maley J, Dana LP, Novak I, Pellegrini MM, Caputo A (2019) Pathways of SME internationalization: a bibliometric and systematic review. Small Bus Econ 55:1–21

Dana LP (2017) International entrepreneurship research: how it evolved and directions for the future. Int J Entrep Small Bus 30(4):477–489

Dana LP, Dana TE (2005) Expanding the scope of methodologies used in entrepreneurship research. Int J Entrep Small Bus 2(1):79–88
Davidsson P, Gordon SR (2016) Much ado about nothing? The surprising persistence of nascent entrepreneurs through macroeconomic crisis. Entrep Theory Pract 40(4):915–941
Doern R, Williams N, Vorley T (2019) Special issue on entrepreneurship and crises: business as usual? An introduction and review of the literature. Entrepreneurship & Regional Development 31(5–6):400–412
Edward G, Dana L-P (2019) Qualitative methodologies and data collection methods: toward increased rigour in management research, vol 1. World Scientific
ETLA (2020) Etla: Suomen bkt voi supistua tänä vuonna jopa 5% koronaviruspandemian takia. Available at https://www.etla.fi/ajankohtaista/etla-suomen-bkt-voi-supistua-tana-vuonna-jopa-5-koronaviruspandemian-takia/
Fillis I (2007) A methodology for researching international entrepreneurship in SMEs. J Small Bus Enterp Dev 14(1):118–135
Flanagan JC (1954) The critical incident technique. Psychol Bull 51(4):327
Ivanova-Gongne M, Torkkeli L (2018) No manager is an island: culture in sensemaking of business networking. J Bus Ind Mark 33(5):638–650
Jones MV, Coviello N, Tang YK (2011) International entrepreneurship research (1989–2009): a domain ontology and thematic analysis. J Bus Ventur 26(6):632–659
Kauppalehti (2020) "Olemme palanneet kymmenen vuotta ajassa taaksepäin" – Pk-yritysten kansainvälistyminen tyssäsi koronakriisiin. Available at https://www.kauppalehti.fi/uutiset/olemme-palanneet-kymmenen-vuotta-ajassa-taaksepain-pk-yritysten-kansainvalistyminen-tyssasi-koronakriisiin/a0d40202-50bb-4cc4-86ea-6b1f0bf3aea7
Kuckertz A, Brändle L, Gaudig A, Hinderer S, Reyes CAM, Prochotta A et al (2020) Startups in times of crisis – a rapid response to the COVID-19 pandemic. J Bus Ventur Insights 13:e00169
Kuivalainen O, Saarenketo S, Torkkeli L, Puumalainen K (2015) International entrepreneurship among finnish SMEs. In: Handbook of research on international entrepreneurship strategy. Edward Elgar Publishing
McDougall PP, Oviatt BM (2000) International entrepreneurship: the intersection of two research paths. Acad Manag J 43(5):902–906
Nummela N, Paavilainen-Mäntymäki E (2014) International entrepreneurship research in Finland: past, present, and future. In: Laaksonen M, Arslan A, Kontkanen M (eds) Contributions to international business: essays in honour of professor Jorma Larimo. ACTA WASAENSIA 303
Nummela N, Saarenketo S, Puumalainen K (2004) A global mindset – a prerequisite for successful internationalization? Canadian Journal of Administrative Sciences/Revue Canadienne des Sciences de l'Administration 21(1):51–64
Oviatt BM, McDougall PP (2005) Defining international entrepreneurship and modeling the speed of internationalization. Entrep Theory Pract 29(5):537–553
Paul J, Rosado-Serrano A (2019) Gradual internationalization vs born-global/international new venture models: a review and research agenda. Int Mark Rev 36(6):830–858
Peiris IK, Akoorie ME, Sinha P (2012) International entrepreneurship: a critical analysis of studies in the past two decades and future directions for research. J Int Entrep 10(4):279–324
Perälä H (2020) Korona kolauttaa kovaa. Helsingin Seudun Kauppakamari. Available at https://helsinki.chamber.fi/korona-kolauttaa-kovaa/
Ratten V (2020) Coronavirus and international business: an entrepreneurial ecosystem perspective. Thunderbird Int Bus Rev 62:629–634
Schwens C, Zapkau FB, Bierwerth M, Isidor R, Knight G, Kabst R (2018) International entrepreneurship: a meta-analysis on the internationalization and performance relationship. Entrep Theory Pract 42(5):734–768
Servantie V, Cabrol M, Guieu G, Boissin JP (2016) Is international entrepreneurship a field? A bibliometric analysis of the literature (1989–2015). J Int Entrep 14(2):168–212
Talouselämä (2020) Analyysi: Suomeen iski Pohjoismaiden pahin konkurssiaalto koronan vuoksi – Ravintolat kärsineet pahasti monessa maassa. Available at https://www.talouselama.fi/uutiset/

analyysi-suomeen-iski-pohjoismaiden-pahin konkurssiaalto-koronan-vuoksi-ravintolat-karsineet-pahasti-monessa maassa/0944571a-0168-4461-b44f-cb7fc8a5337d
Terjesen S, Hessels J, Li D (2016) Comparative international entrepreneurship: a review and research agenda. J Manag 42(1):299–344
Torkkeli L, Nummela N, Saarenketo S (2018) A global mindset–still a prerequisite for successful SME internationalisation? In: Dominguez N, Mayrhofer U (eds) Key success factors of SME internationalisation: a cross-country perspective. International Business and Management, Vol. 34. Emerald Publishing Limited, pp 7–24
Vaara E, Tienari J (2002) Justification, legitimization and naturalization of mergers and acquisitions: a critical discourse analysis of media texts. Organization 9(2):275–304
Vaara E, Tienari J (2004) Critical discourse analysis as a methodology for international business studies. In: Handbook of qualitative research methods for international business. Edward Elgar, Cheltenham
Vadana II, Torkkeli L, Kuivalainen O, Saarenketo S (2019) The internationalization of born-digital companies. In: The changing strategies of international business. Palgrave Macmillan, Cham, pp 199–220
van Burg E, Cornelissen J, Stam W, Jack S (2020) Advancing qualitative entrepreneurship research: leveraging methodological plurality for achieving scholarly impact. In: Entrepreneurship: theory and practice. Macmillan Education UK, London
Volchek D, Jantunen A, Saarenketo S (2013) The institutional environment for international entrepreneurship in Russia: reflections on growth decisions and performance in SMEs. J Int Entrep 11(4):320–350
Zahra SA (2005) A theory of international new ventures: a decade of research. J Int Bus Stud 36 (1):20–28

Lasse Torkkeli is an Adjunct Professor of International Business in the Turku School of Economics at the University of Turku, and Associate Professor at the School of Business and Management at LUT University at Lappeenranta, Finland. Torkkeli's research interests are in the international entrepreneurship and international business domains and include SME internationalisation, capabilities and business models, and sustainable entrepreneurship. He has previously published in the International Business Review, International Marketing Review, and the Journal of International Entrepreneurship, among other journals and publishers.

Maria Ivanova-Gongne is an Assistant Professor in International Marketing at Åbo Akademi University. Her research interests include business-to-business interaction, managerial sensemaking and an individual level perspective on culture in international business, as well as migrant entrepreneurship. Her works have appeared in such journals as Industrial Marketing Management, Critical Perspectives on International Business, European Management Journal, Journal of Business and Industrial Marketing, and Scandinavian Journal of Management.

Anna Vuorio (nee Kunttu) is a Post-doctoral Researcher at the School of Business and Management at LUT University at Lappeenranta, Finland. Her research interests are in the fields of entrepreneurship and sustainability and include entrepreneurial opportunities, entrepreneurial cognition, values and decision-making.

Ignat Kulkov is a doctoral student at the Laboratory of Industrial Management, Åbo Akademi University, Finland. His research interests centre around entrepreneurship, management of new technologies, and industry transformation.

Barriers to Entrepreneurial Internationalisation for Ukrainian Creative and Cultural Industries (CCI)

Richard Tomlins, Arun Sukumar, Oksana Malynka, and Nataliia Bartkiv

1 Introduction

Creative industries have been receiving increased attention in recent years (Collins 2018). Our notion of what constitutes creative industries has changed over the last 20 years. Initially, the term 'Cultural Industries' was used to describe a range of activities that had strong cultural roots, such as visual arts, dance, music, film and the heritage sector (Towse 2020). The term underwent a metamorphosis when a further range of creative activities, including those using digital technology for artistic endeavours, created significant employment and contributed widely to economic development (Newbigin 2019; Sadraei et al. 2018). Today, the term 'creative industries' denotes a broad range of creative activities that has increasing importance to the economy of many countries (Boix et al. 2016). Some countries have started measuring the impact of the sector and have actively set up policies and mechanisms to promote entrepreneurial behaviour among individuals involved in the sector (Ayob and Dana 2017; Bazalgette 2017).

Although not easily identified as an industrial sector, creative industries are heavily dependent on individual creative talents and their entrepreneurial behaviour. The generation of intellectual property is a vital aspect of creative industries and a key activity of entrepreneurs involved in this sector (Landoni et al. 2019). The

R. Tomlins · A. Sukumar (✉)
International Centre for Transformational Entrepreneurship, Coventry University, Coventry, UK
e-mail: aa3252@coventry.ac.uk; ac2780@coventry.ac.uk

O. Malynka
Ivano-Frankivsk National Technical University of Oil and Gas, Ivano-Frankivsk, Ukraine

N. Bartkiv
Ivano-Frankivsk Chamber of Commerce and Industry, Ivano-Frankivsk, Ukraine

V. Jafari-Sadeghi et al. (eds.), *Empirical International Entrepreneurship*, Contributions to Management Science,
https://doi.org/10.1007/978-3-030-68972-8_12

creative talents of individuals have contributed to a variety of industries and professions from tourism to advertising, and there is a growing recognition that the skills and work patterns of the creative sector have an impact on other industries and national economies (Beheshti et al. 2016; Mahmoudi et al. 2019; Newbigin 2019).

In the EU, the cultural and creative industries (CCIs) is a recognised sector that has been integrated into policy documents and programs for more than a decade (Ratten et al. 2007; Farinha 2017). The contribution of CCIs to national economies has been recognised, which has resulted in the development of favourable policies and entrepreneurial ecosystems that aim to exploit the creative talents of individuals and propel the industry (Newbigin 2019). According to the latest statistics, core creative industries generated 558 billion Euros in the EU and accounted for nearly 8.3 million full-time equivalent jobs (Farinha 2017). The statistics also show that most of the CCIs had a high proportion of youth in employment and were resilient compared to other industries and sectors during the financial crisis of 2008 (Farinha 2017). In the non-European context, CCIs generate approximately 2250 billion dollars in revenue and provide nearly 30 million jobs worldwide (Farinha 2017; Hajiagha et al. 2013, 2015, 2018).

In the EU-Eastern partnership, socio-political changes in former Soviet Bloc countries including Ukraine, Georgia and Belarus have resulted in a conducive climate for the expansion of creative industries. Among these, Ukraine has been proactive in the promotion of its creative and cultural industries. In 2016, the government released its Long-Term National Culture Strategy 2025 solely aimed at the development of CCIs in Ukraine (Farinha 2017). In terms of national cultural products, film sector development has been prioritised and decentralisation has made it possible for local authorities to invest resources in the creative sector. A recent UNESCO Culture for Development indicator noted that CCIs have made relevant contributions to the economic and social development of Ukraine (Farinha 2017). Further plans are in place to promote cross-border networking and alliances of creative entrepreneurs (Farinha 2017). Efforts are also underway to integrate the competitive advantage of CCIs into regional development by promoting creativity, innovation and socio-economic development (Felsenstein et al. 2019).

While there have been considerable positive changes in the promotion of CCIs and cross-border trade, Ukrainian creative enterprises still find it difficult to internationalise their business. Small and medium-sized firms especially are not reaping the benefits of promotional policies, increased investment and favourable conditions to seek opportunities abroad (Dana 1987; Amin Moghadasi et al. 2017; Jafari-Sadeghi et al. 2019). In this context of cross-border trade, this chapter explores the barriers that prevent Ukrainian firms in CCIs to internationalise their business. It explores the motivations to go abroad (Jafari-Sadeghi 2020), the process of internationalisation (Jafari-Sadeghi et al. 2020), the major barriers to internationalisation and how the barriers have been overcome.

2 Research Approach

Case studies were the main mode of data collection for this study. Before the case studies, the researchers conducted a systematic literature review to understand the landscape of creative industries in Ukraine. Existing policy documents and the literature on creative and cultural industries were examined to build the historical and current status of creative industries in Ukraine. The review also explored the current support offered by agencies in developing the creative and cultural sector. The next section of the methodology consisted of conducting four case studies with creative entrepreneurs to understand their journey of internationalisation. The case studies involved interviews with the owners of the firms to ascertain the barriers to the internationalisation of firms in Ukrainian creative and cultural industries. Also, they involved document analysis regarding the strategies and motivations for internationalisation and interviews with the owners of the firms to explore the need for moving abroad, the issues the entrepreneurs had to deal with, the reconciliation of creative inputs in the context of international demand and market expectations and wider networking aspects that led to competitive advantage (Biancone and Jafari-Sadeghi 2016; Mahdiraji et al. 2011, 2019, 2020; Sukumar et al. 2020).

3 Creative Industries

Creative industries have been identified as a separate sector of the economy (United Nations Conference on Trade and Development (UNCTAD) 2018a). Millions of people work and realise their creative potential in this field while supporting a country's economy on the world stage and its culture. The importance of creative and creative industries to Ukrainian and global economies can be seen through the successful adoption of 2021 by the United Nations (UN) as the International Year of Creative Economy for Sustainable Development (UN 2019). The internationalisation of the creative entrepreneurship sector in Ukraine is intended to obtain competitive advantages and improve its position in international trade (Ushkarenko et al. 2018). The Ukrainian economy is integrated into the global system of foreign trade, which is seen as extremely important for the economic development of this country (SlovoiDilo 2019).

Open access of the society to entrepreneurship gives entrepreneurs the opportunity to express their creative potential and boldly implement their ideas while fulfilling one of the main functions of entrepreneurship: to make money, gain profit and achieve social impact from the sale of goods and services. The UN (2019) resolution refers to 'the creative economy', which is called the 'orange economy' in a number of countries. It includes although is not limited to 'knowledge-based economic activities and the interplay between human creativity and ideas, knowledge and technology, as well as cultural values or artistic, cultural heritage and other individual or collective creative expressions'. However, the resolution also refers to 'creative industries' and 'cultural and creative industries' as well as to the 'creative economy', although they are not specifically differentiated within the resolution.

The term 'creative industries' is used in this chapter to reflect the initial journey of the six case studies whilst the authors are cognisant of the wider role of the creative economy and creative clusters. These terms have varying interpretations. Indeed, UNCTAD (2020) argues that the creative economy is not a fixed concept—limiting the scope for a precise definition whilst attempting some scoping. The United Nations Conference on Trade and Development's categorisation can be seen as simultaneously reducing and expanding the definition of the creative economy. It is reduced to 'the mix of human creativity, ideas, intellectual property, knowledge and technology' that are seen as producing 'the knowledge-based economic activities upon which the "creative industries" are based'. Within a paragraph or two, the expanded creative economy becomes the 'sum of all the parts of the creative industries, including trade, labour and production'.

The nomenclature is of more than definitional interest, as it frames the economic size and potential of the 'sector' and potential policy responses accordingly. This team of authors also notes the importance of a wider economic and social ecosystem of professional services that are supported by and facilitate creative industries. The interaction between these firms alongside the scope to enable Landry's 'creative cities' is of further research interest as well as creative hubs and clusters within the spatial context of Ukraine (Warm 2020) and globally (Zanna Creative 2019). There is a clear link in the UN resolution (2019) to the wider economic and more 'significant' concept of creativity as a core driver of social value (Tomlins 2015; Taghavifard et al. 2018; Mokhtarzadeh et al. 2018) and societal change. In turn, this has further echoes of Landry's (2012) creative city and creative space concepts. Neelands et al. (2015) demonstrate the interconnectedness between culture and the creative industries in the description of a 'dynamic flow and exchange' between them, which resulted in their use of the term 'Cultural and Creative Industry Ecosystem'.

The United Nations Conference on Trade and Development (2020) adopts an indicative approach to identifying creative industries with its broad statement that they include 'advertising, architecture, arts and crafts, design, fashion, film, video, photography, music, performing arts, publishing, research & development, software, computer games, electronic publishing, and TV/radio'. Operationally, and in the context of this chapter's focus on internationalisation, UNCTAD notes that the trade in creative and related goods is categorised as 'the cycle of creation, production and distribution of a tangible product with creative content, economic and cultural value and a market objective' (Kuku et al. 2018: 13). Ukrainian creative industries might expect this profiling to generate support from the government accentuated not only by the economic impact but also by the potential of creative industries to generate greater economic and social inclusivity (UNCTAD 2018a).

3.1 Creative Industries in Ukraine

Ukraine borders three former Soviet states (Russia, Belarus and Moldova) and four countries in the European Union (Poland, Slovakia, Hungary and Romania) and has a coastline along the Black Sea at its southern edge. In Ukraine, the definition of 'creative industries' is included in the basic legislation of Ukraine on 'Culture'. The creative economy is about freedom and ideas and the possibilities of their realisation, networking, interaction and cooperation. However, starting a business or expanding operations into the country is an arduous process and an administrative issue that is swamped in bureaucracy and costly procedures, which reveals the need for local help (TMF Group 2019). Despite the improvement of Ukraine's ease of doing business ranking according to a recent World Bank and International Finance Corporation report, challenges remain for local entrepreneurs, with the country ranked among the bottom 20% of economies in five of 10 areas of regulation measured by the report. Indeed, Ukraine has the worst rankings in Eastern Europe and Central Asia on registering property and resolving insolvency. It takes 2.9 years to resolve insolvency, which is well above the Organisation for Economic Co-operation and Development (OECD) average. Costing 42% of the estate, it is also an expensive process (TMF Group 2019).

Starting a business in Ukraine involves several procedures and a cost of $1262, which is well above the OECD average of $78.7 (TMF Group 2019). Getting electricity can take up to 285 days and cost 192.3% of the income per capita. The wait of 53 days for the completion and approval of the external connection design by a private electrical design company is the most drawn-out task. Ukraine jumped 15 places for the ease of registering a property in the most recent World Bank study, although the improvement still left it in 149th place (TMF Group 2019). At 70 days and 10 procedures, registering a property takes considerably more time than the OECD norm (TMF Group 2019). Obtaining credit is the easiest step to setting up a business in Ukraine, relative to the other tasks. The country ranks 23rd in the world and runs a relatively developed financial system. Behind obtaining credit, enforcing contracts is one of the most streamlined processes in Ukraine. It takes 343 days compared to the 510-day OECD average, although the associated costs are quite steep. However, paying taxes is by far the most laborious task for businesses in Ukraine, as it requires 28 payments per year and 491 hours. Unified social contribution and corporate income tax take a considerable amount of time compared to OECD counterparts (TMF Group 2019).

The United Nations Conference on Trade and Development (2018b) notes that many small businesses, including creative ones, face many challenges in reaching export markets accessing services such as logistics for shipping goods abroad, knowledge of regulatory requirements in the exporting and importing countries and trade finance (Alon et al. 2009; Rezaei et al. 2020; Sadeghi et al. 2017, 2018). For example, trading across Ukraine's borders is a complicated ordeal. It requires six documents and 30 days to export product, with heavy costs associated with both importing and exporting containers. This is exacerbated by the lack of a convenient connection between cities, including small towns and regional centres. Ukraine remains centralised, although the government has declared decentralisation (TMF Group 2019). Regional centres that have airports in Ukraine are connected with Kyiv, but not with each other. For example, from cultural and artistic Lviv, a person can fly to the research and production centre Kharkiv only through Kyiv.

Most European creative companies (95%) are micro-enterprises (employed less than 10 people), which provide 35% of the jobs in the sector (Protogeroua et al. 2016). In Ukraine, entrepreneurs need to engage in business with low levels of trust and a relatively weak rule of law as well as political and economic instability. These long-term circumstances have a strong impact on both public governance and business management and the ability of these firms to internationalise. Whilst OECD refers to North Korea as the last transition economy (Koen and Beom 2020), Ukraine appears to rival its status. There is a need to reorient existing pre-Soviet influences, especially in areas such as alternative education, contemporary art, new economy and urban planning. Positive initiatives include the physical symbolism of old factories in Lviv and Ivano-Frankivsk (Western Ukraine) being transformed into creative clusters, and co-working spaces being opened in the building of a former factory in Kharkiv, Eastern Ukraine (Mykolaienko 2019). Teams of creative people who are individual creative entrepreneurs are driving these initiatives to provide a platform for sustainability and internationalisation. Large-scale forums, festivals, lectures, workshops and training courses are taking place on the topic of the creative economy and creative industries. The Ministry of Culture usually holds an international forum titled 'Creative Ukraine', but it lacks external visibility (Humenna 2018).

Unlike traditional sectors, creative industries are characterised by low capital intensity, which in combination with the heterogeneity of the market creates low barriers to entry into the market and encourages start-ups. Its importance is such that Ukraine's government investment agency profiles it as a specific opportunity to highlight national expertise and growth. It positions Ukraine as part of the echelon of most creative countries through its 'huge talent potential, high level of education, and the development of innovative technologies' (Ukraine Invest 2020). This builds on the founding of the Department of Cultural and Creative Industries in 2016 by the Ministry of Culture. An indication of the health of the creative industries is seen in the increase in the contribution of arts, sports, entertainment and recreation by 3.7% towards the nation's GDP in 2019. Presenting more recent data, Ukraine Invest 2020 articulates a noticeably more 'upbeat' ecosystem for Ukrainian creative industries and wider entrepreneurship. The United Nations Conference on Trade and Development (2018) recognises Ukraine as the second-largest exporter of creative goods of the transition economies despite the marginal significance of these exports on the sector's global economy. Roughly, 2.8% of the working population work in the creative economy and 3.17% in cultural employment according to the UNESCO Culture for Development indicators (Skavronska 2017).

Experts of the World Economic Forum in Davos say that over the last decade, the creative economy can be considered as a new model of growth (Humenna 2018). This is not just about creative industries, but also about the way in which a creative environment and skills might be a platform for the implementation and development of innovative and creative thinking (Tomlins et al. 2020). In this context, innovation and a creative approach to problem-solving is an efficient development strategy for both the enterprise and the state. Since creativity combines aesthetics, technological and commercial and management activities, it can be considered a competitive advantage, philosophy, motivation or even a strategic weapon for companies and states (Skavronska 2017).

3.2 The Operationalisation of the Creative Economy in Ukraine

The 'direction of travel' for creative industries in Ukraine can be characterised around three related spatial themes: (1) regeneration initiatives, (2) information technology clusters and (3) cultural clusters (Skavronska 2019).

Regeneration initiatives include the renewal of former industrial plants and factories such as in Ivano-Frankivsk (Promprylad), Lviv (ReZavod) and Kharkiv (Fabrika.space). This is not only an economic initiative through developing former industrial sites into hubs of creativity and knowledge, but the projects also have a qualitative focus including non-formal education and aiming at long-term cohesion of citizens, businesses, NGOs and local authorities.

Information technology (IT) clusters have been launched in more than eleven Ukrainian cities, including Lviv, Lutsk, Ternopil, Ivano-Frankivsk, Vinnytsia, Odessa, Mykolaiv, Cherkasy, Dnipro, Kharkiv and Kyiv. These clusters are intended to improve the quality of IT education by assisting universities to bring syllabus changes according to ongoing trends. In doing so, they are tasked with creating the conditions for the development of new IT projects, sharing expertise, organising events, promoting the IT-industry and creating jobs. More widely the number of IT clusters in Ukraine has at least doubled, and we are interested in this both as a process and as a dynamic. Skavronska (2019) notes that the Kyiv IT cluster accommodates about 47% of all IT specialists in the city with the intention of maximising communication among IT businesses, educational institutions and authorities (Mateos-Garcia and Bakhshi 2016).

Cultural clusters have huge growth potential in Ukraine, although it should be noted that there are limits to how far they can be planned. Ukraine's creative economy reflects its rich cultural traditions and history and seeks to preserve its national identity and uniqueness whilst developing new creative ideas. The most developed types of handicrafts include pottery, blacksmithing and weaving. Nowadays, the fastest-growing cultural clusters are clusters of folk artistic crafts 'Suzirya' (Ivano-Frankivsk region) and Krolevets Creative Cluster (Sumy region). There are also different cultural projects such as the Interregional Cluster of Folk Textile Crafts (Lviv, Ivano-Frankivsk, Kyiv and Poltava regions), the 'Gogol places of Poltava region' cluster and the Cluster for Rural Development 'Sorochinsky Yarmarok' (Poltava region).

Creative industries represent a dynamic sector of the national economy with a high development rate. The biggest issue of the Ukrainian creative sector is that creativity is considered equal to culture (Skavronska 2019). The main issue is that foreigners do not regularly purchase handmade products, especially "ethnic" ones. The cultural and historical value of Ukrainian decorations or colours is unknown or irrelevant to customers from abroad, so the goods must be attractive in themselves. Besides, the range of products is limited reducing the likelihood of further purchases even if the buyer is completely satisfied with the product. Other trade barriers include inexperience, tough competition and internal procedural barriers.

3.3 Internationalisation Processes for Small and Medium-Sized Businesses in Ukraine

Two major concepts of export-oriented small and medium-sized businesses have been observed in Ukraine (Centre for Economic Strategy and IER 2019):

1. Outsourcing. This model means integration with the business process of a major foreign company (or companies). It is well developed in the IT sector. However, outsourcing can be more complicated for traditional industries (i.e. enterprises working with raw materials supplied by their customers). Such a business model is highly dependent on the demand of the customers (who are suppliers at the same time), although it can be profitable due to the low cost of resource and the ease of scaling up. The core value is a cheap workforce that can perform simple orders.
2. Building a brand. Another way to build an international business is to develop a company's brand. In this case, a unique brand is created and efforts are made to develop values associated with the brand. In comparison to the previous concept, the brand-building allows more independence, but it also puts pressure on resources. The core advantage of this strategy is a high-end value created by the business and the possibility to grow from a local to a global champion.

Through these known mechanisms, internationalisation is attempted. However, an in-depth understanding of the journey taken by Ukrainian creative entrepreneurs is lacking. Especially a focus on motivations, the barriers faced and how entrepreneurs 'achieved it' is lacking. Creative industries and creative entrepreneurs are important for the Ukrainian economy, as internationalisation offers a rich scope not only to expand a business but also as a valuable source for foreign exchange and an outlet for creative talent. Using six short cases, we explored the journey of creative enterprises in their efforts to internationalise. Within this journey, we found interesting anecdotes that shed light on the efforts of entrepreneurs and how they overcame obstacles.

3.4 Motivations

When analysing the data from the case studies, it was evident that the primary motivations to move abroad was to increase revenue. One of the earlier entrepreneurs who started the internationalisation journey noted that the decision-making criteria for choosing an international market included customer's interest in their product and market purchasing power. The main motivation to go abroad was business expansion and an increase in foreign currency earnings. However, of all the entrepreneurs we interviewed, there was an underlying message about sustainability. Many of the case studies entrepreneurs expanded abroad because they believed that the product they were involved in would be better suited for markets abroad. For example, one of the interviewees noted, *'There is no market for sustainable clothes in Ukraine (or it is very small). Such clothes are expensive in their costs and therefore the final price is high. Consequently, the only option for the enterprise's existence is its exporting story.'* In another case, the entrepreneur stated that the reason for exporting was mainly to do with sending messages of ecological sustainability. They believe that the international markets better understand the messages associated with the ethical and ecological aspects of their product and have better attitudes towards sustainability.

3.5 Implementation

When it comes to implementing the internationalisation plans, the data revealed that each of the case study companies followed their journey differently. One of the firms highlighted that they went about internationalising their business through participation in international profile exhibitions in this country and abroad, in B2B platforms, pieces of training and trade missions. Another firm noted they went about internationalising their business by running a PR campaign in Western mass media, emailing buyers and interacting with marketplaces. They also hired experts to help with the internationalisation. Some of the other entrepreneurs relied on social networks to get their business into other countries. They used their networks and friends to display their products/services and reached foreign clients through freelance exchanges such as "UpWork" (an on-demand freelance platform).

3.6 Barriers

When analysing the barriers, our case study organisations seemed detached from the ecosystem that might drive entrepreneurial change. In general, they acted 'on intuition' and had no state support: just some support from the Chambers of Commerce and a specific NGO. It is not clear that these are gateways to a more comprehensive ecosystem even in locations where high-profile cultural hubs are functioning. Structural and macro-barriers that prevent internationalisation include a lack of skills and know-how within the CCI community for international networking and fundraising, in particular, to maximise the potential of the Creative Europe Programme. The need for greater compliance with the EU's audio-visual legislation hinders the full participation in the media subprogram of Creative Europe. Inconclusive discussions on the legislation of certification of national product/film hinder international co-productions. Random and fragmented support for international mobility prevents the long-term maintenance of international links and partnerships (UNCTAD 2020).

During this examination of the internationalisation efforts and strategies of Ukrainian small and micro firms, it became evident that while there are opportunities and encouragement from agencies to promote creative industries, issues remain that prevent the full-fledged participation of the cultural sector. The main barriers associated with internationalisation include a lack of familiarity with the international environments, language issues and more traditional issues associated with cost, overseas brand building and advertisement. The lack of signposting and dedicated support for creative industries was also cited as impediments for local artisan businesses to expand abroad. From a broader context, Ukraine's sponsorship with other nations of the UN International Year of Creative Economy for Sustainable Development 2021 (UN 2019) frames the economic importance of the creative economy globally as well as domestically. It profiles the scope of international collaboration as a catalyst for the economic diversification of transition economies for and through creative economy development.

4 Conclusion

Case studies were the main mode of data collection for this study. Six in-depth case studies were completed to ascertain the barriers for the internationalisation of firms in Ukrainian creative and cultural industries. The case studies involved document analysis examining the strategies and motivations for internationalisation and in-depth interviews with the owners of the firms. They explored the need for moving abroad, the issues the entrepreneurs had to deal with, the reconciliation of creative inputs in the context of international demand and market expectations and wider networking aspects that led to competitive advantage. The analysis of the data revealed interesting themes that explain some of the unique motivations prompting creative entrepreneurs to look for business abroad. The data also revealed the role played by the remnants of the Soviet era of decision-making and its influence in the current generation of creative entrepreneurs. When it came to barriers, the major issues were (1) the lack of support in signposting entrepreneurs to undertake the process related to internationalisation and (2) information asymmetry, which prevented them making decisions regarding trust and access to local markets.

References

Alon I, Dana LP, Jenkins A (2009) International business by SMEs: empirical findings from New Zealand. Journal of International Business and Economy 10(2):59–78

Amin Moghadasi M, Derakhshandeh B, Ferdosi M, Jafari Sadeghi V (2017) Organizational conformity as an entrepreneurial response to the changes in internationalization process: a study of IT-oriented firms in Saveh. World Journal of Accounting, Finance and Engineering 1 (1):53–64

Ayob AH, Dana LP (2017) Product strategies for export ventures: an empirical investigation among SMEs in an emerging economy. Jurnal Pengurusan (UKM Journal of Management) 50

Bazalgette P (2017) Independent review of the creative industries. Department for Digital, Culture, Media and Sport, London

Beheshti M, Mahdiraji HA, Zavadskas EK (2016) Strategy portfolio optimisation: a copras g-modm hybrid approach. Transform Bus Econ 15(3C):500–519

Biancone PP, Jafari-Sadeghi V (2016) Risk Management in Export Compliance: concepts, procedures, and solutions. In: Cantino V, De Vincentiis P, Racca MG (eds) Risk management: perspectives and open issues. McGraw-Hill, London, UK, pp 64–78

Boix R, Capone F, De Propris L, Lazzeretti L, Sanchez D (2016) Comparing creative industries in Europe. European Urban and Regional Studies 23(4):935–940

Centre for Economic Strategy (CES) and IER (2019) *How can Ukrainian SME grow into national and global champions?* (online). Available at https://ces.org.ua/wp-content/uploads/2019/06/CES-EN-1.pdf. Accessed 10 Sept 2020

Collins H (2018) Creative research: the theory and practice of research for the creative industries. Bloomsbury Publishing

Dana LP (1987) Evaluating policies promoting entrepreneurship – a cross-cultural comparison of entrepreneurship case study: Singapore and Malaysia. Journal of Small Business & Entrepreneurship 4(3):36–41

Farinha C (2017) Developing creative and cultural industries in Ukraine. European Union, Brussels

Felsenstein C, Deans KR, Dana LP (2019) Small firms in regional clusters: local networks and internationalization in the southern hemisphere. J Small Bus Manag 57(2):496–516

Hajiagha SHR, Mahdiraji HA, Hashemi SS (2013) Multi-objective linear programming with interval coefficients. Kybernetes 42:482–496

Hajiagha SHR, Hashemi SS, Mahdiraji HA, Azaddel J (2015) Multi-period data envelopment analysis based on Chebyshev inequality bounds. Expert Syst Appl 42(21):7759–7767

Hajiagha SHR, Mahdiraji HA, Tavana M, Hashemi SS (2018) A novel common set of weights method for multi-period efficiency measurement using mean-variance criteria. Measurement 129:569–581

Humenna O (2018) *Rozvytokklasterukreatyvnykhindustrii v Ukraini* (online). Available at http://ukraine2030.org/uk/blog/view/104-Rozvitok-klasteru-kreativnih-industrij-v-Ukrayini. Accessed 20 Sept 2020

Jafari-Sadeghi V (2020) The motivational factors of business venturing: opportunity versus necessity? A gendered perspective on European countries. J Bus Res 113:279–289

Jafari-Sadeghi V, Nkongolo-Bakenda JM, Anderson RB, Dana LP (2019) An institution-based view of international entrepreneurship: a comparison of context-based and universal determinants in developing and economically advanced countries. Int Bus Rev 28(6):101588

Jafari-Sadeghi V, Dutta DK, Ferraris A, Del Giudice M (2020) Internationalisation business processes in an under-supported policy contexts: evidence from Italian SMEs. Bus Process Manag J 26(5):1055–1074

Koen V, Beom J (2020) OECD Economics Department working papers No. 1607 North Korea: the last transition economy? (online). Available at https://www.oecd-ilibrary.org/docserver/82dee315-en.pdf?expires=1599865387&id=id&accname=guest&checksum=5458DF417C659D7B5B0FD7651E31E49D. Accessed 11 Sept 2020

Kuku P, Quintana C, Shelver A, Henderson M (2018) Creative economy outlook: trends in international trade in creative industries. UNCTAD, Zurich

Landoni P, Dell'era C, Frattini F, Petruzzelli AM, Manelli L (2019). Business model innovation in cultural and creative industries: insights from three leading mobile gaming firms. *Technovation*, p 102084

Landry C (2012) The creative city: a toolkit for urban innovators. Earthscan, London, UK

Mahdiraji HA, Hajiagha SHR, Pourjam R (2011, September) A Grey mathematical programming model to time-cost trade-offs in Project Management under uncertainty. In: IEEE 2011 international conference on Grey systems and intelligent services. IEEE, pp 698–704

Mahdiraji HA, Kazimieras Zavadskas E, Kazeminia A, Abbasi Kamardi A (2019) Marketing strategies evaluation based on big data analysis: a CLUSTERING-MCDM approach. Econ Res-Ekonomskaistraživanja 32(1):2882–2892

Mahdiraji HA, Hafeez K, Kord H, Kamardi AA (2020) Analysing the voice of customers by a hybrid fuzzy decision-making approach in a developing country's automotive market. *Management Decision*

Mahmoudi M, Mahdiraji HA, Jafarnejad A, Safari H (2019) Dynamic prioritization of equipment and critical failure modes. Kybernetes 48(9):1913–1941

Mateos-Garcia J, Bakhshi H (2016) The geography of creativity in the UK: creative clusters, creative people and creative networks. NESTA, London

Mokhtarzadeh NG, Mahdiraji HA, Beheshti M, Zavadskas EK (2018) A novel hybrid approach for technology selection in the information technology industry. Technologies 6(1):34

Mykolaienko N (2019) *(Napiv) revitalizovani: 4 prykladypereosmyslenniaindustrialnykhprostoriv v Ukraini* (online). Available at https://mistosite.org.ua/ru/articles/napivrevitalizovani 4 pryklady-pereosmyslennia-industrialnykh-prostoriv-v-ukraini. Accessed 11 Sept 2020

Neelands J, Belfiore E, Firth C, Hart N, Perrin L, Brock S, Holdaway D, Woddis J (2015) Enriching Britain: culture, creativity and growth. The 2015 report by the Warwick commission on the future of cultural value. University of Warwick, Coventry

Newbigin J (2019) W*hat is creative economy?* British Council. Available at https://creativeconomy.britishcouncil.org/guide/what-creative-economy/. Accessed 11 Sept 2020

Protogeroua A, Kontolaimoua A, Caloghirou Y (2016) *Innovation in the European creative industries: a firm-level empirical approach* (online). Available at <https://www.researchgate.net/publication/311929795_Innovation_in_the_European_creative_industries_a_firm-level_empirical_approach. Accessed 11 Sept 2020

Ratten V, Dana LP, Han M, Welpe I (2007) Internationalisation of SMEs: European comparative studies. Int J Entrep Small Bus 4(3):361–379

Rezaei M, Jafari-Sadeghi V, Bresciani S (2020) What drives the process of knowledge management in a cross-cultural setting: the impact of social capital. Eur Bus Rev 32(3):485–511

Sadeghi V, Biancone PP, Giacoma C, Secinaro S (2017) Export compliance: a missing component of international entrepreneurship. International Journal of Business and Management 12 (11):103–110

Sadeghi V, Biancone PP, Giacoma C, Secinaro S (2018) How does export compliance influence the internationalization of firms: is it a thread or an opportunity? J Glob Entrep Res 8(3):1–15

Sadraei R, Jafari Sadeghi V, Sadraei M (2018) Biotechnology revolution from academic entrepreneurship to industrial: chemo-entrepreneurship. Biometrics & Biostatistics International Journal 7(6):546–550

Skavronska IV (2017) Creative industries in Ukraine: analysis and prospects of the development. Econ Soc 10(2):87–106

Skavronska IV (2019) *Creative clusters and the position of Ukraine in the market of creative products* (online). Available at https://unctad.org/meetings/en/Contribution/cep2019-22-10-contribution_en_Ukraine.pdf. Accessed 10 Sept 2020

SlovoiDilo (2019) *Zovnishniatorhivlia: z kym ta chymnaibilshetorhuvala Ukraina v 2019 rotsi* (online). Available at https://www.slovoidilo.ua/2020/02/20/infografika/ekonomika/zovnishnya-torhivlya-kym-ta-chym-najbilshe-torhuvala-ukrayina-2019-roczi. Accessed 10 Sept 2020

Sukumar A, Jafari-Sadeghi V, Garcia-Perez A, Dutta DK (2020) The potential link between corporate innovations and corporate competitiveness: evidence from IT firms in the UK. J Knowl Manag 24(5):965–983

Taghavifard MT, Amoozad Mahdiraji H, Alibakhshi AM, Zavadskas EK, Bausys R (2018) An extension of fuzzy SWOT analysis: an application to information technology. Information 9 (3):46

TMF Group (2019) *Top challenges of doing business in Ukraine* (online). Available at https://www.tmf-group.com/en/news-insights/business-culture/top-challenges-ukraine/. Accessed 10 Sept 2020

Tomlins R (2015) Social value today. HouseMark, Coventry

Tomlins R, Cuthill H, Richards A, Sukumar A, Malynka O (2020) *Sprinting for creative economy growth – a case study of a business planning and rapid prototyping toolkit for the Brazilian creative economy sector* (online). Available at https://easychair.org/publications/preprint_open/mSbV. Accessed 10 Sept 2020

Towse R (2020) Creative industries. In: Handbook of cultural economics, 3rd edn. Edward Elgar Publishing

Ukraine Invest (2020) *Creative industries* (online). Available at https://ukraineinvest.gov.ua/investment-opportunities/creative-industries/. Accessed 10 Sept 2020

United Nations (2019) *Economic and Financial Committee (Second Committee) status of draft proposals for the 74th session growth* (online). Available at https://www.un.org/en/ga/second/74/proposalstatus.shtml. Accessed 31 Aug 2020

United Nations Conference on Trade and Development (UNCTAD) (2018a) Creative economy outlook: trends in international trade in creative industries. UNCTAD, Zurich

United Nations Conference on Trade and Development (UNCTAD) (2018b) *Summary report* (online). Available at https://unctad.org/meetings/en/SessionalDocuments/dtl_eWeek2018_summary_en.pdf. Accessed 31 July 2020

United Nations Conference on Trade and Development (UNCTAD) (2020) *Creative economy programme* (online). Available at https://unctad.org/en/Pages/DITC/CreativeEconomy/Creative-Economy-Programme. Accessed 31 July 2020

Ushkarenko YV, Chmut AV, Syniakova KM (2018) *Kreatyvnaekonomika: sutnistponiattia ta znachenniadliaUkrainy v umovakhyevropeiskoiintehratsii* (online). Available at http://www.economyandsociety.in.ua/journal/18_ukr/10.pdf. Accessed 10 Sept 2020

Warm (2020) *Prompryladrenovation* (online). Available at https://warm.if.ua/en/projects/promprylad. Accessed 22 Aug 2020

Zanna Creative (2019) *The anatomy of a creative cluster – inspiration from global creative initiatives* (online). Available at https://static1.squarespace.com/static/5d926839e372ee532397e570/t/5d94bf222eb88a6b2368a093/1570029438212/The+Anatomy+of+a+Creative+Cluster++Zanna+Creative.pdf. Accessed 23 Aug 2020

Richard Tomlins is an Assistant Professor at the International Centre for Transformational Entrepreneurship (ICTE) Coventry University and a Visiting Professor at the Department of Energy Management and Technical Diagnostics at Ivano-Frankivsk National Technical University of Oil and Gas, Ukraine. He is an internationally recognised expert in creative economy, social value and entrepreneurial innovation, social enterprise, community cohesion, regeneration, equalities and social inclusion as well as driving business and social gains through commissioning, procurement and social impact measurement.

Arun Sukumar is an Associate Professor of Research in ICTE, Coventry University. His research interests are in in the field of technology entrepreneurship, exploring entrepreneurial ecosystems, technology and sustainability in developing economies. He has published extensively and is an editor and reviewer for journals associated with entrepreneurship. He has secured funding in the areas of social entrepreneurship and has completed projects for Coventry City Council, Africa Union, World Technologies Network, Enterprise Educators UK and British Council.

Oksana Malynka is an Associate Professor of Entrepreneurship and Marketing Department, Ivano-Frankivsk National Technical Oil and Gas University, Ukraine, an expert in marketing, marketing management and brand management, recently involved in the projects on creative economy and entrepreneurship. Oksana has experience of working at four universities of Ivano-Frankivsk. Besides, she is a freelance translator (Ukrainian–English–Russian). She speaks five languages: Ukrainian; Russian; English—fluent; French—reading, writing, speaking with a vocabulary; German—basics. Oksana is also known as a trainer of business literacy projects.

Nataliia Bartkiv works in the Chamber of Commerce as an advisor to the President. She has also established the fashion project Kraika, its online platform, fashion shows, event and courses from young designers and the fashion community. Nataliia is an expert and trainer on export goods and services to Canada and the EU and has organised more than 10 online and offline events for regional entrepreneurs. In the Chamber, she has established a Women's Committee and developed educational courses and events. Nataliia is currently involved in various projects aimed at supporting the creative industries.

Part IV
Quantitative Research Streams: Applied Statistics

Early Internationalising Ventures Facing Ageing and Sizing: International Growth, Entrepreneurial, and Market Orientation

Antonio Daood, Luciano Fratocchi, Vincenza Odorici, and Manuela Presutti

1 Introduction

In the current age of globalisation and advanced technology, evidence shows how small firms can become more and more global and at the same time that internationalisation is becoming a tool of survival, growth, and sustainability for small firms facing globalisation (Alon et al. 2009; Acs et al. 2003).

Internationalisation of small and medium companies can be considered as a dynamic process in which a company involves more and more within foreign markets over time (Welch and Luostarinen 1988). As a consequence, the timing factor is a relevant issue in the studies on a small and medium firm's internationalisation process (Buckley and Casson 1991; Melin 1992; Jones and Coviello 2005; Dana 2002, 2005). In this context environment, time-delayed models, such as the stages theory, do not provide an adequate scenario for either survival or growth. Smaller firms may have neither the prerequisite resources to internationalise nor unlimited time in which to acquire such resources (Ratten et al. 2007; Ayob and Dana 2017).

More specifically, two different concepts have been developed (Ancona et al. 2001; Eden 2009; Autio et al. 2000): (a) The first one is the earliness of the internationalisation (EOI; Autio et al. 2000; Khavul et al. 2010; Oviatt and McDougall 1994; Zhou 2007), that is, the elapsed time that passes from the year

A. Daood · V. Odorici · M. Presutti (✉)
Department of Management, University of Bologna, Bologna, Italy
e-mail: manuela.presutti@unibo.it

L. Fratocchi
Department of Industrial and Information Engineering & Economics, University of L'Aquila, L'Aquila, Italy
e-mail: luciano.fratocchi@univaq.it

V. Jafari-Sadeghi et al. (eds.), *Empirical International Entrepreneurship*, Contributions to Management Science,
https://doi.org/10.1007/978-3-030-68972-8_13

the new venture was established to the year of its first entry into international markets. Hilmersson and Johanson (2016: 72) refer to this concept as "the speed of beginning international," while other authors use the term "venture age" at the first foreign market entry (Autio et al. 2000; Jones and Coviello 2005). Finally, Zucchella et al. (2007) refer to this issue with the term "precocity;" (b) The second concept regards the speed at which a company spreads its activities internationally (Hilmersson and Johanson 2016; Casillas and Acedo 2013). This issue is also called "post-entry speed" (Casillas and Acedo 2013) or "rapidity" (Zucchella et al. 2007).

This paper is focused on the EOI concept; more specifically, its relationship (if any) with the firm's internationalisation growth is investigated (Dana et al. 1999). In this respect, the internationalisation growth of the firm is conceptualised in terms of the scale and geographic scope. While earlier international entrepreneurship scholars have been deeply investigated the impact of EOI on firm's performance (Rodríguez-Serrano and Martín-Armario 2017; Amin Moghadasi et al. 2017; Li et al. 2012; Zhou and Wu 2014; Zhou et al. 2012), the impact on internationalisation growth has not been analysed neither under the theoretical perspective nor the empirical one (Hitt et al. 2016). In other words, whether newness represents a liability, or an advantage remains a controversial issue in this extant literature (Zahra et al. 2018). Consequently, Romanello and Chiarvesio (2019) recently recommended that future studies investigate whether EOI has a real impact on company performance. In this respect, the relationship between EOI and international performance is not static, but it depends on specific contingent elements, which can differently influence the EOI effects. These contingent elements are not limited to firm-specific attributes and they include exogenous contextual factors, such as under-supporting national policies (Jafari-Sadeghi et al. 2020). Moreover, it can depend on the different measures of international growth that are taken into consideration, particularly from a longitudinal perspective of analysis. While extant research has extensively explored structural contingent variables, such as age and size, it has focused less on strategic variables, such as market orientation (MO) and entrepreneurial orientation (EO).

This article improves our understanding of EOI, as it (1) studies the interaction effects of two different and very significant contingent variables (i.e. age and size) on the direct effect of EOI on the international growth of small and medium enterprises (SMEs); (2) distinguishes how age and size effect change according to different levels of both, MO and EO; (3) adopts a longitudinal perspective, capturing not only the growth of the internationalisation process in terms of scale (i.e. foreign sales as a percentage of total sales) but also of scope (i.e. the number of foreign markets served); and (4) defines, measures and analyses the EOI operations conducted by high-tech SMEs located in central Italy.

The paper is organised as follows: In the next section, we develop the theoretical context and the hypotheses. Then, we present the empirical context and applied methods. Subsequently, we present and discuss the main findings, proposing some theoretical and managerial implications. In the final section, we discuss the main limitations of the study and define future research directions.

2 Theoretical Framework and Hypotheses Development

While traditionally, the international business literature focused on large multinational corporations (Dana et al. 1999), in recent decades, a growing amount of evidence has emerged related to companies that began to be international at their inception or during their first years of activity. The debate on SMEs, internationalisation, and globalisation can be traced back to more than 40 years ago and since then, it has received increased attention (Dabić et al. 2019; Presutti et al. 2016).

There has been continuing research in the areas of internationalisation of small businesses especially in the area of exporting (Sadeghi et al. 2017; Wright and Dana 2003; Alon et al. 2009). Such companies have been referred as by several different labels, among them "International New Ventures" (INVs) (McDougall et al. 1994; Oviatt and McDougall 1994, 1997), and "Born Globals" (BG) (Knight 1997; Knight and Cavusgil 1996; Madsen and Servais 1997) are the most used and are often used synonymously. In the next sections of the paper, we will adopt the broader label "Earlier Internationalising Firms" (EIFs), which refers to all firms achieving early internationalisation. Regardless of the label used, studies on EIFs have created a significant research stream that is now recognised as a sub-field within the international entrepreneurship literature (Jones et al. 2011; Rialp et al. 2005; Aspelund et al. 2007; Romanello and Chiarvesio 2019). Dana and Wright (2009) emphasised that entrepreneurship research and international business research were no longer mutually exclusive. Bridging entrepreneurship and international business—two formerly disparate fields—and facilitating their fusion, was the fertile new research field of international entrepreneurship (Dana 2017; Presutti et al. 2020).

Earlier internationalisation behaviour is mainly explained on the basis of "Learning Advantage of Newness" (LAN), which allows younger companies to acquire market knowledge needed to improve their early internationalisation process (Autio et al. 2000). These advantages derive from the less rigid organisational routines and organisational structures characterising younger companies relative to older ones (Dana et al. 2005).

Different general performance measures have been usually used to discuss the consequences of internationalisation speed; Trudgen and Freeman (2014: 555, citing Huit et al. 2008) argues that "...the BG literature has applied an arbitrary mix of financial performance, operational performance, and overall effectiveness measures as performance measures." For example, Mohr and Batsakis (2017) discuss the firm profitability, while Meschi et al. (2017) study the different effects of both age and pace at internationalisation on the survival rate. In the Khavul et al. (2010) no evidence of any significant positive or negative tie between international speed and self-reported general performance scales has been founded. Also, the work of Zhou and Wu (2014) verified that EOI is positively associated with overall sales growth but not with profitability. In a very recent empirical work (Fariborzi and Keyhani 2018: 621), the authors found that "...early internationalisation is better for post-internationalisation survival than late internationalisation," although Trudgen and Freeman (2014: 569) concluded that rapid internationalisation slows BG evolution through the early international entry-development step. At a general level, exports boost profitability, improve capacity utilisation, provide employment and improve trade balances (Dana et al. 2009). More recently, D'Angelo and Buck (2019) noted that exporting is used very rarely as a performance variable for evaluating the positive consequences of EOI. In any case, their work verified a positive connection between the firm's earliness of exporting and its exporting performance. In summary, there exists an open debate in the international entrepreneurship literature about the advantages or disadvantages of EOI (Zahra et al. 2018; D'Angelo and Presutti 2019; Zahra et al. 2000). Following these different approaches, we decide to formulate the first hypothesis as follows:

HP1 *A firm's EOI positively relates to its international growth.*

This positive relationship might be influenced by several potential contingency variables, such as stage industry life cycle, diversity between foreign and domestic cultures, the foreign political context, the international orientation of domestic partners, the degree of centralisation of the firm, its emphasis on deliberate learning, its performance level with respect to aspiration, its pre-internationalisation endowment, and the international exposure of managers (Zahra et al. 2018). Some empirical studies have investigated the relationship between LANs and performance and verified how it can be modified according to specific factors that can mitigate or reinforce it. In this respect, specific interest has recently been devoted to the role of age (Romanello and Chiarvesio 2019), since, as the firm ages, it loses its LAN (i.e. "liability of ageing") (Zhou and Wu 2014). In this respect, Paul and Gupta (2014) found that younger EIFs can count on faster international growth. At the same time, Zhou and Wu (2014) found a strong confirmation of the moderating role of age with respect to the positive relationship between EOI and sales growth. However, this finding has found weak support in recent work by D'Angelo and Buck (2019), which investigated the impact of firm EOI on its export intensity. According to these argumentations, we pass to formulate the second hypothesis:

HP2 *Firm age moderates the way a firm's EOI affects its international growth.*

Another firm dimension generally analysed in international business studies is size. More specifically, many scholars have assumed that firm size is an enabling factor for success in foreign markets (e.g. Buckley 1997) because it is a proxy of available resources (Berra et al. 1995; Haveman 1993; Verbeke and Kenworthy 2008). However, some empirical investigations did not confirm this association (Calof 1994; McNaughton 2003) or obtained mixed results (Coviello and McAuley 1999). Furthermore, when considering EIFs, one must keep in mind that the small dimension increases the firm's organisational flexibility and, in turn, its rapid internal communication and decision-making processes. Moreover, the absence of middle management in entrepreneurial small firms makes the link between top management cognition and capability deployment direct, significantly enhancing firms' ability to proactively adjust (Autio et al. 2011). In other words, as the firm gets larger, it loses its LAN (i.e. "liability of sizing"). From an empirical viewpoint,

Jiménez Naharro et al. (2010) found that the micro-companies (That is, the ones with fewer than 10 employees) were the largest group of EIFs among the Spanish sample they analysed. On the other hand, Amorós et al. (2016) found a positive relationship between the proportion of foreign customers and the firm's size. Moreover, Li et al. (2012) postulated and empirically confirmed that size has an inverted-U-shaped relationship with the positive slope for smaller companies and with the negative one for very large companies. Finally, a recent study by D'Angelo and Buck (2019) verified the moderating effect of the firm's size. The above discussion leads to the formulation of the following hypothesis:

HP3 *Firm size moderates the way a firm's EOI affects its international growth.*

The three hypotheses proposed earlier have already been investigated by international business scholars, with different results, and the relationships among related variables are quite established. From here, our theoretical model advances the existing body of research by considering two other strategic variables, namely, entrepreneurial orientation (EO) and market orientation (MO), that may impact the moderating effects of age and size on the way EOI affects international growth.

EO and MO have been considered two relevant dimensions of strategic orientation influencing the foreign performance of SMEs (Presutti and Odorici 2019; Covin and Miller 2014; Lee et al. 2001; McDougall and Oviatt 2000) and their possibility to compete despite the direct competition with the large and resource-rich corporation (Ayob and Dana 2017; Mokhtarzadeh et al. 2020a). EO is the set "organising principles" by which decisions are taken; therefore, it relates to the strategy-making processes that allow companies to take those risky decisions that can qualify as proactive and innovative (Covin and Slevin 1989; Naman and Slevin 1993; Rauch et al. 2009; Wales et al. 2013; Wales 2016; Karami and Tang 2019). In contrast, MO is the "degree to which the business unit obtains and uses information from customers, develops a strategy that will meet customer needs, and implements that strategy by being responsive to customers' needs and wants" (Raju et al. 2011: 13; Ruekert 1992).

The firm's EO characterises the ability of a company to assure learning processes in a new foreign market. For example, the propensity to proactively search for new business partners (which is one of EO's components; Lumpkin and Dess 1996) will induce the company to find foreign suppliers and customers. This, in turn, will allow the company to more intensively exchange valuable knowledge with foreign partners and improve its strategic competitiveness abroad (Sapienza et al. 2006). Therefore, the EO provides resource-constrained SMEs with the requested amount of capabilities required to adequately compete abroad (Wiklund and Shepherd 2003, 2005). A pristine example of EO-related capabilities is those related to networking (e.g. Mokhtarzadeh et al. 2020b), which not only are critical for the very innovation performance of firms but also for its internationalisation, and knowledge foresight (Jafari-Sadeghi et al. 2019), which are key when seeking international opportunities. In this respect, Sapienza et al. (2006) found that EO has a positive impact on the intensity of the learning effort the company carries out in the international market. Similar findings have emerged in, among others, Knight and Cavusgil (2004),

Gerschewski et al. (2015), Kuivalainen et al. (2007), and Jantunen et al. (2008). Finally, D'Angelo and Buck (2019) investigated the level of decision-making centralisation, one of the EO dimensions (i.e. high levels of decentralisation are correlated with high levels of EO—cf. Bouchard and Basso 2011; Merz and Sauber 1995) and found that the higher the centralisation is, the higher the moderating effect of the firm's age and size on the relationship between EOI and the internationalisation process.

We recall that EOI is positively connected with international export performance primarily because of LAN, which, in turn, is expected to decrease as the firm gets older and larger. Considering that EO expresses the intensity of learning effort employed by a firm during internationalisation, probably it is realistic that higher levels of EO would lessen both liabilities of ageing and liability of sizing. In other words, the firms that are able to maintain high levels of EO over time might limit the loss of LANs deriving by higher age and size. Therefore, we can formulate the following hypotheses:

HP4(a) *The moderating effect of a firm's age on the relationship between the EOI and its international growth is greater for firms featuring a lower EO than those with a higher EO.*

HP5(a) *The moderating effect of a firm's size on the relationship between the EOI and its international growth is greater for firms featuring a lower EO than those with a higher EO.*

Regarding MO, Zhou et al. (2012) suggest that early internationalisation allows companies to develop market-specific capabilities that allow EIFs to succeed and to realise rapid internationalisation. More specifically, marketing capabilities (Day 1994; Fang and Zou 2009; Vorhies and Morgan 2005) embedded in the firm's entrepreneurial process allow the company to discover the quality of information regarding international markets (Zhou et al. 2012; Sadeghi et al. 2019a), which, in turn, makes it possible to bypass the scarcity of absorptive capacity, with the latter needed to transform knowledge-based processes in value-generation activities (Zahra 2005). In other words, "the timing of international market entry has an impact on a young firm's marketing capabilities, which in turn drives its international growth" (Zhou et al. 2012: 26). Considering that MO expresses the firm's ability to innovate in order to respond to different evolutions of the market, it seems reasonable to speculate that those firms that decide to invest in high levels of MO when ageing and growing in size might limit the losses in LAN associated with the processes of ageing and sizing (Majocchi and Presutti 2009).

Notably, it is reasonable to expect MO to have an impact on this relation, which is similar to the one expected for EO, as evidence suggests that both EO and MO have a positive effect on firm performance (Presutti and Odorici 2019) and that firms able to align high levels of EO and MO maximise their performance (Boso et al. 2013, 2014). In other words, we expect that the effect of EOI on international growth will be weaker for firms with low MO than for firms with high MO as firms become older and larger. This consideration leads to the formulation of the following hypotheses:

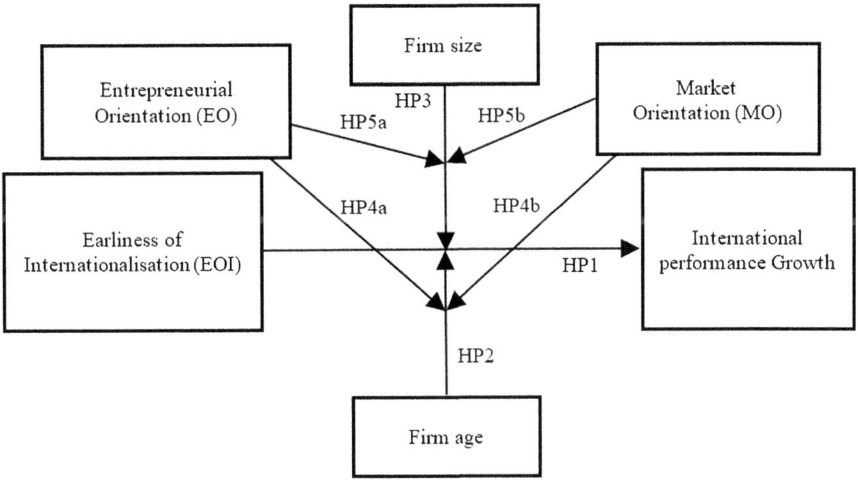

Fig. 1 Hypothesised model

HP4(b) *The moderating effect of a firm's age on the relationship between the EOI and its international growth is greater for firms featuring a lower MO than for those featuring a higher MO.*

HP5(b) *The moderating effect of a firm's size on the relationship between the EOI and its international growth is greater for firms featuring a lower MO than for those featuring a higher MO.*

Figure 1 summarises the hypotheses of the selected model.

3 Data and Methodology

3.1 Empirical Setting

To test the previously discussed hypotheses, we investigated a sample of high-tech SMEs exporting and operating abroad located inside a cluster in Rome (D'Angelo and Presutti 2019; Presutti et al. 2019).

To select the sample, we used the Chamber of commerce data on high-tech companies during two different periods of analysis. Specifically, we collected data on the computer, electronics, telecommunications, and the new economy industries. During the two analysed periods (2007 and 2018, respectively we collected data from October to December). According to the Chamber of Commerce database, the total population comprised 550 companies at the end of October 2007 and we collected responses from 290. In 2018, only 198 (of the 290) had survived and we collected 168 responses. In order to realise a dynamic analysis, we included only

Table 1 Descriptive statistics of the untransformed variables (average values)

	2007	2018
Firm total foreign sales (K€)	265	345
Number of served foreign markets	5	7
Total sales (K€)	505	620
Firm age (years)	7	16

these 168 companies to test the hypotheses and discuss the results from both observation periods.

We used a structured questionnaire with Likert scales to collect any necessary information submitted to entrepreneurs considered representative of all small firms. In the case of more than one entrepreneur per firm (only for 3% of the sample), we weighted the average of the experience values considering the number of total entrepreneurs. We collected additional firm-specific information to complete our dataset.

Table 1 describes the statistics of the variables. The investigated sample increased both its total foreign revenues in the two considered periods (going from 265 to 345 million euros) and the number of served foreign markets (on average 5 in 2007 and 7 at the end of 2018). In 2018, the average sales of companies are €620,000 (more than 50% of which accounts for foreign sales), and their average age is 16 years (7 years in 2007).

3.2 Variables and Measures

Dependent Variable. The international growth is analysed by focusing on the dimension of the scale and the scope of the process (Yli-Renko et al. 2001. To assure a dynamic analysis, we measured the scale of international growth including the growth rate of foreign annual sales of the firms between the two observation periods (2007 and 2018). To measure the scope of international growth, we considered the difference between the number of foreign markets served at the end of 2007 and 2018 according to many previous studies (Lu and Beamish 2001; Tallman and Li 1996).

Independent Variable. The EOI is measured as the amount of time (expressed in years) that passed from the year the new venture was started to the year it invested in its first international market (Autio et al. 2000; Khavul et al. 2010; Oviatt and McDougall 1994; Zhou 2007). This variable is considered fixed in both the analysed periods.

Moderating Variables. We adopted moderating variables, namely, size, age, MO and EO. We used the logarithm of total sales at the end of the two periods to measure the firm's size (Yli-Renko et al. 2001; Laforet 2013). We measured the firm's age as the number of years the firm has been created (Zahra and Hayton 2008). Moreover, we measured EO by adopting the scale proposed by Lumpkin and Dess (1996) which considers five issues (proactiveness, innovativeness, risk propensity, proclivity to be competitive/aggressive, and autonomy). However, only three dimensions are significant in our research: innovativeness (measured with three items), proactiveness (three items), and risk propensity (two items). Having assumed a dynamic perspective, we used the difference between the values of the items at the two observation periods. Finally, to measure MO, we included an index characterised by three different dimensions: market intelligence generation, dissemination, and responsiveness (Boso et al. 2013; Jaworski and Kohli 1993). We used two items each to measure market intelligence generation and dissemination, and three for market responsiveness. To capture a dynamic perspective, we calculated the difference in the values of the items between the observation periods.

Control Variables. We consider two main categories of control variables. The first category was chosen to consider previous entrepreneurial experience; therefore, we used the following two: (a) the number of companies launched before the company's foundation (as a proxy for the generic entrepreneurial experience) and (b) the number of companies launched in the same sectors before the company's foundation (as a proxy for the industry-specific entrepreneurial experience). In this way, we differentiated the novice and the habitual entrepreneur according to the specific level of experience of habitual entrepreneurs within the industry. We included the growth rates of the four analysed sectors during analysed periods.

3.3 Reliability and Validity

The validity and reliability of data are assured in this research. First of all, we improved the survey by pretesting the questionnaire to check potentially critical items. Second, only validated measurement items have been selected in our research to discuss our research's problem. At the same time, as many variables are measured by considering the personal opinions of entrepreneurs and thus could be affected by common method variance, we develop Harman's one-factor test to partially solve this problem. We obtained three factors with eigenvalues greater than one, with the first factor accounting for only 23% of the total variance and for the dependent and independent variables loading on different factors. Thus, we verified that common method variance is not a problem for our data. Finally, for EO and MO, we used measures featuring multiple items.

To validate the selected variables to measure EO and MO, we used the factor analysis (Churchill 1979) for both periods of analysis. This analysis confirms a high degree of internal reliability of the data as all the coefficient alphas in both analysed periods were all greater than 0.75. In a second step, we applied the LISREL system to realise the confirmatory factor analysis (CFA) on the data. As shown in Table 2, the model performs very well: The standardised factors are all above the recommended minimum of 0.40 and the goodness-of-fit index (GFI) is greater than 0.85 in each period.

Finally, we addressed the endogeneity problem. In particular, to identify the endogeneity of the explanatory variable, EOI, we used the Durbin–Wu–Hausman

Table 2 Model measurement in both analysed periods

	Measurement item	Standardised loading 2007	Standardised loading 2018	Cronbach's alpha 2007	Cronbach's alpha 2018
Market orientation (MO)	We generate a large amount of information concerning trends in our target markets	0.62**	0.72**		
	We are quick to detect fundamental shifts in our target markets	0.72***	0.70***	0.75**	0.82***
	Information that can influence the way we serve our customers takes a long time to reach relevant personnel	0.69***	0.70***		
	Important information about our customers is often "lost in the system"	0.62***	0.67***		
	Information about our competitors' activities often reaches relevant personnel too late to be of any use	0.71***	0.72***		
	We are quick to respond to important changes in our competitors' price structures in target markets	0.72***	0.77***		
	We rapidly respond to competitive actions that threaten us in our target markets	0.70***	0.80***		
Entrepreneurial orientation (EO)	Our company is known as an innovator among businesses in our industry	0.68**	0.73***		
	We promote new, innovative products/services in our company	0.72***	0.77***		
	Our company provides leadership in developing new products/services	0.68***	0.72***		
	Top managers of our company generally tend to invest in high-risk projects	0.72***	0.73***	0.72**	0.77**
	This company shows a great deal of tolerance for high-risk projects	0.70***	0.72***		
	We seek to exploit anticipated changes in our target market ahead of our rivals	0.73***	0.74***		
	We seize initiatives whenever possible in our target market operations	0.70***	0.72***		
	We act opportunistically to shape the business environment in which we operate	0.70***	0.75***		
Goodness-of-fit index (GFI) = 0.84 Adjusted goodness-of-fit index (AGFI) = 0.75					

(continued)

Table 2 (continued)

	Measurement item	Standardised loading		Cronbach's alpha	
		2007	2018	2007	2018

The table summarises the results of confirmatory factor analysis on the different items (second column) selected to measure the independent variables (first column). For each item, the table shows the values of factor loading (third column) for both selected periods. In the last column, the extracted alpha average variance is shown. In the last row of the table, the values of both GFI and AGFI are illustrated. $*p < 0.05$; $**p < 0.01$; $***p < 0.001$

Table 3 Results of the Durbin–Wu–Hausman test

	Scale of international performance	Scope of international performance
EOI	180.3	120.15

Chi-square values are presented in this table

test. Table 3 illustrates the test results, which reveal that EOI does not suffer from endogeneity problems when international growth is considered in both of its dimensions (Table 3).

4 Results

First of all, the multicollinearity problems do not affect our data as the variance inflation factor (VIF) values were below the recommended cut-off point of 2.5 (Allison 1994). Table 4 shows descriptive statistics and zero-order correlations among the variables.

We used the ordinary least squares technique with Stata software to test our hypotheses. In order to check for survivor bias, we applied the Heckman procedure. The results verified that survivorship bias is not a problem in our data. First of all, focusing on the full sample we selected as dependent a binary variable which is equal to one of the firms still exists at the end of 2015 and zero otherwise. The in the model is the "duration of access to local public funding," that is for how many years between 2005 and 2018 the firm has accessed local public funding. We selected this exclusion restriction variable because it is different and independent from "local public funding for international growth" (Messeghem et al. 2017), while they could only increase the likelihood of the companies to grow and thus to survive inside the local context; Indeed as shown in Table 3, the "duration of access to local public funding" is significantly correlated with the survivor but not with international growth. In the next steps, we included the restriction variable as an independent variable to estimate international growth, the robustness check verified the independence between these two variables, confirming again our decision to select the "duration of access to local public funding" as restriction variable. Table 5 shows the results of the probit estimates of the selection equation for our different selected models. We obtained that the likelihood of a firm surviving until 2018 is positively

Table 4 Correlations among variables (2007–2018)

Variables	1	2	3	4	5	6	7	8	9	10	11	12	13	14	15
1. Growth rate of electronic sector	1														
2. Growth rate of computer sector	0.22*	1													
3. Growth rate of telecommunications	0.30*	0.11	1												
4. Growth rate of new economy	0.15*	0.26*	0.21**	1											
5. Firm size	0.11	0.12	0.28	0.18	1										
6. Firm age	0.21	0.28	0.19*	0.10	0.18**	1									
7. Entrepreneurial experience in different industries	0.10	0.25	0.15	0.19*	0.18*	0.25	1								
8. Entrepreneurial experience in similar industries	0.28	0.21	0.03	0.22	0.34*	0.15*	0.19*	1							
9. Earliness of internationalisation	0.23	0.11	0.13	0.33	0.18*	0.21*	0.40*	0.18*	1						
10. EO	0.01	0.34	0.22	0.12	0.14*	0.01*	0.55*	0.22*	0.09	1					
11. MO	0.01	0.34	0.54	0.01	0.23	0.15*	0.56	0.09*	0.11*	0.23*	1				
12. Duration of access to local public funding	0.02	0.55	0.09	0.11	0.23	0.11	0.08	0.09	0.03	0.34	0.23	1			
13. Survivor of companies	0.01	0.08	0.11	0.13	0.23	0.24	0.09	0.22	0.44	0.55	0.22	0.35**	1		
14. Foreign sales	0.55	0.33	0.54	0.07	0.11*	0.33*	0.09	0.11	0.22*	0.34*	0.02*	0.04	0.20	1	
15. Number of served foreign markets	0.11	0.09	0.33	0.40	-0.22	0.09	0.11	0.09	0.02*	0.011*	0.05*	0.12	0.09	0.23	1

The table shows the values of the correlations among all the variables included in the study. $^{*}p < 0.05$; $^{**}p < 0.01$; $^{***}p < 0.001$

Table 5 Results of the fixed effects model (FEM) regression analysis of international performance growth (2007–2018)

	Probit 1	Model 1		Probit 2	Model 2		Probit 3	Model 3		Probit 4	Model 4	
		% of foreign sales	N. of served markets		% of foreign sales	N. of served markets		% of foreign sales	N. of served markets		% of foreign sales	N. of served markets
Duration of access to local public funding	0.34**			0.15**			0.09**			0.23**		
Growth rate of electronic sector	0.15	0.08	0.18	0.09	0.15	0.12	0.12	0.89	0.58	0.11	0.13	−0.15
Growth rate of computer sector	0.09	0.09	0.18	0.23	0.23	0.03	0.08	0.01	0.19	0.07	0.05	0.23
Growth rate of telecommunications	0.44	0.19	0.48	0.09	0.26	0.22	0.02	0.13	0.13	0.02	0.16	0.14
Growth rate of new economy	0.04	0.09	0.27	0.22	0.18	0.11	0.22	0.04	0.15	0.33	0.16	0.25
Firm size	0.23*	−0.15	−0.33	0.25*	−0.35	−0.45	0.35*	−0.69	−0.21	0.09	−0.18	−0.27
Firm age	0.09*	−0.21*	−0.43*	0.14*	−0.30*	−0.27*	0.22*	−0.39*	−0.39*	0.23*	−0.33*	−0.23*
Entrepreneurial experience in different industries	0.01	0.11	0.19*	0.02	0.19	0.08	0.20*	0.23	0.21	0.11*	0.23	0.08
Entrepreneurial experience in similar industries	0.09	0.25*	0.28*	0.08	0.05**	0.01*	0.12	0.06*	0.08*	0.10*	0.05*	0.23*
Earliness of internationalisation				0.15	0.38**	−0.08*	0.09	0.28	−0.24*	0.08	0.18	−0.38*
Earliness of internationalisation*age							0.08	0.18	−0.18*	0.08	0.02	−0.22*
Earliness of internationalisation*size										0.11	0.34	−0.44*
Lambda		0.11	0.43		0.33	0.13		0.09	0.33		0.15	0.20

(continued)

Table 5 (continued)

	Probit 1	Model 1		Probit 2	Model 2		Probit 3	Model 3		Probit 4	Model 4	
		% of foreign sales	N. of served markets		% of foreign sales	N. of served markets		% of foreign sales	N. of served markets		% of foreign sales	N. of served markets
R^2		0.55	0.45		0.62	0.59		0.68	0.63		0.70	0.67
Var R^2					0.07	0.14		0.06	0.04		0.02	0.04
***F* statistic**		40.08**	41.75**		42.05**	42.27*		44.05**	44.07*		46.09**	45.54**

influenced by both the "duration to access to local funding" (2005–2018) and the firm's size and age. Indeed, results show how the coefficients of the inverse Mills ratio coefficient (λ) correction are not significant. In summary, our data are not affected by the survivorship bias. Same considerations are available for Tables 6 and 7.

Moving to the analysis of our hypotheses, Tables 5, 6, 7, 8 and 9 show the results obtained with the regression analysis for the different tested models. Table 5 shows the results for the first three hypotheses of our research, while Tables 6, 7, 8 and 9 show the results for hypotheses 4a, 4b, 5a and 5b. In all the tables, we distinguish the results for the two different selected measures of international growth, namely, international scale and scope.

Table 5 shows four different models; the first one includes all control variables and two moderator variables (size and age), the second introduces the EOI, and the last two introduces the interaction effects. Model 1 shows how the entrepreneurial experience in similar industries influences in a positive way the international growth, and age in a negative way. Model 2 confirms hypothesis 1 for international scale (positive and statistically significant) but not for geographic scope (negative and statistically significant). Thus, hypothesis 1 is only partially confirmed. In Model 3, age reinforces the negative effect of EOI on geographic scope, while it is not significant for international scale. Thus, hypothesis 2 is only partially confirmed. The same results are obtained for the interaction between EOI and size, with the negative effect of EOI on geographic scope increasing with the size of the venture, only partially confirming hypothesis 3.

Table 6 shows the results for hypothesis 4a. In Model 1, we insert the EOI, and in Model 2, we add its interaction with age. The EOI is positive and significant on an international scale only; the age, positively moderates the international scale only in the case of low levels of EO. Thus, hypothesis 4a is partially confirmed.

In Table 7, we report the results for hypothesis 4b. In Model 1, we insert the EOI, and in Model 2, we insert its interaction with age. In this case, we verify how EOI positively and significantly affects the international scale independently of high or low levels of MO. Age reinforces this positive effect only for ventures with a high level of MO, partially confirming hypothesis 4b.

In Table 8, we show the results for hypothesis 5a. In Model 1, we insert the EOI, and in Model 2, we insert its interaction with size. The EOI is positive and significant on both measures of international growth independent of high and low levels of EO, and size reinforces this effect. The effect is higher for a low level of EO. Thus, hypothesis 5a is confirmed.

In Table 9, we show the results for hypothesis 5b. In Model 1, we insert the EOI, and in Model 2, we insert its interaction with size. The EOI always has positive effects on international growth. Size reinforces these effects, but these results are positive only for ventures with a high level of MO. Thus, hypothesis 5b is not confirmed.

Table 6 Results of the fixed effects model (FEM) regression analysis of international performance growth with the interaction between earliness of internationalisation and age for low and high levels of EO (2007–2018)

		Model 1					Model 2			
		% of foreign sales		N. of served markets			% of foreign sales		N. of served markets	
	Probit 1	High EO	Low EO	High EO	Low EO	Probit 2	High EO	Low EO	High EO	Low EO
Duration of access to local public funding	0.55**					0.15***				
Growth rate of electronic sector	0.08	0.10	0.18	0.14	0.15	0.08	0.18	0.11	0.19	0.20
Growth rate of computer sector	0.23	0.23	0.35	0.25	0.14	0.12	0.44	0.14	0.23	0.23
Growth rate of telecommunications	0.03	0.23	0.27	0.20	0.28	0.22	0.25	0.47	0.20	0.26
Growth rate of new economy	0.11	0.35	0.15	0.23	0.13	0.33	0.14	0.12	0.38	0.35
Firm size	0.22*	−0.25	−0.28	0.21	0.11	0.22	−0.11	−0.14	−0.30	−0.23
Firm age	0.11*	−0.30	−0.30*	−0.34*	−0.29*	0.13	−0.40	−0.10*	−0.25	−0.23
Entrepreneurial experience in different industries	0.08	0.14	0.11*	0.39	0.11	0.03	0.28	0.24	0.25	0.18
Entrepreneurial experience in similar industries	0.22	0.28*	0.21*	0.258**	0.04*	0.08	0.05*	0.09*	0.07*	0.13*
Earliness of internationalisation	0.11*	0.20*	0.24*	0.20	−0.13	0.25*	0.25*	0.34*	0.24	−0.33
Earliness of internationalisation*age						0.08	0.11	0.50**	0.20	0.15
Lambda		0.09	0.22	0.08	0.12		0.11	0.55	0.60	0.06
R^2		0.55	0.54	0.56	0.54		0.60	0.66	0.60	0.56
***F* statistic**		40.02*	41.34*	42.02*	40.05*		41.11*	42.23*	40.09*	41.08*

Table 7 Results of the fixed effects model (FEM) regression analysis of international performance growth with the interaction between earliness of internationalisation and age for low and high levels of MO (2007–2018)

	Probit 1	Model 1				Probit 2	Model 2			
		% of foreign sales		N. of served markets			% of foreign sales		N. of served markets	
		High MO	Low MO	High MO	Low MO		High MO	Low MO	High MO	Low MO
Duration of access to local public funding	0.43**					0.11**				
Growth rate of electronic sector	0.11	0.10	0.22	0.15	0.19	0.02	0.12	0.19	0.13	0.22
Growth rate of computer sector	0.08	0.19	0.38	0.24	0.24	0.01	0.29	0.20	0.18	0.25
Growth rate of telecommunications	0.23	0.18	0.20	0.10	0.19	0.05	0.18	0.29	0.18	0.20
Growth rate of new economy	0.10	0.18	0.10	0.27	0.10	0.34	0.20	0.20	0.29	0.10
Firm size	0.14*	0.1	0.15	0.18	−0.16	0.30*	0.28	0.28	0.10	−0.14
Firm age	0.20*	−0.23	−0.07*	−0.11*	−0.22*	0.23*	−0.29	−0.14*	−0.21*	−0.23*
Entrepreneurial experience in different industries	0.09	0.10	0.14*	0.34	0.19	0.09	0.30	0.29	0.28	0.19
Entrepreneurial experience in similar industries	0.02	0.11	0.10*	0.08	0.22	0.11	0.23	0.09	0.11	0.33
Earliness of internationalisation	0.24	0.20*	0.10*	0.25*	0.01*	0.40	0.10**	0.19*	0.35*	0.11*
Earliness of internationalisation*age						0.20	0.09*	0.25**	0.05*	0.24**
Lambda		0.11	0.10	0.09	0.23		0.20	0.03	0.33	0.20
R^2		0.53	0.44	0.66	0.54		0.61	0.65	0.63	0.56
***F* statistic**		40.22*	41.24*	42.12*	41.05*		41.10*	42.26*	40.11*	40.08*

Table 8 Results of the fixed effects model (FEM) regression analysis of international performance growth with the interaction between earliness of internationalisation and size for low and high levels of EO (2007–2018)

		Model 1					Model 2			
		% of foreign sales		N. of served markets			% of foreign sales		N. of served markets	
	Probit 1	High EO	Low EO	High EO	Low EO	Probit 2	High EO	Low EO	High EO	Low EO
Duration of access to local public funding	0.43**					0.11**				
Growth rate of electronic sector	0.11	0.10	0.22	0.15	0.19	0.02	0.12	0.19	0.13	0.22
Growth rate of computer sector	0.08	0.19	0.38	0.24	0.24	0.01	0.29	0.20	0.18	0.25
Growth rate of telecommunications	0.23	0.18	0.20	0.10	0.19	0.05	0.18	0.29	0.18	0.20
Growth rate of new economy	0.10	0.18	0.10	0.27	0.10	0.34	0.20	0.20	0.29	0.10
Firm size	0.14*	0.1	0.15	0.18	−0.16	0.30*	0.28	0.28	0.10	−0.14
Firm age	0.20*	−0.23	−0.07*	−0.11*	−0.22*	0.23*	−0.29	−0.14*	−0.21*	−0.23*
Entrepreneurial experience in different industries	0.09	0.10	0.14*	0.34	0.19	0.09	0.30	0.29	0.28	0.19
Entrepreneurial experience in similar industries	0.02	0.11	0.10*	0.08	0.22	0.11	0.23	0.09	0.11	0.33
Earliness of internationalisation	0.24	0.20*	0.10*	0.25*	0.01*	0.40	0.10**	0.19*	0.35*	0.11*
Earliness of internationalisation*size						0.20	0.09*	0.25**	0.05*	0.24**
Lambda		0.11	0.10	0.09	0.23		0.20	0.03	0.33	0.20
R^2		0.53	0.44	0.66	0.54		0.61	0.65	0.63	0.56
***F* statistic**		40.22*	41.24*	42.12*	41.05*		41.10*	42.26*	40.11*	40.08*

Table 9 Results of the fixed effects model (FEM) regression analysis of international performance growth with the interaction between earliness of internationalisation and size for low and high levels of MO (2007–2018)

	Probit 1	Model 1				Probit 2	Model 2			
		% of foreign sales		N. of served markets			% of foreign sales		N. of served markets	
		High MO	Low MO	High MO	Low MO		High MO	Low MO	High MO	Low MO
Duration of access to local public funding	0.43**					0.11**				
Growth rate of electronic sector	0.11	0.10	0.22	0.15	0.19	0.02	0.12	0.19	0.13	0.22
Growth rate of computer sector	0.08	0.19	0.38	0.24	0.24	0.01	0.29	0.20	0.18	0.25
Growth rate of telecommunications	0.23	0.18	0.20	0.10	0.19	0.05	0.18	0.29	0.18	0.20
Growth rate of new economy	0.10	0.18	0.10	0.27	0.10	0.34	0.20	0.20	0.29	0.10
Firm size	0.14*	0.1	0.15	0.18	−0.16	0.30*	0.28	0.28	0.10	−0.14
Firm age	0.20*	−0.23	−0.07*	−0.11*	−0.22*	0.23*	−0.29	−0.14*	−0.21*	−0.23*
Entrepreneurial experience in different industries	0.09	0.10	0.14*	0.34	0.19	0.09	0.30	0.29	0.28	0.19
Entrepreneurial experience in similar industries	0.02	0.11	0.10*	0.08	0.22	0.11	0.23	0.09	0.11	0.33
Earliness of internationalisation	0.24	0.16*	0.10*	0.05*	0.09*	0.40	0.54**	0.11	0.15*	0.25*
Earliness of internationalisation*size						0.20	0.14**	0.19	0.22*	0.20
Lambda		0.11	0.10	0.09	0.23		0.20	0.03	0.33	0.20
R^2		0.53	0.44	0.66	0.54		0.61	0.65	0.63	0.56
***F* statistic**		40.22*	41.24*	42.12*	41.05*		41.10*	42.26*	40.11*	40.08*

5 Discussion and Main Implications

We verified how the earlier a firm internationalises, the greater the scale of the achieved international presence but the lesser its scope. While a positive relationship between a firm's EOI and its international scale growth (foreign sales) is obtained from this data, a negative one we found between a firm's EOI and its international scope growth (expressed in terms of the number of foreign countries). This result is interesting given that among international entrepreneurship scholars, the success of early internationalised new ventures seems linked to an aggressive multimarket presence that reinforces the ability to identify and exploit market opportunities (Knight and Liesch 2016) and to improve learning and growth (Zahra et al. 2000). The emphasis on learning from different sources of knowledge has induced scholars to assume a relationship between early internationalisation and geographic diversity (Wu and Zhou 2018: 63), even if their understanding of this relationship is limited (Patel et al. 2018; Sui and Baum 2014).

Our results highlight the complexity of the relationship between early internationalisation and post-entry international development, suggesting consideration of different dimensions to measure international performance growth (Dana 2004; Dana and Wright 2009). When the scale and scope of international growth are treated as distinct trajectories of development, the effect of early internationalisation is different. More specifically, the result is definitively negative for geographic scope, confirming the difficulty to grow by simultaneously pursuing both paths (Hashai 2011). This result confirms what Zhou and Wu (2014) suggest about the existence of limits to how well early internationalisation can extend learning advantage. Zahra et al. (2018) suggest that early internationalisation could have limited effects because of the relationship between LAN and cultural differences between markets. The sources to learn for a company could decrease when firms invest resources to invest in foreign markets very similar to domestic ones. Thus, the negative effect of early internationalisation on geographic scope could be justified by a sort of learning slowdown produced by markets' homogeneity (Bayfield et al. 2009). However, we cannot reach this conclusion because we do not distinguish foreign markets in terms of their cultural distance. In a recent paper, Wu and Zhou (2018), who used the Blau index, which measures the number of global regions served by firms and their importance, also found no supposed positive effect between EOI and geographic scope. On the other hand, studies that investigate the effect of international scope on BG survival find a difference between intraregional and interregional geographic diversification: More specifically, while the first one increases survival chances, the latter reduces them (Patel et al. 2018). Thus, the results we observed could depend on the need for early internationalised firms to slow down or to shrink their multimarket exposition to reduce the risk of failure (Biancone and Jafari-Sadeghi 2016). The multimarket approach adopted from inception could be resized by EIF, as these firms could have a harder time combining and pursuing both the exploitation and exploration of foreign markets. While in the stage model, market exploitation is the condition to enter new foreign markets, for early internationalised ventures, things seem to work the other way around. After enlarging their market scope, firms could concentrate their scarce resources on exploiting fewer markets.

An alternative explanation of our result could be that early internationalised ventures, in pursuing a multimarket approach since inception, use parameters different from gradually internationalised firms. Crick and Jones (1999) show that small and medium high-tech firms tend to choose markets according to the perception of growth opportunities rather than cultural distances. They could fall more often into unexpected difficulties, requiring them to slow down a market entry or to abandon market praesidium to avoid compromising firm survival. All these considerations suggest that newness cannot always be considered an advantage but can be a limit for EIFs when international diversification growth is considered.

For hypotheses 2 and 3, our results differ from those of other studies. Age and size negatively influence the relationship between EOI and international growth (D'Angelo and Buck 2019; Zhou and Wu 2014). However, the distinction we made between the scale and scope of international growth allows us to better understand this effect for early internationalised ventures. When factoring in age and size, the positive effect of EOI on international scale growth is no longer significant. One explanation might be ascribed to life cycle dynamics. In fact, as with any other growth process, sales in a new foreign market are expected to grow until a certain threshold, after which stabilisation should arrive with the maturity phase. Given that older and larger firms are likely to be closer to such a maturity phase, the advantages connected to early internationalisation in terms of foreign sales growth could no longer be present in the reference period, and differences with gradual internationalised firms disappear. However, when factoring in age and size, the negative effect of EOI on the geographic scope is reinforced. While age usually increases the geographic scope, the relationship with the size is less clear (McNaughton 2003). In our research, both age and size have a negative influence on the relationships between early internationalisation and international scope. This negative effect is compatible with a reduction in the LAN effect, as routines take over and thus slow down entry into new markets (Zhou and Wu 2014; Wu and Zhou 2018).

The effect on the international growth of the EOI and its interaction with age to high and low levels of EO is positive and significant only for the international scale. Age shows a reinforcing effect of EOI only on foreign sales (scale) and only for ventures with low EO. The effect on the international growth of the EOI and its interaction with size for different levels of EO is always positive. The consideration of different levels of EO does not change the reinforcing effect of size on the relationship between EOI and international scale and scope. However, the reinforcing effect seems to be higher for firms with a low level of EO. Recalling that in our study, firms with a low level of EO are those with a lower increase of EO during the observation period, this result suggests that EIF becoming larger and older can reach higher international growth if they relax their innovative efforts. According to Boso et al. (2013), EO reflects an exploratory learning tension that exposes firms to risks and uncertainties, which often counterbalance their benefits on ventures' growth and performance. Focusing too much on being innovative and proactive following high-risk investments absorbs resources usually made available by larger size (Jafari-Sadeghi and Bianconc 2017; Wiklund and Shepherd 2005; Su et al. 2015), subtracting them from international growth. Moreover, as suggested by Sadraei et al. (2018) and Sukumar et al. (2020) in the high-tech industry, characterised by short product cycles, the effect of innovativeness on competitiveness over time is not linear. However, the different interaction effects of age and size must be deeply considered. While size usually leads ventures to have a higher availability of resources and thus explains its positive effect on both international scale and scope, age is linked to a higher accumulation of experience that reinforces EOI's effect on international growth but only in the form of penetration in the same market (international scale). Following the arguments related to the liability of ageing (Sørensen and Stuart 2000; Zhou and Wu 2014; D'Angelo and Buck 2019), we suggest that the knowledge consolidation produced by ageing can still be positive. In fact, when the effect on international development is limited to increasing market penetration for early internationalised firms that are not distracted by a strong entrepreneurial orientation, becoming older can still be an advantage.

The interaction effect of age on the relationship between EOI and international growth when different levels of MO are considered is positive and significant only for the international scale of ventures with a high MO. When the effect on the international development of EOI and its interaction with the size is analysed by taking into account different levels of MO, it is always positive but not always significant. The effect of EOI on an international scale and scope is reinforced by size when firms have a high level of MO. Firms that keep investing in marketing capabilities during the observed period are able to boost internationalisation. In this case, the size that makes new resources available seems to positively sustain the effect of earliness on international development in firms that are highly oriented to the market. Usually, firms with high MO are less interested in questioning the market setting (Cadogan et al. 2009) and more interested in anticipating market trends (Boso et al. 2013) and in exploiting new market opportunities. The ventures that do not lose their tension towards market orientation can reinforce the positive effect of early internationalisation on their subsequent international growth while maintaining their advantage with respect to gradually internationalised firms.

Our results suggest the importance to focus a lot on the interaction effect of age and size on the relationship between EOI and international growth. D'Angelo and Buck (2019), in a recent study, argue that age together with size produces a sort of "exporting sclerosis," which neutralises the boost given by LAN to EOI and the international growth relationship. We suggest that age and size can reinforce the earliness/international growth relationship according to ventures' strategic orientations. Our findings show that size reinforces all the dimensions of internationalisation growth, but its effect is stronger when firms have low EO and high MO. Such divergence between the effects of EO and MO is consistent with the evidence brought about by Morgan et al. (2014), who found that EO has a positive relationship with firm performance (new product development), and MO negatively moderates such a relationship. Ventures' ageing does not interrupt the positive effect of earliness on international growth, but only if the international scale is considered. Age can reinforce this relationship when firms have low entrepreneurial orientation and high market orientation. Thus, ageing more than sizing seems able to sclerotise early international ventures, thus reducing their ability to enlarge their international scope.

From a managerial point of view, our study has interesting implications. Notably, in light of this study, managers deciding whether their firms should internationalise earlier should be aware of the difficulties involved in simultaneously growing in terms of international scale and geographic scope. Furthermore, they should also consider that early internationalisation has been found to restrain geographic scope. Furthermore, they should acknowledge that the ability of their firm to retain the beneficial effects at the international scale brought about by early internationalisation depends on their firms' levels of EO and MO.

6 Limitations

Some limitations will be now discussed. First, our focus on one country and on companies operating in the high-tech sector limits the generalisability of our findings (Sadeghi et al. 2019b; Dana 1986, 1987) but also constitutes a strength, as it provides managers and entrepreneurs of Italian high-tech firms with a solid basis for their internationalisation decisions, pinpointing the first direction for further research, as new research could replicate these findings in other countries and, most importantly, in another medium- and low-tech sectors. In this regard, new research proving, further advancing, or perhaps disproving our findings might offer important contributions for theoretical development. Second, further studies could analyse other significant boundary conditions influencing the importance of the effect of early internationalisation on international growth. They could also consider the interaction between market and entrepreneurial orientation because we also include a single dimension without considering the interaction effects between them (Armario et al. 2008). Third, the measure of the internationalisation scope does not consider the cultural distance of the geographical markets—only their number. As we suggest in the discussion section, this approach represents a limitation because we were unable to discover if the relationship between EOI and internationalisation growth can be strengthened when learning is fuelled by experiences in distant markets, which accelerate learning and increase learning cost (Wu and Zhou 2018). Finally, this study can be affected by same-source bias as we used self-reported data to measure the evolution of MO and EO. However, this problem is usually in cross-sectional researches (Yli-Renko et al. 2001).

References

Acs Z, Dana LP, Jones MV (2003) Toward new horizons: the internationalisation of entrepreneurship. *J Int Entrep* 1:5–12

Allison PD (1994) Using panel data to estimate the effects of events. *Sociol Methods Res* 23 (2):174–199
Alon I, Dana LP, Jenkins A (2009) International business by SMEs: empirical findings from New Zeland. *J Int Bus Econ* 10(2):59–78
Amin Moghadasi M, Derakhshandeh B, Ferdosi M, Jafari Sadeghi V (2017) Organizational conformity as an entrepreneurial response to the changes in internationalization process: a study of IT-oriented firms in Saveh. *World J Acc Fin Eng* 1(1):53–64. https://doi.org/10.21742/wjafe.2017.1.1.05
Amorós JE, Basco R, Romaní G (2016) Determinants of early internationalization of new firms: the case of Chile. *Int Entrep Manag J* 12(1):283–307
Ancona D, Goodman P, Lawrence B, Tushman M (2001) Time: a new research lens. *Acad Manage Rev* 26(4):645–663
Armario JM, Ruiz DM, Armario EM (2008) Market orientation and internationalization in small and medium-sized enterprises. *J Small Bus Manag* 46(4):485–511
Aspelund A, Koed Madsen T, Moen Ø (2007) A review of the foundation, international marketing strategies, and performance of international new ventures. *Eur J Mark* 41(11/12):1423–1448
Autio E, Sapienza HJ, Almeida JG (2000) Effects of age at entry, knowledge intensity, and imitability on international growth. *Acad Manage J* 43(5):909–924
Autio E, George G, Alexy O (2011) International entrepreneurship and capability development—qualitative evidence and future research directions. *Entrep Theory Pract* 35(1):11–37
Ayob A, Dana LP (2017) Product strategies for export ventures: an empirical investigation among SMEs in an emerging economy. *J Pengurusan* 50:25–33
Bayfield R, Dana LP, Stewart S (2009) Firm characteristics and internationalisation strategies: an empirical investigation of New Zealand exporters. *Int J Glob Small Bus* 3(3):275–287
Berra L, Piatti L, Vitali G (1995) The internationalization process in the small and medium sized firms: a case study on the Italian clothing industry. *Small Bus Econ* 7(1):67–75
Biancone PP, Jafari-Sadeghi V (2016) Risk management in export compliance: concepts, procedures, and solutions. In: Cantino V, De Vincentiis P, Racca MG (eds) *Risk management: perspectives and open issues*. McGraw-Hill, London, UK, pp 64–78
Boso N, Story VM, Cadogan JW (2013) Entrepreneurial orientation, market orientation, network ties, and performance: study of entrepreneurial firms in a developing economy. *J Bus Ventur* 28 (6):708–727
Boso N, Cadogan JW, Story VM (2014) Entrepreneurial orientation and market orientation as drivers of product innovation success: a study of exporters from a developing economy. *Int Small Bus J* 31(1):57–81
Bouchard V, Basso O (2011) Exploring the links between entrepreneurial orientation and intrapreneurship in SMEs. *J Small Bus Enterp Dev* 18(2):219–231
Buckley PJ (1997) International technology transfer by small and medium sized enterprises. *Small Bus Econ* 9(1):67–78
Buckley PJ, Casson M (1991) Multinational enterprises in less developed countries: cultural and economic interactions. In: Buckley PJ, Clegg J (eds) *Multinational enterprises in less developed countries*. Macmillan, London, pp 27–55
Cadogan JW, Kuivalainen O, Sundqvist S (2009) Export market-oriented behavior and export performance: quadratic and moderating effects under differing degrees of market dynamism and internationalization. *J Int Mark* 17(4):71–89
Calof JL (1994) The relationship between firm size and export behavior revisited. J Int Bus Stud 25 (2):367–387
Casillas JC, Acedo FJ (2013) Speed in the internationalization process of the firm. *Int J Manag Rev* 15(1):15–29
Churchill GA Jr (1979) A paradigm for developing better measures of marketing constructs. *J Market Res* 16(1):64–73
Coviello N, McAuley A (1999) Internationalization and the small firms: a review of contemporary empirical research. *Manag Int Rev* 39(3):223–256

Covin JG, Miller D (2014) International entrepreneurial orientation: conceptual considerations, research themes, measurement issues, and future research directions. *Entrep Theory Pract* 38 (1):11–44
Covin JG, Slevin DP (1989) Strategic management of small firms in hostile and benign environments. *Strategic Manag J* 10(1):75–87
Crick D, Jones M (1999) Design and innovation strategies within "successful" high-tech firms. *Mark Intell Plan* 17(3):161–168
D'Angelo A, Buck T (2019) The earliness of exporting and creeping sclerosis? The moderating effects of firm age, size and centralization. *Int Bus Rev* 28(3):428–437
D'Angelo A, Presutti M (2019) SMEs international growth: the moderating role of experience on entrepreneurial and learning orientations. *Int Bus Rev* 28(3):613–624
Dabić M, Maley J, Dana LP, Novak I, Pellegrini MM, Caputo A (2019) Pathways of SME internationalization: a bibliometric and systematic review. *Small Bus Econ*
Dana LP (1986) Evaluating policies promoting entrepreneurship—a cross cultural comparison of entrepreneurship case studies: Singapore and Malaysia. *J Small Bus Entrep* 4(3):36–41
Dana LP (1987) Industrial development efforts in Malaysia and Singapore. *J Small Bus Manag* 25 (3):74–76
Dana LP (2002) Entrepreneurship in a remote sub-arctic community: Nome, Alaska, in N. Krueger (Ed.) Entrepreneurship: critical perspectives on business and management, London: Routledge, Vol. IV, pp.255–275, reprinted from 1995. *Entrep Theory Pract* 20(1):55–72
Dana LP (ed) (2004) The handbook of research on international entrepreneurship. Edward Elgar, Cheltenham, UK
Dana LP (2005) When economies change hands: a survey of entrepreneurship in the emerging markets of Europe from the Balkans to the Baltic states. Haworth Press, Binghamton
Dana LP (2017) International entrepreneurship research: how it evolved and directions for the future, *International Journal of. Entrep Small Bus* 30(4)
Dana LP, Wright RW (2009) International entrepreneurship: research priorities for the future. *Int J Glob Small Bus* 3(1):90–134
Dana LP, Etemad H, Wright RW (1999) The theoretical foundations of international entrepreneurship. In: Wright RW (ed) *International entrepreneurship: globalization of emerging businesses*. JAI Press, Stamford, CN, pp 3–22
Dana LP, Bajramovic MB, Wright RW (2005) The new paradigm of multipolar competition and its implications for entrepreneurship research in Europe. In: Fayolle A, Kyro P, Ulijn J (eds) *Entrepreneurship research in Europe: outcomes and perspectives*. Edward Elgar, Cheltenham, pp 102–121
Dana LP, Grimwood S, William G (2009) Export incentives and international entrepreneurship in New Zealand firms. *J Int Bus Entrep Dev* 4(1/2):1–21
Day GS (1994) The capabilities of market-driven organizations. *J Mark* 58(4):37–52
Eden L (2009) Letter from the editor-in-chief: time in international business. *J Int Bus Stud* 40 (4):535–538
Fang EE, Zou S (2009) Antecedents and consequences of marketing dynamic capabilities in international joint ventures. *J Int Bus Stud* 40(5):742–761
Fariborzi H, Keyhani M (2018) Internationalize to live: a study of the post-internationalization survival of new ventures. *Small Bus Econ* 50(3):607–624
Gerschewski S, Rose EL, Lindsay VJ (2015) Understanding the drivers of international performance for born global firms: an integrated perspective. *J World Bus* 50(3):558–575
Hashai N (2011) Sequencing the expansion of geographic scope and foreign operations by "born global" firms. *J Int Bus Stud* 42(8):995–1015
Haveman HA (1993) Organizational size and change: diversification in the savings and loan industry after deregulation. *Adm Sci Q* 38(1):20–50
Hilmersson M, Johanson M (2016) Speed of SME internationalization and performance. *Manag Int Rev* 56(1):67–94

Hitt MA, Li D, Xu K (2016) International strategy: from local to global and beyond. *J World Bus* 51 (1):58–73
Jafari-Sadeghi V, Biancone PP (2017) Shariah compliant international entrepreneurship: a study of Islamic Finance in Europe. Eur J Islam Finance (8)
Jafari-Sadeghi V, Kimiagari S, Biancone PP (2019) Level of education and knowledge, foresight competency and international entrepreneurship. *Eur Bus Rev* 1:46–68
Jafari-Sadeghi V, Dutta DK, Ferraris A, Del Giudice M (2020) Internationalisation business processes in an under-supported policy contexts: evidence from Italian SMEs. *Bus Process Manag J* 26(5):1055–1074
Jantunen A, Nummela N, Puumalainen K, Saarenketo S (2008) Strategic orientations of born globals—do they really matter? *J World Bus* 43(2):158–170
Jaworski BJ, Kohli AK (1993) Market orientation: antecedents and consequences. *J Mark* 57 (3):53–70
Jiménez Naharro F, Palacín Sánchez MJ, Pérez López C, Trujillo Ponce A (2010) A financial analysis of born-global firms: evidence from Spain. *Probl Perspect Manag* 8(3):36–47
Jones MV, Coviello NE (2005) Internationalization: conceptualising an entrepreneurial process of behaviour in time. *J Int Bus Stud* 36(3):284–303
Jones MV, Coviello N, Tang YK (2011) International entrepreneurship research (1989–2009), a domain ontology and thematic analysis. *J Bus Ventur* 26(6):632–659
Karami M, Tang J (2019) Entrepreneurial orientation and SME international performance: the mediating role of networking capability and experiential learning. *Int Small Bus J* 37 (2):105–124
Khavul, Susanna & PÕrez-Nordtvedt, Liliana & Wood, Eric, 2010. "Organizational entrainment and international new ventures from emerging markets," Journal of Business Venturing, Elsevier, vol. 25(1), pages 104-119, January
Knight GA (1997) Emerging paradigm for international marketing: the born global firm, PhD dissertation. East Lansing: Department of Marketing and Supply Chain Management, Michigan State University
Knight GA, Cavusgil ST (1996) The born-global firm: a challenge to traditional internationalization theory. In: Cavusgil ST, Madsen T (eds) *Advances in international marketing*, vol 8. JAI Press, Greenwich
Knight GA, Cavusgil ST (2004) Innovation, organizational capabilities, and the born-global firm. *J Int Bus Stud* 35(2):124–141
Knight GA, Liesch PW (2016) Internationalization: from incremental to born global. *J World Bus* 51(1):93–102
Kuivalainen O, Sundqvist S, Servais P (2007) Firms' degree of born-globalness, international entrepreneurial orientation and export performance. *J World Bus* 42(3):253–267
Laforet S (2013) Organizational innovation outcomes in SMEs: effects of age, size, and sector. *J World Bus* 48(4):490–502
Lee C, Lee K, Pennings JM (2001) Internal capabilities, external networks, and performance: a study on technology-based ventures. *Strategic Manag J* 22(6–7):615–640
Li L, Qian G, Qian Z (2012) Early internationalization and performance of small high-tech "born-globals". *Int Mark Rev* 29(5):536–561
Lu JW, Beamish PW (2001) The internationalization and performance of SMEs. *Strategic Manag J* 22(6–7):565–586
Lumpkin GT, Dess GG (1996) Clarifying the entrepreneurial orientation construct and linking it to performance. *Acad Manage Rev* 21(1):135–172
Madsen TK, Servais P (1997) The internationalization of born globals: an evolutionary process? *Int Bus Rev* 6(6):561–583
Majocchi A, Presutti M (2009) Industrial clusters, entrepreneurial culture and the social, environment: the effects on FDI distribution. Int Bus Rev 18(1):76–88
McDougall PP, Oviatt BM (2000) International entrepreneurship: the intersection of two research paths. *Acad Manage J* 43(5):902–906

McDougall PP, Shane S, Oviatt BM (1994) Explaining the formation of international new ventures: the limits of theories from international business research. *J Bus Ventur* 9(6):469–487
McNaughton RB (2003) The number of export markets that a firm serves: process models versus the born-global phenomenon. *J Int Entrep* 1(3):297–311
Melin L (1992) Internationalization as a strategy process. *Strategic Manag J* 13:99–118
Merz RG, Sauber MH (1995) Profiles of managerial activities in small firms. *Strategic Manag J* 16 (7):551–564
Meschi PX, Ricard A, Moore ET (2017) Fast and furious or slow and cautious? the joint impact of age at internationalization, speed, and risk diversity on the survival of exporting firms. *J Int Manag* 23(3):279–291
Messeghem K, Bakkal C, Sammut S, Swalhi A (2017) Measuring nonprofit incubator performance: toward an adapted balanced scorecard approach. *J Small Bus Manag* 56(4):658–680
Mohr A, Batsakis G (2017) Internationalization speed and firm performance: a study of the market-seeking expansion of retail MNEs. *Manag Int Rev* 57(2):153–177
Mokhtarzadeh NG, Mahdiraji HA, Jafarpanah I, Jafari-Sadeghi V, Cardinali S (2020a) Investigating the impact of networking capability on firm innovation performance: using the resource-action-performance framework. *J Intellect Cap* 21(6):1009–1034
Mokhtarzadeh NG, Mahdirji HA, Jafari-Sadeghi V, Soltani A, Kamardi AA (2020b) A product-technology portfolio alignment approach for food industry: a multi-criteria decision making with z-numbers. *Br Food J* 122(12):3947–3967
Morgan T, Anokhin S, Kretinin A, Frishammar J (2014) The dark side of the entrepreneurial orientation and market orientation interplay: a new product development perspective. *Int Small Bus J* 33(7):731–751
Naman JL, Slevin DP (1993) Entrepreneurship and the concept of fit: a model and empirical tests. *Strategic Manag J* 14(2):137–153
Oviatt BM, McDougall PP (1994) Toward a theory of international new ventures. *J Int Bus Stud* 25 (1):45–64
Oviatt BM, McDougall PP (1997) Challenges for internationalization process theory: the case of international new ventures. *Manag Int Rev* 37(2):85–99
Patel PE, Criaco G, Naldi L (2018) Geographic diversification and the survival of born-globals. *J Manag* 44(5):2008–2036
Paul J, Gupta P (2014) Process and intensity of internationalization of IT firms—evidence from India. *Int Bus Rev* 23(3):594–603
Presutti M, Odorici V (2019) Linking entrepreneurial and market orientation to the SME's performance growth: the moderating role of entrepreneurial experience and networks. *Int Entrep Manag J* 15(3):697–720
Presutti M, Boari C, Fratocchi L (2016) The evolution of inter-organisational social capital with foreign customers: its direct and interactive effects on SMEs' foreign performance. *J World Bus* 51:760–773
Presutti M, Boari C, Majocchi A, Molina Morales X (2019) Distance to customers, absorptive capacity, and innovation in high-tech firms: the dark face of geographical proximity. *J Small Bus Manag* 57(2):343–361
Presutti M, Cappiello G, Johanson M (2020) Analysing social capital and product innovativeness in the relationship evolution of born-global companies the mediating role of knowledge acquisition. *Int Entrep Manag J*. https://doi.org/10.1007/s11365-020-00663-0
Raju PS, Lonial SC, Crum MD (2011) Market orientation in the context of SMEs: a conceptual framework. *J Bus Res* 64(12):1320–1326
Ratten V, Dana L-P, Han M, Welpe I (2007) Internationalisation of SMEs: European comparative studies. *Int J Entrep Small Bus* 4(3):361–379
Rauch A, Wiklund J, Lumpkin GT, Frese M (2009) Entrepreneurial orientation and business performance: an assessment of past research and suggestions for the future. *Entrep Theory Pract* 33(3):761–787

Rialp A, Rialp J, Knight GA (2005) The phenomenon of early internationalizing firms: what do we know after a decade (1993–2003) of scientific inquiry? *Int Bus Rev* 14(2):147–166
Rodríguez-Serrano MA, Martín-Armario E (2017) Born-global SMEs, performance, and dynamic absorptive capacity: evidence from Spanish firms. *J Small Bus Manag* 57(2):298–326
Romanello R, Chiarvesio M (2019) Early internationalizing firms: 2004–2018. *J Int Entrep* 17 (2):172–219. https://doi.org/10.1007/s10843-018-0241-8
Ruekert RW (1992) Developing a market orientation: an organizational strategy perspective. Int J Res Mark 9(3):225–245
Sadeghi VJ, Biancone PP, Giacoma C, Secinaro S (2017) Export compliance: a missing component of international entrepreneurship. *Int J Bus Manag* 12(11):103–110
Sadeghi VJ, Biancone PP, Anderson RB, Nkongolo-Bakenda JM (2019a) International entrepreneurship by particular people "on their own terms": a study on the universal characteristics of entrepreneurs in evolving economies. *Int J Entrep Small Bus* 37(2):288–308
Sadeghi VJ, Nkongolo-Bakenda JM, Anderson RB, Dana LP (2019b) An institution-based view of international entrepreneurship: a comparison of context-based and universal determinants in developing and economically advanced countries. *Int Bus Rev* 28(6):101588
Sadraei R, Jafari Sadeghi V, Sadraei M (2018) Biotechnology revolution from academic entrepreneurship to industrial: chemo-entrepreneurship. *Biom Biostat Int J* 7(6):546–550
Sapienza HJ, Autio E, George G, Zahra SA (2006) A capabilities perspective on the effects of early internationalization on firm survival and growth. *Acad Manage Rev* 31(4):914–933
Sørensen JB, Stuart TE (2000) Aging, obsolescence, and organizational innovation. *Adm Sci Q* 45 (1):81–112
Su Z, Xie E, Wang D (2015) Entrepreneurial orientation, managerial networking, and new venture performance in China. *J Small Bus Manag* 53(1):228–248
Sui S, Baum M (2014) Internationalization strategy, firm resources and the survival of SMEs in the export market. *J Int Bus Stud* 45(7):821–841
Sukumar A, Jafari-Sadeghi V, Garcia-Perez A, Dutta DK (2020) The potential link between corporate innovations and corporate competitiveness: evidence from IT firms in the UK. *J Know Manag* 24(5):965–983
Tallman S, Li J (1996) Effects of international diversity and product diversity on the performance of multinational firms. *Acad Manage J* 39(1):179–196
Trudgen R, Freeman S (2014) Measuring the performance of born-global firms throughout their development process: the roles of initial market selection and internationalisation speed. *Manag Int Rev* 54(4):551–579
Verbeke A, Kenworthy TP (2008) Multidivisional vs metanational governance of the multinational enterprise. *J Int Bus Stud* 39(6):940–956
Vorhies DW, Morgan NA (2005) Benchmarking marketing capabilities for sustainable competitive advantage. *J Mark* 69(1):80–94
Wales WJ (2016) Entrepreneurial orientation: a review and synthesis of promising research directions. *Int Small Bus J* 34(1):3–15
Wales W, Wiklund J, McKelvie A (2013) What about new entry? Examining the theorized role of new entry in the entrepreneurial orientation–performance relationship. *Int Small Bus J* 33 (4):351–373
Welch LS, Luostarinen R (1988) Internationalization: evolution of a concept. *J Gen Manag* 14 (2):34–55
Wiklund J, Shepherd D (2003) Knowledge-based resources, entrepreneurial orientation, and the performance of small and medium-sized businesses. *Strategic Manag J* 24(13):1307–1314
Wiklund J, Shepherd D (2005) Entrepreneurial orientation and small business performance: a configurational approach. *J Bus Ventur* 20(1):71–91
Wright RW, Dana LP (2003) Changing paradigms of international entrepreneurship strategy. *J Int Entrep Strategy* 1(1):135–152
Wu A, Zhou L (2018) Understanding earliness of internationalization and its impact on postentry geographic diversity of international young ventures. *J Int Mark* 26(2):62–79

Yli-Renko H, Autio E, Sapienza HJ (2001) Social capital, knowledge acquisition, and knowledge exploitation in young technology-based firms. *Strategic Manag J* 22(6–7):587–613

Zahra SA (2005) A theory of international new ventures: a decade of research. *J Int Bus Stud* 36 (1):20–28

Zahra SA, Hayton JC (2008) The effect of international venturing on firm performance: the moderating influence of absorptive capacity. *J Bus Ventur* 23(2):195–220

Zahra SA, Ireland RD, Hitt MA (2000) International expansion by new venture firms: international diversity, mode of market entry, technological learning, and performance. *Acad Manage J* 43 (5):925–950

Zahra SA, Zheng C, Yu J (2018) Learning advantages of newness: a reconceptualization and contingent framework. *J Int Entrep* 16(1):12–37

Zhou L (2007) The effects of entrepreneurial proclivity and foreign market knowledge on early internationalization. *J World Bus* 42(3):281–293

Zhou L, Wu A (2014) Earliness of internationalization and performance outcomes: exploring the moderating effects of venture age and international commitment. *J World Bus* 49(1):132–142

Zhou L, Wu A, Barnes BR (2012) The effects of early internationalization on performance outcomes in young international ventures: the mediating role of marketing capabilities. *J Int Mark* 20(4):25–45

Zucchella A, Palamara G, Denicolai S (2007) The drivers of the early internationalization of the firm. *J World Bus* 42(3):268–280

Antonio Daood is a PhD in Management at the Sapienza University of Rome, Antonio Daood is a Postdoctoral Research Fellow at the University of Bologna. His current research interests are focused on organisational change and growth, business model innovation, and Made in Italy industries. So far, he has been awarded several prizes for his academic career, such as the "Excellent Graduate Award" by Sapienza University of Rome, and the "Best Student Paper Award" by the University of Berkeley, California at the sixth World Open Innovation Conference (WOIC 2019).

Luciano Fratocchi earned his Bachelor in Management from the Luiss Guido Carli University of Rome (Italy). He obtained a PhD in Management at the University of Bologna (Italy), Department of Management. He was Visiting PhD Student at the School of Management University of Bath (UK; Supervisor Prof. Charles Baden-Fuller) and at the Department of Business Studies University of Uppsala (Sweden, Supervisor Prof. Jan Johansson). He is a Full Professor of Management Engineering at the Department of Industrial and Information Engineering and Economics of the University of L'Aquila. During the last years, her research interest has included the relocations of the second degree (back-shoring, near-shoring, and further off-shoring) and the internationalisation process of small and medium firms. On these topics, he has several Scopus indexed publications.

Vincenza Odorici is an Associate Professor of Management at the University of Bologna, Italy, where she teaches General Management and International Business. After a period as Visiting Scholar at the Business School of Texas A & M University (College Station, Texas, USA) where she conducted her research on rivalry and cognitive strategic groups, she received her PhD in Management at the University of Bologna. She is the author of articles on the intermediaries fostering the convergence of supply and demand in market exchanges. She studies the role of corporate governance and ownership's type on internationalisation. Moreover, she is working on the relationship between born-global start-up, habitual entrepreneurship, and founding teams' strategic orientation.

Manuela Presutti earned her Bachelor in Management from the Luiss Guido Carli University of Rome. She took a PhD in Management at the University of Bologna, Department of Management, joining the Department of Business Studies, University of Uppsala, as Visiting Scholar, where she conducted research on the impact of social capital on the internationalisation process, together with prof. Mats Forsgren. From 2005 to 2010 she was an Assistant Professor at the Faculty of Economy of the University of Bologna. Since 2010 she is an Associate Professor of Management and now, she teaches Strategy and Management at the Faculty of Economy of Rimini (Bologna). She is the Director of the International Second Degree of Tourism at the Campus of Rimini. Most of her scientific production is about Internationalisation, New Business Development, Entrepreneurship, and Social Capital. On these topics, she has publications in national journals and international journals.

To Internationalise Entrepreneurially from Low-Tech Emerging Market: The Role of International Entrepreneurial Capability and Orientation in Early Internationalising Firms from Bangladesh

Anisur R. Faroque, Hasan Mahmud, Lasse Torkkeli, and Sami Saarenketo

1 Introduction

The export entry of small firms has been recognised as an entrepreneurial act in entrepreneurship literature (Ibeh 2003). Johanson and Vahlne (2009), the advocates of internationalisation stage theory, acknowledge that 'internationalisation has much in common with entrepreneurship' (p. 1423). Thus, developing a holistic understanding of what it means for small firms to internationalise entrepreneurially across different contexts is essential.

Since the 1990s, globalisation and technological advances such as the Internet have allowed small firms new access to customers, suppliers, and other business partners and stakeholders across the world (Dana et al. 1999), and since firms of all sizes are increasingly competing at an international and global arena (Dana 2001), it remains important to shed light on the factors that enable successful entrepreneurial internationalisation. The main focus of studies related to these phenomena in the international entrepreneurship (IE) literature is that of early internationalising firms such as international new ventures (INVs; see Oviatt and McDougall 1994) or born globals (Knight and Cavusgil 2004; Weerawardena et al. 2007).

As opposed to traditional internationalising firms, these firms follow an early internationalisation path from inception or soon thereafter. Since the 1990s, early internationalising firms have been the main research focus in IE literature (e.g., Jones

A. R. Faroque · H. Mahmud · S. Saarenketo
School of Business and Management, LUT University, Lappeenranta, Finland
e-mail: Anisur.Faroque@lut.fi; Hasan.Mahmud@student.lut.fi; Sami.Saarenketo@lut.fi

L. Torkkeli (✉)
School of Business and Management, LUT University, Lappeenranta, Finland

Turku School of Business, University of Turku, Turku, Finland
e-mail: Lasse.Torkkeli@lut.fi

V. Jafari-Sadeghi et al. (eds.), *Empirical International Entrepreneurship*, Contributions to Management Science,
https://doi.org/10.1007/978-3-030-68972-8_14

et al. 2011), and their increasing prevalence and importance in international business indicate a need for greater understanding of these ventures (Oviatt and McDougall 2004). Research has called for more elaboration on the distinctiveness of early internationalising firms and how they develop distinct capabilities (Dana and Wright 2009). However, the literature on capabilities in international entrepreneurship has tended to remain either conceptual (e.g., Al-Aali and Teece 2014) or qualitative (Mort and Weerawardena 2006; Autio et al. 2011; Glavas and Mathews 2014). Literature reviews on the international entrepreneurship domain have also often found the field to be permeated by primarily qualitative methods (e.g., Jones et al. 2011; Peiris et al. 2012). However, the few quantitative studies linking capabilities to performance, profitability, and other types of successful internationalisation have tended to find significant relationships between the two (e.g., Torkkeli 2014; Pinho and Prange 2016). These results indicate that quantitative assessment of the dynamic capabilities leading to successful entrepreneurial internationalisation is both necessary and underresearched. Moreover, these few quantitative studies have been conducted mostly in a relatively narrow empirical context of high-technology ventures originating from developed economies; indeed, most empirical research in IE is skewed towards the high-tech industries in the developed world, and therefore knowledge surrounding early internationalising firms in traditional industries from emerging economies has been lacking (Rialp et al. 2005; Kiss et al. 2012). This has been an issue since a multitude of phenomena related to international business and entrepreneurship in the emerging market, for instance, environmental institutions (Sadeghi et al. 2019), can be distinct to those in developed economies. A recent review of studies related to the internationalisation of small and medium enterprises in general (Dabić et al. 2019) came to a similar conclusion, highlighting the lack of studies on capabilities of emerging market firms as a gap in internationalisation research. Thus, research conducted in the latter context may not be applicable to the emerging market context.

Taken together, it seems logical that the field of international entrepreneurship would benefit increasingly from quantitative methodology in explaining the relevant capability-performance relationships, and from doing so also in low-technology and developing markets contexts. This chapter aims to respond to these methodological and contextual gaps in the literature, by conducting a quantitative study on the capabilities of early internationalising firms from Bangladesh. While recognising that to become successful in international business, these firms rely more heavily on entrepreneurial capabilities and skills, which reduce their resource constraints and liability of newness and foreignness (cf. Zaheer 1995). Studies of early internationalising firms confirmed that such firms possess a strong entrepreneurial orientation (EO) (Freeman et al. 2006). Rasmussen and Madsen (2002) maintain that IE as a new field of academic enquiry supplements the huge stream of internationalisation research by explicitly focusing on the role of the entrepreneur. However, IE researchers are predominantly obsessed with few capabilities of international entrepreneurs (e.g., prior international business experience). This parochial view of capabilities has limited our understanding of the topic. The relationship between entrepreneurial capability and entrepreneurial orientation (EO), more specifically how entrepreneur-level entrepreneurial capability drives firm-level EO and performance outcomes in early internationalising firms, has not been investigated in IE, and a study illustrating their joint dynamics can thus help in the further theoretical development of the IE research domain.

Despite entrepreneurial capability being recognised as the most influential determinant in early internationalisation, empirical research examining this in terms of breadth of capabilities and number of studies has been lacking. We note in this study that prior experience constitutes only a subset of broader entrepreneurial 'capability set', and we argue that this narrow and parochial view of entrepreneurial capability has until fallen short of reporting a valid association between international entrepreneurial capability and early internationalisation. More specifically, in this chapter, we examine international entrepreneurial capability and the type of EO that influence the internationalisation of early internationalising firms in a developing country low-tech industry context. Consequently, this study posits that entrepreneurial internationalisation involves the adoption and application of both entrepreneurial capability and orientation simultaneously. In this way, the study adds to the scientific knowledge on what it means to internationalise entrepreneurially and in part helps in confirming the assertion by Johanson and Vahlne (2009) that internationalisation and entrepreneurship are indeed tightly intertwined. Simultaneously, it emphasises the important role that quantitative research methods have in IE in general, as well as for developing markets and low-tech industries in particular.

2 Theoretical Framework and Hypotheses

The conceptual model guiding our study is presented in Fig. 1. The model draws on the capability perspective (Sen 1985; Anand and Van Hees 2006; Gries and Naudé 2011), and strategy-making process literature (Miller 1983). The model positions international entrepreneurial capability as a crucial component for driving international EO, which in turn enhances the international performance of early internationalising firms. It also supposes an indirect relationship between international entrepreneurial capability and performance.

2.1 The Capability Approach and International Entrepreneurial Capability

Capability approach pioneered by Sen (1985) has been a hot topic in welfare economics. Capabilities refer to a person's 'ability to achieve a given functioning'. The set of all possible vectors of capabilities that a person can achieve is called the 'capability set' of the person (Anand and Van Hees 2006). From an entrepreneurship viewpoint, 'capability set' might include all possible capabilities that an entrepreneur

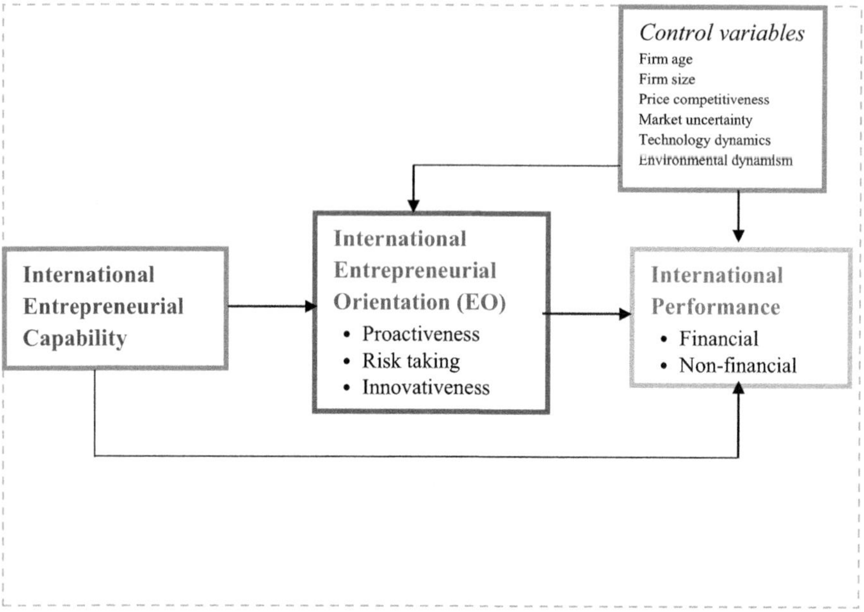

Fig. 1 International entrepreneurial capability, orientation, and performance among early internationalising firms: the direct and mediated paths

can develop or achieve. Capability approach can provide useful insights into IE research with regard to entrepreneurial capabilities.

Entrepreneurial Capabilities refer to the abilities to identify and acquire the necessary resources to act upon opportunities identified in the market or to create new market opportunities (Karra et al. 2008). Zhang et al. (2009) identified five different sets of capabilities which might constitute international entrepreneurial capability. They are international experience, international marketing, learning, networking, and innovative and risk-taking capability. Drawing from human capital theory, Faroque et al. (2020a) grouped entrepreneurial capabilities in two broad categories: general and international. General entrepreneurial capabilities include prior entrepreneurial, managerial, and technical experience, whereas international entrepreneurial capabilities consist of entrepreneurs' international business experience, networking, entrepreneurial orientation, and global vision. Research on the operationalisation of entrepreneurial capabilities rests on a parochial view of capabilities, i.e., entrepreneur's prior experience, ignoring other human and social capital (Faroque et al. 2020a). Therefore, further investigation combining all these capabilities is needed to recognise and understand the roles and characteristics of entrepreneurs in early internationalisation more elaborately (Mort and Weerawardena 2006) and the ways in which they influence early internationalising firms' international behaviour.

2.2 International Entrepreneurial Orientation

Entrepreneurial orientation (EO) is a combination of three dimensions: innovativeness, proactiveness, and risk-taking (Covin and Slevin 1986; Wiklund and Shepherd 2003). This same concept has been adopted in IE with special reference to an international business setting and known as international EO. In an internationalisation context, innovativeness refers to a firm's capacity to generate new ideas, products, and services for foreign markets and its fortitude to develop creative solutions to challenges it faces (Knight 2001). Proactiveness reflects a firm's proclivity to take initiatives, anticipate and pursue new opportunities, and participate in foreign markets (Miller 1983). Risk-taking refers to the proclivity of a firm to undertake risky ventures in foreign markets (Dimitratos and Plakoyiannaki 2003).

On the basis of an extensive literature review and interviews with three general managers and IE academics, Zhang et al. (2009) conceptualise international entrepreneurial capability as the firm-level ability to leverage resources through a combination of innovative, proactive, and risk-seeking activities to explore and exploit international business opportunities. This conceptualisation of international entrepreneurial capability parallels that of EO. EO also represents firm-level behavioural orientation involving innovative, proactive, and risk-seeking activities. Two different constructs representing the same attributes might confuse IE researchers. Rather we believe international entrepreneurial capability relates to entrepreneur and this is in line with Karra et al. (2008) who position it as entrepreneur-level capability. According to Karra et al. (2008), entrepreneurial capabilities stem from experience in international markets, international network connections, and from the ability of opportunity exploration.

2.3 International Entrepreneurial Capability, EO, and Early Internationalising Firm Performance

In the present study, we posit four main hypotheses for linking entrepreneurial capabilities, IEO, and international performance of early internationalising firms. First, most research relating to EO in entrepreneurship and IE is concerned with a direct relationship between EO and performance. The theoretical discussion and empirical evidence on the antecedents of EO is not comprehensive in both fields. According to Lumpkin and Dess (1996), while all the dimensions of EO may be present when a firm engages in a new entry, it is not the necessary pre-condition of such entry. Rather, a successful new entry may be realised with some of these factors being operational. They further posit that some external factors, such as the industry or business environment, or internal factors, such as the characteristics of founders or top managers may also influence the extent to which each of these dimensions of EO is useful for predicting the nature and success of a new entry. This argument implies that the capabilities of entrepreneurs might determine the EO of the firm, even in an international context. We can extend this argument to early internationalising firm creation and success. International entrepreneurial capabilities such as innovative, proactive, and risk-taking behaviour of entrepreneurs must have bearing on the similar behaviour and attitudes of top managers in these firms. In addition, the entrepreneur's prior international experience and networking capability might positively impact an early internationalising firm's EO. Early internationalising firms, due to their earliness, lack substantial financial and human resources (Knight et al. 2004), and tend to rely heavily on the entrepreneur and his resource endowments to proactively locate opportunities in international markets and exploit them. Therefore, we have hypothesised that:

Hypothesis 1 *There is a positive association between the international entrepreneurial capability of entrepreneur and IEO of early internationalising firms.*

Second, the background and characteristics of the entrepreneur may have a great influence on the speed of learning, internationalisation (Madsen and Servais 1997; Oviatt and McDougall 1997), and development of such early internationalising firms. Early internationalisation approach virtually requires entrepreneurs to develop distinctive entrepreneurial capabilities and prudence, in their past career, to recognise the opportunity in international markets (Knight and Cavusgil 1996; Madsen and Servais 1997; McDougall et al. 1994).

McDougall et al. (2003) argued that the entrepreneur's international experience plays an important role in the internationalisation of early internationalising firms. Many founders and managers of early internationalising firms have gained international experience and competence during previous work experiences (Madsen and Servais 1997; Oviatt and McDougall 1997; Reuber and Fischer 2002; Sharma and Blomstermo 2003), which help the firm to enter foreign markets successfully (Jones 2001; Reuber and Fischer 1997).

According to Gabrielsson et al. (2008), resource commitment (in other words, risk-taking) is necessary and sufficient condition for firms' early internationalisation and success. Based on the case studies of eight early internationalising firms in Greece, Norway, Finland, and Italy, they propose that sustainable early internationalising firms have an effective commitment to enter and penetrate international markets rapidly. This indicates a direct relationship of the risk-taking attitude of entrepreneurs with early internationalising firms' international growth and performance.

Andersson (2000) found that an international proactive entrepreneur was the most important factor explaining why early internationalising firms expanded internationally. Furthermore, these firms require entrepreneurs and top managers to meet with their overseas customers. It is the individuals, not the organisational routines, that play the most significant role in decision-making in these firms (Oviatt and McDougall 1997). This emphasises the entrepreneurial capability of the entrepreneur of the early internationalising firm in market entry and success. Based on the discussion above, we have hypothesised that:

Hypothesis 2 *There is a positive association between international entrepreneurial capability and performance of early internationalising firms.*

Third, early internationalising firms are found to be characterised by an organisational culture that is proactive, risk-taking, and innovative (Freeman et al. 2006). More than five decades ago, Schumpeter (1942: 194) stated that 'the opening of a new market is an innovation, which positions internationalisation as an innovative entrepreneurial activity (Andersson 2000; Casson 2005; Knight and Cavusgil 2004). A firm with innovative capabilities and culture possesses a superior ability to both recognise and exploit opportunities in foreign markets (Jantunen et al. 2005). This indicates that innovativeness is central to international performance (Frishammar and Andersson 2009).

The second component of IEO is proactiveness, which implies an increased speed of international development, a criterion necessary for success (Frishammar and Andersson 2009). Internationalisation process and export marketing literature frequently refer to proactiveness with regard to international strategies. The early internationalisation perspective also underlines the significance of proactive and opportunity-seeking attitude. Proactiveness is an important factor explaining why some firms are international from inception and how they achieve superior international performance (Andersson and Wictor 2003). Pla-Barber and Escribá-Esteve (2006) claimed that a proactive attitude of managers regarding internationalisation activities facilitates the rapidness of the internationalisation process.

The third component of IEO is risk-taking which occurs along a continuum ranging from relatively low risks (e.g., exporting) to very high risks (e.g., joint venture or foreign direct investment). Early internationalising firms, considering their resource constraints, often use direct export or sales through representatives. Luo and Tung (2007) argue that firms from emerging markets, as latecomers in the global market, need to hug more aggressive and risk-taking measures in order to combat their competitive weaknesses.

Though much research has been done on the EO—international performance relationship (Jantunen et al. 2005; Dimitratos et al. 2004; Zahra and Garvis 2000; Ibeh 2003, McAulcy 1999; and Robertson and Chetty 2000), few studies have been conducted on the IEO—international performance relationship in IE. Acosta et al. (2018) and Swoboda and Olejnik (2016) found that international performance of SMEs is influenced by IEO. In another study on Romanian small and medium firms, Emoke-Szidónia (2015) found a significant positive impact of IEO on the international performance of these firms. Based on a study on Turkish manufacturing firms, Kaya and Ağca (2009) found that though all of the three dimensions of IEO affect international performance, the effect of risk-taking is not significant. Again Hernández-Perlines et al. (2016) found a positive relationship between EO and international performance of the family-owned business. In summary, we can assert that three dimensions of IEO positively influence the performance of early internationalising firms. Therefore, we have hypothesised that:

Hypothesis 3 *There is a positive association between international EO and performance of early internationalising firms.*

Finally, we posit that international EO can act as a mediator. The independent study of the relationship between international entrepreneurial capability and performance (Zhang et al. 2009, 2017; Karra et al. 2008) largely ignores the very important concept of IE: international EO. However, to date, the vast majority of the studies assume a direct effect of entrepreneurial capabilities of EO on performance. No research in entrepreneurship and IE investigated the mediating mechanisms of IEO that link international entrepreneurial capabilities and performance in early internationalising firms. Relationship between international entrepreneurial capability and performance is context-specific, which indicates moderating and/or mediating effects on performance. Simply examining the direct entrepreneurial capability-performance relationship provides an incomplete picture of the phenomenon. The international entrepreneurial capability could elicit more performance outcome if the firm possesses a greater degree of risk-taking propensity, proactiveness, and innovativeness; the three core dimensions of IEO. Therefore, our next hypothesis that will be tested in this study is:

Hypothesis 4 *The positive relationship between international entrepreneurial capabilities and performance is partially mediated by international EO of early internationalising firms.*

3 Research Methodology

Our investigation rides on early internationalising firms in the apparel export industry of a South Asian developing country Bangladesh. Bangladesh, the world's 44th largest economy (IMF 2012), is one of the Next 11 (N-11) countries identified by Goldman Sachs, which combined with its 150 million populations, economic, and political conditions could greatly impact the global economy. It has become an export powerhouse, second only to China in global apparel exports (Yardley 2012). Cheap labour and capacity have helped Bangladesh become a hot spot for global apparel brands seeking the cheapest labour, especially in the face of rising wages in China. Bangladesh, once Kissinger's 'basket case' and irrelevant to the global economy, is now seen as the 'next China'. McKinsey and Co (2011), a global management consulting firm, has predicted that Bangladeshi apparel exports, now about $18 billion a year, could triple by 2020. The industry has emerged as very critical to the country's economy, accounting for 80 per cent of national exports, 13 per cent of gross national product, and more than three million jobs. It has given birth to about 5000 early internationalising firms in the industry. To be eligible for government export promotion schemes companies are required to be early internationalising firms by law and are not allowed to sell their products in domestic markets.

The phenomenal growth of apparel exports from Bangladesh has generally been attributed to favourable external conditions by researchers, most notably due to the Multi-Fibre Arrangement (MFA)—the bilateral quota system imposed by developed countries—supportive government policy, and low wages in the country (Rashid 2006). However, the role of apparel entrepreneurs and their entrepreneurial capabilities in the dynamic growth of this industry has always been overlooked. Thus, the industry offers a very lucrative setting of research to investigate the role of entrepreneurial capability and orientation in early internationalising firm's performance in the industry.

3.1 Survey Design and Data Source

Mail survey has recently become the sexiest data collection method for its cost-effectiveness and ease of implementation. Considering the low response rate in a developing country like Bangladesh, we decided to conduct a face-to-face survey using a structured questionnaire. A sample of 800 exporters was randomly generated from two existing members' directories in the industry: Bangladesh Garments Manufacturers and Exporters Association (BGMEA) and Bangladesh Knitwear Manufacturers and Exporters Association (BKMEA). We collected 718 questionnaires filled-up, a response rate of about 90%. After going through a rigorous normality test in SPSS 24, we finally got 647 usable cases.

The structured questionnaire used for the survey was developed through a comprehensive literature review and was written originally in English and translated into Bengali. Four academic experts familiar with the topic assessed the content validity of the items. The questionnaire was then pretested with 15 managers. Subsequently, we revised the questionnaire based on their feedback. We then back-translated the questionnaire into English and checked for consistency with the original version to prove 'translation equivalence' (Van de Vijver and Leung 1997).

We have taken several steps to minimise common method bias, including the protection of respondent and firm; reducing item ambiguity by pre-testing the survey on entrepreneurs; ensuring items relating to the dependent variables were not located close to the independent variables on the questionnaire. The Harman's one-factor test (Podsakoff et al. 2003) was conducted. All the statements relating to the endogenous and exogenous variables were entered in a single Principal Component Analysis (PCA) in SPSS 24 to check whether one component accounted for most of the variance. Four components with eigenvalues greater than 1.00 were identified. These components accounted for 59.11% of the variance, with the largest component accounting for only 17.94%. No evidence of common method bias was detected. Furthermore, we also checked common method bias by using a confirmatory factor analytic approach in which common method bias is detected if a single latent factor accounts for all observed variables. The single factor model produced poor model fit ($\chi^2 = 937.399$, df $= 90$; χ^2/df $= 10.416$; the goodness-of-fit index (GFI) $= 0.810$, adjusted GFI (AGFI) $= 0.747$, comparative fit index (CFI) $= 0.684$, Tucker-Lewis Index (TLI) $= 0.631$, incremental fit index (IFI) $= 0.686$, normed fit index (NFI) = 0.664, root mean square error of approximation (RMSEA) = 0.121). This suggests that common method bias is not a problem in this study.

3.2 Development of Measures

All items were measured on a seven-point Likert scale and asked respondents to report what happened in the last three years of the company's operation.

International Entrepreneurial Capability. This construct is developed based on the items used by Faroque et al. (2020a, b), Zhang et al. (2009) and the discussion of Karra et al. (2008). While Zhang et al. (2009) developed multidimensional measures of capability, we considered this as unidimensional. Our entrepreneurial capability construct includes six specific capabilities of entrepreneurs: prior international business experience, global vision, networking, innovative, proactive, and risk-taking capabilities.

International EO. Previously validated scales were adopted for the three dimensions of international EO. These represent several commonly used items for the construct—as previously used by Covin and Slevin (1986), Knight and Cavusgil (2004), and Lumpkin and Dess (1996). We have refined innovativeness construct to reflect the product, market, behavioural, strategic, and process innovations based on the discussion and operationalisation of Wang and Ahmed (2004). The established construct of innovativeness is mainly focused on product innovativeness which cannot truly reflect innovativeness of the whole organisation.

International Performance. Export performance is a complex multi-dimensional construct, relying on a number of different and interrelated variables internal and external to the firm (Katsikeas et al. 2000). In line with contemporary literature, we have included some financial as well as non-financial measures. Financial measures include export sales volume, export sales growth, and export profitability (Katsikeas et al. 2000) whereas non-financial measures include new market entry/number of export countries (Katsikeas et al. 2000), the company's overall satisfaction with the quality of key suppliers' critical components, quality of the company's relationship with key overseas customers, and key customers' overall satisfaction with the quality of the company's products/services (Lages et al. 2009).

Control Variables. In their theoretical arguments on the EO-performance relationship as well as on the determinants of export performance, scholars (e.g. Achrol and Stern 1988; Joshi and Campbell 2003; Lumpkin and Dess 2001; Zhou et al. 2010) emphasised the importance of control variables. We have included following control variables to allow for a better delineation of the relationships proposed in this study: firm age (operationalised as the number of years since the establishment), firm size (number of employees), market uncertainty (vulnerability to the change in trade policies across borders), technology dynamics (change to technology relating to early internationalising firm's main product/industry), price competitiveness (competitive advantage of early internationalising firm's product price in relation to major competitors in international markets), and environmental dynamism (change in overseas customers' demand and preferences, competitors' new product introduction rate and new selling strategies).

3.3 Analysis Methods

For the analytical purpose, we used structural equation modelling (SEM). This technique is deemed appropriate when a series of regressions are performed and the dependent variable for one regression analysis is also the independent variable for another (Hair et al. 1998). SEM also enables to measure indirect effects between the constructs. SEM constitutes two components: (a) the measurement model, which reduces observed variable to a smaller number of latent factors, and (b) the structural model, which defines causal relationships among latent variables. A number of software programs such as LISREL, AMOS, and EQS are available for such analysis. We used AMOS 24 in this study.

3.4 Results and Analyses

Data were analysed following three-step paradigm advocated by Gerbing and Hamilton (1996): exploratory factor analysis (EFA) in SPSS 24, confirmatory factor analysis (CFA), and SEM in AMOS 18. Prior to AMOS analyses, we performed EFA and reliability analysis to identify any poorly performing items of the measurement construct. In this exploratory stage, we excluded several items with low factor loadings, high cross-loadings, or low item-to-total correlations. The remaining items were entered in CFA to verify the hypothesised factor structure and to assess convergent validity and discriminant validity. In EFA, international entrepreneurial capability emerged as unidimensional and international performance as two dimensional as expected. International EO emerged as unidimensional as opposed to our expectation of conventional three-dimensional outcomes in entrepreneurship and IE literature. However, from a literature review on EO-performance relationship, Rauch et al. (2009) conclude that it is premature to suggest EO as a multidimensional rather than a unidimensional concept based on how the dimensions relate to performance. We, therefore, treated international EO as unidimensional based on EFA results.

3.5 Measurement Model

The measurement model with all 15 items is analysed as a CFA. The covariance matrix for the 15 items is used for the analysis, and parameter estimates are made under the maximum likelihood (ML) method. Table 1 shows the correlation matrix and descriptive statistics for the constructs. Table 2 shows the standardised loadings

Table 1 Correlation between constructs, means, and standard deviation

Construct	Mean	SD	(1)	(2)	(3)	(4)
(1) International entrepreneurial capability	5.156	1.049	**0.714**			
(2) International entrepreneurial orientation (IEO)	5.154	0.995	0.628	**0.730**		
(3) International performance: financial	5.012	0.989	0.466	0.459	**0.700**	
(4) International performance: non-financial	5.429	0.950	0.444	0.411	0.536	**0.721**

Note: Diagonal is the square root of the variance extracted

Correlations greater than 0.13 are significant at the 0.05 level. Correlations greater than 0.17 are significant at the 0.01 level

obtained from the estimation of the CFA model. Factor loadings in the measurement model are all significant and greater than 0.50 which indicates convergent validity. For adequate discriminant validity, the diagonal elements of the correlation matrix should be greater than the off-diagonal elements (Fornell and Larcker 1981). Table 1 shows that the measurement model demonstrates adequate discriminant validity which implies that the four constructs used in the model belong to distinct and separate entities.

Construct reliability was estimated by Cronbach's alpha, composite reliability (CR), and average variance extracted (AVE). Alpha values and CR scores of all constructs exceed the recommended threshold of 0.70, which suggests that high internal reliability exists in the constructs (Fornell and Larcker 1981). In addition, the AVE coefficients are all greater than 0.50 (the AVE of financial performance construct is 0.49 which is very close to 0.50), suggesting that the items are able to explain the variance in the constructs (Fornell and Larcker 1981). Finally, the measurement model shows acceptable fit indices for RMSEA, GFI, AGFI, CFI, TLI, IFI, and NFI which provides sufficient proof of model fit. Therefore, this model has been used as the basis of the structural model.

3.6 *Structural Model*

The conceptual framework of the study is simultaneously estimated in a structural equation model using ML estimation in AMOS 18. The overall chi-square for the model exhibited in Fig. 2 was significant due to a large sample size ($\chi^2 = 327.086$, df $= 133$, $p < 0.00$; χ^2/df $= 2.459$). Other fit indices, for example, GFI $= 0.948$, AGFI $= 0.926$, CFI $= 0.944$, TLI $= 0.928$, IFI $= 0.944$, RMSEA $= 0.048$ provide sufficient proof of model fit (Browne and Cudeck 1993). Thus, the conceptual model fits the data well and does a good job of explaining the relationships among the latent variables. Direct, indirect, and total effects of the exogenous variables on the relevant endogenous variables were estimated with 90% confidence level and are reported in Table 3.

Figure 2 shows the empirically tested structural model.

Table 2 Measurement scales and properties

Constructs/items	Standardised loadings	β	CR	AVE
International entrepreneurial capability		0.713	0.806	0.510
1. The founder(s) has prior international business experience before starting this business. (prior international experience)	0.694			
2. The founder(s) has networking capability to build a relationship with suppliers, customers, and other network partners abroad.	0.654			
3. The founder(s) actively explores new business opportunities in international markets (proactiveness).	0.791			
4. The founder(s) of the firm has undertaken significant and risky resource commitments for international business.[a]				
5. The founder(s) is very innovative (in terms of creative ideas, products, process, problem-solving, etc. in international business) (innovativeness).	0.711			
International entrepreneurial orientation		0.783	0.850	0.530
Proactiveness				
1. Our top managers have regularly attended local/foreign trade fairs.[a]				
2. Our top managers have usually spent some time abroad to visit.[a]				
3. Our top management actively seeks contact with suppliers or clients in international markets.	0.720			
4. Our top management regularly monitors the trend of export markets.[a]				
Risk-taking				
5. Our top management focuses more on opportunities than risks abroad.	0.744			
6. When confronted with decisions about exporting or other international operations, our top management is always tolerant of potential risks.[a]				
7. Our top managers have shared vision towards the risks of foreign markets.	0.751			
8. Our top management believes that owing to the nature of the international business environment, it is best to explore opportunities abroad gradually via cautious, incremental steps.[a]				
9. When confronted with international decision-making situations, we typically adopt a cautious, 'wait-and-see' posture in order to minimise the chance of making costly mistakes.[a]				
Innovativeness				
10. We are willing to try new ways of doing things and seek unusual novel solutions.	0.745			
11. We constantly search for new overseas customers.[a]				

(continued)

Table 2 (continued)

Constructs/items	Standardised loadings	β	CR	AVE
12. We always try to serve our existing/new overseas customers with new products/service offerings.	0.675			
13. Our new products and services are often perceived as a novel by our overseas customers.[a]				
14. We are constantly improving our business processes.[a]				
15. We have the ability to harmonise ambitious international business objectives with existing resources.[a]				
International performance				
Financial		0.724	0.735	0.490
1. Export sales volume	0.736			
2. Export sales growth	0.794			
3. Export profitability	0.536			
Non-financial		0.720	0.764	0.520
1. Newmarket entry/number of export countries	0.738			
2. Our key customers' overall satisfaction with the quality of our products/services	0.762			
3. Quality of our company's relationship with key overseas customers	0.658			
4. Our overall satisfaction with the quality of key suppliers' critical components[a]				

Measurement model fit indices are as follows: $\chi^2 = 294.783$, df = 150; $\chi^2/df = 1.965$; GFI = 0.957; AGFI = 0.934; CFI = 0.960; TLI = 0.944; IFI = 0.960; NFI = 0.923, RMSEA = 0.039
Note: All standardised coefficient loadings are significant at $p < 0.01$
CR = Composite reliability; AVE = Average variance extracted
[a]Indicates the item that was dropped in the scale purification process in Exploratory Factor Analysis (EFA) in SPSS

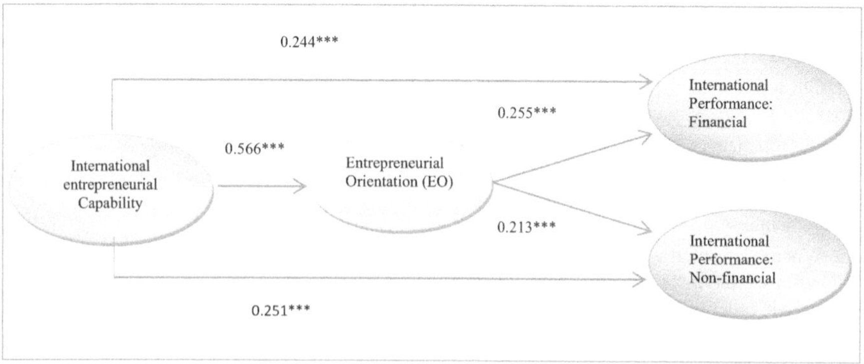

Fig. 2 Results of structural equation modelling (SEM) on the hypothesised model

Table 3 Standardised direct, indirect, and total effects of exogenous variables in the model

		Endogenous variables					
		International entrepreneurial orientation (IEO)		International performance: financial		International performance: non-financial	
Exogenous variables	Type of effects	Beta	c.r.	Beta	c.r.	Beta	c.r.
International entrepreneurial capability	Direct effect	0.566***	7.968	0.244***	3.308	0.251***	3.358
	Indirect effect	–	–	0.145***	2.900	0.121***	2.327
	Total effect	0.566***	7.968	0.389***	6.208	0.372***	5.685
International entrepreneurial orientation (IEO)	Direct effect	–	–	0.255***	3.763	0.213***	3.136
	Indirect effect	–	–	–	–	–	–
	Total effect	–	–	0.255***	3.763	0.213***	3.136

Critical ratios (c.r.) are significant: $^{***}p \leq 0.01$; $^{**}p \leq 0.05$; $^{*}p \leq 0.10$

Consistent with hypotheses H1, the results indicate that there is a significant positive relationship between the international entrepreneurial capability of entrepreneurs and international EO of the firm ($\beta = 0.566$, $p < 0.01$). Similarly, as predicted by H2, the international entrepreneurial capability of entrepreneurs is positively associated with both financial ($\beta = 0.244$, $p < 0.01$) and non-financial ($\beta = 0.251$, $p < 0.01$) performance measures. Supporting findings for H3 indicate that international EO of the firm is positively associated with both financial ($\beta = 0.255$, $p < 0.01$) and non-financial ($\beta = 0.213$, $p < 0.01$) performance outcomes.

In terms of indirect (mediated) effects of international EO (H4), we found that the relationship between the international entrepreneurial capability of entrepreneurs and international performance is partially mediated by international EO across both dimensions of performance measures: financial ($\beta = 0.145$, $p < 0.01$) and non-financial ($\beta = 0.121$, $p < 0.01$). In terms of total effects, international entrepreneurial capability exerts significant and larger effects on both financial ($\beta = 0.389$, $p < 0.01$) and non-financial ($\beta = 0.372$, $p < 0.01$) performance measures.

In relation to controlling variables, environmental dynamism ($\beta = 0.108$, $p < 0.05$) and firm age ($\beta = 0.143$, $p < 0.01$) are positively associated with financial performance. In addition, environmental dynamism ($\beta = 0.141$, $p < 0.01$), market uncertainty ($\beta = 0.134$, $p < 0.01$), and technology dynamics ($\beta = 0.118$, $p < 0.05$) have a positive relationship with non-financial performance. None of the control variables showed any significant association with international EO of early internationalising firms.

4 Discussion and Conclusion

The point of departure for this study was to argue for the applicability and usefulness of quantitative methods in explaining the role of capabilities in entrepreneurial internationalisation in general while focusing on a neglected empirical context of low-tech manufacturing in developed economies in particular. In doing so, we investigated the relationships between international entrepreneurial capability, IEO, and international performance in the low-technology context of early internationalising firms originating from Bangladesh. In addition, we also explored the mediating role of IEO in the relationships between international entrepreneurial capability and international performance. We found that our hypotheses linking international entrepreneurial capabilities to increased entrepreneurial orientation and, consequently, to increased international performance were by and large supported by the quantitative empirical analysis. The present study, therefore, adds an important piece of knowledge to empirical IE research. First, it highlights the applicability of quantitative methods in explaining capability development in IE, while earlier research in the domain has been mostly conceptual or qualitative in nature (Mort and Weerawardena 2006; Autio et al. 2011; Glavas and Mathews 2014). Second, by taking the approach of examining early internationalising firms from low-technology and developing market context, the present study further argues for the applicability of quantitative approaches in a domain where most quantitative studies have been conducted almost exclusively in developed market high-technology contexts (e.g., Raymond and St-Pierre 2013; Torkkeli 2014; Pinho and Prange 2016). This study therefore further advocates that IE scholars should strongly consider quantitative approaches when aiming to shed light on the role of capabilities and orientations in entrepreneurial and early internationalisation; and to do so regardless of the market or industry context that they deem the most suitable as their empirical basis.

This study also makes several contributions to the theoretical development of IE, most specifically to early internationalising firm literature. First, while the capabilities perspective is expected to underlie early internationalisation (Cavusgil and Knight 2015), this study is among the few studies that empirically tested the impact of international entrepreneurial capability on the performance of early internationalising firms. To the best of our knowledge, there is no other study in IE that empirically tested the relationship between international entrepreneurial capability and EO. How an entrepreneur's capability influences EO of early internationalising firms is an important research area considering the crucial role of the entrepreneur in early internationalising firm internationalisation and success. Second, it also suggests an indirect link between international entrepreneurial capability and performance, in addition to a direct relationship between the two. Therefore, the present study is not just an argument for the applicability of quantitative methodology across market and industry contexts in IE but also helps extend the theoretical discussion on the role of international entrepreneurial capabilities as important antecedents of successful internationalisation.

Third, it sheds light on an emerging market traditional industry, which is a specific 'context contribution' to IE. Fourth, our findings indicate that EO scale needs further refinement in an international setting. Although EO scale achieved cross-cultural validity, replicating the previously developed scales for studies in the United States without enough investigation of the validity of these measures in an international setting is becoming increasingly problematic (Kreiser et al. 2002). While pretesting the EO scale in a cross-cultural setting, Kreiser et al. (2002) reported significant cross-loadings between some items and due to the same problem, we have deleted some items from the EO scale. Knight and Cavusgil (2004) also reported the same problem regarding international EO construct even in their study of US early internationalising firms.

Fifth, we have used different measures of firm international performance, i.e., both financial and non-financial performance measures. Most previous studies in IE used either financial or non-financial measures. While each of the measures has its own strengths and limitations, using both of them in the same study gives more reliable results (Tang et al. 2008). Finally, we have positioned entrepreneurial capability as an entrepreneur level phenomenon, as opposed to firm-level positioning by Zhang et al. (2009). While EO itself is a firm-level capability construct and consists of innovative, proactive, and risk-taking capabilities, positioning international entrepreneurial capability as firm-level with similar capability dimensions would make no difference. This clear distinction in our study, we hope, will encourage researchers to further develop the construct and examine its impact on IEO and performance.

4.1 Implications

Several implications can be extracted from the findings for practitioners. First, for early internationalising firms' entrepreneurs, this study highlights the fact that entrepreneurs need to have certain entrepreneurial capabilities both to induce entrepreneurial orientation of the firm and to achieve superior financial and strategic performance outcomes in international markets. More specifically, prior international experience, proactive and innovative attitude, and networking capabilities of entrepreneurs help build managers' entrepreneurial orientation and influence performance. Entrepreneurs in early internationalising firms should, therefore, develop and upgrade such entrepreneurial capabilities to build managers' entrepreneurial orientation and realise entrepreneurial success.

Second, it also suggests that while the range of capabilities is diverse, an entrepreneurial team be built to ensure the presence of all these capabilities. Having been successful in domestic markets does not necessarily guarantee the existence of entrepreneurial capabilities necessary to create an early internationalising firm and become successful. In addition to the same entrepreneurial capabilities necessary in domestic entrepreneurship, IE requires some specific capabilities in order to take challenges prevailing in the international environment (Karra et al. 2008). Third, for managers in existing early internationalising firms, this study suggests that to achieve international performance managers need to capitalise on the entrepreneur's capabilities. Building on the entrepreneur's prior international experience, proactive and innovative attitude, and networking capabilities, managers can develop their own proactiveness, risk-taking, and innovative attitude and perform these activities to achieve higher performance advantage.

This study provides some important guidelines for public policymakers responsible for promoting international entrepreneurship. For one, it suggests that it is the entrepreneur who drives entrepreneurial orientation and international performance of early internationalising firms. Therefore, public policymakers need to provide support in the areas in which entrepreneurs need to develop their entrepreneurial capabilities. According to Lefebvre et al. (2003), government assistance programs should target the most powerful determinants of export performance. In this study, for achieving financial performance, the contribution of international EO is greater than the contribution of international entrepreneurial capability.

In contrast, international entrepreneurial capability seems to be more influential than international EO in achieving non-financial performance outcomes. This suggests that financial outcomes are achieved through internal orientation and operations of early internationalising firms and that is why international entrepreneurial capability needs to be mediated through international EO. By contrast, non-financial outcomes may be obtained by the direct influence of international entrepreneurial capability because the entrepreneur himself is actively involved in building long-term beneficial relationship with customers, in ensuring overseas customers' satisfaction reflected in quality products, and in seeking out new markets and customers. Therefore, policymakers should have specific programs targeting entrepreneurs at the individual level and managers at the firm level.

In sum, this study has sought to respond to recent calls (Dabić et al. 2019) for conducting small-firm internationalisation research, considering the capabilities of emerging market firms. By linking international entrepreneurial capability to entrepreneurial orientation and successful internationalisation simultaneously, it helps to bring added insight on what it means to internationalise entrepreneurially, and empirically this study has contributed in illustrating these dynamics in a neglected context of low-tech developing countries context.

4.2 Limitations and Future Research

This study has some potential limitations. First, the measures we developed to assess international entrepreneurial capability showed sufficient reliability and validity but need to be cross-validated in other studies and can include some other entrepreneurial capabilities to make a wider and complete 'capability set'. In addition, the scale of international EO we used in this study retained only five items out of 15 most used measures in the pertinent literature. Therefore, a more comprehensive and customised scale is required to the best capture of the rich meanings of IEO construct in emerging economy setting. Second, regardless of the entrepreneur's capabilities and the firm's strategic orientations, other entrepreneur and firm-specific factors could have an impact on early internationalising firms' performance. While we controlled some key firm and international market factors, other factors relating to entrepreneur's capabilities, environmental changes, and industry dynamics (Lumpkin and Dess 2001) could also be considered in future studies. Third, IEO may play different roles at different stages of early internationalising firms (Zhou et al. 2010) and this is worth investigating in future studies. Fourth, one possible limitation of this study is the lack of generalisability of findings because of its focus on a particular industry of a particular country. The proposed model should be replicated in other countries as well as in another industry setting to establish greater generalisability. Finally, this study employed a cross-sectional research design which cannot fully capture the dynamic aspects of the constructs used in this study. A longitudinal research design is therefore recommended.

References

Achrol RS, Stern LW (1988) Environmental determinants of decision-making uncertainty in marketing channels. J Mark Res 25(1):36–50

Acosta AS, Crespo ÁH, Agudo JC (2018) Effect of market orientation, network capability and entrepreneurial orientation on international performance of small and medium enterprises (SMEs). Int Bus Rev 27(6):1128–1140

Al-Aali A, Teece DJ (2014) International entrepreneurship and the theory of the (Long–lived) international firm: a capabilities perspective. Entrep Theory Pract 38(1):95–116

Anand P, Van Hees M (2006) Capabilities and achievements: an empirical study. J Soc Econ 35 (2):268–284

Andersson S (2000) The internationalization of the firm from an entrepreneurial perspective. Int Stud Manag Organ 30:63–92

Andersson S, Wictor I (2003) Innovative internationalisation in new firms: born globals–the Swedish case. J Int Entrep 1(3):249–275

Autio E, George G, Alexy O (2011) International entrepreneurship and capability development—qualitative evidence and future research directions. Entrep Theory Pract 35(1):11–37

Browne MW, Cudeck R (1993) Alternative ways of assessing model fit. In: Bollen KA, Long JS (eds) Testing structural equation models. Sage, Newbury Park, CA, pp 136–161

Casson M (2005) Entrepreneurship and the theory of the firm. J Econ Behav Organ 58(2):327–348

Cavusgil ST, Knight G (2015) The born global firm: an entrepreneurial and capabilities perspective on early and rapid internationalization. J Int Bus Stud 46(1):3–16

Covin JG, Slevin DP (1986) The development and testing of an organizational-level entrepreneurship scale. Frontiers of entrepreneurship research 1:626–639

Dabić M, Maley J, Dana LP, Novak I, Pellegrini MM, Caputo A (2019) Pathways of SME internationalization: a bibliometric and systematic review. Small Bus Econ:1–21

Dana LP (2001) Networks, internationalization & policy. Small Bus Econ 16(2):57–62

Dana LP, Wright RW (2009) International entrepreneurship: research priorities for the future. IJGSB 3(1):90–134

Dana LP, Etemad H, Wright RW (1999) The impact of globalization on SMEs. Glob Focus 11 (4):93–106

Dimitratos P, Plakoyiannaki E (2003) Theoretical foundations of an international entrepreneurial culture. J Int Entrep 1(2):187–215

Dimitratos P, Lioukas S, Carter S (2004) The relationship between entrepreneurship and international performance: the importance of domestic environment. Int Bus Rev 13(1):19–41
Emoke-Szidónia F (2015) International entrepreneurial orientation and performance of Romanian small and medium-sized firms: empirical assessment of direct and environment moderated relations. Procedia Econo Fin 32(15):186–193
Faroque AR, Mostafiz MI, Faruq MO, Bashar MFB (2020a) Revisiting entrepreneurial capabilities and export market orientation: a multi-scale investigation in an emerging economy. Int J Emerg Mark. https://doi.org/10.1108/IJOEM-08-2019-0644
Faroque AR, Mostafiz MI, Kuivalainen O, Sundqvist S (2020b). Prior experience and export performance: the missing link of global vision. https://www.senatehall.com/entrepreneurship?article=651
Fornell C, Larcker DF (1981) Evaluating structural equation models with unobservable variables and measurement error. J Mark Res 18(1):39–50
Freeman S, Edwards R, Schroder B (2006) How smaller born-global firms use networks and alliances to overcome constraints to rapid internationalization. J Int Mark 14(3):33–63
Frishammar J, Andersson S (2009) The overestimated role of strategic orientations for international performance in smaller firms. J Int Entrep 7(1):57–77
Gabrielsson M, Kirpalani V, Dimitratos P, Solberg CA, Zucchella A (2008) Born globals: propositions to help advance the theory. Int Bus Rev 17(4):385–401
Gerbing DW, Hamilton JG (1996) Viability of exploratory factor analysis as a precursor to confirmatory factor analysis. Struct Equ Model Multidiscip J 3(1):62–72
Glavas C, Mathews S (2014) How international entrepreneurship characteristics influence internet capabilities for the international business processes of the firm. Int Bus Rev 23(1):228–245
Gries T, Naudé W (2011) Entrepreneurship and human development: a capability approach. J Public Econ 95(3):216–224
Hair J, Anderson R, Tatham R, Black W (1998) Multivariate data analysis, 5th edn. Prentice Hall, Upper Saddle River, NJ
Hernández-Perlines F, Moreno-García J, Yañez-Araque B (2016) The mediating role of competitive strategy in international entrepreneurial orientation. J Bus Res 69(11):5383–5389
Ibeh KIN (2003) Toward a contingency framework of export entrepreneurship: conceptualizations and empirical evidence. Small Bus Econ 20(1):49–68
IMF (2012) World economic outlook database, October 2012. http://www.imf.org
Jantunen A, Puumalainen K, Saarenketo S, Kyläheiko K (2005) Entrepreneurial orientation, dynamic capabilities and international performance. J Int Entrep 3(3):223–243
Johanson J, Vahlne JE (2009) The Uppsala internationalization process model revisited: from liability of foreignness to liability of outsidership. J Int Bus Stud 40(9):1411–1431
Jones MV (2001) First steps in internationalisation: concepts and evidence from a sample of small high-technology firms. J Int Manag 7(3):191–210
Jones MV, Coviello N, Tang YK (2011) International entrepreneurship research (1989–2009): a domain ontology and thematic analysis. J Bus Ventur 26(6):469–492
Joshi AW, Campbell AJ (2003) Effect of environmental dynamism on relational governance in manufacturer-supplier relationships: a contingency framework and an empirical test. J Acad Mark Sci 31(2):176
Karra N, Phillips N, Tracey P (2008) Building the born global firm: developing entrepreneurial capabilities for international new venture success. Long Range Plan 41(4):440–458
Katsikeas CS, Leonidou LC, Morgan NA (2000) Firm-level export performance assessment: review, evaluation, and development. J Acad Mark Sci 28(4):493–511
Kaya H, Ağca V (2009) Entrepreneurial orientation and performance of Turkish manufacturing FDI firms: an empirical study
Kiss AN, Danis WM, Cavusgil ST (2012) International entrepreneurship research in emerging economies: a critical review and research agenda. J Bus Ventur 27(2):266–290
Knight GA (2001) Entrepreneurship and strategy in the international SME. J Int Manag 7 (3):155–171

Knight GA, Cavusgil ST (1996) The born global firm: a challenge to traditional internationalization theory. Adv Int Mark 8:11–26

Knight GA, Cavusgil ST (2004) Innovation, organizational capabilities, and the born-global firm. J Int Bus Stud 35(2):124–141

Knight G, Madsen TK, Servais P (2004) An inquiry into born-global firms in Europe and the USA. Int Mark Rev 21(6):645–665

Kreiser PM, Marino LD, Weaver KM (2002) Assessing the psychometric properties of the entrepreneurial orientation scale: a multi-country analysis. Entrep Theory Pract 26(4):71–94

Lages LF, Silva G, Styles C, Pereira ZL (2009) The NEP scale: a measure of network export performance. Int Bus Rev 18(4):344–356

Lefebvre E, Bourgault M, Prefontaine L, Lefebvre LA (2003) Understanding the driving forces behind the internationalisation process of fast-moving SMEs: implications for export assistance programmes. Int J Entrep Innov Manag 3(5–6):447–467

Lumpkin GT, Dess GG (1996) Clarifying the entrepreneurial orientation construct and linking it to performance. Acad Manag Rev 21:135–172

Lumpkin GT, Dess GG (2001) Linking two dimensions of entrepreneurial orientation to firm performance: the moderating role of environment and industry life cycle. J Bus Ventur 16 (5):429–451

Luo Y, Tung RL (2007) International expansion of emerging market enterprises: a springboard perspective. J Int Bus Stud 38(4):481–498

Madsen TK, Servais P (1997) The internationalization of born globals: an evolutionary process? Int Bus Rev 6(6):561–583

McAuley A (1999) Entrepreneurial instant exporters in the Scottish arts and crafts sector. J Int Mark 7:67–82

McDougall P, Shane S, Oviatt BM (1994) Explaining the formation of international new ventures: the limits of theories from international business research. J Bus Ventur 9(6):469–487

McDougall PP, Oviatt BM, Shrader RC (2003) A comparison of international and domestic new ventures. J Int Entrep 1(1):59–82

McKinsey, and Co (2011) Bangladesh's ready-made garments landscape: the challenge of growth, pp 1–24

Miller D (1983) The correlates of entrepreneurship in three types of firms. Manag Sci 29 (7):770–791

Mort GS, Weerawardena J (2006) Networking capability and international entrepreneurship: how networks function in Australian born global firms. Int Mark Rev 23(5):549–572

Oviatt BM, McDougall PP (1994) Toward a theory of international new ventures. J Int Bus Stud 25 (1):45–64

Oviatt BM, McDougall PP (1997) Challenges for internationalization process theory: the case of international new ventures. Manage Int Rev:85–99

Oviatt BM, McDougall PP (2004) Toward a theory of international new ventures. J Int Bus Stud 36 (1):29–41

Peiris IK, Akoorie ME, Sinha P (2012) International entrepreneurship: A critical analysis of studies in the past two decades and future directions for research. J Int Entrep 10(4):279-324

Pinho JC, Prange C (2016) The effect of social networks and dynamic internationalization capabilities on international performance. J World Bus 51(3):391–403

Pla-Barber J, Escribá-Esteve A (2006) Accelerated internationalisation: evidence from a late investor country. Int Mark Rev 23(3):255–278

Podsakoff PM, MacKenzie SB, Lee JY, Podsakoff NP (2003) Common method biases in behavioral research: a critical review of the literature and recommended remedies. J Appl Psychol 88 (5):879

Rashid MA (2006) Rise of readymade garments industry in Bangladesh: entrepreneurial ingenuity or public policy, paper presented at the workshop on governance and development. Organized by the World Bank and BIDS, Dhaka

Rasmussen ES, Madsen TK (2002). The born global concept. Paper presented at the paper presented at the 28th EIBA conference, Athens, Greece
Rauch A, Wiklund J, Lumpkin GT, Frese M (2009) Entrepreneurial orientation and business performance: an assessment of past research and suggestions for the future. Entrep Theory Pract 33(3):761–787
Raymond L, St-Pierre J (2013) Strategic capability configurations for the internationalization of SMEs: a study in equifinality. Int Small Bus J 31(1):82–102
Reuber AR, Fischer E (1997) The influence of the management team's international experience on the internationalization behaviors of SMEs. J Int Bus Stud 28:807–825
Reuber AR, Fischer E (2002) Foreign sales and small firm growth: the moderating role of the management team. Entrep Theory Pract 27(1):29–45
Rialp A, Rialp J, Knight GA (2005) The phenomenon of early internationalizing firms: what do we know after a decade (1993–2003) of scientific inquiry? Int Bus Rev 14(2):147–166
Robertson C, Chetty SK (2000) A contingency-based approach to understanding export performance. Int Bus Rev 9(2):211–235
Sadeghi VJ, Nkongolo-Bakenda JM, Anderson RB, Dana LP (2019) An institution-based view of international entrepreneurship: a comparison of context-based and universal determinants in developing and economically advanced countries. Int Bus Rev 28(6):101588
Schumpeter JA (1942) Capitalism, socialism and democracy. Harper and Row, New York
Sen AK (1985) Commodities and capabilities. North-Holland, Amsterdam
Sharma DD, Blomstermo A (2003) The internationalization process of born globals: a network view. Int Bus Rev 12(6):739–753
Swoboda B, Olejnik E (2016) Linking processes and dynamic capabilities of international SMEs: the mediating effect of international entrepreneurial orientation. J Small Bus Manag 54 (1):139–161
Tang J, Tang Z, Marino LD, Zhang Y, Li Q (2008) Exploring an inverted U-shape relationship between entrepreneurial orientation and performance in Chinese ventures. Entrep Theory Pract 32(1):219–239
Torkkeli L (2014) Profitable SME internationalisation: the influence of cross-relational and relationship-specific network competence. Int Procure Manage 7(6):677–694
Van de Vijver F, Leung K (1997) Methods and data analysis of comparative research. In: Berry JW, Poortinga YH, Pandey J (eds) Handbook of cross-cultural psychology. Allyn and Bacon, Boston, MA
Wang CL, Ahmed PK (2004) The development and validation of the organisational innovativeness construct using confirmatory factor analysis. Eur J Innov Manag 7(4):303–313
Weerawardena J, Mort GS, Liesch PW, Knight G (2007) Conceptualizing accelerated internationalization in the born global firm: a dynamic capabilities perspective. J World Bus 42(3):294–306
Wiklund J, Shepherd D (2003) Knowledge-based resources, entrepreneurial orientation, and the performance of small and medium-sized businesses. Strateg Manag J 24(13):1307–1314
Yardley J (2012). Made in Bangladesh: export powerhouse feels pangs of labor strife, The New York times, Retrieved from http://www.nytimes.com
Zaheer S (1995) Overcoming the liability of foreignness. Acad Manag J 38(2):341–363
Zahra SA, Garvis DM (2000) International corporate entrepreneurship and firm performance: the moderating effect of international environmental hostility. J Bus Ventur 15(5):469–492
Zhang M, Tansuhaj P, McCullough J (2009) International entrepreneurial capability: the measurement and a comparison between born global firms and traditional exporters in China. J Int Entrep 7(4):292–322
Zhang M, Gao Q, Cho HS (2017) The effect of sub-national institutions and international entrepreneurial capability on international performance of export-focused SMEs: evidence from China and South Korea. J Int Entrep 15(1):85–110
Zhou L, Barnes BR, Lu Y (2010) Entrepreneurial proclivity, capability upgrading and performance advantage of newness among international new ventures. J Int Bus Stud 41(5):882–905

Anisur R. Faroque is a post-doctoral researcher at the School of Business and Management at LUT University, Finland. Anisur's research interests are in the international entrepreneurship and international business areas and include opportunity exploration and exploitation, entrepreneurial capabilities, and internationalization. He has published in International Business Review, Journal of Business and Industrial Marketing, Asia Pacific Journal of Marketing and Logistics, and International Journal of Emerging Markets, among others.

Hasan Mahmud is an M.Sc. student in international business and entrepreneurship at LUT Business School and Management, LUT University, Finland. His research interests include entrepreneurship, international business, and organizational behaviour. He has written many textbooks on marketing and banking in Bengali. His research has been published in the European Journal of Business and Management.

Lasse Torkkeli is an Adjunct Professor of International Business in the Turku School of Economics at the University of Turku and Associate Professor at the School of Business and Management at LUT University at Lappeenranta, Finland. Torkkeli's research interests are in the international entrepreneurship and international business domains and include SME internationalisation, capabilities and business models, and sustainable entrepreneurship. He has previously published in the International Business Review, International Marketing Review, and the Journal of International Entrepreneurship, among other journals and publishers.

Sami Saarenketo is a professor of International Marketing at the School of Business and Management, at LUT University, Finland. His primary areas of research interest are international entrepreneurship and international marketing. He has published in Journal of World Business, Management International Review, International Business Review, European Journal of Marketing and Journal of International Entrepreneurship, among others.

The Study of Leaders Navigating Institutional on Female International Entrepreneurship in Emerging Economies

Sepideh Khavarinezhad and Paolo Pietro Biancone

1 Introduction

A phenomenon that keeps puzzling researchers and policymakers alike is the persistently lower rate of female entrepreneurs across the globe. Since women entrepreneurs play a significant role in the growth process of a country (Minniti et al., 2007) and make an important contribution to the development of the world economy (Allen et al. 2007), the interest to examine this founder group has increased dramatically over the years. Work collected so far mainly focuses on four different aspects: (1) the process why some women become entrepreneurs, (2) the consequences of doing so, (3) the psychological and contextual factors that facilitate or inhibit their entrepreneurial activity, and (4) differences in these three areas as compared to their male counterparts (Jennings and Brush 2013). A fundamental contribution to research that female entrepreneurship studies have yielded so far is that entrepreneurship is not a gender-neutral phenomenon and is thus influenced by systems of socially constructed and widely shared beliefs about characteristics typically associated with women and men, and the behaviours and roles deemed appropriate for the members of each sex (Hmieleski and Sheppard 2019; Jennings and Brush 2013; Malmström et al. 2017). International entrepreneurship includes internationalisation and entrepreneurship, which requires recognising opportunities for the coordination of scarce resources across international borders (Sadeghi et al. 2017, 2019; Dana 2017).

Institutions are one of the factors influencing international entrepreneurship. According to institutional theory, one of the factors affecting the internationalisation of entrepreneurs is institutional factors. The internationalisation element shows the

S. Khavarinezhad (✉) · P. P. Biancone
Department of Management, University of Turin, Turin, Italy
e-mail: sepideh.khavarinezhad@unito.it; paolo.biancone@unito.it

V. Jafari-Sadeghi et al. (eds.), *Empirical International Entrepreneurship*,
Contributions to Management Science,
https://doi.org/10.1007/978-3-030-68972-8_15

level of the entrepreneur's internationalisation of the country (Etemad et al. 2010; Sadeghi and Biancone 2017, 2018). At the individual level, it is measured by the "export" potential of businesses and at the institutional level by the "degree of economic complexity". "Exports" require capabilities beyond the capabilities of manufacturing businesses for the domestic market. The institutional dimension of this element reflects the level of openness of the country to women international entrepreneurs (Jafari Sadeghi et al. 2018, 2020). Drawing from the role of institutional theory, this study investigates the stereotypes women hold about female entrepreneurs and how they can respond to these to deal with existing role conflicts in the international environment. The increasing participation of women in creating jobs and businesses in the domestic and international environment has attracted the attention of researchers to the role of gender and differences in this field (Jafari-Sadeghi et al. 2019; Beheshti et al. 2016).

Female entrepreneurs play an important role in the growth process of a country, yet female entrepreneurs are underrepresented across the globe, as they face various obstacles during the founding process. Therefore, it is important to consider the factors that influence the rate of female international entrepreneurship. This research is exploratory and seeks to generate a more accurate view of how institution roles are perceived by women entrepreneurs from different countries and how female entrepreneurs respond to stereotyping based on these roles and about which little is known. We take advantage of quantitative research design with a sample of 30 emerging economies which were extracted from different databases in 2018: Global Entrepreneurship Monitor (GEM), Adult Population Survey (APS), Ease of Doing Business Index (EDBI) published by the World Bank, Heritage Foundation, United Nations Conference on Trade and Development (UNCTAD, 2016), World Economic Situation and Prospects, Business Insights on Emerging Markets, and International Monetary Fund (IMF DATA).

The construct of the analysis consists of these factors: legal factors (freedom of business, property rights, ease of starting a business, ease of doing business); cognitive factors (understanding the opportunity, knowing an entrepreneur, skills); normative elements (entrepreneurial reputation, media attention); guiding factors (ICT rules, university–industry collaboration, access to VC, access to the latest technology); and moderate variable (risk-taking).

For the analysis of the data related to indicators and test the hypotheses, partial least squares structural equation modelling (PLS-SEM) will be used with SmartPLS software. International entrepreneurship rate in each country (dependent variable) with average customer ratio of female entrepreneurs and adolescents living abroad is measured. To evaluate the institutional environment (independent variables) the tools presented by Stenholm (2013) will be used.

The political and economic conditions and institutional relationships and access to various resources in emerging economies have provided a different context for studying the phenomenon of international entrepreneurship in these countries. In emerging economies, institutions face challenges and risks, and it can be claimed that there is an institutional void. Reforming the institutional environment is usually complex and time-consuming; therefore, entrepreneurs must be prepared to operate in an inappropriate institutional climate. In this regard, in this study, considering the interaction between institutions and entrepreneurship strategy (Peng, 2001; Peng, 2003), risk-taking is considered as one of the organisational mechanisms that entrepreneurs choose in inappropriate institutional conditions. According to the above explanation, the primary purpose of this study is to assess the impact of institutional factors on the rate of female international entrepreneurship in emerging economies, considering the moderating role of risk-taking. Moreover, we seek to understand the role of institutions in providing conditions for international female entrepreneurs to deal with existing conflicts despite the existence of gender differences stereotypes in emerging economies. In these areas, women may refrain from doing entrepreneurship because of difficulties in obtaining adequate legal protection.

The defect of institutions in one country can be partially compensated by organisational mechanisms; in this respect, due to deficient institutions in emerging economies, in this study, we evaluate the impact of institutional factors on women's international entrepreneurship rates in these countries by considering the interaction between the institutional environment and entrepreneurial strategy.

2 Theoretical Framework

Institutional theory has been associated with entrepreneurial research (Bruton et al., 2010), especially in helping to examine the elements that shape entrepreneurial success (Ahlstrom and Bruton, 2002). In this section, we present our theoretical argument regarding the role of institutional determinants in attracting women to establish their businesses. Institutional theory has been applied in entrepreneurship to realise the tendency of nations to be entrepreneurial (Ahlstrom and Bruton, 2002). Institutional theory is a progressively employed theoretical lens for entrepreneurship research (Bruton et al., 2010; Mahmoudi et al. 2019). In numerous articles, it refers to the study of economic performance and the impact of institutions on financial performance. The institutional theory explores a wide range of topics in various fields ranging from institutional economics and political science to organisational theory. The institutional approach has proven to be especially useful in entrepreneurial research (Ahlstrom and Bruton, 2002; Hajiagha et al. 2013, 2015, 2018). Institutional theory has also been very strong in investigating pertinent international issues (Jafari Sadeghi et al., 2019). This chapter regards existing entrepreneurial literature that utilises institutional theory to address the current state of the field, its current shortcomings, and where we need to move in the future. The success of entrepreneurs in an international environment generates not only economic benefits but also social and cultural benefits (Rezaei et al. 2020). Entrepreneurship has a variety of reasons, including unemployment and wage reduction, and dissatisfaction with their previous jobs. One of the most important criteria for measuring a country's development is the degree of importance and credit that women have in that country. The role of entrepreneurship in development depends directly on the purpose of social and economic development and is a fundamental factor in the evolution of all human societies. In this concept, gender has not been considered an unusual feature that could affect business results, since men have traditionally played the business role (Amin Moghadasi et al. 2017; Boudlaie et al. 2020; Mahdiraji et al. 2011, 2019, 2020). However, currently, analysing the differences and similarities between men and women which affect the performance of a business is of concern to many researchers in explaining case studies from different countries.

International women entrepreneurship is a process in which female entrepreneurs carry out business across national borders. The main objective of this study is to observe women entrepreneurship and its implementation in domestic entrepreneurship and evaluate their performance in export and international entrepreneurship to study the nature and consequences of a firm's risk-taking behaviour as it ventures into international markets (Covin and Muller, 2014; Mokhtarzadeh et al. 2018, 2020). Government policies can provide a context that is beneficial for productive entrepreneurship. Therefore, the government should emphasise the creation of an environment that is beneficial for the division of labour, the commercialisation of inventions, and the exchange.

Meanwhile, the degree of economic development in the country is important, and the relationship between government policies and female entrepreneurial activity will vary across countries. Overall, according to government mechanisms, activists must always balance their desire for innovation with pressures to conform to public order (Jafari Sadeghi and Biancone 2017; Sukumar et al. 2020). The mechanisms and policies put forward by the government should also be commensurate with the country's growth stage and not only hinder entrepreneurship but also implement policies that accelerate productive entrepreneurship. Because the government plays a vital role in shaping the rules of the game for entrepreneurs, government efforts at the social level can reduce entrepreneurship constraints by reducing opportunity costs for new businesses. For this reason, many scholars seek to explain the role of government policies in the entrepreneurial space. By looking at some of the entrepreneurial failures, we can see the positive effects of government policies on reducing the losses of entrepreneurs, which encourages risk-taking by entrepreneurs. Government policies towards entrepreneurs to provide financial support through subsidies and preferential loans or favourable financial policies that they call the "regulatory environment" for entrepreneurship increase the opportunities (Jafari-Sadeghi 2020) available to existing businesses and new businesses. Countries where entrepreneurship training programmes are commonplace and people know how to finance and manage a new business will have the ability to manage their business successfully. The existence of such conditions refers to the "cognitive environment" for entrepreneurship. Finally, in countries where entrepreneurial activities are valued, more people will be motivated to find a new business or manage a new business. The existence of such conditions refers to the "normative environment". Regulatory, cognitive, and normative environments constitute the three pillars or bases for supporting a country's entrepreneurial activities. According to economic experts, governments that adopt the approach of promoting domestic entrepreneurial business will succeed if they implement policies to strengthen all three of these foundations.

3 Literature Review

McDougall (1989) presented the first definition of international entrepreneurship (Keupp and Gassmann 2009; Taghavifard et al. 2018), developing new businesses or start-ups that have been involved in the international market since its inception and consider their operational domain to be international from the early stages of the company's operations (McDougall 1989). This definition limits international entrepreneurship to low-risk ventures, but this definition is still used in some recent research Keupp and Gassmann 2009. Zahra expanded the domain of international entrepreneurship to corporate entrepreneurship. Under the influence of this approach, the definitions presented hereafter are independent of the size and age of the company (North 1990; Zahra and George 2002). They discovered and exploited opportunities in the international entrepreneurial literature, thereafter considered as the main elements of this issue. In this study, based on McDougall's studies of novice entrepreneurs, the initial definition was provided by McDougall (1989).

There have been few experimental studies on the role of institutional factors in entrepreneurial activism. Ruta Aidis et al. (2008), in an article entitled "Institutions and Entrepreneurship Development in Russia", used a comparative perspective to examine how institutions influence entrepreneurial development. They applied statistical data (GEM) to study the effects of weak institutions on entrepreneurship in Russia, first compared it with the countries in examples of GEM, and then compared it with Brazil and Poland in more detail. The results showed that Russia's institutional environment is important in explaining the relatively low level of entrepreneurial development. They stated that the business environment plays a unique role among institutional factors.

Sobel (2008), in a study entitled "Baumol Theory Test: The Quality of Institutions and Entrepreneurial Productivity", tested Baumol's productive and unproductive entrepreneurship theory, which is one of the most important literature on entrepreneurship from an economic perspective. In this study, he endorsed Baumol's theory that entrepreneurs, depending on the economic, political, and legal institutions that govern society, make their efforts in different directions. He also examined the relationship between the quality of legal and political institutions in the USA and productive and unproductive entrepreneurship, concluding that the appropriate institutional structure increases risky investments, patents, and firm rates, and thus, raising the level of entrepreneurship provides a high rate of economic growth. Chienwattanasook and Jermsittiparsert (2019), in a study entitled "Impact of entrepreneur education on entrepreneurial self-employment : a study from Thailand" , examines the role of institutional variables in explaining the large gap observed in the self-employment rate of emerging economies. The model presented in this study is dedicated to the analysis of the role of tax situation and tax evasion opportunities. In this model, based on the relevant theoretical foundations, it is expected that tax evasion opportunities will have a positive effect on the self-employment rate.

International entrepreneurship in emerging economies is the collection of growing and extensive research (Yamakawa et al. 2008). Women's entrepreneurship is also a hot topic in the entrepreneurial literature (Kiss et al. 2012). In this vein, the rule of law does not affect gender; in fact, women's entrepreneurship is more prevalent in countries with more substantial state sectors (Jafari-Sadeghi et al. 2020). To examine the impact of institutions on the internationalisation of entrepreneurs in emerging economies, Stenholm et al. (2013) developed the model in measuring the institutional dimensions of the entrepreneurial activity environment and, in addition to institutional factors, also included the cultural environment and industry-based factors as independent variables in the model. The results of the analysis using secondary data and structural equation modelling showed that with the per capita variable control of GDP, there is a positive relationship between the legal environment and the international entrepreneurship rate and a negative correlation between the normative environment and the international entrepreneurship rate (Terjesen and Hessels, 2013;Volchek et al. 2015). Terjesen and Hessels (2009) examined the impact of institutions (industrial relations, vocational training, intra-corporate relations, corporate governance, and labour relations) on the internationalisation of entrepreneurs in Asian countries. Jafari-Sadeghi et al. (2019a) pointed to the scarce resources at international borders that require arbitration decisions, and this is very important for women's international entrepreneurship.

Stenholm et al. (2013), based on the institutional approach, have presented a multidimensional scale for the entrepreneurial environment. With this scale, they have examined the effect of institutional arrangements on the entrepreneurship rate and the type of entrepreneurial activity, including international entrepreneurship. In the conceptual model of this research, the independent variables are legal, cognitive, normative, and environmental dimensions.

The collected secondary data related to 63 countries and the results of the analysis using structural equation modelling show that by controlling the per capita variable GDP, the legal dimension of the environment has a positive effect on the entrepreneurship rate and the environmental aspect has a positive impact on the type of women entrepreneurship.

4 Hypothesis Development

According to the existing literature, international entrepreneurship is influenced by institutional factors (Zahra & George, 2002; Jafari-Sadeghi et al. 2019b). One of the frameworks for measuring the institutional environment affecting entrepreneurial activity is the framework provided by Stenholm et al. (2013). They place the institutional environment into four categories: legal, normative, cognitive, and guiding. Accordingly, these four dimensions have been used as an independent

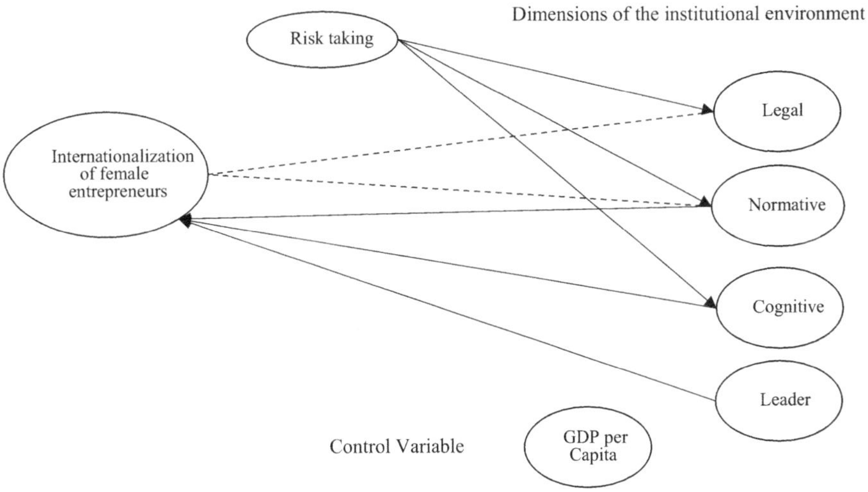

Fig. 1 Conceptual framework of research

variable to measure the institutional environment, and the international entrepreneurship rate variable has been considered as a dependent variable. Also, the risk-taking variable, mediator variables in the relationship between institutional factors and international entrepreneurship rates, is considered, because when institutions are not developed, risk-taking is one of the mechanisms used by entrepreneurs.

The conceptual model of the research is presented in Fig. 1.

According to the conceptual model of the study, the research hypotheses are as follows:

H1
Legal factors do not affect the rate of female international entrepreneurship in emerging economies.

H2
Normative factors do not affect the rate of female international entrepreneurship in emerging economies.

H3
Cognitive factors affect the rate of female international entrepreneurship in emerging economies.

H4
Guiding factors affect the rate of female international entrepreneurship rates in emerging economies.

H5
Risk-taking negatively moderates the relationship between the legal entity and the female international entrepreneurship rate in emerging economies.

H6
Risk-taking negatively moderates the relationship between the normative institution and the female international entrepreneurship rate in emerging economies.

H7
Risk-taking negatively moderates the relationship between the cognitive institution and the female international entrepreneurship rate in emerging economies.

H8
Risk-taking negatively moderates the relationship between the governing institution and the female international entrepreneurship rate in emerging economies.

5 Methodology

This research applied a quantitative research design in terms of purpose and collection. We selected emerging economies to examine the role of institutions in women's international entrepreneurship. We consider countries that are not classified as advanced in the IMF report. The IMF classifies a transition or developing economy based on its high level of income, diverse economic structure, and improved financial institutions. We recognise that this represents a diverse range of countries in terms of geography as well as the level of development (Kiss et al. 2012). But it does not use these criteria as an absolute criterion. According to this definition, emerging economies refer to countries that are rapidly growing and industrialising through social and commercial activities. As a result, the research sample is countries that have participated in the Global Entrepreneurship Monitor programme. The sample countries are in Asia (32%), Africa (31%), South and North America (34%), and Oceania (3%).

To collect data, reports for 2014, 2015, and 2016 containing research variables were extracted from the websites of the Global Entrepreneurship Monitor, Heritage Foundation, World Bank, and Global Competitiveness Index, according to Table 1. To calculate these variables in the reports, survey data were used, which is collected through a network of local partners based in different countries. The research data source is presented in Table 1.

6 Measurement

The variables for the research sample countries were extracted from these reports and recorded in Excel and transferred to SmartPLS3 software. The rate of international entrepreneurship in each country (dependent variable) is measured by the average proportion of young female entrepreneurs living abroad (GEM 2016). To measure the institutional environment (independent variables), tools provided by Stenholm et al. (2013) are used.

Table 1 Research data source and descriptive indicators of variables

Institutions	Variable	Database	Average	Standard Deviation
Dependent variable	Internationalisation of nascent entrepreneurs	Global entrepreneurship monitor	0/22	0/21
Legal institution	Business freedom		0/42	0/22
	Property rights		0/37	0/21
	Ease of doing business	World Bank	0/64	0/21
	Ease of business termination		0/50	0/27
Cognitive institution	Opportunity perception		0/55	0/19
	Recognising an entrepreneur		0/44	0/22
	Skills	Global entrepreneurship monitor	0/60	0/21
Normative institution	Entrepreneurial position		0/54	0/22
	Media attention		0/52	0/22
Guiding institution	ICT rules		0/47	0/21
	University–industry cooperation		0/46	0/21
	VC access	Global competitiveness index	0/29	0/24
	Access to the novel technology		0/44	0/23
Moderator variable	Risk-taking	Global entrepreneurship monitor	0/69	0/20

The legal dimension of the institutional environment is measured by four indicators. The Business Freedom Scale is a general indicator of the effectiveness of government laws in the area of business. This index is calculated from the average scores related to the number of procedures, time, cost, and minimum capital to start a business, the number of procedures, time and cost to obtain a licence, and time, cost, and rate of return for the termination of business. The Property Rights Scale is used to assess the ability of individuals to collect private property. The two scales of ease of starting a business and ease of closing business from the ease of doing business index are also used to emphasise the importance of these two indicators in measuring the legal dimension (Stenholm et al. 2013).

To measure the normative dimension of the institutional environment, two indicators of the percentage of the adult population of women between 16 and 64 years old who believe that successful entrepreneurs have a high status in their country and the percentage of adults between the ages of 16 and 64 who believe they often see stories of successful female entrepreneurs in their country's public media (Indeed). To measure the cognitive dimension of the institutional environment from three indicators of the percentage of the adult population of women between 16 and

Table 2 Reliability and validity of measuring instruments

Index	Variable	Fa-Load > 0/5	Coe-alpha > 0/7	CR > 0/7	AVE > 0/5
	Business freedom	0/83	0/72	0/84	0/64
	Property rights	0/60			
Legal	Ease of doing business	0/71			
	Ease of business termination	−0/02 0/88		Variable deleted	
Cognitive	Opportunity perception	0/89			
	Recognising an entrepreneur	0/74	0/81	0/88	0/71
	Skills				
Normative	Entrepreneurial position	0/85		1/00	
	Media attention	−0/31		Variable deleted	
Leader	ICT rules	0/92	0/91	0/93	0/78
	University–industry cooperation	0/85 0/82			
	VC access	0/93			
	Access to the novel technology				

64 years old who see excellent business opportunities in their area of life, percentage of adult women between the ages of 16 and 64 who believe they have the skills and knowledge needed to start a business, and the percentage of the adult population of women between the ages of 16 and 64 who know someone who has started a business in the last two years.

To evaluate the dimension of leader, the variable indicators of communication and information technology laws, the cooperation of the University of Industry, access to venture capital, and access to the latest technology are used. Risk variability is also measured based on the percentage of women between the ages of 16 and 64 in each country where fear of failure does not prevent them from starting a new business (Acs and Virgill 2010; Acs et al. 2016; Garousi Mokhtarzadeh et al. 2020; Sadraei et al. 2018). Most of the data collected were from 2016, but while the latest available data on the dependent variable of the international entrepreneurship rate for a country were related to a year other than 2016, additional research data for that country are also collected from the same year. In this vein, the data for 28 countries are for 2016, for 10 countries are for 2015, and 21 countries are for 2014 (according to the method of data collection in the research of Stenholm et al. 2013). Also, the measurement model used by Stenholm et al. (2013) has been developed. The convergent reliability and validity of the measurement tool are also shown in Table 2.

According to the results of reliability analysis, the indicators of ease of business termination and media attention have a factor load of 0.02 and 0.31. Therefore, they are removed from the measurement model. The results of divergent validity tests are also presented in Table 3. Also, considering that the indicators of the measurement

Table 3 Divergent validity and linearity between indicators (Fornell and Larcker test)

	Reciprocal factor loads				Fornell and Larcker test				
Index	Legal	Cognitive	Normative	Leader	Legal	Cognitive	Normative	Leader	VIF < 0/5
Business freedom	0/887	−0/330	−0/004	0/497	0/803				1/734
Ease of doing business	0/779	−0/300	−0/233	0/491					1/721
Property rights	0/734	−0/137	−0/217	0/586					1/220
Ease of business termination	−0/213	0/884	0/234	−0/219	−0/317	0/841			1/937
Opportunity perception	−0/340	0/894	0/044	−0/225					1/750
Recognising an entrepreneur	−0241	0/736	0/148	−0/197					1/623
Entrepreneurial position	−0/155	0/157	1/000	−0119	−0/155	0/157	1/000		1/000
ICT rules	0/611	−0/257	−0/145	0/922	0/646	– 0/252	– 0/119	0/882	7/229
University–industry cooperation	0/430	−0/229	−0/274	0/854					4/731
VC access	0/405	−0/256	−0/114	0/822					2/415
Access to the novel technology	0/686	−0/193	−0/065	0/927					2/411

model are a separate concept for each of the structures and do not overlap with each other, the measurement model is of the constructive type. As a result, the alignment between the indices is checked so that if the criterion of the variance rate increase factor for an index is equal to or greater than 5, that index will be removed from the measurement model (Duarte and Raposo 2010).

As shown in Table 3, the amount of correlation between the indices with their respective structures is greater than the correlation between them and other structures. Also, according to Fornell and Larcker tests, the principal diameter of the matrix is more substantial than its underside, which indicates the appropriate divergent validity of the measurement model. Besides, the variance rate increase factor of the ICT rules index is more than 5. Therefore, this indicator is removed from the measurement model.

The structural equation model with the PLS approach is used to calculate the path coefficients and to present the final model and test the hypotheses because this approach is superior to sample size, data distribution, and measurement models (Vinzi et al. 2010).

7 Findings

In this section, we will present the findings from our analysis. Descriptive indicators of research variables are shown in Table 1. All variables are normalised. Therefore, they are between 0 and 1. The standard coefficient and significance coefficients were calculated in the initial structural model. Criterion R2 is equal to 0.416, and Q2 (the predictive power index of the model) is 0.090. As a result, the predictive power of the initial model is lower than the average. To modify the model, first, the impact size (f2) of the moderator variables was calculated, and the moderator variables with a lower impact size were removed until the predictive power of the model at least moderately increased. Thus, by removing the two modifier variables from the initial Q2 model, it was equal to 0.162, which indicates the average predictive power of the model.

The standard path coefficients and the significant coefficients of the final model are shown in Fig. 2. The GoF criterion controls the overall section fit after fitting the measurement section and the structural section of the overall research model (Jafari-Sadeghi et al. 2020; Tenenhaus et al. 2004). The result of calculating this index is shown in Table 4. Three values of 0.01, 0.25, and 0.36 are introduced as weak, medium, and strong values for GoF (Akter et al. 2011).

$$GOF = \sqrt{\text{Communalities} \times \text{R}^2}$$

GOF = 0/57

Therefore, the overall fit of the model is considered strong.

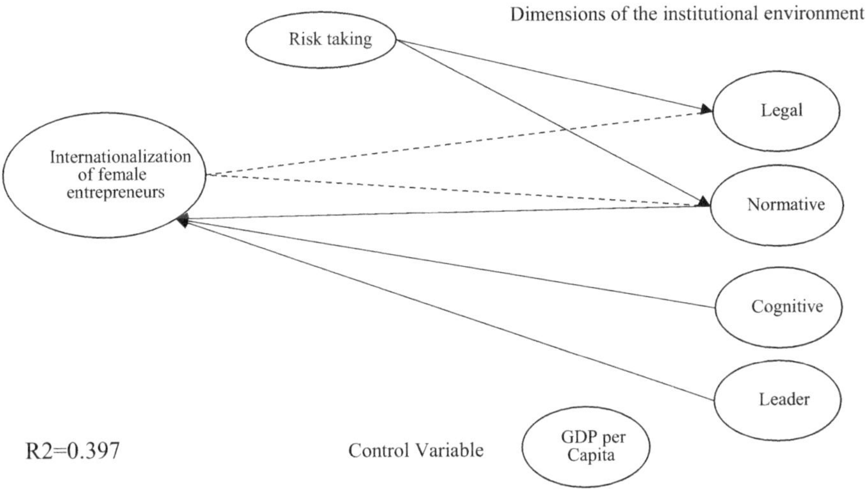

Fig. 2 Standard path coefficients and significance coefficients of the final model

Table 4 Calculation of cumulative index of structures

Variable	Cumulative index	Variable	Cumulative index
International women entrepreneurship rate	1/000	Risk-taking	1/000
Cognitive	0/55	Cognitive*risk-taking	1/000
Normative	1/000	Legal*risk-taking	1/000
Legal	0/49	GDP per capita	1/000
Leader	0/24	Average	0/81

8 Discussion

The hypothesis test results are presented in Table 5. As shown in Table 5, in Hypotheses 1, 2, and 3, the effect of legal, normative, and cognitive dimensions on women's international entrepreneurship rates is not significant at the 95% confidence level. Therefore, Hypotheses 1 and 2 are confirmed, and Hypothesis 3 is rejected. In contrast, Hypothesis 4 is confirmed, and then the institutional environment leader explains 15.2% of the changes in women's international entrepreneurship rates. In the field of hypotheses related to the moderating role of the risk-taking variable according to the significance coefficients, Hypotheses 5 and 7 are confirmed. Therefore, increasing the risk-taking variable by one standard deviation from its average, reducing the coefficient related to the relationship between the legal dimension and women's international entrepreneurship rate by 0.472, and decreasing the path coefficient related to the relationship between cognitive dimension and

Table 5 The result of testing hypotheses

Hypothesis	t-value	Path code	Test result
1. Legal factors do not affect women's international entrepreneurship rates in emerging economies	0/306	−0/035	ACCEPT
2. Normative factors do not affect women's international entrepreneurship rates in emerging economies	1/128	−0/131	ACCEPT
3. Cognitive factors affect women's international entrepreneurship rates in emerging economies	0/894	−0/110	REJECT
4. Leader factors affect women's international entrepreneurship rates in emerging economies	2/281	−0/390	ACCEPT
5. Risk-taking negatively modulates the relationship between the legal institution and the international entrepreneurship rate of women in emerging economies	2/698	−0/472	ACCEPT
6. Risk-taking negatively modulates the relationship between the normative institution and the international entrepreneurship rate of women in emerging economies	0/691	−0/105	REJECT
7. Risk-taking negatively modulates the relationship between the cognitive institution and the international entrepreneurship rate of women in emerging economies	2/563	−0/253	ACCEPT
8. Risk-taking negatively modulates the relationship between the leader institution and the international entrepreneurship rate of women in emerging economies	0/734	−0/109	REJECT

international entrepreneurship rate leads to −0.253. The final model is presented in Fig. 2.

9 Conclusion and Implication

The main purpose of this study is to evaluate the impact of institutional factors on women's international entrepreneurship rate in emerging economies by considering the role of risk mediating. The first four hypotheses are regarded as the impact of each dimension of the institutional environment on the rate of international women entrepreneurship. Also, the moderating role of the risk-taking variable in the relationship between each of the aspects of the institutional environment and women's international entrepreneurship rate has been tested in the first four hypotheses. The results of testing the hypotheses show that among the four dimensions of the institutional environment, only the leading institution has a positive effect on the rate of international entrepreneurship in developing countries, which is consistent with the results of a study by Stenholm et al. (2013). In the mentioned research, only the effect of the leading institution on the type of entrepreneurship is positive and significant. The correlation studied by Stanholm et al. (2013) is the statistical population in developing countries and this variable depends on the type of entrepreneurship. But this study evaluates the rate of international female entrepreneurship in emerging economies. This result is consistent with the research of Bowen and De Clercq (2008) in which the legal framework of the country is not significantly related to the allocation of entrepreneurial activities to growth-oriented activities. Stenholm et al. (2013) argue that the lack of legal and normative dimension on the type of entrepreneurship is due to the sensitivity of indicators of these dimensions to the rate of women entrepreneurship and not international entrepreneurship (Peiris et al. 2012). In other words, as legal and normative conditions improve, entrepreneurs are more likely to choose an activity that is less risky. The importance of the impact of cognition on the rate of women's international entrepreneurship can be assessed as the lack of recognition of opportunities in the entrepreneurial environment may ultimately harm women's international entrepreneurship. In the conceptual model of this study, in addition to measuring the direct impact of institutions on the international entrepreneurship rate, the risk-taking strategy also modulates the effects of institutions on the international entrepreneurship rate, which has not been considered in previous research. The results of testing the hypotheses related to the role of the risk-taking variable in the field of the impact of institutional factors on women's international entrepreneurship rate show that with the increasing level of risk-taking, the effect of cognitive and legal institutions on international entrepreneurship rate decreases significantly.

The weakness of cognitive and legal institutions in a country for entrepreneurial activity in foreign markets can be compensated by this entrepreneurial mechanism, because, when institutions do not function properly, the risk of entrepreneurial activity is high (Biancone and Jafari Sadeghi 2016; Peng et al. 2008). Therefore, high risk-taking is fruitful. For this reason, the more complex the environment, the higher the risk-taking among successful female entrepreneurs (Jafari-Sadeghi 2020). Increased risk-taking causes female entrepreneurs to consider foreign markets in an unsuitable institutional environment for entrepreneurial activity. Therefore, to strengthen women's international entrepreneurship, due to the time-consuming and costly reform of the institutional environment, it is suggested to enhance the risk-taking ability of entrepreneurs based on existing models. The statistical population of this study is emerging economies. But these countries are different in terms of economic, social, and political structure. Therefore, it is suggested that the conceptual model of this research be repeated in homogeneous groups of countries, such as resource-based and efficiency-oriented economies. Since the effect of the cognitive construct in this study and similar studies on the rate and type of entrepreneurial activity has not been significant, it seems that the measurement indices of this variable do not adequately reflect the concept of cognitive institution. As a result, it is suggested that better measurement tools for this concept be provided in future research.

References

Acs ZJ, Szerb L, Autio E (2016) The global entrepreneurship and development index. In: Global entrepreneurship and development index 2015. Springer International Publishing, New York, pp 11–31

Acs ZJ, Virgill N (2010) Entrepreneurship in developing countries. In: Handbook of entrepreneurship research. Springer, New York, pp 485–515

Ahlstrom D, Bruton GD (2002) An institutional perspective on the role of culture in shaping strategic actions by technology-focused entrepreneurial firms in China. Entrep Theory Pract 26 (4):53–68

Akter, S., D'Ambra, J., & Ray, P. (2011). An evaluation of PLS based complex models: the roles of power analysis, predictive relevance and GoF index.

Allen, E., Elam, A., Langowitz, N., & Dean, M. (2007). Report on women and entrepreneurship. *Global Entrepreneurship Monitor*

Amin Moghadasi M, Derakhshandeh B, Ferdosi M, Jafari Sadeghi V (2017) Organizational conformity as an entrepreneurial response to the changes in internationalization process: a study of IT-oriented firms in Saveh. World Journal of Accounting, Finance and Engineering 1 (1):53–64

Beheshti M, Mahdiraji HA, Zavadskas EK (2016) Strategy portfolio optimisation: a COPRAS G-MODM hybrid approach. Transform Bus Econ 15(3C):500–519

Biancone PP, Jafari Sadeghi V (2016) Risk Management in Export Compliance: concepts, procedures, and solutions. In: Cantino V, De Vincentiis P, Racca MG (eds) Risk management: perspectives and open issues. McGraw-Hill, London, UK, pp 64–78

Boudlaie H, Mahdiraji HA, Shamsi S, Jafari-Sadeghi V, Garcia-Perez A (2020) Designing a human resource scorecard: an empirical stakeholder-based study with a company culture perspective. Journal of Entrepreneurship, Management and Innovation 16(4):113–147

Bowen HP, De Clercq D (2008) Institutional context and the allocation of entrepreneurial effort. J Int Bus Stud 39(4):747–767

Bruton GD, Ahlstrom D, Li HL (2010) Institutional theory and entrepreneurship: where are we now and where do we need to move in the future. Entrep Theory Pract 34(3):421–440

Chienwattanasook K, Jermsittiparsert K (2019) Impact of entrepreneur education on entrepreneurial self-employment: a study from Thailand. Pol J Manag Stud 19

Covin JG, Miller D (2014) International entrepreneurial orientation: conceptual considerations, research themes, measurement issues, and future research directions. Entrep Theory Pract 38 (1):11–44

Dana LP (2017) International entrepreneurship research: how it evolved and directions for the future. Int J Entrep Small Bus 30(4):477–489

Duarte PAO, Raposo MLB (2010) A PLS model to study brand preference: an application to the mobile phone market. In: Handbook of partial least squares. Springer, Berlin, Heidelberg, pp 449–485

Etemad H, Wilkinson I, Dana LP (2010) Internetization as the necessary condition for internationalization in the newly emerging economy. J Int Entrep 8(4):319–342

Garousi Mokhtarzadeh N, Amoozad Mahdiraji H, Jafari-Sadeghi V, Soltani A, Abbasi Kamardi A (2020) A product-technology portfolio alignment approach for food industry: a multi-criteria decision making with z-numbers. Br Food J 122(12):3947–3967

GEM (2016). GEM 2016 Global Report. Recuperado 16/06/2015 de http://gemconsortium.org/docs

Hajiagha SHR, Mahdiraji HA, Tavana M, Hashemi SS (2018) A novel common set of weights method for multi-period efficiency measurement using mean-variance criteria. Measurement 129:569–581

Hajiagha SHR, Hashemi SS, Mahdiraji HA, Azaddel J (2015) Multi-period data envelopment analysis based on Chebyshev inequality bounds. Expert Syst Appl 42(21):7759–7767

Hajiagha SHR, Mahdiraji HA, Hashemi SS (2013) Multi-objective linear programming with interval coefficients. Kybernetes

Hmieleski KM, Sheppard LD (2019) The yin and Yang of entrepreneurship: gender differences in the importance of communal and agentic characteristics for entrepreneurs' subjective Well-being and performance. J Bus Ventur 34(4):709–730

Jafari-Sadeghi V (2020) The motivational factors of business venturing: opportunity versus necessity? A gendered perspective on European countries. J Bus Res 113:279–289

Jafari Sadeghi V, Biancone PP (2017) Exploring the drivers of gender entrepreneurship: focus on the motivational perspectives in USA, Italy, and France. In: Ratten V, Ramadani V, Dana L-P, Hisrich RD, Ferreira J (eds) Gender and family entrepreneurship. Routledge, London, UK, pp 124–141

Jafari Sadeghi V, Biancone PP, Giacoma C, Secinaro S (2018) How does export compliance influence the internationalization of firms: is it a thread or an opportunity? J Glob Entrep Res 8(3):1–15

Jafari-Sadeghi V, Dutta DK, Ferraris A, Del Giudice M (2020) Internationalisation business processes in an under-supported policy contexts: evidence from Italian SMEs. Bus Process Manag J 26(5):1055–1074

Jafari-Sadeghi V, Kimiagari S, Biancone PP (2019) Level of education and knowledge, foresight competency and international entrepreneurship: a study of human capital determinants in the European countries. Eur Bus Rev 32(1):1

Jafari-Sadeghi V, Nkongolo-Bakenda JM, Anderson RB, Dana LP (2019a) An institution-based view of international entrepreneurship: a comparison of context-based and universal determinants in developing and economically advanced countries. Int Bus Rev 28(6):1

Jafari-Sadeghi V, Nkongolo-Bakenda JM, Dana LP, Anderson RB, Biancone PP (2019b) Home country institutional context and entrepreneurial internationalization: the significance of human capital attributes. J Int Entrep 2020(18):165–195

Jennings JE, Brush CG (2013) Research on women entrepreneurs: challenges to (and from) the broader entrepreneurship literature? Acad Manag Ann 7(1):663–715

Keupp MM, Gassmann O (2009) The past and the future of international entrepreneurship: a review and suggestions for developing the field. J Manag 35(3):600–633

Kiss AN, Danis WM, Cavusgil ST (2012) International entrepreneurship research in emerging economies: a critical review and research agenda. J Bus Ventur 27(2):266–290

Mahdiraji HA, Kazimieras Zavadskas E, Kazeminia A, Abbasi Kamardi A (2019) Marketing strategies evaluation based on big data analysis: a CLUSTERING-MCDM approach. Economic research-Ekonomska istraživanja 32(1):2882–2892

Mahdiraji, H. A., Hajiagha, S. H. R., & Pourjam, R. (2011, September). A Grey Mathematical Programming model to Time-Cost Trade-offs in Project Management under Uncertainty. In *IEEE 2011 International Conference on Grey Systems and Intelligent Services* (pp. 698–704). IEEE

Mahdiraji, H. A., Hafeez, K., Kord, H., & Kamardi, A. A. (2020). Analysing the voice of customers by a hybrid fuzzy decision-making approach in a developing country's automotive market. *Management Decision*

Mahmoudi M, Mahdiraji HA, Jafarnejad A, Safari H (2019) Dynamic prioritization of equipment and critical failure modes. Kybernetes 48(9):1913–1941

Malmström M, Johansson J, Wincent J (2017) Gender stereotypes and venture support decisions: how governmental venture capitalists socially construct entrepreneurs' potential. Entrep Theory Pract 41(5):833–860

McDougall PP (1989) International versus domestic entrepreneurship: new venture strategic behavior and industry structure. J Bus Ventur 4(6):387–400

Mokhtarzadeh NG, Mahdiraji HA, Beheshti M, Zavadskas EK (2018) A novel hybrid approach for technology selection in the information technology industry. Technologies 6(1):34

Mokhtarzadeh N, Amoozad Mahdiraji H, Jafarpanah I, Jafari-Sadeghi V, Cardinali S (2020) Investigating the impact of networking capability on firm innovation performance: using the resource-action-performance framework. J Intellect Cap 21(6):1009–1034
North DC (1990) Institutions, institutional change and economic performance. Cambridge University Press, Cambridge
Peiris IK, Akoorie ME, Sinha P (2012) International entrepreneurship: a critical analysis of studies in the past two decades and future directions for research. J Int Entrep 10(4):279–324
Peng MW (2001) How entrepreneurs create wealth in transition economies. Acad Manag Exec 15 (1):95–108
Peng MW (2003) Institutional transitions and strategic choices. Acad Manag Rev 28(2):275–296
Peng MW, Wang DY, Jiang Y (2008) An institution-based view of international business strategy: a focus on emerging economies. J Int Bus Stud 39(5):920–936
Rezaei M, Jafari-Sadeghi V, Bresciani S (2020) What drives the process of knowledge management in a cross-cultural setting: the impact of social capital. Eur Bus Rev 32(3):485–511
Sadeghi VJ, Biancone PP (2017) Shariah compliant international entrepreneurship: a study of Islamic finance in Europe. European Journal of Islamic Finance 8:1
Sadeghi VJ, Biancone PP (2018) How micro, small and medium-sized enterprises are driven outward the superior international trade performance? A multidimensional study on Italian food sector. Res Int Bus Financ 45:597–606
Sadeghi VJ, Biancone PP, Anderson RB, Nkongolo-Bakenda JM (2019) International entrepreneurship by particular people 'on their own terms': a study on the universal characteristics of entrepreneurs in evolving economies. Int J Entrep Small Bus 37(2):288–308
Sadeghi VJ, Biancone PP, Giacoma C, Secinaro S (2017) Export compliance: a missing component of international entrepreneurship. International Journal of Business and Management 12 (11):103–110
Sadraei R, Jafari Sadeghi V, Sadraei M (2018) Biotechnology revolution from academic entrepreneurship to industrial: chemo-entrepreneurship. Biometrics & Biostatistics International Journal 7(6):546–550
Sobel RS (2008) Testing Baumol: institutional quality and the productivity of entrepreneurship. J Bus Ventur 23(6):641–655
Stenholm P, Acs ZJ, Wuebker R (2013) Exploring country-level institutional arrangements on the rate and type of entrepreneurial activity. J Bus Ventur 28(1):176–193
Sukumar A, Jafari-Sadeghi V, Garcia-Perez A, Dutta DK (2020) The potential link between corporate innovations and corporate competitiveness: evidence from IT firms in the UK. J Knowl Manag 24(5):965–983
Taghavifard MT, Amoozad Mahdiraji H, Alibakhshi AM, Zavadskas EK, Bausys R (2018) An extension of fuzzy SWOT analysis: an application to information technology. Information 9 (3):46
Tenenhaus, M., Amato, S., & Esposito Vinzi, V. (2004, June). A global goodness-of-fit index for PLS structural equation modelling. In *Proceedings of the XLII SIS scientific meeting*, 739–742
Terjesen S, Hessels J (2009) Varieties of export-oriented entrepreneurship in Asia. Asia Pac J Manag 26(3):537–561
Terjesen S, Hessels J, Li D (2013) Comparative international entrepreneurship a review and research agenda. J Manag 42(1):299–344
UNCTAD. (2016). UNCTADSTAT. Retrieved from http://unctadstat.unctad.org/wds/ReportFolders/reportFolders.aspx
Vinzi VE, Trinchera L, Amato S (2010) PLS path modeling: from foundations to recent developments and open issues for model assessment and improvement. In: Handbook of partial least squares. Springer, Berlin, Heidelberg, pp 47–82
Volchek D, Saarenketo S, Jantunen A (2015) Structural model of institutional environment influence on international entrepreneurship in emerging economies. In: Institutional impacts on firm internationalization. Palgrave Macmillan, London, UK, pp 190–216

Yamakawa Y, Peng MW, Deeds DL (2008) What drives new ventures to internationalize from emerging to developed economies? Entrep Theory Pract 32(1):59–82

Zahra, S. A., & George, G. (2002). International entrepreneurship: The current status of the field and future research agenda. *Strategic entrepreneurship: Creating a new mindset*, 255–288

Sepideh Khavarinezhad is a doctoral research fellow at the Università degli Studi di Torino. Her research interests are international entrepreneurship, female entrepreneurship, and internationalisation. she has published papers in several international journals and publications such as European Journal of Islamic Finance, International Journal of Applied Research in Management and Economics and as a PhD student has some papers in process of Publishing. Sepideh is a member of editorial board and reviewer of scientific journals.

Paolo Pietro Biancone is a Full Professor in Business Administration at the University of Turin. He is a chartered accountant, a freelance journalist and author of numerous publications on accounting, entrepreneurship, and Islamic finance field. He is Editor in Chief of the European Journal of Islamic Finance. He is the scientific coordinator of the University of Turin team of the European project H2020 Avangard on the electric business model. He promoted research in new technologies within all the research topics interested.

The Impact of International Networking Capability on International Performance: The Mediating Role of Dynamic Entrepreneurship Capabilities

Nima Garousi Mokhtarzadeh, Ismail Jafarpanah, and Ali Zamani Babgohari

1 Introduction

Scholars have acknowledged that huge changes have taken place in what businesses are and how they are internationalised (Dana et al. 2020; Jafari Sadeghi et al. 2019; Taghavifard et al. 2018). Today, even the firm size is no longer a prerequisite for entering global markets. Studies show that small and medium-sized enterprises have become the most important international business players (Jafari Sadeghi and Biancone 2018; G. Knight and Cavusgil 2005; Mokhtarzadeh et al. 2020a, b; Solano Acosta et al. 2018; Torres-Ortega et al. 2015) Internationalisation is the most complex strategy that any company can adopt to gain a sustainable competitive advantage (Ayob and Dana 2017; Jafari Sadeghi and Biancone 2018; Mahdiraji et al. 2019). Due to the globalisation of the world economy and the digital transformation in recent decades, many growth opportunities have been made available to companies operating in local markets to improve their performance by developing strategic capabilities to gain international competitive advantage (Fitzgerald 2014; Hajiagha et al. 2013; Melgarejo Duran and Stephen 2020). Globalisation processes, such as ICT development, have facilitated business operations and changed global value chains. Thus, more local businesses have expanded their operations internationally (Covin and Miller 2014; Angulo-Ruiz et al. 2020). Companies operating in local markets can play an important role in economic growth and job creation by entering international markets (Falahat et al. 2020; Mahdiraji et al. 2019). Therefore, various authors have emphasised the need for research on the internationalisation of local firms (Musteen et al. 2014).

N. G. Mokhtarzadeh (✉) · I. Jafarpanah · A. Z. Babgohari
Faculty of Management, University of Tehran, Tehran, Iran
e-mail: mokhtarzadeh@ut.ac.ir; jafarpanah@ut.ac.ir; Zamania@ut.ac.ir

V. Jafari-Sadeghi et al. (eds.), *Empirical International Entrepreneurship*,
Contributions to Management Science,
https://doi.org/10.1007/978-3-030-68972-8_16

International entrepreneurship is a new area of research focusing on activities related to the internationalisation of local firms. This phenomenon indicates the globalisation and technological advances that have led to the rapid geographical expansion of emerging companies or their globalisation, which has led to an increase in competition at the international level (Felzensztein 2016). Research shows that international entrepreneurship is the main driver of companies operating in the local market (Boehe 2013; Z. Tang et al. 2010; Jafari-Sadeghi et al. 2020). International entrepreneurship is essential to accelerate local firms' growth in the international market (Dimitratos et al. 2010). It can even play a significant role in the internationalisation of latecomer and emerging firms and enhance their ability to overcome resource constraints (Y. K. Tang 2011). On one hand, recently, the importance of this phenomenon in continuous growth and sustainable competitive advantage has led business managers to pay special attention to international entrepreneurship (Danneels 2002; Verbeke and Yuan 2007). On the other hand, a review of the academic literature confirms that international entrepreneurship research has progressed significantly over the past two decades (Beheshti et al. 2016; Dimitratos et al. 2012; Gabrielsson and Gabrielsson 2013; Jafari-Sadeghi et al. 2019). Therefore, in general, it can be argued that these conditions have made international entrepreneurship one of the hot topics of entrepreneurship management research.

Based on the above, an entrepreneurial firm's success in the local market will not guarantee its successful entry into the international market. Since entering an international market is practically a fundamental change, the local market's entrepreneurial capabilities are different from international entrepreneurship (Rothaermel 2016; Mokhtarzadeh et al., 2020a). International entrepreneurship requires developing dynamic capabilities and implementing related mechanisms and routines in the firm (Dimitratos et al. 2012; Keupp and Gassmann 2009). These capabilities and mechanisms vary in different markets, industries, and firms. Entrepreneurial management thematic literature refers to a wide range of dynamic capabilities, including foreign market knowledge capability, international entrepreneurial opportunity recognition capability, and adaptive capability. Firms looking to enter international markets need to be well aware of these capabilities and understand how they affect each other and how they affect their performance improvement.

The contribution of this study is significant for the international entrepreneurship literature stream from two perspectives. First, few studies have looked at international entrepreneurship from a dynamic capability perspective (Dabić et al. 2020). To cover this theoretical gap, in this study, we examine the impact of international entrepreneurship and its capabilities that play a key role in global competition (Dabić et al. 2020) from the dynamic capabilities' perspective. Second, as noted earlier, international entrepreneurship requires a wide range of dynamic capabilities. Despite the fundamental role of these capabilities in improving the firm's performance, few studies have examined these capabilities' effect on their internationalisation (Zhu et al. 2017). For example, little attention has been paid to the relationship between international opportunity recognition capability and international performance (Karami and Tang 2019). Research also shows that there are very few studies on the relationship between international networking capability and international opportunity recognition capability and foreign market knowledge capability (Tayauova 2012). Therefore, we generally argue that dynamic entrepreneurial capabilities' mediating role contributes to the relationship between international networking capability and international performance. Besides, addressing the common ground of dynamic capabilities and international entrepreneurship can lead to both fields' theoretical development.

This study investigates the effect of international networking capability on firm's international performance by considering the mediating role of foreign market knowledge capability, international entrepreneurial opportunity recognition capability, and adaptive capability. The focus of this study is software development companies that have succeeded in developing new international markets. The study's results will help companies properly design and implement their path to internationalisation. Besides, international entrepreneurship researchers can also provide the ground for the theoretical development of the international entrepreneurship literature stream by considering other dynamic entrepreneurial capabilities. Accordingly, the present study is organised as follows: Section 2 provides a literature review, including the subsections of dynamic capability and international entrepreneurship, international networking capability, and dynamic entrepreneurial capabilities. Section 3 will thoroughly discuss the research conceptual model and hypotheses. The measurement tool development and hypothesis testing will be described in Sects. 4 and 5. Finally, the research findings will be presented in Sect. 6.

2 Basics and Literature Review

2.1 Dynamic Capability View and International Entrepreneurship

To fully understand the nature of international entrepreneurship and its development, we need to look at its fundamental roots in international entrepreneurship and business. Entrepreneurship is defined as "the scientific study of how, by whom, and with what effects opportunities to create goods and services are discovered, evaluated, and exploited" (Shane and Venkataraman 2000b). Contrary to the common misconception that entrepreneurship is limited to new and small companies, the above definition does not make such a reference to the company's context. Indeed, it follows from the concept that entrepreneurship is a mindset and insight (Haynie et al. 2010) that enables the identification and pursuit of opportunity (Hajiagha et al. 2015; Short et al. 2010). In general, the literature review shows that entrepreneurship can take place at both local and international levels (Mainela et al. 2018). The focus of this research is on international entrepreneurship. International entrepreneurship is rooted in the concept of international business. Research on international entrepreneurship emerged in the late 1980s when new activities were carried out internationally. They were inconsistent with traditional international business (Jones et al.

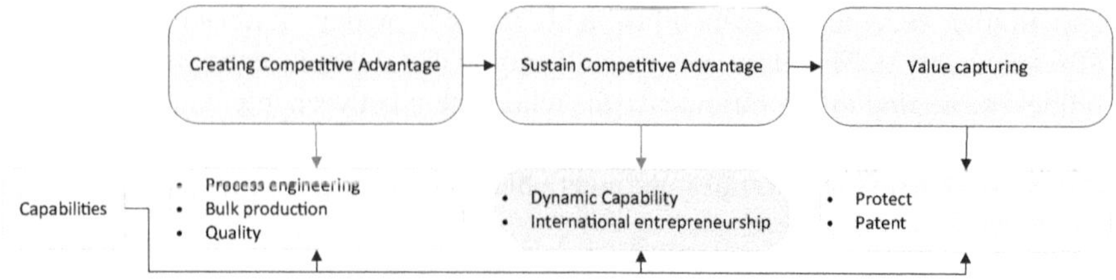

Fig. 1 The value creation process and its dynamic capability position (adapted from Grant 2016)

2011; Keupp and Gassmann 2009; Rialp et al. 2014; Servantie et al. 2016). Subsequently, this initial definition was revised to focus on transnational corporations' new and innovative activities (McDougall and Oviatt 1996). More recently, international entrepreneurship has been recognised as the discovery, adoption, evaluation, and exploitation of transnational opportunities (Ahsan and Fernhaber 2019). In other words, as defined by Buckley and Casson (2009), companies are created when entrepreneurs identify more profitable opportunities and create companies to take advantage of them.

We first need to have a clear understanding of the resource-based view (RBV) to recognise the concept of dynamic capabilities. This view focuses on the idea that an organisation has access to a set of resources to pave the way for a competitive advantage (J. B. Barney 1986). Criticising the static nature of RBV, D. J. Teece et al. (1997) proposed a new dynamic capability (DC) approach to achieving change in the business environment. According to this view, DC is "the ability of a company to integrate, create, and reconfigure internal and external competencies to address rapidly changing environments" (D. J. Teece et al. 1997). DC is the firm's potential to systematically solve problems that are formed by being close to opportunities and threats to make timely and market-oriented decisions and change its resources (Barreto 2010). As shown in Fig. 1, DC is the key to create, sustain, and value capturing for customers.

Recent studies argue that understanding opportunities by the entrepreneur or key decision-maker in a company is consistent with the creation and use of DCs (Zahra et al. 2006). Therefore, recognising international opportunities is a dynamic capability. It refers to discovering, evaluating, and exploiting opportunities to create goods and provide services in the future that make the international market competitive (Shane and Venkataraman 2000a). Accordingly, it can be concluded that DCs facilitate international entrepreneurship and ultimately achieve a competitive advantage. DC is a potential resource for companies with international entrepreneurship (Zahra et al. 2006). These capabilities facilitate the recognition and exploitation of international entrepreneurial opportunities and enhance the firm's ability to produce goods or provide services at the local market level to the international market level (D. Teece et al. 2016; D. J. Teece 2007). DC research, in turn, points to the interrelationship between DC and international entrepreneurship and, ultimately, a positive impact on firm performance (D. J. Teece 2016).

2.2 International Networking Capability

In recent years, relationships and networks have been extensively analysed with a special focus on small and medium-sized companies and due to the lack of resources needed to compete in the international environment. Walter et al. (2006) define networking capability (NC) as "the ability of a company to develop and use inter-organisational relationships to access the diverse resources maintained by other existing firms". Gulati (1998) defines international NC as a company's ability to obtain resources from the environment by creating social alliances for use in its activities in international markets. Therefore, NC is conceived as a dynamic capability because it allows the company to quickly identify opportunities and respond to them (G. A. Knight and Liesch 2016; Weerawardena et al. 2007).

NC is a dynamic capability that creates interdependencies inside and outside the organisation (Battistella et al. 2017). By reviewing the literature on this concept, it can be acknowledged that NCs enable companies to access different resources, identify opportunities, and rapidly change the market and customers (Gulati et al. 2000; Solano Acosta et al. 2018). Due to their limited size, small and medium-sized companies must rely on foreign relations to overcome their debts and enter international markets (Zacca et al. 2015). Therefore, international NC is a key driver and determinant of the long-term success of small and medium-sized companies operating in the local market and seeking to enter international markets (Parida and Örtqvist 2015). Some scholars have argued that NC helps companies succeed internationally by identifying new market opportunities and creating market knowledge (Chetty and Blankenburg Holm 2000; N. Coviello and Munro 1997; Madsen and Servais 1997).

2.3 Dynamic Entrepreneurship Capabilities

Thematic literature on international entrepreneurship introduces various DCs that help companies enhance their operations from the local market to the international market. This study addresses three main capabilities: foreign market knowledge capability, international entrepreneurial opportunity recognition capability, and adaptive capability. Each of these concepts will be explained in detail below (Amin Moghadasi et al. 2017; Hajiagha et al. 2013, 2015, 2018).

2.4 Foreign Market Knowledge Capability

Based on the assumptions of the knowledge-based view (KBV), knowledge is a key and strategic resource for the firm (Nonaka 1994). Knowledge is an intangible resource for achieving sustainable competitive advantage (J. Barney 1991).

Knowledge improves the company's ability to deal with uncertainties. Foreign market knowledge capability is the firm's knowledge base that helps it continue its business in the international market. The specific knowledge bases that intend to operate in international markets include foreign business knowledge, foreign institutional knowledge, and internationalisation knowledge (Eriksson et al. 2015a). Foreign business knowledge refers to the empirical knowledge of customers, markets, and competitors. Lack of empirical knowledge of customer needs for goods and services is problematic for an international company. It is costly for the company to spend resources to identify and take advantage of international market opportunities. External institutional knowledge refers to the empirical knowledge of government, institutional framework, laws, norms, and values (Eriksson et al. 2015b; Mokhtarzadeh et al. 2016). Lack of this knowledge also causes many problems because it is difficult for the company to adequately understand the technical and commercial rules and regulations applied in the foreign market (Ling-yee 2004; Sadeghi et al. 2017, 2018). Foreign market knowledge is gained through corporate foreign and international business communications (Denis and Depelteau 1985), interpretation of information in a specific corporate context (Carlson 1974), and access to new empirical knowledge.

2.5 *International Entrepreneurial Opportunity Recognition Capability*

As research emphasises, opportunities play an essential role in the international entrepreneurship process and improve it (Baron 2006; Shane 2000; Shane and Venkataraman 2000b). Newmarket penetration is an entrepreneurial process because it involves searching for opportunities, recognising them, and building exchanges in new locations with previously unknown partners (Chandra et al. 2009; Zahra et al. 2005). Recognising international opportunities is one of the basic dimensions of entrepreneurship (Kiss et al. 2012). Although some opportunities may exist, only if an entrepreneur recognises this opportunity and understands its value, he/she can take advantage of these opportunities and operate internationally (Dabić et al. 2020; Shane 2000). Entering a foreign market involves risk, resource commitment, and trading in new markets (Biancone and Jafari Sadeghi 2016; Dimitratos and Jones 2005; McDougall and Oviatt 2000). Recent studies show that international entrepreneurial opportunity recognition is one of the key components of international market presence strategy. It relates to how firms identify and use new opportunities in international markets for better performance (Chandra et al. 2009; Dimitratos et al. 2012; Shane and Venkataraman 2000a; Zahra et al. 2006).

A substantial body of literature has shown that entrepreneurial opportunity recognition capability is strongly influenced by cultural factors. Given that the role of culture in entrepreneurship is so clear, it is obvious that cultural issues are more critical in international entrepreneurship (Light and Dana 2013). Capturing this thinking, cultural perception affects the firm's ability to identify an international business opportunity. Thus, entrepreneurial opportunity recognition capability cannot receive the same response in all cultures and countries; nor should it be expected to. Along this vein, Dana (1996) suggests that identification of or response to opportunity is linked to the culture. Thus, businesses should recognise the impact of culture on market development, especially international ones (Dana 2007). Furthermore, according to Weber (2010) and Dana (1995), the success of the entrepreneur could be traced to cultural values such as asceticism, deferred gratification, frugality, and thrift fundamentals of protestant culture. This suggests that entrepreneurial opportunity recognition capability is culture-bound (Dana 1996). Consequently, we can imply that the culture has a different but critical role in entrepreneurial opportunity recognition in each context (Mahdiraji et al. 2011, 2019, 2020).

2.6 Adaptive Capability

Emerging markets are fraught with changes in the industry, structural uncertainty, and unreliable market information (Gu et al. 2008; Luo 2007). These factors highlight the need to develop adaptive capability. This capability is a competitive advantage for a firm in unstable environments, a hallmark of transition economies (Gu et al. 2008; K. Z. Zhou and Li 2010). In such circumstances, the firm must be able to adapt to turbulent markets to improve its performance in international markets. Thus, a firm has adaptive capability when it is prominently adaptable, accountable, and responsive (Grewal and Tansuhaj 2001; Tripsas and Gavetti 2000). Adaptive capability refers to the firm's flexibility in adapting to market changes. It particularly demonstrates the firm's ability to align internal resources with external demand (C. L. Wang and Ahmed 2007; K. Z. Zhou and Li 2010). Adaptive capability occurs for two reasons. First, adaptive capability focuses on flexibly regulating resources and exploiting them effectively (Staber and Sydow 2002; C. L. Wang and Ahmed 2007) by efficiently searching and balancing exploration and exploitation strategies (Ambrosini et al. 2009). Second, the adaptive capability is at the top of the company's dynamic capability hierarchy. Thus, it allows the firm to use several other low-level DCs to improve its performance and achieve its goals.

3 Research Model and Hypotheses

Figure 2 shows the study's conceptual model. Since this study's theoretical framework is a DC perspective, the conceptual model variables are also divided based on the logic of the DC process, i.e. sensing, seizing, and orchestrating (D. Teece et al. 2016). Sensing refers to the recognition and classification of opportunities through continuous review, filtering, and exploring technologies and markets (D. J. Teece

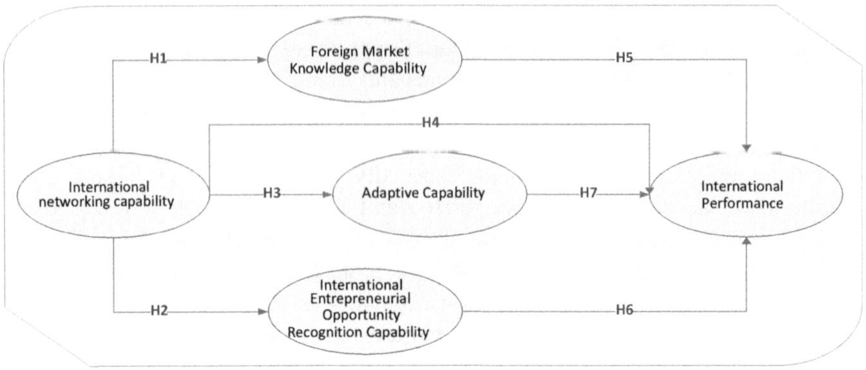

Fig. 2 Conceptual model

2007). Sensing also refers to the ability to evaluate the external environment and identify new opportunities (D. J. Teece et al. 1997). Companies can also identify new business opportunities through continuous control over markets and technologies (Day and Schoemaker 2016; Sadraei et al. 2018). This capability also includes exploring the business ecosystem's information activities (Cullen et al. 2005). According to D. J. Teece 2016 and D. J. Teece 2007's conceptualisation, seizing is the second part of DCs that enables the firm to compete in the international market. Once new opportunities are identified, companies should take advantage of them to improve their performance (Karimi-Alaghehband and Rivard 2020). Orchestrating is the third dimension of DCs, which includes increasing, combining, and protecting tangible and intangible assets and reconfiguring and reorganising them to maintain competitiveness and gain a competitive advantage.

Firms that intend to enter international markets through local markets and develop new businesses must first use NCs to establish relationships with international partners. Then, they need to strengthen their knowledge of new international markets by deepening relationships with these partners. Communicating with partners and acquiring their related knowledge helps assess the foreign market environment. Besides, these firms must work with their international partners to look for new business cases in the target country to turn them into new business lines. It is achieved using entrepreneurial opportunity recognition capabilities. This capability prepares the firm to take advantage of the entrepreneurial opportunity. Ultimately, the firm must adapt to the new foreign market environment to succeed. This adaptation requires reorganising the firm's resources and reconfiguring its routines. Adapting to new market requirements by reorganising existing and new resources will improve the firm's international performance.

3.1 International Networking Capability and Foreign Market Knowledge Capability

According to KBV, knowledge is considered a vital source of sustainable competitive advantage and sustainable competitive performance (Grant 2016). Lack of knowledge acquisition from foreign markets is the main obstacle to internationalisation and international market activities (Loane and Bell 2006). Given the importance of knowledge, firms cannot guarantee the necessary knowledge for internationalisation only by relying on internal resources. Thus, they can take advantage of international networking capabilities and overcome their knowledge constraints in emerging markets by gaining relevant international experiences (Chetty and Blankenburg Holm 2000; Loane and Bell 2006).

In this context, Nahapiet and Ghoshal (1998) suggest that business partners can share information and create new knowledge by developing joint ventures and frequent international interactions in global networks. Johanson and Vahlne (2006) also state that international interactions affect knowledge development and the acquisition of new knowledge about foreign markets by using networking capabilities, which help make decisions about the international market. Foreign market knowledge acquisition is very important for firms operating in local markets and intending to enter international markets, ultimately leading to a firm's competitive advantage and better performance (Altinay and Wang Catherine 2006; Beamish and Lupton 2009; Dimitratos et al. 2014). Therefore, this study concludes that:

H1
There is a positive and significant relationship between international networking capability and foreign market knowledge capability.

3.2 International Networking Capability and International Entrepreneurial Opportunity Recognition Capability

International networking capability is an entrepreneurs' ability to build relationships with foreign counterparts to create and develop a firm's international exports (Mainela and Puhakka 2011). International networking capability is very important at every stage of business development and new partnerships. It plays a decisive role in improving its performance (Anwar et al. 2018). Internal and external organisational networks facilitate the international opportunity recognition process and strengthen communication between different groups both inside and outside the organisation. International networking capability is the ability to innovate new communications and acquire new resources (Mostafiz et al. 2019). In their study, Mort and Weerawardena (2006) have shown that international networking capabilities help companies seize global market opportunities. They pointed out that international networking capability development is a continuous process for international companies. Entrepreneurs develop their previous network from the beginning of their business and for operating in international markets. Networking increases the likelihood of creating international opportunities through innovative ideas and knowledge (Mostafiz et al. 2020). Strong international networking can reduce the likelihood of resource scarcity, expand internationalisation, gain relevant market knowledge, and seize the opportunity to enter a new international market sooner than competitors seize (Reuber and Fischer 1997). Accordingly, this study argues that:

H2
There is a positive and significant relationship between international networking capability and international entrepreneurial opportunity recognition capability.

3.3 International Networking Capability and Adaptive Capability

The impact of international networking capability on adaptive capability can be examined from both technology and market perspectives. First, the high-tech turmoil in export markets forces firms to adapt to gradual and fundamental changes in the environment by their searches and trial and error (Mu and Benedetto 2012). Firms with stronger networking capabilities can effectively establish their technological relationships and respond more quickly to technological changes in new markets by acquiring new technologies (Yu et al. 2014). Communicating with suppliers, technical advisors, and universities in the target markets will provide the firm's technological resources. International networking capability provides valuable information that can facilitate technological decision-making, reduce export market uncertainty, and increase the firm's chances of success (Lin et al. 2020). Therefore, it can be argued that in export markets with higher technological turbulence, NC will have a significant impact on international performance. Second, international networks help build long-term relationships between firms in the global market. Therefore, organisations can create and exploit social capital, access external resources, and meet customers' needs and wants (Danso et al. 2016; Peng and Luo 2000). These resources can help businesses identify new opportunities and use them to adapt to customers' changing needs. In this regard, Freeman et al. 2006 stated that international networking capability helps companies understand customer needs and respond to complex international markets. Therefore, it can be argued that meeting customers' needs and wants is a positive factor affecting the firm's performance improvement globally and internationally. For example, a distributor must quickly adapt its resources to customer's changing demands to conform to the changing market and compete with superior performance (Zhu et al. 2017). In particular, the higher the level of demand uncertainty is, the more prominent the role of adaptive capability in the firm's performance improvement becomes. Therefore, it is concluded that:

H3
There is a positive and significant relationship between international networking capability and adaptive capability.

3.4 International Networking Capability and International Performance

International networking capability reflects a firm's transnational relationship with two or more independent international firms that use each other's key resources and competencies. Networking is one of the main resources for creating value and improving performance (Park and Luo 2001). A firm's international networking capability is considered a strategic capability that enables the firm to acquire key external resources and core competencies (Mu and Benedetto 2012; Vesalainen and Hakala 2014). International networking capability also improves the quality of access to companies and builds close strategic relationships with international partners (Rowley et al. 2000; Mokhtarzadeh and Faghei 2019). The interaction between international networking capability and international performance can lead to competitive advantage and competition in the international market (Solano Acosta et al. 2018).

Several studies have demonstrated the direct impact of networking capability on firms' performance in both local and international markets. For example, Ostgaard and Birley (1996) found a positive relationship between the firm's international networking capability and international performance. Hu and Stanton (2011) reported that five aspects of NC, i.e. quality building, variety diversifying, resource sharing, exercising power, and focusing, positively affect business performance. Li et al. (2013) identified a significant positive relationship between in-house (local) and extra-organisational (international) networks and the firm's performance. Empirical evidence shows that local networking capability (Boehe 2013) and international networking capability (Babakus et al. 2006; Leckel et al. 2020) also directly and positively affect a firm's export performance indicating improved performance. Similarly, Antonio Belso-Martínez (2006) explained that international networks positively affect increasing exports and corporate performance satisfaction. As mentioned earlier, the existing literature on international enterprises has largely identified a positive relationship between international networking capability and international performance (Stoian et al. 2017). Therefore, we argue that:

H4
There is a positive and significant relationship between international networking capability and international performance.

3.5 Foreign Market Knowledge Capability and International Performance

Knowledge influences decisions about market entry, market expansion, and market selection (Eriksson et al. 2000). Therefore, it can be acknowledged that extensive knowledge acquisition provides the basis for presence in international markets and, thus, better performance. Therefore, foreign market knowledge capability can play an important role in corporate performance, leading to competitive advantage. Foreign market knowledge is often acquired by collaborating with firms that hold this knowledge (Chetty and Blankenburg Holm 2000). The firm gains access to various information resources by collaborating with other companies in an internationally competitive environment. Therefore, it has more opportunities to learn instead of relying on internal knowledge (Grabher 1993). The firm's new information and knowledge in these relationships will enable it to improve its understanding of international business partners in foreign markets and learn how to work with them (Eriksson and Chetty 2003). Foreign market knowledge is considered one of the main resources in the internationalisation process (Autio et al. 2000; Johanson and Vahlne 2003). It leads to opportunity recognition and dealing with uncertainties and potential risks (Liesch et al. 2014). Lack of foreign market knowledge is a major obstacle to corporate internationalisation and improved performance (Eriksson et al. 2015a). Numerous studies confirm this hypothesis. They show evidence that lack of foreign market knowledge directly or indirectly affects international markets' corporate performance, both for international companies (Mogos Descotes and Walliser 2013) and emerging companies (Musteen et al. 2014). For example, Musteen and Datta (2011) argue that gaining knowledge from competitive and external environments leads to competitive advantage, improves firms' performance, and allows them to compete effectively in international markets. Also, foreign market knowledge includes knowledge of local culture, competitive conditions, customer needs, and broader institutional space, which will lead to superior firm performance (Musteen and Datta 2011; Mokhtarzadeh et al. 2018). International literature shows that foreign market knowledge is a basic concept that also provides the firm's internationalisation. Based on the arguments outlined, we conclude that:

H5
There is a positive and significant relationship between foreign market knowledge capability and international performance.

3.6 International Entrepreneurial Opportunity Recognition Capability and International Performance

Entrepreneurial opportunity recognition leads to identifying new product/service ideas and the development of new business lines for the organisation. It develops the firm's international revenue streams, enhances international performance, and achieves a sustainable competitive advantage (Bianchi et al. 2017; Mahmoudi et al. 2019; Rezaei et al. 2020). International opportunity recognition is one of the main aspects of entrepreneurship. It is especially important for start-ups that want to operate and compete in international markets rather than local markets, as this can improve their performance (Song et al. 2017; Hajiagha et al. 2013; Alon et al. 2009). Newmarket penetration is an entrepreneurial process that involves looking for opportunities, recognising them, and interacting in new locations with previously unknown partners (Chandra et al. 2009; Zahra et al. 2005). Recent studies show that international entrepreneurial opportunity recognition is one of the key strategic components of international markets' presence. It is related to how firms recognise and use new opportunities to participate in international markets for better performance (Chandra et al. 2009; Dimitratos et al. 2012; Shane and Venkataraman 2000a; Zahra et al. 2005). Accordingly, international entrepreneurial opportunity recognition capability creates a leap in the firm's performance. It means that the firm can take advantage of these opportunities to participate and compete in international markets. Therefore, based on the evidence explained, we conclude that:

H6
There is a positive and significant relationship between international entrepreneurial opportunity recognition capability and international performance.

3.7 Adaptive Capability and International Performance

Adaptive capability is at a high level. It is a highly important dynamic capability that should be given special attention in each company (Chryssochoidis et al. 2016). Adaptive capability with external changes allows organisations to gain a competitive advantage through a set of short-term benefits (D'aveni and Gunther 1995). Firms with high adaptive capability seem to perform better than other companies perform in international competition. Changes in demand and competitive environments require organisations to not only respond continuously to external challenges but do so more quickly and creatively (Lavie 2006; Taghavifard et al. 2018). The adaptive capability plays a crucial role in corporate networking and the firm's performance improvement (Sheng et al. 2011). It is also essential for the firm's survival and success and good performance in the international market (Lu et al. 2010; K. Z. Zhou and Li 2010). It can be concluded that an organisation which is able to understand and anticipate rapidly changing environments makes informed decisions on time and implements changes in its processes and resources quickly can gain a competitive advantage that means superior performance in the international market (C. L. Wang and Ahmed 2007). Therefore, our hypothesis is that:

H7
There is a positive and significant relationship between adaptive capability and international performance.

4 Data and Sample

This research is a cross-sectional survey study investigating the effect of international networking capabilities on international performance through the mediating role of dynamic entrepreneurial capabilities. The research environment is software offshoring and export development. Today, information and communication technologies have crossed geographical boundaries and turned the world into a global village. The software industry has also become an international industry due to the facilitation of global communications. Various firms are transferring their development and sales activities to other countries (Lehdonvirta et al. 2018) because moving from domestic markets to export markets has a more significant impact on the competitiveness of firms operating in the software industry (Heeks and Nicholson 2004; Sukumar et al. 2020).

On the other hand, the ease of access to the Internet and electronic devices, such as computers and mobile phones, has led many small technology companies to engage in innovative entrepreneurship in the software industry with large companies (Tomy and Pardede 2017). Such trends have led to an increase in international entrepreneurship and new businesses in the software industry. Iran is one of the countries which has been trying to enter regional and international software markets for many years (Nicholson and Sahay 2003). The country currently has leading companies, large and small, in software development, which in the last decade have begun extensive efforts to enter regional and international markets. In recent years, these companies have significantly improved their international performance through networking and international cooperation, both in the development phase and in the marketing phase (WTO 2020). This study intends to test the proposed conceptual model in the context of Iranian firms that have succeeded in software offshoring and export development at the international level.

Based on the above, the study population includes the Iranian Informatics Association, the Iranian Mobile Software Manufacturer Association, and the Iranian Software Manufacturer and Exporter Association. The member companies of these associations were first contacted by telephone, and their entry into international markets was confirmed. Power analysis method (Cohen 1988) and G * Power software were used to calculate the sample size. According to this rule, there must be a sample at least ten times the number of paths in the structural model (Hair Jr et al. 2017). The minimum sample size required to achieve a 75% coefficient of determination is 140 companies at a 95% confidence level. However, the sampling process continued until reaching 200 valid questionnaires to increase the research results' quality. A total of 140 managers of Iranian software industry companies participated in this study. These people were at senior organisational levels, such as CEO, Senior Marketing Manager, or Senior Project/Product Manager. In terms of gender, there were 106 (76%) male respondents and 34 (24%) female respondents. In terms of education, 57 (41%) had a bachelor's degree, and 83 (59%) had a postgraduate degree. In terms of business, 98 companies (70%) were from the Iranian Informatics Association, 28 companies (20%) were from the Mobile Software Manufacturer

Table 1 Sample profile

Variable		Frequency	Percentage
Respondents' gender	Male	106	76%
	Female	34	24%
Education	Undergraduate	57	41%
	Postgraduate	83	59%
Firms' business field	Iranian informatics association	98	70%
	Mobile software manufacturer association	28	20%
	Software manufacturer and exporter association	14	10%
Firms' age	Less than 10 years	33	24%
	Between 10 and 15 years	60	43%
	More than 20 years	47	34%

Association, and 14 companies (10%) were from the Software Manufacturer and Exporter Association. In terms of age, 33 companies (24%) had less than ten years of experience, 60 companies (43%) had between 10 and 15 years of experience, and 47 companies (34%) had more than 20 years of experience. The results are shown in Table 1.

4.1 Measurement Tool

The items related to the five main constructs of this study are adapted from the thematic literature. These items are international networking capability (Mostafiz et al. 2020), foreign market capability (Ciszewska-Mlinaric and review 2016), international entrepreneurial opportunity recognition capability (Bianchi et al. 2017), adaptive capability (Lu et al. 2010), and international performance (Karami and Tang 2019). Accordingly, the instrument of this survey consists of 26 items whose scale is a five-point Likert spectrum.

In a pilot study, the overall Cronbach's alpha coefficient was 0.912. The average variance extracted (AVE) and discriminant validity methods are used to evaluate validity. The value of AVE must be greater than 0.5 for all variables. The results show that the AVE value for all constructs is greater than 0.5. Discriminant validity is another measure of the goodness of fit (GOF) of the PLS method's measurement models. Heterotrait-Monotrait (HTMT) ratio is used to assess discriminant validity. The HTMT limit is between 0.85 and 0.9. If its value is less than 0.9, discriminant validity is acceptable (Henseler et al. 2015). The composite reliability (CR) and Cronbach's alpha coefficient of each construct are also calculated to determine the reliability. The composite reliability and Cronbach's alpha of all constructs must be greater than 0.7 (Hair et al. 2010; Kock 2015). The findings confirm that all factor loadings are greater than 0.7. Therefore, the reliability of the measurement tool is confirmed. The validity and reliability test results of the measurement model are given in Tables 2, 3, and 4.

Table 2 Factor loadings of the measurement tool's item

Constructs	Items	Loadings
International networking capability	Links with customers in international markets	0.924
	Links with suppliers in international markets	0.956
	Entrepreneurial collaborations with external partners	0.906
Foreign market knowledge capability	The foreign law and industry regulations	0.849
	The policies and actions of foreign competitors	0.846
	The expectations of foreign customers	0.813
	The effectiveness of foreign distribution channels	0.829
	Business opportunities in foreign markets such as opportunities for partnering or potential new customers	0.816
International entrepreneurial opportunity recognition capability	Our firm actively seeks out new international market opportunities	0.878
	When we see a new international market opportunity, we invest resources to exploit the new international opportunity	0.877
	We pursue international opportunities regardless of the resources the firm may have	0.911
	The firm has many formal or informal processes that evaluate the effectiveness of its activities in international markets	0.905
Adaptive capability	Adaptive to meet foreign customer demands	0.916
	Adaptive to tailor products/services according to foreign customer requests	0.912
	Adaptive to respond quickly to a change in product prices	0.921
International performance	International sales volume	0.778
	International sales growth	0.724
	International profitability	0.771
	Overall international performance	0.796
	Return on investment (ROI) from international business	0.768
	Market share in international markets	0.799
	New product/service introduction in international markets	0.777
	Time to market for new products/services internationally	0.861
	The international reputation of the firm	0.847
	Gaining a foothold in international markets	0.812
	The success of your main international business	0.883

Table 3 Measurement model and measurement fit indices

Indicators	CR	Cronbach's alpha	AVE	Mean	SD
INC	0.940	0.905	0.840	2.969	1.203
FMKC	0.918	0.888	0.690	3.699	0.811
IEORC	0.940	0.915	0.796	3.513	0.889
AC	0.950	0.920	0.863	3.574	1.008
IP	0.944	0.933	0.589	3.714	0.782

Table 4 Discriminant validity based on Heterotrait-Monotrait ratio

Indicators	INC	FMKC	IEORC	AC	IP
INC					
FMKC	0.676				
IEORC	0.737	0.665			
AC	0.658	0.826	0.632		
IP	0.418	0.551	0.460	0.346	

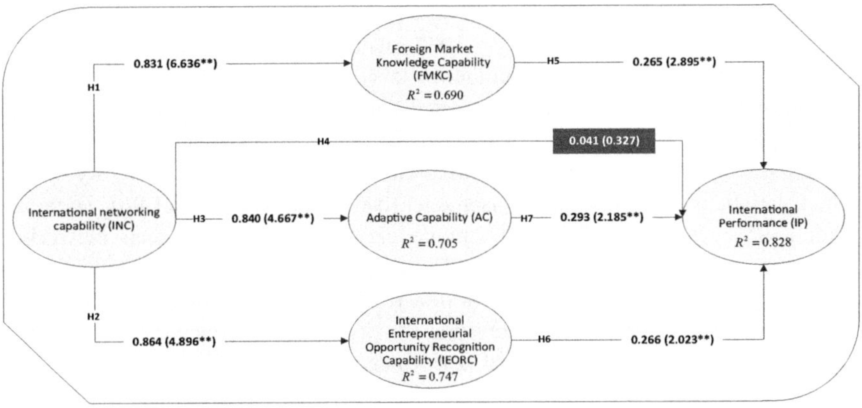

Fig. 3 The evaluation results of the study's conceptual model

4.2 *Hypothesis Testing*

In this study, the partial least squares (PLS) method with Smart PLS software has been used to test the hypotheses. For this purpose, the size and significance of the relationships between construct paths were evaluated. Thus, the changes explained in each path were identified. The bootstrapping procedure was used to test the significance level, according to Hair et al. (2013). The factor loading is between zero and one. If the factor loading is less than 0.3, there is a weak correlation, and it is ignored (Barkus et al. 2006). A factor loading between 0.3 and 0.6 is acceptable. If the factor loading is greater than 0.6, it is very good (Kline 2011). If the test statistic, i.e. t-statistic, is greater than the critical value of t0.05, i.e. 1.96, then the observed factor loading is significant. Figure 3 is the product of the complete implementation of the model in Smart PLS software.

Table 5 The test results of the research hypotheses

Hypothesis	Independent variables	Dependent variables	Loading	Bootstrapping (t)	Result
H1	INC	FMKC	0.831	6.636	Accepted
H2	INC	IEORC	0.864	4.896	Accepted
H3	INC	AC	0.840	4.667	Accepted
H4	INC	IP	0.041	0.327	Rejected
H5	AC	IP	0.293	2.185	Accepted
H6	FMKC	IP	0.265	2.895	Accepted
H7	IEORC	IP	0.266	2.023	Accepted

The effect of international networking capability on foreign market capability is 0.831. The t-statistic is also 6.636, which is greater than the critical value (1.96). Therefore, with a 95% confidence level, it can be claimed that international networking capability affects foreign market capability. The effect of international networking capability on international entrepreneurial opportunity recognition capability is 0.864. The t-statistic is also 4.896, which is greater than the critical value (1.96). Therefore, with a 95% confidence level, it can be argued that international networking capability affects international entrepreneurial opportunity recognition capability.

The effect of international networking capability on adaptive capability is 0.84. The t-statistic is also 4.667, which is greater than the critical value (1.96). Therefore, with a 95% confidence level, it can be claimed that international networking capability affects adaptive capability. The effect of international networking capability on international performance is 0.041. The t-statistic is 0.327, which is less than the critical value (1.96). Therefore, this hypothesis is rejected. The effect of adaptive capability on international performance is 0.293. The t-statistic is 2.185, which is greater than the critical value (1.96). Therefore, with a 95% confidence level, it can be said that adaptive capability affects international performance. The effect of foreign market capability on international performance is 0.265. The t-statistic is also 2.895, which is greater than the critical value (1.96). Therefore, with a 95% confidence level, it can be said that foreign market capability affects international performance. The impact of international entrepreneurial opportunity recognition capability on international performance is 0.266. The t-statistic is also 2.023, which is greater than the critical value (1.96). Therefore, with a 95% confidence level, it can be said that international entrepreneurial opportunity recognition capability affects international performance. Table 5 summarises the test results of the research hypotheses.

In this study, the structural model's fit is performed using the coefficient of determination (R^2), redundancy, and GOF statistics. R^2 is a measure that indicates the number of changes in each one of the dependent variables, which is explained by independent variables. It should be noted that R^2 is presented only for endogenous variables, and it is zero for exogenous constructs. The higher the R^2 for endogenous constructs is, the better the model's GOF is. Chin (1998) defined three values of

Table 6 R^2 related to the model's endogenous constructs

Constructs	Communality	Redundancy	R^2	GOF
AC	0.451	0.322	0.705	0.522
FMKC	0.301	0.172	0.690	
IEORC	0.407	0.278	0.747	
INC	0.474	0.345	–	
IP	0.200	0.071	0.828	

0.19, 0.33, and 0.67 as criteria for the weak, medium, and strong values of the structural model's fit by R^2. Besides, the Stone-Geisser or Q^2 criterion determines the prediction power of the model. Regarding the model's prediction power for endogenous constructs, Henseler and Sarstedt (2013) determined three values of 0.02, 0.15, and 0.35 as a weak, medium, and strong prediction power. Suppose Q^2 equals zero or less than zero for an endogenous construct. In that case, it indicates that the relationship between the other constructs of the model and the endogenous construct is not well explained. The blindfolding technique was used to calculate Q^2 in PLS software. Positive numbers indicate the good quality of the model. In this study, based on two indicators of cross-validated communality and cross-validated redundancy, blindfolding values for all research constructs were positive and greater than 0.35. Finally, GOF is the main indicator of the model fit in the PLS technique. Therefore, in this study, the GOF value is as follows:

$$\mathrm{GOF} = \sqrt[2]{0.743 \times 0.367} = 0.522$$

The GOF index is 0.696. Therefore, the model has a good fit. The results of the model's fit quality are reported in Table 6. According to this table, the reported coefficients for the research variables are at moderate and strong levels.

5 Discussion and Conclusion

Expanding international businesses is crucial for the survival, success, and growth of firms operating in the local market (Dikova et al. 2016; Majocchi et al. 2005). Internationalisation requires firms to communicate with different actors to develop international entrepreneurship (Jafari Sadeghi et al. 2019). These international communications with international partners strengthen firms' technological innovation capabilities (Mokhtarzadeh et al., 2020b), help identify international entrepreneurial opportunities (Chang and Chen 2020), gain foreign market knowledge, and pave the way for adapting to these markets (Shu et al. 2018; Geramian et al. 2017).

Classical international entrepreneurship research focused more on early or rapid internationalisation (McDougall and Oviatt 2000). These studies considered the main internationalisation components as firm size, global perspective, and international entrepreneurial networks (Yiu et al. 2007). This narrow view has led to criticism of international entrepreneurship research for not paying enough attention to dynamic entrepreneurial capabilities (Hoskisson et al. 2011; Y.-K. Wang et al. 2015). However, in the existing literature, dynamic capabilities have been considered necessary to achieve a sustainable competitive advantage (N. E. Coviello et al. 2011; Shu et al. 2018; L. Zhou 2007). Few studies have examined their role in enhancing the firms' international performance. By covering the above research gap, this study contributes significantly to the theoretical development of the international entrepreneurship literature and introduces firms' capabilities for internationalisation. In this study, the effect of international networking capability on the firm's international performance was evaluated from dynamic entrepreneurial capabilities, namely, adaptive capability, foreign market knowledge capability, and international opportunity recognition capability. The conceptual model presented by this study has a significant contribution to international entrepreneurship literature.

This study analysed the effect of international networking capability and dynamic entrepreneurial capabilities on firm performance through the mediating role of adaptive capability, foreign market knowledge capability, and international entrepreneurial opportunity recognition capability. The results indicated that hypothesis 1 (H_1), the positive effect of networking capability on foreign market knowledge capability, was supported. However, Musteen et al. (2014) also supported a similar hypothesis in their research. Hypothesis 2 (H_2), the effect of international networking capability on international opportunity recognition capability, was also supported. This result was consistent with Mostafiz et al. (2020)'s study. Hypothesis 3 (H_3) argued that international networking capability had a positive effect on adaptive capability. The results supported this hypothesis. This result was also consistent with Lu et al. (2010)'s study. However, hypothesis 4 (H_4) was not supported. Unlike some similar studies (Bai et al. 2016; Karami and Tang 2019) that confirmed the impact of networking capability on international performance, this study did not find a significant relationship between the two variables. Studies have shown that merely international communications without leveraging dynamic entrepreneurial capabilities cannot enhance international performance. International communications will be useful when it helps the firm develop foreign market knowledge, recognise international entrepreneurial opportunities, and reconfigure resources to adapt to new foreign markets. Hypothesis 5 (H_5), the positive effect of foreign market knowledge capability on firm performance, was also supported. Research supporting this hypothesis has argued that foreign market knowledge capability has a positive effect on firm performance. It can lead to globalisation, internationalisation, and sustainable competitive advantage for the firm (Ciszewska-Mlinaric and review 2016; Madhok 1997; L. Zhou 2007). Hypothesis 6 (H_6) suggested that international entrepreneurial opportunity recognition develops the firm's international performance. The findings supported this hypothesis. Andersson and Wictor (2003) and Kontinen and Ojala (2011) have also argued that international entrepreneurial opportunity recognition provides the basis for performance improvement. It is also an intangible source for local firms seeking to compete in the international market. The last hypothesis, Hypothesis 7 (H_7), suggested a positive effect of adaptive capability on the firm's performance. The study's findings also supported this hypothesis. Wei and Lau (2010) and Eshima and Anderson (2017) also confirmed this hypothesis. They argued that quick response capability in a competitive business environment could lead to a firm's growth and international performance.

The results showed that companies operating in the local market and intending to participate and compete in the international market should develop international networking capabilities and dynamic international entrepreneurial capabilities and improve their international performance. This study draws international entrepreneurship artisans and researchers' attention towards creating international networking capability and dynamic entrepreneurial capability (Mainela et al. 2018). It depends on managers' mindset, whether they are willing to support international entrepreneurship or not. However, it is suggested that corporate executives should take appropriate internationalisation and international entrepreneurship measures to achieve a sustainable competitive advantage (Gerschewski et al. 2015). They provide opportunities for organisational members to gain new experiences on internationalisation (Karami and Tang 2019).

This study makes some suggestions for researchers and those interested in this field to be considered in future studies. First, the capabilities examined in the conceptual model or other dynamic entrepreneurial capabilities that were not addressed in this study can be evaluated in terms of dynamic capability (sensing, seizing, and reconfiguration). The study's cross-sectional implementation was one of its limitations. Therefore, researchers are recommended to do this longitudinally in future studies, which is likely to increase the results' validity. Third, since the SEM-PLS approach has limitations, it is suggested that future researchers consider these limitations in their studies (Karami and Tang 2019). This study's main limitation may be related to the compatibility of the results, as the compatibility of the path coefficients specified in the final conceptual model may also differ with the smaller sample sizes (Sosik et al. 2009). Thus, it is suggested to consider a larger sample size for data collection in future research. Fourth, the conceptual model's variables also include other metrics. Therefore, it is recommended to increase the model's validity and generalisability by confirmatory factor analysis and identifying more metrics for each variable.

References

Ahsan M, Fernhaber SA (2019) Multinational enterprises: leveraging a corporate international entrepreneurship lens for new insights into subsidiary initiatives. J Int Manag 25(1):51–65

Alon, I., Dana, L.-P., Jenkins, A. J. J. o. I. B., & Economy. (2009). International business by SMEs: empirical findings from New Zealand. 10(2), 59 78

Altinay L, Wang Catherine L (2006) The role of prior knowledge in international franchise partner recruitment. Int J Serv Ind Manag 17(5):430–443

Ambrosini V, Bowman C, Collier N (2009) Dynamic capabilities: an exploration of how firms renew their Resource Base. Br J Manag 20(s1):S9–S24

Amin Moghadasi M, Derakhshandeh B, Ferdosi M, Jafari Sadeghi V (2017) Organizational conformity as an entrepreneurial response to the changes in internationalization process: a study of IT-oriented firms in Saveh. World Journal of Accounting, Finance and Engineering 1 (1):53–64

Andersson S, Wictor I (2003) Innovative internationalisation in new firms: born Globals–the Swedish case. J Int Entrep 1(3):249–275

Angulo-Ruiz F, Pergelova A, Dana LP (2020) The internationalization of social hybrid firms. J Bus Res 113:266–278

Antonio Belso-Martínez J (2006) Do industrial districts influence export performance and export intensity? Evidence for Spanish SMEs' internationalization process. Eur Plan Stud 14 (6):791–810

Anwar M, Rehman Atiq U, Shah Syed Zulfiqar A (2018) Networking and new venture's performance: mediating role of competitive advantage. Int J Emerg Mark 13(5):998–1025

Autio E, Sapienza HJ, Almeida JG (2000) Effects of age at entry, knowledge intensity, and imitability on international growth. Acad Manag J 43(5):909–924

Ayob, A. H., & Dana, L.-P. J. J. P. (2017). Product strategies for export ventures: An empirical investigation among SMEs in an emerging economy. 50

Babakus E, Yavas U, Haahti A (2006) Perceived uncertainty, networking and export performance: a study of Nordic SMEs. Eur Bus Rev 18(1):4–13

Bai W, Holmström Lind C, Johanson M (2016) The performance of international returnee ventures: the role of networking capability and the usefulness of international business knowledge. Entrepreneurship & Regional Development 28(9–10):657–680

Barkus, E., Yavorsky, C., Foster, J. J. F. o. H., & Sciences-Papers, B. (2006). Understanding and Using Advanced Statistics. 393

Barney J (1991) Firm resources and sustained competitive advantage. J Manag 17(1):99–120

Barney JB (1986) Organizational culture: can it be a source of sustained competitive advantage? Acad Manag Rev 11(3):656–665

Baron RA (2006) Opportunity recognition as pattern recognition: how entrepreneurs "connect the dots" to identify new business opportunities. Acad Manag Perspect 20(1):104–119

Barreto I (2010) Dynamic capabilities: a review of past research and an agenda for the future. J Manag 36(1):256–280

Battistella C, De Toni AF, De Zan G, Pessot E (2017) Cultivating business model agility through focused capabilities: a multiple case study. J Bus Res 73:65–82

Beamish PW, Lupton NC (2009) Managing joint ventures. Acad Manag Perspect 23(2):75–94

Beheshti M, Mahdiraji HA, Zavadskas EKJT i B, Economics (2016) Strategy portfolio optimisation: a Copras G-Modm hybrid approach. Transform Bus Econ 15:1

Bianchi C, Glavas C, Mathews S (2017) SME international performance in Latin America: the role of entrepreneurial and technological capabilities. J Small Bus Enterp Dev 24(1):176–195

Biancone PP, Jafari Sadeghi V (2016) Risk Management in Export Compliance: concepts, procedures, and solutions. In: Cantino V, De Vincentiis P, Racca MG (eds) Risk management: perspectives and open issues. McGraw-Hill, London, UK, pp 64–78

Boehe D (2013) Collaborate at home to win abroad: how does access to local network resources influence export behavior? J Small Bus Manag 51(2):167–182

Buckley PJ, Casson MC (2009) The internalisation theory of the multinational enterprise: a review of the progress of a research agenda after 30 years. J Int Bus Stud 40(9):1563–1580

Carlson S (1974) International transmission of information and the business firm. Ann Am Acad Pol Soc Sci 412(1):55–63

Chandra Y, Styles C, Wilkinson I (2009) The recognition of first time international entrepreneurial opportunities: evidence from firms in knowledge-based industries. Int Mark Rev 26(1):30–61

Chang, Y.-Y., & Chen, M.-H. (2020). Creative entrepreneurs' creativity, opportunity recognition, and career success: Is resource availability a double-edged sword? *European Management Journal*

Chetty S, Blankenburg Holm D (2000) Internationalisation of small to medium-sized manufacturing firms: a network approach. Int Bus Rev 9(1):77–93
Chin, W. W. J. M. m. f. b. r. (1998). The partial least squares approach to structural equation modeling. 295(2), 295–336
Chryssochoidis G, Dousios D, Tzokas N (2016) Small firm adaptive capability, competitive strategy, and performance outcomes: competing mediation vs. moderation perspectives. Strateg Chang 25(4):441–466
Ciszewska-Mlinaric, M. J. E. b., & review, e. (2016). Foreign market knowledge and SME's international performance: Moderating effects of strategic intent and time-to-internationalization. 4(4), 51–66
Cohen J (1988) Statistical power analysis for the behavioral sciences, 2nd edn. Erbaum Press, Hillsdale, NJ, Á/L. IN
Coviello N, Munro H (1997) Network relationships and the internationalisation process of small software firms. Int Bus Rev 6(4):361–386
Coviello NE, McDougall PP, Oviatt BM (2011) The emergence, advance and future of international entrepreneurship research — an introduction to the special forum. J Bus Ventur 26(6):625–631
Covin JG, Miller D (2014) International entrepreneurial orientation: conceptual considerations, research themes, measurement issues, and future research directions. Entrep Theory Pract 38 (1):11–44
Cullen S, Seddon PB, Willcocks LP (2005) IT outsourcing configuration: research into defining and designing outsourcing arrangements. J Strateg Inf Syst 14(4):357–387
D'aveni, R. A., & Gunther, R. E. (1995). Hypercompetitive rivalries: Competing in highly dynamic environments: Free Pr
Dabić M, Maley J, Dana L-P, Novak I, Pellegrini MM, Caputo A (2020) Pathways of SME internationalization: a bibliometric and systematic review. Small Bus Econ 55(3):705–725
Dana L-P (1995) Entrepreneurship in a remote sub-Arctic community. Entrep Theory Pract 20 (1):57–72
Dana L-P (2007) A comparison of indigenous and non-indigenous enterprise in the Canadian sub-Arctic. Int J Bus Perform Manag 9(3):278–286
Dana LP (1996) Self-employment in the Canadian sub-Arctic: an exploratory study. Canadian Journal of Administrative Sciences / Revue Canadienne des Sciences de l'Administration 13 (1):65–77
Dana L-P, Gurau C, Light I, Muhammad N (2020) Family, community, and ethnic capital as entrepreneurial resources: toward an integrated model. J Small Bus Manag 58(5):1003–1029
Danneels E (2002) The dynamics of product innovation and firm competences. Strateg Manag J 23 (12)
Danso A, Adomako S, Damoah JO, Uddin M (2016) Risk-taking propensity, managerial network ties and firm performance in an emerging economy. J Entrep 25(2):155–183
Day GS, Schoemaker PJH (2016) Adapting to fast-changing markets and technologies. Calif Manag Rev 58(4):59–77
Denis J-E, Depelteau D (1985) Market knowledge, diversification and export expansion. J Int Bus Stud 16(3):77–89
Dikova D, Jaklič A, Burger A, Kunčič A (2016) What is beneficial for first-time SME-exporters from a transition economy: a diversified or a focused export-strategy? J World Bus 51 (2):185–199
Dimitratos P, Amorós JE, Etchebarne MS, Felzensztein C (2014) Micro-multinational or not? International entrepreneurship, networking and learning effects. J Bus Res 67(5):908–915
Dimitratos P, Jones MV (2005) Future directions for international entrepreneurship research. Int Bus Rev 14(2):119–128
Dimitratos P, Plakoyiannaki E, Pitsoulaki A, Tüselmann HJ (2010) The global smaller firm in international entrepreneurship. Int Bus Rev 19(6):589–606

Dimitratos P, Voudouris I, Plakoyiannaki E, Nakos G (2012) International entrepreneurial culture—toward a comprehensive opportunity-based operationalization of international entrepreneurship. Int Bus Rev 21(4):708–721

Eriksson K, Chetty S (2003) The effect of experience and absorptive capacity on foreign market knowledge. Int Bus Rev 12(6):673–695

Eriksson K, Johanson J, Majkgård A, Sharma DD (2015a) Experiential knowledge and cost in the internationalization process. In: Forsgren M, Holm U, Johanson J (eds) Knowledge, networks and power: the Uppsala School of International Business. Palgrave Macmillan UK, London, pp 41–63

Eriksson, K., Johanson, J., Majkgård, A., & Sharma, D. D. (2015b). Experiential knowledge and cost in the internationalization process. In Knowledge, networks and power (pp. 41–63): Springer

Eriksson K, Majkgård A, Sharma DD (2000) Path dependence and knowledge development in the internationalization process. MIR: Management International Review 40(4):307–328

Eshima Y, Anderson BS (2017) Firm growth, adaptive capability, and entrepreneurial orientation. Strateg Manag J 38(3):770–779

Falahat M, Ramayah T, Soto-Acosta P, Lee Y-Y (2020) SMEs internationalization: the role of product innovation, market intelligence, pricing and marketing communication capabilities as drivers of SMEs' international performance. Technol Forecast Soc Chang 152:119908

Felzensztein C (2016) International entrepreneurship in and from emerging economies. J Int Entrep 14(1):5–7

Fitzgerald M (2014) Audi puts its future into high(tech) gear. MIT Sloan Manag Rev 55(4):1–4

Freeman S, Edwards R, Schroder B (2006) How smaller born-global firms use networks and alliances to overcome constraints to rapid internationalization. J Int Mark 14(3):33–63

Gabrielsson P, Gabrielsson M (2013) A dynamic model of growth phases and survival in international business-to-business new ventures: the moderating effect of decision-making logic. Ind Mark Manag 42(8):1357–1373

Geramian A, Mehregan Mohammad R, Garousi Mokhtarzadeh N, Hemmati M (2017) Fuzzy inference system application for failure analyzing in automobile industry. International Journal of Quality & Reliability Management 34(9):1493–1507

Gerschewski S, Rose EL, Lindsay VJ (2015) Understanding the drivers of international performance for born global firms: an integrated perspective. J World Bus 50(3):558–575

Grabher, G.J.T.e.f.O.t.s.o.i.n. (1993). Rediscovering the social in the economics of interfirm relations. 1–31

Grant, R. M. (2016). Contemporary strategy analysis: Text and cases edition: John Wiley & Sons

Grewal R, Tansuhaj P (2001) Building organizational capabilities for managing economic crisis: the role of market orientation and strategic flexibility. J Mark 65(2):67–80

Gu FF, Hung K, Tse DK (2008) When does Guanxi matter? Issues of capitalization and its dark sides. J Mark 72(4):12–28

Gulati R (1998) Alliances and networks. Strateg Manag J 19(4):293–317

Gulati R, Nohria N, Zaheer A (2000) Strategic networks. Strateg Manag J 21(3):203–215

Hair, J. F., Black, W. C., Anderson, R. E., & Tatham, R. L. (2010). Multivariate data analysis with readings

Hair JF, Ringle CM, Sarstedt MJL r p (2013) Partial least squares structural equation modeling: rigorous applications, better results and higher acceptance. Theoretical Economics Letters 46 (1–2):1–12

Hair Jr, J. F., Sarstedt, M., Ringle, C. M., & Gudergan, S. P. (2017). Advanced issues in partial least squares structural equation modeling: SAGE publications

Hajiagha SHR, Mahdiraji HA, Tavana M, Hashemi SS (2018) A novel common set of weights method for multi-period efficiency measurement using mean-variance criteria. Measurement 129:569–581

Hajiagha SHR, Hashemi SS, Mahdiraji HA, Azaddel J (2015) Multi-period data envelopment analysis based on Chebyshev inequality bounds. Expert Syst Appl 42(21):7759–7767

Hajiagha, S. H. R., Mahdiraji, H. A., & Hashemi, S. S. (2013). Multi-objective linear programming with interval coefficients. Kybernetes

Haynie JM, Shepherd D, Mosakowski E, Earley PC (2010) A situated metacognitive model of the entrepreneurial mindset. J Bus Ventur 25(2):217–229

Heeks R, Nicholson B (2004) Software export success factors and strategies in 'follower' nations. Competition & Change 8(3):267–303

Henseler J, Ringle CM, Sarstedt M (2015) A new criterion for assessing discriminant validity in variance-based structural equation modeling. J Acad Mark Sci 43(1):115–135

Henseler J, Sarstedt M (2013) Goodness-of-fit indices for partial least squares path modeling. Comput Stat 28(2):565–580

Hoskisson RE, Covin J, Volberda HW, Johnson RA (2011) Revitalizing entrepreneurship: the search for new research opportunities. J Manag Stud 48(6):1141–1168

Hu J, Stanton J (2011) A study of how mainland Chinese small and medium privately owned businesses engage in networking. Ind Mark Manag 40(4):534–539

Jafari-Sadeghi V, Dutta DK, Ferraris A, Del Giudice M (2020) Internationalisation business processes in an under-supported policy contexts: evidence from Italian SMEs. Bus Process Manag J 26(5):1055–1074

Jafari-Sadeghi V, Kimiagari S, Biancone Paolo P (2019) Level of education and knowledge, foresight competency and international entrepreneurship: a study of human capital determinants in the European countries. Eur Bus Rev 32(1):46–68

Jafari Sadeghi V, Biancone PP (2018) How micro, small and medium-sized enterprises are driven outward the superior international trade performance? A multidimensional study on Italian food sector. Res Int Bus Financ 45:597–606

Jafari Sadeghi V, Nkongolo-Bakenda J-M, Anderson RB, Dana L-P (2019) An institution-based view of international entrepreneurship: a comparison of context-based and universal determinants in developing and economically advanced countries. Int Bus Rev 28(6):101588

Johanson J, Vahlne J-E (2003) Business relationship learning and commitment in the internationalization process. J Int Entrep 1(1):83–101

Johanson, J., & Vahlne, J.-E. J. M. I. R. (2006). Commitment and opportunity development in the internationalization process: A note on the Uppsala internationalization process model. 46(2), 165–178

Jones MV, Coviello N, Tang YK (2011) International entrepreneurship research (1989–2009): a domain ontology and thematic analysis. J Bus Ventur 26(6):632–659

Karami M, Tang J (2019) Entrepreneurial orientation and SME international performance: the mediating role of networking capability and experiential learning. Int Small Bus J 37 (2):105–124

Karimi-Alaghehband F, Rivard S (2020) IT outsourcing success: a dynamic capability-based model. J Strateg Inf Syst 29(1):101599

Keupp MM, Gassmann O (2009) The past and the future of international entrepreneurship: a review and suggestions for developing the field. J Manag 35(3):600–633

Kiss AN, Danis WM, Cavusgil ST (2012) International entrepreneurship research in emerging economies: a critical review and research agenda. J Bus Ventur 27(2):266–290

Kline, R. B. J. N. Y., NY: Guilford. (2011). Principles and practice of structural equation modeling (3. Baskı)

Knight G, Cavusgil T (2005) A taxonomy of born-global firms. Manag Int Rev 1:15–35

Knight GA, Liesch PW (2016) Internationalization: from incremental to born global. J World Bus 51(1):93–102

Kock, N. J. L., TX: ScriptWarp Systems. (2015). WarpPLS 5.0 user manual

Kontinen T, Ojala A (2011) International opportunity recognition among small and medium-sized family firms. J Small Bus Manag 49(3):490–514

Lavie D (2006) The competitive advantage of interconnected firms: an extension of the resource-based view. Acad Manag Rev 31(3):638–658

Leckel A, Veilleux S, Dana LP (2020) Local open innovation: a means for public policy to increase collaboration for innovation in SMEs. Technol Forecast Soc Chang 153:119891
Lehdonvirta V, Kässi O, Hjorth I, Barnard H, Graham M (2018) The global platform economy: a new offshoring institution enabling emerging-economy microproviders. J Manag 45 (2):567–599
Li W, Veliyath R, Tan J (2013) Network characteristics and firm performance: an examination of the relationships in the context of a cluster. J Small Bus Manag 51(1):1–22
Light I, Dana LP (2013) Boundaries of social Capital in Entrepreneurship. Entrep Theory Pract 37 (3):603–624
Liesch PW, Welch LS, Buckley PJ (2014) Risk and uncertainty in internationalisation and international entrepreneurship studies. In: Buckley PJ (ed) The multinational Enterprise and the emergence of the global factory. Palgrave Macmillan UK, London, pp 52–77
Lin Z, Cao X, Cottam E (2020) International networking and knowledge acquisition of Chinese SMEs: the role of global mind-set and international entrepreneurial orientation. Entrepreneurship & Regional Development 32(5–6):449–465
Ling-yee L (2004) An examination of the foreign market knowledge of exporting firms based in the People's republic of China: its determinants and effect on export intensity. Ind Mark Manag 33 (7):561–572
Loane S, Bell J (2006) Rapid internationalisation among entrepreneurial firms in Australia, Canada, Ireland and New Zealand: an extension to the network approach. Int Mark Rev 23(5):467–485
Lu Y, Zhou L, Bruton G, Li W (2010) Capabilities as a mediator linking resources and the international performance of entrepreneurial firms in an emerging economy. J Int Bus Stud 41 (3):419–436
Luo Y (2007) Are joint venture partners more opportunistic in a more volatile environment? Strateg Manag J 28(1):39–60
Madhok A (1997) Cost, value and foreign market entry mode: the transaction and the firm. Strateg Manag J 18(1):39–61
Madsen TK, Servais P (1997) The internationalization of born Globals: an evolutionary process? Int Bus Rev 6(6):561–583
Mahdiraji HA, Kazimieras Zavadskas E, Kazeminia A, Abbasi Kamardi A (2019) Marketing strategies evaluation based on big data analysis: a CLUSTERING-MCDM approach. Economic research-Ekonomska istraživanja 32(1):2882–2892
Mahdiraji, H. A., Hajiagha, S. H. R., & Pourjam, R. (2011, September). A Grey Mathematical Programming model to Time-Cost Trade-offs in Project Management under Uncertainty. In IEEE 2011 International Conference on Grey Systems and Intelligent Services (pp. 698–704). IEEE
Mahdiraji, H. A., Hafeez, K., Kord, H., & Kamardi, A. A. (2020). Analysing the voice of customers by a hybrid fuzzy decision-making approach in a developing country's automotive market. *Management Decision*
Mahmoudi M, Mahdiraji HA, Jafarnejad A, Safari H (2019) Dynamic prioritization of equipment and critical failure modes. Kybernetes 48(9):1913–1941
Mokhtarzadeh NG, Mahdiraji HA, Beheshti M, Zavadskas EK (2018) A novel hybrid approach for technology selection in the information technology industry. Technologies 6(1):34
Mainela T, Puhakka V, Sipola S (2018) International entrepreneurship beyond individuals and firms: on the systemic nature of international opportunities. J Bus Ventur 33(4):534–550
Mainela T, Puhakka VJIJ o EV (2011) Role of networks in emergence of international new ventures. Int J Entrep Ventur 3(1):5–25
Majocchi A, Bacchiocchi E, Mayrhofer U (2005) Firm size, business experience and export intensity in SMEs: a longitudinal approach to complex relationships. Int Bus Rev 14 (6):719–738
McDougall PP, Oviatt BM (1996) New venture internationalization, strategic change, and performance: a follow-up study. J Bus Ventur 11(1):23–40

McDougall PP, Oviatt BM (2000) International entrepreneurship: the intersection of two research paths. Acad Manag J 43(5):902–906
Melgarejo Duran M, Stephen S-A (2020) Internationalization and the capital structure of firms in emerging markets: evidence from Latin America before and after the financial crisis. Res Int Bus Financ 54:101288
Mogos Descotes R, Walliser B (2013) Foreign market-related knowledge absorption and the international financial performance of SMEs. Management international / International Management / Gestiòn Internacional 17(4):178–193
Mokhtarzadeh, N. G., Ahangari, S. S., & Faghei, M. (2016). Proposing a three dimensional model for selecting a portfolio of R&D projects. Paper presented at the IAMOT 2016 Conference Proceedings
Mokhtarzadeh NG, Faghei M (2019) Technological learning in inter-firm collaborations: a review and research agenda. International Journal of Technological Learning, Innovation Development 11(1):78–96
Mokhtarzadeh NG, Mahdiraji HA, Jafari-Sadeghi V, Soltani A, Kamardi AA (2020a) A product-technology portfolio alignment approach for food industry: a multi-criteria decision making with z-numbers. Br Food J 122(12):3947–3967
Mokhtarzadeh NG, Mahdiraji HA, Jafarpanah I, Jafari-Sadeghi V, Cardinali S (2020b) Investigating the impact of networking capability on firm innovation performance: using the resource-action-performance framework. J Intellect Cap 21(6):1009–1034
Mort GS, Weerawardena JJIMR (2006) Networking capability and international entrepreneurship: how networks function in Australian born global firms. Int Mark Rev 23(5):549–572
Mostafiz, M. I., Sambasivan, M., & Goh, S.K.J.I.J.o.E.M.. (2019). Born Global phenomenon: a critical review and avenues for future research
Mostafiz, M. I., Sambasivan, M., & Goh, S.K.J.I.J.o.E.M. (2020). The performance of export manufacturing firms: roles of international entrepreneurial capability and international opportunity recognition
Mu J, Benedetto AD (2012) Networking capability and new product development. IEEE Trans Eng Manag 59(1):4–19
Musteen M, Datta DK (2011) Learning about foreign markets: a study of Czech SMEs. J Int Entrep 9(2):91–109
Musteen M, Datta DK, Butts MM (2014) Do International networks and foreign market knowledge facilitate SME internationalization? Evidence from the Czech Republic. Entrep Theory Pract 38 (4):749–774
Nahapiet J, Ghoshal S (1998) Social capital, intellectual capital, and the organizational advantage. Acad Manag Rev 23(2):242–266
Nicholson B, Sahay S (2003) Building Iran's software industry: an assessment of plans and prospects. The Electronic Journal of Information Systems in Developing Countries 13(1):1–19
Nonaka IJO s (1994) A dynamic theory of organizational knowledge creation 5(1):14–37
Ostgaard TA, Birley S (1996) New venture growth and personal networks. J Bus Res 36(1):37–50
Parida V, Örtqvist D (2015) Interactive effects of network capability, ICT capability, and financial slack on technology-based small firm innovation performance. J Small Bus Manag 53 (sup1):278–298
Park SH, Luo Y (2001) Guanxi and organizational dynamics: organizational networking in Chinese firms. Strateg Manag J 22(5):455–477
Peng MW, Luo Y (2000) Managerial ties and firm performance in a transition economy: the nature of a micro-macro link. Acad Manag J 43(3):486–501
Reuber AR, Fischer E (1997) The influence of the management Team's international experience on the internationalization Behaviors of SMES. J Int Bus Stud 28(4):807–825
Rezaei M, Jafari-Sadeghi V, Bresciani SJEBR (2020) What drives the process of knowledge management in a cross-cultural setting. Eur Bus Rev 32(3):485–511
Rialp, A., Rialp, J., & Knight, G.A.J.T.R.c.t.i.e. (2014). International entrepreneurship. 7
Rothaermel, F. T. (2016). Strategic management: concepts, 2, McGraw-Hill Education

Rowley T, Behrens D, Krackhardt D (2000) Redundant governance structures: an analysis of structural and relational embeddedness in the steel and semiconductor industries. Strateg Manag J 21(3):369–386

Sadeghi V, Biancone PP, Giacoma C, Secinaro S (2018) How does export compliance influence the internationalization of firms: is it a thread or an opportunity? J Glob Entrep Res 8(3):1–15

Sadeghi V, Biancone PP, Giacoma C, Secinaro S (2017) Export compliance: a missing component of international entrepreneurship. International Journal of Business and Management 12 (11):103–110

Sadraei R, Jafari Sadeghi V, Sadraei M (2018) Biotechnology revolution from academic entrepreneurship to industrial: chemo-entrepreneurship. Biometrics & Biostatistics International Journal 7(6):546–550

Servantie V, Cabrol M, Guieu G, Boissin J-P (2016) Is international entrepreneurship a field? A bibliometric analysis of the literature (1989–2015). J Int Entrep 14(2):168–212

Shane S (2000) Prior knowledge and the discovery of entrepreneurial opportunities. Organ Sci 11 (4):448–469

Shane S, Venkataraman S (2000a) The promise of entrepreneurship as a field of research. Acad Manag Rev 25(1):217–226

Shane S, Venkataraman S (2000b) The promise of entrepreneurship as a field of research. Acad Manag Rev 25(1):217–226

Sheng S, Zhou KZ, Li JJ (2011) The effects of business and political ties on firm performance: evidence from China. J Mark 75(1):1–15

Short JC, Ketchen DJ, Shook CL, Ireland RD (2010) The concept of "opportunity" in entrepreneurship research: past accomplishments and future challenges. J Manag 36(1):40–65

Shu R, Ren S, Zheng Y (2018) Building networks into discovery: the link between entrepreneur network capability and entrepreneurial opportunity discovery. J Bus Res 85:197–208

Solano Acosta A, Herrero Crespo Á, Collado Agudo J (2018) Effect of market orientation, network capability and entrepreneurial orientation on international performance of small and medium enterprises (SMEs). Int Bus Rev 27(6):1128–1140

Song G, Min S, Lee S, Seo Y (2017) The effects of network reliance on opportunity recognition: a moderated mediation model of knowledge acquisition and entrepreneurial orientation. Technol Forecast Soc Chang 117:98–107

Sosik JJ, Kahai SS, Piovoso MJ (2009) Silver bullet or voodoo statistics?: a primer for using the partial least squares data analytic technique in group and organization research. Group Org Manag 34(1):5–36

Staber U, Sydow J (2002) Organizational adaptive capacity: a structuration perspective. J Manag Inq 11(4):408–424

Stoian M c, Rialp J, Dimitratos P (2017) SME networks and international performance: unveiling the significance of foreign market entry mode. J Small Bus Manag 55(1):128–148

Sukumar A, Jafari-Sadeghi V, Garcia-Perez A, Dutta D (2020) The potential link between corporate innovations and corporate competitiveness: evidence from IT firms in the UK. J Knowl Manag 24(5):965–983

Taghavifard MT, Amoozad Mahdiraji H, Alibakhshi AM, Zavadskas EK, Bausys R (2018) An extension of fuzzy SWOT analysis: an application to information technology. Information 9 (3):46

Tang YK (2011) The influence of networking on the internationalization of SMEs: evidence from internationalized Chinese firms. Int Small Bus J 29(4):374–398

Tang Z, Kreiser PM, Marino L, Weaver KMJJ o SBM (2010) Exploring proactiveness as a moderator in the process of perceiving industrial munificence: a field study of SMEs in four countries. J Small Bus Manag 48(2):97–115

Tayauova G (2012) The effect of foreign language knowledge and foreign market knowledge on success of foreign firms doing business in Kazakhstan. Procedia Soc Behav Sci 46:3395–3400

Teece D, Peteraf M, Leih S (2016) Dynamic capabilities and organizational agility: risk, uncertainty, and strategy in the innovation economy. Calif Manag Rev 58(4):13–35

Teece DJ (2007) Explicating dynamic capabilities: the nature and microfoundations of (sustainable) enterprise performance. Strateg Manag J 28(13):1319–1350
Teece DJ (2016) Dynamic capabilities and entrepreneurial management in large organizations: toward a theory of the (entrepreneurial) firm. Eur Econ Rev 86:202–216
Teece DJ, Pisano G, Shuen A (1997) Dynamic capabilities and strategic management. Strateg Manag J 18(7):509–533
Tomy, S., & Pardede, E. J. E. R. J. (2017). Opportunity evaluation using uncertainties in software entrepreneurship. 7(3)
Torres-Ortega R, Rialp-Criado A, Rialp-Criado J, Stoian MC (2015) How to measure born-global firms' orientation towards international markets? Revista Española de Investigación de Marketing ESIC 19(2):107–123
Tripsas M, Gavetti GJS m j (2000) Capabilities, cognition, and inertia: evidence from digital imaging. Strateg Manag J 21(10–11):1147–1161
Verbeke A, Yuan W (2007) Entrepreneurship in multinational enterprises: a Penrosean perspective. Manag Int Rev 47(2):1
Vesalainen J, Hakala H (2014) Strategic capability architecture: the role of network capability. Ind Mark Manag 43(6):938–950
Walter A, Auer M, Ritter T (2006) The impact of network capabilities and entrepreneurial orientation on university spin-off performance. J Bus Ventur 21(4):541–567
Wang CL, Ahmed PK (2007) Dynamic capabilities: a review and research agenda. Int J Manag Rev 9(1):31–51
Wang Y-K, Chung CC, Lim DSK (2015) The drivers of international corporate entrepreneurship: CEO incentive and CEO monitoring mechanisms. J World Bus 50(4):742–753
Weber, M. (2010). Die protestantische Ethik und der Geist des Kapitalismus: CH Beck
Weerawardena J, Mort GS, Liesch PW, Knight G (2007) Conceptualizing accelerated internationalization in the born global firm: a dynamic capabilities perspective. J World Bus 42(3):294–306
Wei L-Q, Lau C-M (2010) High-performance work systems and performance: the role of adaptive capability. Hum Relat 63(10):1487–1511
WTO. (2020). World Trade Statistical Review. World Trade Organization
Yiu DW, Lau C, Bruton GD (2007) International venturing by emerging economy firms: the effects of firm capabilities, home country networks, and corporate entrepreneurship. J Int Bus Stud 38 (4):519–540
Yu B, Hao S, Ahlstrom D, Si S, Liang DJAPJ o M (2014) Entrepreneurial firms' network competence, technological capability, and new product development performance. Asia Pac J Manag 31(3):687–704
Zacca R, Dayan M, Ahrens T (2015) Impact of network capability on small business performance. Manag Decis 53(1):2–23
Zahra SA, Korri JS, Yu J (2005) Cognition and international entrepreneurship: implications for research on international opportunity recognition and exploitation. Int Bus Rev 14(2):129–146
Zahra SA, Sapienza HJ, Davidsson P (2006) Entrepreneurship and dynamic capabilities: a review, model and research agenda. J Manag Stud 43(4):917–955
Zhou KZ, Li CB (2010) How strategic orientations influence the building of dynamic capability in emerging economies. J Bus Res 63(3):224–231
Zhou L (2007) The effects of entrepreneurial proclivity and foreign market knowledge on early internationalization. J World Bus 42(3):281–293
Zhu W, Su S, Shou Z (2017) Social ties and firm performance: the mediating effect of adaptive capability and supplier opportunism. J Bus Res 78:226–232

Nima Garousi Mokhtarzadeh is an associate professor at the University of Tehran, Management Faculty. His research and teaching focus is on Strategic Management of Technology and Innovation (SMOTI), with a particular interest in the areas of Innovation Networks and Inter-Business Collaborations. Nima has a mechanical engineering background, with a MSc and PhD in Operations Management. He is the author of a book entitled Strategic Technology Planning at Firm and Supra-Firm Levels and several peer-reviewed papers published in different academic journals. Moreover, he has presented his academic works at various national and international conferences such as IAMOT and PICMET. Nima has industrial experience in SMOTI consulting and contract research.

Ismail Jafarpanah is a PhD candidate in management of technology and innovation (MOTI) at the University of Tehran. His master-level was also at the same university in the field of MBA-strategic management. During his career in business and management, he has done several consultancy projects for different organisations in the automotive, oil, gas, and petrochemicals industries. He is currently investigating technological catch-up in the Iranian automotive industry. Management of technology and innovation, strategic management, road mapping, and networking are their most important research interests.

Ali Zamani Babgohari is a PhD student of Operations Management at the University of Tehran. He received his bachelor's degree in industrial management from the University of Rafsanjan in 2018 and received his master's degree in the field of Operations Management from the University of Tehran in 2020 respectively. Ali's research areas include Operations and Supply Chain Management, Multiple Criteria Decision Making (MCDM), Data Envelopment Analysis (DEA) and Mathematical Modelling.

How Do Experts Think? An Investigation of the Barriers to Internationalisation of SMEs in Iran

Mojtaba Rezaei, Alberto Ferraris, Elaheh Heydari, and Shahrbanou Rezaei

1 Introduction

In recent years, the importance of small- and medium-sized enterprises (SMEs) in industrialised countries, especially in developing countries, has been increasing. The emergence of new technologies in production and communication has led to fundamental revisions in improving production capacity, improving production methods and distributing and changing the organisational structure of firms, which has generally increased the importance of SMEs (Ng and Kee 2012). Moreover, the reform in the business environment also has a significant impact on all aspects of trade and production. These changes have made a new condition in which the role of SMEs in increasing economic scales and, consequently, improving sustainable development has become more brilliant (Cressy and Olofsson 1997; Cassar and Holmes 2003; Saarani and Shahadan 2013).

Parallel with these major changes, globalisation and its consequences have forced SMEs to pay more attention to their business domain for expanding economics and commercials operations beyond national borders (Jafari-Sadeghi et al. 2019, 2020). As SMEs in many developing countries have started to operate in international markets and extended their presence in the markets of developed countries,

M. Rezaei (✉) · A. Ferraris
Department of Management, University of Turin, Turin, Italy
e-mail: mojtaba.rezaei@unito.it; alberto.ferraris@unito.it

E. Heydari
Department of Management, IA University, Mashhad, Iran
e-mail: heydarie2@mums.ac.ir

S. Rezaei
Department of Industrial Engineering, Sajjad University, Mashhad, Iran
e-mail: sh.rezaei737@sadjad.ac.ir

V. Jafari-Sadeghi et al. (eds.), *Empirical International Entrepreneurship*, Contributions to Management Science,
https://doi.org/10.1007/978-3-030-68972-8_17

therefore, it seems it is not only an optional promotion but also is a mandatory factor so that some international enterprises, such as the United Nations Industrial Development Organisation (UNIDO), recognise integration into the global economy through an open economy and democracy as the best way to overcome poverty and inequality in developing countries; therefore, development of the private sector, especially SMEs, is fundamental for achieving these goals (Soto 2015). The report published by the European Commission (2007) indicates the increase in average global trade by 6% since 1990, which is faster than the global gross domestic product (GDP) (Dana et al. 2011; Hope et al. 2019). In the same way, some new challenges such as open economy, shrinking government and privatisation of more specialised professions, increased competitive pressure and reduced direct assistance and government support (Ferraris et al. 2020), particularly in developing countries, have also changed the corporate sales and marketing policies (Dana et al. 2004; Sukumar et al. 2020). Companies have realised the need to offer newer products and expand into wider markets to maintain survival as well as grow more in a complex business environment (Laudal 2011). As a result, the need for internationalisation among SMEs has become more pronounced. Expanding export activities helps companies in increasing profitability and improving trade balances directly and indirectly helps society deal with the problems of poverty and unemployment (Fliess and Busquets 2006; Karadeniz and Göçer 2007; Sadeghi et al. 2019).

Nowadays, many companies are encouraged by governments to consider internationalisation in their medium- and long-term strategies (Al-Hyari et al. 2012; Hajiagha et al. 2013, 2015, 2018). In addition to the inherent inclination of companies themselves, many researchers have studied this issue from different dimensions, and internationalisation has been the subject of much research in the study of corporate strategy, international trade and entrepreneurship (Fliess and Busquets 2006; Al-Hyari et al. 2012; Jafari-Sadeghi et al. 2020). Along with the expansion of long-term horizons and the entry and involvement of companies in international trade, various problems and obstacles in the path of internationalisation became apparent, and researchers, from different scopes, have examined the background and causes of barriers, which has led to the identification of factors limiting the spread of internationalisation (Dana 2001). These restrictions which limit the ability to initiate, develop and sustain business abroad are caused by a wide range of attitudinal, structural and operational factors. Several restrictions in internationalisation are related to the liability of foreignness and newness (Dana 2001). The challenges become more apparent when target markets have fewer intrinsic features similar to the local market (Lange et al. 2000; Korsakiene 2015). Therefore, companies need new resources to enable them to enter foreign markets. The problem of adapting to international markets seems more acute for SMEs because the problem of providing new resources (and especially financial resources) for these companies is bigger than large companies (Fliess and Busquets 2006; Sox et al. 2014).

In this study, we have tried to consider the significant barriers and problems in the path of internationalisation of SMEs, and by collecting experts' opinions and experiences, we identified a road map for decision-makers in government and SMEs managers.

2 Literature Review

The experience of many developing and developed countries shows that the SME sector plays a pivotal role in economic and industrial development for various reasons (Sadeghi and Biancone 2018; Dabić et al. 2020). SMEs, as the backbone of the economy, are important to almost every economy in the world, especially for developing countries. According to the European Commission in 2008, the number of SMEs operating within the EU reached 60 million businesses, which accounted for 99.8% of all enterprises. In East Asia, the figure is estimated at 20–30 million businesses, accounting for about 95% of all businesses in the region (Demary et al. 2016; Yoshino and Taghizadeh-Hesary 2018). Therefore, SMEs are rapidly becoming major players in global markets, and their role will grow if technological and legal barriers are removed and protectionist policies are increased. Shifting the trade and investing scopes from a limited domestic to global makes new opportunities for SMEs (Senik et al. 2010; Dana and Ramadani 2015; Ratten et al. 2017). Therefore, SMEs have realised the importance of "international business" as the most effective way to increase their commercial activities outside the borders of domestic markets. This exchange process can be done through the export or import of goods, services and technology. As a result, "internationalisation" entered the corporate business literature as the mainstay of the business (Angulo-Ruiz et al. 2020).

In business literature, there are many definitions for internationalisation. According to some definitions, internationalisation is considered as the geographical development of corporate economic activities beyond national borders (Bardhan 2002; Beheshti et al. 2016; Farooqi and Miog 2012). Some researchers defined internationalisation as a process that seeks to describe a company's efforts to expand its economic operations outside the domestic sphere (Labate and Jungaberle 2011; Bang 2013). These common features have led to the internationalisation of companies as a step-by-step process or as a regular and evolutionary process that takes place with increasing international participation and relevant organisational changes (Dana 2004). Meanwhile, some researchers have not accepted these restrictions in the definition of internationalisation to the physical expansion of the company's scope of activity and consider this concept beyond the geographical concept. Welch and Luostarinen (1988) consider internationalisation as a "process of increasing participation in international activities" (Chong et al. 2019; Dabić et al. 2020). By this definition, they emphasise that a company may be involved in international activities, but there is no avoidance for these activities to continue because internationalisation can occur at any stage of the firm's development. Internationalisation is a process in which enterprises both increase their awareness of the direct and indirect effects of international exchanges in their future and establish their exchanges with other countries (Paul et al. 2017; Paul 2020). In some studies, internationalisation is reflected as "the process of adapting corporate processes to international environments" (Sadeghi et al. 2018; Saridakis et al. 2019; Schmid and Morschett 2020). Hollensen (2007) considers "doing business in many countries" to be an important principle of the definition of internationalisation (Harris and Wheeler 2005; Kreutzer et al. 2017; Bowen 2019). Internationalisation is defined as the "process of developing trade relations networks in other countries through expansion, influence, and integration" (Coviello and Munro 1997; Coviello and Martin 1999; Zain and Ng 2006). The focus in this definition is on relationships and connections. Relationships can help companies enter foreign market networks. According to Vahlne and Johanson (2017), connections are an important principle for networking and entering into internationalisation. Mejri and Umemoto (2010) know internationalisation as expanding the company's business operations to foreign markets, which will not necessarily constitute a one-dimensional process (Ribau et al. 2018; Mahmoudi et al. 2019). From an entrepreneurial perspective, Oviatt and McDougall (2005) see internationalisation as the process of discovering, approving, evaluating and exploiting opportunities across borders to build goods and services (Oviatt and McDougall 2005; Coviello et al. 2011).

Internationalisation is found to be an important aspect of the maximisation of business opportunities, and over the last few decades, many SMEs began internationalisation as a requirement for business success (Ratten et al. 2007; Rundh 2007). Internationalisation is a significant description of the outward movement of the international operations of a firm and wildly is applied in international business studies (Ratten et al. 2017). In most studies, internationalisation has been viewed as outward processes that are related to exporting, licensing, franchising and foreign direct investment (Karlsen et al. 2003; Welch and Paavilainen-Mäntymäki 2014).

Considering the advantages of internationalisation is also an important issue for SMEs. SMEs seek to internationalise their business for greater economic and financial benefits, but the practical incentives that motivate them to pursue this process are different (Chiao et al. 2006; Kumar 2008; Landau et al. 2016). Cost is the most important motivation for manufacturers to expand their business and internationalise. Managers of production companies and manufacturers are encouraged to expand their business to enhance competitiveness versus commercial competitors and manufacturers in the market (Mahdiraji et al. 2011, 2019, 2020). Thus, accessing lower labour cost can be a reasonable driver for them. However, for service firms, the prime driver is achieving new knowledge and technology (Doh et al. 2010; Abdul-Aziz et al. 2013). Although it should be noted that market share is also an important driver for firms. When a company feels its business share in the market is decreasing, its knowledge on the domestic markets is not adequate (e.g. Dezi et al. 2019) and the cost of the manufacturing process is increasing, internationalisation can be a good opportunity for expanding the market, accessing new knowledge and finding cheaper material and working labour (Ratten et al. 2007; Paul et al. 2017). These stimuli can also be effective for service companies, but the "time" is more attractive for them than manufacturing firms. Time zone differences enable service providers (SPs) to provide around the clock service. The nonstop operation helps SPs to enjoy benefits of cost reduction and eliminate the role of "time" to market access, in other words, have their customers at all times (Mokhtarzadeh et al. 2018).

However, sometimes, companies do not succeed in internationalisation and may not reach their predicted plans and the expected outcome of the internationalisation because they cannot overcome the barriers faced in the processes (Shaw and Darroch 2004; Rahman et al. 2017). Barriers to internationalisation have been a favourite subject in the context of exporting activities as in an extreme body of study, researchers focused on its causes and effects in both conceptual and empirical approaches (Ghauri et al. 2003; Leonidou and Theodosiou 2004; Leonidou et al. 2011). These barriers, in business literature, are known as restrictions that affect and disturb the firm's capability to start, develop or uphold business operations in overseas markets. Leonidou (2004) defined barriers as the limitations that hinder a firm's ability to initiate, develop or sustain business operations in overseas markets.

Some scholars tried to elaborate on the barrier-related differences for a wide range of firms (Pinho and Martins 2010; Leonidou et al. 2011; Kahiya 2013; Romanello and Chiarvesio 2019). For some firms (that are known domestic firms), the barriers are more related to the management's desire to not change the current business domain that is rooted of their limited communication with the foreign market, lack of sufficient knowledge of exporting procedures, lack of qualified personnel for conducting exports and an intrinsic fear of overseas product acceptance and raising initial investment (Pinho and Martins 2010). However, for internationalised firms, the barriers are different. These firms have more challenges with export procedures, slow payment by foreign buyers, poor economic conditions in foreign markets, etc. that are more operational barriers and relate to market variables (Leonidou 2004; Taghavifard et al. 2018). Despite these differences in obstacles to internationalisation, there are many common challenges which affect companies in the internationalisation process, and given the importance of this issue, identifying and investigating their effects have always been a favourite to researchers. Different classifications have been proposed to categorise different barriers based on their different characteristics. For instance, in some of the literature, barriers are divided into two groups: initial problems which are linked to shortage of experience and knowledge and ongoing problems that are related to greater participation in foreign markets (Bilkey and Tesar 1977; Chong et al. 2019; Dabić et al. 2020; Morais and Ferreira 2020; Treviño and Doh 2020). Some researchers have divided the challenges of internationalisation into two groups: internal and external challenges. Depending on whether the company can control the problems in internationalisation directly or not, barriers are also divided into two main parts: controllable and uncontrollable factors (Buckley 1993; Kahiya 2013; Chandra et al. 2020a; Mueller-Using et al. 2020). Controllable factors, most of which are internal barriers, are related to internal organisational resources and capabilities, including goods and services policies, sales, pricing and distribution plans that are directly under the control and planning of the management of the enterprise. They can formulate and implement legal restrictions, consumer tastes and strategies based on new conditions in international markets and their competitive challenge. Uncontrollable factors are known as external factors, depending on the specific market conditions, the external environment of the company which includes the general policies of the government and especially marketing activities by competitors overseas, the legal structure and internal economic conditions of the country, political and economic situation, technology level, geography and culture (Donthu and Kim 1993; Shoham and Albaum 1995; Leonidou and Theodosiou 2004; Goswami and Agrawal 2019).

According to Cavusgil and Nevin (1981), the real barrier for internationalisation for SMEs is internal barriers (Coudounaris 2018), but Gripsrud and Benito (2005) believed in external barriers. Some researchers studied barriers to internationalisation as both aspects, internal and external obstacles (Tesfom and Lutz 2006; Pinho and Martins 2010; Al-Hyari et al. 2012; Uner et al. 2013; Roy et al. 2016a). Classification of internal and external types of barriers has also been done by many researchers. According to Leonidou (2004), internal barriers consist of functional, informational and marketing, and external barriers are classified as to procedural, governmental, task and environmental. Arteaga-Ortiz and Fernández-Ortiz (2010) believed barriers can be categorised into four groups: knowledge, resource, procedure and exogenous. Al-Hyari et al. (2012) studied the barriers to internationalisation in Jordanian SMEs, in four categories, informational and financial as internal barriers and environmental and governmental as external. However, in many studies on this subject, internal barriers have been classified more into four groups, informational, financial, marketing and functional, and external barriers have come more in the form of procedural, governmental, environmental and tariff and non-tariff barriers (Muhammad Azam Roomi and Parrott 2008; Hutchinson et al. 2009; Kahiya 2013; Roy et al. 2016b; Pavlák 2018).

In this study, we examined internal barriers as informational, financial, marketing and functional obstacle and external barriers in procedural, governmental, environmental and tariff and non-tariff barriers to examine a wider range of barriers to internationalisation.

3 Methodology

This study is a developmental research based on a systematic approach to designing, developing and evaluating instructional processes. It is also considered applied research because of addressing the issue of barriers to internationalisation. Also, we applied a descriptive research method that consists of a set of methods designed to describe the conditions or phenomena in a study. So, we identified the dimension and barrier indicators through a Delphi survey, and then we analysed the “barriers of internationalization” by using the structural equation modeling and confirmatory factor analysis—to examine the construct validity of factors.

3.1 Delphi Method

Delphi method is a systematic approach or method of research to extract opinions from a group of experts on a topic or a question or to reach a group consensus through a series of questionnaire rounds while maintaining the anonymity of the respondents and feedback: comments to panel members (Toma and Picioreanu 2016). Delphi is a process which makes use of professional judgments from heterogeneous and independent experts on a specific topic at a large geographical level using questionnaires that are repeated continuously until a consensus is reached. Delphi is a multi-step study method for gathering opinions on the subjectivity of the subject and using written answers instead of bringing together a group of experts; the goal of the consensus is to be able to freely express and revise ideas with numerical estimates (Linstone and Turoff 1975). Delphi's main goal was to predict the future, but it is also used in decision-making, increasing effectiveness, judgment, facilitating problem-solving, needs assessment, goal setting, planning assistance and prioritisation. In the Delphi method, the repetition or iteration of the questionnaire, the expert group, controlled feedback, anonymity, analysis of results, consensus, time and the coordinating team are the main components. According to Gordon (1994), Delphi is a useful communication tool between a group of experts that facilitates the formulation of group members' opinions. Delphi is a way of organising a group communication process so that it enables all members of the group to effectively tackle a complex problem (Toma and Picioreanu 2016). Hsu and Sandford (2007), in their article on the Delphi method, believe this method can be conducted in three or four rounds based on previous successful research using Delphi (Hjarnø et al. 2007; Hsu and Sandford 2007; Steurer 2011).

3.2 The Panel of Experts

Delphi participants are experts or panellists. They need four characteristics: knowledge and experience in the subject, willingness, sufficient time to participate and effective communication skills, and the key parameters of the study are the competence of the panellists, the size of the panel and the method of their selection. This method is based on finding and gathering experts' opinions in a short term; therefore, final results depend on the expertise of the individuals, the quality and accuracy of the responses and their ongoing involvement and participation during the study period (Steurer 2011). The Delphi panel of experts should have sufficient knowledge and mastery of the subject matter, be involved in the discussion and influence each step of the process outcome. Respondents should be relatively neutral, and the information gained reflects their knowledge and understanding. In addition to the participants' ability, interest and commitment to the subject, continuous involvement in all rounds is also required. We applied the judgmental method and snowball sampling method as a non-probability sampling method to identify the panel

Table 1 Panel member composition

	Educational level				Quantity	
	Diploma	Bachelors	Masters	PhD	Male	Female
(Industrial experts) executes	5	10	5	4	17	7
Total	24				24	

members (Etikan and Bala 2017). Therefore, in a preliminarily step, a shortlist of professional investigators and managers was prepared, and then they completed this panel by introducing and adding more members which are known as experts. Therefore, 24 members were selected. Table 1 shows the panel member composition.

As a pre-start activity, which involves developing a research question and a pretest for the appropriateness of words such as ambiguity, the pilot should be conducted outside of the research process and to identify ambiguities and estimate time; of course, researchers may pretest or pilot the questionnaire at the beginning or at each stage to keep the questions clear and focus on the purpose of the research. To identify the barriers, a detailed study was conducted in the research literature to extract important concepts and variables which is finally applied in the Delphi questionnaire. For example, panellists were asked: "To what extent do you agree or disagree that lack of financial resources is a barrier for internationalisation?" A 5-point Likert scale was used for the measure. The questionnaire, also, consisted of open-ended questions that asked participants to improve the questionnaire if they thought the factor or other concepts might have ethical challenges but were not mentioned in the questionnaire; as such, participants were asked: "Please provide other indicators relevant to the barrier of internationalisation." After collecting the first-round questionnaires, the scores of each of the variables of the questionnaire were determined, and their mean, standard deviation and Kendall's coefficient of concordance (W) were calculated. For each round, the results of the previous round are analysed and the variables that have an average of less than 3 removed and the other variables presented to the participant in the next round questionnaire. In the second round, the respondents also were informed about the group feedback in the first round and the migraine responses individually. In the third round, this trend was repeated, and finally, by expert consensus, 31 variables were obtained. Diagram 1 illustrates the steps of the Delphi method (Fig. 1).

Table 2 shows the descriptive statistics for three rounds of Delphi synthesis ($M > 3$). This analysis has been done by SPSS software. The important issue in the study of the consensus in the Delphi method is the central tendency measures (such as means and standard deviation) in the descriptive statistics because low variation in consecutive rounds is called success.

After three rounds of the research process and based on the results, it was proved that there was a good consensus among the members, and thus the repetition of the rounds ended. In almost all factors, the proportion of members who ranked the order of importance of the challenges according to the group, as a whole, was more than

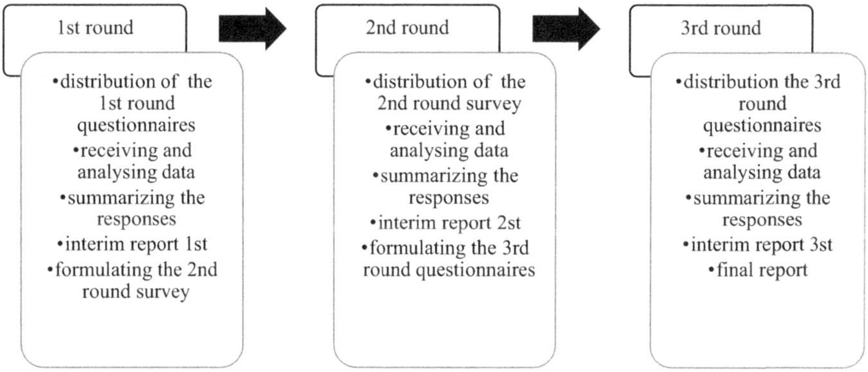

Fig. 1 The steps of the Delphi method

50%, and the standard deviation of members' responses to the importance of success factors in the third round was lower than in the first and second rounds. As mentioned, Kendall's coefficient of concordance (W) also indicates the extent of the members' collective agreement on the factors. Kendall's W ranges between "0" reflecting "no agreement" and "1" indicating the "complete agreement". After three rounds of research, this coefficient has increased to an optimal figure of 0.6, which confirms that agreement on the degree of importance of ethical challenges has been increased and reached to 60% between experts and panellists (Table 3).

3.3 *Factor Analysis*

After identifying the most important ethical challenges arising from the use of digital technologies in the health sector, the correlation coefficients of the variables are tested. Consequently, the results of the Delphi technique were provided as a second questionnaire to the interviewers in the second statistical sample. The second statistical community includes a wide range of decision-makers in business such as owners and top managers of export manufacturing companies, senior business managers related to the commercial activities and senior employees of marketing, sales and business departments of companies involved in international business activities. Based on the Cochran formula, for the population at the error level of 0.05, we determined the appropriate sample size on $n = 200$ members. Therefore, 380 questionnaires, which were set up by Likert Scales, were distributed, and finally, by considering all received responses, 212 questionnaires were accepted, which reflects over 60 per cent response rate (Table 4). For the next step, we determined the reliability of the questionnaire by Cronbach's alpha coefficient. Therefore, in a pretesting of 54 questionnaires, the Cronbach's alpha was 0.902 that indicates the method employed has an acceptable level of confidence.

Table 2 Descriptive statistics of Delphi rounds

	Barriers	1st Round		2nd Round		3rd Round	
		M	SD	M	SD	M	SD
1	Difficulty to identify foreign business opportunity	3.23	0.652	3.23	0.652	3.35	0.485
2	Limited info to analysing market	4.14	0.777	4.24	0.779	4.88	0.494
3	Unreliable data about market	4.00	0.980	4.38	0.804	4.58	0.452
4	Limited info and inability to connect with overseas customers	4.45	0.495	4.55	0.498	4.65	0.501
5	Shortage of funds to finance working capital	3.92	0.989	4.22	0.849	4.72	0.532
6	Lack of financial resource	4.46	0.842	4.60	0.489	4.75	0.475
7	Shortage of insurance for internationalisation	3.35	0.562	3.35	0.562	3.42	0.571
8	Difficulty in developing new products for foreign markets	3.22	0.721	3.32	0.729	3.52	0.524
9	Lack of competitive price to costumers in foreign markets	3.32	0.919	3.34	0.921	3.56	0.594
10	Complexity of foreign distribution and finding reliable foreign representative	3.55	0.562	3.55	0.562	3.62	0.571
11	High transportation costs	3.36	0.938	3.54	0.518	3.56	0.558
12	Lack of managerial time to deal with exports	3.58	0.942	4.38	0.814	4.58	0.452
13	Lack of export skills	4.45	0.474	4.55	0.491	3.64	0.424
14	Lack of new technology	4.25	0.843	4.35	0.774	4.59	0.514
15	Insufficient or lack of trained personnel for internationalization	4.44	0.642	4.41	0.638	4.49	0.514
16	Unfamiliarity with the procedures and documentations requirement process	3.68	0.578	3.82	0.562	4.48	0.575
17	Inadequate communications with foreign costumers	3.36	0.938	3.54	0.979	3.48	0.572
18	Slow collection of payment from abroad	4.13	0.805	4.19	0.811	4.36	0.518
19	Difficulty in enforcing contract and resolving disputes	4.38	0.641	4.48	0.633	4.17	0.442
20	Lack of home government supports and incentives and complex foreign bureaucracy	4.62	0.713	4.84	0.412	4.91	0.432
21	Restriction rules on foreign ownership	3.44	0.520	3.78	0.520	3.80	0.527
22	Restriction on movement of people/business persons (such as visa)	4.54	0.588	4.65	0.523	4.72	0.525
23	Unfair treatment compared to domestic firms	4.29	0.875	4.69	0.726	4.60	0.582
24	International sanction	4.72	0.486	4.72	0.498	4.91	0.337
25	Poor economic condition abroad	4.44	0.632	4.45	0.635	4.65	0.524
26	Currency fluctuation	4.04	0.704	4.14	0.725	4.89	0.499
27	Language and cultural differences	4.07	0.704	4.31	0.684	4.54	0.529
28	Arbitrary tariff classification and reclassification	3.23	0.705	3.41	0.795	3.55	0.485
29	High tariff barriers	3.23	0.652	3.23	0.655	3.55	0.455
30	Inadequate property right (e.g. copyright)	4.21	0.827	4.33	0.825	4.46	0.528
31	Restrictive health, safety and technical standards	4.24	0.812	4.23	0.805	4.49	0.543

Table 3 Kendall's coefficient of concordance (W)

	Q	Kendall W	DF	Sig.
1st round	32	0.325	31	0.000
2nd round	32	0.472	31	0.000
3rd round	32	0.609	31	0.000

Table 4 Descriptive of the second survey community

	Educational level				Gender		
	Diploma	Bachelor	Master	PhD	Male	Female	Total
Owner and top managers	6	6	4	0	14	2	16
Senior managers	0	19	29	11	47	12	59
Senior employees	28	53	54	2	99	38	137
Total	34	78	85	13	160	52	212

3.4 *Confirmatory Factor Analysis of the Conceptual Model of Research*

After identifying the most significant barriers to internationalisation, we applied the Factor analysis to recognise and detect factors. By factor analysis, variables are classified into two factors at least. According to this method, each factor can be considered as a hypothetical variable combining several variables that have similarities in appearance (Rezaei et al. 2020). The factor analysis method facilitates analysing by data reduction and detects structure by measuring the validity and reliability of the questionnaire. In other words, the research variables are restricted by two or more categories based on their common characteristics, and these categories are called factors, and the relationships between the factors are obtained; in each factor, the relations between its variables are calculated, and ultimately the main objective of the research, which is the relationship between the variables of the research, is calculated. For measuring the validity and reliability of the questionnaire, factor analysis identifies whether the items are placed inside the factors (Bandalos and Finney 2018).

Factor analysis approaches can be divided into two general categories: exploratory factor analysis (EFA) and confirmatory factor analysis (CFA). In this study since we have already determined the structure of the factors, therefore, the CFA analysis is used (Sadeghi and Biancone 2018). The most important goal of confirmatory factor analysis is to determine the adaptability of the predefined conceptual model with a set of observed data. In other words, confirmatory factor analysis seeks to determine whether the number of measured variable loads on these factors corresponds to what was expected based on the theoretical model.

3.5 Goodness of Fit

In a general description, by the goodness of fit, the researcher can find how well its model fits a set of observations. These measures typically indicate the discrepancy between observed values and the values expected under the designed model in the survey (Marsh et al. 2005). It should be noted that there is no general agreement about these tests and several indicators are used to measure model fit. Usually, three to five indices are sufficient to confirm the model. Some of the goodness of fit indexes are the chi-square test (x 2/df), the goodness of fit index (GFI), the adjusted goodness of fit index (AGFI), and the root mean square error of approximation (RMSEA) (Mulaik et al. 1989). However, the two most prominent indices that are visible in the LISREL output are the chi-square test (x 2/df) and the RMSEA.

3.6 Confirmatory Factor Analysis

To confirm the validity of the questionnaire and the structure and to measure barriers, second-order confirmatory factor analysis has been implemented, and, as mentioned, to measure these 8 factors, 31 items are considered. Table 5 shows the second-order confirmatory factor analysis, while Table 6 presents the fitness indices.

According to Table 5, since the path coefficient and t values for all factors exceed at the level of $p < 0.05$, it is found the correlations are significant ($p < 0.05$) and positive.

4 Results and Discussion

The CFA outputs show that among the factors of this test, the most important obstacle for the internationalisation of Iranian SMEs is the financial factor (Cronbach's alpha 95%). The second obstacle was marketing-related issues, and informational and environmental are in the next category by $R^2 = 0.81$. The results also demonstrate the procedural and tariff and non-tariff are not as important as the other barriers are in internationalisation for SMEs. Despite the increasing role of SMEs in globalisation, the World Trade Organisation (WTO) statistics show a slowdown in internationalisation in developing countries (Jafari-Sadeghi et al. 2020). This downward trend indicates a lack of courage in SMEs to enter international markets. As a result, exploring the reasons and obstacles to the internationalisation of companies has been a fascinating topic for researchers. Informational, financial, marketing, functional, governmental, environmental and

Table 5 Second-order confirmatory factor analysis

Second-order variable	First-order factors	Items	λ Coefficients	δ (Measurement errors)	t-Value*	R^2
Barriers	Informational	Q1–Q4	0.90	0.43	7.16	0.81
	Financial	Q5–Q7	0.95	0.33	7.45	0.90
	Marketing	Q8–Q11	0.91	0.47	7.25	0.83
	Functional	Q12–Q15	0.89	0.35	6.90	0.79
	Procedural	Q16–Q19	0.70	0.27	5.94	0.49
	Governmental	Q20–Q23	0.89	0.29	6.88	0.79
	Environmental	Q24–Q27	0.90	0.31	7.14	0.81
	Tariff and non-tariff	Q28–Q31	0.60	0.39	5.41	0.36

*$p < 0.05$

Table 6 Fitness indices

Fit indices	Reference value (good fit)	Model value
χ^2/df	χ^2/df < 3	1.3799
P-value	P-value<0.05	0.0000
RMSEA	RMSEA<0.05	0.042
GFI	More than 0.9	0.92
AGFI	More than 0.9	0.91

tariff and non-tariff are some of the main barriers which reduce the firm's desire to internationalise.

Concerning external-related barriers, in general, the results show internal-related barriers are a more considerable issue for experts as their average of the coefficient is higher than external barriers. According to the resource-based theory, the resources are the key factors for firms in expanding their market into a foreign market. One of these essential resources is financial resources. According to the findings, financial barriers are identified as a significant barrier to SMEs internationalisation by 0.81. This barrier is recognised in financing resources, working capital and insurance cost for internationalisation. Financing is a common considerable issue for SMEs for many centuries. SMEs are faced with this problem from starting out up to growing their business. As the major sources of financing sectors, banks are reluctant to invest in companies due to the lack of adequate collateral and the uncertainty of debt repayment. Besides, the regional and global economic crises impact corporate investment negatively (Arndt et al. 2009). Our findings are consistent with the results of Camra-Fierro et al. (2012); Chandra et al. (2020b); and Rahman et al. (2017). Marketing is another key factor that can hinder the implementation of the international process. Globalisation and international marketplaces have made it easier for everyone to access international markets which simply means companies' competitions have become closer (Dana et al. 1999). Therefore, they should improve the quality of their products while providing a more reasonable price. In parallel with the product cost, they also should find the cheapest distribution ways to reduce their overhead expenses. Difficulty in developing new products, lack of competitive price in a foreign market, problems in goods distribution and representation and high transport cast in and to foreign markets are some issues that compose marketing barrier. Our findings are in line with some previous studies (Raymond et al. 2001; Rutashobya et al. 2005; Singh et al. 2010; Roy et al. 2016b). Information is perhaps the most crucial device for firms in internationalisation. Informational barriers, which are categorised as an internal challenge, refer to those problems that are rooted in lack or insufficient information, knowledge and data for analysing and identifying foreign market and customers. According to some studies of barriers to internationalisation, the information plays a vital role in the success or failure of companies on the path to internationalisation (Su¡rez-Ortega 2003; Pinho and Martins 2010; Kahiya 2018; Felzensztein et al. 2019). Among the external challenges of internationalisation, environmental factors have the highest correlation. Environmental barriers refer to macroeconomic, political, cultural, social and financial constraints that exist regardless of the inherent company's ability for internationalisation which included international sanctions, poor economic conditions abroad, currency fluctuations and cultural and linguistic differences. Environmental problems such as economic and political instability and the global imposed limitation are the major risk for export and international trade for SMEs. In studies which are conducted by Camra-Fierro et al. (2012) and Al-Hyari et al. (2012), the political and economic uncertainty as an environmental issue is an important barrier for SMEs.

SMEs need significant government support to succeed in entering international markets, and the government's lack of attention and incentives has been one of their main obstacles to internationalisation. Governmental barriers are associated with the action and inactions that arise from the economic decisions of home governments and their policies in internationalisation. These barriers are related to unfavourable and restriction rules and regulations. According to Ahmed et al. (2008); Al-Hyari et al. (2012); and Korsakiene (2015) which conducted their studies in Lebanon, Jordan and Lithuania, respectively, lack of government assistant causes a lot of problem for SMEs in internationalisation. It is also argued that the government complex bureaucracy has a positive impact on internationalising the SMEs (Freeman and Reid 2006).

Among internal barriers, the functional problem has the same correlation as governmental has in external barriers. This challenge is related to the insufficiencies of human resource management dealing with the internationalisation process (Boudlaie et al. 2020). Without allocating sufficient time, sources (e.g. expert employees) and energy, SMEs will face a lot of difficulties in their process into international markets. Our results are parallel with some research in considering SMEs' barriers to internationalisation (e.g. Leonidou 2004; Green 2007; Shah et al. 2013; Narayanan 2015; George et al. 2019).

Procedural barriers are associated with the operational aspects of transactions with foreign customers. Internationalisation is affected by procedural challenges such as being unfamiliar with techniques and procedures, failure in communication and the problem about the slow collection of payments and difficulty in enforcing contracts which finally has a deep impact on export behaviour. Our result shows this barrier is not as important as internal challenges for Iranian SMEs. According to Uner et al. (2013), the procedural barrier is the most important barrier for Turkish SMEs. Roy et al. (2016b) found, for Indian SMEs, that the procedural barrier is the most important obstacle. Based on Mendy and Rahman's (2019) study, legal procedural complexity is known as a factor in the path to internationalisation. Tariff and non-tariff barriers are associated with foreign government policies on exporting and internationalising. High tariff rate, inadequate property rights protection, restrictive rules in health and safety standards, arbitrary tariff classification and high costs of customs administration are some of tariff and non-tariff barriers which impose challenges in internationalisation process for SMEs (Shaw and Darroch 2004; Leonidou et al. 2011). Based on outputs, the Cronbach's alpha for this relationship is the lowest among all analysed barriers.

5 Limitations

Interpretation of the findings and conclusions should be made in light of some limitations. Since the challenges for SMEs in internationalization have not been properly studied in Iran, we are limited to examining some parts of barriers which do not cover all aspects of the impact of obstacles on internationalisation. On the other hand, collecting data via the questionnaire has an inherent risk of common method bias. Participants may aim at consistency rather than accuracy, therefore introducing undue variance in the variables. Survivorship bias is another limitation for this research; our sample is limited; thus, by changing the sample size or society, the result may have different outputs. Furthermore, the scope of this research was limited to a two-step method to identify the barriers in internationalization procedures for SMEs. However, for such a complex challenge, we call for more research, which use practical cases to verify and enrich the outcome of this research. In this regard, by using a combined Delphi-CFA method in this research, the identified outcomes could predict the challenges in future studies in internationalization and demonstrate the significant role of each problem.

References

Abdul-Aziz A-R et al (2013) Internationalization of construction-related consultants: impact of age and size. J Prof Issues Eng Educ Pract. American Society of Civil Engineers 139(2):148–155

Ahmed ZU, Julian CC, Mahajar AJ (2008) Export barriers and firm internationalisation from an emerging market perspective. J Asia Bus Stud. Emerald Group Publishing Limited

Al-Hyari K, Al-Weshah G, Alnsour M (2012) Barriers to internationalisation in SMEs: evidence from Jordan. Mark Intell Plan 30(2):188–211

Angulo-Ruiz F, Pergelova A, Dana LP (2020) The internationalization of social hybrid firms. J Bus Res. Elsevier 113:266–278
Arndt C, Buch CM, Mattes A (2009) Barriers to internationalization: firm-level evidence from Germany. IAW Diskussionspapiere
Arteaga-Ortiz J, Fernández-Ortiz R (2010) Why don't we use the same export barrier measurement scale? An empirical analysis in small and medium-sized enterprises. J Small Bus Manag 48 (3):395–420
Bandalos DL, Finney SJ (2018) Factor analysis: exploratory and confirmatory. In: The reviewer's guide to quantitative methods in the social sciences. Routledge, pp 110–134
Bang Y (2013) Internationalization of higher education: a case study of three Korean private universities. University of Southern California
Bardhan P (2002) Decentralization of governance and development. J Econ Perspect 16 (4):185–205
Beheshti M, Mahdiraji HA, Zavadskas EK (2016) Strategy portfolio optimisation: a copras g-modm hybrid approach. Transform Bus Econ 15(3C):500–519
Bilkey WJ, Tesar G (1977) The export behavior of smaller-sized Wisconsin manufacturing firms. J Int Bus Stud. Springer 8(1):93–98
Boudlaie H, Mahdiraji HA, Shamsi S, Jafari-Sadeghi V, Garcia-Perez A (2020) Designing a human resource scorecard: an empirical stakeholder-based study with a company culture perspective. W. Kucharska (ed), p 113
Bowen R (2019) Motives to SME internationalisation. Cross Cult Strateg Manag. Emerald Publishing Limited
Buckley PJ (1993) Barriers to internationalization. In: Perspectives on strategic change. Springer, pp 79–106
Camra-Fierro J et al (2012) Barriers to internationalisation in SMEs: evidence from Jordan. Mark Intell Plan. Emerald Group Publishing Limited
Cassar G, Holmes S (2003) Capital structure and financing of SMEs: Australian evidence. Acct Fin. Wiley Online Library 43(2):123–147
Cavusgil ST, Nevin JR (1981) Internal determinants of export marketing behavior: an empirical investigation. J Mark Res. SAGE Publications Sage CA: Los Angeles, CA 18(1):114–119
Chandra A, Paul J, Chavan M (2020a) Internationalization barriers of SMEs from developing countries: a review and research agenda. Int J Entrep Behav Res. Emerald Publishing Limited
Chandra A, Paul J, Chavan M (2020b) Internationalization barriers of SMEs from developing countries: a review and research agenda. Int J Entrepreneurial Behav Res 26(6):1281–1310
Chiao Y-C, Yang K-P, Yu C-MJ (2006) Performance, internationalization, and firm-specific advantages of SMEs in a newly-industrialized economy. Small Bus Econ. Springer 26 (5):475–492
Chong P et al (2019) Internationalisation and innovation on balanced scorecard (BSC) among Malaysian small and medium enterprises (SMEs). Manag Sci Lett 9(10):1617–1632
Coudounaris DN (2018) Typologies of internationalisation pathways of SMEs: what is new? Rev Int Bus Strateg. Emerald Publishing Limited
Coviello NE, Martin KA-M (1999) Internationalization of service SMEs: an integrated perspective from the engineering consulting sector. J Int Mark. SAGE Publications Sage CA: Los Angeles, CA 7(4):42–66
Coviello N, Munro H (1997) Network relationships and the internationalisation process of small software firms. Int Bus Rev. Elsevier 6(4):361–386
Coviello NE, McDougall PP, Oviatt BM (2011) The emergence, advance and future of international entrepreneurship research—an introduction to the special forum. J Bus Ventur. Elsevier 26 (6):625–631
Cressy R, Olofsson C (1997) European SME financing: an overview. Small Bus Econ. Springer 9 (2):87–96
Dabić M et al (2020) Pathways of SME internationalization: a bibliometric and systematic review. Small Bus Econ. Springer 55(3):705–725

Dana LP (2001) Networks, internationalization & policy. Small Bus Econ. Springer 16(2):57–62
Dana LP (2004) Handbook of research on international entrepreneurship. Edward Elgar Publishing
Dana LP, Ramadani V (2015) Family business in transition economies: management, succession and internationalization
Dana L-P, Etemad H, Wright RW (1999) The impact of globalization on SMEs. Glob Focus 11 (4):93–106
Dana L-P, Etemad H, Wright RW (2004) Back to the future: international entrepreneurship in the new economy. In: Emerging paradigms in international entrepreneurship. Edward Elgar Publishing, p 19
Dana L-P et al (2011) 32 internationalization of European entrepreneurs. In: World encyclopedia of entrepreneurship. Edward Elgar Publishing, p 274
Demary M, Hornik J, Watfe G (2016) SME financing in the EU: moving beyond one-size-fits-all. IW-Report
Dezi L, Ferraris A, Papa A, Vrontis D (2019) The role of external embeddedness and knowledge management as antecedents of ambidexterity and performances in Italian SMEs. IEEE Trans Eng Manag. https://doi.org/10.1109/TEM.2019.2916378
Doh J et al (2010) Issues in services offshoring research: a multidisciplinary. Citeseer
Donthu N, Kim SH (1993) Implications of firm controllable factors on export growth. J Glob Mark. Taylor & Francis 7(1):47–64
Etikan I, Bala K (2017) Sampling and sampling methods. Biom Biostat Int J 5(6):149
Farooqi F, Miog R (2012) Influence of network forms on the internationalization process: a study on Swedish SMEs
Felzensztein C, Deans KR, Dana L (2019) Small firms in regional clusters: local networks and internationalization in the southern hemisphere. J Small Bus Manag. Taylor & Francis 57 (2):496–516
Ferraris A, Santoro G, Pellicelli AC (2020) "Openness" of public governments in smart cities: removing the barriers for innovation and entrepreneurship. Int Entrep Manag J:1–22
Fliess B, Busquets C (2006) The role of trade barriers in SME internationalisation. OECD Pap 6 (13):1–19
Freeman S, Reid I (2006) Constraints facing small western firms in transitional markets. Eur Bus Rev. Emerald Group Publishing Limited
George, A. D., Mathew, L. S. and Chandramohan, G. (2019) 'Internationalization of SMEs: a Darwinian perspective', in Transnational entrepreneurship. Springer, pp 363–378
Ghauri P, Lutz C, Tesfom G (2003) Using networks to solve export-marketing problems of small- and medium-sized firms from developing countries. Eur J Mark. MCB UP Ltd
Gordon, T. J. (1994) 'The Delphi method', Futures research methodology. American Council for the United Nations University: Washington, DC, 2(3), 1–30
Goswami AK, Agrawal RK (2019) Explicating the influence of shared goals and hope on knowledge sharing and knowledge creation in an emerging economic context. J Knowl Manag. Emerald Publishing Limited
Green, M. F. (2007) 'Internationalizing community colleges: barriers and strategies', New directions for community colleges. Wiley Subscription Services, Inc., A Wiley Company San Francisco, 2007(138), 15–24
Gripsrud G, Benito GRG (2005) Internationalization in retailing: modeling the pattern of foreign market entry. J Bus Res. Elsevier 58(12):1672–1680
Hajiagha SHR, Mahdiraji HA, Hashemi SS (2013) Multi-objective linear programming with interval coefficients. Kybernetes
Hajiagha SHR, Hashemi SS, Mahdiraji HA, Azaddel J (2015) Multi-period data envelopment analysis based on Chebyshev inequality bounds. Expert Syst Appl 42(21):7759–7767
Hajiagha SHR, Mahdiraji HA, Tavana M, Hashemi SS (2018) A novel common set of weights method for multi-period efficiency measurement using mean-variance criteria. Measurement 129:569–581

Harris S, Wheeler C (2005) 'Entrepreneurs' relationships for internationalization: functions, origins and strategies'. Int Bus Rev. Elsevier 14(2):187–207
Hjarnø L, Syed A, Aro A (2007) Report of interview summaries and Delphi rounds. p 3
Hollensen S (2007) Global marketing: a decision-oriented approach. Pearson Education
Hope, K. et al. (2019) Annual report on European SMEs 2018/2019: research & development and innovation by SMEs
Hsu C-C, Sandford BA (2007) The Delphi technique: making sense of consensus. Pract Assess Res Eval 12(1):10
Hutchinson K, Fleck E, Lloyd-Reason L (2009) An investigation into the initial barriers to internationalization. J Small Bus Enterp Dev. Emerald Group Publishing Limited
Jafari-Sadeghi V et al (2019) Home country institutional context and entrepreneurial internationalization: the significance of human capital attributes. J Int Entrep. Springer:1–31
Jafari-Sadeghi V et al (2020) Internationalisation business processes in an under-supported policy contexts: evidence from Italian SMEs. Bus Process Manag J. Emerald Publishing Limited
Kahiya ET (2013) Export barriers and path to internationalization: a comparison of conventional enterprises and international new ventures. J Int Entrep. Springer 11(1):3–29
Kahiya ET (2018) Five decades of research on export barriers: review and future directions. Int Bus Rev. Elsevier 27(6):1172–1188
Karadeniz EE, Göçer K (2007) Internationalization of small firms. Eur Bus Rev. Emerald Group Publishing Limited
Karlsen T et al (2003) Knowledge, internationalization of the firm, and inward–outward connections. Ind Mark Manag. Elsevier 32(5):385–396
Korsakiene R (2015) Internationalization of Lithuanian SMEs: investigation of barriers and motives. Econ Bus 26:54
Kreutzer RT, Neugebauer T, Pattloch A (2017) Digital business leadership. In: Digital transformation–Geschäftsmodell-innovation–agile organisation–change-management. Springer
Kumar N (2008) Internationalization of Indian enterprises: patterns, strategies, ownership advantages, and implications. Asian Econ Pol Rev. Wiley Online Library 3(2):242–261
Labate BC, Jungaberle H (2011) The internationalization of Ayahuasca. LIT Verlag Münster
Landau C et al (2016) Institutional leverage capability: creating and using institutional advantages for internationalization. Glob Strateg J. Wiley Online Library 6(1):50–68
Lange T, Ottens M, Taylor A (2000) SMEs and barriers to skills development: a Scottish perspective. J Eur Ind Train. MCB UP Ltd
Laudal T (2011) Drivers and barriers of CSR and the size and internationalization of firms. Soc Responsib J 7(2):234–256. https://doi.org/10.1108/17471111111141512
Leonidou LC (2004) An analysis of the barriers hindering small business export development. J Small Bus Manag. Taylor & Francis 42(3):279–302
Leonidou LC, Theodosiou M (2004) The export marketing information system: an integration of the extant knowledge. J World Bus. Elsevier 39(1):12–36
Leonidou LC, Palihawadana D, Theodosiou M (2011) National export-promotion programs as drivers of organizational resources and capabilities: effects on strategy, competitive advantage, and performance. J Int Mark. SAGE Publications Sage CA: Los Angeles, CA 19(2):1–29
Linstone HA, Turoff M (1975) The Delphi method. Addison-Wesley, Reading, MA
Mahdiraji HA, Hajiagha SHR, Pourjam R (2011) A Grey mathematical programming model to time-cost trade-offs in Project Management under uncertainty. In: IEEE 2011 international conference on Grey systems and intelligent services. IEEE, pp 698–704
Mahdiraji HA, Kazimieras Zavadskas E, Kazeminia A, Abbasi Kamardi A (2019) Marketing strategies evaluation based on big data analysis: a CLUSTERING-MCDM approach. Econ Res-Ekonomska istraživanja 32(1):2882–2892
Mahdiraji HA, Hafeez K, Kord H, Kamardi AA (2020) Analysing the voice of customers by a hybrid fuzzy decision-making approach in a developing country's automotive market. Manag Decis

Mahmoudi M, Mahdiraji HA, Jafarnejad A, Safari H (2019) Dynamic prioritization of equipment and critical failure modes. Kybernetes 48(9):1913–1941
Marsh HW, Hau K-T, Grayson D (2005) Goodness of fit in structural equation models. Lawrence Erlbaum Associates Publishers
Mejri K, Umemoto K (2010) Small-and medium-sized enterprise internationalization: towards the knowledge-based model. J Int Entrep. Springer 8(2):156–167
Mendy J, Rahman M (2019) Application of human resource management's universal model: an examination of people versus institutions as barriers of internationalization for SMEs in a small developing country. Thunderbird Int Bus Rev. Wiley Online Library 61(2):363–374
Mokhtarzadeh NG, Mahdiraji HA, Beheshti M, Zavadskas EK (2018) A novel hybrid approach for technology selection in the information technology industry. Technol 6(1):34
Morais F, Ferreira JJ (2020) SME internationalisation process: key issues and contributions, existing gaps and the future research agenda. Eur Manag J. Elsevier 38(1):62–77
Mueller-Using S, Urban W, Wedemeier J (2020) Internationalization of SMEs in the Baltic Sea region: barriers of cross-national collaboration considering regional innovation strategies for smart specialization. Growth Chang. Wiley Online Library
Muhammad Azam Roomi and Parrott G (2008) Barriers to development entrepreneurship in Pakistan.Pdf. J Entrep 17(1):59–72
Mulaik SA et al (1989) Evaluation of goodness-of-fit indices for structural equation models. Psychol Bull. American Psychological Association 105(3):430
Narayanan V (2015) Export barriers for small and medium-sized enterprises: a literature review based on Leonidou's model. Entrepreneurial Bus Econ Rev. Uniwersytet Ekonomiczny w Krakowie 3(2):105–123
Ng HS, Kee DMH (2012) The issues and development of critical success factors for the SME success in a developing country. Int Bus Manag 6(6):680–691
Oviatt BM, McDougall PP (2005) Defining international entrepreneurship and modeling the speed of internationalization. Entrep Theory Pract. SAGE Publications Sage CA: Los Angeles, CA 29 (5):537–553
Paul J (2020) SCOPE framework for SMEs: a new theoretical lens for success and internationalization. Eur Manag J. Elsevier
Paul J, Parthasarathy S, Gupta P (2017) Exporting challenges of SMEs: a review and future research agenda. J World Bus. Elsevier 52(3):327–342
Pavlák M (2018) Barriers to the internationalization of Czech SMEs. Eur Res Stud J 21(2):453–462
Pinho JC, Martins L (2010) Exporting barriers: insights from Portuguese small-and medium-sized exporters and non-exporters. J Int Entrep. Springer 8(3):254–272
Rahman M, Uddin M, Lodorfos G (2017) Barriers to enter in foreign markets: evidence from SMEs in emerging market. Int Mark Rev 34(1):68–86. https://doi.org/10.1108/IMR-10-2014-0322
Ratten V et al (2007) Internationalisation of SMEs: European comparative studies. Int J Entrep Small Bus. Inderscience Publishers 4(3):361–379
Ratten V et al (2017) Family entrepreneurship and internationalization strategies. Rev Int Bus Strateg. Emerald Publishing Limited
Raymond MA, Kim J, Shao AT (2001) Export strategy and performance: a comparison of exporters in a developed market and an emerging market. J Glob Mark. Taylor & Francis 15(2):5–29
Rezaei M, Jafari-Sadeghi V, Bresciani S (2020) What drives the process of knowledge management in a cross-cultural setting. Eur Bus Rev. Emerald Publishing Limited
Ribau CP, Moreira AC, Raposo M (2018) SME internationalization research: mapping the state of the art. Canadian J Adm Sci/Revue Canadienne des Sciences de l'Administration. Wiley Online Library 35(2):280–303
Romanello R, Chiarvesio M (2019) Early internationalizing firms: 2004 2018. J Int Entrep. Springer 17(2):172–219
Roy A, Sekhar C, Vyas V (2016a) Barriers to internationalization: a study of small and medium enterprises in India. J Int Entrep 14(4):513–538. https://doi.org/10.1007/s10843-016-0187-7

Roy A, Sekhar C, Vyas V (2016b) Barriers to internationalization: a study of small and medium enterprises in India. J Int Entrep. Springer 14(4):513–538
Rundh B (2007) International marketing behaviour amongst exporting firms. Eur J Mark. Emerald Group Publishing Limited
Rutashobya L, Mukasa D, Jaensson J-E (2005) Networks, relationships and performance of small and medium enterprises in the shipping sub-sector in Tanzania, in IMP Conference at Rotterdam
Saarani AN, Shahadan F (2013) The determinant of capital structure of SMEs in Malaysia: evidence from enterprise 50 (E50) SMEs. Asian Soc Sci. Canadian Center of Science and Education 9 (6):64
Sadeghi VJ, Biancone PP (2018) How micro, small and medium-sized enterprises are driven outward the superior international trade performance? A multidimensional study on Italian food sector. Res Int Bus Financ. Elsevier 45:597–606
Sadeghi VJ et al (2018) How does export compliance influence the internationalization of firms: is it a thread or an opportunity? J Glob Entrep Res. Springer 8(1):3
Sadeghi VJ et al (2019) An institution-based view of international entrepreneurship: a comparison of context-based and universal determinants in developing and economically advanced countries. Int Bus Rev. Elsevier 28(6):101588
Saridakis G et al (2019) 'SMEs' internationalisation: when does innovation matter?'. J Bus Res. Elsevier 96:250–263
Schmid D, Morschett D (2020) Decades of research on foreign subsidiary divestment: what do we really know about its antecedents? Int Bus Rev. Elsevier 29(4):101653
Senik ZC et al (2010) Influential factors for SME internationalization: evidence from Malaysia. Int J Econ Manag 4(2):285–304
Shah TH, Javed S, Syed S (2013) Internationalization of SMES in Pakistan: a brief theoretical overview of controlling factors. J Manag Sci 7(2)
Shaw V, Darroch J (2004) Barriers to internationalisation: a study of entrepreneurial new ventures in New Zealand. J Int Entrep 2(4):327–343. https://doi.org/10.1007/s10843-004-0146-6
Shoham A, Albaum GS (1995) Reducing the impact of barriers to exporting: a managerial perspective. J Int Mark. SAGE Publications Sage CA: Los Angeles, CA 3(4):85–105
Singh G, Pathak RD, Naz R (2010) Issues faced by SMEs in the internationalization process: results from Fiji and Samoa. Int J Emerg Mark. Emerald Group Publishing Limited
Soto JLG (2015) Annual report 2014. Revista de Educacion 368:274–286
Sox CB, Kline SF, Crews TB (2014) Identifying best practices, opportunities and barriers in meeting planning for generation Y. Int J Hosp Manag. Elsevier Ltd 36:244–254
Steurer J (2011) The Delphi method: an efficient procedure to generate knowledge. Skelet Radiol 40 (8):959–961
Su¡rez-Ortega, S. (2003) Export barriers: insights from small and medium-sized firms. Int Small Bus J. SAGE Publications 21(4):403–419
Sukumar A, Jafari-Sadeghi V, Garcia-Perez A, Dutta DK (2020) The potential link between corporate innovations and corporate competitiveness: evidence from IT firms in the UK. J Knowl Manag. Emerald Publishing Limited
Taghavifard MT, Amoozad Mahdiraji H, Alibakhshi AM, Zavadskas EK, Bausys R (2018) An extension of fuzzy SWOT analysis: an application to information technology. Info 9(3):46
Tesfom G, Lutz C (2006) A classification of export marketing problems of small and medium sized manufacturing firms in developing countries. Int J Emerg Mark. Emerald Group Publishing Limited
Toma C, Picioreanu I (2016) The Delphi technique: methodological considerations and the need for reporting guidelines in medical journals. Int J Public Health Res 4(6):47–59
Treviño LJ, Doh JP (2020) Internationalization of the firm: a discourse-based view. J Int Bus Stud. Springer:1–19
Uner MM et al (2013) Do barriers to export vary for born globals and across stages of internationalization? An empirical inquiry in the emerging market of Turkey. Int Bus Rev. Elsevier 22 (5):800–813

Vahlne J-E, Johanson J (2017) From internationalization to evolution: the Uppsala model at 40 years. J Int Bus Stud. Springer 48(9):1087–1102
Welch LS, Luostarinen R (1988) Internationalization: evolution of a concept. J Gen Manag. SAGE Publications Sage UK: London, UK 14(2):34–55
Welch C, Paavilainen-Mäntymäki E (2014) Putting process (back) in: research on the internationalization process of the firm. Int J Manag Rev. Wiley Online Library 16(1):2–23
Yoshino N, Taghizadeh-Hesary F (2018) The role of SMEs in Asia and their difficulties in accessing finance. Asian Development Bank Institute
Zain M, Ng SI (2006) 'The impacts of network relationships on SMEs' internationalization process. Thunderbird Int Bus Rev. Wiley Online Library 48(2):183–205

Mojtaba Rezaei is a PhD candidate in Business and Management at the Università degli Studi di Torino, Italy. His research interests are knowledge management, digitalisation, and entrepreneurship. He has contributed to different research projects with various scholars and universities.

Alberto Ferraris, PhD in Business and Management, is currently working as a Senior Researcher at the University of Turin—Department of Management. He obtained the qualification of Full Professor at the National Scientific Evaluation (ASN) in Italy in 2020. He is an active member and Research Fellow of the Laboratory for International and Regional Economics, Graduate School of Economics and Management, Ural Federal University (Russia) and he is Fellow (F-EMAB) of the EuroMed Research Business Institute. He is the author of many academic and scientific articles published in international journals and he is in the Editorial Board and serves as Guest Editor for special issues in several prestigious international journals. During the last years, he got several international awards such as the "2015 Emerald/EMRBI Business Research Award for Emerging Researchers" and the "Best Reviewer Award" for different conferences as well as for Journal of Intellectual Capital (2018).

Elaheh Heydari has a master's degree in management and a bachelor's in accounting. Her background includes finance, executive management experience in healthcare and advisor in marketing. She works as a customer satisfaction analyst at the Ministry of Health and Medical Education in Iran. Her main research interests are related to customer satisfaction in SMEs and entrepreneurship.

Shahrbanou Rezaei is a marketing researcher at Sajjad University in Iran-Mashhad. She has a master's degree in industrial engineering and a bachelor's in IT engineering. Her main research interests are related to customer clustering, in particular, the credit scoring model and entrepreneurship. She is also a marketing and entrepreneurship consultant for several SMEs in Iran.

Part V
Quantitative Research Streams: MCDM

A Hybrid Best-Worst Method and Multi-criteria Decision-Making Methods for Location Selection in the International Entrepreneurial Ecosystem. Case Study: Medical Tourism Start-Up

Shide Sadat Hashemi and Mostafa Azari

1 Introduction

The global village is the concept of recent decades; however its indications are rarely observed in real problems. In this regard, many products and services are presented regardless of their negative environmental, social, and economic long-term effects. Although the corporates use some costing and scarce resources to benefit and create value, they leave the destructive effects. Businesses may have impacts and contaminate air, water, wildlife, and inhabitant ecosystems. Many factors can lead to these undesired results. One of these effective factors is the location of corporates or plants. Wrong location selection can cause environmental and social problems, in addition to increasing the cost of supplying raw materials and delivering the finished products (Kheybari et al. 2019). Some parts of these costs are imposed on society and the environment. Therefore, managers should eliminate these extra costs and provide the environment more benefits considering the corporate internal situations, too. International businesses have been more noticed, and their main and side effects are seriously monitored by different associations all around the world, recently (Sadeghi et al. 2017, 2018). They should balance these costs logically, which seems a multi-criteria problem including several conflicting criteria (Devi and Yadav 2013). Many studies indicate that MCDM methods are suitable tools to select a firm's location based on multiple criteria (Karaşan et al. 2018; Kaul et al. 2020; Wang et al. 2018). Many selection methods are developed for decision-making,

S. S. Hashemi (✉)
Saramadan Andishe Avina Co., Science, and Technology Park of Tarbiat Modares, Tehran, Iran

M. Azari
Faculty of Management, University of Tehran, Tehran, Iran
e-mail: mostafa.azari@ut.ac.ir

V. Jafari-Sadeghi et al. (eds.), *Empirical International Entrepreneurship*,
Contributions to Management Science,
https://doi.org/10.1007/978-3-030-68972-8_18

while multiple criteria decision-making methods are the best approaches to compare the alternatives regarding multiple conflict criteria (Hashemi et al. 2016).

Since location selection has long-term effects on business performance and future situation, it became an important and strategic initial decision at the first step of business planning (Govindan et al. 2016). Accordingly, start-ups as growing corporates need to manage their expenditures crucially, because about only 50% of start-ups can survive beyond the first 5 years (Cader and Leatherman 2011). Many previous studies claim that businesses can survive based on some factors such as industry field, location, economic and environmental condition, etc. (Lueg et al. 2014; Beheshti et al. 2016), but these factors may change across different countries (Jafari Sadeghi et al. 2019). Innovation is the key for organisational and market survival and development and is essential for the sustainable development of companies, countries, and economic systems (Dana et al. 2021; Mahmoudi et al. 2019; Sukumar et al. 2020). Internal entrepreneurship leads to pursuing internal entrepreneurial opportunities including more profit creation, developing the market, personal desires, and achieving social status (Jafari-Sadeghi et al. 2020). During the past decade, society has changed due to demographic change and the increased usage of information technology. This has affected the type of entrepreneurship of people in their businesses (Sadraei et al. 2018; Vanessa and Leo-Paul 2019). In order to reduce the risk of bankruptcy, start-ups should concentrate on making decision about these factors like location selection and try to find the most appropriate and effective criteria for location selection and employ the suitable methodology to prioritise the location alternatives based on these criteria.

In the few last decades, patients have travelled overseas to have surgeries, medical visits, and diagnoses. It was due to high-tech healthcare services in destination countries, lack of enough updated resources at home, and some unique facilities or natural features in the destination region (Connell 2006; Biancone and Jafari Sadeghi 2016; Mahdiraji et al. 2011, 2019, 2020). In the past, the tourism industry depended only on tourist packages; however medical tourism can rely on and grow based on private healthcare services and benefits from quick healthcare and tourism globalisation together (Connell 2006). Medical tourism is a term that indicates the treatment process in another country or outsourcing medical operations (Jones and Keith 2006; Hajiagha et al. 2013, 2015, 2018). This section is faced with an extended market including medical surgeries, eye care, dental services, cosmetic surgeries, and implants. They might be high-tech and expensive or, on the contrary, non-developed in the origin country. Regardless of the level of development of the destination country, many patients travel from developed countries to developing countries due to various reasons (Ahmed and Yeasmeen 2016). Medical tourism predictions implied this industry is growing at 15–25% per year. The older report published by the official magazine of the Medical Tourism Association indicates India, Brazil, Malaysia, Thailand, Turkey, Mexico, Costa Rica, Taiwan, South Korea, and Singapore are the more popular alternatives for Americans (Berdine 2019). It was estimated this market value will reach about 1.9 million American medical tourists in 2019 that spend an average of 3.410 $ per trip and suggests the Americans are about 10% of the world market (Berdine 2019; Mokhtarzadeh et al.

2018). According to a report of "medical tourism.com" in 2016, the top destination score of America is 76.62, for Asia it is 73.56, for Europe it reaches 71.90, in the Middle East it is 67.54, and finally, for Africa, it is calculated 62.60.[1] The number of medical tourists to all destinations was predicted about 14–16 million in 2017, and the average cost of each visit in this industry could be about $3800–6000 per visit (Dalen and Alpert 2019). Before coronavirus crisis, the global medical tourism market size was estimated to rise about $179 billion by 2026.[2] It can lead to foreign exchange income and contribute to the overall development of any economy by providing job positions and employment chance for locals. However, it depends deeply on healthcare growth, governments' regulations and supports, general reputation, social security and protection, international relationships, and insurance protections which are key factors to become a tourism destination region (www.businesswire.com/new). Medical tourism growth has increased significantly during the past two decades (Khan et al. 2016).

About 14 million people spent $68 billion on medical tourism in 2016.[3] Until December 2019, the amount of global online medical tourism was 137 companies around the world that most of them are start-ups.[4] They provide various services such as searching, booking, and arranging medical travels; creating a platform to compare services and find a clinic; searching medical beauty and aesthetic services in certain countries or globally; etc. Now, one of the most popular destinations in the world is India with prominent physicians and, of course, the low cost of treatments and surgeries compared with many developed origin countries. Some other countries such as the Philippines, Singapore, Thailand, etc. are growing in this field too. These services in different countries are managed based on platforms generated by start-ups. Figure 1 demonstrates ten reasons why start-ups fail.

Along with other countries, medical tourism start-ups have grown in Iran's entrepreneurship ecosystem and reached more than 15 corporates as they need a lot of time and efforts to:

- Take certificates
- Identify suitable medical resources and services
- Identify suitable accommodation resources and services
- Develop platforms, application, or gadget
- Find an accelerator or co-founder
- Establish a team
- Find a location, etc.

[1]https://www.medicaltourism.com/mti/2016-2017/overview

[2]https://www.businesswire.com/news/home/20190225005696/en/Worldwide-Market-Medical-Tourism-2019-2026-Size-Share

[3]https://www.bloomberg.com/news/articles/2018-07-12/startups-look-to-mainstream-medical-tourism

[4]https://tracxn.com/d/trending-themes/Startups-in-Online-Medical-Tourism

Fig. 1 Ten reasons for start-ups' failure

Therefore, it seems wise to consider the limitations of time and cost to run the invulnerable corporate to survive during the first 5 years and grow remarkably towards its goals and mission. There is a combination of medical tourism start-ups that fail, while others emerge confidently in the industry. Some points should be considered by start-up managers to prevent failure and to smooth the path to success.

There are two types of factors to motivate this market: the factors related to patients and the origin country and the factors related to host country and healthcare service providers (Fetscherin and Stephano 2016). In this regard, the destination country and healthcare service providers need to consider the whole effective elements and factors to facilitate the process of incoming and supplementary services. The importance of location factor may vary in different industries (Felzensztein et al. 2019), but in this field, the location is one effective and critical factor to provide reliably the services more comfortable and welcoming. This research focuses on location selection for medical tourism start-ups according to well-defined and suitable criteria.

The remainder of the paper is organised as follows: Sect. 2 involves the literature review which the criteria can be extracted. In Sect. 3 the methodology is explained, and then in Sect. 4 the real-world problem is solved in medical tourism start-up location problem. Finally, the conclusions are presented in Sect. 5.

2 Literature Review

Entrepreneurship is an important feature of today's societies. Many factors affect the entrepreneurial characteristics of people. In this regard, education significantly affects entrepreneurship, which assumes that investing in education can lead to personal growth and the development of business ventures by the individual (Jafari-Sadeghi 2020; Sadeghi and Biancone 2017). Moreover, education changes the foresight skills of entrepreneurs (Jafari-Sadeghi et al. 2019a). In this section, we first review existing MCDM applications in the field of entrepreneurship and start-ups and then focus on variables influencing location decisions of entrepreneurs and start-ups.

2.1 Multi-criteria Decision-Making in Entrepreneurship and Start-Up

Although several studies are focusing on location factors and criteria, few of them analyse entrepreneurship and start-ups. In this part, we examine some applications of MCDM methods in the field of entrepreneurship, start-ups, and innovation. Also, many multi-criteria decision-making problems in those fields are considered as well. Some of them used a single method or a hybrid/combination of MCDM methods to rank effective factors and elements in case of entrepreneurship-, innovation-, and start-up-related decisions. Tsai and Kuo (2011) proposed a hybrid approach that combines the DEMATEL, ANP, and zero-one goal programming methods to evaluate entrepreneurship policies for SMEs in Taiwan, using the criteria such as "reducing entry and exit barriers", "promotion", "entrepreneurship knowledge", and "financing and business support". The results of this assessment show that three alternatives such as platforms for sharing the knowledge, incubator centre, and financial support are selected considering cost limitations and it provides an effective solution to assist the senior decision-makers to assess and choose possible entrepreneurship policy combinations. Mouzakitis et al. (2013) proposed a multi-criteria method, based on the PROMETHEE method for evaluation and ranking of a selected set of companies in which to invest, considering the business angels' point of view. They determined criteria according to the business angels' viewpoint and performance of the company. They finally suggested implementing the proposed method using a web-based system to enhance the networks of modern business angels. Rostamzadeh et al. (2014) proposed a multi-criteria method based on fuzzy analytical hierarchy process (FAHP), VIKOR, and TOPSIS methods to assess and rank the entrepreneurial capability and intention of the SMEs. As the results show, VIKOR and TOPSIS ranking methods provide different rankings. Afful-Dadzie et al. (2015) proposed an intuitionistic fuzzy TOPSIS framework to illustrate the selection of start-up businesses in government-run public venture capital (GPVC). They used the intuitionistic fuzzy weighted averaging (IFWA) operator to aggregate personal ratings and reach consensus and make group decisions. Results indicate this framework provides useful means to examine the selection of start-ups' fields. Jafari-Moghadam et al. (2017) proposed a model to create an entrepreneurship tourism policy interacting with economic development using an entrepreneurship development framework. Thus, entrepreneurship policy aspects are weighted and ranked by tourism entrepreneurs, policymakers, and specialists through DEMATEL and ANP techniques. Findings indicate that initial entrepreneurship development elements in tourism need to be considered. Additionally, efficiency strengthener criteria should be improved along with innovation incentive criteria. Zhao et al. (2019) proposed a hybrid MCDM to assess strategies of service innovation to improve China's sustainable banking industry along with the Fintech new circumstances. They determined the related weights of criteria by DEMATEL and DEMATEL-ANP (DANP) techniques and then assess the performance gaps in different fields of service innovation by the modified VIKOR method as an MCDM technique. In conclusion, they reported innovative strategies for the paper aims and perform the changes in response to the influence of the Fintech revolution. Nilashi et al. (2019) proposed a hybrid MCDM model by combining DEMATEL and fuzzy TOPSIS, to ascertain the interactions among the elements and to find the comparative importance of these elements in the decision-making model. They concluded that human and technology-based elements are more important than organisational and environmental factors in the field of medical tourism in Malaysia. Büyüközkan and Güler (2020) proposed a model combining the SAW method with HFLTS data and ARAS method to decide on innovative products. This decision is made in an uncertain environment. Golghamat Raad and Akbarpour Shirazi (2020) employed a combination of DEMATEL-based ANP and MODM methods to rank and implement the projects which lead to entrepreneurial universities. Dhochak and Doliya (2020) used fuzzy AHP to prioritise the strategic theories to measure and determine the value of a new corporate and start-up. This method helps venture capitalists to decide on their investment in the initial steps of the start-up lifecycle. Some of the other researchers have employed this methodology to rank and make decisions about managerial elements such as location selection in businesses. Cheng et al. (2005) employed MCDM methods to determine the most appropriate place for a shopping mall. Their model can provide a powerful and comprehensive framework to decide on this area. Chou (2007) for purpose of transhipment cost reduction used the fuzzy MCDM method and then ranked and selected the most appropriate container ports. This method led to a quick selection process. Żak and Węgliński (2014) presented a model to select the location for logistic centres of business regard to multiple significant criteria through ELECTRE III/IV methodologies. Erol et al. (2014) to decide about the location of the nuclear power plants for future projects employed the fuzzy MCDM method and ranked the alternative sites in Turkey. To support decision-makers in overcoming the uncertain environment for developing the intermodal transport terminal in Belgrade and its location, Zečević et al. (2017) used a hybrid MCDM model combining fuzzy Delphi, fuzzy ANP, and fuzzy VIKOR. They considered a variety of conflicting criteria by different stakeholders. C.-N. Wang et al. (2018) proposed a hybrid MCDM model by combining FAHP, DEA, and TOPSIS to find the best region for locating a solar power plant based on different criteria.

Table 1 summarises the above-mentioned literature and various applications. The review implies less focus on location selection of entrepreneurship and start-ups; therefore, this necessitates the need for deeper analyses in this area.

Table 1 Categorisation of MCDM in entrepreneurship and start-up literature

No.	Author(s)	Method(s)	Case study	Objective
1	Cheng et al. (2005)	MCDM	Shopping mall	Location
2	Chou (2007)	Fuzzy MCDM	Transhipment	Rank and select the most appropriate container ports
3	Tsai and Kuo (2011)	DEMATEL ANP Zero-one goal programming	SME	Evaluate entrepreneurship policies for SME
4	Mouzakitis et al. (2013)	PROMETHEE	–	Evaluation and ranking companies to invest in
5	Rostamzadeh et al. (2014)	FAHP VIKOR TOPSIS	SME	Evaluate and prioritise the entrepreneurial intensity
6	Żak and Węgliński (2014)	ELECTRE III/IV	–	Select the location for logistic centres
7	Erol et al. (2014)	Fuzzy MCDM	Nuclear power plants	Location
8	Afful-Dadzie et al. (2015)	PROMETHEE	Start-up businesses	Selecting start-ups in GPVCs
9	Jafari-Moghadam et al. (2017)	DEMATEL ANP	Tourism	Prioritise entrepreneurship tourism policy
10	Zečević et al. (2017)	Fuzzy Delphi Fuzzy ANP Fuzzy VIKOR	Intermodal transport terminal	Location
11	C.-N. Wang et al. (2018)	FAHP DEA TOPSIS	Solar power plant	Finding the best location of a power plant
12	Zhao et al. (2019)	DEMATEL DEMATEL-ANP (DANP) VIKOR	Banking industry along with the Fintech new circumstances	Assess strategies of service innovation
13	Nilashi et al. (2019)	DEMATEL Fuzzy TOPSIS	Medical tourism	Prioritise the importance of elements in an organisation
14	Büyüközkan and Güler (2020)	SAW ARAS HFLTS	Smart watch production line	Decide on innovative products
15	Golghamat Raad and Akbarpour Shirazi (2020)	DEMATEL ANP MODM	Entrepreneurial universities	Rank and implement the projects
16	Dhochak and Doliya (2020)	Fuzzy AHP	Evaluation of a new corporate and start-up value	Prioritise the strategic theories

2.2 Factors Influencing Location Selection Problems

Selecting a location for a start-up is a crucial component in the eventual success or failure of the start-up. Location decisions of knowledge-based entrepreneurs and start-ups are influenced by factors that are both internal and external to the firm (Lafuente et al. 2010; Rezaei et al. 2020). There are many specific influencing factors for location selection. Thus, some scholars have analysed or summarised these factors (Table 2). Athawale et al. (2012) proposed a PROMETHEE-II method to solve two real-time facility location selection problems, considering eight factors that affect the facility location selection decisions. Sánchez-Lozano et al. (2013) used geographic information system (GIS), AHP, and TOPSIS to obtain the evaluation of the optimal placement of photovoltaic solar power plants in Spain. First, they evaluated criteria weights by using AHP and GIS. Further, they prioritise sites based on the degree of adequacy using the TOPSIS method. Silva et al. (2014) combined the use of a GIS to manage and process spatial information with the flexibility of multi-criteria decision aid (MCDA) to assess factual information with more subjective information. They used ELECTRE TRI in their analysis. Ray et al. (2015) proposed a hybrid MCDM model with TOPSIS, SAW, GRA, and MOORA to determine the best location of the manufacturing industry. Finally, an outranking MCDM approach (ELECTRE-I) is applied to find an appropriate plant location. Cebi et al. (2016) proposed a hybrid MCDM model for the most appropriate location of biomass power plant location in Turkey, using fuzzy sets, AHP, opinion aggregation method, and Information Axiom method. Finally, the authors performed a sensitivity analysis to show the reliability of the obtained results. Jha et al. (2018) proposed a model based on critical success factors (CSFs) for the selection of sustainable warehouse for Indian chemical industries. They used the interpretive structural modelling (ISM) technique to create interrelationship among the parameters which were defined and also to specify the key criteria with high driving power. Kheybari et al. (2019) proposed a model for a bioethanol production province selection in Iran by using the best-worst method (BWM). Their evaluation framework is proposed based on the three dimensions of sustainability (economic, environmental, and social). Seker and Aydin (2020) applied interval-valued Pythagorean fuzzy (IVPF) method and used fuzzy interval values to overcome the vagueness of human decisions to select the best location for the decomposition plant in Turkey. Amin Moghadasi et al. (2017) and Yücenur et al. (2020) proposed an MCDM model that affects the evaluation of the alternatives to select a suitable city in Turkey for biogas production. SWARA and COPRAS methods are used for selecting an appropriate city to establish a biogas facility. They found that as the use of environmentally friendly energy resources increases, research activities on new energy sources will increase.

Literature review proves that location selection is a complex decision-making problem and existing literature reveals that many criteria affect the optimal location of entrepreneurs and start-ups.

Table 2 The literature review applying MCDM methods for the location selection problem

No.	Author(s)	MCDM method(s)	Industry/sector/area	Criteria
1	Athawale et al. (2012)	PROMETHEE II	Facility location	Cost of land Cost of energy Cost of raw materials Cost of transportation and cost of labour
2	Sánchez-Lozano et al. (2013)	AHP TOPSIS	Photovoltaic solar power plant location	Environmental Orographical Location Climate
3	Silva et al. (2014)	GIS ELECTRE TRI	Biogas plant	Environmental Economic social Social and safety
4	Ray et al. (2015)	TOPSIS SAW GRA MOORA ELECTRE-I	Plant location	Skilled workers Expansion possibility Availability of material Investment cost Risks imposed on the site
5	Cebi et al. (2016)	AHP Opinion aggregation method Information axiom	Biomass power plant	Biomass produced in the region The energy potential of the region Capacities of energy production Setup and operating costs
6	Jha et al. (2018)	ISM	Sustainable warehouse	Energy-saving provisions Strategic geographic location The climate of the region The overall cost of the warehouse Availability of the sustainable skilled workforce Availability of the safety measures Ease of transportation Government policies and regulations Warehouse capacity Availability of the technology Parking facilities
7	Kheybari et al. (2019)	BWM	Bioethanol production	Social Environmental Economic
8	Seker and Aydin (2020)	TOPSIS IVPF	Decomposition plant	Economical Socio-economic Technical Environmental

(continued)

Table 2 (continued)

No.	Author(s)	MCDM method(s)	Industry/sector/area	Criteria
9	Yücenur et al. (2020)	SWARA COPRAS	Biogas production	Distance to the city centre The productivity of the land Profitability Labour costs Transportation costs Investment cost Corrosion Risk of earthquake Risk of terror Selection of raw material Distance to raw material Raw material cost

3 Research Methodology

According to the above, rare researches are focusing on medical tourism start-ups and entrepreneur's location selection problems, considering the key factors effectively. In this regard, the literature review is performed to extract and achieve the appropriate criteria to examine the location alternatives based on applicable and responsive methodologies. For this purpose, this paper aims to employ multi-criteria decision-making methods to make the optimal selection with reasonable features. This paper methodology is proposed as below.

Step 1. Calculation of the weights of criteria and sub-criteria. After literature review and determining the criteria and sub-criteria, it is required to determine the weight of them. The importance of the criteria and sub-criteria is different in the point of view of experts. Therefore, the BWM method is used to determine the weight of the criteria in the decision-making process.

Step 2. Decision matrix establishment. Then, the research team should establish the decision matrix and complete it by gathering data.

Step 3. Normalisation. The matrix consists of different criteria with various units. Therefore, it seems necessary to normalise them and make the criteria units standard. It transforms different data measurement units into a compatible unit. There are several normalisation techniques in which some of them are particularly used in MCDM methods regardless if they are suitable for this method (Chakraborty and Yeh 2007). As this study aims to employ several multi-criteria decision-making methods, it is important to use appropriate normalisation techniques for each method. Therefore, in this step, the linear or nonlinear (Euclidean) normalisation methods following different methods are suggested.

Step 4. Calculation of weighted normalised matrix. In this part, the weights of the criteria and sub-criteria are considered in the decision matrix.

Step 5. Ranking the alternatives. The MCDM methods are employed to prioritise and rank the alternatives based on criteria and sub-criteria.

The used methods for weighting the criteria and ranking the alternatives are introduced in the section.

3.1 BWM

BWM is a new and efficient pairwise comparison-based multi-criteria decision-making method (Mahdiraji et al. 2019). In this method, the best and worst criteria are selected among a specific set of criteria by decision-makers to find consistency radio (CR) and the optimal weights using an optimisation model (Mahdiraji et al. 2019; Mokhtarzadeh et al. 2020). To determine the weights of the criteria using BWM, the following steps should be followed (Rezaei 2015):

1. Determine a set of decision criteria $\{c_1; c_2 \ldots ; c_n\}$.
2. Determine the best (most desirable/important) and the worst (least desirable/important) criteria.
3. Use a number between 1 and 9 to prioritise the best criterion against all the other criteria. The resulting best-to-others vector would be

$$A_B = (a_{B1}, a_{B2}, \ldots, a_{Bn}),$$

where the preference of the best criterion B over criterion j is illustrated by a_{Bj}.

4. Use a number between 1 and 9 to specify the preference of all the other criteria over the worst criterion. The resulting others-to-worst vector would be

$$A_W = (a_{1W}, a_{2W}, \ldots, a_{nW})^T,$$

where a_{jW} illustrates the preference of the criterion j over the worst criterion W.

5. Calculate the optimal weights $(w_1^*; w_2^*; \ldots; w_n^*)$.

The optimal criteria weight can be calculated as one, while for each pair of w_B/w_j and w_j/w_w, we have $w_B/w_j = a_{Bj}$ and $w_j/w_w = a_{jW}$. To meet these conditions for all j, we should recognise a way which minimises the maximum absolute differences $\left|\frac{w_B}{w_j} - a_{Bj}\right|$ and $\left|\frac{w_j}{w_w} - a_{jW}\right|$ for all j. Given the non-negativity and considering sum condition for the weights, the following problem results:

$$\min \max_{j} \left\{ \left| \frac{w_B}{w_j} - a_{Bj} \right|, \left| \frac{w_j}{w_w} - a_{jW} \right| \right\}$$

$$\text{s.t.}$$

$$\sum_j w_j = 1$$

$$w_j \geq 0, \text{for all j} \tag{1}$$

Equation (1) can be transferred into

$$min\xi$$

$$\text{s.t.}$$

$$\left| \frac{w_B}{w_j} - a_{Bj} \right| \leq \xi, \text{for all } j$$

$$\left| \frac{w_j}{w_w} - a_{jW} \right| \leq \xi, \text{for all } j$$

$$\text{s.t.}$$

$$\sum_j^n w_j = 1$$

$$w_j \geq 0, \text{for all } j \tag{2}$$

The optimal weights and ξ can be calculated by solving the model (Rezaei 2015).

4 MCDM Methods' Steps

In this study, to compare the results of different decision-making methods and selecting the most suitable location, four various MCDM methods including TOPSIS, VIKOR, WASPAS, and SAW are used (see Fig. 2). As multi-criteria methods results are satisfying than optimal (Ramesh and Zionts 2001), therefore, it seems essential to perform a comparison of results obtained by different methods. In this part, we illustrate these methods briefly to provide more information.

4.1 TOPSIS

TOPSIS was proposed by Chen and Hwang (1992), concerning Hwang and Yoon (1981) to determine the best alternative based on the concepts of the compromise

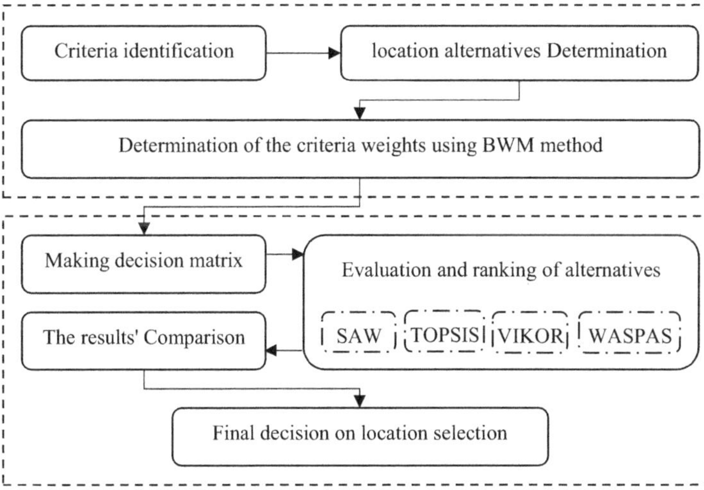

Fig. 2 Decision-making process by proposed methods and selection of the best alternative

solution. It is one of the well-known and widely used MADM techniques (Jahanshahloo et al. 2006). In this method, the selected solution is the alternative that simultaneously is near to the positive ideal solution (PIS) and far from the negative ideal solution (NIS) (Wang and Lee 2009). Each alternative with a greater closeness coefficient has higher priority (Taghavifard et al. 2018). This method is performed in steps as illustrated in Box 1.

Box 1 TOPSIS Algorithm (Hwang and Yoon 1981)

– Establishing an evaluation matrix $D[\mathrm{x_{ij}}]_{m \times n}$ involving m alternatives and n criteria. $\mathrm{x_{ij}}$ indicates the amount of alternative i in criterion j.

$$D = [\mathrm{x_{ij}}]$$

– Vector normalisation of the decision variables:

$$\mathrm{r_{ij}(x)} = \frac{\mathrm{x_{ij}}}{\sqrt{\sum_{\mathrm{i=1}}^{\mathrm{m}} \mathrm{x_{ij}^2}}} \tag{3}$$

– Calculation of the weighted normalised matrix:

(continued)

Box 1 (continued)

$$v_{ij}(x) = w_j r_{ij}(x), i = 1, \ldots, m; j = 1, \ldots, n.$$

- Determination of the positive ideal (PIS) and negative ideal (NIS) solutions:

$$\begin{aligned} PIS &= \left(v_1^+, v_2^+, \ldots, v_j^+, \ldots, v_n^+\right) \\ &= \left\{\left(\max_i v_{ij}(x) | j \in j_1\right), \left(\min_i v_{ij}(x) | j \in j_2\right) | i = 1, \ldots, m\right\}, \end{aligned}$$

$$\begin{aligned} NIS &= \left(v_1^-, v_2^-, \ldots, v_j^-, \ldots, v_n^-\right) \\ &= \left\{\left(\min_i v_{ij}(x) | j \in j_1\right), \left(\max_i v_{ij}(x) | j \in j_2\right) | i = 1, \ldots, m\right\}, \end{aligned}$$

- Calculation of the distance of each alternative from positive ideal solution:

$$d_i^+ = \sqrt{\sum_{j=1}^{n} \left(v_{ij}(x) - v_j^+(x)\right)^2}, i = 1, 2, \ldots, m \tag{4}$$

- Calculation of the distance of each alternative from negative ideal solution:

$$d_i^- = \sqrt{\sum_{j=1}^{n} \left(v_{ij}(x) - v_j^-(x)\right)^2}, i = 1, 2, \ldots, m. \tag{5}$$

- Calculation of the closeness coefficient of each alternative CC_i:

$$CC_i = \frac{d_i^-}{d_i^- + d_i^+}, i = 1, 2, \ldots, m. \tag{6}$$

4.2 VIKOR

The VIKOR method was developed as a multi-criteria decision-making method to solve discrete decision problems (Opricovic and Tzeng 2004). VIKOR focuses on selecting and ranking a set of alternatives to determine compromise solutions for a problem with conflicting criteria (Opricovic and Tzeng 2007). This method can maximise advantages for a large group while it minimises losses for the "opponent" (Opricovic 1998). The compromise ranking algorithm VIKOR is illustrated in Box 2.

Box 2 VIKOR Algorithm

– Determination of the most desirable and undesirable values:

$$f_j^* = \max_j f_{ij}, i = 1, 2, \ldots, m$$

$$f_j^- = \min_j f_{ij}, i = 1, 2, \ldots, m$$

where the most desirable value is f_j^* and the most undesirable value is f_j^-.

– Computing the distance between alternatives and ideal solution:

$$S_i = \sum_{j=1}^{n} w_j \left(f_j^* - f_{ij} \right) / \left(f_j^* - f_j^- \right) \tag{7}$$

$$R_i = \max_j \left[w_j \left(f_j^* - f_{ij} \right) / \left(f_j^* - f_j^- \right) \right] \tag{8}$$

- where S_i indicates the distance rate of the alternative i to the PIS (best combination) and R_i shows the distance rate of the alternative i to the NIS (worst combination)
- Calculation of Q_i:

$$Q_i = v \left[\frac{S_i - S^*}{S^- - S^*} \right] + (1 - v) \left[\frac{R_i - R^*}{R^- - R^*} \right] \tag{9}$$

- where $S^- = \max_i S_i, S^* = \min_i S_i$, $R^- = \max_i R_i, R^* = \min_i$, R_i and v indicates the weight of the approach of "the most of criteria" (or "the maximum advantages for a large group")
- Ranking of the alternatives based on Q_i, S_i and R_i values ascending. It leads to three ranking lists.

(continued)

Box 2 (continued)

- Then, the following two conditions should be considered:

Alternative *á* is the best compromising solution following these conditions for the measure Q (minimum):

C1. "Acceptable advantage":

$$Q(a'') - Q(a') \gg DQ \tag{10}$$

Here a'' is ranked as the second option by Q considering: $DQ = 1/(J - 1)$; J indicates the number of alternatives.

C2. "Acceptable stability in decision-making":

It is supposed that alternative a' is ranked as the best according to S, R, or one of them. This will be a stable compromise solution during the decision-making procedure, with $v > 0.5$ as the rule of voting by majority or reaching consensus with $v \approx 0.5$ or $v < 0.5$ as ignoring vote. According to what is mentioned above, v can be considered as the weight of decision policy "the most of criteria" or maximum advantages for a large group.

If one of those conditions is not fulfilled, it is proposed that:

- Alternatives a' and a'' are compromise solutions if condition C2 is the only unfulfilled condition.
- Alternatives $a', a'', \ldots a^{(M)}$ are compromise solutions if C1 is not met; and $a^{(M)}$ can be specified by $Q(a^{(M)}) - Q(a') < DQ$ for maximum M (the closeness is the base for decision-making).

Ranking based on Q determines the lowest value of Q as the best alternative. This ranking list leads to the compromise solution considering the "benefit rate".

4.3 WASPAS

The WASPAS algorithm is an optimal search algorithm based on two optimisation procedures known as the weighted sum model (WSM) and the weighted product model (WPM). This technique is introduced by Zavadskas et al. (2012). This method provides the highest accuracy to estimate in the optimisation of weighted aggregated function. It has been successfully applied in location selection problems (Zavadskas et al. 2014). The calculation method of WASPAS is illustrated in Box 3.

Box 3 WAPAS Algorithm (Zavadskas et al. 2012)

– Linear normalisation of the decision variables:

$$r_{ij} = \begin{cases} \dfrac{x_{ij}}{Max(x_{ij})} & \textit{for a benefit criteria} \\ \dfrac{Min(x_{ij})}{x_{ij}} & \textit{for cost criteria} \end{cases} \tag{11}$$

Determination of the total relative importance of the alternative i following WSM:

$$Q_i^{(1)} = \sum_{j=1}^{n} r_{ij} w_j \tag{12}$$

– Determination of the total relative importance of the alternative i following WPM:

$$Q_i^{(2)} = \prod_{j=1}^{n} (r_{ij})^{w_j} \tag{13}$$

– Calculation of the joint generalised criterion for weighted aggregation:

$$Q_k = \lambda Q_i^{(1)} + (1-\lambda) Q_i^{(2)} = \lambda \sum_{j=1}^{n} r_{ij} w_j + (1-\lambda) \prod_{j=1}^{n} (r_{ij})^{w_j} \tag{14}$$

4.4 SAW

The simple additive weighting (SAW) method is generally known as the weighted summing method. This method aims to find the weighted sum of performance ratings on each alternative on all attributes (Nurmalini and Rahim 2017; Afshari et al. 2010). The calculation method of SAW is illustrated in Box 4.

Box 4 SAW Algorithm

– Linear normalisation of the decision variables as seen in (11)
– Determining the weights of criteria
– Calculate V_i:

(continued)

Box 4 (continued)

$$V_i = \sum_{j-1}^{n} = 1\, w_j\, r_{ij} \tag{15}$$

5 The Case Study

The low cost of surgeries and medical treatments in Iranian hospitals and healthcare centres compared to other countries makes it attractive for medical tourists. It goes back to 2003 that the Iran Ministry of Health and Medical Education paid attention to medical tourism significantly for the first time, and it became important in 2004 as a separate health industry (Rezaee and Mohammadzadeh 2016).

In addition to many Iranian attractive opportunities in the field of medical tourism such as the reasonable price with an acceptable level of medical treatment quality, there are many approximately well-equipped hospitals and medical centres that are significantly increasing these years. Along with the mentioned advantages for attracting medical tourists, it is worth mentioning the geopolitical location of Iran with vast borders and historical background which includes various climates (Rezaee and Mohammadzadeh 2016) and can help tourists to take a journey all year round and even use the holidays for medical treatments in mild weather. In this regard, many companies are trying to achieve more market share in the medical tourism industry using IT infrastructures and communication technologies to reduce the costs and increase the availability of foreign medical treatment applicants. Accordingly, IT-based businesses and start-ups benefit more due to fewer assets and more agility. Therefore, they should find the most appropriate location to minimise the costs and maximise the accessibility and benefits. For this purpose, the TMT group is going to set up a start-up to manage medical surgeries for foreigners and tourists from all around the world. As they are experienced in plastic surgery, it is reasonable to target this service for more medical tourists. Thus, they have to decide about the city for the location of the central office to manage their services in five zones of the country: North-west, Centre, North-east, West, and South branch of Iran. Figure 3 shows the location of these alternatives.

In this regard, the research team identified a group of criteria and categorised them into three categories based on literature review and finalised them as demonstrated in Table 3; and then the TMT founder and colleagues as expert people implied their opinion about the importance of each criterion on "health tourism start-up's location selection" process using 5-point Likert scale, a type of categorised response that helps responders to imply their level of agreement based on typically five points:

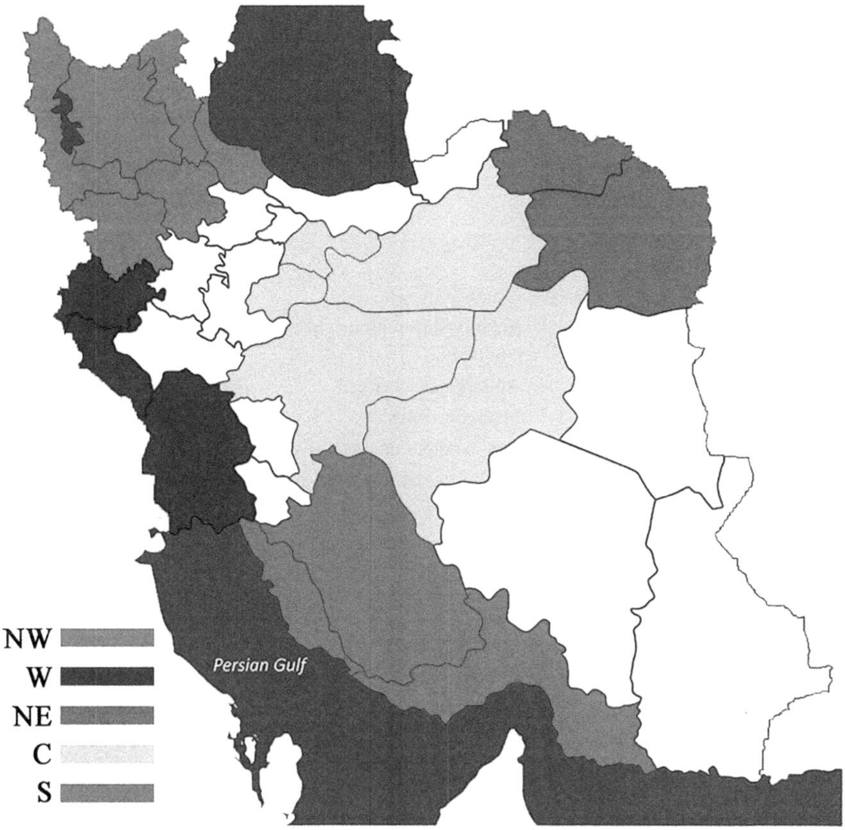

Fig. 3 Alternatives for medical tourism *start-up* location in Iran

1. Strongly disagree
2. Disagree
3. Neither agree nor disagree
4. Agree
5. Strongly agree (Preedy and Watson 2010)

Step 1. Calculation of the weights of criteria and sub-criteria. Considering experts' opinions, the weights of the criteria are calculated using the BWM method. As the criteria include three levels, the method is employed to calculate the weight in the level of criteria, sub-criteria level 2 and level 3 using Eqs. (1) and (2). To reach a consensus, experts' opinions should be aggregated. For this purpose, the average of the scores assigned to the criteria is calculated. This is illustrated in Table 4.

To determine the best location for the medical tourism start-up, we evaluated five alternatives based on three dimensions. Table 5 shows the weight of those three dimensions. The column of CR is the consistency ratio of pairwise comparisons. According to experts' opinion, the economic dimension is the most important, followed by social and environmental dimensions.

Table 3 The criteria resulted from the literature review and experts' opinion

Categories	Criteria	Sub-criteria	Experts' opinion No. 1	No. 2	No. 3	No. 4
Economical	Investment costs	–	5	3	5	5
	Operation costs	–	4	4	3	5
	Profitability	–	5	4	5	3
	Labour costs	–	5	2	2	3
Social	Social acceptance	–	5	5	4	2
	Government laws and policies	Issuance of visa	2	4	2	3
		Relationship with origin countries	5	4	2	2
		Authorised services	5	5	1	2
		Insurance rules	2	2	1	1
		Tax exemptions, incentives	5	4	5	1
	Language and communication	Health tourist language support	5	4	4	2
		Contract	5	4	5	3
		Transportation agencies	4	4	3	4
		Accommodation facilities	5	5	3	–
	Specialists	–	5	3	5	3
	Market features	Market attractiveness	3	5	3	2
		Market share	3	3	3	2
		Market growth	3	4	3	4
		Barriers to competitors entry and exit of the market	2	4	2	4
Technologic	Efficient information systems	Access to medical tourism information resource and networks	3	2	5	3
		Related ecosystems, accelerators, and incubator	4	3	5	3
	Medical technology	Access to healthcare	4	5	3	3
		Medical specialties	4	5	–	3
	Appropriate Internet infrastructures	Quality of Internet service	5	3	5	2
		Quality of transportation system	3	4	3	2
		Hotels and accommodation	3	4	3	3

Tables 6, 7, and 8 demonstrate the weights of sub-criteria of the three categories economic, social, and technologic level 2 respectively. As shown in Table 6, investment costs were identified as the most important factor in the economic category.

The weights of sub-criteria for social dimension are presented in Table 7, the specialist was selected as the most important sub-criteria, and this is due to the need of start-up enterprises for knowledge and skills (Jafari-Sadeghi et al. 2019b). The Islamic Republic of Iran combines factors of democracy with an Islamic theocracy. Hence, business activities of Iranian firms should be Shariah (Islamic law) compliant

Table 4 Experts' opinion to calculate criteria weights

Criteria	Aggregated scores
Investment costs	4.50
Operation costs	4.00
Profitability	4.25
Labour costs	3.00
Social acceptance	4.00
Government laws and policies	2.90
Language and communication	3.93
Specialists	4.00
Market features	3.12
Efficient information systems	3.50
Medical technology	3.75
Appropriate Internet infrastructures	3.33

Table 5 The weight of categories

Criteria	Weight	Rank	CR
Economic	0.5	1	0.1
Social	0.3	2	
Technologic	0.2	3	

Table 6 Sub-criteria weight for economic dimension in level 2

Sub-criteria	Weight	Rank	CR
Investment costs	0.452	1	0.129
Operation costs	0.194	3	
Profitability	0.290	2	
Labour costs	0.065	4	

Table 7 Sub-criteria weight for social dimension in level 2

Sub-criteria	Weight	Rank	CR
Social acceptance	0.302	2	0.075
Government laws and policies	0.038	5	
Language and communication	0.189	3	
Specialists	0.377	1	
Market features	0.094	4	

Table 8 Sub-criteria weight for technologic dimension in level 2

Sub-criteria	Weight	Rank	CR
Efficient information systems	0.292	2	0.041
Appropriate internet infrastructures	0.542	1	
Medical technology	0.167	3	

(Jafari Sadeghi and Biancone 2017) which is the same all around the country and could be the reason that government law and policies were indicated as the least important factor.

The weights of the sub-criteria level 2 for the technologic dimension are presented in Table 8. Appropriate Internet infrastructures were identified by the

Table 9 Sub-criteria weight for social dimension in level 3

Category	Sub-criteria	Weight	Rank	CR
Social acceptance	–	0.302	–	–
Policy and legal support	Issuance of visa	0.137	4	0.041
	Relationship with origin countries	0.205	2	
	Authorised services	0.205	2	
	Insurance rules	0.082	5	
	Tax exemptions, incentives	0.370	1	
Language and communication	Health tourist language support	0.088	4	0.066
	Contract	0.288	2	
	Transportation agencies	0.115	3	
	Accommodation facilities	0.509	1	
Specialists	–	0.377	–	–
Market features	Market attractiveness	0.259	2	0.051
	Market share	0.103	4	
	Market growth	0.172	3	
	Barriers to competitor's entry and exit of the market	0.466	1	

Table 10 Sub-criteria weight for technologic dimension in level 3

Category	Sub-criteria	Weight	Rank	CR
Efficient information systems	Access to medical tourism information resource and networks	0.333	2	–
	Related ecosystems, accelerators, and incubator	0.667	1	
Medical technology	Access to healthcare	0.333	2	–
	Medical specialties	0.667	1	
Appropriate Internet infrastructure	Quality of Internet service	0.542	1	0.041
	Quality of transportation system	0.167	3	
	Hotels and accommodation	0.292	2	

experts as being the most influential factor in the technologic category. It concurs with previous findings illustrating the importance of "Internetisation" (i.e. the firm's ability to adopt Internet-based technologies) for entrepreneurs (Etemad et al. 2010).

Then, the weights of sub-criteria level 3 of social and technologic criteria are calculated through the BWM method as shown in Tables 9 and 10.

According to the experts, the barriers to competitors' entry and exit of the market is the most important criterion in market features; to enter a new market and achieve a position in a severely competitive market, start-up enterprises must have a good product or service strategy (Tien et al. 2020).

Based on the tables above, the overall weights of sub-criteria are calculated in Table 11 to provide an appropriate situation for deciding about five zones as the decision alternatives through considering the weights overall.

Table 11 The overall weights of sub-criteria

Row	Code	Sub-criteria	Weight	Rank
1	C11	Investment costs	0.226	1
2	C12	Operation costs	0.097	4
3	C13	Profitability	0.145	2
4	C14	Labour costs	0.032	9
5	C21	Social acceptance	0.060	6
6	C221	Issuance of visa	0.001	25
7	C222	Relationship with origin countries	0.002	23
8	C223	Authorised services	0.002	23
9	C224	Insurance rules	0.001	26
10	C225	Tax exemptions, incentives	0.003	21
11	C231	Health tourist language support	0.003	19
12	C232	Contract	0.011	14
13	C233	Transportation agencies	0.004	18
14	C234	Accommodation facilities	0.019	12
15	C24	Specialists	0.075	5
16	C251	Market attractiveness	0.005	17
17	C252	Market share	0.002	22
18	C253	Market growth	0.003	20
19	C254	Barriers to competitor's entry and exit of the market	0.009	15
20	C311	Access to medical tourism information resource and networks	0.029	10
21	C312	Related ecosystems, accelerators, and incubator	0.058	7
22	C321	Health services	0.054	8
23	C322	Medical specialties	0.108	3
24	C331	Quality of Internet service	0.027	11
25	C332	Quality of transportation system	0.008	16
26	C333	Hotels and accommodation	0.015	13

Step 2. Decision matrix establishment. Following the sub criteria weight calculation, the decision matrix is established in Table 12 to be considered as the basis for multiple decision-making methods. This matrix is completed using the recent and valid data and information at the Statistical Centre of Iran website.

Step 3. Normalisation. In this part, the matrix should be normalised; while various normalisation techniques are suitable for different methods, this step is performed using linear normalisation technique (Eq. 11) for SAW and WASPAS methods and nonlinear technique (Euclidean) (Eq. 3) for TOPSIS method. The results of linear normalisation are illustrated in Table 13.

Table 14 shows the nonlinear (Euclidean) normalisation technique results.

Step 4. Calculation of weighted normalised matrix. In this part, the importance of criteria and sub-criteria is considered as a weighted normalised matrix. As there are two types of normalisation matrices in this research, the weighted normalised matrices for linear normalisation and Euclidean normalisation are shown in Tables 15 and 16, respectively.

Table 12 The decision matrix of five alternatives regarding each criterion

Criteria	Unit	North-west	West	North-east	Centre	South
C11	$	60,135	45,611	44,455	316,953	89,776
C12	$	53,122	41,133	21,030	93,425	53,980
C13	$	10,795	7652	4738	9688	18,505
C14	$	195,581	151,616	217,098	750,215	238,056
C21	5-point Likert scale	4	3	2	5	5
C221	5-point Likert scale	4	4	2	1	2
C222	5-point Likert scale	5	4	1	5	2
C223	5-point Likert scale	5	4	1	2	4
C224	5-point Likert scale	3	2	5	3	4
C225	5-point Likert scale	4	4	5	1	5
C231	5-point Likert scale	5	5	1	5	4
C232	5-point Likert scale	4	5	4	5	5
C233	$	83	190	312	742	411
C234	$	319	695	402	2108	1570
C24	$	5620	4212	3008	12,482	7661
C251	5-point Likert scale	4	4	2	5	5
C252	5-point Likert scale	5	4	4	1	5
C253	5-point Likert scale	3	3	2	4	2
C254	5-point Likert scale	2	2	3	4	3
C311	5-point Likert scale	3	3	3	5	4
C312	5-point Likert scale	2	2	2	5	4
C321	5-point Likert scale	4	4	3	5	5
C322	5-point Likert scale	3	3	2	5	5
C331	5-point Likert scale	2	2	2	5	4
C332	5-point Likert scale	3	3	2	5	4
C333	5-point Likert scale	3	2	2	5	4

Step 5. Ranking the alternatives. In this section, the above calculations are employed in MCDM methods to prioritise and rank the five zones of the country to locate the central office of the TMT medical tourism company. At first, the TOPSIS method is used and its results are presented in Table 17.

Then, the VIKOR method is employed and the results are shown in Table 18.

SAW method as a scoring MCDM method is used to prioritise and rank the locations as the decision alternatives. Its results are shown in Table 19.

Finally, the WASPAS method is employed to rank five-country zones to solve the medical tourism start-up location problem. The result is in Table 20.

The results obtained by TOPSIS, VIKOR, WASPAS, and SAW methods are presented in Table 21.

As can be seen, the results of different methods emphasise on South of the country as the most appropriate zone for the location of medical tourism start-up. Also, the majority implies the Centre of the country is considered as the least desirable zone for this purpose.

Table 13 Normalisation results for linear normalisation technique matrix of five alternatives

Criteria	North-west	West	North-east	Centre	South
C11	0.739	0.975	1	0.140	0.495
C12	0.396	0.511	1	0.225	0.390
C13	0.583	0.414	0.256	0.524	1
C14	0.775	1	0.698	0.202	0.637
C21	0.8	0.6	0.4	1	1
C221	1	1	0.5	0.25	0.5
C222	1	0.8	0.2	1	0.4
C223	1	0.8	0.2	0.4	0.8
C224	0.6	0.4	1	0.6	0.8
C225	0.8	0.8	1	0.2	1
C231	1	1	0.2	1	0.8
C232	0.8	1	0.8	1	1
C233	0.112	0.256	0.420	1	0.554
C234	0.151	0.330	0.191	1	0.745
C24	0.450	0.337	0.241	1	0.614
C251	0.8	0.8	0.4	1	1
C252	1	0.8	0.8	0.2	1
C253	0.75	0.75	0.5	1	0.5
C254	1	1	0.667	0.5	0.667
C311	0.6	0.6	0.6	1	0.8
C312	0.4	0.4	0.4	1	0.8
C321	0.8	0.8	0.6	1	1
C322	0.6	0.6	0.4	1	1
C331	0.739	0.975	1	0.140	0.495
C332	0.396	0.511	1	0.225	0.390
C333	0.583	0.414	0.256	0.524	1

6 Conclusion

The gradual revolution in business models and the emergence of start-ups in various industries and services, and the lucrative and high turnover of this type of business have caused the youth generation tendency to this direction. Despite the start-up's advantages, there are many traps to failure. One of the most effective concepts on failure and success is correct decision-making on different dimensions of a start-up business model. The location selection as an expensive dimension should be considered very carefully due to its conflict criteria. For this purpose, decision-making on location is met as a multiple-criteria problem.

In this research, the location selection for a medical tourism start-up is considered as a multi-criteria decision-making problem because the business should select a county and zone to locate to reduce the costs and increase the turnover. For this purpose, we identified the important criteria that could affect the location of a medical tourism start-up, by reviewing related literature; finally, 26 criteria were selected to evaluate the alternatives. The five zones of the country are considered as

Table 14 Normalisation results for nonlinear normalisation (Euclidean) technique matrix of five alternatives

Criteria	North-west	West	North-east	Centre	South
C11	0.167	0.220	0.226	0.032	0.112
C12	0.038	0.049	0.097	0.022	0.038
C13	0.085	0.060	0.037	0.076	0.145
C14	0.025	0.032	0.023	0.007	0.021
C21	0.048	0.036	0.024	0.060	0.060
C221	0.001	0.001	0.001	0.000	0.001
C222	0.002	0.001	0.000	0.002	0.001
C223	0.002	0.001	0.000	0.001	0.001
C224	0.000	0.000	0.001	0.000	0.000
C225	0.002	0.002	0.003	0.001	0.003
C231	0.003	0.003	0.001	0.003	0.003
C232	0.009	0.011	0.009	0.011	0.011
C233	0.000	0.001	0.002	0.004	0.002
C234	0.003	0.006	0.004	0.019	0.014
C24	0.034	0.025	0.018	0.075	0.046
C251	0.004	0.004	0.002	0.005	0.005
C252	0.002	0.002	0.002	0.000	0.002
C253	0.002	0.002	0.002	0.003	0.002
C254	0.009	0.009	0.006	0.004	0.006
C311	0.018	0.018	0.018	0.029	0.023
C312	0.023	0.023	0.023	0.058	0.047
C321	0.043	0.043	0.033	0.054	0.054
C322	0.065	0.065	0.043	0.108	0.108
C331	0.011	0.011	0.011	0.027	0.022
C332	0.005	0.005	0.003	0.008	0.007
C333	0.009	0.006	0.006	0.015	0.012

location alternatives. An online survey is used to collect expert points of view; they scored these alternatives to indicate the importance of the criteria. Then, these zones are ranked by MCDM methods As MCDM methods do not provide the optimum result, therefore, the research team decided to run several methods to compare the results and make the final selection.

In this paper, TOPSIS, SAW, VIKOR, and WASPAS are used and their results are compared; the comparison shows that most of the methods rank South of the country as the most suitable zone for this start-up and Centre and North-east of the country as the most inappropriate sections.

Theoretical conclusion. The MCDM methods do not prepare a situation which leads to the optimum response; therefore, the research team decided to use multiple methods to reach comparable results and select the response based on the most appropriate response in more methods. For this purpose, to consider the importance of criteria, BWM method is used to calculate the weights of criteria. This method is suitable to do the pairwise comparison and determine the weights of criteria and sub-criteria. Therefore, the weights are highly reliable and accepted. On the other

Table 15 The weighted normalisation results for linear normalisation technique matrix of five alternatives

Criteria	North-west	West	North-east	Centre	South
C11	0.167	0.220	0.226	0.032	0.112
C12	0.038	0.049	0.097	0.022	0.038
C13	0.085	0.060	0.037	0.076	0.145
C14	0.025	0.032	0.023	0.007	0.021
C21	0.048	0.036	0.024	0.060	0.060
C221	0.001	0.001	0.001	0.000	0.001
C222	0.002	0.001	0.000	0.002	0.001
C223	0.002	0.001	0.000	0.001	0.001
C224	0.000	0.000	0.001	0.000	0.000
C225	0.002	0.002	0.003	0.001	0.003
C231	0.003	0.003	0.001	0.003	0.003
C232	0.009	0.011	0.009	0.011	0.011
C233	0.000	0.001	0.002	0.004	0.002
C234	0.003	0.006	0.004	0.019	0.014
C24	0.034	0.025	0.018	0.075	0.046
C251	0.004	0.004	0.002	0.005	0.005
C252	0.002	0.002	0.002	0.000	0.002
C253	0.002	0.002	0.002	0.003	0.002
C254	0.009	0.009	0.006	0.004	0.006
C311	0.018	0.018	0.018	0.029	0.023
C312	0.023	0.023	0.023	0.058	0.047
C321	0.043	0.043	0.033	0.054	0.054
C322	0.065	0.065	0.043	0.108	0.108
C331	0.011	0.011	0.011	0.027	0.022
C332	0.005	0.005	0.003	0.008	0.007
C333	0.009	0.006	0.006	0.015	0.012

hand, using four multi-criteria decision-making methods leads to comparable results and more dependable response.

Managerial conclusion. Deciding start-ups seems approximately different from traditional business companies. According to very restricted resources in the initial steps of start-ups, it is so important to plan and organise the business elements with regard to cost reduction and high productivity. The location of the central office includes a significant part of the investment. Therefore, the managerial team tends to minimise it through correct decision-making. In this regard, they need to use various criteria to comprehensively review the situations and select the most suitable zone for selection. Here, the criteria are divided into three categories and sub-criteria into two levels which are adapted from the literature review and cover the selection situations.

Practical conclusion. Although, there are many types of research on location selection; it is rarely seen for start-up location, while the criteria and their weights for location selection can be remarkably different due to the start-up nature and business

Table 16 The weighted normalisation results for nonlinear normalisation (Euclidean) technique matrix of five alternatives

Criteria	North-west	West	North-east	Centre	South
C11	0.040	0.030	0.029	0.210	0.059
C12	0.040	0.031	0.016	0.070	0.041
C13	0.062	0.044	0.027	0.056	0.107
C14	0.007	0.006	0.008	0.028	0.009
C21	0.027	0.020	0.014	0.034	0.034
C221	0.001	0.001	0.000	0.000	0.000
C222	0.001	0.001	0.000	0.001	0.000
C223	0.001	0.001	0.000	0.000	0.001
C224	0.000	0.000	0.000	0.000	0.000
C225	0.001	0.001	0.002	0.000	0.002
C231	0.002	0.002	0.000	0.002	0.001
C232	0.004	0.005	0.004	0.005	0.005
C233	0.000	0.001	0.001	0.003	0.002
C234	0.002	0.005	0.003	0.015	0.011
C24	0.026	0.019	0.014	0.057	0.035
C251	0.002	0.002	0.001	0.003	0.003
C252	0.001	0.001	0.001	0.000	0.001
C253	0.002	0.002	0.001	0.002	0.001
C254	0.003	0.003	0.004	0.005	0.004
C311	0.011	0.011	0.011	0.018	0.014
C312	0.016	0.016	0.016	0.040	0.032
C321	0.023	0.023	0.017	0.028	0.028
C322	0.038	0.038	0.026	0.064	0.064
C331	0.007	0.007	0.007	0.019	0.015
C332	0.003	0.003	0.002	0.005	0.004
C333	0.006	0.004	0.004	0.010	0.008

Table 17 The closeness coefficient and rank of five alternatives by the TOPSIS method

Alternative	d_i^+	d_i^-	CC_i	Rank
North-west	0.073	0.179	0.710586	2
West	0.086	0.187	0.685795	3
North-east	0.106	0.190	0.642399	4
Centre	0.197	0.075	0.276867	5
South	0.046	0.182	0.797839	1

Table 18 The S_i, R_i, Q_i, rankings, and the compromise solution of five alternatives by VIKOR method (for $\nu = \mathbf{0.5}$)

	N-W	W	N-E	C	Ranking	Compromise solution
S_i	0.482	0.081	0.281	3	S ≻ C ≻ NW ≻ W ≻ NE	S
R_i	0.507	0.114	0.388	4	S ≻ NW ≻ W ≻ NE ≻ C	S
Q_i	0.637	0.145	0.553	5	S ≻ NW ≻ W ≻ NE ≻ C	S

Table 19 The score and ranks of five alternatives by SAW method

Alternative	Score	Rank
North-west	0.610	4
West	0.639	2
North-east	0.592	5
Centre	0.626	3
South	0.745	1

Table 20 Rankings of five alternatives by the WASPAS method

Alternative	$Q_i^{(1)}$	$Q_i^{(2)}$	Q_k ($\lambda = 0.5$)	Rank
North-west	0.610	0.582	0.596	3
West	0.639	0.594	0.616	2
North-east	0.592	0.510	0.551	4
Centre	0.626	0.472	0.549	5
South	0.745	0.705	0.725	1

Table 21 Rankings of five alternatives by different methods

Alternative	TOPSIS	VIKOR S	VIKOR R	VIKOR Q	WASPAS	SAW
North-west	2	3	2	2	3	4
West	3	4	3	3	2	2
North-east	4	5	4	4	4	5
Centre	5	2	5	5	5	3
South	1	1	1	1	1	1

Methods		Ranking
TOPSIS		S ≻ NW ≻ W ≻ NE ≻ C
VIKOR	S_i	S ≻ C ≻ NW ≻ W ≻ NE
	R_i	S ≻ NW ≻ W ≻ NE ≻ C
	Q_i	S ≻ NW ≻ W ≻ NE ≻ C
WASPAS	$Q_i^{(1)}$	S ≻ W ≻ C ≻ NW ≻ NE
	$Q_i^{(2)}$	S ≻ W ≻ NW ≻ NE ≻ C
	Q_k	S ≻ W ≻ NW ≻ NE ≻ C
SAW		S ≻ W ≻ NW ≻ NE ≻ C

model. Therefore, many start-up founders can use the criteria and rely on these results for decision-making on location for their early-stage businesses.

Limitations. The research is performed based on quantitative measures, and also the data is estimated for each zone, while the accurate data for each city in these zones is more desirable. As it was a costly and time-consuming procedure, the managers preferred to save time and perform the research process economically.

Future studies. The literature review indicates very few researches on medical tourism start-up location, and it seems necessary for founders to avoid waste of resources; therefore, future researches can concentrate on more qualitative and quantitative criteria and also consider ambiguity and uncertainty using non-determinant data.

Acknowledgement This research was partially supported by TebMedTourism Company and Safiran Salamat Co.

References

Afful-Dadzie E, Oplatkova ZK, Nabareseh S, Senkeřík R (2015) Selecting start-up businesses in a public venture capital with intuitionistic fuzzy TOPSIS. Lect Notes Eng Comput Sci 2219:471–476

Afshari A, Mojahed M, Yusuff R (2010) Simple additive weighting approach to personnel selection problem. Int J Innov Manag Technol 1(5):511–515

Ahmed Z, Yeasmeen F (2016) First world healthcare by third world provider: position of Bangladesh. J Health Sci Res 1(2):29–33

Amin Moghadasi M, Derakhshandeh B, Ferdosi M, Jafari Sadeghi V (2017) Organizational conformity as an entrepreneurial response to the changes in internationalization process: a study of IT-oriented firms in Saveh. World J Account Financ Eng 1(1):53–64

Athawale VM, Chatterjee P, Chakraborty S (2012) Decision making for facility location selection using PROMETHEE II method. Int J Ind Syst Eng 11(1–2):16–30

Beheshti M, Mahdiraji HA, Zavadskas EK (2016) Strategy portfolio optimisation: a copras g-modm hybrid approach. Transform Bus Econ 15(3C):500–519

Berdine G (2019) Medical tourism. Southwest Resp Crit Chronicles 7(28):53–54

Biancone PP, Jafari Sadeghi V (2016) Risk Management in Export Compliance: concepts, procedures, and solutions. In: Cantino V, De Vincentiis P, Racca MG (eds) Risk management: perspectives and open issues. McGraw-Hill, London, pp 64–78

Büyüközkan G, Güler M (2020) Smart watch evaluation with integrated hesitant fuzzy linguistic SAW-ARAS technique. Meas J Int Meas Confederation:107353

Cader HA, Leatherman JC (2011) Small business survival and sample selection bias. Small Bus Econ 37(2):155–165

Cebi S, Ilbahar E, Atasoy A (2016) A fuzzy information axiom based method to determine the optimal location for a biomass power plant: a case study in Aegean region of Turkey. Energy 116:894–907

Chakraborty S, Yeh C-H (2007) A simulation based comparative study of normalization procedures in multiattribute decision making. Proceedings of the 6th Conference on 6th WSEAS Int Conf on Artificial Intelligence, Knowledge Engineering and Data Bases 6:102–109

Chen S-J, Hwang C-L (1992) Fuzzy multiple attribute decision making methods. In: Fuzzy multiple attribute decision making. Springer, Berlin, pp 289–486

Cheng EWL, Li H, Yu L (2005) The analytic network process (ANP) approach to location selection: a shopping mall illustration. Constr Innov 5(2):83–97

Chou CC (2007) A fuzzy MCDM method for solving marine transshipment container port selection problems. Appl Math Comput 186(1):435–444

Connell J (2006) Medical tourism: sea, sun, sand and . . . Surgery. Tour Manag 27(6):1093–1100

Dalen JE, Alpert JS (2019) Medical tourists: incoming and outgoing. Am J Med 132(1):9–10

Dana L-P, Gurău C, Hoy F, Ramadani V, Alexander T (2021) Success factors and challenges of grassroots innovations: learning from failure. Technol Forecast Soc Chang: 164(C):119600

Devi K, Yadav SP (2013) A multicriteria intuitionistic fuzzy group decision making for plant location selection with ELECTRE method. Int J Adv Manuf Technol 66:1219–1229

Dhochak M, Doliya P (2020) Valuation of a startup: moving towards strategic approaches. J Multi-Criteria Decis Anal 27(2):1–11

Erol I, Sencer S, Özmen A, Searcy C (2014) Fuzzy MCDM framework for locating a nuclear power plant in Turkey. Energy Policy 67:186–197

Etemad H, Wilkinson I, Dana LP (2010) Internetization as the necessary condition for internationalization in the newly emerging economy. J Int Entrep 8(4):319–342

Felzensztein C, Deans KR, Dana L (2019) Small firms in regional clusters: local networks and internationalization in the southern hemisphere. J Small Bus Manag 57(2):496–516

Fetscherin M, Stephano RM (2016) The medical tourism index: scale development and validation. Tour Manag 52:539–556

Golghamat Raad N, Akbarpour Shirazi M (2020) A project portfolio selection framework for transforming Iranian universities into entrepreneurial institutions. J Ind Univ Collaboration 2(1):2–21

Govindan K, Garg K, Gupta S, Jha PC (2016) Effect of product recovery and sustainability enhancing indicators on the location selection of manufacturing facility. Ecol Indic 67:517–532

Hajiagha SHR, Mahdiraji HA, Hashemi SS (2013) Multi-objective linear programming with interval coefficients. Kybernetes 42(3):482–496

Hajiagha SHR, Hashemi SS, Mahdiraji HA, Azaddel J (2015) Multi-period data envelopment analysis based on Chebyshev inequality bounds. Expert Syst Appl 42(21):7759–7767

Hajiagha SHR, Mahdiraji HA, Tavana M, Hashemi SS (2018) A novel common set of weights method for multi-period efficiency measurement using mean-variance criteria. Measurement 129:569–581

Hashemi SS, Hajiagha SHR, Zavadskas EK, Mahdiraji HA (2016) Multicriteria group decision making with ELECTRE III method based on interval-valued intuitionistic fuzzy information. Appl Math Model 40(2):1554–1564

Hwang C-L, Yoon K (1981) Multiple criteria decision making. Lect Notes Econ Math Syst 186:58–191

Jafari Sadeghi V, Biancone P (2017) Shariah compliant international entrepreneurship: a study of islamic finance in europe. Eur J Islamic Financ 8:1–7

Jafari Sadeghi V, Nkongolo-Bakenda J-M, Anderson RB, Dana L-P (2019) An institution-based view of international entrepreneurship: a comparison of context-based and universal determinants in developing and economically advanced countries. Int Bus Rev 28(6):101588

Jafari-Moghadam S, Zali MR, Sanaeepour H (2017) Tourism entrepreneurship policy: a hybrid MCDM model combining DEMATEL and ANP (DANP). Decision Sci Lett 6(3):233–250

Jafari-Sadeghi V (2020) The motivational factors of business venturing: opportunity versus necessity? A gendered perspective on European countries. J Bus Res 113:279–289

Jafari-Sadeghi V, Kimiagari S, Biancone P (2019a) Level of education and knowledge, foresight competency and international entrepreneurship. Eur Bus Rev 32(1):46–68

Jafari-Sadeghi V, Nkongolo-Bakenda J-M, Dana L-P, Anderson RB, Biancone PP (2019b) Home country institutional context and entrepreneurial internationalization: the significance of human capital attributes. J Int Entrep 2020(18):165–195

Jafari-Sadeghi V, Dutta DK, Ferraris A, Del Giudice M (2020) Internationalisation business processes in an under-supported policy contexts: evidence from Italian SMEs. Bus Process Manag J 26(5):1055–1074

Jahanshahloo GR, Lotfi FH, Izadikhah M (2006) An algorithmic method to extend TOPSIS for decision-making problems with interval data. Appl Math Comput 175:1375–1384

Jha MK, Raut RD, Gardas BB, Raut V (2018) A sustainable warehouse selection: an interpretive structural modelling approach. Int J Procurement Manag 11(2):201–232

Jones CA, Keith LG (2006) Medical tourism and reproductive outsourcing: the dawning of a new paradigm for healthcare. Int J Fertil Womens Med 51(6):251–255

Karaşan A, Kaya İ, Erdoğan M (2018) Location selection of electric vehicles charging stations by using a fuzzy MCDM method: a case study in Turkey. Neural Comput Applic 32:4553–4574

Kaul A, Darbari JD, Jha PC (2020) A fuzzy MCDM model for facility location evaluation based on quality of life. In: Soft computing for problem solving. Springer, Berlin, pp 687–697

Khan MJ, Chelliah S, Haron MS (2016) Medical tourism destination image formation process: a conceptual model. Int J Healthcare Manag 9(2):134–143

Kheybari S, Kazemi M, Rezaei J (2019) Bioethanol facility location selection using best-worst method. Appl Energy 242:612–623

Lafuente E, Vaillant Y, Serarols C (2010) Location decisions of knowledge-based entrepreneurs: why some Catalan KISAs choose to be rural? Technovation 30(11–12):590–600

Lueg R, Malinauskaite L, Marinova I (2014) The vital role of business processes for a business model: the case of a startup company. Probl Perspect Manag 12(4):213–220

Mahdiraji HA, Hajiagha SHR, Pourjam R (2011, September) A grey mathematical programming model to time-cost trade-offs in project management under uncertainty. In IEEE 2011 international conference on grey systems and intelligent services, pp 698–704. IEEE

Mahdiraji HA, Kazimieras Zavadskas E, Kazeminia A, Abbasi Kamardi A (2019) Marketing strategies evaluation based on big data analysis: a CLUSTERING-MCDM approach. Econ Res 32(1):2882–2892

Mahdiraji HA, Hafeez K, Kord H, Kamardi AA (2020) Analysing the voice of customers by a hybrid fuzzy decision-making approach in a developing country's automotive market. Manag Decis. https://dx.doi.org/10.1108/MD-12-2019-1732

Mahmoudi M, Mahdiraji HA, Jafarnejad A, Safari H (2019) Dynamic prioritization of equipment and critical failure modes. Kybernetes 48(9):1913–1941

Mokhtarzadeh NG, Mahdiraji HA, Beheshti M, Zavadskas EK (2018) A novel hybrid approach for technology selection in the information technology industry. Technologies 6(1):34

Mokhtarzadeh NG, Mahdiraji HA, Jafari-Sadeghi V, Soltani A, Kamardi AA (2020) A product-technology portfolio alignment approach for food industry: a multi-criteria decision making with z-numbers. Br Food J 122(12):3947–3967

Mouzakitis S, Karamolegkos G, Ntanos E, Psarras J (2013) A fuzzy multi-criteria outranking approach in support of business angels' decision-analysis process for the assessment of companies as investment opportunities. J Optim Theory Appl 158(1):274–283

Nilashi M, Samad S, Manaf AA, Ahmadi H, Rashid TA, Munshi A et al (2019) Factors influencing medical tourism adoption in Malaysia: a DEMATEL-fuzzy TOPSIS approach. Comput Ind Eng 137:106005

Nurmalini N, Rahim R (2017) Study approach of simple additive weighting for decision support system. Int J Sci Res Sci Technol 3(3):541–544

Opricovic S (1998) Multicriteria optimization of civil engineering systems. Faculty Civil Eng Belgrade 2(1):5–21

Opricovic S, Tzeng G-H (2004) Compromise solution by MCDM methods: a comparative analysis of VIKOR and TOPSIS. Eur J Oper Res 156(2):445–455

Opricovic S, Tzeng G-H (2007) Extended VIKOR method in comparison with outranking methods. Eur J Oper Res 178(2):514–529

Preedy VR, Watson RR (2010) Handbook of disease burdens and quality of life measures. Springer, New York

Ramesh R, Zionts S (2001) Multiple criteria decision making. In: Gass SI, Harris CM (eds) encyclopedia of operations research and management science. Springer, New York, pp 33–57

Ray A, De A, Dan PK (2015) Facility location selection using complete and partial ranking MCDM methods. Int J Ind Syst Eng 19(2):262–276

Rezaee R, Mohammadzadeh M (2016) Effective factors in expansion of medical tourism in Iran. Med J Islam Repub Iran 30:409–420

Rezaei J (2015) Best-worst multi-criteria decision-making method. Omega 53:49–57

Rezaei M, Jafari-Sadeghi V, Bresciani S (2020) What drives the process of knowledge management in a cross-cultural setting: the impact of social capital. Eur Bus Rev 32(3):485–511

Rostamzadeh R, Ismail K, Bodaghi Khajeh Noubar H (2014) An application of a hybrid MCDM method for the evaluation of entrepreneurial intensity among the SMEs: a case study. Sci World J 2(3):24–44

Sadeghi VJ, Biancone P (2017) Exploring the drivers of gender entrepreneurship: focus on the motivational perspectives in USA, Italy, and France. In: Gender and family entrepreneurship. Routledge, New York, pp 124–141
Sadeghi V, Biancone PP, Giacoma C, Secinaro S (2017) Export compliance: a missing component of international entrepreneurship. Int J Bus Manag 12(11):103–110
Sadeghi V, Biancone PP, Giacoma C, Secinaro S (2018) How does export compliance influence the internationalization of firms: is it a thread or an opportunity? J Glob Entrep Res 8(3):1–15
Sadraei R, Jafari Sadeghi V, Sadraei M (2018) Biotechnology revolution from academic entrepreneurship to industrial: chemo-entrepreneurship. Biometrics Biostat Int J 7(6):546–550
Sánchez-Lozano JM, Teruel-Solano J, Soto-Elvira PL, Socorro García-Cascales M (2013) Geographical information systems (GIS) and multi-criteria decision making (MCDM) methods for the evaluation of solar farms locations: case study in South-Eastern Spain. Renew Sust Energ Rev 24:544–556
Seker S, Aydin N (2020) Hydrogen production facility location selection for Black Sea using entropy based TOPSIS under IVPF environment. Int J Hydrog Energy 45(32):15855–15868
Silva S, Alçada-Almeida L, Dias LC (2014) Biogas plants site selection integrating multicriteria decision aid methods and GIS techniques: a case study in a Portuguese region. Biomass Bioenergy 71:58–68
Sukumar A, Jafari-Sadeghi V, Garcia-Perez A, Dutta DK (2020) The potential link between corporate innovations and corporate competitiveness: evidence from IT firms in the UK. J Knowl Manag 24(5):965–983
Taghavifard MT, Amoozad Mahdiraji H, Alibakhshi AM, Zavadskas EK, Bausys R (2018) An extension of fuzzy SWOT analysis: an application to information technology. Information 9 (3):46
Tien, N. H., Dana, L. P., Jose, R. J. S., Van Dat, N., & Duc, P. M. (2020) Analysis of McDonalds' entry strategy into Vietnam market 5(3):23–29
Tsai WH, Kuo HC (2011) Entrepreneurship policy evaluation and decision analysis for SMEs. Expert Syst Appl 38(7):8343–8351
Vanessa R, Leo-Paul D (2019) Societal entrepreneurship and competitiveness. In: Dana L-P, Ratten V (eds) Societal entrepreneurship and competitiveness, pp 1–4
Wang TC, Lee HD (2009) Developing a fuzzy TOPSIS approach based on subjective weights and objective weights. Expert Syst Appl 36(5):8980–8985. https://doi.org/10.1016/j.eswa.2008.11.035
Wang C-N, Nguyen VT, Thai HTN, Duong DH (2018) Multi-criteria decision making (MCDM) approaches for solar power plant location selection in Viet Nam. Energies 11(6)
Yücenur GN, Çaylak Ş, Gönül G, Postalcıoğlu M (2020) An integrated solution with SWARA&COPRAS methods in renewable energy production: City selection for biogas facility. Renew Energy 145:2587–2597
Żak J, Węgliński S (2014) The selection of the logistics center location based on MCDM/a methodology. Transport Res Proc 3:555–564
Zavadskas EK, Turskis Z, Antucheviciene J, Zakarevicius A (2012) Optimization of weighted aggregated sum product assessment. Elektronika Ir Elektrotechnika 122(6):3–6
Zavadskas EK, Antucheviciene J, Hajiagha SHR, Hashemi SS (2014) Extension of weighted aggregated sum product assessment with interval-valued intuitionistic fuzzy numbers (WASPAS-IVIF). Appl Soft Comput 24:1013–1021
Zečević S, Tadić S, Krstić M (2017) Intermodal transport terminal location selection using a novel hybrid MCDM model. Int J Uncertainty Fuzziness Knowl Based Syst 25(6):853–876
Zhao Q, Tsai PH, Wang JL (2019) Improving financial service innovation strategies for enhancing China's banking industry competitive advantage during the fintech revolution: a hybrid MCDM model. Sustainability (Switzerland) 11(5):1419

Shide Sadat Hashemi is the executive manager of Saramadan Andishe Avina Co. She post-graduated from Allameh Tabataba'i University in 2008 and for about 6 years worked as a self-employed management consultant. Since 2014, she worked as the master management consultant in different managerial projects in SA-AVINA; she simultaneously manages the teams' members and coaches them. Shide is interested in research and has contributed to more than 40 papers as author and co-author. She extracts some papers based on her performed managerial projects. Most of her published papers are categorised in multi-criteria decision-making and start-up subject. She has published in expert systems with applications, applied soft computing, *Kybernetes*, etc.

Mostafa Azari is the business specialist of Saramadan Andishe Avina Co. Mostafa and is currently finishing his Master of Industrial Management in Operation Research at the University of Tehran. Mostafa has experiences in business model implementation, business process management, strategic implementation, and company collaboration. He has managed projects at National Cartographic Centre; Apiculture Industry Development and Advocacy Fund; Social Insurance Fund Farmers, Villagers & Nomads; and PMP industry.

A Hybrid Interval-Valued Intuitionistic Fuzzy Aggregation Operator-Based Algorithm for Team Member Selection of International Entrepreneurs

Seyed Hossein Razavi Hajiagha and Niloofar Ahmadzadeh Kandi

1 Introduction

The emergence of start-ups and their increasing expansion is one of the salient features of economic growth in any society, and due to various spatial and temporal factors and the special needs of each society, the evolution and development of start-ups are increasing every day. Every young organisation is designed for a purpose that requires some kind of management according to its structure. Entrepreneurship development research shows that entrepreneurs before starting a business must have the necessary capital, technology, and facilities to produce goods or services and, most importantly, appropriate team members (Hisrich and Drnovsek 2002). Therefore, entrepreneurs of start-ups and small, immature firms are always looking for achieving transformational members which is one of the big concerns of start-ups. The importance of having strong team members to manage a start-up is so crucial that it can lead to inefficiency in the organisation and failure to achieve organisational goals if chosen incorrectly. The teams play a crucial role in corporate governance (Gurău and Dana 2020), and they have an important role in the advancement of the start-ups. Hence, entrepreneurs are looking for decision-making models that can select capable people as members of their team to help the organisation achieve its goals.

S. H. Razavi Hajiagha (✉)
Department of Management, Faculty of Management and Finance, Khatam University, Tehran, Iran
e-mail: h.razavi@khtam.ac.ir

N. Ahmadzadeh Kandi
Department of Business and Law, University of Wollongong, Sydney, NSW, Australia
e-mail: nak127@uowmail.edu.au

V. Jafari-Sadeghi et al. (eds.), *Empirical International Entrepreneurship*, Contributions to Management Science,
https://doi.org/10.1007/978-3-030-68972-8_19

The selection of team members is the process of selecting people who have the necessary qualifications to do the job in the best way. Increasing competition in global markets has forced organisations to place more emphasis on the team member selection process. With high levels of business competition, having a flexible team of members who can adapt to working conditions is critical. Important topics such as changes in organisations, work, society, rules and regulations, and marketing have had an impact on team selection (Dursun and Karsak 2010).

Moreover, the growth of start-ups and young organisations disproportionately contributes to creating jobs, innovation, and the dynamics of the economy. Wealth distribution and economic growth are among the benefits of developing entrepreneurial companies (Brouthers et al. 2015; Sukumar et al. 2020). Start-ups are much more responsive to market demand than larger organisations and, therefore, lead to more job creation in advanced economies. The development of business frontiers and its activity in the foreign market, which is known as internationalisation, is one of the most important ways to achieve success for businesses (Kuivalainen et al. 2012; Sadeghi and Biancone 2017, 2018). Therefore, it is not surprising that the essential factors in the international success of small and medium-sized businesses are of great importance to researchers as well as entrepreneurs (Love and Roper 2015). Thus, the process of internationalisation has intensified in the last decade due to the growth of globalisation, the Internet, and communication innovations) Eurofound 2012).

One of the significant attributes of start-ups and small firms is that they can internationalise without moving their resources abroad (Dana 2017), while in large, well-matured companies, Dana and Wright (2009) acknowledged that resource shifts lead to loss of advantages and lack of complementary resources for operating abroad; hence, this is one of the advantages of international entrepreneurship of start-ups than larger organisations. However, entrepreneurs confront many obstacles at their initial activities, which affect both their performance and their survival rate. In addition to the compatibility and flexibility that these organisations have, they also face more problems than larger organisations. The results of many studies show that the failure rate of start-ups in the first 5 years is more than 50% (Decker et al. 2016). Also, 20% of venture businesses fail in the first year and 66% in the first 6 years (Timmons and Spinelli 1994). Therefore, it is critical to examine the reasons for the failure of venture businesses to provide vital information to stakeholders, entrepreneurs, venture investors, and government policymakers (Liao et al. 2009).

Interesting results from past research have suggested that there are differences between mature and entrepreneurial organisations. Also, among these findings is the relationship between capabilities and performance of organisations) Autio et al. 2011). Many entrepreneurship researchers believe that the lack of fully developed capabilities can be a source of entrepreneurial advantage, especially in rapidly changing environments and uncertain conditions (McMullen and Shepherd 2006). One of the important characteristics of studies in the field of entrepreneurship and organisation is the ability of organisations to respond to uncertainty through structural and strategic adaptations and capacity development (Autio et al. 2011). With this in mind, start-ups and emerging organisations that are more structurally compatible with environmental uncertainty can make their entrepreneurial goals a reality if they survive in a highly competitive market.

According to the definition of Su et al. (2015), an entrepreneur is someone who participates in innovative, risky activities and financial investments to create value for an organisation and to create economic growth. Also, international entrepreneurship involves discovering, approving, evaluating, and exploiting opportunities across national borders to create future goods and services. International entrepreneurship is sometimes driven by demand for corporate products across international borders. International entrepreneurship and domestic entrepreneurship are similar (Fernhaber et al. 2008). Internal entrepreneurship involves pursuing internal entrepreneurial opportunities, such as creating more profits, developing the market and personal desires, and achieving social status, while international entrepreneurship involves pursuing international entrepreneurial opportunities, such as developing relations with international partners and maintaining relations with industrial authorities (Jafari-Sadeghi et al. 2020). The location of an opportunity determines whether the opportunity is exploited domestically or internationally (Oyson and Whittaker 2010; Sadeghi et al. 2017, 2018).

Entrepreneurship and internationalisation play a significant role in effectively creating a business toward global markets and thus facilitating its economic growth (Jafari-Sadeghi et al. 2019b). Therefore, due to the increasing speed of globalisation and competition, entrepreneurs tend to participate in global markets and international opportunities to be able to develop their capabilities and ultimately achieve more profit, and to this end, the entrepreneur cannot achieve the vision without forming an efficient team, so forming a capable and efficient team, as well as the effective selection of a cofounder, has a great impact on the rapid growth of the organisation.

Greiner's growth model describes the various stages of organisational growth, which can be used as a tool that entrepreneurs can employ to understand the current problems in the organisation's growth that they encounter. It is possible to predict problems before they happen. This model includes six growth phases and also shows the root causes of problems that are likely to occur at the end of each phase. These crises can occur for various reasons, such as changes in organisational structure, leadership, management practices, etc., which are essential factors for organisational growth. These six stages include growth through creativity, growth through direction, growth through delegation, growth through coordination, growth through collaboration, and growth through extra-organisational solutions (Greiner 1972).

The Greiner model, in general, can provide an efficient framework to entrepreneurs for identifying and exploring team members of an entrepreneurial organisation at specific evolutionary stages also identifies how processes over time change. Also, through the life cycle of team members, the phases of maturity, decline, reconfiguration, and recovery of entrepreneurial organisations can be considered (Gedajlovic et al. 2013). According to Delmar et al. (2003) study, the growth of entrepreneurial venture capital is irregular, so steps need to be taken to revitalise declining organisations, for example, by creating new links and selecting new team members and leaders (Zahra et al. 2009).

One of the requirements for growth, creativity, and entrepreneurship in society is to study the failure of organisations. Undoubtedly, with the increasing trend of globalisation, entrepreneurs and small businesses are playing a pivotal role in global trade. In this increasingly interconnected world, learning from each other is of more significance (Etemad and Wright 2003). This study aims to focus on one of the causes of failure in start-ups due to team member selection based on various criteria. Some of the reasons for start-up's failure in the early years of their development include low productivity, lower levels of legitimacy than larger organisations, and high capital costs (Gibb 1993). To increase the efficiency and evaluate the probability of start-up survival, it is necessary to examine a comprehensive understanding of the factors influencing the success and failure of start-ups, focusing more on selecting team members in this research.

Some criteria play a more significant role in reviewing the literature on the factors influencing the failure of start-ups. Some researchers have classified influential factors into two categories: individual factors that are controlled by humans and environmental factors that are not controlled by humans. Ooghe and De Prijcker (2008) mentioned that four groups of factors, including the characteristics of the founding teams, resources, structural features and strategy of the organisation, and environmental factors, were important in the failure of businesses (Ooghe and De Prijcker 2008).

In previous studies, the focus has been more on the entrepreneurial characteristics of creating new venture businesses, but founding teams, which themselves include entrepreneurs and founding team members, play a key role in developing new businesses (Chandler et al. 2005).

Extensive reasons for start-up failures can be the source of the external environment or internal factors of the business. While external factors cannot be overestimated, internal factors of start-up failure can be predicted in many cases. In some cases, the combination of these two factors leads to the failure of start-ups in the early years (Arasti et al. 2014).

Selecting team members and a business partner that fits the organisation's goals can lead to the success of the organisation, while the wrong selection of people leads to the failure of organisations. The selection directly affects the effectiveness and performance of the business. Selecting team members based on the personal judgment of entrepreneurs may lead to poor selection. Therefore, it is necessary to adopt a method that considers the multi-criteria selection approach through the views of several experts for the appropriate selection. Selecting team members who have an entrepreneurial orientation will lead to the success of emerging start-ups. Entrepreneurial orientation is the process of creating a strategy that leads the company to continuous innovation, helps the company to position itself in the market, and empowers the company to transform risky investments (Shirokova et al. 2016). The alignment of entrepreneurial orientation in team members has a positive impact on the expansion of businesses and their internationalisation (Amin Moghadasi et al. 2017; Biancone and Jafari Sadeghi 2016; Peschken et al. 2016).

Thus, the basic steps in the process of selecting team members and one of the significant and complex issues that selection faces are providing the attributes and indicators needed for the candidate, selecting the most appropriate criteria, and weighting them (Lin 2010).

Due to the excessive complexity of such issues and the multiplicity of influential variables in this process, there is a need to use multi-criteria decision-making methods that can help us to solve decision-making problems systematically. To this end, the multi-criteria decision-making method, to manage the uncertainty in expert decisions, is examined in the MCDM process as well as ranking among team members in this study.

Entrepreneurs' approach to the procedures and budgets allocated to team selection is different. Some to select the best candidate use costly, challenging, and complicated procedures; they make strategic decisions, while others decide to allocate positions quickly and cheaply based on subjectivity. However, the growing importance associated with the team selection process has paved the way for analytical decision-making approaches. In general, the issue of team members' selection is very complicated, even when in the simplest case it contains only one criterion and one homogeneous skill. When there are multiple criteria and different skills, the problem becomes much more difficult. Therefore, it will be very arduous, though not impossible, to use conventional mathematical techniques or routine planning to solve the problem. In most matters of selecting team members, the information available cannot be accurate or conclusive. Also, inaccurate and ambiguous information can be expressed as linguistic information in the form of variables, such as beliefs, thoughts, feelings, beliefs, etc.

More broadly, decision-making is a process that involves selecting one choice from a variety of options in line with specific goals and determines the best option among several options for specific goals. The selection of individuals is also a multi-criteria decision-making issue. Multi-criteria decision-making problems deal with more than one variable or criterion and are tools that include integrated or hybrid methods used to solve complex problems. Also, decisions can sometimes be imprecise, so intuitive fuzzy sets which are a developed traditional fuzzy set method can cover these weaknesses and are, therefore, a more appropriate tool than standard fuzzy sets (Büyüközkan et al. 2018).

This chapter aims to propose a rational and formalised (Simons 2013 Razavi Hajiagha et al. 2018) framework for selecting team members considering the uncertainty of this problem. The proposed framework consists of forming a multi-criteria structure that includes team member alternative candidates and their evaluation criteria, first. Then, the criteria weight vectors are obtained using the best-worst method (Rezaei 2015). Finally, different aggregation operators are used to appraising the candidate, and the best candidate is chosen by the reconciliation of the obtained ranks from different aggregation operators.

This chapter is organised as below. First, the relevant literature is reviewed in Sect. 2. The criteria used to select team members are then examined in Sect. 3. A brief review of the required preliminaries is then discussed in Sect. 4. The proposed framework of team member selection and its application in a real-world case study is then detailed in Sect. 5, respectively. Finally, this chapter is concluded in Sect. 6.

2 Literature Review

Many factors affect the entrepreneurial personality of people. For example, education directly affects entrepreneurship, and the theory of human capital in entrepreneurship studies also assumes that investing in education can lead to personal growth and the development of business ventures by the individual (Jafari-Sadeghi and Biancone 2017; Beheshti et al. 2016). Moreover, education promotes the foresight skills of entrepreneurs (Jafari-Sadeghi et al. 2019a). The criteria of evaluation and selection of team members include the characteristics of the current members who have performed well in their job positions. Without a list of key factors, the selection will probably be made incorrectly. Besides, if the list of required characteristics is very extensive, there is no possibility of selecting any team member (Golec and Kahya 2007; Mahmoudi et al. 2019). Therefore, there are many criteria and indicators for selecting team members. Now the question arises that among the many criteria and characteristics available, how and what appropriate tools and indicators are used? And which criteria for selecting team members are more critical and effective for different jobs? On the other hand, the multiplicity and diversity of jobs require the utilisation of attributes appropriate to the type of each job and the consideration of different practical factors for the success and effective performance of human resources. Furthermore, to select team members for a similar role in industry and organisations, depending on the type of organisation, different criteria may be considered. All of these unanswered questions show the great importance and breadth of team member selection criteria, which highlights the need for research in this area.

Many researchers have explored the issue of selecting team members using a variety of techniques and skills. A review of the literature revealed that the indicators used as a criterion for selecting team members are very wide and often different; however, some indicators have also been selected jointly in different studies.

In different studies, various characteristics and features are considered as bellow:

- Age, gender, educational background, marital status, work history (Lin 2010; Golec and Kahya 2007; Hajiagha et al. 2013, 2015, 2018)
- Personality, emotional stability, self-confidence, social responsibility, effective use of time (Golec and Kahya 2007; Dursun and Karsak 2010; Lin 2010; Aggarwal 2014; Zhang and Liu 2011)
- Listening and writing skills, the ability to persuade others (Golec and Kahya 2007; Kilic et al. 2020; Goyal and Gupta 2020)
- The ability of analysis, risk-taking, innovation, organisational sensitivity and organisational superiority (Goyal and Gupta 2020; Golec and Kahya 2007)
- Skills related to planning, organising, controlling, risk management, strategy formulation (Golec and Kahya 2007), in several studies, leadership capacity, adaptability, marketing capability, learning (Aggarwal 2014; Wang 2010; Dursun and Karsak 2010)

- Characteristics such as technical knowledge, professional efficiency, use of new technologies (Lin 2010; Sadeghi 2016; Kilic et al. 2020; Sadraei et al. 2018)

As can be seen, various criteria have been reviewed and candidate team members have been evaluated considering these criteria.

The study, conducted by Wu et al. (2008), examined four factors influencing the formation of effective team members in technology-based start-ups in Taiwan, including entrepreneurial resources, the commitment of founding partners, trust, and competitive advantage of start-ups. Finally, according to theories of resource-based (RBV) and social capital view, in technology-based start-ups, entrepreneurs can prevent the failure of venture activities by supporting start-up founding partners as well as increasing the competitive advantage of start-ups. Effective founding partners also need to provide complementary and important resources, which can increase the collaborative commitments of venture business team partners to start-ups (Wu et al. 2008).

In a research conducted by Gungor et al. (2009), general job characteristics such as work experience, academic record, and skills; complementary job characteristics such as decision-making, teamwork, effective use of time, and long-term and satisfactory learning; and individual characteristics such as key ability, appearance, culture, and communication are considered, and the most appropriate individual is selected throughout fuzzy analytic hierarchy process (Gungor et al. 2009; Rezaei et al. 2020).

Wang (2010) used the grey theory and the TOPSIS multi-criteria decision-making method to select the members of the R&D team. He obtained the weight and ranking of the indicators for the options by the linguistic variables expressed in grey numbers (Wang 2010; Mahdiraji et al. 2011, 2019, 2020).

Dursun and Karsak (2010) utilised a fuzzy multi-criteria decision-making algorithm to evaluate linguistic and numerical scales of individual attributes such as the ability to organise personality creativity and leadership (Dursun and Karsak 2010). Zhang and Liu (2011) applied grey relational analysis (GRA)-based intuitionistic fuzzy (IF) multi-criteria group decision-making method to select the most appropriate team member toward organisational success. Using this method, they could combine both subjective and objective opinions to maximise the efficiency of decision-making in team member selection (Zhang and Liu 2011).

Arasti et al. (2012) surveyed 158 unsuccessful start-ups and four groups of individual factors, where motivation, skills, capabilities, and characteristics, were examined. The result of this study showed that a lack of management skills in a crisis condition and the lack of human resource management skills and financial and marketing management skills were among the most important individual factors influencing the failure of start-ups (Arasti et al. 2012).

In another research, Afshari et al. (2012) employed fuzzy simple additive weighting (SWA) method, linguistic variables method, as well as Delphi method to select people in the organisation so that decision-makers can increase the effectiveness of the decision-making process (Afshari et al. 2012). Rouyendegh and Erkan (2012) used the fuzzy ELECTERE method to select the professional academic staff of the training unit. In their case, there were ten qualitative criteria for selecting the best candidates among the five applicants (Rouyendegh and Erkan 2012; Mokhtarzadeh et al. 2018).

A study conducted by Arasti et al. (2014) compared successful entrepreneurs and unsuccessful entrepreneurs and looked at the reasons for start-up failures. In their study, they categorised the causes of failure into three main dimensions: individual, the general environment, and immediate environment. They then ranked the collected samples from 120 entrepreneurs in Iranian start-ups. According to their research, individual factors such as lack of motivation due to crises, lack of management skills, and personal circumstances and problems are the main causes of start-up failure in the individual dimension (Arasti et al. 2014; Taghavifard et al. 2018).

Aggarwal (2014) described a model based on the Delphi method and the fuzzy AHP for employee selection (Aggarwal 2014). In a study conducted by Bogdanovic and Miletic (2015), an organisation used an integrated multi-criteria decision-making approach employing AHP and PROMETHEE approach to reduce team members from five to three for downsizing, to make decision apart from subjectivity and personal judgment and bias (Bogdanovic and Miletic 2015).

Salehi (2016) used a fuzzy hybrid multi-criteria decision-making approach with a combination of AHP and VIKOR to solve the problem of decision-makers' preferences to use linguistic sets to evaluate and select team members (Salehi 2016).

To respond quickly to environmental changes, managers and entrepreneurs must select team members who have the essential knowledge, skills, and competencies to be able to achieve the goals of the organisation with timely decisions and optimal performance. Therefore, Urosevic et al. (2017) conducted a study to select sales team members in the tourism industry, using the SWARA and WASPAS methodologies (Urosevic et al. 2017).

In another article, Sadeghi et al. (2018) examined the impact of 47 factors on the success of technology-based SMEs in Iran and ranked those factors, using a fuzzy analytic network process method (ANP). These success factors were classified by considering critical success factors (CSFs), and then the performance of technology-based SMEs was evaluated by the fuzzy TOPSIS approach according to weighted CSFs. The study also shows that policies and rules, technological factors, and entrepreneurial characteristics are significant success factors (Sadeghi 2016).

In the process of selecting people in the organisation, Nabeeh et al. (2019) used the integrated neutrosophic AHP and TOPSIS technique to classify preferences, to find the ideal solution among the different alternatives in managing the resources of a smart village (Nabeeh et al. 2019).

In another research, Petridis et al. (2019) examined the selection of individuals based on analytical and non-analytical skills using the TOPSIS technique. The AHP method has been applied to identify the weights of each criterion, and by prioritising skills in this study, the potentials for member selection have been identified (Petridis et al. 2019).

Based on a study conducted by Goyal and Gupta in 2020, a multi-attribute group decision-making approach (MAGDM) was presented to identify and select team members for the development of global software. In this study, using intuitionistic fuzzy numbers and then through a multi-criteria decision support system, it has been used to effectively select members of a team and to rank the aggregated opinion from different experts (Goyal and Gupta 2020).

In a study conducted by Kilic et al. (2020), an integrated multi-criteria decision-making method was used to select team members in organisations under consideration of the uncertainty. In this method, the synergy of the two methods of ELECTRE and DEMATEL was performed under increased intuitive fuzzy environmental constraints, and then, after collecting the opinions of experts, the weights of the criteria were calculated by the IF-DEMATEL method and ranked by the IF-ELECTRE method (Kilic et al. 2020).

As a result, due to the many studies that are conducted every year with different approaches in this field, the necessity and importance of examining the issue of team member selection becomes apparent; however, reviewing the research literature and articles, it became clear that in studies and surveys, the method and basis for selecting the criteria used are not clear. On the other hand, the focus of previous articles and reviews is more on the use of different techniques to select the most appropriate team members, rather than developing a model to provide appropriate indicators for selection. No comprehensive and appropriate model can meet all the criteria for selecting employees. In the present study, an attempt has been made to provide a practical and usable framework for selecting and evaluating team members by categorising all the criteria used to select employees in recent years.

According to Table 1, the following conclusions can be drawn:

1. Among the considered studies, almost all of them are classified as multi-criteria decision-making problems. This theme illustrates that the nature of team member selection is a multi-criteria-type problem that required considering several, sometimes conflicting, criteria. Therefore, the method proposed in this chapter is also classified as a multi-criteria team member selection method. Also, several advantages are reported for these methods.
2. Among different MCDM methods, some of the well-known methods, e.g. AHP, ANP, TOPSIS, VIKOR, ELECTRE, etc., have been used. This might be due to the wide application of the considered method in different fields and also the credibility they acquired in their long application history. For instance, ELECTRE was proposed in the 1960s, AHP was introduced in the 1970s, TOPSIS dates back to the 1980s, and ANP and VIKOR were introduced in the 1990s. This background, along with different successful applications, caused researchers to admit the considered method.
3. Since the context of multi-criteria team member selection deals with evaluating a set of candidate members regarding a finite set of criteria, usually these criteria are of subjective type. Therefore, they cannot be evaluated as crisp numbers. In this regard, researchers handle the problem of partial and incomplete information by using uncertainty frameworks. Among the proposed frameworks, fuzzy sets (Zadeh 1965) and intuitionistic fuzzy sets (Atanassov 1986) are used extensively. Fuzzy sets are a generalisation of classic set theory where a membership function

Table 1 Previous related researches

Researcher	Nature		Uncertainty consideration			Solution method	Criteria
	Single criterion	Multi-criteria	None	Fuzzy	IF		
Kilic et al. (2020)		Integrated MCDM			✓	DEMATEL and ELECTRE	• Personal characteristics and skills • Knowledge and experience • Technical skills and requirements • Education • Foreign language • Physical wellness and demographic features • Salary request • Vocational flexibility and capability • References
Goyal and Gupta (2020)		MCDM			✓	IF and Muirhead mean (IFMM)	Criteria based on three categories: **1. Individual past experience** • Programmer experienced in project domain • Language and tool experience • Technical skills and requirements • Contribution to team effort **2. Individual performance based on old projects** • Completing tasks fully and on time • Creativity in approach to problem • Determination and effort **3. Team work-related** • Contributing to discussions • Communicate with team and stakeholders • Effective use of time Leadership
Petridis et al. (2019)		MCDM	✓			AHP, TOPSIS, and non-linear programming	• Knowledge and experience • Personal characteristics and skill • Oral assessment • Technical skills and requirements

Nabeeh et al. (2019)		MCDM		✓		Neutrosophic AHP, and TOPSIS	• Knowledge and experience • Personal characteristics and skills • Vocational flexibility and capability
Sadeghi et al. (2018)		MCDM		✓		ANP	• Policies and regulations • Technological factors • Entrepreneur's characteristics
Urosevic et al. (2017)		Hybrid MCDM			✓	SWARA and WASPAS	• Communication skills • Leadership skills • Flexibility • Decision-making • Negotiating skills • Analytic skills • Consistency
Sadeghi (2016)		Integrated MCDM		✓		AHP and VIKOR	• Knowledge and experience • Personal characteristics and skills • Strategic thinking • Fluency in a foreign language • Technical skills and requirements
Bogdanovic and Miletic (2015)		Integrated MCDM		✓		AHP and PROMETHEE	• Computer skills • Experience • Good cooperation • Strategic thinking • Fluency in a foreign language • Oral communication skills • Project management knowledge • Willingness
Aggarwal (2014)		MADM		✓		Delphi and FAHP	• Knowledge and experience • Technical skills and requirements • Contribution to team effort • Emotional steadiness • Job training • Oral communication skill

(continued)

Table 1 (continued)

Researcher	Nature		Uncertainty consideration			Solution method	Criteria
	Single criterion	Multi-criteria	None	Fuzzy	IF		
Afshari et al. (2012)		MCDM		✓		SAW method, fuzzy linguistic evaluation, and Delphi method	• Knowledge and experience • Personal characteristics and skills • Education • Technical skills and requirements
Rouyendegh and Erkan (2012)		MCDM		✓		Fuzzy ELECTRE	• Foreign language • Education • Oral communication • Past experience • Technical skills and requirements • Teamwork • Self-confidence • Compatibility • Age • Research abilities
Zhang and Liu (2011)		MCDM			✓	IF weighted averaging (IFWA) and Grey relational analysis (GRA)	• Emotional steadiness • Oral communication skill • Personality • Experience • Self-confidence
Dursun and Karsak (2010)		MCDM			✓	Ordered weighted averaging (OWA) and TOPSIS	• Emotional steadiness • Leadership • Self-confidence • Oral communication skill • Personality • Experience • General aptitude • Comprehension

Wang (2010)		MCDM		✓		Grey theory and TOPSIS	• Education • Work experience • Job training • Title level • Job performance • Age • Innovation capability • Loyalty

is assigned to each element of a set. On the other hand, IF can be considered as a generalisation of ordinal fuzzy sets where a non-membership degree is also specified for each element, beyond its membership degree. The main difference between fuzzy and IF sets is that while the ordinal fuzzy sets required the sum of membership and non-membership degrees to be equal to 1, the IF allowed this sum to be less than 1.

Considering the above points, the main contribution of this study can be drawn as developing a multi-criteria team member selection for entrepreneurs and start-ups using interval-valued intuitionistic aggregation operators. Considering the abilities of interval-valued intuitionistic fuzzy sets (IVIFs) in dealing with uncertainty, where membership and non-membership degrees are expressed as intervals, along with the wide acceptance and usage of aggregation operators in multi-criteria decision-making, the proposed method is expected to be a reliable and applicable framework to aid in selecting the appropriate team members.

3 A Review of Team Member Selection Criteria

Regardless of the method used to select team members, either in a single criterion or multi-criteria, the main question is to identify the set of criteria to be used as decision-making criteria. According to Triantaphyllou (2000), defining an MCDM problem, meaning identification of alternatives and criteria can be considered as a critical step where no standard procedure is available, and it usually deals with the artistic rather than the scientific aspect of MCDM. Since identifying decision criteria plays a vital role in this section, an overview of team member selection criteria is represented.

According to Table 1, various criteria are used in different studies. Figure 1 illustrates the frequency distribution of the considered criteria.

The considered criteria can be classified into three distinct categories of knowledge, skills, and attitude (KSA). Figure 2 illustrates the classification of the extracted criteria from the literature.

4 Preliminaries

4.1 Interval Valued Intuitionistic Fuzzy Sets: An Overview

Information plays a vital role in decision-making. A multi-attribute decision-making problem can be defined as a means to evaluate a finite set of alternatives, i.e. $A = \{A_1, A_2, \ldots, A_m\}$, according to a set of attributes, i.e. $C = \{C_1, C_2, \ldots, C_n\}$. Accordingly, a decision matrix of $D = [r_{ij}]$ is constructed where r_{ij} denotes the performance of alternative A_i with regard to criterion C_j. Also, an attribute weight

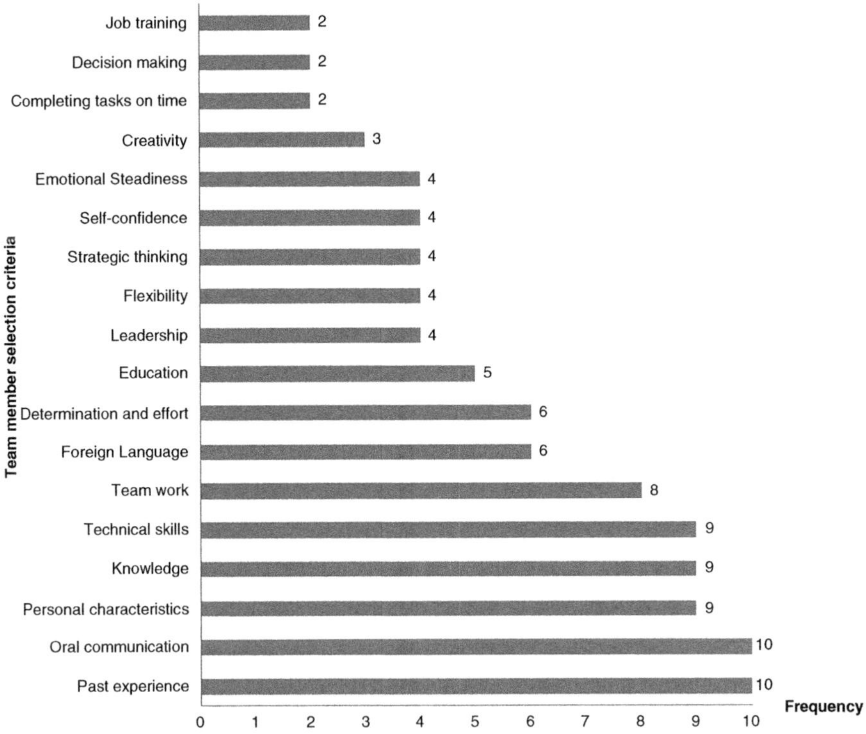

Fig. 1 Frequency distribution of team member selection criteria

vector $W = \{w_1, w_2, \ldots, w_n\}$ is required to represent the importance of each criterion in the considered decision. Therefore, a variety of information is required to formulate the decision problem.

Almost the best knowledge of us about real-world phenomena is partial or approximate. This incomplete information leads researchers toward uncertainty concepts. Liu and Lin (2006) introduced probability theory, fuzzy sets theory, and grey systems theory as three major uncertainty handling frameworks.

A fuzzy set is a well-known and widely used theory dealing with uncertainty, introduced by Zadeh (1965). Fuzzy sets can be used to deal with approximate rather than precise information (Taghavifard et al. 2018). The foundation of this theory is to attend the concept of membership function to the classic notion of sets in mathematic. Beyond its advantageous features, some researchers try to improve and enhance the fuzzy sets theory. Grattan-Guinness (1976) and Gau and Buehrer (1993) expressed that determining an exact degree of membership for the elements of a set without considering any hesitancy can be challenging for decision-makers. Atanassov (1986) developed the intuitionistic fuzzy sets (IFSs) as a generalisation of the classic fuzzy sets. IFS assigned a non-membership degree along with a membership degree to each element of the set, in a way that the sum of membership and

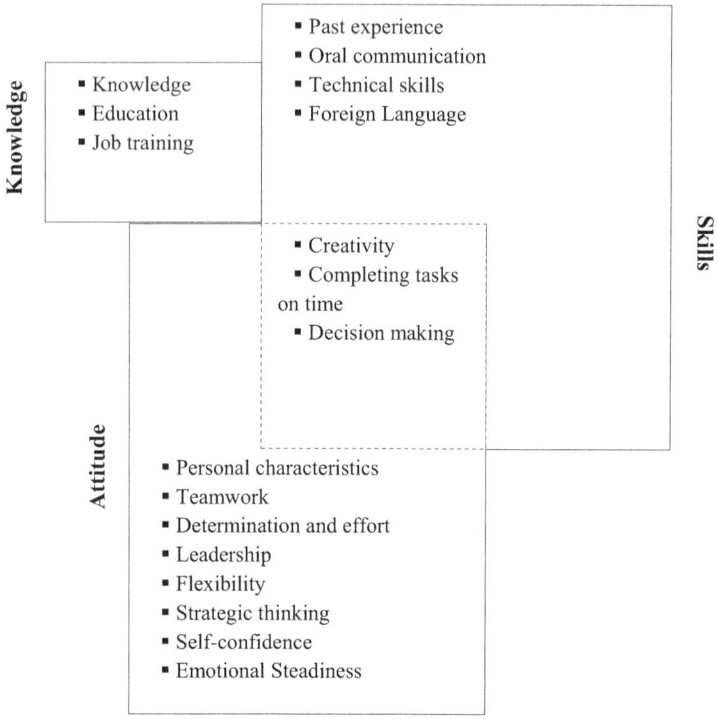

Fig. 2 Classification of the team member selection criteria into KSA

non-membership degrees are lower than the unity. Also, there remains a hesitancy degree for each element.

Later, Atanassov and Gargov (1989) extended the interval-valued intuitionistic fuzzy sets (IVIFS) as below. In this section, a brief overview of the definition and operations of IVIFS is presented. For a more discussion, readers can see Atanassov (1999) and Jian et al. (2010) (Jian et al. 2010).

Definition 1
Let $D[0, 1]$ be the set of all closed subintervals defined in the interval $[0, 1]$ and X be a given non-empty set. An IVIFS in X is defined as $\widetilde{A} = \left\{ \left\langle x, \mu_{\widetilde{A}}(x), \nu_{\widetilde{A}}(x) | x \in X \right\rangle \right\}$, where $\mu_{\widetilde{A}} : X \to D[0, 1]$, $\nu_{\widetilde{A}} : X \to D[0, 1]$, and $0 < sup_x \mu_{\widetilde{A}}(x) + sup_x \nu_{\widetilde{A}}(x) \leq 1$.

The intervals $\mu_{\widetilde{A}}(x)$ and $\nu_{\widetilde{A}}(x)$ illustrate the degrees of membership and non-membership of x to the set A. if $\mu_{AL}(x)$, $\mu_{AU}(x)$ represented the upper and lower bound membership, and $\nu_{AL}(x)$, $\nu_{AU}(x)$ are lower and upper bound non-membership, respectively. The IVIFS A can be denoted by:

$$\widetilde{A} = \{\langle x, [\mu_{AL}(x), \mu_{AU}(x)], [\nu_{AL}(x), \nu_{AU}(x)]\rangle | x \in X\} \tag{1}$$

where $0 < \mu_{AU}(x) + \nu_{AU}(x) \leq 1$, $\mu_{AL}(x)$, $\nu_{AL}(x) \geq 0$.

For simplicity of notation, an IVIFS value is denoted by $\widetilde{A} = ([\mu_{AL}, \mu_{AU}], [\nu_{AL}, \nu_{AU}])$ and called as an interval-valued intuitionistic fuzzy number (IVIFN).

The operational laws of IVIFNs are defined as follows – if $\widetilde{A} = ([\mu_{AL}, \mu_{AU}], [\nu_{AL}, \nu_{AU}])$ and $\widetilde{B} = ([\mu_{BL}, \mu_{BU}], [\nu_{BL}, \nu_{BU}])$ be any two IVIFNs, then (Xu 2007; Zhang and Xu 2015):

$$\widetilde{A} + \widetilde{B} = ([\mu_{AL} + \mu_{BL} - \mu_{AL}\mu_{BL}, \mu_{AU} + \mu_{BU} - \mu_{AU}\mu_{BU}], [\nu_{AL}\nu_{BL}, \nu_{AU}\nu_{BU}]) \tag{2}$$

$$\widetilde{A} \cdot \widetilde{B} = ([\mu_{AL}\mu_{BL}, \mu_{AU}\mu_{BU}], [\nu_{AL} + \nu_{BL} - \nu_{AL}\nu_{BL}, \nu_{AU} + \nu_{BU} - \nu_{AU}\nu_{BU}]) \tag{3}$$

$$\lambda\widetilde{A} = \left(\left[1 - (1 - \mu_{AL})^{\lambda}, 1 - (1 - \mu_{AU})^{\lambda}\right], \left[\nu_{AL}{}^{\lambda}, \nu_{AU}{}^{\lambda}\right]\right), \lambda \geq 0 \tag{4}$$

$$\widetilde{A}^{\lambda} = \left(\left[\mu_{AL}{}^{\lambda}, \mu_{AU}{}^{\lambda}\right], \left[1 - (1 - \nu_{AL})^{\lambda}, 1 - (1 - \nu_{AU})^{\lambda}\right]\right), \lambda \geq 0 \tag{5}$$

For an IVIFN like $\widetilde{A} = ([\mu_{AL}, \mu_{AU}], [\nu_{AL}, \nu_{AU}])$, its score function is defined as

$$S\left(\widetilde{A}\right) = \frac{1}{2}(\mu_{AL} - \nu_{AL} + \mu_{AU} - \nu_{AU}) \tag{6}$$

And its accuracy function as

$$h\left(\widetilde{A}\right) = \frac{1}{2}(\mu_{AL} + \nu_{AL} + \mu_{AU} + \nu_{AU}) \tag{7}$$

Then, for two IVIFNs $\widetilde{A}$ and $\widetilde{B}$ (Xu 2007; Zhang and Xu 2015):

1. If $S\left(\widetilde{A}\right) < S\left(\widetilde{B}\right)$, then $\widetilde{A}$ is smaller than $\widetilde{B}$, i.e. $\widetilde{A} < \widetilde{B}$.
2. If $S\left(\widetilde{A}\right) = S\left(\widetilde{B}\right)$, then:
3. 2–1) If $h\left(\widetilde{A}\right) = h\left(\widetilde{B}\right)$, then $\widetilde{A} < \widetilde{B}$.
4. 2–2) If $h\left(\widetilde{A}\right) < h\left(\widetilde{B}\right)$, then $\widetilde{A}$ is smaller than $\widetilde{B}$, $\widetilde{A} < \widetilde{B}$.

4.2 IVIFN Aggregation Operators and Their Application in Multi-attribute Decision-Making

IVIFNs are widely used in the framework of MADM problems. Researchers extended different methodologies to handle this type of decision-making problems

(Razavi Hajiagha et al. 2013; Zavadskas et al. 2014, 2015; Hashemi et al. 2016; Wang and Chen 2017; Garg and Arora 2018; Wu et al. 2019; Zeng et al. 2020).

Aggregation operators are a class of accepted methodologies that can be used in multi-attribute decision-making. Simply putting, aggregation operators can be defined as a real-valued function defined over a vector input. These operators receive an n-dimensional input vector and transformed it into a real number.

Definition 2
An n-array aggregation operator AO_n is defined as a mapping from n-dimensional space X^n to a corresponding value in a one-dimensional space X, i.e. (Calvo et al. 2002):

$$AO_n : X^n \rightarrow X \tag{8}$$

If the input arguments of AO_n are defined as IVIFNs, then X^n is a vector of IVIFN entries of the AO_n and X resulting from applying the operator over the X^n will be itself an IVIFN.

Aggregation operators as defined in Definition 2 are widely used in the field of MADM. Generally speaking, any alternative A_i can be defined as an n-dimensional vector identified according to its performance on different decision-making attributes, e.g. $A_i \equiv \{r_{i1}, r_{i2}, \ldots, r_{in}\}$. Applying an aggregation operator, each alternative can be represented by a single value of R_i. That is to say:

$$R_i : \{r_{i1}, r_{i2}, \ldots, r_{in}\} \rightarrow R_i \tag{9}$$

In the context of interval-valued intuitionistic fuzzy MADM, a similar pattern can be deducted. In this case, the alternatives can be represented as an n-dimensional IVIF vector representing their performance on decision-making attributes. Therefore, $A_i \equiv \{\tilde{r}_{i1}, \tilde{r}_{i2}, \ldots, \tilde{r}_{in}\}$, where $\tilde{r}_{in} = \left(\left[\mu_{ijL}, \mu_{ijU}\right], \left[\nu_{ijL}, \nu_{ijU}\right]\right)$. Similarly, any IVIF aggregation operator can be defined as:

$$R_i : \{\tilde{r}_{i1}, \tilde{r}_{i2}, \ldots, \tilde{r}_{in}\} \rightarrow \tilde{R}_i \tag{10}$$

where the aggregation operator R_i received an n-dimensional IVIF input vector and produces an IVIF output. According to Wang et al. (2012), the R_i will be an aggregation function if it is monotone and $R_i\left(\tilde{0}, \tilde{0}, \ldots, \tilde{0}\right) = \tilde{0}$, and $R_i\left(\tilde{1}, \tilde{1}, \ldots, \tilde{1}\right) = \tilde{1}$ where $\tilde{0} = \langle [0, 0], [1, 1] \rangle$, and $\tilde{1} = \langle [1, 1], [0, 0] \rangle$.

Suppose that there is a set of IVIFNs, i.e. $\tilde{r}_{ij} = \left(\left[\mu_{ijL}, \mu_{ijU}\right], \left[\nu_{ijL}, \nu_{ijU}\right]\right), j = 1, 2, \ldots, n$, and a vector of associated weights, i.e. $W = (w_1, w_2, \ldots, w_n)$. In the context of MADM, $\tilde{r}_{ij}, j = 1, 2, \ldots, n$ can be considered as the performance of alternative i (i.e. the ith candidate team member), while W is the weight vector of decision attributes. A variety of aggregation operators are proposed for IVIFNs.

Definitions 3 and 4 illustrate two operators using addition and multiplication operations. Equations (2)–(3) are called interval-valued intuitionistic fuzzy weighted averaging (IVIFWA) and geometric averaging (IVIFWGA) operators.

Definition 3
The IVIFWA operator concerning weight vector W is defined as (Xu 2007):

$$IVIFWA_W = \sum_{j=1}^{n} w_j \widetilde{r}_{i1} = \left\langle \left[1 - \prod_{j=1}^{n} (1 - \mu_{ijL})^{w_j}, 1 - \prod_{j=1}^{n} (1 - \mu_{ijU})^{w_j} \right], \left[\prod_{j=1}^{n} v_{ijL}{}^{w_j}, \prod_{j=1}^{n} v_{ijU}{}^{w_j} \right] \right\rangle \quad (11)$$

Definition 4
The IVIFWGA operator for weight vector W is defined as (Xu 2007):

$$IVIFWGA_W = \prod_{j=1}^{n} \widetilde{r}_{ij}^{w_j} = \left\langle \left[\prod_{j=1}^{n} \mu_{ijL}{}^{w_j}, \prod_{j=1}^{n} \mu_{ijU}{}^{w_j} \right], \left[1 - \prod_{j=1}^{n} (1 - v_{ijL})^{w_j}, 1 - \prod_{j=1}^{n} (1 - v_{ijU})^{w_j} \right] \right\rangle \quad (12)$$

Xu and Chen (2007) introduced the IVIF ordered weighted averaging (IVIFOWA) and geometric averaging (IVIFOWGA) operators. In these two operators, using score and accuracy function, Eqs. (6)–(7), respectively, the IVIFNs are ordered as $\left(\widetilde{r}_{ij}^1 > \widetilde{r}_{ij}^2 > \ldots > \widetilde{r}_{ij}^n\right)$. Then:

Definition 5
For a vector of ordered IVIFNs $\widetilde{r}_{ij}^1 > \widetilde{r}_{ij}^2 > \ldots > \widetilde{r}_{ij}^n$, the IVIFOWA and IVIFOWGA are defined as $IVIFOWA_W = \sum_{k=1}^{n} w_j \widetilde{r}_{ij}^k$ and $IVIFOWGA_W = \prod_{K=1}^{n} \left(\widetilde{r}_{ij}^k\right)^{w_j}$. Using the IVIFNs operators, it can be shown that:

And

$$IVIFOWA_W = \left\langle \left[1 - \prod_{k=1}^{n} \left(1 - \mu_{ijL}^k\right)^{w_k}, 1 - \prod_{k=1}^{n} \left(1 - \mu_{ijU}^k\right)^{w_k} \right], \left[\prod_{k=1}^{n} \left(v_{ijL}^k\right)^{w_k}, \prod_{k=1}^{n} \left(v_{ijU}^k\right)^{w_k} \right] \right\rangle \quad (13)$$

$$IVIFOWGA_W = \left\langle \left[\prod_{k=1}^{n} \left(\mu_{ijL}^k\right)^{w_k}, \prod_{k=1}^{n} \left(\mu_{ijL}^k\right)^{w_k} \right], \right.$$

$$\left[1-\prod_{k=1}^{n}\left(1-v_{ijL}^{k}\right)^{w_k},1-\prod_{k=1}^{n}\left(1-v_{ijU}^{k}\right)^{w_k}\right]\Bigg\rangle \tag{14}$$

A general class of parametric aggregation operators is proposed by Zhao et al. (2010). They generalised the previously mentioned aggregation operators as described in the following definitions:

Definition 6
For a collection of IVIFNs $\widetilde{r}_{ij}=\left(\left[\mu_{ijL},\mu_{ijU}\right],\left[v_{ijL},v_{ijU}\right]\right), j=1,2,\ldots,n$, associated weight vector $W=(w_1,w_2,\ldots,w_n)$, and $\lambda>0$,

$$GIVIFWA_W(\widetilde{r}_{i1},\widetilde{r}_{i2},\ldots,\widetilde{r}_{in})=\left(\sum_{j=1}^{n}w_j\widetilde{r}_{ij}^{\lambda}\right)^{\frac{1}{\lambda}}$$

$$=\left\langle\left[\left(1-\prod_{j=1}^{n}\left(1-\mu_{ijL}^{\lambda}\right)^{w_j}\right)^{\frac{1}{\lambda}},\left(1-\prod_{j=1}^{n}\left(1-\mu_{ijU}^{\lambda}\right)^{w_j}\right)^{\frac{1}{\lambda}}\right],\right.$$

$$\left[1-\left(1-\prod_{j=1}^{n}\left(1-(1-v_{ijL})^{\lambda}\right)^{w_j}\right)^{\frac{1}{\lambda}},\right.$$

$$\left.\left.1-\left(1-\prod_{j=1}^{n}\left(1-(1-v_{ijU})^{\lambda}\right)^{w_j}\right)^{\frac{1}{\lambda}}\right]\right\rangle \tag{15}$$

Definition 7
The generalised interval-valued intuitionistic fuzzy ordered weighted averaging (GIVIFOWA) operator is defined as:

$$GIVIFOWA_W(\widetilde{r}_{i1},\widetilde{r}_{i2},\ldots,\widetilde{r}_{in})=\left(\sum_{k=1}^{n}w_k\left(\widetilde{r}_{ij}^{k}\right)^{\lambda}\right)^{\frac{1}{\lambda}}$$

$$=\left\langle\left[\left(1-\prod_{j=1}^{n}\left(1-\left(\mu_{ijL}^{k}\right)^{\lambda}\right)^{w_j}\right)^{\frac{1}{\lambda}},\right.\right.$$

$$\left.\left(1-\prod_{j=1}^{n}\left(1-\left(\mu_{ijU}^{k}\right)^{\lambda}\right)^{w_j}\right)^{\frac{1}{\lambda}}\right],$$

$$\left[1-\left(1-\prod_{j=1}^{n}\left(1-\left(1-v_{ijL}^{k}\right)^{\lambda}\right)^{w_j}\right)^{\frac{1}{\lambda}},\right.$$

$$1-\left(1-\prod_{j=1}^{n}\left(1-\left(1-v_{ijL}^{k}\right)^{\lambda}\right)^{w_j}\right)^{\frac{1}{\lambda}}\Bigg]\Bigg\rangle \tag{16}$$

Among the latest studies, Liu and Wang (2018) proposed IVIF Schweizer-Sklar weighted average (IVIFSSPWA) operator as:

$$IVIFSSPWA(\widetilde{r}_{i1},\widetilde{r}_{i2},\ldots,\widetilde{r}_{in})=\left\langle\left[1-\left(\sum_{j=1}^{n}\xi_{ij}(1-\mu_{ijL})^{\gamma}\right)^{\frac{1}{\gamma}},1-\left(\sum_{j=1}^{n}\xi_{ij}(1-\mu_{ijU})^{\gamma}\right)^{\frac{1}{\gamma}}\right],\right.$$

$$\left.\left[\left(\sum_{j=1}^{n}\xi_{ij}v_{ijL}^{\gamma}\right)^{\frac{1}{\gamma}},\left(\sum_{j=1}^{n}\xi_{ij}v_{ijU}^{\gamma}\right)^{\frac{1}{\gamma}}\right]\right\rangle \tag{17}$$

where $\xi_{ij}(j=1,2,\ldots,n)$ is the collection of integrated weights as below:

$$\xi_{ij}=\frac{w_j\left(1+T\left(\widetilde{r}_{ij}\right)\right)}{\sum_{j=1}^{n}w_jT\left(\widetilde{r}_{ij}\right)} \tag{18}$$

and

$$T\left(\widetilde{r}_{ij}\right)=\sum_{\substack{h=1\\h\neq j}}^{n}\mathrm{Sup}\left(\widetilde{r}_{ij},\widetilde{r}_{ih}\right) \tag{19}$$

In Eq. (19),

$$\mathrm{Sup}\left(\widetilde{r}_{ij},\widetilde{r}_{ih}\right)=1-\mathrm{d}\left(\widetilde{r}_{ij},\widetilde{r}_{ih}\right) \tag{20}$$

$\mathrm{d}\left(\widetilde{r}_{ij},\widetilde{r}_{ih}\right)$ is the normalised Hamming distance between two IVIFNs $\widetilde{r}_{ij}$ and $\widetilde{r}_{ih}$:

$$\mathrm{d}\left(\widetilde{r}_{ij},\widetilde{r}_{ih}\right)=\frac{\left|\mu_{ijL}-\mu_{ihL}\right|+\left|\mu_{ijU}-\mu_{ihU}\right|+\left|v_{ijL}-v_{ihL}\right|+\left|v_{ijL}-v_{ihU}\right|}{4} \tag{21}$$

Similarly, the IVIF Schweizer-Sklar weighted geometric (IVIFSSPWG) operator is:

$$IVIFSSPWG(\widetilde{r}_{i1},\widetilde{r}_{i2},\ldots,\widetilde{r}_{in})=\left\langle\left[\left(\sum_{j=1}^{n}\xi_{ij}\mu_{ijL}{}^{\gamma}\right)^{\frac{1}{\gamma}},\left(\sum_{j=1}^{n}\xi_{ij}\mu_{ijU}{}^{\gamma}\right)^{\frac{1}{\gamma}}\right],\right.$$

$$\left[1-\left(\sum_{j=1}^{n}\xi_{ij}\left(1-v_{ijL}\right)^{\gamma}\right)^{\frac{1}{\gamma}},\right.$$

$$\left.1-\left(\sum_{j=1}^{n}\xi_{ij}\left(1-v_{ijU}\right)^{\gamma}\right)^{\frac{1}{\gamma}}\right]\Bigg\rangle \tag{22}$$

4.3 Team Member Selection Framework

As it is mentioned in the introduction section, choosing non-appropriate members to participate in a team can have destructive effects on a start-up and is one of the main reasons for start-up failures. Therefore, empowering entrepreneurs to select their team members with a structured and formalised procedure can be very beneficial. Considering this aim, a methodology consisting of three stages and ten steps is proposed in this chapter as depicted in Fig. 3.

4.3.1 Stage 1. Problem Formulation

Before anything is done, the main step is to define the problem as exactly as possible. The abstract definition of a team member selection problem can be defined as below: An entrepreneur or investor has an idea and is decided to form a team to operationalise the idea. The main steps to formally define the problem consist of the following:

Step 1-1. Forming the selection committee. Team member selection problem requires a panel of experts or idea owners to evaluate a set of candidate members. Therefore, the first step is to form the evaluation committee. The committee members must be chosen with special considerations. There is no general rule or method to select this committee. The selection committee members can be selected according to the previous knowledge of the main decision-maker. Otherwise, purposive sampling can be used to form a selection committee. Purposive sampling means to select participants intentionally according to the purpose (Macnee and McCabe 2008). Therefore, considering the aim of team member selection, a committee including one or several experts is formed. Suppose that this committee consists of l members. In this step, the main decision-maker, i.e. entrepreneur or investor, also declared a weighting vector $\lambda = (\lambda_1, \lambda_2, \ldots, \lambda_L)$ for the committee members. This vector can be specified by subjective or objective methods as described in Step 3-1.

Step 2-1. Identifying alternatives. A major part of team member selection using MCDM methods is to identify the list of alternatives, i.e. the candidate members to be evaluated and selected as a member of the team. Often, there is a specified and predetermined list of candidates being introduced by the entrepreneur. Sometimes, the entrepreneur is required to search and inquire about the list of candidates.

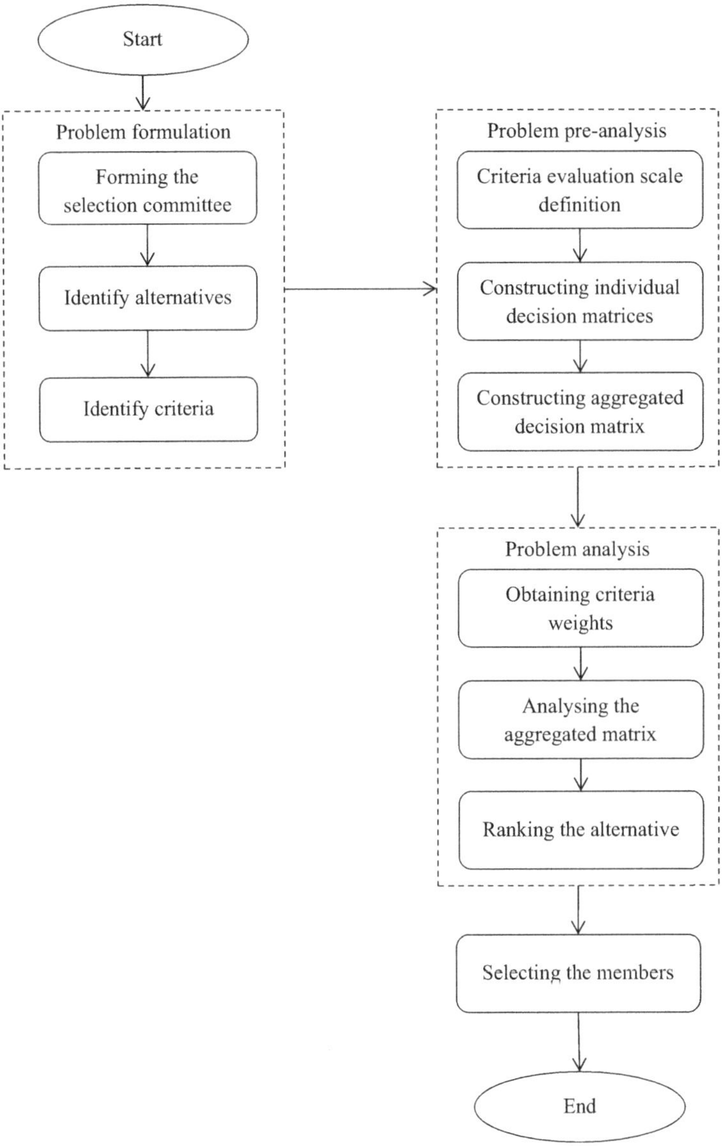

Fig. 3 Team member selection methodology

Regardless of the method used, finally, a set of candidates $A = \{A_1, A_2, \ldots, A_m\}$ are identified.

Step 3-1. Identify criteria. Another part of the team member selection process deals with the identification of selection criteria. While there isn't any standard method of criteria identification, however, some guidelines can be proposed.

Again, sometimes the criteria are proposed and specified directly by the entrepreneur as the main decision-maker. If there isn't any predetermined criteria list, the criteria can be identified using any explanatory method. One of the fruitful identification methods is the literature review, as described in Sect. 6 and also in Delphi (Dalkey and Helmer 1963; Schniederjans et al. 2004; Hsu and Sandford 2007). Suppose that the identified criteria are shown as the finite set of $C = \{C_1, C_2, \ldots, C_n\}$.

4.3.2 Stage 2. Problem Pre-analysis

Since the proposed methodology is designed to use MCDM methods in selecting team members, in this stage, the required elements are prepared to analyse the problem.

Step 1-2. Criteria evaluation scale definition. To construct a decision matrix, all of the alternatives are evaluated against all of the criteria. The criteria can be classified as quantitative and qualitative. Usually, quantitative criteria can be evaluated easily using exact and ration scales. However, a majority of criteria are of the qualitative type in decision-making problems, especially in the case of team member selection. Triantaphyllou (2000) reviewed a series of available scales to evaluate these criteria. However, decision-makers are rather preferred to express their judgments on qualitative variables using linguistic variables (Zadeh 1975; Wang 2010; Musani and Jemain 2013). To comply with this feature of qualitative criteria, the fuzzy sets theory is proposed by Zadeh (1975). However, in this chapter, IVIFS is used to quantify the linguistic evaluations of the candidates. To achieve the flexibility of evaluators in expressing their judgments, several scales are proposed to transform the linguistic evaluations of the committee members into equivalent IVIFNs. Table 2 illustrates the proposed scale (Hashemi et al. 2014; Mousavi et al. 2019).

It should be noted that although the scale represented in Table 2 is used in this chapter, however, any other scale proposed in the literature, e.g. Razavi Hajiagha et al. (2015), can be applied and the proposed method is not sensitive to the applied scale.

Step 2-2. Constructing individual decision matrices. At this step, each committee member completes an individual decision matrix $D^l = \left[\tilde{r}_{ij}^l\right]$ where $\tilde{r}_{ij}^l, i = 1, 2, \ldots, m; j = 1, 2, \ldots, n$ is the IVIF score or performance of the candidate A_i

Table 2 IVIF scale for transforming linguistic variable

Linguistic term	IVIFN
Very important/good (VI) (VG)	[(0.80,0.90), (0.05,0.10)]
Important/good (I) (G)	[(0.60,0.75), (0.10,0.20)]
Medium (M)	[(0.30,0.50), (0.25,0.45)]
Unimportant/poor (UI) (P)	[(0.20,0.35), (0.45,0.60)]
Very unimportant/poor (VUI) (VP)	[(0.00,0.10), (0.70,0.90)]

Hashemi et al. (2014)

regarding criterion C_j as evaluated by the lth committee member. Therefore, at the end of this step, a group of L individual decision matrices is available.

Step 3-2. Constructing aggregated decision matrix. In this step, the individual decision matrices of the previous step, i.e. D^1, D^2, ..., D^L, are aggregated into a single decision matrix $D = \left[\widetilde{r}_{ij}\right]$. The elements of matrix D are obtained using IVIFWA. In fact, $\widetilde{r}_{ij}$ is calculated applying IVIFWA over $\left(\widetilde{r}_{ij}^1, \widetilde{r}_{ij}^2, \ldots, \widetilde{r}_{ij}^L\right)$ using λ as its weight vector.

4.3.3 Stage 3. Problem Analysis

During stages 1 and 2, the main elements of the multi-criteria team member selection problem, including candidate alternatives, evaluation criteria, and the aggregated decision matrix, are identified. In this stage, the problem is analysed.

Step 1-3. Obtaining criteria weights. Criteria weight vector $W = (w_1, w_2, \ldots, w_n)$ is an important element of the decision-making process. This weighting vector can be determined using different methods. The criteria weight determination methods can be classified into two classes of objective and subjective methods. The subjective methods inquire the vector W according to decision-maker opinion. The objective methods extract the weights from the decision-making data structure (Zoraghi et al. 2013). Simple multi-attribute rating technique (SMART) (Edwards 1977), Simos procedure (Simos 1990), pairwise comparison (Saaty 1977, 1987), stepwise weight assessment ratio analysis (SWARA) (Keršuliene et al. 2010), and best-worst method (BWM) (Rezaei 2015) are some of the subjective weight determination methods. On the other hand, linear programming techniques for multidimensional analysis of preferences (LINMAP) (Srinivasan and Shocker 1973), entropy method (Hwang and Yoon 1981), criteria importance through inter-criteria correlation (CRITIC) (Diakoulaki et al. 1995), principal component analysis (Fan 1996), and simultaneous evaluation of criteria and alternatives (SECA) (Keshavarz-Ghorabaee et al. 2018) are some of the well-known objective methods.

In the proposed approach of the current study, the subjective weight determination methods are proposed since team member selection is rather a personal decision with a variety of behavioural and social aspects affecting the preferences of decision-makers. Therefore, implying the viewpoints of the main decision-maker is crucial. To this aim, the BWM method is proposed as an accepted and widely used method. In this step, the method is described to elicit the weights of decision criteria. However, as noted in Step 1-1, this method can be used to determine the weights of the committee member.

Consider the criteria vector $C = \{C_1, C_2, \ldots, C_n\}$. The question is to determine a criteria weight vector $W = \{w_1, w_2, \ldots, w_n\}$ such that $w_j \geq 0$, $j = 1, 2, \ldots, n$ and $\sum_{j=1}^{n} w_j = 1$. According to the BWM method, the decision-maker must first specify the most important (best), C_B, $B \in \{1, 2, \ldots, n\}$, and the least important (worst), C_W, $W \in \{1, 2, \ldots, n\}$, criteria. Then, the decision-maker expressed the preference of the best criterion over other remaining criteria, i.e. best-to-other vector. Suppose that

Table 3 Pairwise comparison scale

Linguistic judgment	Numerical equivalent
Absolutely more important	9
Much more important	7
More important	5
Slightly more important	3
Equal importance	1
Slightly less important	1/3
Less important	1/5
Much less important	1/7
Absolutely minor importance	1/9

Abildtrup et al. (2006)

$A_B = \{a_{B1}, a_{B2}, \ldots, a_{Bn}\}$ is the considered vector. The elements $a_{Bj}, j \in \{1, 2, \ldots, n\}$ illustrate the preference of the best criterion C_B to other criteria C_j. These preferences can be specified using any value; however, the Saaty (1980) ratio scale can be used (Table 3).

It is notable that $a_{WW} = 1$, and $a_{jW} \geq 1$, $\forall$ j, j $\in \{1, 2, \ldots, n\}$. On the other hand, decision-maker provided the other-to-worst vector $A_W = \{a_{1W}, a_{2W}, \ldots, a_{nW}\}$ that represents the preference of all criteria over the worst one. Here again, a_{jW} is the preference of criterion j with regard to the worst criterion w. In this vector, $a_{WW} = 1$, and $a_{jW} \geq 1$, $\forall$ j, j $\in \{1, 2, \ldots, n\}$. In the BWM method, the optimal weights of criteria are then determined by solving the non-linear model of Eq. (23).

$$\begin{aligned}
&\min \xi \\
&\text{st}: \\
&\left|\frac{W_B}{W_j} - A_{bj}\right| \leq \xi; \quad \text{for all j} \\
&\left|A_{jw} - \frac{W_j}{W_W}\right| \leq \xi; \quad \text{for all j} \\
&\sum W_j = 1, \\
&W_j \geq 0
\end{aligned} \tag{23}$$

Solving the above model, an optimal weight vector $W = \{w_1, w_2, \ldots, w_n\}$ is determined. The model can be solved using any optimisation package, e.g. general algebraic modelling system (GAMS) or LINGO.

Solving the model, the optimal objective value of ξ^* is determined. This value is used to determine the consistency of the decision-maker in expressing the preferences. The consistency ratio is calculated as:

$$CR = \frac{\xi^*}{CI} \tag{24}$$

where CI is the consistency index calculated by Rezaei (2015). If $CR \leq 0.1$, the credibility of preferences and obtained weights are approved. Otherwise, the judgments could be revised to improve consistency.

At the end of this step, the criteria weight vector is available.

Step 2-3. Analysing the aggregated matrix. In this step, the aggregated decision matrix, Step 3-2, and criteria weight vector, Step 1-3, are available. Now, the aggregated performance of candidate alternatives is calculated using the introduced IVIF aggregation operators in Sect. 5. To this aim, suppose that $\{\widetilde{r}_{i1}, \widetilde{r}_{i2}, \ldots, \widetilde{r}_{in}\}$ is the IVIF performance vector of candidate A_i. Also, the criteria weight vector is $W = \{w_1, w_2, \ldots, w_n\}$. Then, the IVIFWA, IVIFWGA, IVIFOWA, IVIFOWGA, GIVIFWA, GIVIFOWA, and IVIFSSPA operators are applied to the considered performance vectors. Applying any one of the operators, a given score vector $\{\widetilde{s}_1^o, \widetilde{s}_2^o, \ldots, \widetilde{s}_m^o\}$ is obtained where o is a given operator, i.e.:

$$o \in \{\text{IVIFWA}, \text{IVIFWGA}, \text{IVIFOWA}, \text{IVIFOWGA}, \text{GIVIFWA}, \text{GIVIFOWA}, \text{ and IVIFSSPA}\}.$$

Step 3-3. Ranking the alternatives. After calculating the score of alternatives using different aggregating operators at Step 2-3, it might be possible to rank the alternatives according to different operators. Using the score and accuracy functions, Eqs. (6)–(7), the obtained ranking from different operators is transformed into associated ranking vectors. Suppose that R_i^o is the rank obtained by alternative A_i, applying the operator o. Therefore, based on the operators used to aggregate the performance of alternatives, different ranking vectors will be on hand. The result of this step is a set of the ranking vector $R^o = \{R_1^o, R_2^o, \ldots, R_m^o\}$.

4.3.4 Stage 3. Selecting the Members

At the end of stage 2, several ranking vectors are obtained for alternatives. This stage aims to aggregate the rankings to achieve a final ranking vector.

Step 1-3. Selecting the members. In this step, different rankings obtained by different aggregation operators are aggregated. Different aggregating methods are proposed to find a final ranking from a set of elementary rankings. Among classic methods of ranking aggregation, BORDA and Copeland laws are popular (Pomerol and Barba-Romero 2012). However, these methods consider similar weights for different rankings. To overcome this shortcoming, in this study, the ensemble ranking of Mohammadi and Rezaei (2020) is used to find the final ranking. They proposed the following optimisation model to find the overall ranking, R^*, of alternatives:

$$\min_{R^*} \frac{1}{2} \sum_{o=1}^{O} g\left(\|R^o - R^*\|_2\right) \tag{25}$$

where O is the number of aggregation operators used in Step 2-3 to evaluate the alternatives and $g(\cdot)$ is a half-quadratic function. Then, an algorithm is proposed to find the overall ranks as illustrated below.

Algorithm 1 Ensemble Ranking (Mohammadi and Rezaei 2020)
Input: Rankings R^o, $o = 1, 2, \ldots, O$
While *not converged* do

$$\alpha_o = \delta\left(\|R^o - R^*\|_2\right), o = 1, 2, \ldots, O$$

$$w_o = \frac{\alpha_o}{\sum_{r=1}^{O} \alpha_r}, o = 1, 2, \ldots, O$$

$$R^* = \sum_{o} w_o R^o$$

End while
Output final ranking R^*, R^*

In the above algorithm, $\delta(\cdot)$ is a minimiser function that can be adopted from Mohammadi and Rezaei et al. (2020). These minimiser functions are derived for the associated half-quadratic functions, i.e. $g(\cdot)$ is used in the model of Eq. (21). For simplicity of use, some of these functions are represented in Table 4. In this table, β is a positive constant, and σ and γ are the parameters of HQ functions.

Mohammadi and Rezaei (2020) especially proposed using the Welsch function due to its robustness. Therefore, in this study, this function is also proposed. The

Table 4 Minimiser function to find the overall ranking of alternatives

Estimator	Minimiser function $\delta(s)$
$l_1 - l_2$	$\frac{1}{\sqrt{\beta + s^2}}$
Fair	$\frac{1}{\beta(\beta + \lvert s \rvert)}$
Log-cosh	$\frac{\beta}{s} \tanh(\beta s)$
Welsch	$\exp\left(-\frac{s^2}{\sigma^2}\right)$
Huber	$\begin{cases} 1, \lvert s \rvert \le \gamma \\ \frac{\gamma}{\lvert s \rvert}, \lvert s \rvert > \gamma \end{cases}$

Mohammadi and Rezaei (2020)

parameter σ of this estimator can be updated recursively at each iteration K as (Mohammadi and Rezaei 2020; He et al. 2014):

$$\sigma = \frac{\sum_{o=1}^{O} \|R^o - R^*\|_2^2}{2K^2} \tag{26}$$

Starting with $K = 1$ and running the algorithm 1 until it reached the convergence, the final ranking of alternatives, $R^* = \left(R_1^*, R_2^*, \ldots, R_m^*\right)$ is determined. According to this final ranking, the decision-maker can select the appropriate member to complete the team.

5 Case Study

In this section, a real-world case study of team member selection is illustrated to justify the application of the proposed methodology. A chemistry graduate is going to start a business producing a Nano-product entitled "grapheme oxide" with several industrial applications. This researcher is qualified enough in chemistry and Nano-based knowledge; however, he needs more management, finance, and marketing knowledge. In this regard, the researcher tries to establish a team of prominent people as marketing manager, technical assistant, and financial manager. For this purpose, it seems better that they should understand the business goals, organisational principles, structural hierarchy, and managerial skills and have appropriate interactions and relationships. In this account, the researcher or the main founder knows any technical requirements and is sufficiently ready to treat every Nano-technology problem, while the business includes many other challenges that the founder should struggle with. As an instance, the feasibility study should be performed to extract the probable risks and success chance. It needs a managerial and financial expert to analyse the results and make the appropriate decision to plan the further excellence programs; the market share of the product should be monitored, and the company needs to budget and assign the resources to different growth projects. These activities should be performed by qualified personnel and compromised with appropriate wages. Hiring the staff is a critical, time-consuming, and long-term effecting activity which includes a major part of company costs. Therefore, it is necessary to be done under the supervision of a human resource expert. On the other hand, the production as a manufacturing process should be transformed from a laboratory process into a mass production process and needs to be organised and prepared to respond to market demand. It requires a technician to plan the production process, to supply the raw materials, and to determine the quality levels and characteristics. Generally, the researcher needs a team to run the business and survive among other competitors. These team members will significantly affect the company and its future programs; therefore, it is emphasised to select the business partners very carefully. In this regard, the founder intends to concentrate on the most critical partners to pass the initial steps successfully and with lower costs. He decided to select three experts to assist him in finance, marketing, and production operations as his business partners. The proposed approach is performed on the above-mentioned team member selection problem as described below.

5.1 Forming the Selection Committee

Since the considered entrepreneur decided to choose a team consisting of different fields of experience, including financial, marketing, and operation assistants, the selection committee is formed by the entrepreneur, a financial expert, and a marketing expert. Therefore, a committee of three experts is formed to select the appropriate candidate. Considering the different expertise of committee members, different weights are assigned to them. To select the financial assistant, the entrepreneur (λ_1) and financial (λ_2) and marketing (λ_3) experts are assigned a weight vector $\lambda^1 = (\lambda_1, \lambda_2, \lambda_3) = (0.2,0.6,0.2)$, respectively. The associated weights of committee members to select a marketing assistant is $\lambda^2 = (\lambda_1, \lambda_2, \lambda_3) = (0.2,0.2,0.6)$ and to select operational assistant is $\lambda^3 = (\lambda_1, \lambda_2, \lambda_3) = (0.6,0.2,0.2)$.

5.2 Identify Alternatives

The candidate alternatives are identified using different channels. First, the entrepreneur asked his colleague in university to introduce him to the considered persons. Also, the committee searched through LinkedIn as a complementary tool. Considering the expertise of the committee, a list of candidates is identified. Through this initial examination, four candidates $\{F_1, F_2, F_3, F_4\}$ are selected to be evaluated as a financial assistant; four candidates $\{M_1, M_2, M_3, M_4\}$ are chosen as marketing assistant candidates and three candidates $\{O_1, O_2, O_3\}$ as operational assistant candidates.

Table 5 Team member selection criteria used in the case study

	Financial assistant	Marketing assistant	Operational assistant
Knowledge	• Education • Job training	• Education • Job training	• Education • Job training
Skills	• Experience	• Experience • Oral communication • Foreign language	• Technical skills
Attitude	• Completing tasks on time	• Emotional steadiness • Flexibility	• Completing tasks on time • Teamwork

5.3 *Identify Criteria*

The main consideration to select the appropriate team members is to determine a set of evaluation criteria. Considering the KSA framework, Fig. 2, and using a focus group of committee members, the criteria listed in Table 5 are chosen to appraise different team members.

5.4 *Criteria Evaluation Scale Definition*

To appraise the candidate, they are invited to interview meetings, and the committee members individually interview with any one of the alternatives. A set of 11 interviews are done by each committee member, and the performance of alternatives is appraised using the scale in Table 2.

5.5 *Constructing Individual Decision Matrices*

After each interview, committee members completed their decision matrix regarding their evaluation of the considered candidate regarding the defined criteria.

Table 6 Individual matrices of evaluating financial assistant candidates

Financial expert	Education	Job training	Experience	Completing tasks on time
F1	M	P	P	G
F2	G	M	P	M
F3	P	G	G	M
F4	P	M	M	G
Operational expert	Education	Job training	Experience	Completing tasks on time
F1	P	M	M	G
F2	G	M	P	M
F3	P	G	G	G
F4	P	M	G	M
Marketing expert	Education	Job training	Experience	Completing tasks on time
F1	G	M	P	G
F2	G	M	M	M
F3	M	G	G	G
F4	P	G	G	M

Table 6 illustrates the completed decision matrices of four financial assistant candidates. In the case of the financial assistance, the education is appraised considering the quality of candidate education, job training is appraised based on the professional courses the applicant participated in, the experience is appraised based on the previous work experience of candidates, and completing tasks on time is appraised by assigning work to candidates and asking them to complete the job in a specific time.

5.6 Constructing Aggregated Decision Matrix

To construct the aggregated matrix, first, the linguistic variables of Table 6 are transformed to equivalent IVIFNs according to Table 2. Then, using the committee member's weight vector $\lambda^1 = (0.2,0.6,0.2)$, the aggregated matrix is constructed as Table 7.

Table 7 Aggregated decision matrix to select the financial assistant

Financial expert	Education	Job training	Experience	Completing tasks on time
F1	[(0.357,0.541), (0.234,0.405)]	[(0.242,0.415), (0.356,0.535)]	[(0.221,0.338), (0.4,0.566)]	[(0.6,0.75), (0.1,0.2)]
F2	[(0.6,0.75), (0.1,0.2)]	[(0.3,0.5), (0.25,0.45)]	[(0.221,0.338), (0.4,0.566)]	[(0.3,0.5), (0.25,0.45)]
F3	[(0.221,0.338), (0.4,0.566)]	[(0.6,0.75), (0.1,0.2)]	[(0.6,0.75), (0.1,0.2)]	[(0.44,0.621), (0.173,0.325)]
F4	[(0.2,0.35), (0.45,0.6)]	[(0.374,0.565), (0.208,0.383)]	[(0.44,0.621), (0.173,0.325)]	[(0.5,0.67), (0.144,0.277)]

Table 8 Best-to-other vector

	Education	Job training	Experience	Completing tasks on time
Past experience	5	2	1	1

Table 9 Other-to-worst vector

	Education
Education	1
Job training	2
Experience	5
Completing tasks on time	5

5.7 Obtaining Criteria Weights

To find a suitable candidate, the criteria weight vector must be determined. To determine the criteria weight vector, each committee member is assigned to determine the weights of criteria associated with his or her field. The financial expert believed experience as the most important and education as the least important criterion in evaluating the financial assistant candidates. The best-to-other vector is expressed by the financial expert as illustrated in Table 8.

Also, the other-to-worst vector is determined as illustrated in Table 9.

The corresponding BWM model is formulated as below.

$$\begin{gathered}
\min \xi \\
\text{st}: \\
\left|\frac{W_3}{W_1} - 5\right| \leq \xi \\
\left|\frac{W_3}{W_2} - 2\right| \leq \xi \\
\left|\frac{W_3}{W_4} - 1\right| \leq \xi \\
\left|2 - \frac{W_2}{W_1}\right| \leq \xi \\
\left|5 - \frac{W_3}{W_1}\right| \leq \xi \\
\left|5 - \frac{W_4}{W_1}\right| \leq \xi \\
W_1 + W_2 + W_3 + W_4 = 1 \\
W_j \geq 0, j = 1, 2, 3, 4
\end{gathered} \tag{27}$$

Solving the model in Eq. (27), the weight vector is obtained as $W = (0.078, 0.171, 0.375, 0.375)$ and $\xi^* = 0.193$. Therefore, the consistency ratio is approximated as $CR = 0.193/1.63 = 0.118$. This consistency ratio is not acceptable and the committee member required revising the vectors. The financial expert revised the preference of experience and completing the task on time to education from 5 to 4. Solving the model, the weight vector is corrected as $W = (0.091, 0.182, 0.364, 0.364)$ with complete consistency. This weight vector is used in the following steps:

Table 10 IVIF aggregation operator's result to select the financial assistant

	IVIFWA	IVIFWGA	GIVIFWA($\lambda = 2$)	IVIFSSWPA and IVIFSSWPG ($\gamma = 1$)	IVIFSSWPA ($\gamma = 2$)	IVIFSSWPG ($\gamma = 2$)
1	[(0.402,0.572), (0.225,0.372)]	[(0.337,0.512), (0.28,0.435)]	[(0.429,0.588), (0.218,0.358)]	[(0.366,0.529), (0.274,0.421)]	[(0.344,0.501), (0.305,0.452)]	[(0.405,0.554), (0.262,0.398)]
2	[(0.308,0.493), (0.273,0.455)]	[(0.286,0.512), (0.297,0.478)]	[(0.323,0.502), (0.269,0.447)]	[(0.297,0.479), (0.291,0.471)]	[(0.290,0.470), (0.304,0.481)]	[(0.312,0.489), (0.285,0.462)]
3	[(0.52,0.684), (0.139,0.262)]	[(0.49,0.659), (0.159,0.289)]	[(0.528,0.689), (0.137,0.259)]	[(0.511,0.657), (0.151,0.275)]	[(0.498,0.657), (0.171,0.294)]	[(0.523,0.681), (0.147,0.268)]
4	[(0.434,0.612), (0.183,0.334)]	[(0.417,0.596), (0.2,0.351)]	[(0.439,0.615), (0.181,0.331)]	[(0.430,0.606), (0.192,0.341)]	[(0.424,0.597), (0.208,0.352)]	[(0.438,0.612), (0.188,0.335)]

Table 11 Aggregated decision matrix to select the operational assistant

Operational assistants	Education	Job training	Technical skills	Completing tasks on time	Teamwork
O1	[(0.6,0.75), (0.1,0.2)]	[(0.281,0.473), (0.281,0.477)]	[(0.553,0.713), (0.12,0.235)]	[(0.44,0.621), (0.173,0.325)]	[(0.262,0.445), (0.316,0.505)]
O2	[(0.8,0.9), (0.05,0.1)]	[(0.826,0.856), (0.066,0.132)]	[(0.6,0.75), (0.1,0.2)]	[(0.3,0.5), (0.25,0.45)]	[(0.2,0.35), (0.45,0.6)]
O3	[(0.8,0.9), (0.05,0.1)]	[(0.6,0.75), (0.1,0.2)]	[(0.868,0.88), (0.057,0.115)]	[(0.221,0.383), (0.4,0.566)]	[(0.163,0.306), (0.492,0.651)]

5.8 *Ranking the Alternatives*

Constructing the aggregated decision matrix in Table 7 and determining the criteria weight vector in the previous step, the IVIF aggregation operators are applied. Table 10 illustrates the results of applying different aggregation operators on the information about selecting the financial assistant. To rank the candidates, the score functions of the obtained aggregation functions are calculated, and the alternatives are ranked based on the descending order of these scores. Since a similar ranking is obtained in different aggregation operators, there is no need to aggregate the ranking. The obtained ranking is $F_3 \succ F_4 \succ F_1 \succ F_2$. This means that the candidate F_3 is selected as the financial assistant of the entrepreneur.

The above-mentioned steps also are done to find suitable operational and marketing assistants. Table 11 illustrates the aggregated decision matrix of the operational assistant. The table is completed for three candidates.

Also, the operational expert determined the technical skills as the most important (best) and teamwork as the least important (worst) criteria. Using BWM, the weight vector of criteria is obtained as $W = (0.14, 0.218, 0.388, 0.175, 0.079)$ and the consistency ration is $CR = 0.222/2.30 = 0.097$. Using this information, the alternatives are ranked by aggregation operators. In this case, different aggregation operators resulted in a non-similar ordering of alternatives as represented in Table 12.

Applying the HQ function-based aggregation, the final ranking is obtained as $O_3 \succ O_2 \succ O_1$ and the third operational assistant candidate is selected.

Finally, the aggregated decision matrix of marketing assistant candidates is constructed as Table 13. To determine the criteria weight vector, the BWM method is used. At the first iteration, the achieved consistency ratio is obtained as $CR = 0.887/3.73 = 0.238$ that is unacceptable. Revising the best-to-other and other-to-worst vectors, at the sixth iteration, $CR = 0.298/3.73 = 0.08$ is obtained. The obtained weight vector is $W = (0.167, 0.167, 0.167, 0.285, 0.084, 0.045, 0.084)$. Using this weighting vector and the aggregated decision matrix, the final ranking is obtained as $M_4 \succ M_1 \succ M_2 \succ M_3$.

Therefore, the entrepreneur can form a team consisting $\{F_3, O_3, M_4\}$ as his or her financial, operational, and marketing assistants.

6 Conclusion

Selecting team members is one of the most challenging issues facing the organisation, and just as the right choice can have many potential benefits for the organisation, the wrong choice can have devastating effects and cause financial loss and loss of valuable time of the organisation, which will lead to loss of competitive advantage. Many factors influence team member selection; these include personality traits, environmental characteristics, and other elements. Judgment-based decision-making

Table 12 Ordering of candidates to select the operational assistant

Operational assistants	IVIFWA	IVIFWGA	GIVIFWA	IVIFSSWPA($\gamma = 1$)	IVIFSSWPA($\gamma = 2$)	IVIFSSWPG($\gamma = 2$)
O1	3	3	3	3	3	3
O2	2	1	2	2	1	2
O3	1	2	1	1	2	1

Table 13 Aggregated decision matrix to select the marketing assistant

Marketing assistants	Education	Job training	Experience	Oral communication	Foreign Language	Emotional steadiness	Flexibility
O1	[(0.221,0.383), (0.4,0.566)]	[(0.541,0.697), (0.135,0.249)]	[(0.44,0.621), (0.173,0.325)]	[(0.652,0.792), (0.087,0.174)]	[(0.221,0.383), (0.4,0.566)]	[(0.6,0.75), (0.1,0.2)]	[(0.652,0.792), (0.087,0.174)]
O2	[(0.322,0.491), (0.296,0.455)]	[(0.248,0.438), (0.307,0.517)]	[(0.652,0.792), (0.087,0.174)]	[(0.44,0.621), (0.173,0.325)]	[(0.272,0.427), (0.364,0.522)]	[(0.455,0.638), (0.181,0.333)]	[(0.44,0.621), (0.173,0.325)]
O3	[(0.44,0.621), (0.173,0.325)]	[(0.553,0.731), (0.12,0.235)]	[(0.374,0.565), (0.208,0.383)]	[(0.3,0.5), (0.25,0.45)]	[(0.6,0.75), (0.1,0.2)]	[(0.374,0.565), (0.208,0.383)]	[(0.186,0.342), (0.437,0.614)]
O4	[(0.697,0.827), (0.076,0.152)]	[(0.44,0.621), (0.173,0.325)]	[(0.6,0.75), (0.1,0.2)]	[(0.3,0.5), (0.25,0.45)]	[(0.553,0.713), (0.12,0.235)]	[(0.553,0.713), (0.12,0.235)]	[(0.541,0.697), (0.135,0.249)]

will also always be problematic. Using quantitative methods to stay away from personal judgments can prevent potential harm of subjectivity.

In this study, a hybrid multi-criteria decision-making methodology under interval-valued intuitionistic fuzzy numbers (IVFNs) is developed to deal with environmental uncertainty. While previous studies deal with the issue of uncertainty in selecting team members, however, the application of IVIF sets in this field is almost rare. Through the proposed methodology, after determining the criteria for selecting team members based on the literature review, the opinions of the experts' committee regarding the performance of candidate alternatives are gathered using linguistic variables that are transformed to IVIFN. After developing individual decision matrices, they are aggregated in a single aggregated matrix, representing the overall evaluation of alternatives based on different criteria. Also, the criteria weight vector is extracted using the best-worst method (BWM). Several aggregation operators are then applied to determine the total performance of alternatives. Since different operators provide non-similar rankings, different rankings are finally integrated using the half-quadratic-based aggregation. This hybrid methodology seems to be a suitable and trustworthy methodology to select team members.

The trustworthiness of the proposed method can be analysed through Saaty and Ergu (2015) framework. They proposed 15 features of a decision-making method as below:

- The simplicity of use. For the proposed method, the simplicity of the proposed algorithm seems medium since it required decision-maker to put some effort into learning it.
- The comprehensive structure: breadth and depth. Since the criteria used in the proposed methodology cannot be decomposed, the comprehensiveness of the methodology is rated low.
- The comprehensive structure consists of merit substructures. Since no limitation is imposed to define the criteria, the methodology can be rated high in this feature.
- Logical, mathematical procedure. The method can be rated high in this feature since it used pairwise comparison in determining criteria weights.
- Justification of the approach justifiable axioms. The proposed methodology is constructed using accepted and well-known mathematical procedures. Therefore, its justification is rated high.
- Scales of measurement. The proposed method is developed based on IVIF sets to transform linguistic (ordinal) scales into IVIFNs. Therefore, the method is rated low in this feature. However, the ability to deal with linguistic variables can adjust its weakness in this feature.
- Synthesis of judgments with merging functions. Since the individual judgments are aggregated using a formal aggregation operator, the method is rated high in this feature.
- Ranking of tangibles. As can be seen from the case study, the proposed methodology provides a final ranking of alternatives and, therefore, is rated high in this feature.

- The generalisation to the ranking of intangibles. Intangible factors are handled using IVIFNs. Based on this ability, the method is rated high in this feature.
- Rank preservation and reversal. The method can be rated high in this feature since it uses different aggregation operators and is not dependent only on a single method.
- Sensitivity analysis. Since the proposed method uses several aggregation operators and also the BWM method can improve the consistency of decision-makers in its iterations, the method is rated high in this feature.
- Validation of decision problems. The proposed method can be easily used in real-world problems, as illustrated in the case study. Therefore, the method is rated high in this feature.
- Prediction of the outcome of decisions with intangibles (the capability to predict preferences). The method is proposed to rank the alternatives without any sense of predicting the results. Therefore, the method is rated low.
- Generalisability to dependence and feedback. Dependence among criteria can be imposed into the proposed methodology by using the analytic network process (ANP) or any network-based weight elicitation method instead of BWM. However, this dependence and feedback are not handled directly in the proposed methodology. Therefore, the method is rated medium in this feature.
- Applicability to conflict resolution. Since the proposed method used a weighted aggregation operator to aggregate individual judgments, the method is rated high in this feature.
- Trustworthiness and validity of the approach. Considering the importance of the findings for decision-makers and its mathematical axioms and foundations, the method is rated high in this feature.

From a managerial perspective, the findings of this study help entrepreneurs to focus on the key factors in selecting team members through which they can improve the overall performance of the entrepreneurship while avoiding subjectivity. This research can also be a general guide for entrepreneurs and start-ups to be able to save time and money in selecting team members and make optimal decisions. Besides, identifying important variables in selecting team members in start-ups will lead to the success of the organisation in the short term and long term.

This study can be considered as the first research that has used interval-valued intuitionistic fuzzy sets for team member selection. However, the method can be empowered by enabling it to handle interdependence among criteria. Also, the method can be generalised into large-scale group decision-making (LSGDM) problems of selecting people for large and mature organisations. Providing a software package to aid entrepreneurs to facilitate using the proposed methodology also can be considered.

References

Abildtrup J, Audsley E, Fekete-Farkas M, Giupponi C, Gylling M, Rosato P, Rounsevell M (2006) Socio-economic scenario development for the assessment of climate change impacts on agricultural land use: a pairwise comparison approach. Environ Sci Pol 9(2):101–115

Afshari, A., Yusuff, R., & Derayatifar, A. (2012). Project manager selection by using fuzzy simple additive weighting method. 2012 International Conference on Innovation Management and Technology Research

Aggarwal R (2014 Identifying and prioritizing human capital measurement indicators for personnel selection using fuzzy MADM. Proceedings of the third international conference on soft computing for problem solving, 427–439

Amin Moghadasi M, Derakhshandeh B, Ferdosi M, Jafari Sadeghi V (2017) Organizational conformity as an entrepreneurial response to the changes in internationalization process: a study of IT-oriented firms in Saveh. World Journal of Accounting, Finance and Engineering 1 (1):53–64

Arasti Z, Zandi F, Talebi K (2012) Exploring the effect of individual factors on business failure in Iranian new established small businesses. Int Bus Res 5(4)

Arasti Z, Zandi F, Bahmani N (2014) Business failure factors in Iranian SMEs: do successful and unsuccessful entrepreneurs have different viewpoints? J Glob Entrep Res 4(1)

Atanassov KT (1986) Intuitionistic fuzzy sets. Fuzzy Sets Syst 20(1):87–96

Atanassov KT (1999 Interval valued intuitionistic fuzzy sets. In: Atanassov K (ed.) Intuitionistic fuzzy sets. Studies in Fuzziness and Soft Computing, 35, Physica, Heidelberg

Atanassov K, Gargov G (1989) Interval valued intuitionistic fuzzy sets. Fuzzy Sets Syst 31 (3):343–349

Autio E, George G, Alexy O (2011) International entrepreneurship and capability development-qualitative evidence and future research directions. Entrep Theory Pract 35(1):11–37

Beheshti M, Mahdiraji HA, Zavadskas EK (2016) Strategy portfolio optimisation: a copras g-modm hybrid approach. Transform Bus Econ 15(3C):500–519

Biancone PP, Jafari Sadeghi V (2016) Risk management in export compliance: concepts, procedures, and solutions. In: Cantino V, De Vincentiis P, Racca MG (eds) Risk management: perspectives and open issues. McGraw-Hill, London, UK, pp 64–78

Bogdanovic D, Miletic S (2015) Personnel evaluation and selection by multicriteria decision making method. Economic Computation and Economic Cybernetics Studies and Research 48(3)

Brouthers KD, Nakos G, Dimitratos P (2015) SME entrepreneurial orientation, international performance, and the moderating role of strategic alliances. Entrep Theory Pract 39 (5):1161–1187

Büyüközkan G, Göçer F, Karabulut Y (2018) A new group decision making approach with IF AHP and IF VIKOR for selecting hazardous waste carriers. Measurement 10:41–51

Calvo T, Kolesárová, Komorniková M, Mesia R (2002) Aggregation operators: properties, classes and construction method. In: Calvo T, Mayor G, Mesia R (eds) Aggregation operators: new trends and applications. Physica-Verlag, Heidelberg, Germany, pp 3–104

Chandler G, Honig B, Wiklund J (2005) Antecedents, moderators, and performance consequences of membership change in new venture teams. J Bus Ventur 20:705–725

Dalkey NC, Helmer O (1963) An experimental application of the Delphi method to the use of experts. Manag Sci 9(3):458–467

Dana LP (2017) International entrepreneurship research: how it evolved and directions for the future. Int J Entrep Small Bus 30(4):477

Dana LP, Wright RW (2009) International entrepreneurship: research priorities for the future. International Journal of Globalisation and Small Business 3(1):90

Decker R, Haltiwanger J, Jarmin R, Miranda J (2016) Where has all the skewness gone? The decline in high-growth (young) firms in the U.S. Eur Econ Rev 86:4–23

Delmar F, Davidsson P, Gartner WB (2003) Arriving at the high-growth firm. J Bus Ventur 18(2): 189–216

Diakoulaki D, Mavrotas G, Papayannakis L (1995) Determining objective weights in multiple criteria problems: the critic method. Comput Oper Res 22(7):763–770
Dursun M, Karsak E (2010) A fuzzy MCDM approach for personnel selection. Expert Syst Appl 37 (6):4324–4330
Edwards W (1977) How to use multiattribute utility measurement for social decision-making. IEEE Trans Syst Man Cybern 7(5):326–340
Etemad H, Wright RW (2003) Internationalization of SMEs: Toward a New Paradigm. Small Bus Econ 20(1):1–4
Eurofound (2012) Born global: the potential of job creation in new international businesses. Publications Office of the European Union, Luxembourg
Fan ZP (1996 Complicated multiple attribute decision making: theory and applications, Ph.D. Dissertation, Northeastern University, Shenyang, P.R.C.
Fernhaber SA, Gilbert BA, McDougall PP (2008) International entrepreneurship and geographic location: an empirical examination of new venture internationalization. J Int Bus Stud 39 (2):267–290
Garg H, Arora R (2018) A nonlinear-programming methodology for multi-attribute decision-making problem with interval-valued intuitionistic fuzzy soft sets information. Appl Intell 48 (8):2031–2046
Gau W-L, Buehrer DJ (1993) Vague sets. IEEE Trans Syst Man Cybern 23(2):610–614
Gedajlovic E, Honig B, Moore C, Payne G, Wright M (2013) Social capital and entrepreneurship: a schema and research agenda. Entrep Theory Pract 37(3):455–478
Gibb A (1993) Key factors in the design of policy support for the small and medium enterprise development process: an overview. Entrep Reg Dev 5(1):1–24
Golec A, Kahya E (2007) A fuzzy model for competency-based employee evaluation and selection. Comput Ind Eng 52:143–161
Goyal M, Gupta C (2020) Intuitionistic fuzzy decision making towards efficient team selection in global software development. Journal of Information Technology Research 13(2):75–93
Grattan-Guinness I (1976) Fuzzy membership mapped onto intervals and many-valued quantities. Zeitschrift Für Mathematische Logik Und Grundlagen Der Mathematik 22(1):149–160
Greiner L (1972) Evolution and revolution as organizations grow. Harv Bus Rev 50(4):37–46
Gungor Z, Serhadlıoglu G, Erhan Kesen S (2009) A fuzzy AHP approach to personnel selection problem. Appl Soft Comput 9:641–646
Gurău C, Dana LP (2020) Financing paths, firms' governance and corporate entrepreneurship: accessing and applying operant and operand resource in biotechnology firms. Technological Forecasting and Social Change 153
Hajiagha SHR, Mahdiraji HA, Hashemi SS (2013) Multi-objective linear programming with interval coefficients. Kybernetes
Hajiagha SHR, Hashemi SS, Mahdiraji HA, Azaddel J (2015) Multi-period data envelopment analysis based on Chebyshev inequality bounds. Expert Syst Appl 42(21):7759–7767
Hajiagha SHR, Mahdiraji HA, Tavana M, Hashemi SS (2018) A novel common set of weights method for multi-period efficiency measurement using mean-variance criteria. Measurement 129:569–581
Hashemi H, Bazargan J, Mousavi SM, Vahdani B (2014) An extended compromise ratio model with an application to reservoir flood control operation under an interval-valued intuitionistic fuzzy environment. Appl Math Model 38(14):3495–3511
Hashemi SS, Razavi Hajiagha SH, Zavadskas EK, Amoozad Mahdiraji H (2016) Multicriteria group decision making with ELECTRE III method based on interval-valued intuitionistic fuzzy information. Appl Math Model 40(2):1554–1564
He R, Zheng W-S, Tan T, Sun Z (2014) Half-quadratic-based iterative minimization for robust sparse representation. IEEE Trans Pattern Anal Mach Intell 36(2):261–275
Hisrich RD, Drnovsek M (2002) Entrepreneurship and small business research—a European perspective. J Small Bus Enterp Dev 9(2):172–222

Hsu CC, Sandford BA (2007) The Delphi te8chnique: making sense of consensus. Pract Assess Res Eval 12(10):1–7
Hwang CL, Yoon K (1981) Multiple attribute decision making: methods and applications. Springer-Verlag, New York
Jafari-Sadeghi V, Biancone PP (2017) Exploring the drivers of gender entrepreneurship: focus on the motivational perspectives in USA, Italy and France. In: Ratten V, Ramadani V, Dana L-P, Hisrich RD, Ferreira J (eds) Gender and family entrepreneurship. Routledge Taylor & Francis Group, London, pp 124–141
Jafari-Sadeghi V, Kimiagari S, Biancone PP (2019a) Level of education and knowledge, foresight competency and international entrepreneurship: a study of human capital determinants in the European countries. Eur Bus Rev 32(1):46–68
Jafari-Sadeghi V, Nkongolo-Bakenda J-M, Dana L-P, Anderson RB, Biancone PP (2019b) Home country institutional context and entrepreneurial internationalization: the significance of human capital attributes. J Int Entrep 2020(18):165–195
Jafari-Sadeghi V, Dutta DK, Ferraris A, Del Giudice M (2020) Internationalisation business processes in an under-supported policy contexts: evidence from Italian SMEs. Bus Process Manag J 26(5):1055–1074
Jian Y, Tang Y, Chen Q, Liu H, Tang J (2010) Interval-valued intuitionistic fuzzy soft sets and their properties. Comput Math Appl 60(3):906–918
Keršuliene V, Zavadskas EK, Turskis Z (2010) Selection of rational dispute resolution method by applying new stepwise weight assessment ratio analysis (SWARA). J Bus Econ Manag 11 (2):243–258
Keshavarz-Ghorabaee M, Amiri M, Zavadskas EK, Turskis Z, Antucheviciene J (2018) Simultaneous evaluation of criteria and alternatives (SECA) for multi-criteria decision-making. Informatica 29(2):265–280
Kilic H, Demirci A, Delen D (2020) An integrated decision analysis methodology based on IF-DEMATEL and IF-ELECTRE for personnel selection. Decis Support Syst
Kuivalainen O, Sundqvist S, Saarenketo S, McNaughton R (2012) Internationalization patterns of small and medium-sized enterprises. Int Mark Rev 29(5):448–465
Liao J, Welsch H, Moutray C (2009) Start-up resources and entrepreneurial discontinuance the case of nascent entrepreneurs. J Small Bus Strateg 19(2):1–15
Lin H (2010) Personnel selection using analytic network process and fuzzy data envelopment analysis approaches. Comput Ind Eng 59(4):937–944
Liu S, Lin Y (2006) Grey information: theory and practical applications. Springer, London
Liu P, Wang P (2018) Some interval-valued intuitionistic fuzzy Schweizer-Sklar power aggregation operators and their application to supplier selection. Int J Syst Sci 49(6):1188–1211
Love, M.B., & Roper, S. (2015). SME innovation exporting and growth: a review of existing evidence. Int Small Bus J, 33(1), 28–48
Macnee CL, McCabe S (2008) Understanding nursing research: using research in evidence-based practice. Lippincott Williams & Wilkins, New York
Mahdiraji HA, Hajiagha SHR, Pourjam R (2011) A Grey mathematical programming model to time-cost trade-offs in project management under uncertainty. In: IEEE 2011 International Conference on Grey Systems and Intelligent Services. IEEE, pp 698–704
Mahdiraji HA, Kazimieras Zavadskas E, Kazeminia A, Abbasi Kamardi A (2019) Marketing strategies evaluation based on big data analysis: a CLUSTERING-MCDM approach. Economic Research-Ekonomska istraživanja 32(1):2882–2892
Mahdiraji HA, Hafeez K, Kord H, Kamardi AA (2020) Analysing the voice of customers by a hybrid fuzzy decision-making approach in a developing country's automotive market. Manag Decis
Mahmoudi M, Mahdiraji HA, Jafarnejad A, Safari H (2019) Dynamic prioritization of equipment and critical failure modes. Kybernetes 48(9):1913–1941
McMullen JS, Shepherd DA (2006) Entrepreneurial action and the role of uncertainty in the theory of the entrepreneur. Acad Manag Rev 31(1):132–152

Mohammadi M, Rezaei J (2020) Ensemble ranking: aggregation of rankings produced by different multi-criteria decision-making methods. Omega 96:article 102254
Mokhtarzadeh NG, Mahdiraji HA, Beheshti M, Zavadskas EK (2018) A novel hybrid approach for technology selection in the information technology industry. Technologies 6(1):34
Mousavi SM, Antucheviciene J, Zavadskas EK, Vahdani B, Hashemi H (2019) A new decision model for cross-docking center location in logistics networks under interval-valued intuitionistic fuzzy uncertainty. Transport 34(1):30–40
Musani S, Jemain AA (2013) A fuzzy MCDM approach for evaluating school performance based on linguistic information. IP Conference Proceedings 1571(December):1006–1012
Nabeeh N, Smarandache F, Abdel-Basset M, El-Ghareeb H, Aboelfetouh A (2019 An integrated Neutrosophic-TOPSIS approach and its application to personnel selection: a new trend in brain processing and analysis. IEEE Access
Ooghe H, De Prijcker S (2008) Failure process and causes of company bankruptcy, a typology. Manag Decis 46(2):223–242
Oyson M, Whittaker DH (2010 An opportunity-based approach to international entrepreneurship: pursuing opportunities internationally through prospection. Proceedings of the eighteenth annual high technology small firms conference (The Netherlands)
Peschken T, Shukla P, Lennon J, Rate S (2016) The role of information alignment and entrepreneurial traits on SME internationalization: a conceptual framework. Manag Res Rev 39 (2):196–214
Petridis K, Drogalas G, Zografidou E (2019) Internal auditor selection using a TOPSIS/non-linear programming model. Ann Oper Res. https://doi.org/10.1007/s10479-019-03307-x
Pomerol JC, Barba-Romero S (2012) Multicriterion decision in management: principles and practice. Springer, New York
Razavi Hajiagha SH, Hashemi SS, Zavadskas EK (2013) A complex proportional assessment method for group decision making in an interval-valued intuitionistic fuzzy environment. Technol Econ Dev Econ 19(1):22–37
Razavi Hajiagha SH, Amoozad Mahdiraji H, Hashemi SS, Zavadskas EK (2015) Evolving a linear programming technique for MAGDM problems with interval valued intuitionistic fuzzy information. Expert Syst Appl 42(23):9318–9325
Razavi Hajiagha SH, Amoozad Mahdiraji H, Tavana M, Hashemi SS (2018) A novel common set of weights method for multi-period efficiency measurement using mean-variance criteria. Measurement 129:569–581
Rezaei J (2015) Best-worst multi-criteria decision-making method. Omega 53:49–57
Rezaei M, Jafari-Sadeghi V, Bresciani S (2020) What drives the process of knowledge management in a cross-cultural setting: the impact of social capital. Eur Bus Rev 32(3):485–511
Rouyendegh B, Erkan T (2012) An application of the fuzzy ELECTRE method for academic staff selection. Human Factors and Ergonomics in Manufacturing & Service Industries 23 (2):107–115
Saaty TL (1977) A scaling method for priorities in hierarchical structures. J Math Psychol 15 (3):234–281
Saaty TL (1980) The analytic hierarchy process. McGraw-Hill, New York
Saaty TL (1987) The analytic hierarchy process-what it is and how it is used. Mathematical Modelling 9(3–5):161–176
Saaty TL, Ergu D (2015) When is a decision-making method trustworthy? Criteria for evaluating multi-criteria decision-making methods. Int J Inf Technol Decis Mak 14(6):1171–1187
Sadeghi A (2016) Success factors of high-tech SMEs in Iran: a fuzzy MCDM approach. J High Technol Managem Res 29(1):71–87
Sadeghi VJ, Biancone PP (2017) Shariah compliant international entrepreneurship: a study of Islamic finance in Europe. European Journal of Islamic Finance 8(1):23–32
Sadeghi VJ, Biancone PP (2018) How micro, small and medium-sized enterprises are driven outward the superior international trade performance? A multidimensional study on Italian food sector. Res Int Bus Financ 45:597–606

Sadeghi VJ, Biancone PP, Giacoma C, Secinaro S (2017) Export compliance: a missing component of international entrepreneurship. International Journal of Business and Management 12 (11):103–110
Sadeghi VJ, Biancone PP, Giacoma C, Secinaro S (2018) How does export compliance influence the internationalization of firms: is it a thread or an opportunity? J Glob Entrep Res 8(3):1–15
Sadraei R, Jafari Sadeghi V, Sadraei M (2018) Biotechnology revolution from academic entrepreneurship to industrial: chemo-entrepreneurship. Biometrics & Biostatistics International Journal 7(6):546–550
Salehi K (2016) An integrated approach of fuzzy AHP and fuzzy VIKOR for personnel selection problem. Global Journal of Management Studies and Researches 3(3):89–95
Schniederjans MJ, Hamaker JL, Schniederjans AM (2004) Information technology investment: decision-making methodology. World Scientific Publishing, Singapore
Shirokova G, Bogatyreva K, Beliaeva T, Puffer S (2016) Entrepreneurial orientation and firm performance in different environmental settings: contingency and configurational approaches. J Small Bus Enterp Dev 23(3):703–727
Simons R (2013) Performance measurement and control systems for implementing strategy: text and cases. Pearson Education Limited, New Jersey
Simos J (1990) L'évaluation environnementale: Un processus cognitif négocié. DGF-EPFL These de doctorat, Lausanne
Srinivasan V, Shocker AD (1973) Linear programming techniques for multidimensional analysis of preferences. Psychometrika 38(3):337–369
Su J, Zhai Q, Landström H (2015) Entrepreneurship research in China: internationalization or contextualization? Entrep Reg Dev 27(1/2):50–79
Sukumar A, Jafari-Sadeghi V, Garcia-Perez A, Dutta DK (2020) The potential link between corporate innovations and corporate competitiveness: evidence from IT firms in the UK. J Knowl Manag 24(5):965–983
Taghavifard MT, Amoozad Mahdiraji H, Alibakhshi AM, Zavadskas EK, Bausys R (2018) An extension of fuzzy SWOT analysis: an application to information technology. Information 9:46
Timmons J, Spinelli S (1994) New venture creation: entrepreneurship for the 21st century, vol 4. Irwin, Boston
Triantaphyllou E (2000) Multi-criteria decision making methods. In: Multi-criteria decision making methods: a comparative study. Applied optimization, vol 44. Springer, Boston, MA
Urosevic S, Karabasevic D, Stanujkic D, Maksimovic M (2017) An approach to personnel selection in the tourism industry based on the SWARA and the WASPAS methods. Econ Comput Econ Cyberns Stud Res 51(1): 75–88
Wang WP (2010) A fuzzy linguistic computing approach to supplier evaluation. Appl Math Model 34:3130–3141
Wang CY, Chen SM (2017) Multiple attribute decision making based on interval-valued intuitionistic fuzzy sets, linear programming methodology, and the extended TOPSIS method. Inf Sci 397–398:155–167
Wang W, Liu X, Qin Y (2012) Interval-valued intuitionistic fuzzy aggregation operators. Journal of Systems Engineering end Electronics 23(4):574–580
Wu L, Wang C, Tseng C, Wu M (2008) Founding team and start-up competitive advantage. Int J Organ Anal 16:138–151
Wu L, Gao H, Wei C (2019) VIKOR method for financing risk assessment of rural tourism projects under interval-valued intuitionistic fuzzy environment. J Intell Fuzzy Syst 37(6):1–8
Xu ZS (2007) Methods for aggregating interval-valued intuitionistic fuzzy information and their application to decision making. Control and Decision 22:215–219
Xu ZS, Chen J (2007) An approach to group decision making based on interval-valued intuitionistic judgment matrices. Systems Engineering-Theory & Practice 27(4):126–133
Zadeh LA (1965) Fuzzy Sets. Inf Control 8(3):338–353
Zadeh LA (1975) The concept of a linguistic variable and its application to approximate reasoning—I. Inf Sci 8(3):199–249

Zahra S, Filatotchev I, Wright M (2009) How do threshold firms sustain corporate entrepreneurship? The role of boards and absorptive capacity. J Bus Ventur 24:248–260

Zavadskas EK, Antuchevicience J, Razavi Hajiagh SH, Hashemi SS (2014) Extension of weighted aggregated sum product assessment with interval-valued intuitionistic fuzzy numbers (WASPAS-IVIF). Appl Soft Comput 24:1013–1021

Zavadskas EK, Antuchevicience J, Razavi Hajiagh SH, Hashemi SS (2015) The interval-valued intuitionistic fuzzy MULTIMOORA method for group decision making in engineering. Math Probl Eng 13:560690

Zeng S, Chen SM, Fan KY (2020) Interval-valued intuitionistic fuzzy multiple attribute decision making based on nonlinear programming methodology and TOPSIS method. Inf Sci 506:424–442

Zhang S, Liu S (2011) A GRA-based intuitionistic fuzzy multi-criteria group decision making method for personnel selection. Expert Syst Appl 38(9):11401–11405

Zhang F, Xu S (2015) Remarks to 'Fuzzy multicriteria decision making method based on the improved accuracy function for interval-valued intuitionistic fuzzy sets'. Soft Comput 21 (9):2263–2268

Zhao H, Xu ZS, Ni MF (2010) Generalized aggregation operators for intuitionistic fuzzy sets. Int J Intell Syst 25:1–30

Zoraghi N, Amiri M, Talebi G, Zowghi M (2013) A fuzzy MCDM model with objective and subjective weights for evaluating service quality in hotel industries. Journal of Industrial Engineering International 9(1):1–13

Seyed Hossein Razavi Hajiagha is an Assistant Professor at the Department of Management, Khatam University, Tehran, Iran. He has received his PhD from Faculty of Management and Accounting of Allameh Tabatabaei University. His research and teaching interests span the fields of multi-criteria decision-making, business process management, data envelopment analysis, fuzzy sets theory, and response surface methodology. He has published more than 50 papers in various indexed journals including Expert Systems with Applications, Applied Soft Computing, Applied Mathematical Modelling, Annals of Operations Research, The International Journal of Advanced Manufacturing Technology, and Supply Chain Management: An International Journal, and Kybernetes. Dr. Razavi Hajiagha is the Editorial Board Member of Technological and Economic Development of Economy (SSCI).

Niloofar Ahmadzadeh Kandi, a co-author of the current book chapter, received his MBA in Strategy in 2016 and is currently an MBA student in Business Analytics specialisation at the Business School of the University of Wollongong. After presenting her thesis in 2016 with a high distinction, she has continued her research and has collaborated as a co-author in international journals.

Part VI
Quantitative Research Streams: Optimisation

International Entrepreneurship Rate Prediction Using Neural Networks

María de las Mercedes Barrachina Fernández, María del Carmen García Centeno, and Carmen Calderón Patier

1 Introduction

Entrepreneurship is of great importance in the economy and the global society and is being a hot topic for interested public decision-makers due to its growing importance in economic activity (Thurik 2014). According to various studies, entrepreneurship creates employment, boosts competitiveness and actively participates in the modernisation of the economy (Romero and Milone 2016; Hoskisson et al. 2011; Bird et al. 2012; Carlsson et al. 2013). The importance of business activity has increased in recent decades, centring the entrepreneurial spirit as one of the main causes of economic growth. Audrestch and Thurik (2001) identified the fact of going from an "administered" economy to an "entrepreneurial" economy. This is mainly because the "managed" economy is characterised by large, static companies and bureaucratic hegemony, while these factors have been replaced by innovation, knowledge, and dynamic company structures throughout the years. Thus, both in public debate and in research, the entry and exit of companies and their rapid adaptation to new productive forms, technological changes and the incessant evolution of demand. Therefore, entrepreneurial activity, self-employment, small businesses, microenterprises and SMEs have become the epicentre of economic life and public policy and the main agent of job creation. Specifically, job creation has been relevant in the European Union in the last 25 years, due to the different difficulties of combining higher productivity with job creation (Martí and García Tabuenca 2006).

The number of people in a country who would be willing to become an entrepreneur depends on very different factors. One way to explain them is by using a supply and demand scheme, as it is done with the other productive factors (Verheurl

M. de las Mercedes Barrachina Fernández (✉) · M. del Carmen García Centeno · C. C. Patier
San Pablo CEU University (CEINDO), Law and Economics Program, Madrid, Spain
e-mail: mar.barrachina.ce@ceindo.ceu.es; garcen@ceu.es; calder@ceindo.ceu.es

V. Jafari-Sadeghi et al. (eds.), *Empirical International Entrepreneurship*, Contributions to Management Science,
https://doi.org/10.1007/978-3-030-68972-8_20

et al. 2001). The conjunction of both functions determines the level of entrepreneurial activity that is observed in the economy. This level may be different from that of long-term equilibrium, in which case forces arise within the system itself that take it to it. If the level of entrepreneurial activity is below the equilibrium level, the risk of failure will be low and the returns observed by the entrepreneurs will be particularly attractive, which will induce the appearance of new entrepreneurs. On the contrary, if it exceeds the equilibrium level, in the long term the reduction in profitability and the greater risk will stop the entry of new entrepreneurs. The supply of entrepreneurial activity is latent in society and is materialised by the individual considerations that potential entrepreneurs always make of the market situation. It is determined by the characteristics of the population from which it arises, including both purely demographic and human capital aspects. It is, therefore, a perspective of the labour market in which supply is defined as the entrepreneurial activity that underlies society. The determinants of supply are fundamentally individual, but there are certain socioeconomic aspects that influence the "raw material" from which entrepreneurs can emerge (Boudlaie et al. 2020; Martí and García Tabuenca 2006).

International entrepreneurship defines the process of creating products and services in a creative way, so they can be considered interesting material by other markets, and at the same time being a competitive advantage. There are several studies in the literature focused on evaluating and identifying the factors, from different perspectives (geographical, economical, educational, gender, social, etc.) that influence entrepreneurship and international entrepreneurship.

The main goal of this study is to propose an original approach, mainly based on using a machine learning algorithm to predict the rate of entrepreneurship, considering data from the OECD countries. Basically, the data will be economic variables, fiscal variables and educational variables. Overall, the chapter has been organised as follows. First, the literature review supporting the research provided. Then, the research methodology and data collection have been highlighted along with the main results of this study, together with the discussion. Finally, conclusions, as well as limitations and future lines of research have been proposed.

2 Literature Review

Small and medium-sized companies are key in projecting inclusive and sustainable growth, also considering factors such as social cohesion. More specifically, in OECD countries, these types of companies, also known as SMEs, represent 99% of companies, 60% of employment, and are the main drivers in some cities and regions (OECD 2019). According to the mentioned report (OECD 2019), the structure of SMEs is stable in all OECD countries; however, there are a huge number of strategic changes taking place, especially in the areas that are directly exposed to digital transformation. Likewise, the productivity and international competitiveness of these companies are highly dependent on the sector, as well as on the region where it is located.

The analysis of innovative start-ups in the different OECD countries (Breschi et al. 2018) reports that there are significant differences between countries in the education of start-ups. Likewise, it is stated that the political priority in all OECD countries aims to create the right conditions for innovative companies to grow and prosper. Various researchers consider entrepreneurship as a way to transform knowledge into knowledge with economic value, thus becoming a key factor in the modern economic gear (Jafari-Sadeghi et al. 2019; Lupiañez et al. 2014), conceptualising both the company as a growth engine and source of wealth and job creation. Furthermore, during the last 40 years, there has been a significant change in the status and political weight of female entrepreneurs, as well as a rapid increase in interest and research on the subject. The first articles were published in the 1970s, expanding to various disciplines, methods and countries (Minniti and Naude 2010; Ramadani et al. 2013; Palalic et al. 2017; Jafari-Sadeghi 2020). Women-owned businesses are known to tend to be smaller and to grow less than men-owned businesses (Minniti 2009; Sadeghi and Biancone 2017). Moreover, there is a specific analysis that evaluates the impact of the different created policies on entrepreneurial activities (Dana 1987).

Regarding the study of entrepreneurship, several data sources used in the literature have been identified. One of the main ones has been the GEM (Global Entrepreneurship Monitor) database, which is the world's most important observatory on entrepreneurship. It started in 1999 and since then, it measures the entrepreneurial dynamics in more than 100 countries thanks to a common methodology, with which it evaluates characteristics, attitudes and motivations (Asociación RED GEM España 2019). Specifically, the GEM was created in September 1997 as a joint research initiative between Babson College and London Business School. Its main objective was to bring together the best academics in the world in entrepreneurship and create a database that would allow analysing the relationship between entrepreneurship and economic growth. Initially, GEM focused on the G7 countries (Canada, France, Germany, Italy, Japan, the United Kingdom and the United States) and three more countries were added, due to the origin of the selected academics (Denmark, Finland and Israel) (Reynolds 1999).

There are three characteristics that uniquely identify this database worldwide:

1. There is no other data source that contains information on entrepreneurship from so many countries.
2. Contains information on any type of entrepreneurship.
3. Analyse the entrepreneurship from its most initial phase (nascent entrepreneurship).

The GEM provides a strong framework in which national governments can develop a set of effective policies to improve entrepreneurship. The sources of information that feed the GEM observatory (Bergmann et al. 2014; Asociación RED GEM España 2019) are the following:

1. *APS*: Survey of the adult population. This survey is carried out on more than 2000 adult individuals (18–64 years) from the country analysed and mainly analyses

the business aspirations of the country's population. It takes place between April and July in all participating nations and regions. NES: National Survey of Experts. This survey is carried out by a group of experts, at least 36 business and academic experts from the country analysed and focuses on analysing the country's institutional factors. Each participating country or region selects a representative sample of experts in different fields: financing, government policies, political programmes, education, R&D transfer, the opening of the internal market, social regulations, etc. These experts are interviewed between the months of March and July through a questionnaire designed by GEM.

2. *Secondary sources*: Every year the GEM project collects information, from July to September, from different sources that provide information on fundamental economic variables: economic development, demography, labour market, innovation, competitiveness, etc.

The two mentioned surveys are subjected to rigorous quality controls in relation to their translation and fieldwork in order to guarantee that the responses obtained in all the participating countries are comparable.

Multiple articles have been found in the literature that analyses different aspects of entrepreneurship based on the GEM database. According to the study performed by Faghih et al. (2019), they proposed three new indices with the aim of investigating the attitude and capacity of communications, proposing a non-linear regression approach and delving into the relationship between these indices. In addition, it develops a ranking list of countries, showing that the entrepreneurial attitude dispersion index can improve the economic categorisation of countries. Considering the importance of agriculture in Southern Europe, the article by Lekovi and Petrovi (2019) is also interesting, which focuses on analysing the determinants that influence business activity in the early stages of the agricultural sector in the countries of the Southeast Europe region (SEE). The determinants analysed are the national culture, individual business characteristics and also business aspirations such as growth, innovation and internalisation.

Articles based on studying gender differences in entrepreneurship have also been found. Zinger and Lebrasseur (2007) also examine the differences between women and men entrepreneurs in the early stages of small business development, finding as to the main result that women entrepreneurs were much more likely to establish a commercial or consumer services company. They also found that they had significantly lower incomes than men. Additionally, women were less likely than men to work full time in their companies, to use new technologies and to anticipate new opportunities in the short term. Thus, it is concluded that the differences between genders in the variables related to the business are strengthened as the company evolves from nascent to new and subsequently the differences related to personal attitudes decrease during this progression. Other authors, for example, the authors Boudreaux et al. (2019) argue that using data from 43 countries, the results reflect those female entrepreneurs have fewer growth aspirations than men. Specifically, the results indicate that improving the quality of the credit market is associated with a lower gender difference in growth aspirations in the early stages.

There are also researchers who focus their study on analysing temporally and geographically different aspects related to entrepreneurship. Beynon et al. (2016) present a novel longitudinal study of entrepreneurship attitudes and activities, using data from the GEM database, covering a total of 54 countries. Khyareh and Torabi (2019) study the effect of elements of Iran's entrepreneurial ecosystem, examining the ecosystem problems that hampered economic growth.

Sustainable development is increasingly important in the studies that are carried out on entrepreneurship. Moya-Clemente et al. (2019) use the GEM database to analyse, using data from 50 countries, sustainable entrepreneurship over time, focusing on the identification of combinations of environmental factors, such as clean water and sanitation, affordable clean energy, urgent action to combat climate change etc., and also factors of economic development, such as job quality and economic growth. The most important conclusion of the mentioned study is that the protection and sustainable use of terrestrial ecosystems always have a positive enough effect to guarantee a high level of sustainable entrepreneurship. Furthermore, they argue that high levels of sustainable use of terrestrial ecosystems, sustainable growth and quality work are related to good access to affordable and sustainable energy, as well as promoting sustainable entrepreneurship.

Lately, entrepreneurship in emerging economies and developing countries is also a very studied topic. Several articles based on GEM data have been found that are focused on studying entrepreneurship from different approaches. Klimis (2019) examines the characteristics that relate to the business attitudes, perceptions, intentions and aspirations of 17 developing and emerging economies during the period between 2002 and 2016. As a key factor, it is highlighted that many of these countries have registered high rates of economic growth and have become increasingly outward-oriented in terms of both export activities and direct investment abroad. The main results obtained show that there has been an increase in the general index of entrepreneurial attitude on average, but the trend is different between countries. Likewise, the results show that the improved entrepreneurial attitudes do not explain the growing international commercial orientation that has been observed during the sample period.

Another well-known database used in this study has been the World Bank Database. The World Bank has a tool, "TC Data 360", that provides data on trade and competitiveness of many nations. Specifically, there is an initiative of the World Bank Group's Global Macroeconomics, Trade and Investment Practice, whose objective is to help countries achieve the Bank Group's objectives, with the aim of eradicating extreme poverty and promoting prosperity. This tool aggregates data from multiple sources and presents them with other resources, allowing data to be viewed at the country, subject or point level, to display current and historical data, to use integrated tools to create and share data visualisation, etc. Currently, the site contains around 2400 indicators from a multitude of sources, for example, African Development Indicators, Industrial Competitiveness Performance Index, Gender Statistics, OECD Innovation Indicators, Investment Index, the Global Innovation Index, etc.

These data are also used in different articles found in the reviewed literature. For example, the study performed by Torres and Godinho (2019) aims to improve the understanding of the conditions that can lead to high and low opportunity entrepreneurship in countries where the oil industry is a preferential sector. It uses various data sources (GEM database, World Bank database, KOF Swiss Economic Institute data). The main results obtained show that the control of corruption is important to achieve high levels of entrepreneurship opportunities in any type of country (regardless of whether one of its main industries is oil). Likewise, they postulate that high corruption control or low taxes must be produced to achieve high levels of entrepreneurship opportunities.

Data from the OECD (Organisation for Economic Cooperation and Development) database that contains multiple indicators from different countries on agriculture, development, energy, environment, health, innovation and technology, society, government, have also been used. Regarding the analysis techniques used in the literature, different methodologies have been found, especially those related to machine learning techniques to study different characteristics of entrepreneurship. Researches based on linear regression have been found (Levie 2007; Guerrero and Peña 2013; Urbano and Turró 2013), in decision trees (Cinar et al. 2018) or clusterisation (Chuang et al. 2019; Canestrino et al. 2020). Analysing the usage of neural networks to study different economic phenomena, it was found that it has been used to predict time series problems, for example, to predict stock market price indices (Wang et al. 2016) or forecast types of change (Chaudhuri and Ghosh 2016). The characteristics of entrepreneurs (fear of failure, meeting other entrepreneurs, level of education, gender, age, etc.) have recently been analysed through a neural network (Mezulic et al. 2019). Machine learning techniques have also been used to analyse the influence of the cultural values defined by Hofstede, that is, individualism–collectivism, masculinity–femininity and avoidance of uncertainty in entrepreneurship using an artificial neural network, specifically multilayer perceptron techniques, MLP (Morales-Alonso et al. 2020). Specifically, for the neural network, it is a very interesting technique to analyse entrepreneurship as it remembers all the information that it might need to be used later and to learn from the past data. This means that time series can be utilised to learn the characteristics from the past data and predict the outcome of the network.

In 1990, international entrepreneurship was starting to become a notable emerging research area. The economist J.F. Morrow (1988) was one of the key academics in collaborating in the definition of the term "International Entrepreneurship", highlighting the technological progress that induces the opening of new markets. In the same decade, there are other authors, also collaborating in the formal definition (Kohn 1988; McDougall 1989). Related to setting up the boundaries of international entrepreneurship, different studies can be found in the literature. Some authors focus on new ventures, having as an example Zahra (1993) analysis, and others centre their analysis in the entrepreneurial behaviour (Wright and Ricks 1994), suggesting that international entrepreneurship is observable at the organisational behaviour level, mainly focusing on the relationship between business and the international environment in which those organisations are operating.

Keupp and Gassmann (2009) understood the international entrepreneurship as the intersection between entrepreneurship and international business theories. During the last 25 years, this research area has been developed very intensely; however, it is still under-investigated (Wach and Wehrmann 2014) even though it has been gaining importance over the years.

According to Gartner (1989), international entrepreneurship is summarised as an internationally oriented creative process that includes the generation of new ventures and combinations of goods and services, methods of production, markets and supply chains. Some researchers relate the "international entrepreneurship" concept with three different terms: entrepreneurship, international business and strategic management (Wach and Wehrmann 2014). Four concepts are the base for the international entrepreneurship concept: (1) international new ventures, (2) born global, (3) rapid internalisation and (4) general model of international entrepreneurship.

The key drivers of international entrepreneurship are (Zucchella and Scabini 2007): shrinking transportation and communication costs, have better access to knowledge, enhanced knowledge creation and exploitation, achieve public support, manage international value chains and enhanced speed of growth and value creation process. Other studies have found theoretical inconsistencies, potential wrong predictions and important gaps related to the knowledge (Keupp and Gassmann 2009; Rezaei et al. 2020). Recent studies (Jones et al. 2011) focused their analysis in providing categorisation on the existing literature review, mainly based on (1) entrepreneurial internationalisation, (2), international comparison of entrepreneurship and (3) comparative internationalisation. In international markets, there is evidence of a positive relationship between several indicators of international performance and orientation to international entrepreneurship, showing that engaging in cross-border business could be driven by the international entrepreneurial spirit (Covin and Miller 2014).

Related to the internalisation process, there are several studies in the literature, but the first known process was known as the "Uppsala" internationalisation process, and the companies perform a step-by-step process focusing on exporting their key business activities (Johanson and Vahlne 1977). This process was later suggested to be less important as considered because it does not consider the speed to enter foreign markets (Ferreira et al. 2017). Other scholars developed a model considering the speed of internalisation (Oviatt and McDougall 2005), considering that this speed would be dependent on technology, competition and international network of the firm. Immigration is another subarea analysed when studying entrepreneurial activities and internalisation. There are some studies that focus on the gender differences in migrating and becoming entrepreneurs (Ribeiro et al. 2012), mainly cantered on identifying the reasons for migrating and for performing entrepreneurial activities.

Family is an important topic analysed within the literature, specifically to evaluate the factors that influence the internationalisation of family businesses and gender differences (Ratten et al. 2017). Other interesting aspects are the characteristics of the succession in family businesses (Ramadani et al. 2018). Motivation, general attitude, orientation, adequate experience to start a business and networking in a

growing interesting topic when studying the international development of businesses (Andersson 2004; Sadeghi et al. 2017). Another important topic to analyse is the influence of the home country human capital on entrepreneurial internalisation and according to the literature found (Jafari-Sadeghi et al. 2020), there is a positive relationship between the entrepreneurial intentions of the country´s non-entrepreneurs and effective business creation and therefore, it has a positive impact in the level of internationalisation.

Comparative internalisation is the most recent research area being developed related to international entrepreneurship. The main characteristics analysed in this kind of analysis are based on the venture type, the internationalisation patterns, the internalisation influences as well as on organisational issues (Jones et al. 2011; Jafari-Sadeghi et al. 2019a, 2019b), confirming that there is a pattern in international entrepreneurship in which national culture directly affects the individual entrepreneurial behaviour (Amin Moghadasi et al. 2017; Hayton et al. 2002). Other authors (Andersson and Evangelista 2006) found that a factor key for affecting the cross-border orientation of a business is the entrepreneurial team characteristics.

Age is a relevant factor when analysing the internationalisation of a business. There are several authors (Kautonen et al. 2011) focused on analysing the age factor in entrepreneurial intentions. Moreover, there are plenty of studies evaluating the reasons to become international. One of the main reasons to go international is to have a unique set of resources, including competencies, knowledge, capabilities, attitudes, relationships and reputation (Bloodgood et al. 1996).

SME is an important part of the international entrepreneurship area; however, the most common models of internalisations refer primarily to large firms. Nowadays, the internationalisation of small and medium firms had to spark the development of new research are to study this phenomenon (Ratten et al. 2007; Alon et al. 2009; Ayob and Dana 2017; Jafari-Sadeghi and Biancone 2018). There are authors who confirm that SME operates in a different way than large firms when deciding to become international and they do not have, in general, such a long decision-making process, and they do not follow such a complex theoretical model (Ahlert et al. 2007). Some studies report that the internationalisation paths of some SMEs were quicker when not considering the incremental models of internalisation (Oviatt and McDougall 2005), considering that the key factors influencing the rapid internalisation are knowledge and having international networking. Specifically, to SMEs, there are specific patterns, for example, that small and medium companies expand to nearby countries, considering geographic or cultural factors, not considering markets that could be interesting from a strategic or financial purpose (Wolf 2011).

3 Data and Methodology

The purpose of this work is to create a neural network that could be used to predict the value of the rate of entrepreneurship, conditioned to a group of independent economic, fiscal and educational variables. With this objective, information has been extracted from different databases, reaching a total of 26 countries and in the sample period between 2001 and 2019. First, the data from the Global Entrepreneurship Monitor (GEM) is used for the years 2001–2019 at the country level, to extract the variable related to the entrepreneurship rate (TEA), which is the independent variable of the approximated model in this analysis. Second, the OECD database is used to extract the data for the gross domestic product (GDP), the household saving rate (HOUS_SAV), research and development spending (GDP_ID), taxes on benefits (TAX_REV), income taxes (TAX_INC), social security contributions (SOC_CON), percentage of the population (ages 25–34) with tertiary education (POP_TER), and unemployment rate (UNEMPLOY). Third, the World Bank database will be used to extract the corresponding cost of establishing a business (COST_STARTUP) and net household income (ADJ_NET_INC) data.

The countries analysed in this study have been: Spain, Italy, Portugal, Ireland, Germany, France, United States, Canada, United Kingdom, Belgium, Denmark, Estonia, Finland, Greece, Hungary, Japan, Luxembourg, Latvia, Mexico, Netherlands, Norway, Poland, Slovakia, Slovenia, Sweden. In total, 318 records have been taken as input.

It is appropriate to highlight that one of the main limitations of the analysis carried out is the lack of availability of the data, which has meant that the sample of countries has been reduced, as well as the sample period under study. For the same reason, countries such as China or Japan could not be included in the study.

In the development of this work, three different data sources have been used, although the initial intention was to consider the last 25 years in at least 100 different countries, the following limitations were found:

1. The data from the GEM database are available from the year 2000 and not for all countries, so this variable has been the "central" variable, conditioning the results obtained in the different databases.
2. Data from the OECD and World Bank databases had limitations at the country level for years in which the information was available.

Table 1 shows the variables that have been considered in this study.

These variables have been selected, according to the results obtained in the reviewed literature, mainly due to their strong relationship with entrepreneurship. The reason for selecting each variable is briefly indicated below:

1. *Gross Domestic Product and Adjusted National Income (GDP and ADJ_NET_INC)*: They are used to measure the economic growth of an economy. Various studies analyse the impact of entrepreneurial activity and the competitiveness of the represented economy with the gross domestic product (GDP) per capita (Van Stel et al. 2010; Harmina 2016). Other authors analyse how

Table 1 Variables considered in this study

Group	Variable	Description	Source
Dependent variable	TEA	Total Early-Stage Entrepreneurship Activity (TEA): Percentage of 18–64 population who are either a nascent entrepreneur or owner-manager of a new business	GEM Database
Economics	GDP	Gross Domestic Product (GDP) (per capita in dollars)	OECD Database
	HOUS_SAV	Net household savings (percentage of household disposable income)	OECD Database
	GDP_ID	Gross domestic expenditure on Research and Development (percentage of total GDP)	OECD Database
	UNEMPLOY	Unemployment rate (percentage of the total workforce)	OECD Database
	COST_STARTUP	Cost of business procedures (percentage of GNI per capita)	World Bank Database
	ADJ_NET_INC	Adjusted Net National Income per capita (current US $)	World Bank Database
Taxes	TAX_REV	Tax revenue (percentage of total GDP)	OECD Database
	TAX_INC	Income taxes (percentage of GDP)	OECD Database
	SOC_CON	Contributions to social security	OECD Database
Education	POP_TER	Percentage of population (between 25 and 34 years) with tertiary education	OECD Database

entrepreneurial activities affect GDP per capita (Doran et al. 2018), highlighting the influence of different types of entrepreneurial activities (rate of high growth potential, rate of activity by need, rate of activity by opportunity and general activity rate), finding that entrepreneurship with high growth potential has a significant impact on economic growth (represented by the Gross Domestic Product (GDP), Coduras and Autio 2013).

2. *Household net savings (HOUS_SAV)*: Saving is considered a basic instrument to accumulate capital and that enables economic development through investment in different activities. Various articles that analyse its development have been found in the literature. Rikwentische et al. (2015) examined the effects of saving on entrepreneurial development in Nigeria. Other studies focus on studying the consequences of increased savings and investment in entrepreneurship (Gentry and Hubbard 2004). Carter (2011) states that entrepreneurs tend to save more money than other types of workers, among other reasons, because their income is more irregular.
3. *Gross domestic spending on research and development (GDP_ID)*: Various studies evaluate the relationship between research spending, represented by innovation and entrepreneurship. Specifically, the innovation that leads to higher

productivity is the main source of increased wealth in an economy; therefore, the level of research and development is essential for innovation to advance (Sukumar et al. 2020; Yasar Akcali and Sismanoglu 2015). Ülkü (2004) analysed the relationship between spending on research and development (R&D), innovation and economic growth through different studies relating panel data for 30 countries and a specific period of 26 years, concluding that there is a positive relationship between the innovation created by the R&D sector and the GDP per capita.

4. *Unemployment rate (UNEMPLOY)*: There are articles in the literature that directly relate unemployment to entrepreneurship (Gaweł 2010). There are studies that maintain that higher levels of entrepreneurship reduce unemployment, while others affirm that the increase in unemployment reduces entrepreneurship (Kum and Karacaoğlu 2012; Van Stel et al. 2007).
5. *Cost of business procedures (COST_STARTUP)*: It is assumed that by reducing the costs of creating a business, the creation of companies and, therefore, entrepreneurship is encouraged. Evidence has been found in the literature that the costs of starting a business are directly related to the rates of entrepreneurship (Cullen and Gordon 2007; Braunerhjelm and Eklund 2014; Block 2016; Gentry and Hubbard 2000). On the other hand, it has also been studied how the high initial costs of creating a business can lead to the positive selection of those individuals who have high doses of motivation and who expect high incomes from entrepreneurial activity (Darnihamedani et al. 2018). Likewise, there are works that justify how the low costs of setting up a company or the low level of regulation attract entrepreneurs who expect low returns in their business (Monteiro and Assunção 2012; Branstetter et al. 2014; Rostam-Afschar 2014).
6. *Taxes*: Including the variables of tax income (TAX_REV), income taxes (TAX_INC) and contributions to social security (SOC_CON). In general, high taxes discourage entrepreneurship (Saez et al. 2012). Different studies analyse the different fiscal measures that affect the entrepreneurial spirit (Bedard and Brookes 2018). There are studies investigating the effect of taxes on entrepreneurship, having a clear example in the study performed by Baliamoune-Lutz and Garello (2014), showing the effects of taxes and fiscal progressivity on entrepreneurship in a group of specific European countries, discovering that tax progressivity at higher than average income has an effect solid negative in nascent entrepreneurship.
7. *Tertiary education (POP_TER)*: Different studies show that higher education level means higher entrepreneur motivations (Formichella 2004). Other investigations add psychological aspects to the education variable such as the increased need for achievement, decreased fear of failure or decision to take risks (Ndofirepi 2020).

The algorithm used in this work is based on neural networks. Neural networks are a widely used machine learning method for decision-making, mainly due to the power to perform predictive analysis. The biological concept of the neural network is imitated in this algorithm, through which it is intended to replicate the structure of

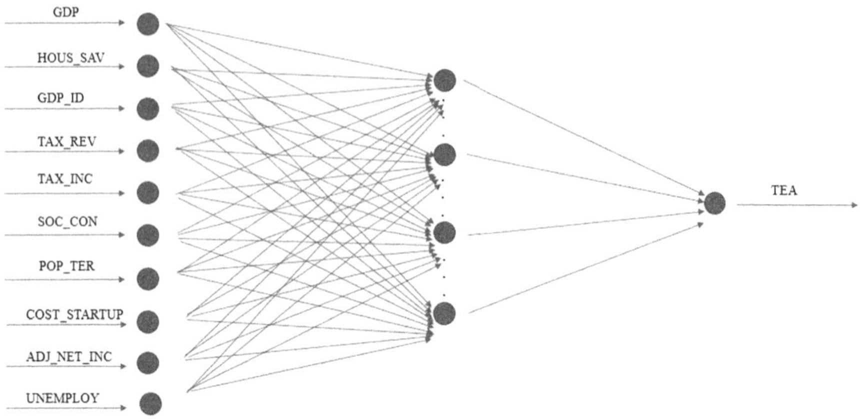

Fig. 1 Neural network diagram

the human brain, simulating the distributed processing model. In 1974, the field of neural network research was advanced thanks to the development of the multilayer perceptron network (MLP) and thanks to the identification of the backpropagation algorithm in 1986. Currently, neural networks are used to solve problems of different fields such as finance, medicine, engineering, marketing, etc. It has been widely used in activities related to classification, association, grouping, optimisation, prediction and control (Paliwal and Kumar 2009). One of the main advantages of the neural network is the ability to learn and model relationships that are not linear and highly complex, as well as that it does not impose any restrictions on the input variables (such as, for example, that these variables have to be equally distributed). Likewise, it has been found in the reviewed literature that comparing an MLP network with an ARIMA model, the former usually has better results (Olawoyin and Chen 2018).

A neuron is defined as the minimum processing unit that receives weighted information from other variables. Its main function is to transform the inputs, depending on the selected activation function and send those outputs to other variables (Gurney 1997; Nielsen 2015). There are multiple types of neural networks with different complexities. The Multilayer Perceptron (MLP for Multilayer Perceptron) is a specific type of neural network that is made up of different layers: the input layer (formed by the neurons that introduce the input patterns), the hidden layers (the layers that have connections with other neurons as inputs and outputs) and the output layer (made up of neurons that have the network's own output as output values). This type of network only considers one event at a time and assumes that all inputs are temporarily independent of each other. For example, Fig. 1 shows the topology of an MLP.

However, recurrent neural networks are indeed designed to manage this type of dependencies and are widely used in voice recognition, time series forecasting, translations, etc. (Weytjens et al. 2019). Also, more specifically, in this analysis, we are going to use a short-term memory network or LSTM network (Long Short-Term Memory, which is a type of recurrent neural network frequently used in deep learning) and that allows solving time series prediction problems since they can remember not only short-term dependencies but also long-term dependencies.

The neural network used in this study has been an RNN-LSTM network consisting of five layers of neurons: the input layer, three internal layers of 80 nodes each, and the output layer, all of them using the activation function "relu". The neural network has been implemented using the Keras framework. Once the network has been trained, it is necessary to evaluate its performance. The measures used to assess network performance are the Root Mean Squared Error (RMSE) and Mean Absolute Error (MAE). The RMSE is calculated by taking the square root of the average of the squared differences between the predicted and observed values. The MAE is calculated considering the average of all the absolute error values of the predictions.

Neural networks are based on two basic phases: the training phase and the testing phase. The data must be divided into two subsets so that they can be used in these phases. Seventy percent of the data has been used to train the constructed neural network and the remaining 30% to test and evaluate its operation. The main question established in this study is if it is possible to use machine learning techniques to predict, with specific precision, entrepreneurship rate considering different input variables. The contribution of this work will focus on the prediction of the rate of entrepreneurship by applying the neural network, described above, using variables of an economic, fiscal and educational nature, which, to the best knowledge of the authors, have not been used simultaneously in previous works.

4 Results

Once the data set to be analysed was loaded, the code for the creation of the neural network in Python was written, and subsequently, the training and testing of the data was carried out, taking as independent inputs the 10 characteristics referred to, above. Before deciding on the final neural network architecture to use, a total of 35 different neural network configurations have been tested, changing the number of internal layers, the internal nodes, the activation functions, the number of epochs and the size of the batch used. Finally, the network used in this analysis is obtained, being the one with the best performance and prediction capacity (evaluated using the RMSE and MAE parameters). The summary of the structure of the implemented model can be seen in Table 2.

Table 2 shows that the total parameters of the created network are 180,881, having the same number of trainable parameters, where for each layer, the number of input variables is 10, and counts and a total of 80 neurons.

Figure 2 shows the comparison between the real value of the entrepreneurship rate and the estimated value of mentioned variable with the set of test data.

In order to evaluate the result obtained with the use of the neural network, the parameters RMSE (defined as the mean square error) and MAE (defined as the mean absolute error) are utilised. The results obtained are identified in Table 3.

Table 2 Structure summary

Layer (type)	Output shape	Param #
lstm_5 (LSTM)	(None, 10, 80)	26,240
dropout_5 (Dropout)	(None, 10, 80)	0
lstm_6 (LSTM)	(None, 10, 80)	51,520
dropout_6 (Dropout)	(None, 10, 80)	0
lstm_7 (LSTM)	(None, 10, 80)	51,520
dropout_7 (Dropout)	(None, 10, 80)	0
lstm_8 (LSTM)	(None, 80)	51,520
dropout_8 (Dropout)	(None, 80)	0
dense_2 (Dense)	(None, 1)	81
Total parameters		1,80,881
Trainable parameters		1,80,881
Non-trainable parameters		0

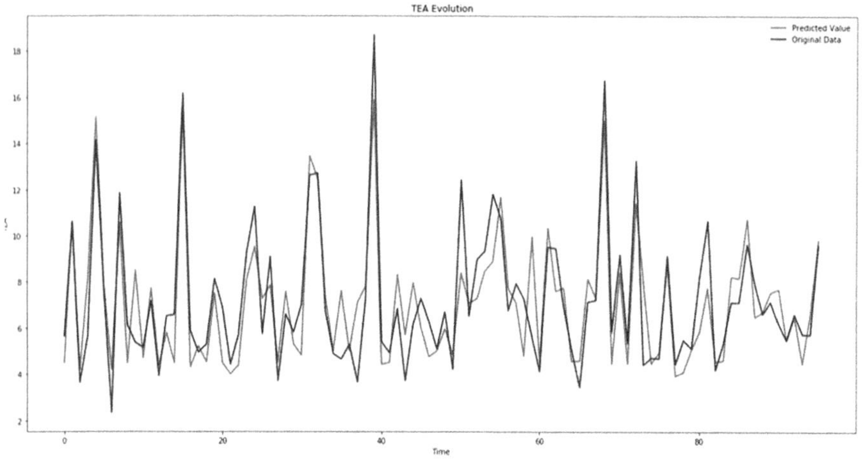

Fig. 2 TEA predicted value and original value

Table 3 Variables used for measuring error

Parameters	Description	Value
RMSE	Root Mean Square Error	1.51
MAE	Mean Absolute Error	1.18

It can be seen in Table 3, the value of the root means a square error, RMSE, reaches a value of 1.51, while the value of the mean absolute error is 1.18. Values that are small, which shows that the trained neural network is capable of obtaining good predictions about the entrepreneurship rate of a country by using economic variables such as gross domestic product, net saving household, unemployment rate, cost of business procedures, net income per capita; with variables of a fiscal nature such as tax income, income taxes and contributions to social security and with the percentage of the population with tertiary education.

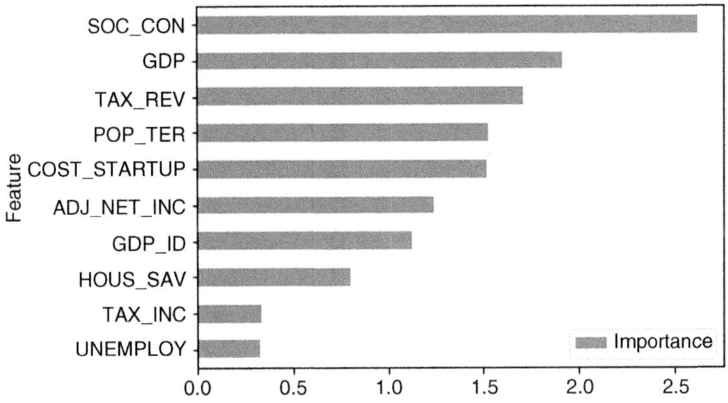

Fig. 3 Importance of the variables

Additionally, the importance of the variables used has been calculated. This importance is reflected in Fig. 3. For this, the input data and the prediction of the dependent variable are taken into account. To perform this analysis, each of the input variables has been disturbed with a normal distribution, and the prediction is calculated from it. Subsequently, the effect of the disturbance will be calculated from the RMS between the predicted variable and the variable obtained after the disturbance. A larger RMS error will mean a "more important" variable.

Not all the variables used to predict the entrepreneurship rate in the countries under analysis have the same importance or weight. In Fig. 3, it is observed that the most relevant variables for the prediction of mentioned rate are, contributions to social security, gross domestic product and tax revenue. Of these, social security contributions and tax revenues are fiscal variables, while the gross domestic product has an economic nature. On the other hand, the least relevant are the unemployment rate and the income tax. This contribution is very relevant since it can help the authorities or economic agents when formulating policies or making decisions, fundamentally, in the economic and fiscal field to facilitate the growth of entrepreneurship and thus contribute to the growth and development of a country.

5 Discussion

This study proposes an original approach, mainly based on using a machine learning algorithm to predict the rate of entrepreneurship according to a series of input variables: economic (gross domestic product, household savings rate, research and development spending, cost of starting a business, net household income, and unemployment rate), tax (income taxes, taxes on income, taxes corresponding to social security) and education (percentage of the population with tertiary education). After testing different types of neural networks, this study has proposed a recurrent neural network, specifically an LSTM to predict the evolution of entrepreneurship (quantified with the TEA variable). The main findings are explained in detail below.

The first and most relevant finding is that the proposed model provides promising results to predict the entrepreneurship rate based on the economic, fiscal and educational variables utilised. Acceptable results have been obtained, considering that the amount of data used, based on availability, has not been very high. The neural network results are expected to be improved when feeding it with large sets; therefore, the obtained results could be improved if more data is utilised, including geographical indications, quality of life indicators, development indicators, migration or social protection indicators. This novel approach, to the best of the authors' knowledge, is the first neural network model using economic data to predict the entrepreneurship rate, at the national level. The model designed is a first step contribution to the entrepreneurship literature combining the usage of a machine learning model with entrepreneurship indicators with the purpose of being able to precisely orient the government decisions in improving national and regional economic status.

The second finding is that the architecture of the proposed model is reasonable since the LSTM network maintains the previous information and contributes to learning from the time series. Constantly adding information about the released time series published related to the utilised data into the model would help to improve the results obtained. The third finding is that the model designed can be used by researchers, public managers and policymakers to promote entrepreneurship and to design, depending on the related variables, how the economic, social and fiscal environment is going to affect the entrepreneurship phenomenon.

6 Conclusions

The main aim of this research was to identify a machine learning model to predict the entrepreneurship rate, considering different economic, fiscal and educational variables, so that policies can be articulated based on the continuous entrepreneurship target value. In this work, the importance of entrepreneurship in the economy has been exposed, which makes it extremely useful to know how it will evolve depending on the different decisions made in other fields, especially to promote entrepreneurship in different sectors, executing different economic policies.

This analysis contributes to the literature in two ways. The first contribution is related to validate the usage of neural networks to predict entrepreneurship processes, more concretely, to predict the entrepreneurship rate when specific economic, fiscal and education variables are available. Second, the authors consider that this analysis contributes to extend the existing entrepreneurship literature and generates awareness of the huge potential that machine learning techniques could have when designing the entrepreneurship policies at the national or regional level, so policymakers and economic stakeholders could consider this contribution an interesting tool for producing predictions related to the entrepreneurship level.

There are several limitations to the results of this study. This analysis is subject to the limitations found during the execution, mainly related to the number of countries in the scope with information available. Even though the initial idea was to consider the last 25 years in at least 100 different countries, the data from the GEM databases was not available for all the countries, and the data from the OECD and the World Bank Databases had limitations at the country level in different years. Based on the results obtained and considering that the topic of entrepreneurship is booming due to its relationship with economic growth, for future research, it would be interesting to extend this model in the future with the aim of improving its predictive performance. A possible extension of this work would consist of updating the database with each new set of data that is released annually, in order to refine the network created, further reducing the error obtained and having the most precise possible characterisation of the level of entrepreneurship based on the economic, fiscal and educational decisions that are made in the coming years. Additionally, other factors, not considered in this study, could be added in order to improve the precision of the estimations.

Extending the potential future research and specifically related to international entrepreneurship, it would be interesting to use the introduced model as a seed and increment the entry variables with the internalisation rates per each country in scope, the limitations in the internationalisation process or the government support in becoming international. It would be possible to create a model for predicting the probabilities of a company to become international after a specific period of time of being created. This would be useful for policymakers and even for researchers and entrepreneurs to define the company's next steps accordingly to its strategic internalisation purposes. Finally, it is important to highlight the importance that economic variables such as gross domestic product tax or contributions to social security have in the development and growth of the rate of entrepreneurship in the different countries under study.

References

Ahlert D, Große-Vehne R, Kruse P (2007) Internationale Markenführung in Dienstleistungsnetzwerken – case study: Internationalisierung im Speditionsgewerbe am Beispiel des KMU (IMADI-Projektbericht), vol 6. Münster

Alon I, Dana L, Jenkins A (2009) International business by SMEs: empirical findings from New Zealand. *J Int Bus Econ* 2(2):59–78

Amin Moghadasi M, Derakhshandeh B, Ferdosi M, Jafari Sadeghi V (2017) Organizational conformity as an entrepreneurial response to the changes in internationalization process: a study of IT-oriented firms in Saveh. World J Acc Fin Eng 1(1):53–64

Andersson S (2004) Internationalization in different industrial contexts. *J Bus Ventur* 19 (6):851–875

Andersson S, Evangelista F (2006) The entrepreneur in the born global firm in Australia and Sweden. *J Small Bus Enterp Dev* 13(4):642–659

Asociación RED GEM España (2019) Informe global entrepreneurship (GEM) España 2018–2019

Audrestch D, Thurik AR (2001) Capitalism and democracy in the 21st century: from the managed to the entrepreneurial economy. *J Evol Econ* 10:17–34

Ayob A, Dana LP (2017) Product strategies for export ventures: an empirical investigation among SMEs in an emerging economy. *Jurnal Pengurusan* 50:25–33. https://doi.org/10.17576/pengurusan-2017-50-03

Baliamoune-Lutz M, Garello P (2014) Tax structure and entrepreneurship. *Small Bus Econ* 42 (1):165–190

Bedard M, Brookes K (2018) Entrepreneurship and fiscal policy – how taxes affect entrepreneurial activity. MEI. Ideas for a more prosperous society

Bergmann H, Mueller S, Schrettle T (2014) The use of global entrepreneurship monitor data in academic research: a critical inventory and future potentials. *Int J Entrep Ventur* 6(3):242–260

Beynon MJ, Jones P, Pickernell D (2016) Country-based comparison analysis using fsQCA investigating entrepreneurial attitudes and activity. *J Bus Res* 69(4):1271–1276

Bird B, Schjoedt L, Baum JR (2012) Editor's introduction. Entrepreneurs' behaviour: elucidation and measurement. *Entrep Theory Pract* 36(5):889–913

Block J (2016) Corporate income taxes and entrepreneurship activity. IZA World of Labour

Bloodgood JM, Sapienza HJ, Almeida JG (1996) The internationalization of new high potential U.S. ventures: antecedents and outcomes. *Entrep Theory Pract* 20(4):61–76

Boudlaie H, Mahdiraji HA, Shamsi S, Jafari-Sadeghi V, Garcia-Perez A (2020) Designing a human resource scorecard: an empirical stakeholder-based study with a company culture perspective. *J Entrep Manag Innov* 16(4):113–147

Boudreaux CJ, Nikolaev BN, Klein P (2019) Socio-cognitive traits and entrepreneurship: the moderating role of economic institutions. *J Bus Ventur* 34(1):178–196

Branstetter L, Lima F, Taylor LJ, Venâncio A (2014) Do entry regulations deter entrepreneurship and job creation? Evidence from recent reforms in Portugal. *Econ J* 124(577):805–832

Braunerhjelm P, Eklund JE (2014) Taxes, tax administrative burdens and new firm formation. *Kyklos* 67(1):1–11

Breschi S, Lassébie J, Menon C (2018) A portrait of innovative start-ups across countries. OECD Science, Technology and Industry Working Papers, No. 2018/02, OECD Publishing, Paris

Canestrino R, Cwiklicki M, Magliocca P, Pawelek B (2020) Understanding social entrepreneurship: a cultural perspective in business research. *J Bus Res* 110:132–143

Carlsson B, Braunerhjelm P, McKelvey M, Olofsson CH, Persson L, Ylinenpää H (2013) The evolving domain of entrepreneurship research. *Small Bus Econ* 41:913–930

Carter S (2011) The rewards of entrepreneurship: exploring the incomes, wealth, and economic wellbeing of entrepreneurial households. *Entrep Theory Pract* 35(1):39–55

Chaudhuri TD, Ghosh I (2016) Artificial neural network and time series modelling based approach to forecasting the exchange rate in a multivariate framework. *J Ins Fin Manag* 1(5):92–123

Chuang LM, Yeh C, Lin C (2019) Applying the self-organizing maps to analyse and interpret the clustering and characteristics of nascent entrepreneurs: a cross-country study. Bus Entrep J 8 (1):1–3

Cinar M, Du Y, Hienkel T (2018) Chinese entrepreneurship attributes: a comparative GEM data analysis. *J Entrep Emerging Econ*

Coduras A, Autio E (2013) Comparing subjective and objective indicators to describe the national entrepreneurial context: the global entrepreneurship monitor and the global competitiveness index contributions, Investigaciones Regionales, 47–74, ISSN: 1695-7253

Covin JG, Miller D (2014) International entrepreneurial orientation: conceptual considerations, research themes, measurement issues, and future research directions. *Entrep Theory Pract* 38 (1):11–44

Cullen JB, Gordon RH (2007) Taxes and entrepreneurial risk-taking: theory and evidence for the U.S. *J Public Econ* 91(7–8):1479–1505

Dana LP (1987) Evaluating policies promoting entrepreneurship – a cross-cultural comparison of entrepreneurship case study: Singapore and Malaysia. *J Small Bus Entrep* 4:36–41

Darnihamedani P, Block JH, Hessels J, Simonyan A (2018) Taxes, start-up costs, and innovative entrepreneurship. *Small Bus Econ* 51:355–369

Doran J, McCarthy N, O'Connor M (2018) The role of entrepreneurship in stimulating economic growth in developed and developing countries. *Cogent Econ Fin* 6(1)

Faghih N, Bonyadi E, Sarreshtehdari L (2019) Global entrepreneurship capacity and entrepreneurial attitude indexing based on the Global Entrepreneurship Monitor (GEM) dataset. Globalization and Development

Ferreira JJ, Fernandes CI, Ratten V (2017) International entrepreneurship research: mapping and cognitive structures. *Int J Entrep Small Bus* 30:545–566

Formichella MM (2004) El concepto de emprendimiento y su relación con la educación, empleo y el desarrollo local. Chacra Experimental Integrada Barrow (Convenio MAAyP-INTA). Tres Arroyos

Gartner WB (1989) Who is an entrepreneur? Is the wrong question. *Entrep Theory Pract* 13 (4):47–68

Gaweł A (2010) The relationship between entrepreneurship and unemployment in the business cycle. *J Int Stud* 3:59–69

Gentry W, Hubbard G (2000) Tax policy and entrepreneurial entry. *Am Econ Rev* 90(2):283–287

Gentry W, Hubbard R (2004) Entrepreneurship and household saving. Adv Econ Anal Policy 4 (1):1053–1053

Guerrero M, Peña I (2013) The effect of intrapreneurial experience on corporate venturing: evidence from developed economies. *Int Entrep Manag J* 9:397–416

Gurney K (1997) An introduction to neural networks. University College London (UCL) Press, 1997. ISBN: 1-85728-673-1 HB

Harmina A (2016) The role of entrepreneurship in explaining the real gross domestic product per capita: regression model selection. *Croatian Rev Econ Bus Social Stat* 2(1):24–38

Hayton JC, George G, Zahra SA (2002) National culture and entrepreneurship: a review of behavioural research. *Entrep Theory Pract* 26(4):33–52

Hoskisson RE, Covin J, Volberda HW, Johnson RA (2011) Revitalizing entrepreneurship: the search for new research opportunities. *J Manag Stud* 48(6):1141–1168

Jafari-Sadeghi V (2020) The motivational factors of business venturing: opportunity versus necessity? A gendered perspective on European countries. *J Bus Res* 113:279–289

Jafari-Sadeghi V, Biancone P (2018) How micro, small and medium-sized enterprises are driven outward the superior international trade performance? A multidimensional study on Italian food sector. *Res Int Bus Financ* 45:597–606

Jafari-Sadeghi V, Kimiagari S, Biancone PP (2019) Level of education and knowledge, foresight competency and international entrepreneurship: a study of human capital determinants in the European countries. *Eur Bus Rev* 32(1):46–68

Jafari-Sadeghi V, Biancone P, Anderson RB, Nkongolo-Bakenda JM (2019a) International entrepreneurship by particular people 'on their own terms': a study on the universal characteristics of entrepreneurs in evolving economies. Int J Entrep Small Bus 37(2):288–308

Jafari-Sadeghi V, Nkongolo-Bakenda JM, Anderson R, Dana LP (2019b) An institution-based view of international entrepreneurship: a comparison of context-based and universal determinants in developing and economically advanced countries. Int Bus Rev 28(6)

Jafari-Sadeghi V, Nkongolo-Bakenda J, Dana L, Anderson R, Biancone P (2020) Home country institutional context and entrepreneurial internationalization: the significance of human capital attributes. *J Int Entrep* 18:165–195

Johanson J, Vahlne JE (1977) The internationalization process of a firm – a model of knowledge foreign and increasing market commitments. *J Int Bus Stud* 8:23–32

Jones MV, Coviello N, Tang YK (2011) International entrepreneurship research (1989–2009): a domain ontology and thematic analysis. *J Bus Ventur* 26:632–659

Kautonen T, Tornikoski ET, Kibler E (2011) Entrepreneurial intentions in the third age: the impact of perceived age norms. *Small Bus Econ* 37(2):219–234

Keupp MM, Gassmann O (2009) The past and the future of international entrepreneurship: a review and suggestions for developing the field. *J Manag* 35(3):600–633

Khyareh M, Torabi H (2019) Investigating the role of entrepreneurship ecosystem in Iran's economic growth. *IUP J Entrep Devel* 15(4):7–25

Klimis V (2019) Do entrepreneurial attitudes explain the rising international business orientation in developing and emerging economies? *Stud Bus Econ* 14(2):245–256

Kohn TO (1988) International entrepreneurship: foreign direct investment by small U.S.-based manufacturing firms, Unpublished DBA Thesis, Harvard University, Ann Arbor, MI (University Microfilms)

Kum H, Karacaoğlu K (2012) Relationship between entrepreneurship and unemployment in Turkey: a dynamic analysis. *Actual Prob Econ* 138:399–405

Lekovi B, Petrovi M (2019) Characteristics of agro-entrepreneurs in Southeast Europe. In: Handbook of research on agricultural policy. Rural Development and Entrepreneurship in Contemporary Economies

Levie J (2007) Immigration, in-migration, ethnicity and entrepreneurship in the United Kingdom. *Small Bus Econ* 28:143–169

Lupiañez L, Priede T, López-Cózar C (2014) El emprendimiento como motor del crecimiento económico. Boletín Económico del ICE, Issue 3048

Martí F, García Tabuenca A (2006) Dimensión y características de la actividad emprendedora en España. Ekonomiaz: Revista vasca de economía, ISSN: 0213-3865, Issue 62, 2006 (Ejemplar dedicado a: La actividad emprendedora como motor de desarrollo económico), pp 264–289

McDougall PP (1989) International versus domestic entrepreneurship: new venture strategic behaviour and industry structure. *J Bus Ventur* 4(6):387–400

Mezulic P, Has A, Koprivnjak T (2019) Profiling nascent entrepreneurs in Croatia – neural network approach. *Rev Contemporary Bus Entrep Econ Issues* 32(2):335–347

Minniti M (2009) Gender issues in entrepreneurship. *Found Trends Entrep* 5(7–8)

Minniti M, Naude W (2010) What do we know about the patterns and determinants of female entrepreneurship across countries? *Eur J Dev Res* 22(3):277–293

Monteiro JCM, Assunção JJ (2012) Coming out of the shadows? Estimating the impact of bureaucracy simplification and tax cut on formality in Brazilian microenterprises. *J Devel Econ* 99(1):105–115

Morales-Alonso G, Núñez Guerrero Y, Aguilera J, Rodríguez-Monroy C (2020) Entrepreneurial aspirations: economic development, inequalities and cultural values. *Eur J Innov Manag*

Morrow JF (1988) International entrepreneurship: a new growth opportunity. *New Manag* 3:59–61

Moya-Clemente I, Ribes-Giner G, Pantoja-Diaz G (2019) Configurations of sustainable development goals that promote sustainable entrepreneurship overtime. *Sust Devel*

Ndofirepi TM (2020) Relationship between entrepreneurship education and entrepreneurial goal intentions: psychological traits as mediators. *J Innov Entrep* 9(2)

Nielsen AM (2015) Neural networks and deep learning. Determination press, San Francisco

OECD (2019) SME and entrepreneurship outlook 2019

Olawoyin A, Chen Y (2018) Predicting the future with artificial neural network. *Procedia Comp Sci* 140:383–392

Oviatt BM, McDougall PP (2005) Defining international entrepreneurship and modelling the speed of internationalization. *Entrep Theory Pract* 29(5):537–554

Palalic R, Ramadani V, Dana LP (2017) Entrepreneurship in Bosnia and Herzegovina: focus on gender. Eur Bus Rev 29(4):476–496

Paliwal M, Kumar UA (2009) Neural networks and statistical techniques: a review of applications. *Expert Sys App* 36(1):2–17

Ramadani V, Gerguri S, Dana L, Tašaminova T (2013) Women entrepreneurs in the Republic of Macedonia: waiting for directions. *Int J Entrep Small Bus* 19

Ramadani V, Dana L, Sadiku-Dushi N, Ratten V, Welsh D (2018) Decision-making challenges of women entrepreneurs in the family business succession process. *J Enterp Culture* 25

Ratten V, Dana L, Han M, Welpe I (2007) Internationalisation of SMEs: European comparative studies. Int J Entrep Small Bus 4:361–379

Ratten V, Dana L, Ramadani V (2017) Women entrepreneurship in family business: an overview

Reynolds P (1999) Global entrepreneurship monitor: 1999 executive report

Rezaei M, Jafari-Sadeghi V, Bresciani S (2020) What drives the process of knowledge management in a cross-cultural setting: the impact of social capital. *Eur Bus Rev* 32(3):485–511

Ribeiro A, Rezaei S, Dana L (2012) Gender and family in transnational entrepreneurship. *Int J Bus Globalisation* 8:409–420

Rikwentische R, Pulka B, Kaku Msheliza S (2015) The effects of saving and saving habits on entrepreneurship development. *Eur J Bus Manag* 7(23):111–118

Romero AM, Milone M (2016) El emprendimiento en España: Intención emprendedora, motivaciones y obstáculos. *J Globalization, Competitiveness Governability* 10(1):95–109

Rostam-Afschar D (2014) Entry regulation and entrepreneurship: a natural experiment in German craftsmanship. *Emp Econ* 47(3):1067–1101

Sadeghi V, Biancone PP (2017) Exploring the drivers of gender entrepreneurship: focus on the motivational perspectives in USA, Italy, and France. In: Ratten V, Ramadani V, Dana L-P, Hisrich RD, Ferreira J (eds) *Gender and family entrepreneurship*. Routledge, London, UK, pp 124–141

Sadeghi V, Biancone PP, Giacoma C, Secinaro S (2017) Export compliance: a missing component of international entrepreneurship. *Int J Bus Manag* 12(11):103–110

Saez E, Slemrod J, Giertz S (2012) The elasticity of taxable income with respect to marginal tax rates: a critical review. *J Econ Lit* 50(1):3–50

Sukumar A, Jafari-Sadeghi V, Garcia-Perez A, Dutta DK (2020) The potential link between corporate innovations and corporate competitiveness: evidence from IT firms in the UK. *J Know Manag* 24(5):965–983

Thurik R (2014) Entrepreneurship and the business cycle. *IZA World of Labour* 2014:90

Torres P, Godinho P (2019) Opportunity entrepreneurship, oil rents and control of corruption. J Enter Comm: People Places Global Econ 13(5):647–667

Ülkü H (2004) R&D, innovation and economic growth: an empirical analysis, *IMF Working Paper*, W/P/04/185

Urbano D, Turró A (2013) Conditioning factors for corporate entrepreneurship: an in(ex)ternal approach. *Int Entrep Manag J* 9(3):379–396

Van Stel A, Thurik R, Verheul I, Baljeu L (2007) The relationship between entrepreneurship and unemployment in Japan. Tinbergen Institute Discussion Papers 07-080/3, Tinbergen Institute, revised 14 Jul 2008

Van Stel A, Thurik R, Hartog C, Parker S (2010) The two-way relationship between entrepreneurship and economic performance, No H200822, Scales Research Reports, EIM Business and Policy Research

Verheurl I, Wennekers S, Audretsch D, Thurik R (2001) An eclectic theory of entrepreneurship. Timbergen Institute Discussion Paper

Wach K, Wehrmann C (2014) Entrepreneurship in international business: international entrepreneurship as the intersection of two fields [w:] A.S. Gubik, K. Wach (Eds.), International entrepreneurship and corporate growth in Visegrad countries, Miskolc, University of Miskolc, pp 9–22

Wang J, Wang WF, Niu H (2016) Financial time series prediction using Elman recurrent random neural networks. *Comput Intell Neurosci* 2016:1–14

Weytjens H, Lohmann E, Kleinsteuber M (2019) Cash flow prediction: MLP and LSTM compared to ARIMA and Prophet. *Electronic Commerce Research*: 1–21

Wolf K (2011) Internationalisierungs strategien von deutschen Familienunternehmen. Lohmar

Wright R, Ricks D (1994) Trends in international business research: twenty-five years later. *J Int Bus Stud* 25:687–701

Yasar Akcali B, Sismanoglu E (2015) Innovation and the effect of Research and Development (R&D) expenditure on growth in some developing and developed countries. *Procedia Soc Behav Sci* 195:768–775
Zahra SA (1993) Environment, corporate entrepreneurship and company performance: a taxonomic approach. *J Bus Ventur* 8:319–340
Zinger T, Lebrasseur R (2007) Stages of small business development: a comparison of female and male entrepreneurs. *J Enterp Culture* 15(2):107–131
Zucchella A, Scabini P (2007) International entrepreneurship: theoretical foundations and empirical analysis. Palgrave Macmillan, Basingstoke

María de las Mercedes Barrachina Fernández studied BSc and MSc in Telecommunications Engineering and developed her master thesis in the German Aerospace Centre in Germany. She also completed a BSc in Economics and she is completing her PhD now. She has led different technological projects in many different countries such as Japan, the United Arab Emirates, Russia, Peru, Switzerland and France. She also has a strong background working with Big Data and developing neural networks for predicting purposes. She has attended different courses related to Data Science, Machine Learning, Blockchain and Innovation in prestigious international schools (IE Business School (Spain), MIT (Boston, USA), Berkeley (San Francisco, USA)).

María del Carmen García Centeno studied Economic and Business Sciences at the Complutense University of Madrid. She obtained her PhD with an extraordinary award in Economic Sciences from the CEU San Pablo University. She has published articles in national and international research journals and obtained research awards from the Ministry of Defense and the Spanish Association of University Teachers of Mathematics. Since 1995, she has been a professor at the Faculty of Economic and Business Sciences of the CEU San Pablo University in the Department of Mathematics and Statistics.

Carmen Calderón Patier studied Economic and Business Sciences and she finished her PhD in Economic and Business Sciences. She is an Associate Professor of Public Economics at CEU San Pablo University, where she combines her teaching activity at the University with research work. She has published numerous articles in the field of Public Economy where to focus their main lines of research, both from the perspective of spending (analysis of the efficiency of public policies with micro techniques and macroeconomic) as well as income (family business and direct taxation Spanish and European Union). Moreover, she has published many articles in national and international research journals and written several chapters in books related to fiscal economy, entrepreneurship and corporate governance.

Introducing New Products to International Markets Using Green Entrepreneurial Supply Chain Optimisation

Mohammadreza Taghizadeh-Yazdi, Nikta Babakhani, Seyed Mojtaba Sajadi, and Amir Hosein Ebrahimi

1 Introduction

Lately, population growth has led to an increase in food demand. The food industry is one of the primary vital industries in the world. The goal of Supply Chain Management (SCM) is to manage and coordinate all input/output flows (of materials, information and funds) so that producing and distributing products delivers in the right quantity to the right location. In the current competitive industry, responsiveness and competitive advantages are considered important factors for differentiation. So companies must consider the rapid changes in the marketing situation as well as the needs of the consumers. Healy et al. (2015) defined supply chain management as the integration between different entities to achieve predefined common goals. 'A supply chain may be defined as an integrated process in which several different entities (e.g. suppliers, manufacturers, distributors and retailers) work together to (1) obtain raw materials, (2) convert these raw materials into specified products and (3) provide these products to retailers'. Similarly, Chopra and Meindl (2007) stated that a supply chain includes all parties directly or indirectly involved in fulfilling a customer request. The supply chain includes not only manufacturers and suppliers but also shipping, warehousing, retailers and even the customer.

M. Taghizadeh-Yazdi (✉) · N. Babakhani · A. H. Ebrahimi
Department of Industrial Management, Faculty of Management, University of Tehran, Tehran, Iran
e-mail: mrtaghizadeh@ut.ac.ir; nikta.babakhani@ut.acir; amirh.ebrahimi@ut.ac.ir

S. M. Sajadi
New Business Department, Faculty of Entrepreneurship, University of Tehran, Tehran, Iran
e-mail: msajadi@ut.ac.ir

V. Jafari-Sadeghi et al. (eds.), *Empirical International Entrepreneurship*, Contributions to Management Science,
https://doi.org/10.1007/978-3-030-68972-8_21

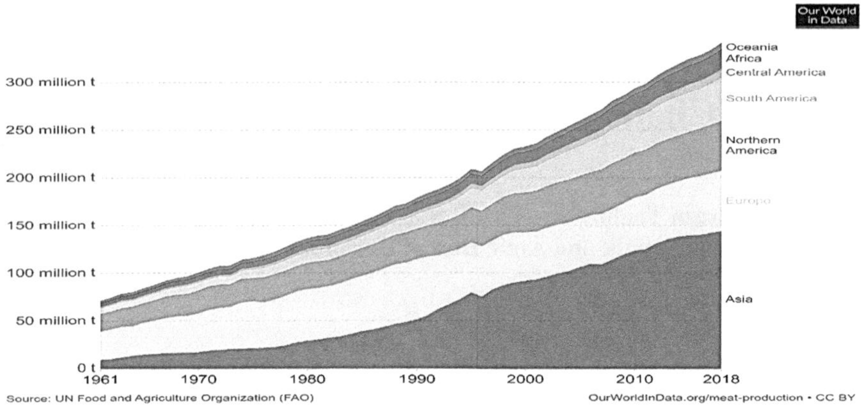

Fig. 1 Global meat production, 1961 to 2018

Physical flow includes the flow of goods (the transfer of materials from a supplier to a producer by truck) as well as the flow of information (a producer sharing his inventory status with his suppliers). Supply chain stages and subsystems are heterogeneous; they have different needs, goals and decision-making behaviours. They also have different geographic locations, unique cultures and various technological capabilities (Krejci et al. 2016; Sadraei et al. 2018). In today's competitive market, economic and manufacturing enterprises, in addition to paying attention to the company and internal resources, have required themselves to manage and monitor related resources and elements outside the company. Accordingly, the procurement of materials, production, maintenance, warehousing of goods, inventory control, distribution, delivery and customer service, which were previously performed at the company level, have now been transferred to the supply chain level (Sadeghi et al. 2019). Recently, rapid population growth has led to a significant increase in demand for food, which is why the food industry is one of the most important and noteworthy industries in all countries. Therefore, food supply chain management plays a crucial role to satisfy the increasing demand for food all around the world.

Food supply has been considered as one of the main concerns of human beings as well as one of their basic needs. In particular, the supply chain of short-lived and perishable goods, especially food, has always been one of the paramount and challenging management issues at different times.

Finding a sustainable way to satisfy the world's food demand would be one of the most concerning challenges in the coming decades. Meat, as an important source of nutrition for many people around the world, has an undeniable position in food demand. Global demand for meat is growing insofar as meat production quadrupled over the past 50 years. The world now produces more than 320 million tons each year. Global meat production has increased rapidly in recent decades; as can be seen in the following figure, the total production quadrupled since 1961. Figure 1 depicts global meat production by region.

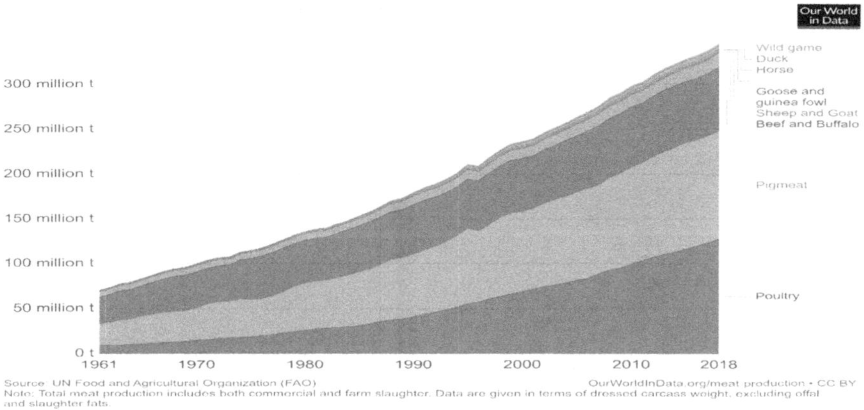

Fig. 2 Meat production by livestock type, world, 1961 to 2018

Asia is the largest meat producer in the world and produces about 40–45% of total meat. The share of continents in producing meat has changed significantly in recent decades. In 1961, Europe and North America were the dominant meat producers, 42 and 25% of total meat production respectively. In 1961, Asia produced only 12%; however, by 2013, Europe and North America's share had plunged to 19 and 15% respectively. At the global level, the dominant livestock types are poultry, cattle (which includes beef and buffalo meat), pig and sheep & goats to a lesser extent. However, the distribution of meat types varies significantly across the world; in some countries, other meat types such as a wild game, horse and duck can account for a significant share of total production. Although the production of all major meat types has been increasing in absolute terms, in relative terms the share of global meat types has changed significantly over the last 50 years. In 1961, poultry meat accounted for only 12% of global meat production; by 2013, its share has approximately tripled to around 35%. In comparison, beef and buffalo meat as a share of total meat production has nearly halved and this production is around 22% now. Pig meat's share has remained more constant at approximately 35–40% (Fig. 2).

2 Beef and Buffalo (Cattle) Meat Production

As Fig. 3 depicts, cattle meat production has more than doubled since 1961—increasing from 28 million tons in 1961 to 68 million tons in 2014. The United States is the world's largest beef and buffalo meat producer, producing 11–12 million tons in 2014. Other major producers are Brazil, China, Argentina, Australia and India.

Figure 4 depicts the Beef production in Iran.

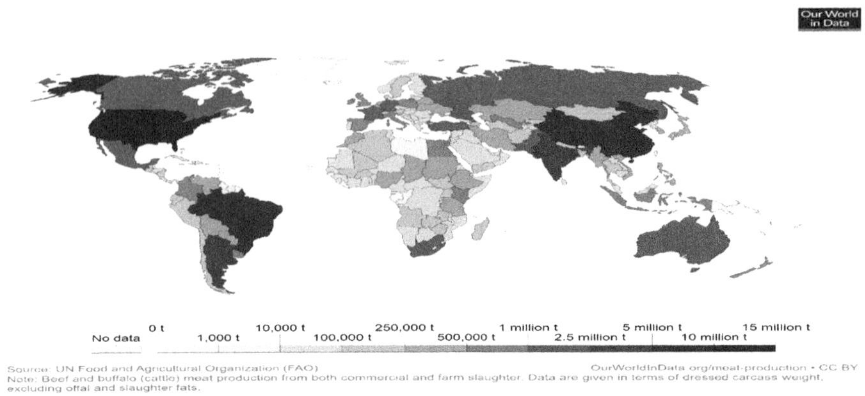

Fig. 3 World beef production, 2018

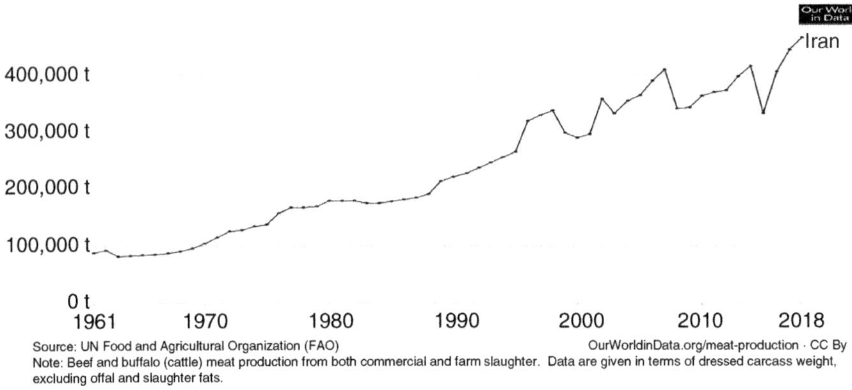

Fig. 4 Beef production in Iran, 1961 to 2018

3 Poultry Production

Global production of poultry meat has increased rapidly over the last 50 years, growing more than 12 times between 1961 and 2014. Global trends in poultry production have been shown in Fig. 5. Like cattle production, the United States is the world's largest producer, producing more than 20 million tons in 2014. China and Brazil are also large poultry producers at 18 and 13 million tons respectively. Collectively, Europe is also a major poultry producer with an output in 2014 of approximately 19 million tons—just below the output of the United States.

Figure 6 shows Poultry production in Iran.

Food supply chain management plays a crucial role in addressing high food demand. The efficacy of the food supply chain network (FSCN) depends on strategic and tactical decisions as to the location and allocation of related facilities in the network as well as the optimisation of product quantities (Mohebalizadehgashti et al.

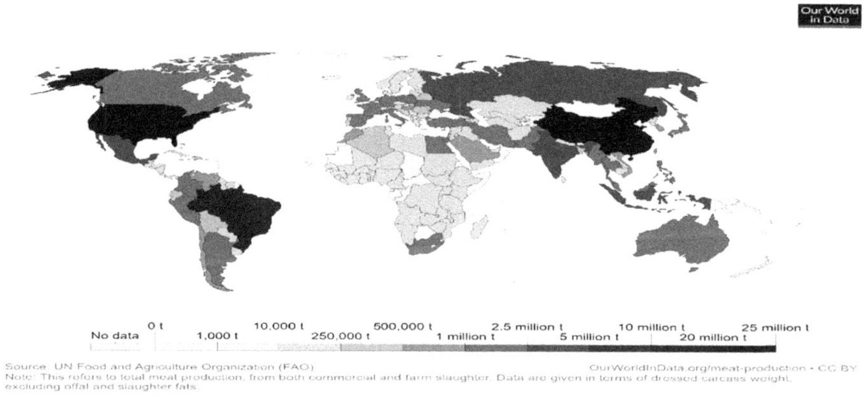

Fig. 5 World poultry production, 2018

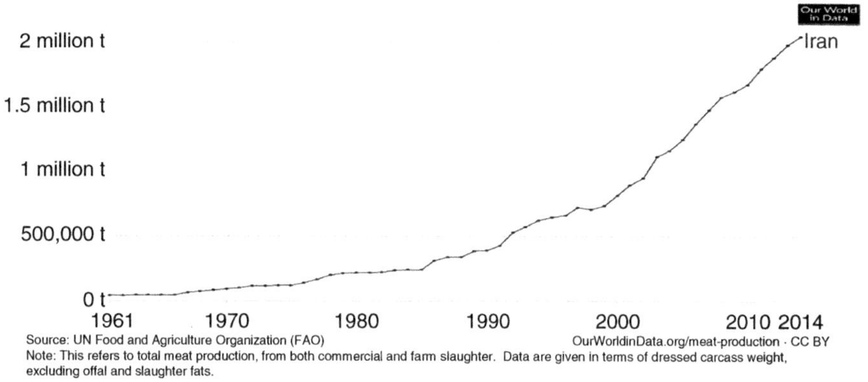

Fig. 6 Poultry production in Iran, 1961 to 2014

2020). Perishable products require special measures that may have social and environmental effects in addition to their known economic aspects (Jouzdani and Govindan 2020). Production of meat has large environmental impacts, for instance, increasing greenhouse gas emissions and misuse of agricultural land as well as freshwater. One of the world's most pressing challenges is to produce and consume meat, dairy and other protein products in a way that reduces its environmental impacts (Hajiagha et al. 2013, 2015, 2018).

Supply chain issues are becoming more and more important every day, in addition to the increasing complexity of the market, other factors such as environmental issues add more complexity. Greenhouses and other environmental matters could potentially lead to the extinction of humanity. Therefore, environmental protection and related strategies soon became a priority of programs in organisational innovations. On the one hand, the organisation had to pay attention to profitability and competitive advantage; on the other hand, they had to eliminate

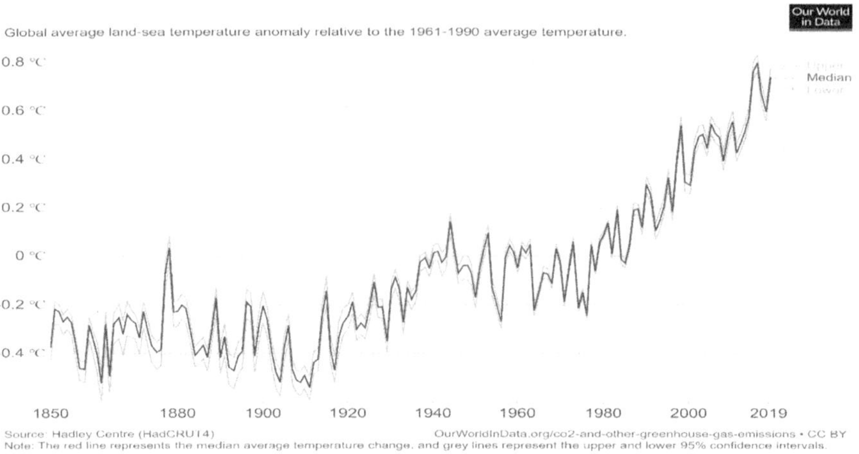

Fig. 7 Average temperature anomaly, global

or minimise waste, including energy, greenhouse gas, chemical/hazardous and solid waste. This illustrates why the idea of a green supply chain came up and soon caught everyone's eye. Therefore, all actions from the supplier to the customer should be in such a way that, in addition to maximising the profit of each level, environmental concerns are minimised. Organisations have to pay attention to these issues to retain customers and to survive in today's dynamic and competitive environment.

Climate change is one of the most important challenges in the world. Since pre-industrial production, emissions of greenhouse gases and carbon dioxide (CO_2), nitrous oxide, methane and other pollutant substance have raised global temperatures by about 1 °C per year. Climate change has a wide range of potential environmental, physical and health effects, including severe weather events (such as floods, droughts, hurricanes and heatwaves), rising sea levels and disruption of systems. Figure 7 shows the global average temperature relative to the period between 1961 and 1990.

Figure 7 shows global temperatures have risen sharply. It reached approximately 0.7 above 0°C in 1961. In general, it can be seen that the average temperature has increased by 1.1°C. Likewise, the concentration of CO_2 in the atmosphere is at its highest level in the last 800,000 years. This increase in global average temperature is attributed to the increase in greenhouse gas emissions. This relationship between global temperature and the concentration of greenhouse gases, especially CO_2, has been true throughout Earth's history. Figure 8 shows the average CO_2 concentration in the atmosphere over the past 800,000 years. During this period, you will see constant fluctuations in CO_2 concentration. These periods of increase and decrease of CO_2 coincide with the beginning of glacial (low CO_2) and interglacial (high CO_2) periods. These oscillations are caused by changes in the Earth's orbit around the Sun called the Milankovitch cycles. During this long period, the atmospheric concentration of CO_2 did not exceed 300 parts per million (ppm). Nevertheless, the Industrial

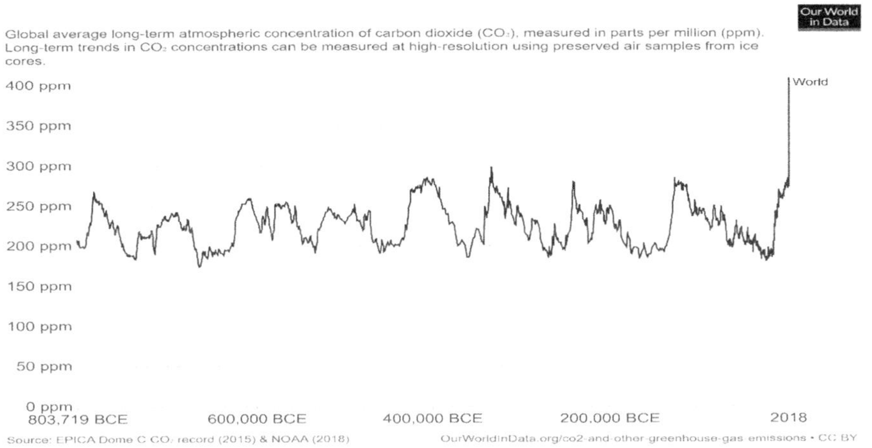

Fig. 8 Atmospheric CO_2 concentration

Revolution and the increase in CO_2 emissions from burning fossil fuels cause a rapid increase in global CO_2 concentrations over the past few centuries, especially in recent decades.

Regarding carbon dioxide emissions, the phenomenon of global warming due to greenhouse gas emissions has faced one of the most important environmental challenges. The dramatic increase in carbon dioxide in the Earth's atmosphere has caused some problems, including global warming, melting glaciers, the destruction of animal and plant habitats, disruption of the water and food supply cycle and sudden changes in water and weather (Töbelmann and Wendler 2020; Mokhtarzadeh et al. 2018; Mahdiraji et al. 2011, 2019, 2020). According to research, every degree of global warming affects the economies of more than three-quarters of the world's countries, widening the gap between rich and poor. If global warming continues to occur due to excessive carbon dioxide emissions and greenhouse effects, global average incomes will decline by 23% (Shaw et al. 2011). Furthermore, the transport vehicles in each part of this supply chain produce a significant amount of pollution that can be reduced by optimising the distribution network in supply chains (Zulfiu et al. 2015). Determining the level of sufficient capacity helps organisations to meet the right amount of product at the right time based on customer demand (Adland et al. 2018). Capacity and facilities utilisation are salient factors that reduce the total costs and increase the efficiency of the logistics network (Jakubovskis 2017).

In the past, due to the lack of competitive markets, the involvement of supply chain members to develop a new product wasn't so important. Afterwards, the only way of successful development of the new product is to actively participate in components (such as suppliers, distributors, customers) and entrepreneurial supply chain management (Filion et al. 2010). Therefore, the alignment and coordination of the components of the entrepreneurial supply chain and new product development (NPD) were discussed. The traditional view of the supply chain focuses mainly on cost, quality and on-time delivery. The entrepreneurial supply chain adds growth, price innovation, quality and delivery. In the new product development process, market opportunities and product technology hypotheses lead to marketable products (Dargahi 2015).

In the new product development process, (a product can be introduced as goods, services and ideas) market opportunities and product technology hypotheses could make the product available. The new product development process consists of six stages: planning, concept development planning, system-level planning, detailed planning, testing and troubleshooting, increasing production quantity. NPD is a discipline that includes marketing management, engineering design and operations management requires the collaboration of all departments of an organisation (Sabzevari et al. 2019). The indicators for evaluating the success of new product development, include new product innovation rate, new product quality, new product development rate, new product sales, market share of a new product and company's profit from selling a new product. This chapter investigates the optimisation of the green entrepreneurial food supply chain, and for doing so, a multi-objective mathematical modelling approach has been used.

4 Literature Review

There are several studies on food supply chain design using the multi-objective optimisation model. These researches focus on a variety of issues, including maximising product quality and safety (James et al. 2006; Mahmoudi et al. 2019; Soysal et al. 2014) and minimising the cost of the entire supply chain network. Literature (Paksoy et al. 2012; Beheshti et al. 2016; Biancone and Jafari Sadeghi 2016; Rajabalipour Cheshmehgaz et al. 2013; Sadeghi et al. 2017, 2018; Dabić et al. 2020; Mohsen et al. 2020; Mohsen et al. 2020) proposed a multi-objective linear planning model to minimise transportation costs between different parts of the vegetable oil supply chain network. Teimoury et al. (2013) examined the food and vegetable supply chain in Tehran. They proposed a multi-objective mathematical model and a simulation-based solution approach.

García-Flores et al. (2014) focused on the meat industry in North Australia and developed a mathematical model to achieve the optimal number of products in various supply chains. Walker (2017) proposed a multi-objective mathematical model for halal meat to minimise total investment costs and maximise return on investment (ROI) in a meat supply chain. They used the Petri nets model, which is a crop simulation model, to show how their proposed network behaves. Mohammed and Wang (2016) proposed a mathematical model of complex integer linear programming to solve four objective functions simultaneously to minimise total cost and maximise profit, maintain freshness and quality and consumer satisfaction. Mohammed and Wang (2017a) introduced a multi-objective function model in the meat supply chain network to minimise total transportation costs, the number of vehicles in transportation and delivery time. To solve their multi-objective model, they used three solution methods, including the Tchebycheff technique, ε-constraint and the LP-Metrics technique. Furthermore, they showed that the ε-constraint method was better than the other two methods.

Mohammed and Wang (2017b) implemented a multi-objective mathematical programme model in a three-echelon meat supply chain network to minimise the total cost (including shipping and operating costs), maximise product quality and maximise customer satisfaction. They used three solution methods to solve the model, including goal programming (GP), adaptive planning and the Chebycheff weighting method. The results showed that the adaptive planning approach was better than the other two approaches. Mohebalizadehgashti et al. (2020) also improved a multi-period, multi-product, multi-objective and multi-echelon mixed linear integer programmer optimisation model for meat supply chain design in Canada. This improvement includes three inconsistent objective functions: minimising fixed costs and transportation at supply chain levels, the amount of carbon dioxide emitted in each transport between different levels of the supply chain and maximising the use of supply capacity. In this study, they used the augmented ε-constraint approach which was an improved model of ε-constraint (Song et al. 2019; Sadiku-Dushi et al. 2019; Sadeghi et al. 2019).

In recent decades, environmental issues have become one of the biggest challenges in supply chain network design. Green supply chain management by incorporating environmental factors into traditional supply chain management, which focuses mainly on the financial aspects of supply chain management, such as the costs of the entire supply chain network (Srivastava 2007). Environmental factors are just as important as the economic aspects of supply chain networks (Mohammed and Wang 2017c; Sadeghi and Biancone 2018; Jafari-Sadeghi et al. 2020; Jafari-Sadeghi et al. 2019).

In general, the studies discussed above have made a significant contribution to the development of optimisation models under uncertainty in different supply chain networks. However, they did not address environmental concerns such as greenhouse gas emissions. Several studies have considered these two factors in the design of green logistics networks (Sadeghi et al. 2018). Soysal et al. (2012) provided an overview of sustainable food supply chain management (SFSCM). A complex integer linear programming model to minimise total logistics costs and greenhouse gas (GHG) emissions in a closed-loop supply chain, including five supply chain echelons, suppliers, manufacturers, distribution centres, customers and recycling centres ((Jafari-Sadeghi 2019; Ramudhin et al. 2012; Taghizadeh-Yazdi and Mohammadi-Balani 2020). However, uncertainty is not included in their proposal. Soysal et al. (2014) developed a multi-objective linear programming model (MOLP) concerning transport emissions. They used the ε-constraint method to solve their proposed model. However, they did not consider several products; they focused only on beef. Unwantedly, the effects of uncertainty were not analysed. Besides, customers, who are an important factor in their attention, are not addressed. Bortolini et al. (2016) focused on fresh food supply chain networks and presents a multi-objective mathematical model to minimise operating costs, carbon dioxide emissions and product delivery times. However, they considered uncertainty in the model.

Hu et al. (2016) examined the time of transportation in the provision of transportation services, which was carried out by carriers using auctions to purchase transportation services from transportation companies in the planning stage is done. Shorter shipping times indicate better shipping services. To minimise the total cost and time of transportation, the problem is providing bi-objective transportation services with transportation time. To solve this problem, they introduced a bi-objective integer programming model that can include some important business constraints. Mohammed and Wang (2017c) optimised a meat supply chain network, introduce a fuzzy multi-objective planning model with four incompatible goals, including minimising the total supply chain cost, minimising carbon dioxide emissions, minimising product distribution time at each echelon of the supply chain and the average delivery time rate. Then, they use three methods to solve their proposed model: goal programming (GP), ε-constraint and comprehensive measure (LP-Metrics). They showed that the ε-constraint method has better performance than the other two methods. However, this study does not consider the production of several products and their proposed model is not multi-period. Also, they do not include customers in their supply chain network; they are focused only on farms and retailers.

Babbar and Amin (2018) designed a two-stage model including quality function deployment (QFD) and a multi-objective mathematical model in the beverage industry. The purpose of the first stage is to select a supplier, while the second stage focuses on quantifying the order using weighted sum, ε-constraints and distance techniques. In the second phase of their study, five target dates were examined, which include minimising the total cost of the supply chain, minimising defects, minimising carbon dioxide emissions and maximising on-time delivery. Mohebalizadeh and Hafezalkotob (2018) by introducing an integer multi-objective linear programming model, they created a sustainable supply chain network in a fuzzy environment that minimises the total supply chain cost, energy consumption and delivery time. Then, they used standard weighted methods and modified fuzzy parametric programming (MFPP) as two solution methods to solve the multi-objective problem. In providing transportation services by truck, transportation time is an important factor that is considered by carriers. In addition to transportation costs, shipping time is expected to be minimised to improve service quality and transport efficiency.

Zhang and Hu (2019) studied the problem of procuring full truck transportation services with transportation time and developed a two-phase multi-objective evolutionary algorithm to discover the Pareto front. The algorithm uses a set of winning carriers to encrypt an individual's chromosome to reduce decision space. Nayeri et al. (2020) developed a multi-objective mathematical model for configuring a sustainable closed-loop supply chain network (SCLSC) for a water reservoir taking into account sustainability measures. The objectives of the proposed model are to optimise the financial, environmental and social impacts of SCLSC. In general, there is uncertainty in configuring the SCLSC network problem due to changes in the business environment (such as shipping costs and demand). As a result, robust fuzzy optimisation (FRO) has been used to deal with the uncertainty in this study. Then, the proposed model is solved using the GP approach. The numerical results show some observations about planning and strategic decisions for SCLSC network design. Finally, several sensitivity analyses have been performed on some important parameters.

Turan et al. (2020) modelled and solved a strategic fleet modernisation problem to meet future operational needs in uncertain circumstances. To this end, they developed a hybrid simulation model combining system dynamics (SD) and discrete event simulation (DES) approaches. Independent use of this model enables decision-makers to analyse the effects of short-term and long-term decisions by simulating the process by which the fleet makes its life cycle available through asset acquisition to retirement. However, the simulation does not suggest or seek the best renewal strategy. To alleviate this difficulty, they proposed a simulation-based optimisation that uses a genetic algorithm (GA) to effectively search for a very wide range of fleet renewal strategies and develop a hybrid simulation model. The finding is used to evaluate the candidate strategies found by GA. Finally, the robustness of optimised strategies in uncertainty is tested using sensitivity analysis and mapping between implemented strategies and fleet performance is made by scenario discovery analysis to gain the insight needed to make a decision (Sajadi et al. 2020).

Several studies on entrepreneurial food supply chain design are describing a value that is created for customers by providing a better good and service. Sajadi et al. (2015) ranked entrepreneurial supply chain management contents on the new product development process in entrepreneurial firms of Iran detergent industry by using descriptive survey. According to the results of the analytical hierarchy process (AHP) method, the Profitability criterion from the new product and market share have the most importance weighed 0.257 and 0.249, respectively. According to the results given of the Topsis method, sales and marketing, the market growth of detergent industry chain and organisational factors (human resources) are prioritised 0.868, 0.779 and 0.757, respectively.

Akbar et al. (2012) investigated the impact of five factors indirectly on entrepreneurial Supply chain management competence and two other factors SCM strategies and performance of the firm. They showed that innovativeness Orientation, Risk-taking characteristics, Proactiveness, relational capital, coordination capability, SCM strategies and performance are the multi-dimensional factors affecting entrepreneurial SCM competence. They used regression analysis to analyse the data and their results provide empirical evidence for manufacturing SMEs that possess a high level of entrepreneurial Supply Chain Management competence to perform better in their supply chain. They also claimed that SMEs could enhance their performance by linking up and skillfully managing their entrepreneurial SCM competence (Amin Moghadasi et al. 2017; Taghavifard et al. 2018; Boudlaie et al. 2020; Sadeghi et al. 2019; Ramadani et al. 2019; Taghizadeh-Yazdi et al. 2020; Sukumar et al. 2020).

Nguyen and Pham (2020) proposed a method to assess the impact of corporate entrepreneurship on organisational culture, supply chain management performance and business performance by using the partial least squares structural equation modeling (PLS-SEM) technique. The results indicate that organisational culture and company size had a moderating role effected positively by corporate entrepreneurship to business performance through organisational culture and supply chain management performance. Kloep (2020) provides a review of the relevant factors for achieving performance as an entrepreneur in the position of supply chain manager. They suggested that at least five factors play a major role in entrepreneurial supply chain management competence, namely innovation orientation, risk-taking characteristics, proactiveness orientation, relational capital and coordination capability. Several potential causes of business failure are also identified, including lack of scheduling and problems with the suppliers. According to the aforementioned literature, this chapter proposed a model which is a multi-product, multi-period, multi-objective and multi-echelon green entrepreneurial supply chain. The mathematical model considered three conflicting objectives simultaneously, including minimising total costs, minimising total CO_2 emission and maximising utilisation of capacities; also, it investigates production and export of new products to neighbouring countries.

5 Problem Statement

Several aspects are considered simultaneously in this study in three conflicting objectives such as minimising total transportation and fixed costs, minimising total CO_2 emissions released from transportation and maximising total capacity utilisation in each echelon of the supply chain. Considering these objectives simultaneously has not been applied in previous research papers in the food supply chain especially in the meat industry. The proposed model was able to determine the optimal quantities of products to be transported in every echelon of the supply chain and find the optimum suppliers and retailers. The main research contributions of this study are summarised as follows:

- Employing real data (Koorosh protein company, Iran).
- Improving a new multi-product, multi-period, multi-echelon and multi-objective mixed-integer linear programming optimisation model in a meat supply chain.
- Applying a solution approach based on the augmented constraint. Pareto-optimal solutions for decision-makers are developed to decide and consider the trade-off between three employed objectives.

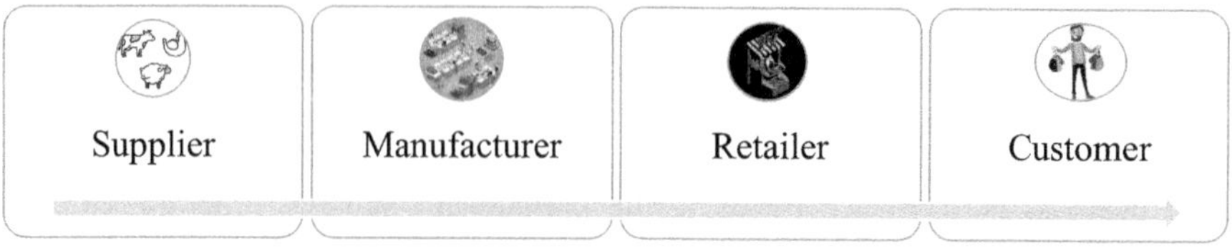

Fig. 9 Schematic four echelon supply chain

In this study, the under-investigation supply chain is a multi-product, multi-period, multi-objective and four echelon food supply chain that starts from producers (such as livestock and poultry) who prepare raw materials and ends with customers who purchase and consume processed products (Fig. 9).

In the production stage, the products are segmented, processed, packaged and turned into semi-finished products. Semi-finished products can then be delivered to supermarkets at later stages and distributed. Finally, the end customer buys and consumes the goods. Therefore, the mainstream of products is between supply (livestock), production (food industry), distribution (retailers) and consumption (customer).

6 Methodology

In conducting any research, choosing the appropriate research method is very important. The research method is a tool to achieve reality, as well the choice of research method depends on factors such as the nature of the research subject, objectives and research questions, the scope of the research subject and executive facilities (Taghizadeh-Yazdi and Mohammadi-Balani 2019). Here are the assumptions of the mathematical model.

- Customer demand is predefined and must be met.
- The maximum capacity of suppliers, manufacturers, and retailers is known.
- The manufacturer and retailer have no initial inventory.
- Retailers can be selected from Iran's neighbouring countries.
- Road transport has been selected to transport products over the network.
- Refrigerated machines with different capacities are used to transport livestock or products.
- Demand is generated by the end-user.

The sets of the mathematical model are as introduced in Table 1.

The parameters of the mathematical model are introduced in Table 2.

The variables of the mathematical model are introduced in Table 3.

The proposed objective functions were as follows:

Table 1 Sets of the mathematical model

S	set of suppliers	$(1...s...S)$
M	set of manufacturers	$(1...m...M)$
R	set of retailers	$(1...r...R)$
C	set of customers	$(1...c...C)$
J	set of products including livestock and product	$(1...j...J)$
T	set of a time	$(1...t...T)$
V	set of vehicles	$(1...v...V)$

Table 2 Parameters of the mathematical model

p_{sjt}	Purchasing cost per ton of livestock j from supplier s in time t.
td_{sm}	Shipping distance (km) from the supplier s to manufacturer m.
td_{mr}	Shipping distance (km) from manufacturer m to retailer r.
td_{rc}	Shipping distance (km) from retailer r to customer c.
tc_{smjt}	Unit shipping cost per kilometre for livestock j from the supplier s to producer m in time t.
tc_{mrjt}	Unit shipping cost per kilometre for product j from producer m to retailer r in time t.
tc_{rcjt}	Unit shipping cost per kilometre for product j from retailer r to customer c in time t.
d_{cjt}	Customer demand (ton) c for product j in time t.
x_{sj}	Maximum supply capacity (number) of suppliers s for livestock j.
v_{mj}	Maximum production capacity (number) of producer m for product j.
u_{rj}	Maximum supply capacity (number) of retailers r for product j.
α_t	CO_2 emission coefficient per kilometre per period t.
$ecap_t$	Maximum carbon emissions per period t.
w_j	Product weight (tons) j.
n_s	Fixed cost of cooperating with the supplier s.
b_m	Fixed cost of constructing a manufacturer m.
e_r	Fixed cost of cooperating with a retailer r.
$Tcap_{smvj}^{max}$	Maximum car capacity v (tons) to send from supplier s to producer m for livestock j.
$Tcap_{smvj}^{min}$	The minimum capacity of car v (tons) to send from supplier s to producer m for livestock j.
$Tcap_{mrvj}^{max}$	Maximum capacity of car v (tons) to send from manufacturer m to retailer r for product j.
$Tcap_{mrvj}^{min}$	The minimum capacity of car v (tons) to send from manufacturer m to retailer r for product j.
$Tcap_{rcvj}^{max}$	Maximum capacity of car v (tons) to send from retailer r to customer c for product j.
$Tcap_{rcvj}^{min}$	Minimum car capacity v (tons) to send from retailer r to customer c for product j.
rp	Fine rate for not using the maximum capacity due to the number of carbon emissions.

Table 3 Variables of the mathematical model

Q_{smjvt}	The number of livestock j transferred from supplier s to producer m in period t by vehicle v.
Q_{mrjvt}	The number of products j transferred from manufacturer m to retailer r in period t by vehicle v.
Q_{rcjvt}	The number of products j transferred from retail r to customer c in period t by vehicle v.
Z_s	The binary variable is equal to 1 if supplier s is selected, otherwise, it is 0.
W_m	The binary variable is equal to 1 if the producer m is selected, otherwise, it is 0.
Y_r	The binary variable, if selected by retailer r, is equal to 1, otherwise, it is 0.
I_{sm}	The binary variable is equal to 1 if sent from supplier s to producer m, otherwise 0.
I_{mr}	The binary variable, if sent from the manufacturer m to the retailer r, is equal to 1, otherwise, it is 0.
I_r	The binary variable is equal to 1 is sent from the retailer to the customer, otherwise, it is 0.
e^+	Amount of carbon emission points that can be purchased according to the environmental policy plan.
e^-	Amount of marketable carbon emission points according to the environmental policy plan.

The proposed objective functions were as follows:

$$Min\ Z_1 = \sum_s \sum_m \sum_j \sum_v \sum_t \left(p_{sjt} \times w_j \times Q_{smjvt} + tc_{smjt} \times td_{sm} \times \frac{Q_{smjvt}}{Tcap_{smvj}^{max}} \right)$$
$$+ \sum_m \sum_r \sum_j \sum_v \sum_t tc_{mrjt} \times td_{mr} \times \frac{Q_{mrjvt}}{Tcap_{mrvj}^{max}}$$
$$+ \sum_r \sum_c \sum_j \sum_v \sum_t tc_{rcjt} \times td_{rc} \times \frac{Q_{rcjvt}}{Tcap_{rcvj}^{max}} + 8\sum_s n_s \times Z_s + \sum_m b_m$$
$$\times W_m + \sum_r e_r \times Y_r \tag{1}$$

$$Min\ Z_2 = \alpha_t \left(\sum_s \sum_m \sum_j \sum_v \sum_t td_{sm} \times \frac{Q_{smjvt}}{Tcap_{smvj}^{max}} + \sum_m \sum_r \sum_j \sum_v \sum_t td_{mr} \right.$$
$$\left. \times \frac{Q_{mrjvt}}{Tcap_{mrvj}^{max}} + \sum_r \sum_c \sum_j \sum_v \sum_t td_{rc} \times \frac{Q_{rcjvt}}{Tcap_{rcvj}^{max}} \right)$$
$$+ \alpha_t * rp \left(\sum_s \sum_m \sum_j \sum_v \sum_t \left(Tcap_{smvj}^{max} \times I_{sm} \right) - Q_{smjvt} \right. \tag{2}$$
$$+ \sum_m \sum_r \sum_j \sum_v \sum_t \left(Tcap_{mrvj}^{max} \times I_{mr} \right) - Q_{mrjvt}$$
$$\left. + \sum_r \sum_c \sum_j \sum_v \sum_t \left(Tcap_{rcvj}^{max} \times I_r \right) - Q_{rcjvt} \right)$$

$$Max\ Z_3 = \sum_s \sum_m \sum_j \sum_v \sum_t \frac{Q_{smjvt}}{x_{sj}} + \sum_m \sum_r \sum_j \sum_v \sum_t \frac{Q_{mrjvt}}{v_{mj}}$$
$$+ \sum_r \sum_c \sum_j \sum_v \sum_t \frac{Q_{rcjvt}}{u_{rj}} \tag{3}$$

s.t.

$$\sum_m \sum_j \sum_v Q_{smjvt} \leq Z_s \times \sum_j x_{sj} \forall s, t \tag{4}$$

$$\sum_r \sum_j \sum_v Q_{mrjvt} \leq W_m \times \sum_j v_{mj} \forall m, t \tag{5}$$

$$\sum_c \sum_j \sum_v Q_{rcjvt} \leq Y_r \times \sum_j u_{rj} \forall r, t \tag{6}$$

$$\sum_s \sum_v Q_{smjvt} \geq \sum_r \sum_v Q_{mrjvt} \forall m, j, t \tag{7}$$

$$\sum_{m}\sum_{v}Q_{mrjvt} \geq \sum_{c}\sum_{v}Q_{rcjvt}\forall r,j,t \tag{8}$$

$$\sum_{r}\sum_{v}Q_{rcjvt} = d_{cjt}\forall c,j,t \tag{9}$$

$$Tcap_{smvj}^{min} \times I_{sm} \leq Q_{smjvt} \leq Tcap_{smvj}^{max} \times I_{sm}\forall s,m,j,v,t \tag{10}$$

$$I_{sm} \leq Z_s\forall s,m \tag{11}$$

$$I_{sm} \leq W_m\forall s,m \tag{12}$$

$$Tcap_{mrvj}^{min} \times I_{mr} \leq Q_{mrjvt} \leq Tcap_{mrvj}^{max} \times I_{mr}\forall m,r,j,v,t \tag{13}$$

$$I_{mr} \leq W_m\forall m,r \tag{14}$$

$$I_{mr} \leq Y_r\forall m,r \tag{15}$$

$$Tcap_{rcvj}^{min} \times I_r \leq Q_{rcjvt} \leq Tcap_{rcvj}^{max} \times I_r\forall r,c,j,v,t \tag{16}$$

$$I_r \leq Y_r\forall r \tag{17}$$

$$\alpha_t\left(\sum_{s}\sum_{m}\sum_{j}\sum_{v}Q_{smjvt} + \sum_{m}\sum_{r}\sum_{j}\sum_{v}Q_{mrjvt} + \sum_{r}\sum_{c}\sum_{j}\sum_{v}Q_{rcjvt}\right) + e^{-} = e^{+} + ecap_t\forall t \tag{18}$$

$$Z_s, W_m, Y_r, I_{sm}, I_{mr}, I_r \in \{0,1\}\forall s,m,r \tag{19}$$

$$Q_{smjvt}, Q_{mrjvt}, Q_{rcjvt}, e^{+}, e^{-} \geq 0\forall s,m,r,c,j,v,t \tag{20}$$

The second objective function (Z2) minimises the amount of CO_2 emissions from transportation distances from supplier to manufacturer, from manufacturer to retailer, and from retailer to customer, according to the maximum possible capacity and carbon dioxide emission per kilometre travelled by the vehicles. There is also a fine cost to minimise the remained capacity which was not used. The last objective function (Z3) maximises capacity utilisation in each segment. The first part considers the function of utilising the supply capacity of the supplier, and the second and third parts consider the utilisation of the production capacities in the production unit and the supply in the retail unit respectively. Constraints (4), (5) and (6) are the maximum capacity limits of suppliers, manufacturers and retailers respectively. Constraints (7) and (8) state that the input and output product must be equal in each of the manufacturers and retailers respectively (for each product in each time). Constraint (9) satisfies customer demand for each product.

Constraint (10) indicates the range of capacity limits for delivery from the supplier to the manufacturer by each vehicle. Constraints (11) and (12) indicate that the shipment is made between the two levels of supplier and manufacturer if the facilities are selected and active at these two levels. Constraint (13) indicates the range of capacity constraints to be sent from the manufacturer to the retailer by each vehicle. Constraints (14) and (15) indicate that the transfer is made between the two levels of producer and retailer if the facilities are selected and active in these two levels. Constraint (16) indicates the range of capacity limitations to be sent from the retailer to the customer by each vehicle. Constraint (17) indicates that the transfer is made between the two levels of the retailer and the customer if the facility is selected and active at this level at the retail level. Constraint (18) indicates the number of allowable carbon emissions based on policy plans along the supply chain. Constraint (19) shows binary variables. Constraint (20) indicates non-negative variables.

The first goal (Z1) is to minimise the total cost of transportation and fixed costs by considering the maximum possible capacity. The first part is related to the cost of purchasing each ton of livestock from the supplier and its transportation cost, taking into account the maximum capacity of the transport machine from supplier to producer. The second and third sections of the first objective function also consider the cost of purchasing products and transporting them from manufacturers to retailers and from retailers to customers respectively. The last part of the first objective function deals with the fixed costs of cooperating with the supplier, establishing the manufacturer and cooperating with the retailer at each level.

6.1 Solution Approach

In this chapter, augmented ε-constraint method, which is an improved version of traditional ε-constraint technique, was employed. The traditional ε-constraint method, which was introduced by Chankong and Haimes (1983), optimises one objective function where the rest of the objective functions are considered as constraints. This method augmented ε-constraint, which was introduced by Mavrotas (2009), has attracted the attention of researchers in recent years because of its advantages. As well as reducing the computational time which is needed for problems with more than two objective functions, this method can guarantee the efficiency of the Pareto-optimal solutions.

6.2 The Augmented ε-Constraint Method

For a problem, there will be the following two mathematical representations:

$$\text{Min } f_1(x)$$

$$\text{Subject to } f_2(x) \leq \varepsilon_2, f_3(x) \leq \varepsilon_3, \ldots, f_p(x) \leq \varepsilon_p, x \in S$$

By changing the values to the right of the new ε constraints, the parting edge of the problem will be obtained. One of the major problems of the ε-method is the high-volume constraint because for each of the objective functions converted to a constraint $p - 1$ several different values of $\varepsilon_i$values must be tested. One of the most common approaches in ε-method, first, obtain the maximum and minimum of each objective function without considering the other objective functions in the $x \in S$ space, and then calculate the interval associated with each of the objective functions using the values obtained from the previous step. If the maximum and minimum values of the objective functions are called f_i^{max} and f_i^{min} respectively, then the interval of each of them is calculated as follows:

$$r_i = f_i^{max} - f_i^{min}$$

The interval r_i is divided by the interval q_i then for ε_i in the following equation, we can get the number $q_i + 1$ of different values that are calculated from the following formula.

$$\varepsilon_i^k = f_i^{max} - \frac{r_i}{q_i} \times k \qquad k = 0, 1, \ldots, q_i$$

In the above relation, k represents the number of the new point corresponding to ε_i. Using the ε-constraint method, the above multi-objective optimisation problem can be converted to $\Pi_{i=2}^{p}(q_i + 1)$ single-objective optimisation problem. Each subproblem has an answer space S as it will be more limited by inequalities related to the objective functions $f_2, \ldots, f_p$.

Each sub-problem leads to a candidate answer to the multi-objective optimisation problem or the so-called Parthian front. Sometimes some of the following issues create an unjustified atmosphere. Finally, after obtaining the optimal Pareto, the decision-maker can choose and use the most appropriate answer in his opinion. The augmented ε-constraint method provides Pareto, efficient optimal solutions. In the ε-constraint method, one of the objective functions is considered as the main objective function to be optimised, while the other objective function is considered as a constraint in the model. The augmented ε-constraint model can be represented by the following equation:

$$Min/Max\left(f_1(x) + \vartheta * \left(\frac{s_2}{r_2} + \frac{s_3}{r_3} + \ldots + \frac{s_i}{r_i} \ldots + \frac{s_n}{r_n}\right)\right)$$

St:

$$f_2(x) - s_2 = \varepsilon_2$$

$$f_3(x) - s_3 = \varepsilon_3$$

$$\ldots\ldots$$

$$i \in [2, n]$$

$$s_i \in R^+$$

According to the above equation, Pareto optimal solutions are obtained in which r_i is the domain of the ith objective function, ϑ is a small number between 0.001 to

Table 4 Objective function values

ε	First objective function	Second objective function	Third objective function
1	2216400	0.479	24.18
2	2304300	0.541	24.41
3	2341300	0.501	24.04
4	2313200	0.642	24.21
5	2331453	0.649	24.51

0.000001 and S_i is an additional non-negative variable. First, the values of NIS_{fi} (worst value) and PIS_{fi} (best value) are obtained for each objective function, then the amplitude value of the *i*th objective function is calculated according to the following equation:

$$r_i = PIS_{fi} - NIS_{fi}$$

$r_i$is then divided into intervals equal to l_i. Then l_i+ 1 points are obtained, which according to the following equation, the value of epsilons is obtained based on these points (Gridpoint).

In this method, for all obtained ε models, the model must be solved that According to the relation η, Gridpoint numbers are obtained.

$$\varepsilon_i^{\eta} = NIS_{f_i} + \frac{r_i}{l_i} * \eta$$

Finally, we solved the augmented ε-constraint model using GAMS software for each of the obtained ε. The set of Pareto optimal answers obtained is as follows (Table 4).

7 Results

There is usually no definite optimal solution to multi-objective problems with this Pareto-based method. Pareto is an evolutionary method proposed for optimising multi-objective problems. In conflicting multi-objective problems that do not simultaneously achieve optimisation, the Pareto-based method creates a set of answers in the form of Pareto points. Based on this set, the decision-maker chooses the Pareto answer, taking into account the priority of the objectives of the final desired answer. Unlike single-objective problems where there is only one optimal point as the answer, a set of optimal solutions is formed in the Pareto-based method, which is the optimal points in the term Pareto points or answers.

The number of j products transferred from supplier s to producer m in period t by vehicle v is introduced in Table 5.

The number of products j transferred from manufacturer m to retailer r in period t by vehicle v is introduced in Table 6.

Table 5 Number of j products transferred from supplier s to producer m by vehicle v in time t

Variables	Values
s1.m1.j1.v1.t1	16
s1.m1.j1.v1.t3	3
s1.m1.j1.v2.t2	3
s1.m1.j2.v1.t1	31
s1.m1.j2.v1.t2	44
s1.m1.j2.v2.t3	44
s2.m1.j2.v1.t2	13
s2.m1.j2.v1.t3	8
s3.m1.j1.v1.t1	31
s3.m1.j1.v1.t2	26
s3.m1.j1.v1.t3	31
s3.m2.j1.v2.t2	18
s3.m2.j1.v2.t3	13

Table 6 Number of products j transferred from manufacturer m to retailer r by vehicle v in time t

Variables	Values
m1.r3.j1.v1.t1	47
m1.r3.j1.v1.t2	29
m1.r3.j1.v1.t3	34
m1.r3.j2.v1.t1	31
m1.r3.j2.v1.t2	57
m1.r3.j2.v2.t3	52
m2.r3.j1.v1.t2	18
m2.r3.j1.v1.t3	13

Table 7 Number of products j transferred from retailer r to customer c by vehicle v in time t

Variables	Values
r3.c1.j1.v1.t1	14
r3.c1.j1.v1.t2	17
r3.c1.j1.v1.t3	16
r3.c1.j2.v1.t1	10
r3.c1.j2.v1.t2	19
r3.c1.j2.v2.t3	20
r3.c2.j1.v1.t2	13
r3.c2.j1.v1.t3	15
r3.c2.j1.v2.t1	15
r3.c2.j2.v1.t1	10
r3.c2.j2.v1.t2	18
r3.c2.j2.v2.t3	15
r3.c3.j1.v1.t2	17
r3.c3.j1.v1.t3	16
r3.c3.j1.v2.t1	18
r3.c3.j2.v1.t1	11
r3.c3.j2.v1.t2	20
r3.c3.j2.v1.t3	17

The number of products j transferred from retail r to customer c in period t by vehicle v is introduced in Table 7.

8 Conclusion

Food supply has been one of the most significant, crucial needs of human beings for all eternity. Meat and poultry are an essential part of any healthy diet and have an undeniable role and a significant share in the food supply. Due to the vast and variety of different activities in the food supply, supply chain networks have paramount and salient effects on the environment since the notion of the green food supply chain has been placed the focal point of attention. However, in today's competitive world, companies need to pay attention to entrepreneurial approaches and new international markets as much as environmental issues to be agile, profitable and alive. In this study, a multi-product, multi-period, multi-objective and four echelon food supply chain was proposed, which had the goal of developing a new product to export to neighbouring countries. A mathematical model with three conflicting objective functions was employed in the present research.

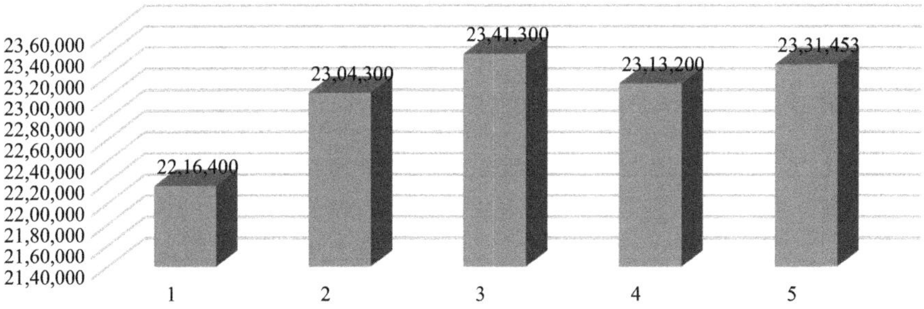

Fig. 10 First objective function values

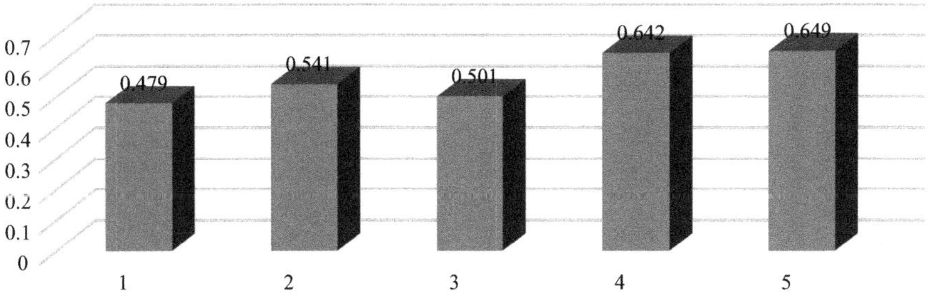

Fig. 11 Second objective function values

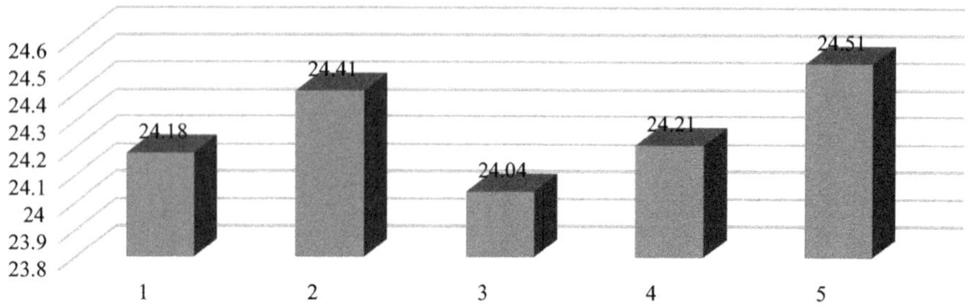

Fig. 12 Third objective function values

The solution approach was augmented ε–constraint to solve the proposed model, and as a result, a Pareto optimal solution was proposed. Figures 10, 11, and 12 depict the values of three objective functions. The best value of the first objective function appeared in the third ε, while the best value of the second objective appeared in the fifth ε, and the best value of the third objective function appeared in the third ε. This Pareto solution can enrich the insight of decision-makers as well as managers and enable them to choose the best solutions according to the trade-off and their priorities. The distribution of goods and services outside the organisation constitutes more than 60% of the total cost of the company. Saving such costs can be done effectively by using strategies to reduce the cost of the product. On the other hand, a large part of the companies' costs that produce perishable products is corrupted products return cost, which causes financial losses in manufacturing companies. Therefore, in this study, a green entrepreneurial four-level supply chain model was presented for the perishable products of Koorosh Protein Company. One of the objectives is to minimise the costs of fixed and transportation costs, and the second objective is to minimise environmental pollution issues and the function of the third objective is to maximise the use of existing capacities of each echelon in the supply chain. Based on the evaluation, the mathematical model was coded in GAMS software, and the optimal answers were analysed and investigated using the augmented ε-constraint method.

The results and their consistency with the actual data depicted the capability and potency of the model. The finding of this chapter can enrich the insight and understanding of the decision-makers and managers as to green entrepreneurial optimal food supply chains and allow them to choose optimal approach in a trade-off between three conflicting objective functions.

According to the results obtained in this research, future research proposals were introduced as follows:

- Considering the lost sales component in the mathematical model: Considering this issue in real environmental conditions, due to problems in the supply chain and production of products, part of customer demand arises as lost sales for the manufacturing company, which is suggested. The issue of lost sales should be considered in the mathematical model.
- It is suggested that due to the existence of a perishable supply chain in the study company, the objective function of minimising supply, and distribution scheduling should be considered in the model which leads to minimisation of delivery time.
- It is suggested to use fuzzy uncertainty theory to investigate the supply chain uncertainty.

References

Adland R, Jia H, Strandenes SP (2018) The determinants of vessel capacity utilization: the case of Brazilian iron ore exports. *Transp Res A Policy Pract 110*:191–201

Akbar, I, Muzaffar M, Cheema K (2012) Entrepreneurial supply chain management competence: performance of manufacturing small and medium enterprises. Available at SSRN 2386969

Amin Moghadasi M, Derakhshandeh B, Ferdosi M, Jafari Sadeghi V (2017) Organizational conformity as an entrepreneurial response to the changes in internationalization process: a study of IT-oriented firms in Saveh. *World J Acc Fin Eng* 1(1):53–64

Babbar C, Amin SH (2018) A multi-objective mathematical model integrating environmental concerns for supplier selection and order allocation based on fuzzy QFD in beverages industry. *Expert Syst Appl 92*:27–38

Beheshti M, Mahdiraji HA, Zavadskas EK (2016) Strategy portfolio optimisation: a copras g-modm hybrid approach. *Transform Bus Econ* 15(3C):500–519

Biancone PP, Jafari Sadeghi V (2016) Risk management in export compliance: concepts, procedures, and solutions. In: Cantino V, De Vincentiis P, Racca MG (eds) *Risk management: perspectives and open issues*. McGraw-Hill, London, UK, pp 64–78

Bortolini M, Faccio M, Ferrari E, Gamberi M, Pilati F (2016) Fresh food sustainable distribution: cost, delivery time and carbon footprint three-objective optimization. *J Food Eng 174*:56–67

Boudlaie H, Mahdiraji HA, Shamsi S, Jafari-Sadeghi V, Garcia-Perez A (2020) Designing a human resource scorecard: an empirical stakeholder-based study with a company culture perspective. *J Entrep Manag Innov* 16(4):113–147

Chankong, V., & Haimes, Y. Y. (1983). Optimization-based methods for multiobjective decision-making-an overview. Large Scale Systems In Information And Decision Technologies, 5(1), 1-33.

Chopra S, Meindl P (2007) Supply chain management. Strategy, planning & operation. Springer. Accessed 29 Aug 2020

Dabić M, Maley J, Dana LP, Novak I, Pellegrini MM, Caputo A (2020) Pathways of SME internationalization: a bibliometric and systematic review. *Small Bus Econ* 55(3):705–725

Dargahi M (2015) Evaluation of the factors of entrepreneurial supply chain management effecting on new product development process

Shaw MR, Pendleton L, Cameron DR, Morris B, Bachelet D, Klausmeyer K, MacKenzie J, Conklin DR, Bratman GN, Lenihan J, Haunreiter E, Daly C, Roehrdanz PR (2011) The impact of climate change on California's ecosystem services. *Clim Chang 109*(suppl. 1):465–484

Filion LJ, Dana LP, Julien PA, Veciana JM, Johannessen T, Raith M (2010) The future of entrepreneurship research: results of a research workshop with invited speakers and discussants at the International Council for Small Business World Conference in Halifax. *Int J Entrep Small Bus* 11(2):105–120

García-Flores R, Higgins A, Prestwidge D, McFallan S (2014) Optimal location of spelling yards for the northern Australian beef supply chain. *Comput Electron Agric 102*:134–145

Hajiagha SHR, Mahdiraji HA, Hashemi SS (2013) Multi-objective linear programming with interval coefficients. *Kybernetes*

Hajiagha SHR, Hashemi SS, Mahdiraji HA, Azaddel J (2015) Multi-period data envelopment analysis based on Chebyshev inequality bounds. *Expert Syst Appl 42*(21):7759–7767

Hajiagha SHR, Mahdiraji HA, Tavana M, Hashemi SS (2018) A novel common set of weights method for multi-period efficiency measurement using mean-variance criteria. *Measurement 129*:569–581

Healy KJ, Withers DH, Fu MC, Dellino G, Kleijnen JPC, Meloni C (2015) International series in operations research & management science handbook of *simulation optimization*. INFORMS J Comput 24:471–484

Hu Q, Zhang Z, Lim A (2016) Transportation service procurement problem with transit time. *Transp Res B Methodol* 86:19–36

Jafari-Sadeghi V (2019) Internationalisation, risk-taking, and export compliance: a comparative study between economically advanced and developing country. *Int J Entrep Small Bus* 37 (2):288–308

Jafari-Sadeghi V, Kimiagari S, Biancone PP (2019) Level of education and knowledge, foresight competency and international entrepreneurship. *Eur Bus Rev* 32(1):46–68

Jafari-Sadeghi V, Dutta DK, Ferraris A, Del Giudice M (2020) Internationalisation business processes in an under-supported policy contexts: evidence from Italian SMEs. *Bus Process Manag J* 26(5):1055–1074

Jakubovskis A (2017) Flexible production resources and capacity utilization rates: a robust optimization perspective. *Int J Prod Econ 189*:77–85

James SJ, James C, Evans JA (2006) Modelling of food transportation systems – a review. *Int J Refrig* 29(6):947–957

Jouzdani J, Govindan K (2020) On the sustainable perishable food supply chain network design: a dairy products case to achieve sustainable development goals. *J Clean Prod* 123060

Kloep M (2020) Innovation and entrepreneurship for supply chain management & logistics. *Int J Supply Chain Manag* 9(1):1088

Krejci CC, Dorneich MC, Stone RT (2016) Hybrid simulation modeling for regional food systems by Anuj Mittal A thesis submitted to the graduate faculty in partial fulfillment of the requirements for the degree of Master of Science Major: Industrial Engineering Program of Study Committee: David

Mahdiraji HA, Hajiagha SHR, Pourjam R (2011) A Grey Mathematical Programming model to time-cost trade-offs in project management under uncertainty. In: *IEEE 2011 International Conference on Grey Systems and Intelligent Services*. IEEE, pp 698–704

Mahdiraji HA, Kazimieras Zavadskas E, Kazeminia A, Abbasi Kamardi A (2019) Marketing strategies evaluation based on big data analysis: a CLUSTERING-MCDM approach. *Econ Res-Ekonomska istraživanja 32*(1):2882–2892

Mahdiraji HA, Hafeez K, Kord H, Kamardi AA (2020) Analysing the voice of customers by a hybrid fuzzy decision-making approach in a developing country's automotive market. *Manag Decis*

Mahmoudi M, Mahdiraji HA, Jafarnejad A, Safari H (2019) Dynamic prioritization of equipment and critical failure modes. *Kybernetes* 48(9):1913–1941

Mavrotas, G. (2009). Effective implementation of the ε-constraint method in multi-objective mathematical programming problems. Applied mathematics and computation, 213(2), 455-465.

Mohammed A, Wang Q (2016) An investment evaluation of a RFID-enabled meat supply chain: a multi-criteria approach. *MATEC Web of Confer 70*

Mohammed A, Wang Q (2017a) Developing a meat supply chain network design using a multi-objective possibilistic programming approach. *Br Food J 119*(3):690–706

Mohammed A, Wang Q (2017b) Multi-criteria optimization for a cost-effective design of an RFID-based meat supply chain. *Br Food J 119*(3):676–689

Mohammed A, Wang Q (2017c) The fuzzy multi-objective distribution planner for a green meat supply chain. *Int J Prod Econ 184*:47–58

Mohebalizadeh M, Hafezalkotob A (2018) Modelling sustainable supply chain management problem with fuzzy demand based on multi-criteria decision making methods. *Int J Ind Syst Eng 30*(3):267–297

Mohebalizadehgashti F, Zolfagharinia H, Amin SH (2020) Designing a green meat supply chain network: a multi-objective approach. *Int J Prod Econ 219*(June 2019):312–327

Mohsen A, Ramadani V, Dana LP (2020) Green entrepreneurship prospects and challenges: the context of Afghanistan. In: *Research handbook on entrepreneurship in emerging economies*. Edward Elgar Publishing

Mokhtarzadeh NG, Mahdiraji HA, Beheshti M, Zavadskas EK (2018) A novel hybrid approach for technology selection in the information technology industry. *Technol 6*(1):34

Nayeri S, Paydar MM, Asadi-Gangraj E, Emami S (2020) Multi-objective fuzzy robust optimization approach to sustainable closed-loop supply chain network design. *Comput Ind Eng 148*:106716

Nguyen T, Pham T (2020) The effect of corporate entrepreneurship, organizational culture on supply chain management and business performance in chemical industry. *Uncertain Supply Chain Manag* 8(1):67–76

Paksoy T, Pehlivan NY, Özceylan E (2012) Application of fuzzy optimization to a supply chain network design: a case study of an edible vegetable oils manufacturer. *Appl Math Model 36* (6):2762–2776

Rajabalipour Cheshmehgaz H, Desa MI, Wibowo A (2013) A flexible three-level logistic network design considering cost and time criteria with a multi-objective evolutionary algorithm. *J Intell Manuf 24*(2):277–293

Ramadani V, Hisrich RD, Abazi-Alili H, Dana LP, Panthi L, Abazi-Bexheti L (2019) Product innovation and firm performance in transition economies: a multi-stage estimation approach. *Technol Forecast Soc Chang* 140:271–280

Ramudhin MA, Supervisor T, Kenné J-P, Gharbi MA (2012) Board of Examiners (PhD thesis). This thesis has been evaluated by the following Board of Examiners. Elsevier. Accessed 30 Aug 2020

Sabzevari M, Sajadi SM, Hadji Molana M (2019) Supply chain reconfiguration for a new product development with risk management approach. *Scientia Iranica 2*(3):20–30

Sadeghi VJ, Biancone PP (2018) How micro, small and medium-sized enterprises are driven outward the superior international trade performance? A multidimensional study on Italian food sector. *Res Int Bus Financ* 45:597–606

Sadeghi V, Biancone PP, Giacoma C, Secinaro S (2017) Export compliance: a missing component of international entrepreneurship. *Int J Bus Manag* 12(11):103–110

Sadeghi V, Biancone PP, Giacoma C, Secinaro S (2018) How does export compliance influence the internationalization of firms: is it a thread or an opportunity? *J Glob Entrep Res* 8(3):1–15

Sadeghi VJ, Nkongolo-Bakenda JM, Anderson RB, Dana LP (2019) An institution-based view of international entrepreneurship: a comparison of context-based and universal determinants in developing and economically advanced countries. *Int Bus Rev* 28(6):101588

Sadiku-Dushi N, Dana LP, Ramadani V (2019) Entrepreneurial marketing dimensions and SMEs performance. *J Bus Res* 100:86–99

Sadraei R, Jafari Sadeghi V, Sadraei M (2018) Biotechnology revolution from academic entrepreneurship to industrial: chemo-entrepreneurship. *Biom Biostat Int J* 7(6):546–550

Sajadi SM, Meigounpoory M, Dargahi M (2015) Evaluation of the factors of entrepreneurial supply chain management effecting on new product development process. *J Entrep Dev* 8(3):513–530

Sajadi SM, Taghizadeh Yazdi M, Aghaee A (2020) Multi objective robust and simulation-based optimization approach for convergent supply chain with continued production despite the fraction of some part. *The 49th International Conference on Computers & Industrial Engineering* (CIE49)

Song Y, Dana LP, Berger R (2019) The entrepreneurial process and online social networks: forecasting survival rate. *Small Bus Econ*. https://doi.org/10.1007/s11187-019-00261-7

Soysal M, Bloemhof-Ruwaard JM, Meuwissen MPM, Van Der Vorst JGAJ (2012) *Int J Food Syst Dyn* 3(2):113–123

Soysal M, Bloemhof-Ruwaard JM, Van Der Vorst JGAJ (2014) Modelling food logistics networks with emission considerations: the case of an international beef supply chain. *Int J Prod Econ 152*:57–70

Srivastava SK (2007) Green supply-chain management: a state-of-the-art literature review. *Int J Manag Rev* 9(1):53–80

Sukumar A, Jafari-Sadeghi V, Garcia-Perez A, Dutta DK (2020) The potential link between corporate innovations and corporate competitiveness: evidence from IT firms in the UK. *J Knowl Manag* 24(5):965–983

Taghavifard MT, Amoozad Mahdiraji H, Alibakhshi AM, Zavadskas EK, Bausys R (2018) An extension of fuzzy SWOT analysis: an application to information technology. *Inform* 9(3):46

Taghizadeh-Yazdi M, Mohammadi-Balani A (2019) A mathematical model for multi-region, multi-source, multi-period generation expansion planning in renewable energy for country-wide generation-transmission planning. *J Inf Technol Manag* 12(4):215–231

Taghizadeh-Yazdi M, Mohammadi-Balani A (2020) A mathematical model for multi-region, multi-source, multi-period generation expansion planning in renewable energy for country-wide generation-transmission planning. *J Inf Technol Manag* 12(4):215–231

Taghizadeh-Yazdi M, Farrokhi Z, Mohammadi-Balani A (2020) An integrated inventory model for multi-echelon supply chains with deteriorating items: a price-dependent demand approach. *J Ind Prod Eng* 37(2–3):87–96

Teimoury, E., Nedaei, H., Ansari, S., & Sabbaghi, M. (2013). A multi-objective analysis for import quota policy making in a perishable fruit and vegetable supply chain: A system dynamics approach. Computers and Electronics in Agriculture, 93, 37–45. https://doi.org/10.1016/j.compag.2013.01.010

Töbelmann D, Wendler T (2020) The impact of environmental innovation on carbon dioxide emissions. *J Clean Prod 244*. https://doi.org/10.1016/j.jclepro.2019.118787

Turan HH, Elsawah S, Ryan MJ (2020) A long-term fleet renewal problem under uncertainty: a simulation-based optimization approach, 145.

Walker N (2017) The Third International Conference on Digital Enterprise and Information Systems (DEIS2015) | Just another WordPress site. Researchgate.Net, April 2015. www.sdiwc.net

Zhang M, Hu Q (2019) An effective evolutionary algorithm for the bi-objective full truckload transportation service procurement problem. In: *Computers and industrial engineering*, vol 127. Elsevier Ltd

Zulfiu V, Ramadani V, Dana LP (2015) Muslim entrepreneurs in secular Turkey: distributors as a source of innovation in a supply chain. *Int J Entrep Small Bus* 26(1):78–95

Mohammadreza Taghizadeh-Yazdi is currently an associate professor in the Department of Industrial Management at the University of Tehran, Iran. He received his B.S. and M.S. in Industrial Engineering and PhD in Productions & Operations Management from the University of Tehran. His research interests centre around Operations Research, Simulation-based Optimisation, Discrete-event Simulation, Agent-based Simulation, and Supply Chain Management. He has also succeeded in both publishing research articles in world-famous journals and presenting some others in accredited international conferences around the world.

Nikta Babakhani has recently received her Master's degree in Supply Chain Management from the Management Department of Tehran University. In her Master's thesis, she proposed a model to optimise a green supply chain of a food company using a combination of multi-objective mathematical model and simulation-based optimisation. She received her bachelor's degree in Industrial Engineering from the Khajeh Nasir Toosi University of Technology in 2016. Her research interests include food supply chain, green supply chain, multi-objective optimisation and simulation. In addition, she is currently working as a Sales and Marketing Expert at Koorosh Protein Company which is one of the biggest FMCG Companies in Iran.

Seyed Mojtaba Sajadi is an Associate Professor at the University of Tehran. He received his PhD, MSc, and BSc in Industrial Engineering from the Amirkabir University of Technology, University of Tehran and Sharif University of Technology respectively. His research interests include Simulation-Based Optimisation, Mathematical Modelling, Artificial Intelligence, Data Science, and Machine Learning. He applies these research methodologies in Supply chain Management, Health Care, Production Control, Truism and Entrepreneurship. His published research articles appear in CIE, IJAMT, Cleaner Production, Simulation Modelling Practice and Theory, Applied Soft Computing, Applied Mathematical Modelling, Journal of Simulation, and Journal of Global Entrepreneurship Research, IJSOM, IJISE, Energy and so forth. He has presented several papers at international conferences such as CIE, INFORMS, ENBIS, ECGBL, IJPR and several national conferences.

Amir Hosein Ebrahimi is a PhD candidate in the management department of Tehran University. He also works as a scientific researcher at the Sharif University of Technology. Amir received his MSc (2017) in Engineering and Construction Management from Sharif University as the first-ranked student. In his Master's thesis, he explored the resilience of the urban infrastructures through the development of simulation software in order to evaluate infrastructures resilience and propose the best rehabilitation option due to the given budget. He received his bachelor's degree in Civil Engineering in 2015 as the first-ranked student. His research interests include resilience, sustainability, green supply chain, simulation, and financial management. In addition to his academic records, he has robust work experience in the industry as a project manager and head of R&D office. He is currently the funder of Green Water and Industry (GWI) startup, one of the pioneer startups in Iran's Industry.

Applying System Dynamics Approach to Modelling Growth Engines in the International Entrepreneurship Era

Zahra Jamshidi, Seyed Mojtaba Sajadi, Kambiz Talebi, and Seyed Hossein Hosseini

1 Introduction and Literature Review

Nowadays, start-ups are known as the economic growth key engine (Fukugawa 2018); significantly, they contribute to societies' development. However, start-ups are highly prone to resource constraints and considerable uncertainty (Eisenmann et al. 2012; Shin 2019), and this affects their decision-making strategies (Amin Moghadasi et al. 2017; Biancone and Jafari Sadeghi 2016) especially when they try to enter foreign markets. This is the main reason for the fact that despite the global movement of start-ups, the majority of start-ups fail within 2 years of establishment (Khanna et al. 2018). For start-ups, achieving the right position in the market and growing in a strongly competitive and dynamic environment demand hard work and a plodding process (Caseiro and Coelho 2019; Dana 2011).

Otherwise, regarding start-ups' significance, it is necessary to know how they can be valuable. According to the literature, a start-up is a company designed to grow fast (Graham 2012), and it is also defined as a mechanism to embrace innovation and high growth (Terho et al. 2015). Also, according to Blank (2017), to become global players, start-ups should be growth-oriented. Consequently, growth is generally known as an important factor of success and one of the goals of all firms (Campos 2017; Geuvers and Dana 2015).

Z. Jamshidi · S. M. Sajadi (✉) · K. Talebi
New Business Department, Faculty of Entrepreneurship, University of Tehran, Tehran, Iran
e-mail: zahra.jamshidi71@ut.ac.ir; msajadi@ut.ac.ir; ktalebi@ut.ac.ir

S. H. Hosseini
Model-Based Management Systems Institute (SAMAM), Tehran, Iran
e-mail: s.h.hosseini@samamsystem.com

V. Jafari-Sadeghi et al. (eds.), *Empirical International Entrepreneurship*, Contributions to Management Science,
https://doi.org/10.1007/978-3-030-68972-8_22

These days, on the one hand, customers have different needs and tastes, and service providers need to create value for them (Mahdiraji et al. 2019); on the other hand, organisations face rapid development of science and technology (Jafari Sadeghi et al. 2014). Thus, rapid growth can provide start-ups with better access to the rapid development of competitive advantage in these markets (Täuscher and Abdelkafi 2016). However, start-ups still often suffer from the lack of a long-term strategy for growth-related decisions, and it is a major issue (Beheshti et al. 2016). They make decisions just relying on impermanent results and parameters, wasting time and resources, and also when the future is unpredictable, their common strategies are not applicable (Taghavifard et al. 2018; Mokhtarzadeh et al. 2018). Thus, a question arises here on how start-ups can achieve sustainable growth under conditions of extreme uncertainty (Bohn and Kundisch 2018).

Start-ups can validate their business model by using the lean start-up approach, a recent set of practices (Ghezzi 2019). Lean start-up, a methodology introduced by Eric Ries, has been largely attracting interest (Frederiksen and Brem 2017) and popular with start-up executives. Also, a new notion called "lean global start-up" has emerged that provides start-ups with the idea of adopting the lean approach as part of their global move (Tanev 2017). According to Ries (2011), the engine of growth is one of the most efficient mechanisms start-ups deploy to reach sustainable growth. It is expressed that there are three ways that old customers can bring about an increase in new customers: (1) word of mouth, (2) the side effect of product consumption and (3) through funded advertising. Further, the repetition of purchase also results in start-ups' growth. These activities can be considered as the power of feedback loops known as growth engines.

There are three growth engines each with particular metrics monitoring start-ups' growth speed (Ries 2011; Täuscher and Abdelkafi 2016; de Medeiros Júnior et al. 2015; Frederiksen and Brem 2017):

1. The sticky engine of growth: highlights on customer retention over the long term. It aids companies in cautiously tracking the acquisition rate and churn rate.
2. The paid engine of growth: focuses on customer lifetime value (CLV), which is the remaining money when variable costs are deducted from a certain amount of money each customer pays during his/her lifetime.
3. The viral engine of growth: refers to the viral coefficient, which is the number of customers attracted by each old customer.

Feedback loops reinforce the engines; hence, they are provided with the opportunity to be considered as dynamic models (Ries 2011). However, a few works of literature have explored the engines' implementation in start-ups. Täuscher and Abdelkafi (2016) developed the dynamics for entrepreneurial growth decisions. The author assigned a coefficient for each engine and, then, analysed the coefficients through two scenarios of the worst and the best. However, they ignored start-ups' post-growth challenges of competitive markets; thus, it lacks any empirical validation. How start-ups make decisions to implement the engines and when they pivot to another were also excluded. To survive in the dynamic market, start-ups have to make decisions on whether to change directions or just stay on the selected ones (Björk et al. 2013; van der Ven and Bosch 2013).

De Medeiros Júnior et al. (2015) in a business model-based case study individually examined the structure and behaviour of the three engines. However, it failed to design feedback loops for each. Although growth engine strategy revolves around the fact that start-ups each time must focus on just one engine of growth and then pivot to another once the prior engine had been thoroughly pursued (Ries 2011), there is no dynamic model for decision-making in this study to help entrepreneurs adopt different strategies.

Therefore, the present research tries to coherently model the three engines to provide start-up decision-makers with a simulation tool deciding when each engine should work and what would be the result. Thus, the system dynamics approach, as the main methodology, is used for designing the engines' feedback loops. The required dynamics is attributed to the dynamic of changes in strategies within time (Chanut-Guieu, Guieun and Dana Chanut-Guieu et al. 2019). Also, there are many interrelated variables influencing start-ups' growth (Huang and Kunc 2012; Larsen et al. 1997), which should be considered as a system. Additionally, further studies are expected in the field of entrepreneurship using such methodologies (Keyhani and Levesque 2016).

An information technology start-up has been analysed that can exhibit applicability and efficiency of the proposed model (Hajiagha et al. 2018; Mahmoudi et al. 2019; Sadraei et al. 2018). Also, empirical scenarios have been proposed for different situations. The proposed integrated model simultaneously analyses the three engines of growth and simulates a real-time case given the abundant growth challenges in the competitive market. Moreover, the pivoting decision-making mechanism under various scenarios has been also studied through the use of functional policies.

The rest of the study is organised as follows. In the next section, a brief explanation of the research methodology and process is presented. Then, the research conceptual framework is explained in terms of the relationships between research main variables by causal loop diagrams. The "Mathematical Model" section gives details about the mathematical expression of the model, where the main equations are mentioned. Then, the model's validity is examined, and simulation results are explained in scenario and policy contexts; and finally, the last part is dedicated to the conclusion and further studies.

2 Research Methodology

In this work, the system dynamics approach is used as the research methodology. As a powerful tool for system reflection, it is an approach used for investigating, analysing, forecasting system behaviour and overcoming the complexities. This approach focuses on developing qualitative and quantitative models of complex situations; and then, it experiments and studies the models' behaviour over time (Forrester 1996; Sterman 2000; Hosseini and Shakouri 2016).

In the mid-1950s, Forrester, from MIT, introduced the system dynamics approach. SD solves problems through five steps which are both qualitative and quantitative, including (1) situation analysis and problem identification and definition (qualitative); (2) constructing a conceptual model (causal loop diagrams, qualitative) and (3) mathematical model (stock-flow diagram, quantitative); (4) model simulation and validation (quantitative); and (5) defining different scenarios and selecting and executing appropriate solutions (qualitative and quantitative) (Sweeney and Sterman 2000; Hosseini et al. 2019). Accordingly, SD provides a framework to consider the relationships between system objectives and various indicators (Hosseini et al. 2019). Also, the qualitative parts can be used to verify the quantitative parts (Dana and Dana 2005).

This study focuses on feedback loops in the lean-approach. Further, some effective factors were also identified examining the so-called "Ostadbank"[1] start-up. Ostadbank is a web-based start-up sharing tutors' resumes to help students and their families in selecting the most matched tutors with strong teaching history. Ostadbank tends to play the effective role of a developer in Iran's education system creating and improving the value and satisfaction of students and teachers within high-quality services in addition to market development. This start-up has been initiated by the accelerator support of the Sharif University of Technology and is still working at the university growth centre with 1800 different tutors. In the competing market, the start-up, with over 13,000 learners, has been significantly interesting. However, it was faced with many limitations, too. The start-up's main challenges included a high exit rate or churn rate and lack of attention and focus on keeping the system customers. An interview with executives revealed that all start-ups in the market face the big dilemma of a firm strategy absence to make decisions on the growth issues. Thus, start-ups were instead seeking temporal and impermanent solutions disregarding practical statistics of business growth. That is why the present research has been largely welcomed by their executives.

The research process is presented in Fig. 1. Research main variables were initially obtained through a literature review of lean start-up and growth engines as start-ups' growth strategy and meetings with the marketing manager and managing director of Ostadbank. The system conceptual model was also obtained by the engines' causal loop diagram. Once the equations were formulated using real decision-making mechanisms and Ostadbank data, the start-up growth engine SD model was completed. By the next step, when the system data of the last 6 months in 2019 were collected, a mathematical model was developed to simulate the current and future growth decisions using Vensim PLE. Finally, different scenarios were developed and optimal policies were proposed.

[1] https://www.ostadbank.com/.

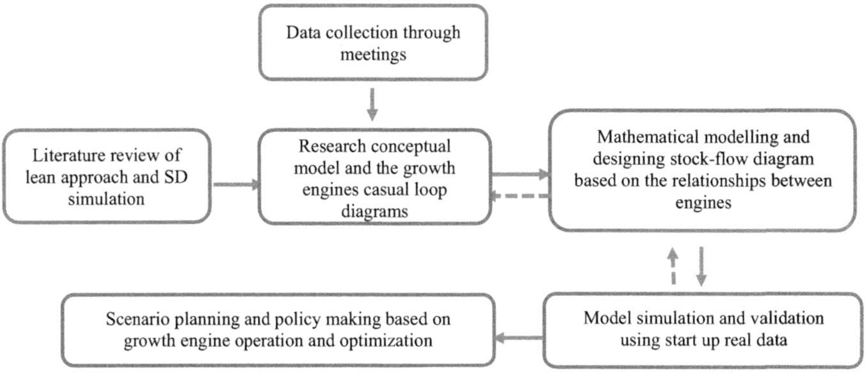

Fig. 1 Research methodology

It is worth to notify that research data were collected with the aid of the start-up staff and executives through checking start-up financial statements and the growth centre reports. Besides, the model was simulated in 24 months.

3 Conceptual Model

In this section, the problem dynamics is presented. It is significantly important for start-ups to apply the right kind of metrics for development evaluation. However, various quantities should be measured. They waste too much time arguing the prioritisation of business development. The company could invest in acquiring new customers, enhancing services to existing customers, boosting the quality or driving down costs, but prioritisation can consume a substantial fraction of the company's time and energy (Ries 2011).

To solve the problem, start-ups may utilise engine growth, defined by Eric Ries (2011) as a mechanism to achieve sustainable growth. Engines of growth are designed to give start-ups a series of metrics on which to focus their energies (Frederiksen and Brem 2017; Pant et al. 2017; Ries 2011). The approach includes three growth engines reinforced by a feedback loop. Technically, at a time, more than one engine of growth can operate in a business, whereas successful start-ups usually focus on just one engine of growth. The engines of the growth framework help start-ups stay focused on the metrics that matter. Identifying which engine of growth a start-up is using can then direct energy toward where it will be the most effective for growing the business (Ries 2011). In this study, two main growth approaches including customer retention and customer acquisition by advertising are identified as the sticky engine and the paid engine, respectively. The other is the viral engine by word of mouth in which the company should invest in the quality of the website or other technical objects.

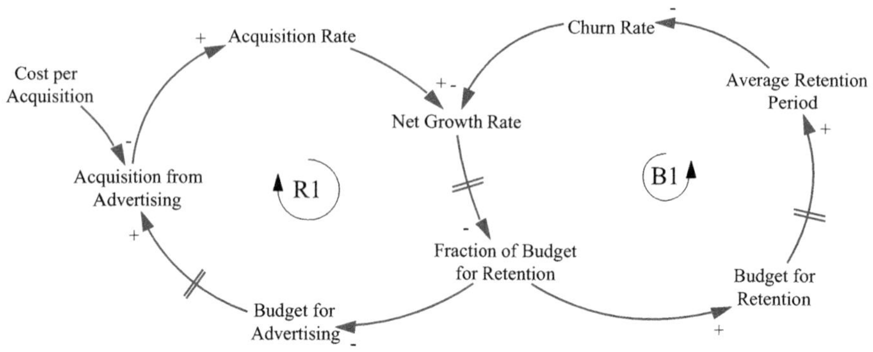

Fig. 2 Casual relations of sticky engine

There has been no effort taken by the understudied start-up to apply the sticky and viral engines excusing customers' high churn rate and low customer lifetime value. Furthermore, the start-up was also challenged as it failed in customer attraction through word of mouth because the existing students avoided referring the tutor to others or the students showed no interest in talking about tutoring. That is why the start-up has only focused on the paid engine. In the following, the engines are outlined relying on the engine implementation in the Ostadbank.

3.1 Sticky Engine

Companies using the sticky engine of growth should monitor the acquisition rate and churn rate very carefully. The speed of growth is measured through the growth rate integration, which is simply the difference between the natural growth rate and the churn rate. Indeed, a start-up mainly focuses on the number of customers joining or leaving the company at a certain period. The purpose of this engine is to improve the rate of customer retention (Ries 2011; de Medeiros Júnior et al. 2015; Täuscher and Abdelkafi 2016). The strategy concentrates on the existing customers and improving the quality of service delivery. A high compounding rate contributes to rapid growth without advertising or viral growth. This engine is effective for the understudied start-up suffering from a high customer churn rate. In practice, the start-up may fail to comprehensively concentrate on the engine if it makes no effort to attract new customers as it is a long-term strategy initially encountering financial shortage. Thus, a decision variable is determined for investment in customer retention or attraction to analyse the variable.

Figure 2 depicts the dynamics of the sticky engine of growth in the lean start-up approach. An increase in the churn rate causes a decrease in the net growth rate, which is the compounding rate in the given month. The rate can be applied as a decision-making tool allocating the revenue to customer retention or advertisement.

The decline in the net growth rate increases the fraction of the customer retention budget. This phenomenon finally brings on less churn rate, and the negative feedback loop B1 is closed.

On the other hand, an increased fraction of the customer retention budget means the company has to spend less money on advertisement, which in turn negatively influences customer acquisition. Hence, it finally decreases the net growth rate, where the loop R1 is formed. The cost per acquisition represents the average cost paid by the company to attract a new customer. Customers are attracted through social media or other means of advertisement. This amount should be deducted from income. Also, it shows the ability of the company to acquire new customers.

3.2 *Viral Engine*

Companies using the viral engine of growth concern person-to-person transmission as a necessary consequence of product consumption. In other words, it mainly concentrates on the word of mouth as a strategy to achieve rapid growth. Customers of the viral engine framework play an important role in marketing. However, they are not necessarily trying to spread the word about the product (Ries 2011). The speed of this engine is determined by the so-called viral coefficient indicating the number of new customers which resulted from other customers' invitations (Ries 2011; Täuscher and Abdelkafi 2016). Start-ups relying on this engine must highlight the growth of the viral coefficient. Facilitating customers' sign-up process and recruiting their friends are an engine acceleration method. As earlier mentioned, Ostadbank failed in applying this engine, too. Improved website services as well as capitalising on the user-friendly order registration process may facilitate the login system for the start-up.

As seen in Fig. 3, the budget for technical items is considered to smoothen the registration of new customers and other services offered by the start-up. Therefore,

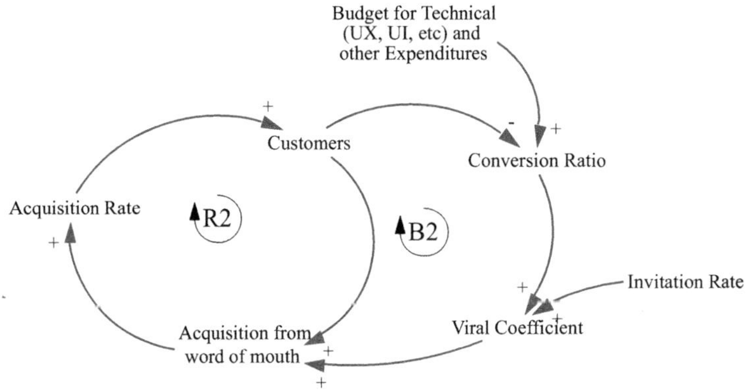

Fig. 3 Casual relations of viral engine

the possibility of conversion of new client invitations, known as conversion ratio, increases. Both invitation rate and conversion ratio are the main variables to measure the viral coefficient. An increase in the viral coefficient may lead to higher customer acquisition and acquisition rates. Finally, when the number of customers multiplies, the company acquires more new customers concerning the viral coefficient (Loop R2). An increased number of customers would reduce technical budget per customer, consequently leading to a decrease in the possibility of conversion of invitations to new customers. As a result, the viral coefficient decreases, and customer acquisition and acquisition rates also drop with a delay (Loop B2, Fig. 3).

3.3 *Paid Engine*

The paid engine of growth determines the amounts of income and costs at a particular period per customer. Companies using this engine can expand their growth rate through increased revenue of each customer or diminishing costs of new customer acquisition. Regarding the paid engine structure, each customer pays a certain amount of money in its lifetime; further, the difference between each customer's average revenues and the variable costs per customer determines the significant variable of customer lifetime value (CLV) (Ries 2011; Täuscher and Abdelkafi 2016). The ability of rapid growth applying this engine depends on the ability of the company to make money from a certain set of customers in competition with other companies (Ries 2011). The results demonstrated the start-up good efforts through continuous price analysis. Hence, it can be expressed that Ostadbank has worked well with the paid engine of growth.

Figure 4 illustrates the dynamics of the paid growth engine. The difference between total lifetime revenue per customer and total lifetime cost per customer

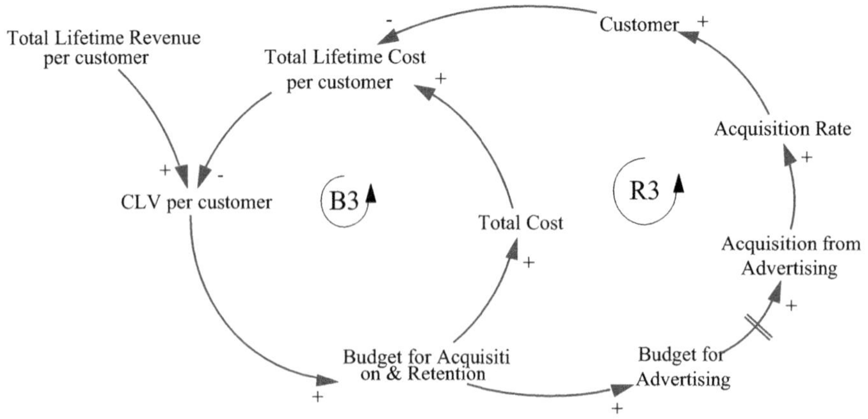

Fig. 4 Casual relations of paid engine

forms the customer lifetime value used for both retention and advertising. The more budget the company allocates, the more cost it pays. The total cost contains all variable costs in the company. Any increase in acquisition and retention budget intensifies advertisement budget; and later, customer acquisition and acquisition rate increase, too. Multiplied number of customers declines total lifetime cost per customer, and the positive loop R3 would be closed.

4 Mathematical Model

In this section, the stock-flow diagram is presented. The diagram shows the causal loops of three engines of growth and the Bass diffusion model. The Bass diffusion model is used as it relies on the two main innovation spreading methods in the market: advertisement and word of mouth (Bass 1969; Sterman 2000). The Bass model represents two stock variables of customers and potential customers connected with the acquisition rate and churn rate determining the market share of the company. As seen, there is another stock variable called financial reserve obtained through subtraction of variable costs from revenue. Payment per customer is another main variable referring to each customer's average payment in a particular period. Ostadbank follows a daily-based payment system in which the fee and the start-up commission are determined according to the grade and/or tutors' rate (tutors are rated based on their working experiences and achievements shown by a "*"). Here, the average number has been computed per month.

The model is mainly characterised by planning how to make a pivot decision, which is known as one of the most important aspects of the lean approach (Pant et al. 2017). It implies that start-up executives must change the right road whenever the wrong strategy road is realised. It is also true about the engines of growth. Companies are allowed to focus only on one engine of growth at a time. So, they require knowing which engine would perform better. Changing acquisition budget fractions, different results are obtained. The fraction determines which strategy of advertisement or retention the start-up prioritises (Fig. 5).

The main relationships between three critical variables of each engine are formulated as follows. One of the main variables is the net growth rate calculated as follows:

$$\text{Net growth rate} = \max\ (0, \text{Acquisition Rate} - \text{Churn Rate}) \tag{1}$$

The maximum function is used to avoid the negative rate. The viral coefficient is the next critical variable:

$$\text{Viral coefficient} = \text{Conversion Ratio} * \text{Invitation Rate} \tag{2}$$

where the invitation rate is multiplied by the conversion ratio. The rates are measured by the website visit and the probability of each visit becoming a purchase.

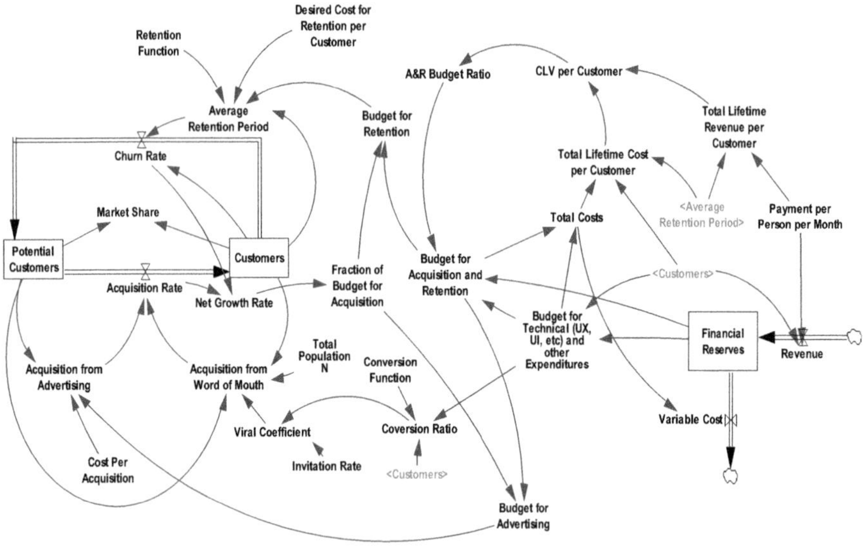

Fig. 5 Stock-flow diagram

$$\text{Customer Lifetime value} = \text{Total Lifetime Revenue per Customer} - \text{Total Lifetime Cost per Customer} \quad (3)$$

It implies the number of customers and customer lifetime cycle, where the costs and revenues are divided into the number of customers and multiplied by the customer lifetime value.

4.1 Model Validation

To analyse or extend the model simulation results, it requires verifying and validation. Model validation, which is an important part of the SD simulation, is a process of model evaluation to find out whether the model components together can lead to authentic results or not. There are various validation methods to verify simulation results and to model reliability in problem analysis (Sterman 2000; Hosseini and Shakouri 2016; Hosseini et al. 2019).

To validate the proposed model, dimensional consistency is initially examined. Next, model behaviour is studied in extreme conditions. As the core validation test, the model behaviour reproduction test is used as the main validation method investigating the model's ability to reproduce the behaviour of the main system variables. The proposed model validation is shown as follows (Figs. 6, 7, 8, and 9):

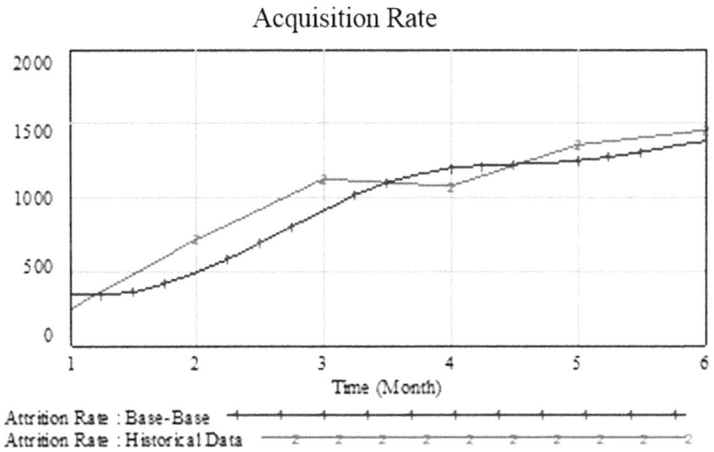

Fig. 6 Simulation results for acquisition rate (person/month)

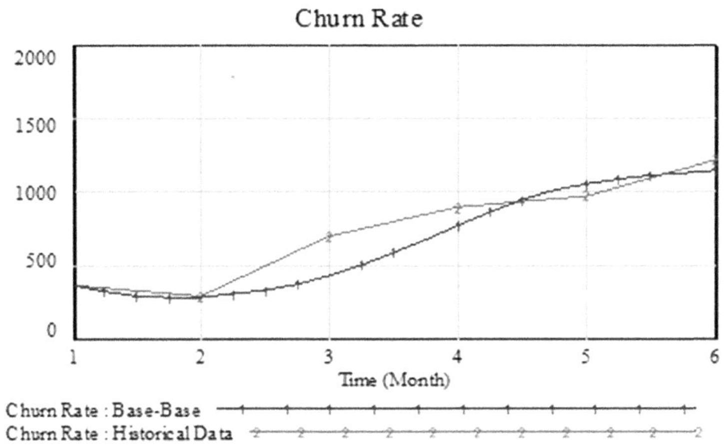

Fig. 7 Simulation results for churn rate (person/month)

As seen, notwithstanding the acquisition rate dramatically growing, the churn rate is increasing, too. One of the major issues the start-up has undergone is the high churn rate as executives ignored customer retention.

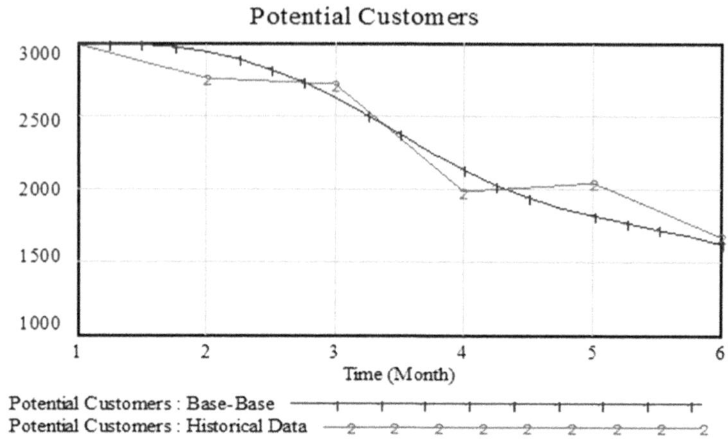

Fig. 8 Simulation results for potential customers (person)

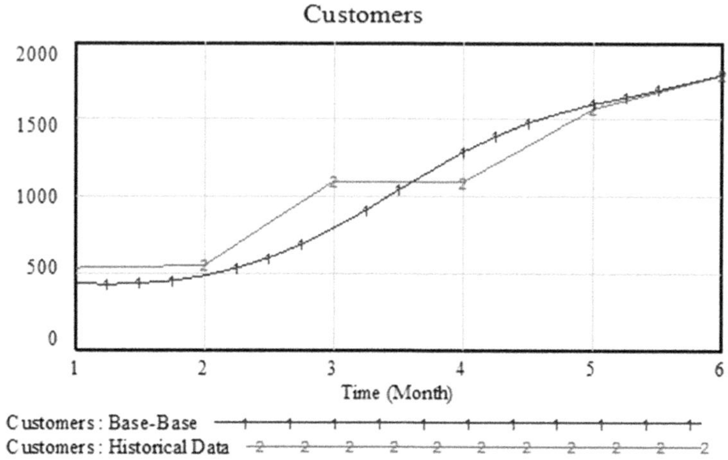

Fig. 9 Simulation results for customers (person)

5 Simulation Results Under Different Scenarios and Policies

In the following, simulation results of five scenarios and proposed policies are discussed. Growth rate depends on three main factors of customer profitability, new customer acquisition cost and purchase repetition rate of existing customers (Ries 2011). Scenarios include an increase or decrease in payment per customer, an increase in the cost of customer acquisition and customer retention and a decline in the conversion ratio.

1. *Base run*: this scenario contains preliminary data of the studied start-up.

Table 1 Parameters' changes in different scenarios

Scenario	Changed parameter	Unit	Value change
Base run	–	–	–
Increased payment	Payment per customer	Dollar/person/month	55%
Decreased payment	Payment per customer	Dollar/person/month	44%
Cost increase	Customer acquisition cost Desired retention cost	Dollar/person Dollar/person/month	15% 33%
Quality competition	The decrease in conversion ratio	Person/month	100%

2. *Increased payment*: it is assumed that start-ups may increase the cost of their services due to inflation or quality improvement.
3. *Decreased payment*: following the previous scenario, payment per customer likely decreases as competition intensifies. Indeed, companies have to follow competitive prices once market competition grows.
4. *Cost increase*: given that growing competitors provide a competitive atmosphere in the market, the cost per acquisition and the retention cost per customer will become larger.
5. *Quality competition*: in the last scenario, the possibility of quality competition is considered implying the declined conversion ratio. When other rivals offer better service quality, the possibility of being selected by customers who have heard about the start-up is lower (Table 1).

According to the lean approach, start-ups should focus on only one engine at a time. It does not mean other engines must stop working; rather, it implies the company's main energy is allocated to the one special engine of growth. Therefore, three main policies of advertising, retention and technologies are designed associated with the paid engine, sticky engine and the viral engine, respectively. Generally, in this article, five scenarios are simulated as follows:

1. *Base*: no data alteration; the simulation merely focuses on the comparison.
2. *Advertisement*: in the policy of advertisement, the advertising allocated budget is enhanced. It means that the paid engine is turning faster comparing other engines, and the revenue can be invested in customer acquisition.
3. *Retention*: the focus of the start-up is on the sticky engine contributing to the increased average retention period.
4. *Technical*: the main factor of the viral engine is the conversion ratio, which indicates what percentage of invitations may lead to new customers. In this policy, the budget for technical objects, like the quality of the website, is heightened, and consequently, the possibility of turning invitations into the customer increases, too.
5. *Combined*: prior policies are simulated here in combination in which attraction and retention budgets were changed up to the 12th month, and then, the technical budget changed.

Then, simulation results are shown in tables, where the scenario and policy results are compared. Simulation results were analysed in terms of three main variables of

Table 2 Parameters' changes in different policies

Policy	Changed parameter	Unit	Value change
Base	–	–	–
Advertisement	Budget for advertising	Dollar/month	20%
Retention	Budget for retention	Dollar/month	20%
Technical	Budget for technical objects	Dollar/month	20%
Combined	All budgets with the time difference	Dollar/month	20%

the engine of growth speed measurement. Net growth rate (NGR) refers to the paid engine per person/month (Table 2). CLV (customer lifetime value) is shown in Table 3 measuring the paid growth rate in dollar/person in Table 4. The viral coefficient of the viral engine of growth per person is represented in Table 5. All changes were from the sixth month on; and by the sixth month, the start-up data were used for simulation.

6 Results

As tables show, the Base run revealed a significant increase of CLV up to the 15th month using customer retention policy in simulation, whereas advertisement policy can be applied after the 15th month ends to improve results in the long term. It is also true with respect to the net growth rate given that the technical policy causes an increase of 50% in the eighth or 13th month. As expected, technical policy significantly improves viral attraction rate results, which is seen in all scenarios. In the decreased payment scenario, where the start-up undergoes complicated conditions, it is observed that the results may increase from 0 at the tenth month to 100,000 through customer retention policy. Such growth emanates from no new customer attraction or no adjustment in the viral attraction. Besides, in the increased customer acquisition and retention cost scenario, CLV heightens up to 80% through investing in technical and viral attraction policies. Also, the results show that the net growth rate tends to zero for all simulations, as customer acquisition cost (CAC) and customer exit will be equal using market potential and the start-up limited potential; hence, at this mode, the optimal number of customers may benefit the system service.

Table 3 Results for customer lifetime valu

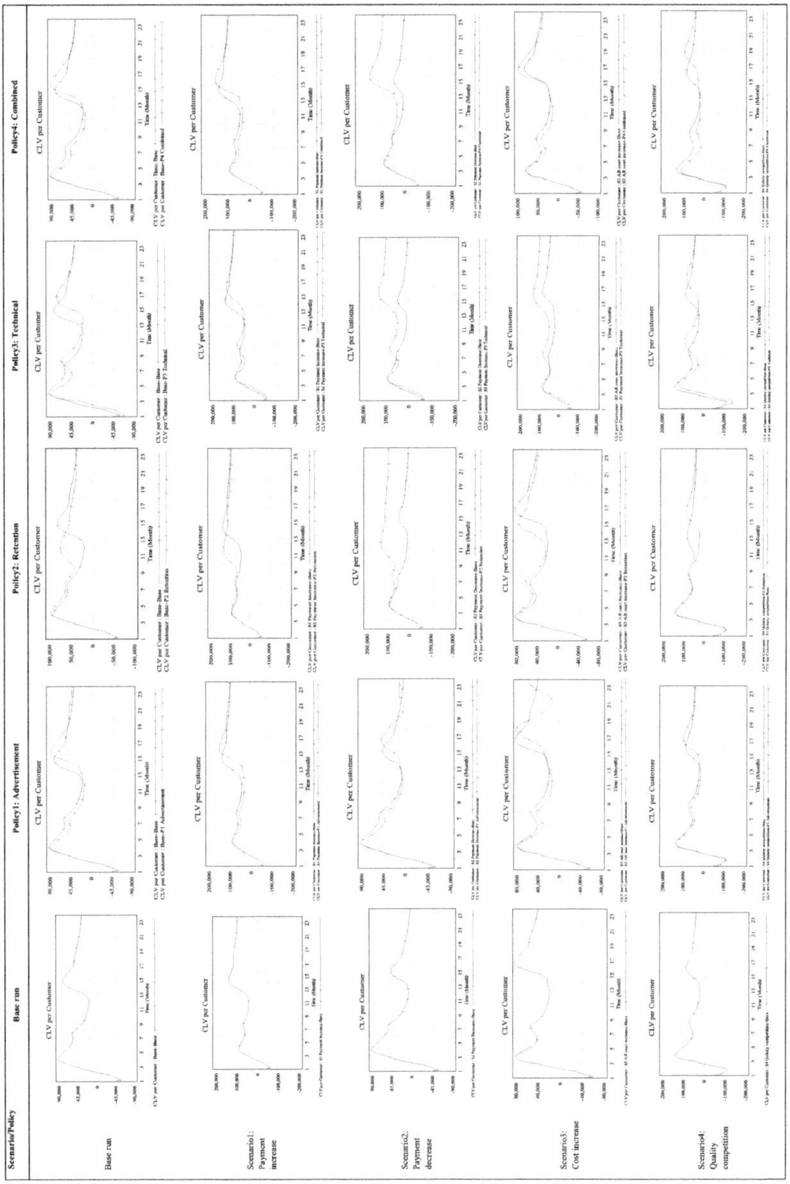

Table 4 Results for net growth rate

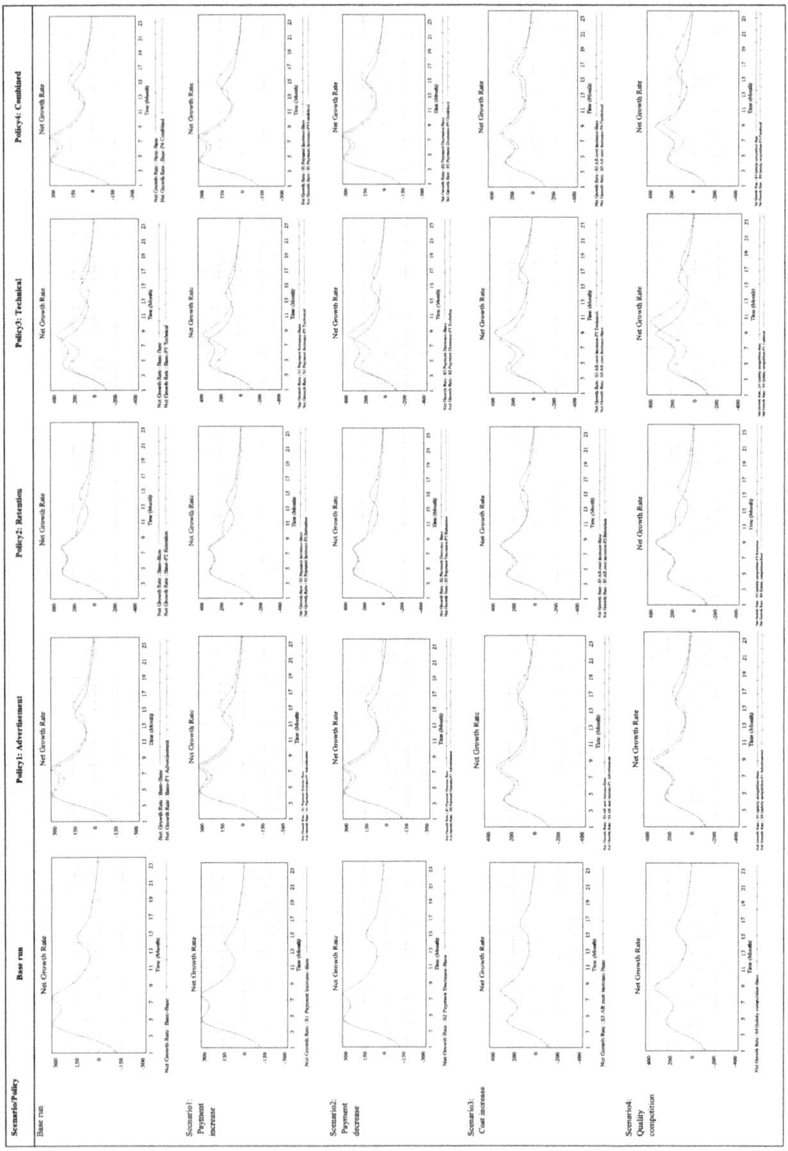

Table 5 Results for viral coefficient

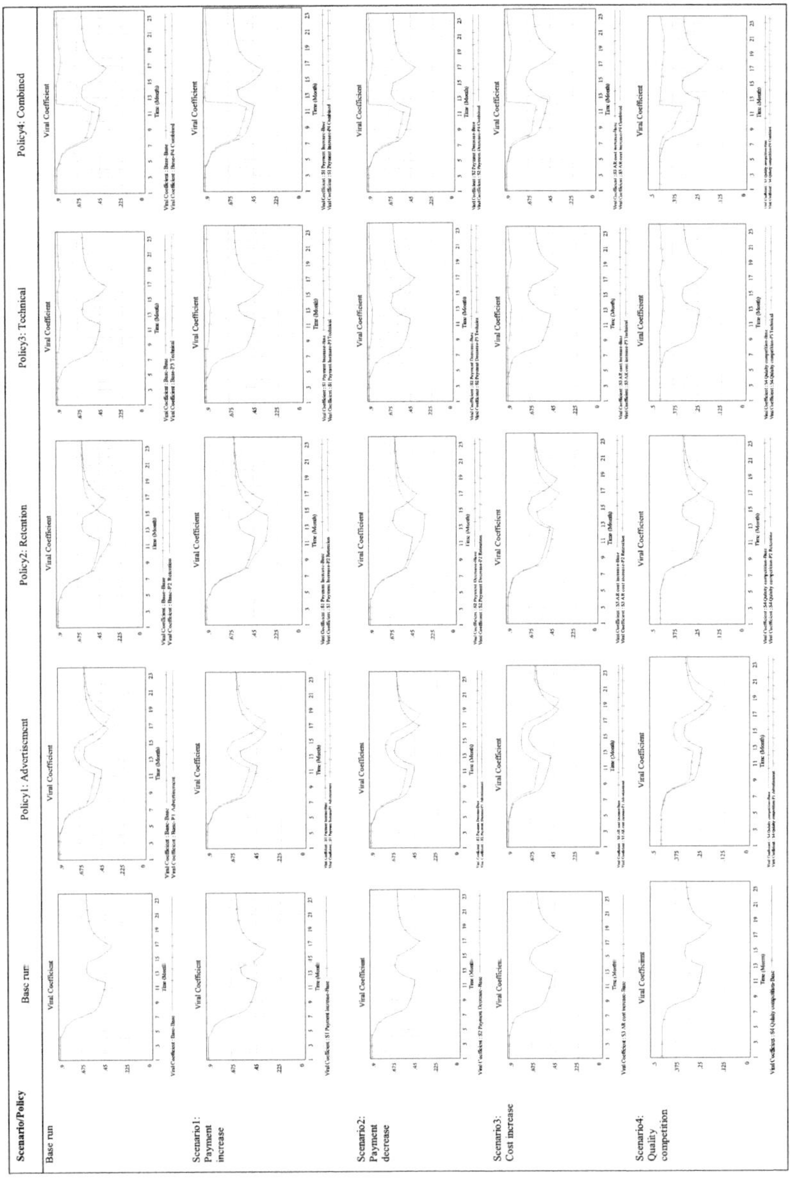

7 Discussion

As earlier mentioned, the understudied start-up lacks concentration on the sticky or viral engine. The base run simulation demonstrated that the start-up CLV reaches zero if a decreased customer payment scenario is implemented. However, the value increases up to 100,000 through implementing customer retention and viral attraction policies. This underlines the significance of selecting the growth direction for start-ups. When no new customer is attracted, the start-up potentials are utilised to deliver better services to existing customers and to gain more revenues by a lower customer exit rate. Moreover, it was also observed that the viral coefficient significantly decreased with respect to customer retention policy. It implies that start-ups must only focus on a particular engine of growth at a time and later try a new engine.

Model simulation results at different scenarios and policies for the acquisition variable are presented in Fig. 10. As shown, the variable continues to grow once it is constrained by the primary market; then, it follows a steady growth or it stops. From this stage on, pivoting becomes more and more significant. By properly tuning the start-up engine, it will even take some steps toward better markets to enjoy more potential customers.

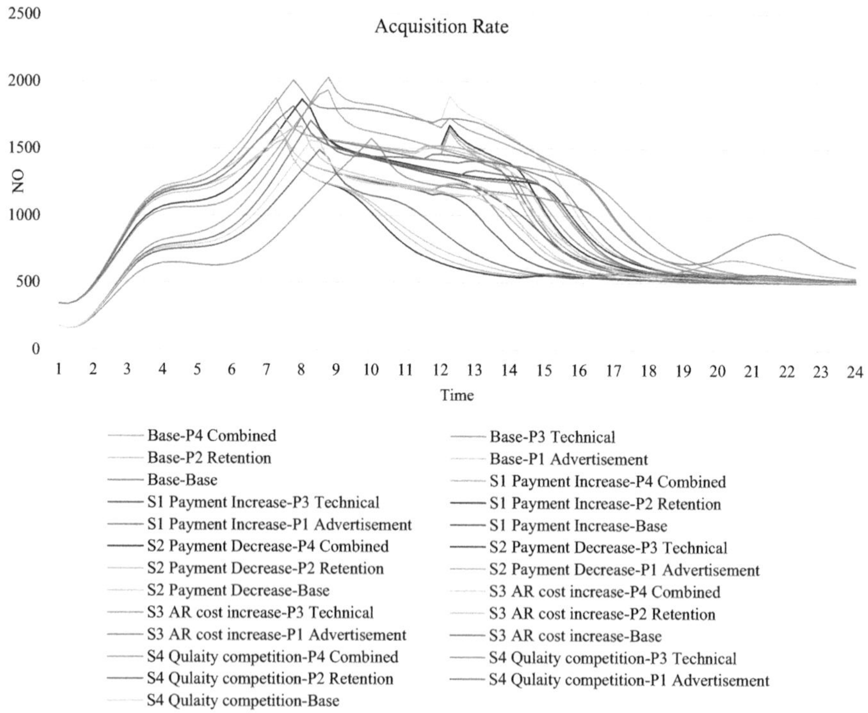

Fig. 10 All runs for the acquisition rate

8 Conclusion

Nowadays, as a result of the global economy and the widespread use of the Internet, enormous internationalisation activities are emerging, and this phenomenon provides great opportunities for entrepreneurs (Etemad et al. 2010; Jafari-Sadeghi et al. 2019). However, internationalisation is complex and challenging (Sadeghi et al. 2018), and competition in international markets makes it hard for small businesses, especially start-ups, to survive and grow (Etemad et al. 2001; Sadeghi and Biancone 2017a, 2017b, 2018; Dabić et al. 2020). Lean strategy as a way of operating start-ups can be an applied strategy for all businesses seeking growth and development. The lean approach in the understudied start-up can be a means of deliverance and, indeed, one way of growth for the upcoming years and of course, international growth in the right age (Sadeghi et al. 2017, 2018; Mahdiraji et al. 2011, 2019, 2020). However, start-ups in the launching phase can also collect the required data for the growth model using the minimum valuable product (MVP). MVP may allow start-up companies to attain real data of the growth model such as invitation rate, conversion ratio and customer lifetime value (Khanna et al. 2018; Ries 2011; Björk et al. 2013).

On the other side, finding a great market also significantly contributes to business success. As observed in the model, primary market constraint means potential customers can challenge start-ups. A market with lots of potential customers can attract start-ups' products. Therefore, the growth engine mechanism is a proper strategy to get to a balanced product and market, and this is the main reason for which this strategy can be used in lean global markets. Since the engine's speed is measured through quantitative variables, it can be a proper suggestion for market product fit (Sadeghi et al. 2019). Thus, it can be expressed that if a business intends to use a viral growth engine, there is no need to concentrate on promotion or sale, whereas a paid growth engine start-up may need extra energy on advertisement and marketing (Ries 2011). The proposed model revealed that an understudied start-up can significantly grow by merely focusing on the current customers; then, it may require pivoting, too. A start-up can invest its energy in finding new customers, servicing existing customers, improved quality or reduced costs every time. So, pivoting decision-making is considered the most significant decision for start-ups (Khanna et al. 2018; Ries 2011). This study tried to inform start-up executives of the prospective pivoting decisions and growth engines for the future of start-up through model simulation. However, the main restriction of such dynamic models is their dependency on knowledge about the future (Hajiagha et al. 2015). So, it is suggested that further studies investigate growth decisions in start-ups with more precise data.

References

Amin Moghadasi M, Derakhshandeh B, Ferdosi M, Jafari Sadeghi V (2017) Organizational conformity as an entrepreneurial response to the changes in internationalization process: a study of IT-oriented firms in Saveh. World Journal of Accounting, Finance and Engineering 1 (1):53–64

Bass FM (1969) A new product growth for model consumer durables. Manag Sci 15(5):215–227

Beheshti M, Mahdiraji HA, Zavadskas EK (2016) Strategy portfolio optimisation: a copras g-modm hybrid approach. Transform Bus Econ 15(3C):500–519

Biancone PP, Jafari Sadeghi V (2016) Risk management in export compliance: concepts, procedures, and solutions. In: Cantino V, De Vincentiis P, Racca MG (eds) Risk management: perspectives and open issues. McGraw-Hill, London, UK, pp 64–78

Björk J, Ljungblad J, Bosch J (2013) Lean product development in early stage startups. IW-LCSP@ ICSOB pp. 19–32)

Blank S (2017) Why the lean start-up changes everything. Harv Bus Rev October

Bohn N, Kundisch D (2018) Much more than 'same solution using a different technology': antecedents and consequences of technology pivots in software startups. Proceedings of the Multikonferenz Wirtschaftsinformatik, Lüneburg

Campos A (2017) The study of the Entrepreneur's values and knowledge: influence in growth expectations. Journal of Evolutionary Studies in Business 2(1):29–65

Caseiro N, Coelho A (2019) The influence of business intelligence capacity, network learning and innovativeness on startups performance. J Innov Knowl 4(3):139–145

Chanut-Guieu C, Guieu G, Dana LP (2019) Leadership, creativity and routine in small businesses experiencing hyper-growth. Revue de lEntrepreneuriat 18(2):147–171

Dabić M, Maley J, Dana LP, Novak I, Pellegrini MM, Caputo A (2020) Pathways of SME internationalization: a bibliometric and systematic review. Small Bus Econ 55(3):705–725

Dana LP, Dana TE (2005) Expanding the scope of methodologies used in entrepreneurship research. Int J Entrep Small Bus 2(1):79–88

Dana LP (ed) (2011) World encyclopedia of entrepreneurship. Edward Elgar Publishing

de Medeiros Júnior JV, de Medeiros Bezerra MH, Calife V (2015) Growth engine strategy analysis based on lean startup approach: case of a Brazilian startup. In Proceedings of the 33rd International Conference of the System Dynamics Society

Eisenmann TR, Ries E, Dillard S (2012) Hypothesis-driven entrepreneurship: the lean startup. Harvard Business School Entrepreneurial Management Case (812-095)

Etemad H, Wright RW, Dana LP (2001) Symbiotic international business networks: collaboration between small and large firms. Thunderbird Int Bus Rev 43(4):481–499

Etemad H, Wilkinson I, Dana LP (2010) Internetization as the necessary condition for internationalization in the newly emerging economy. J Int Entrep 8(4):319–342

Forrester BD (1996) Advanced vibration analysis techniques for fault detection and diagnosis in geared transmission systems (Doctoral dissertation, Swinburne University of Technology)

Frederiksen DL, Brem A (2017) How do entrepreneurs think they create value? A scientific reflection of Eric Ries' lean startup approach. Int Entrep Manag J 13(1):169–189

Fukugawa N (2018) Is the impact of incubator's ability on incubation performance contingent on technologies and life cycle stages of startups?: evidence from Japan. Int Entrep Manag J 14 (2):457–478

Geuvers P, Dana LP (2015) Growth momentum: what entrepreneurial CEOs do to achieve high organic growth (summary). Frontiers of Entrepreneurship Research 35(5):17

Ghezzi A (2019) Digital startups and the adoption and implementation of lean startup approaches: effectuation, Bricolage and opportunity creation in practice. Technol Forecast Soc Chang 146:945–960

Graham P (2012) Startup = growth. Self published online article, article source: http://www.Paulgraham.Com/growth.Html, accessed October

Hajiagha SHR, Mahdiraji HA, Tavana M, Hashemi SS (2018) A novel common set of weights method for multi-period efficiency measurement using mean-variance criteria. Measurement 129:569–581

Hajiagha SHR, Hashemi SS, Mahdiraji HA, Azaddel J (2015) Multi-period data envelopment analysis based on Chebyshev inequality bounds. Expert Syst Appl 42(21):7759–7767

Hosseini SH, Shakouri H (2016) A study on the future of unconventional oil development under different oil price scenarios: a system dynamics approach. Energy Policy 91:64–74

Hosseini SH, Shakouri GH, Kazemi A, Zareayan R, Mousavian HM (2019) A system dynamics investigation of project portfolio management evolution in the energy sector: case study: an Iranian independent power producer. Kybernetes

Huang X, Kunc M (2012) Modeling start-ups using system dynamics: towards a generic model. In Annals do International Conference of the System Dynamics Society, St. Gallen, Switzerland

Jafari Sadeghi V, Jashnsaz A, Honari Chobar M (2014) Organization's conformity assessment with Peter Senge's learning organization principles in municipality of Saveh: a case study. IOSR J Bus Manag 16(5):51–58

Jafari-Sadeghi V, Kimiagari S, Biancone PP (2019) Level of education and knowledge, foresight competency and international entrepreneurship. Eur Bus Rev 32(1):46–68

Keyhani M, Levesque M (2016) The equilibrating and disequilibrating effects of entrepreneurship: revisiting the central premises. Strateg Entrep J 10(1):65–88

Khanna D, Nguyen-Duc A, Wang X (2018) From MVPs to pivots: a hypothesis-driven journey of two software startups. In: International conference of software business. Springer, Cham, pp 172–186

Larsen ER, van Ackere A, Warren K (1997) The growth of service and the service of growth: using system dynamics to understand service quality and capital allocation. Decis Support Syst 19 (4):271–287

Mahdiraji HA, Kazimieras Zavadskas E, Kazeminia A, Abbasi Kamardi A (2019) Marketing strategies evaluation based on big data analysis: a CLUSTERING-MCDM approach. Economic research-Ekonomska istraživanja 32(1):2882–2892

Mahdiraji HA, Hajiagha SHR, Pourjam R (2011) A Grey mathematical programming model to time-cost trade-offs in project management under uncertainty. In: IEEE 2011 International Conference on Grey Systems and Intelligent Services. IEEE, pp 698–704

Mahdiraji HA, Hafeez K, Kord H, Kamardi AA (2020) Analysing the voice of customers by a hybrid fuzzy decision-making approach in a developing country's automotive market. Manag Decis. https://doi.org/10.1108/MD-12-2019-1732

Mahmoudi M, Mahdiraji HA, Jafarnejad A, Safari H (2019) Dynamic prioritization of equipment and critical failure modes. Kybernetes 48(9):1913–1941

Mokhtarzadeh NG, Mahdiraji HA, Beheshti M, Zavadskas EK (2018) A novel hybrid approach for technology selection in the information technology industry. Technologies 6:34

Pant V, Yu E, Tai A (2017) Towards reasoning about pivoting in startups with I-Star. In CEUR Workshop Proceedings

Ries E (2011) The lean startup: how today's entrepreneurs use continuous innovation to create radically successful businesses. Crown Books

Sadeghi V, Biancone PP (2017a) Shariah compliant international entrepreneurship: a study of Islamic finance in Europe. European Journal of Islamic Finance 8. https://doi.org/10.13135/2421-2172/2328

Sadeghi V, Biancone PP (2017b) Exploring the drivers of gender entrepreneurship: focus on the motivational perspectives in USA, Italy, and France. In: Ratten V, Ramadani V, Dana L-P, Hisrich RD, Ferreira J (eds) Gender and family entrepreneurship. Routledge, London, UK, pp 124–141

Sadeghi V, Biancone PP (2018) How micro, small and medium-sized enterprises are driven outward the superior international trade performance? A multidimensional study on Italian food sector. Res Int Bus Financ 45:597–606

Sadeghi VJ, Biancone PP, Giacoma C, Secinaro S (2017) Export compliance: a missing component of international entrepreneurship. International Journal of Business and Management 12 (11):103–110

Sadeghi VJ, Biancone PP, Giacoma C, Secinaro S (2018) How does export compliance influence the internationalization of firms: is it a thread or an opportunity? J Glob Entrep Res 8(1):33–53

Sadeghi VJ, Nkongolo-Bakenda JM, Anderson RB, Dana LP (2019) An institution-based view of international entrepreneurship: a comparison of context-based and universal determinants in developing and economically advanced countries. Int Bus Rev 28(6):101588

Sadraei R, Jafari Sadeghi V, Sadraei M (2018) Biotechnology revolution from academic entrepreneurship to industrial: chemo-entrepreneurship. Biometrics & Biostatistics International Journal 7(6):546–550

Shin SY (2019) Network advantage's effect on exit performance: examining venture capital's inter-organizational networks. Int Entrep Manag J 15(1):21–42

Sterman JD (2000) Business dynamics: systems thinking and modeling for a complex world. McGraw-Hill Higher Education, New York, NY

Sweeney LB, Sterman JD (2000) Bathtub dynamics: initial results of a systems thinking inventory. System Dynamics Review: The Journal of the System Dynamics Society 16(4):249–286

Täuscher K, Abdelkafi N (2016) Modelling the lean startup: a simulation tool for entrepreneurial growth decisions. Model-based strategy assessment in virtual environments for sustainable entrepreneurship. Proceedings of the 16th EURAM Conference, Paris, June 1–4 2016

Taghavifard MT, Amoozad Mahdiraji H, Alibakhshi AM, Zavadskas EK, Bausys R (2018) An extension of fuzzy SWOT analysis: an application to information technology. Information 9:46

Tanev S (2017) Is there a lean future for global startups? Technol Innov Manag Rev 7(5):52–56

Terho H, Eggert A, Haas A, Ulaga W (2015) How sales strategy translates into performance: the role of salesperson customer orientation and value-based selling. Ind Mark Manag 45:12–21

Van der Ven JS, Bosch J (2013) Pivots and architectural decisions: two sides of the same medal. In Proceedings 8th International Conference on Software Engineering Advances (ICSEA) (pp. 310–317)

Zahra Jamshidi studied Industrial Engineering at Iran University of Science and Technology. Studying Industrial Engineering provided a large amount of knowledge to learn about engineering and management, and as she took some courses regarding management, she felt obliged to respond to her question about studying management and business-related subjects in the future. In 2016, she started studying Entrepreneurship at the University of Tehran for her master's degree, and it was a unique experience to learn about the world of businesses. Her research interests are lean start-ups, pivot, growth and innovation, applying mathematical methods to entrepreneurial research, international entrepreneurship, social entrepreneurship and green entrepreneurship and sustainability.

Seyed Mojtaba Sajadi is an Associate Professor at the University of Tehran. He received his PhD, MSc and BSc in Industrial Engineering from the Amirkabir University of Technology, University of Tehran and Sharif University of Technology, respectively. His research interests include simulation-based optimisation, mathematical modelling, artificial intelligence, data science and machine learning. He applies these research methodologies in supply chain management, health care, production control, truism and entrepreneurship. His published research articles appear in CIE, IJAMT, *Journal of Cleaner Production*, *Simulation Modelling Practice and Theory*, *Applied Soft Computing*, *Applied Mathematical Modelling*, *Journal of Simulation*, *Journal of Global Entrepreneurship Research*, IJSOM, IJISE, *Energy* and so forth. He has presented several papers at international conferences such as CIE, INFORMS, ENBIS, ECGBL and IJPR and several national conferences.

Kambiz Talebi is a Full Professor at the Faculty of Entrepreneurship, New Business Department, University of Tehran. He received his MSc and PhD in Industrial Management from the University of Pune, India. His research interest includes entrepreneurship, entrepreneurial strategies, small and medium enterprises, venture creation, business growth and scale-up. He has published several papers in *International Business Research, International Journal of Entrepreneurship and Small Business, International Journal of Gender and Entrepreneurship, Journal of Asia Entrepreneurship and Sustainability* and so forth. He has been a keynote speaker in several international and national conferences.

Seyed Hossein Hosseini received his MSc from Iran University of Science and Technology and PhD from the University of Tehran in Industrial Engineering (Socio-economic Systems Engineering). Currently, he works as the CEO of Model-Based Management Systems Institute (SAMAM: www.samamsystem.com). His research interests include system dynamics modelling, socio-economic systems engineering, model-based policy analysis, strategic planning and policy research in the public sector (including energy, natural resources, environment, urban management, etc.)

9783030689711